GONE TO TEXAS

A HISTORY OF THE LONE STAR STATE

Randolph B. Campbell
University of North Texas

New York Oxford
OXFORD UNIVERSITY PRESS
2003

Oxford University Press

Oxford New York
Auckland Bangkok Buenos Aires Cape Town Chennai
Dar es Salaam Delhi Hong Kong Istanbul Karachi Kolkata
Kuala Lumpur Madrid Melbourne Mexico City Mumbai
Nairobi São Paulo Shanghai Taipei Tokyo Toronto

Published by Oxford University Press, Inc.
198 Madison Avenue, New York, New York, 10016
http://www.oup-usa.org

Library of Congress Cataloging-in-Publication Data
Campbell, Randolph B., 1940–
Gone to Texas : a history of the Lone Star State / Randolph B. Campbell.
p. cm.
Includes bibliographical references (p.) and index.
ISBN 0-19-513842-2 (cloth)—ISBN 0-19-513843-0 (paper)
1. Texas—History. I. Title.
F386.C268 2004
976.4—dc21 2002041657

Printing number: 9 8 7 6 5 4 3 2 1

Printed in the United States of America
on acid-free paper

To the memory of my parents

J. LANDON CAMPBELL AND VIRGINIA L. CAMPBELL

and the memory of

PROFESSOR BERNARD MAYO

Contents

Maps and Illustrations

MAPS

ILLUSTRATIONS

Preface

"Gone to Texas." These three words—often abbreviated "GTT" on the doors of abandoned homesteads across the southeastern United States during the 1830s and 1840s—provide a key to the story of Texas from prehistoric times to the beginning of the twenty-first century. From the arrival of the first humans twelve thousand years ago in the area that is now the Panhandle, the peopling of Texas by immigrants has never ceased. The Caddo and Apache Indians, for example, came during the late prehistoric era. Spanish settlers arrived to stay, as did the Comanches and Wichitas, in the eighteenth century. Anglo-Americans, often bringing African American slaves with them, moved in to dominate during the early nineteenth century, and migration from older states of the United States continued from that time onward. Germans also contributed significantly to population growth in the nineteenth century. Immigrants from Mexico came in large numbers throughout the twentieth century, and Asians became a significant presence by the 1990s.

These immigrants, often in conflict with each other and always in a struggle with the land and climate, shaped a Texas that is widely regarded as a special place. While traveling in the United States or abroad, tell someone that you are from Texas and watch their reaction. It may not always be positive, but few if any will say "where"? The story and idea of Texas appeal to millions of people, many of whom have never been anywhere near the state. Somehow their imaginations have "Gone to Texas" and liked what they found there.

Thus, through the years Texas has attracted millions of diverse immigrants and become well known to countless other people around the world. Its history, therefore, offers a great opportunity both to inform and to entertain. A place without information about its past is like an individual without a memory—it has no identity. How can a people know what they are now if they do not know what they have been? Texans, and those who wish to know about Texas, can draw different lessons from the story of the state's past; however, no one can deny the importance of first knowing what happened in that past. *Gone to Texas* offers an interpretation of the Lone Star State's history, but above all it seeks to provide the information necessary for readers to reach their own conclusions.

Entertainment also fills the pages of Texas history. For many it is found primarily in accounts of adventure and conflict—the stories of Spanish explorers in the sixteenth century, for example, or descriptions of the battles of the Alamo and San Jacinto. But the stories of political struggles such as Sam Houston's courageous battle against secession in 1860–1861 or the antics of "Pa" and "Ma" Ferguson during the second and third decades of the twentieth century make good reading as well. Even economic history, hardly a page-turner in most places, can be exciting in Texas. Consider the story of bringing in the Spindletop gusher in 1901 and then capping the original well just before the sea of crude oil around it caught fire. Texans for the most part have never learned how to be dull. It is fervently hoped that *Gone to Texas* lives up to that standard.

Acknowledgments

A great many Texans love their state's history with a passion that keeps them ready to pounce on factual errors or questionable interpretations in the work of errant historians. Of course, there is often dispute as to what is factually correct and even more bitter disagreement over interpretive matters. No one who enters the thicket of Texas history will emerge unscathed, but those who call on their colleagues for advice and assistance are likely to have fewer scratches than those who do not. Accordingly, I have asked for and received help from many of my colleagues at the University of North Texas and other institutions across the state.

A simple listing of the members of my department who gave their time and energy seems an inadequate recognition of the debt that I owe them, but limitations of space preclude more detailed recognition. Roberto Calderón, Gregg Cantrell, Don Chipman, Pete Lane, Richard Lowe, Ron Marcello, Dale Odom, and Todd Smith read chapters in their fields of specialization. Two of my colleagues in other departments at UNT, Reid Ferring in archeology and Terry Clower in economic development, also critiqued parts of the manuscript. These readers made suggestions that improved my original work, and I truly owe them all.

Academic historians at institutions other than the University of North Texas also provided valuable critiques. Walter L. Buenger of Texas A&M University offered "tough love" on the project from the original prospectus through the final chapter. George N. Green of the University of Texas at Arlington, Carl H. Moneyhon of the University of Arkansas at Little Rock, Harriett Denise Joseph of the University of Texas at Brownsville, and Cecil Harper of North Harris College helped me avoid numerous problems in their areas of specialization. Ron Tyler of the University of Texas encouraged the project from the outset and made helpful suggestions on its interpretive framework.

Robert S. Weddle of Bonham, the author of the most important body of work ever published on the rivalry between Spain and France for control of the Gulf of Mexico and the lands surrounding it, critiqued the chapters on Spanish Texas. Mary C. Ramos, editor of the *Texas Almanac,* gave a close reading to the entire manuscript and offered encouragement that it was on the right track. Patty Lane of Denton also read the manuscript and detected numerous problems of clarity. Philip W. Young of Denton offered helpful comments on the chapter on prehistoric Texas.

Grants from Faculty Research at the University of North Texas and the Nation's Heritage Fund in the Department of History provided funding for the preparation of maps and obtaining permissions for illustrations. I thank Professors Art Goven, Vice Provost for Research, and Harold Tanner, Chair of the Department of History, for their support in obtaining this funding. Chad Maloney of the Center for Media Production at UNT did an outstanding job of producing maps, often from the sketchiest of originals.

This manuscript began with a call from Bruce Borland, an acquisitions editor for Oxford University Press, inviting me to develop a prospectus for a general history of Texas. I had long wanted to undertake such a project, but without Bruce's call, I might never have acted. A large debt of gratitude is also due Peter Coveney of Oxford University Press and Elias Muhanna, his assistant. The book could never have been completed without their patient efforts.

My family also deserves high marks for patience. My wife, Diana, put up with almost-daily whining about how little progress I was making and how much more had to be written. Our sons and daughters-in-law, Landon Campbell and Janice Jacobs and Clay Campbell and Leah Thompson-Campbell, listened politely to progress reports almost every time we got together without ever saying, "So what's new?" I appreciate that.

Finally, as is customary after acknowledging the help of others, I must admit that remaining weaknesses and errors of omission or commission are my own fault. Why one of my friends did not catch them will always remain a mystery. (Just joking, guys.)

Chapter 1

THE FIRST TEXANS

The first people who, figuratively at least, wrote "GTT" on their homes and migrated to Texas probably began the trip eighteen to twenty thousand years ago in Siberia. At that time—known to geologists as the Pleistocene Epoch—vast ice sheets covered the northern parts of the Eurasian and North American continents. More than two miles deep at points, the ice held so much of the earth's water that sea levels were anywhere from 300 to 320 feet below present levels. The result was the exposure of a wide land bridge from Siberia to Alaska at the Bering Strait. Across Beringia, as it is generally called, came the first humans to occupy the Americas.

Fully evolved members of the species *Homo sapiens,* the earliest Americans had the physical form and all the intellectual capabilities of modern man. They were, in the words of one scholar, "the most formidable, vicious, and successful mammal ever to adorn the face of the world." Living in an Ice Age environment that would threaten the most sophisticated twentieth-century man with extinction, these early humans had a culture—a combination of material objects and behavior patterns—that ensured survival. They had fire to warm themselves and cook their food, clothing and shelter to protect against the Arctic climate, and weapons to kill animals and drive off predators. Essentially social beings, they formed small bands whose members worked cooperatively to survive.

These first migrants to America had no idea that they were intercontinental travelers. More than likely, they came simply in pursuit of animals such as the mammoth (a very close relative of the modern elephant) and reindeer that were found in both Asia and North America. Finding good hunting in the cool, humid climate just beyond the edges of the ice sheet, early migrants spread southward from Alaska, a movement that was encouraged by the appearance from time to time of an ice-free corridor along the eastern edge of the Rocky Mountains. Early men thus reached the Great Plains in the heart of North America.

Continuing their southward migration, humans arrived on the South Plains in what is now Texas about twelve thousand years ago. These first Tex-

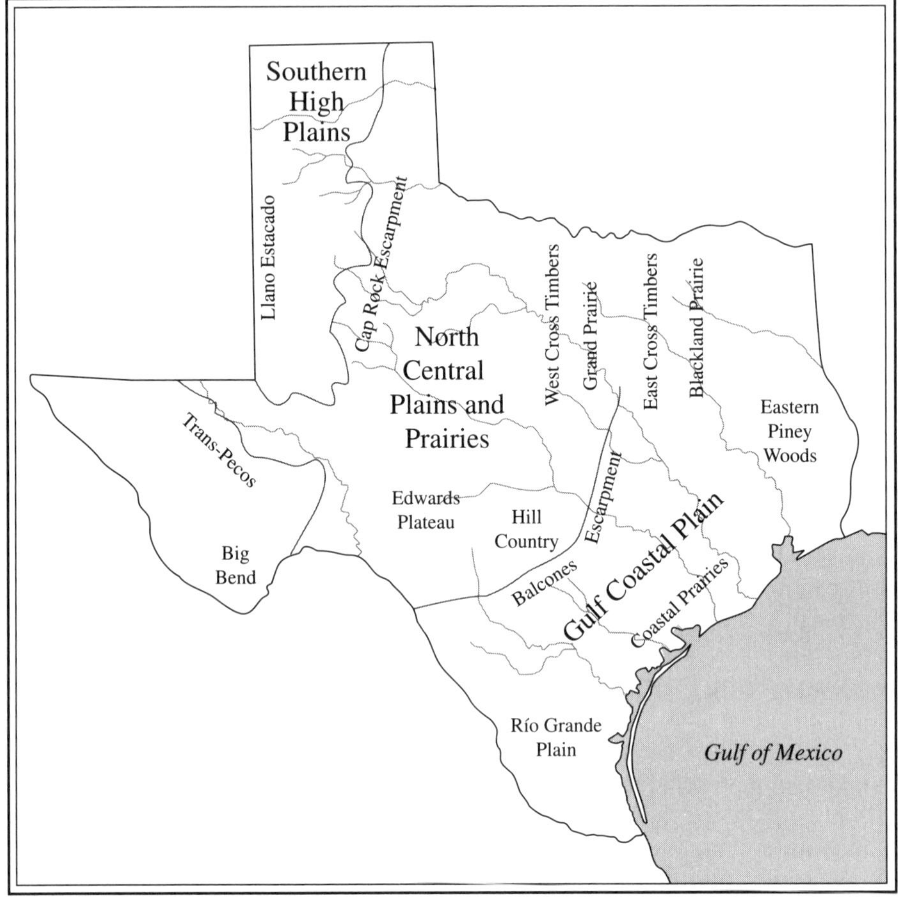

Physiographic Regions of Texas

ans soon extended their domicile from the plains region in the north to the canyon country of the lower Pecos River and across central Texas to the Gulf coast. (See maps: Physiographic Regions and Major Rivers of Texas.) For the next four to five millennia—approximately twelve thousand to seven or eight thousand years before the present—ancient Indians or "Paleo-Indians," in the language of archeologists, populated much of present-day Texas.

The Early Big Game Hunters

Fortunately for them, the first Texans to live on the plains of what is now the Panhandle encountered an environment more favorable to human habitation than that found in the same region at the close of the twentieth century. Temperatures were somewhat cooler in the summer and warmer in the winter, without the extremes of heat and cold now associated with the region. Rain-

Major Rivers of Texas

fall averaged nearly twice the amount of modern times. The level grasslands of today were more of a savanna of grass and sage broken often by broad, shallow valleys that had juniper and oak growing on their slopes. Along the floors of these valleys ran shallow streams connecting small ponds and marshes. This environment was equally attractive, of course, to animal as well as human life, and the earliest Texans lived there primarily as hunters of big game such as mammoth and bison.

Killing a mammoth, the prehistoric elephant whose name became synonymous with "huge," was an awesome challenge for early big game hunters on the Texas plains. Their most useful weapons were spears tipped by four-to-five-inch stone projectile points, primarily the Clovis Fluted point, which received its name from the New Mexico town just west of the Texas Panhandle where it was first discovered. Shaped and flattened by flaking chips from a flint rock core and then fluted by taking longer channels from the base of each side, this point was attached to a handle or shaft and used as a spear. The blunt end of the spear could be placed in a wooden spear thrower called an atlatl that in effect lengthened the arm of the hunter and allowed him to give much greater velocity to his projectile. Even with this weapon, however, men faced great difficulty in killing an animal that could stand twelve to fourteen feet at the shoulder. They had to rely on special circumstances and luck, such as finding a young animal separated from the herd and suffering from illness or injury, and then aim their spears at the thoracic region with the hope of penetrating the heart or spinal column.

Early hunters apparently enjoyed just such a combination of circumstances and good fortune at a site near Miami, about seventy-five miles northeast of Amarillo in the Panhandle, where they killed and butchered five mammoths near or in a small pond. The animals, some mature and some young, probably came to the waterhole suffering from disease or drought and either died there, or in their weakened condition were killed by humans. Archeologists investigating the site recovered bones, tusks, and teeth from the dismembered animals and located three Clovis point spear heads along with a stone scraping tool. The hunters probably took the meat for food and cleaned the hides for other uses.

For some unknown reason, mammoths began to disappear from the South Plains about eleven to twelve thousand years ago, forcing early hunters there to turn primarily to bison as a food source. Actually, by their increasing numbers, bison may have been responsible for the decline of the mammoth population. Early bison were somewhat larger than their modern relatives and were distinguished by large skulls and long, straight horns. Hunters used spears tipped with Folsom Fluted points, which, like the Clovis Fluted point, were named for a town in northeastern New Mexico. Shorter than the Clovis point but more thoroughly worked by the flintsmith, Folsom points generally had flutes on both faces and carefully sharpened edges. Some had rearward projections from the base in the fashion that was common to Indian arrowheads many centuries later.

Early hunters found it easier to kill bison than mammoths. For example, sixteen miles north of the Canadian River in the northeastern Panhandle, more than twenty bison apparently stopped in a depression during a severe snowstorm and were found there by hunters. Some may have died from the cold before the men arrived; others were killed with Folsom point spears. Using flint knives, the men butchered at least nine of the bison, built a fire to cook or smoke some of the meat, and then carried as much as possible away with them. They also cut or cracked open many of the bones to extract the marrow and used flint scrapers to clean the hides. Fourteen animals remained undisturbed to be excavated thousands of years later by archeologists, who named the site the "Lipscomb bison quarry."

Near Plainview in the southern Panhandle, bison hunters relied more on their wits than on the weather in taking their prey. Apparently, they stampeded a herd into a shallow pond situated under a steep bluff on a small creek and then killed the animals that were crippled by those in the rear running over them. These hunters used spears tipped with unfluted flint points known as Plainview points, suggesting that their kill came somewhat later in time than the one near the Canadian. However, they, too, used flint knives and scrapers to butcher the bison on top of the pile and clean their hides.

The men who butchered bison on the Texas plains were remarkably efficient, given the tools with which they worked. They split the skin along the backbone and pulled it away to the front and rear legs. The legs were removed, and the backbone cut in front of and behind the rib cage. Legs, once removed, were taken apart, and the meat stripped from the bones. Ribs were cut into segments. Butchers also removed neck meat from the cervical vertebrae and broke the jawbones as necessary to get at the tongue. They did not break into the skull to remove brains, perhaps because they did not have implements strong enough for that particular job.

After butchering their kills, successful hunters often cooked or smoked part of the meat at the site, but they also carried it to camp sites some distance away. No evidence exists as to whether or not women participated in the hunt, but undoubtedly they had a key role in processing the kills. Camp sites had hearths for the preparation of food—almost exclusively meat it seems from the archeological evidence, although as omnivores early humans probably consumed anything edible. Other necessary functions, such as cleaning and tanning fresh hides and preparing and repairing weapons, also took place in camp.

The manufacture of weapons and tools presented a special challenge for early big game hunters on the South Plains. Flint rock did not abound in the region, but several sites, especially the Alibates quarries on the Canadian River in the northern Panhandle and the Gibson quarry in Coke County north of San Angelo, provided workable stone. Apparently, experienced flintknappers traveled to the quarries and used a hammerstone to split blades of flint from the rock face of the quarry. The knapper then chipped off flakes to trim and shaped the blades to some extent before leaving the quarry. At that point he took some of the blades to his campsite for final preparation and buried others near the quarry or at spots along his route, creating a cache to draw on in the future. Caches of flint blades from the Alibates and Gibson quarries have been discovered as far away as Oklahoma and New Mexico, and some date to the earliest arrival of humans on the South Plains.

This production and transportation of flint for weapons and tools was Texas's first industry—and perhaps its first commercial enterprise as well. Those who went to quarries and produced the blades may have worked for themselves alone. However, the practice of creating caches holding dozens of blades suggests that some were either specialists working for a larger band or were manufacturing for the purpose of trade. Did flintknappers travel the region trading their wares for food? We can only guess.

Within a relatively short time after their arrival on the plains, bison hunters appeared in regions south of the Panhandle. Most of present-day West Texas was also covered with savanna-like grasslands or parklands of grass and trees, but the rougher terrain along the lower Pecos and the Río Grande immediately below Big Bend proved to be especially helpful in the killing of large animals. On at least three occasions about ten thousand years ago, hunters drove herds of giant bison over a cliff into the deep canyon near present-day Langtry. Approximately 120 animals were killed, many by the fall and others by men who found them easy targets due to injuries. Hunters then rolled or dragged the carcasses into a large rock shelter under the canyon wall and butchered them. Bonfire Shelter, as this site is now known, remained a favorite hunting spot for centuries.

Early big game hunters also moved into the central part of the present-day state—defined broadly as the area between the plains region in the north, the Trinity River in the east, the Gulf coast in the south, and the Nueces River in the west—some time between twelve thousand and ten thousand years ago. This region was well watered, especially along the Brazos and Colorado Rivers, and covered with savanna-like grasslands that attracted mammoth and giant bison for at least the first one thousand years of human habitation there. Hunters killed mammoths on the Brazos near Bryan and butchered bison at rock shelters near Waco, Austin, and Kerrville. Near Uvalde on the Sabinal River, one group wounded an animal with at least five Folsom points but it escaped into a shelter under a cliff where it died. More than ten thousand years later, archeologists excavating the Kincaid Shelter discovered the unlucky (or unskilled) hunters' kill.

Early residents of central Texas left a fascinating glimpse into their culture in the form of a burial site on the Brazos River just north of Waco, which was discovered and excavated in the late twentieth century. The shallow grave, dug in the floor of a rock shelter and covered with stone slabs and soil, contained the bodies of an adult male and a child. Grave offerings under the adult's head included seashell beads and perforated canine teeth (seemingly from a necklace), turtle shells (probably used as rattles), red ocher, flint-knapping tools and pieces of flint, and small slabs of sandstone. The child was buried with a small needle made of bone. Another burial site of similar antiquity (nine thousand years ago), discovered at Leander north of Austin, held the remains of a woman placed in a carefully semi-flexed position. Her grave contained a combination grinding tool and chopper, suggesting that her diet included plants as well as animals.

The first humans to reach the coastal plains of Texas twelve thousand to ten thousand years ago found the Gulf of Mexico some 300 to 320 feet below its modern sea level, due to the water frozen in still-existing ice fields in the northern part of the continent. As in other regions of the state, the climate along the coast was cooler and more humid with less seasonal variation than at present. The strip of land nearest the Gulf was covered by marshes; farther inland, forests covered most of the upper coast and savanna-like vegetation characterized the rest. Mastodons, another large mammal resembling the elephant, likely were more numerous on the upper coast than anywhere else in Texas because they were more at home in forests, but the early big game hunters' favorite prey—mammoths and bison—roamed the entire region from the Río Grande to the Sabine River. On the upper coast they were joined by even more exotic animals such as the giant tortoise, dire wolf, and saber-toothed cat.

The woodland environment found inland along the upper coast may have encouraged large animals to disperse rather than form herds. That, plus the absence of natural features such as deep canyons into which they could drive the animals, made it more difficult for big game hunters to kill their prey. Flint spear points found in the region indicate the presence of hunters—who undoubtedly met with enough success to ensure survival—but no kill sites like the Lipscomb Bison Quarry or Bonfire Shelter have been found near the Gulf coast. Moreover, since there were no especially inviting sites for habitation such as rock shelters, early Texans along the coast did not occupy any single spot long enough to leave a significant archeological record. This absence of kill sites and camp sites means that relatively little is known of how the first human residents of the area hunted or lived.

The heavily forested region now known as East Texas, which has always shared more geographic similarities with the southeastern United States than with the rest of Texas, was populated very lightly if at all during the period from twelve thousand to seven thousand years ago. Giant bison, the primary target of early hunters, did not range far enough east to provide subsistence for humans there.

The Hunter-Gatherers

After four to five centuries of survival based primarily on hunting big game, early Texans began to face a decline in the numbers of their favorite prey, as mammoths, long-horned bison, and other large animals became extinct. Reasons for the extinction of "megafauna" in the region remain unknown and therefore debatable. Some scholars blame overkilling by the hunters themselves. A more likely explanation points to changes in climate that became noticeable about eight thousand to seven thousand years ago when the long-term trend toward warmer and drier weather that marked the end of the Ice Age accelerated. The relatively cool, humid climate that had existed year round for centuries was gradually replaced by conditions more like those in modern Texas—less rainfall, greater heat much of the year, and more extreme cold at times in the winter.

Hotter and drier weather and more seasonal variation meant smaller streams and rivers and less vegetation, which in turn decreased the quantity and variety of the food supply for big animals. Apparently, large mammals simply did not have adequate food to remain healthy and reproduce. The larger an animal, the longer its gestation period, when nutritional needs are especially great. Mammoths, for example, are estimated to have had a two-and-one-half year gestation period, far too long a time to survive on the food supply of an environment marked by extremes in hot and cold. Even today no animal with a gestation period longer than one year survives outside the tropics where the climate changes little year round.

This change in climate moved slowly into Texas from the southwest, affecting the lower Pecos River valley first and then covering the whole region from the plains to the Gulf coast. Decreases in the number of big game animals matched changes in the weather. As early as nine thousand years ago, bison began to disappear from the lower Pecos valley, and some one thousand to fifteen hundred years later the same trend appeared on the plains and in central Texas. Archeologists have found virtually no bones of giant bison at sites across the present-day state that date to between eight thousand and forty-five hundred years before the present. Bison reappeared after that period, but they were the smaller animals of modern times rather than the giant bison found by the earliest human habitants of Texas.

Thus, early Texans, like all humans faced with changes in climate and food supply, had to adapt or die. So, adapt they did, primarily by developing a hunter-gatherer approach to subsistence. The change probably came grudgingly, given the usual tendency to hold on to old ways, but it is likely, in spite of a lack of archeological evidence on the matter, that early big game hunters had always supplemented their diets by gathering plants, fruits, berries, and such. The transition probably came more as a matter of a shift in emphasis than as a totally wrenching move from old to new. In any case, eight thousand to seven thousand years ago, the first Texans entered a new stage (the "Archaic" in the language of archeologists) on the road to historic times, a stage that would last about six millennia and end two thousand to fifteen hundred years before the present.

Inhabitants of rock shelters along the canyons of the lower Pecos left the best record available today of how Archaic hunter-gatherers lived. Fossilized feces (coprolites) at Hinds Cave in present-day Val Verde County indicate that occupants six thousand years ago ate at least twenty-three different animals and twenty-two plants. The animals included deer, cottontail and jackrabbits, raccoon, coyotes, fish (especially catfish), snakes, birds, lizards, rats, and mice. Once the animals were cooked and the meat stripped from the bones, the bones themselves were cracked for marrow. Among the plants were hackberries, persimmons, grapes, wild onions, prickly pear stems and fruit (called tuna in Spanish), grass seeds, sotol (a spiny-leafed plant of the lily family), and yucca (a plant of the agave family). Some of the plants were eaten raw, and the fruit of others such as the yucca were dried. Early cooks also baked the bulbs of sotol plants in shallow earthen ovens lined with limestone rocks.

As they foraged for a living, hunter-gatherers in this region added the manufacture of textiles to flintknapping as the first Texas "industries." Hunters, who had not yet invented the bow and arrow, continued to kill larger game with stone-tipped spears thrown with the aid of an atlatl and to take smaller game such as rabbits with clubs. Flintknappers, working in much the same way that they had for thousands of years on the plains (except that on the lower Pecos the necessary raw material was readily at hand), made a variety of spear points, scrapers, and cutting and grinding tools. Gatherers, however, needed carrying containers such as baskets and bags, which could be made from the leaves and fibers of the yucca and sotol plants. Thus developed the manufacture of cords of twisted fibers and the use of such cordage in making baskets, sandals, aprons, snares, and netting. The well-equipped forager some eight thousand years ago could venture out wearing sandals to protect his feet, carrying a throw net to catch fish and string to build snares, and taking a basket or large bag to hold any plants or small animals of value that he might find.

The population of hunter-gatherers on the lower Pecos was small—at any given time an estimated one thousand humans scattered over fourteen thousand square miles—and social units must have been small as well. Most individuals probably lived in bands of twenty-five or thirty extended family members that managed enough stability to create at least semipermanent residences. Occupants of Hinds Cave, for example, compartmentalized their space to include living areas with floors covered by prickly pear stems and hearths for fires; sleeping areas that had shallow pits lined with grass, twigs, and other "mattress" materials; and distinct latrine areas.

Survival undoubtedly required virtually all the energy of these early foragers, and the threat of starvation could never have been far from their minds, especially during the colder months from November to March. But like all humans, they believed that their world also depended on the supernatural, on unseen forces that might somehow be called to their aid. Dramatic evidence of this faith is found in the pictographs created on the walls of caves and rock shelters along the lower Pecos River between forty-five hundred and two thousand years ago. Painted in colors of dark and light red, yellow, and orange (all created from ocher), white (from clay), and black (from carbon)—either by applying the colors in liquid form with a brush or by using a crayon of molded pigment—the pictographs' most striking feature is the appearance of figures representing shamans or medicine men. Some shamans are less than a foot in height, but many are in excess of ten feet. They generally wear elaborate costumes and headdresses and stand with arms outstretched. With them are figures (generally smaller) depicting ordinary humans and pictures of animals such as deer and panthers/cougars. One panther found on the wall of a cave in Val Verde County measures nineteen feet from its head to the tip of its tail. The deer often are pierced with spears, but the cougars are not.

Who created these pictographs, and what do they mean? More than likely, shamans themselves were the artists, painting an account of drug-induced visits to the world of the supernatural. Mescal beans (seeds of the Texas mountain laurel) and peyote (from cactus), both powerful hallucinogens, have been found in many of the caves containing rock art. Apparently, shamans under the influence of these drugs saw visions of successful hunts for deer, hunts on which they were accompanied by cougars. The cougar, which was expert in finding and killing deer, may have been regarded as a source of supernatural aid for hunters and perhaps of power and knowledge in general. Shamans also painted humans killed by spears and darts, visions no doubt of victory in warfare.

Painting from Panther Cave, Val Verde County. The panther is nineteen feet long from its nose to the tip of its tail. Note the shaman beneath the panther and, beneath him, the "hole" through which he traveled to a world beyond the cave. Credit: Photograph by Jim Zintgraff.

Whatever its exact meaning, this rock art is proof that early Texans facing the constant struggle for survival as hunter-gatherers at times enjoyed dramatic ceremonies that brought color and excitement to their lives. Seeing a shaman depict the miraculous world of spirits that explained so much of what lay beyond their own experiences must have been wonderful indeed. Against all odds these first Texans expressed imagination and creativity.

Humans living along the lower Pecos thus adapted with reasonable success to the changes in climate and animal life that ushered in the Archaic stage in Texas. However, those who occupied the plains region found the transition more difficult. Thinning vegetation and the extinction of mammoth and giant bison ended big game hunting and forced a change, but the plains environment, lacking many of the small animals and plants found on the Pecos, proved inhospitable to the development of a hunter-gatherer life style. Archeologists have located sites along the southern part of this region that were created by foragers, but the human population there declined beginning about eight thousand years ago and remained small until the appearance of the modern bison nearly four millennia later. Then, from approximately forty-five hundred to fifteen hundred years before the present (the last three thousand years of the Archaic stage), the first Texans in the plains region lived primarily as nomadic hunters, leaving very little record of their culture.

In contrast to the plains, climatic changes in central Texas made the region more inviting to human inhabitants. Hunters found deer and smaller animals reasonably plentiful, and gatherers located numerous edible roots, seeds, and fruits. Archeological evidence dating to seven or eight thousand years ago, located especially in middens of burned and fire-cracked hearthstones and other camp refuse, is so plentiful that it suggests an increase in population over the earlier big game hunting era. Bands of hunter-gatherers probably ranged over the area and camped along its streams, traveling a good deal more than did their contemporaries in the Pecos region, as they moved from place to place according to the availability of food. Weapons and tools used by these early central Texans included those common elsewhere in the state—spear points, blades, axes, and scrapers made of flint and needles and fish hooks made of bone. However, textile products such as baskets have not been found in central Texas. Perhaps the absence of caves and deep rock shelters meant that discarded textiles rotted quickly, but the kinds of plants that produced workable fibers were not commonly found there either. In any case, hunter-gatherers thrived in central Texas for more than five thousand years.

Early Texans living along the Gulf coast could hardly have noticed the change, but with the warming and drying of their climate that began some seven thousand years ago came a slow rise in sea level. The trend toward higher temperatures all over Eurasia and North America reduced ice packs and during the next three to four centuries raised the level of the Gulf of Mexico 300 to 320 feet. Approximately three thousand years ago the coastline of Texas reached its present-day position.

The rise in sea level covered much archeological evidence from the Archaic period, but it seems likely that the first several thousand years of change in climate brought a great reduction in population. Eventually, however, humans along the coast adjusted and, like their contemporaries in other areas of Texas, lived as hunter-gatherers. Their proximity to the sea provided one resource that could be gathered for food—shellfish—not available in other regions. Middens at open campsites such as one excavated in Harris County during the 1960s are filled with the shells of clams and oysters. Shells as well as stone and bone were used to fashion tools.

Hunter-gatherers also occupied East Texas during the Archaic period, but the soils of that region, which are not conducive to preservation, have yielded relatively little evidence on their lives. The Wolfshead site in San Augustine County, however, provided an assortment of stone spear points, knives, and scrapers comparable to those used elsewhere in Texas at the time. Flint is not common in the region, forcing the use of an available substitute—petrified wood. This material, which was laminated and easily broken into thin sheets, apparently was plentiful in an area that had been heavily forested for millions of years. Texans who pride themselves on the ability to "make do" with what is at hand should be pleased at the thought of early craftsmen chipping weapons and implements out of petrified wood.

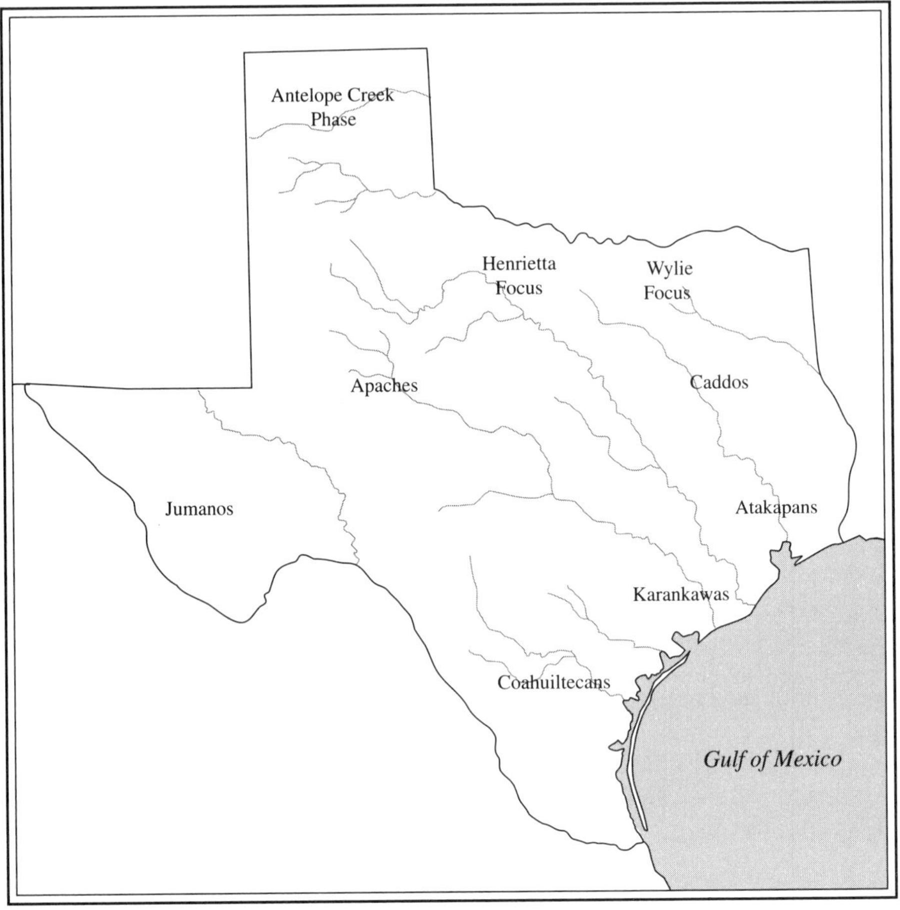

Late Prehistoric Indians of Texas

The Development of Agriculture

The first Texans remained "Archaic" hunter-gatherers for five to six millennia, but approximately fifteen hundred years ago an agricultural revolution began, marking the onset of what archeologists term the Late Prehistoric period. Over the next millennium, the development of farming, accompanied by the creation of pottery and the adoption of the bow and arrow, changed the lives of most early Texans. To point again to the obvious, these changes did not come to all regions of a place as large as Texas at the same time or in precisely the same way. Some of the early Texans whom Europeans would "discover" less than five hundred years ago (in 1528 to be exact) continued to live largely as their forebears had for thousands of years, but many others had developed a far more comfortable life and sophisticated society than they could have built as hunter-gatherers. (For the geographical distribution of these early Texans, see map: Late Prehistoric Indians of Texas.)

The first Texans to adopt a lifestyle based essentially on agriculture lived in the mixed-oak-pine-hickory woodlands of the eastern part of the state. Europeans would call these people the "Caddo," from the French abbreviation of "Kadohadacho," a word that meant "real chief" in the Caddoan language. Their ancestors broke the usual pattern of arrival in Texas by migrating from the east up the tributaries of the Mississippi River rather than from the northwest. They lived at first (some four thousand to twenty-five hundred years ago) as hunter-gatherers, finding abundant food sources in the forested areas along the Red River, but then, like other Indians to the east, they began to cultivate crops such as corn, beans, squash, pumpkins, and sunflowers. Corn—early or "little corn," harvested in July, and "flour corn," harvested in September—became the staple crop. Although hunters continued to kill deer, bear, and small game such as turkeys, squirrels, and rabbits, and gatherers still collected nuts, fruits, and other plant foods, the success of agriculture allowed the Caddos to build an advanced and rich culture that began to flourish in their woodlands environment around 700 A.D. Unlike subsistence-level peoples, they produced enough wealth to permit the development of social classes and a political and religious elite.

Adopting a settlement pattern not unlike that found in much of East Texas to this day, the Caddos lived on scattered farmsteads, in small hamlets, and in a few larger towns. They built permanent, beehive-shaped residences of canes covered with grasses. A completed dwelling averaged forty or fifty feet in height and sixty feet in width, and its construction required the joint efforts of everyone in the community. Elevated beds lined the walls, mats covered the well-swept floor, and a fire always burned in the center.

The Caddos used chipped-stone tools to clear trees and brush and to turn the soil. As in the building of houses, the entire community planted crops, beginning with the fields of the elite and continuing down to those of ordinary members of the community. Women harvested the corn, shelled it, and stored it in strong reed baskets. The best ears were kept as part of a two years' supply of seed corn.

Caddo hunters were armed with stone-tipped arrows and bows made of bois d'arc (also known as Osage orange) wood. They also had a considerable variety of smaller digging, cutting, and scraping implements made of stone, bone, shell, and wood. Craftsmen fashioned reed baskets for use in gathering, but for purposes of cooking, serving, and storing foods Caddos relied on their ability, unsurpassed among Texas Indians, for making ceramics from locally abundant clays. In addition to vessels with practical purposes, some of which were two feet in height and diameter, potters also created beautifully decorated bowls and bottles.

Another important craft, practiced by the women, involved dressing deer, bear, and buffalo skins so that, in the words of one historical observer, they resembled "fine cloth." Finished skins were dyed and bordered with beads or fringe. Women wore skirts and blouses made of this "cloth"; men, a breechcloth in summer and a buffalo skin blanket or robe in winter. Both wore moccasins of deerskin.

The Caddos' successes in agriculture and crafts provided the basis for yet another cultural advance—the development and maintenance of long-distance trade with other Indian groups. Making contacts hundreds of miles from their homeland, they traded hides, ceramics, bows, arrows, baskets, and salt (which was available locally) for marine shells, copper, cotton, and turquoise. Shells obviously came from the coast, but the cotton was grown in the southwest and the turquoise originated in the vicinity of present-day Albuquerque, New Mexico. Clearly, then, the Caddos' economy produced a surplus that, used as trade goods, brought greater comfort and even luxury to their lives.

Caddoan religious and political organization depended on a hierarchy of leaders who inherited their positions. Spiritual leadership in each group or band came from the *xinesi,* who served as intermediaries between ordinary people and the supreme god, the *Caddi Ayo.* The *xinesi* also performed all rites related to the supernatural and presided over harvest and naming ceremonies. Political leadership rested in the hands of a *caddi,* the headman of local communities who, in consultation with advisors called *canahas,* made important civil decisions and decided questions of war and peace. Only men acted as *xinesi* and *caddi,* but interestingly, the line of descent in Caddo society was matrilineal. Hereditary status, including the family name, passed through the mother rather than the father.

Family life among the Caddos tended to depend on the community more than on married couples. Several families occupied each house. First marriages were arranged by parents and the *caddi,* but few couples remained together for life, and second marriages did not require parental consent. Divorce and remarriage were so common that the first Catholic priests to live among the Caddos complained that unions of men and women amounted only to serial monogamy. When couples divorced, children went with their mother, so that for Caddos the most important adult influences, other than their mothers, were maternal aunts and uncles.

Caddo spiritual life centered on belief in a supreme god, a creator of the universe who rewarded good and punished evil. All who died went up to a "House of Death" in the sky where they waited in a state of happiness until the souls of all the tribe had been gathered. Then, all began a new life in another world. Only their enemies' souls went to the house of the devil to be punished.

Like most early Texans, the Caddos engaged in warfare only sporadically, and their military forays amounted to little more than organized raids to take a few prisoners or scalps. War leaders and warriors in each band, called the *amayxoya,* did not inherit their positions; rather, they earned that status by success in battle. War chiefs were elected from among this group.

The Caddos' culture reached its zenith between 800 and 1350. Their prosperity and well-developed religious and political system were reflected in the building of civic-ceremonial centers characterized by huge earthen mounds. One such center, located a little west of present-day Nacogdoches, had two flat-topped mounds, on which spiritual leaders performed religious rites, and a conical burial mound. Generally, the graves of members of the Caddo social elite in burial mounds contained extremely valuable goods such as engraved pottery and conch shells, copper ornaments, clay pipes, quartz crystals, and carefully chipped arrowheads placed in quivers.

Beginning about 1350, a long-term climatic change brought a decline in rainfall that affected the Caddos by making the production of corn and other crops less certain. Those who lived north of the Red River suffered the most from the drought and tended over time to move south to join the groups living along the river and in East Texas. Caddoan culture remained strong in those areas, but even there the building of ceremonial centers with earthen mounds ceased. By 1500, the Caddos were organized into three affiliated kin-based groups often called confederacies—the Natchitoches of northwestern Louisiana, the Kadohadacho of the great bend area of the Red River in far northeastern Texas and southwestern Arkansas, and the Hasinai of the East Texas area along the Sabine, Angelina, and Neches Rivers. The total population of the three confederacies at that time probably numbered 200,000. Their advanced culture entitled them to be recognized, in the words of one scholar, as the "Romans of Texas." Tragically, as residents of America, they had no exposure to European diseases, and their settled lifestyle and lack of immunities would make them especially vulnerable to smallpox, measles, and cholera. It is estimated that during the two centuries following their first contact with Europeans, the Caddos' population declined to about fifteen thousand, a loss of more than 90 percent.

Incidentally, when the Spanish arrived in Texas, they turned the Caddo word *techas,* which means "friend," into "Tejas" and began to use their word as the name for that entire group of Indians. The transition from "Tejas" to "Texas" came easily (since *x* and *j* have the same pronunciation in Spanish—like an English *h*) and appeared as early as 1689. Texas thus derived its name from a Caddo word, and the state's motto, "Friendship," still reflects that heritage.

Any Caddo venturesome enough to travel a few hundred miles south of his woodland home to the Gulf of Mexico and follow the coast southwestward to the Río Grande would have encountered the least culturally developed Indians in late prehistoric Texas—the Atakapans, Karankawas, and Coahuiltecans. Living on the coastal plain, which was largely unsuitable for agriculture because of salt water flooding, infertile soils, and limited rainfall at certain times of the year, these groups could not rely on growing food crops. Instead, they lived largely by hunting, fishing, and gathering and generally moved about rather than settling into permanent residences. They used the bow and arrow effectively, but advances in the manufacture of ceramics and basket making were limited.

The Atakapans lived in southwestern Louisiana and in southeast Texas from the Sabine to the San Jacinto Rivers. Those located farthest inland from the Gulf, especially a subgroup known as the Bidais, engaged in farming to a limited extent. Most Atakapans, however, hunted deer and bear, fished in the shallows with small spears, collected shellfish such as oysters, and gathered birds' eggs along with edible plants. The alligator, which they killed by spearing through the eye, was especially important for its meat and hide and for the oil, which served as an insect repellent. Alligator grease had a terrible odor, but apparently desire to escape the attack of coastal insects easily overcame any objections to the smell.

Because they lived in small dispersed bands that moved often, the Atakapans had only a rudimentary social organization. Each band had a headman, but there was no tribal chief who brought all the groups together for a common meeting. Their spiritual beliefs centered on a creation myth that told of the first men being cast up from the sea in large oyster shells. Men were ordered by a supreme being to do no evil. Those who obeyed went above at death, and those who did not descended under the earth.

"Atakapa" meant "eaters of men" in Choctaw, a description that they deserved. Their cannibalism, however, was of the ritualistic kind practiced by other Texas Indians as well. They believed that a man who was eaten by other men could not enter a second life and was eternally damned. Cannibalism thus served as the ultimate punishment of an enemy. Another purpose of ritualistic cannibalism was to take on the "essence" of the victim—the courage of a particularly brave warrior, for example.

The Karankawas lived southwest of the Atakapans, along the Gulf coast from Galveston Bay to Corpus Christi Bay. "Karankawa" probably meant "dog lovers" or "dog raisers" because the group kept coyote-like dogs. Living amidst the islands, lagoons, and salt marshes close to the coast, the Karankawas did not practice any form of agriculture. Instead, like most of the Atakapans, they subsisted on hunting, fishing, and gathering what their habitat had to offer on a seasonal basis. During the fall and winter Karankawa bands lived on the shorelines of bays and lagoons and relied on fish, especially the black drum and redfish, for food. They also ate shellfish and killed white-tailed deer. In the spring and summer the Karankawas moved short distances inland and established camps along rivers and creeks. There, they gathered summer greens, fruits, pecans, and seeds and also hunted deer and bison.

The Karankawas traveled in canoes made from hollowed-out tree trunks and lived in easily movable wigwams. The dugout canoes, propelled by poles, were large enough to carry a family across shallow lagoons and inlets, but they were unsuited for deep, open water. Wigwams or "ba-aks" consisted of a dozen or so willow poles that could be pushed into the ground at one end, tied together at the other, and covered with skins. Because they seldom had food to store, the Karankawas had relatively little need for pottery. However, they manufactured cooking pots that were coated inside and decorated outside with asphaltum, a tar-like substance found on beaches. Some of their baskets also had asphaltum coatings for waterproofing. Like their coastal neighbors, they smeared their bodies with alligator or shark grease to repel insects.

The Karankawas depended on the bow and arrow for hunting, fishing, and fighting their enemies. They fashioned bows from red cedar and strung them with deer sinew. Their arrows were made of cane, feathered, and fitted with implants of wood at each end, one shaped to hold the arrow head and the other notched to fit the bow string. Bows, which were custom-made according to the height and strength of their users, propelled yard-long arrows with terrific force. One historical observer reported seeing a Karankawa warrior shoot an arrow at a three-year-old bear in the top of a tree and send it through "the brute's body" and "forty or fifty yards beyond."

Unlike most Indians who had a subsistence life style, the Karankawas were magnificent physically. The men were tall and muscular and went nude or wore only a deerskin breechclout. They painted and tattooed their bodies extensively and pierced their nipples and lower lips with small pieces of cane. They loved contests of physical skill and were so adept at wrestling that other Indians referred to them as the Wrestlers. Women also had tattoos and wore skirts of skin or Spanish moss that reached to the knee. European observers recorded that unmarried women had a single stripe of paint running from the forehead across the nose and lips to the chin, and married women painted themselves with designs representing animals, birds, and flowers.

Social organization among the Karankawas depended on kinship-based groups of thirty or forty individuals, each with its own chief. The most basic unit, however, was the family. Men arranged marriages with the parents of their brides who, because of an incest taboo, were usually from other bands. The couple then lived with the husband's family, and an in-law taboo existed between the husband and the bride's family. They never spoke or looked at each other. This taboo probably was meant to prevent conflict between groups. At least it ensured that Karankawa men had no mother-in-law difficulties.

Husbands and wives apparently paid little attention to issues of marital fidelity, but they generally remained together unless they failed to produce children. Parents were especially loving toward their children, in spite of the constant struggle to find food for family members. Europeans reported in amazement that Karankawa children nursed until they were twelve years of age, the reason being that the practice was essential to the health of the young when mature individuals might have to go without food for two or three days at a time. Of course, as soon as they could, children had to contribute to their family's subsistence.

Karankawa spiritual life depended on a belief in two gods with whom shamans served as intermediaries. Several ceremonies or *mitotes* conducted by shamans marked key events of religious significance. After especially successful fishing or hunting expeditions, huge quantities of an intoxicating tea were made from leaves of the yaupon, a shrub-like tree native to south Texas. Men drank and danced for three days; women were prohibited from even passing by the pot while the tea was cooking. Ceremonies of thanksgiving took place immediately and ended in a relatively short time, but rites following deaths took much time. When a boy or young man died, his parents and kin wept for him three times a day for an entire year. Burials, except for those of shamans, were in shallow graves near campsites. Shamans were cremated, and a year later relatives drank their ashes mixed with water, more than likely with the purpose of keeping their magic alive.

Southwest of the Karankawas, in the region stretching from the Guadalupe River southward across the Río Grande and including all of southern Texas, lived yet another group of hunters and gatherers—the Coahuiltecans. The name for these Indians derived from the Spanish adjective meaning "native of Coahuila," but the extent to which they shared any ethnic or cultural unity with each other or with Indians from the Mexican state of Coahuila remains unknown. Divided and subdivided into several hundred autonomous groups, the Coahuiltecans may not even have spoken dialects of the same language. Clearly, however, they had the same basic lifestyle, drawing a crude subsistence from the land.

The Coahuiltecans lived in the poorest part of Texas in terms of natural resources and roved constantly in search of food. Deer and javelina provided meat, but apparently these animals were not numerous and could not be killed without considerable effort or ingenuity. Sometimes the Indians, showing almost unimaginable endurance, simply ran down a deer. On other occasions hunters drove deer into the Gulf where the animals drowned or used encircling fires to drive them to a point where they could easily be killed. Javelina were taken by digging and disguising pitfalls. Plant foods were available, too, including several not generally known to gatherers farther north on the coast. Pecan trees grew along the Guadalupe and Nueces, and mesquite thickets were common from the Nueces to the Río Grande. Coahuiltecans used mesquite beans, which are sweet and nutritious, as a staple in their diet. Pounded into a coarse flour, the beans could be prepared in many ways and stored as well. One recipe called for digging a hole in the ground and using it as a place to pound beans to a flour. The mixture of bean flour and earth that became mixed with it was then put in a container, covered with water, and drunk. Finally, like the first Texas hunter-gatherers in the lower Pecos Valley, the South Texas Indians also ate the fruit or tuna of the prickly pear cactus and the bulb of the sotol plant. The tuna were consumed raw or preserved by drying, and sotol bulbs were roasted in pits and ground into flour.

Regardless of this seemingly broad array of food sources, the Coahuiltecans, either out of necessity or practice, ate virtually anything that the human digestive system could handle. They consumed everything that moved—spiders, worms, lizards, and snakes, for example—and some things that did not, including ant eggs, rotten wood, and deer dung. Uncleaned fish were roasted and then set aside long enough for the larvae of flies and other insects to develop in the rotting meat. Then, the larvae were consumed as a delicacy, along with the rest of the fish. Modern sensibilities are offended by such omnivorous people, but only an adequate food supply stands between most humans and the willingness to eat whatever is available.

Coahuiltecans had few tools and weapons. They lived in small, movable huts made of bent saplings covered with reed mats or hides. Curved sticks served as all-purpose tools used to dig and to throw at small game. Gourds rather than ceramics provided storage for mesquite or sotol flour and water. Large net bags made of plant fibers held most of the things that were transported from place to place. The bow and arrow was their primary weapon.

Social organization and spiritual life among the Coahuiltecans generally resembled that among their fellow hunter-gatherers along the Gulf coast. They spent most of their time in family units, joining others to form larger groups during certain hunting and harvest seasons. Bands had headmen and shamans, but the authority of these leaders was limited, particularly when it came to the "every man for himself" matter of obtaining food. Like the Karankawas, the Coahuiltecans had strong beliefs in the supernatural and celebrated thanksgivings or appealed for approval and assistance from the gods in numerous ceremonies or *mitotes*. They differed from the Karankawas, however, in having the potent hallucinogen, peyote, as a stimulant in their celebrations. A typical *mitote* began around sundown with the arrival of guests from other groups and the building of a fire to cook meat. Men and women, after eating peyote or drinking it as tea, then danced through the night to the rhythm provided by a drum and a gourd rattle. Dancing around the fire in a close-knit circle and continuing to consume peyote, some of the dancers fell into trances from which they were aroused by being scratched with a pointed instrument. The ceremony ended at daybreak. No doubt such *mitotes* were as much a social event as a religious experience, but many peoples blend the two.

Coahuiltecan bands did not have the resources or unity to be warlike, but they constantly feuded with each other and occasionally fought small-scale wars. Conflicts generally arose, as might be expected, over food sources such as tuna cactus grounds. Women goaded and taunted the men of one band into attacking another by chanting and shouting about injuries received at the hands of the other. Men then initiated war by sending an emissary to the camp of the band to be attacked where he shot arrows into a tree and performed a war dance. If the ensuing attack proved successful, the victorious warriors brought scalps or captives back to their camps. The scalps, placed on poles, served as the focal point for a victory dance by the warriors and women. Captives were roasted and eaten.

The poorest of all Indians in late prehistoric Texas, the Coahuiltecans, would be the only group genuinely accepting of missionary efforts by the Spanish. Perhaps their lack of organization and the constant struggle for subsistence made them less secure in their own ways and therefore more susceptible to the promise of a mission lifestyle.

To the northwest of the Coahuiltecans in the region where the Pecos River reaches the Río Grande, Indians continued to live for the last thousand years before the arrival of Europeans essentially as they had for the previous five millennia. Having successfully combined a hunter-gatherer economy with using rock shelters and caves as homes, they made no basic changes such as developing the crop production or ceramics manufacture found elsewhere in Texas. They continued to eat deer, small game, and fish and to collect plants, seeds, and berries. Eventually they began to use the bow and arrow, but in general their implements remained the same. A bag from this era found in Hinds Cave in Val Verde County contained bundles of deer sinew, a buckskin thong, pink pigment, stone blades and projectile points in various states of manufacture, flaking tools made of deer antlers, a hammerstone, a perforated terrapin shell, and more than a hundred mountain laurel and buckeye seeds. These contents amounted to the portable tool kit of a lower Pecos River valley hunter-gatherer about a thousand years ago.

No historic name such as Caddo or Karankawa can be given to these Indians of the lower Pecos in the late prehistoric years. By the time Europeans arrived, they had disappeared as a distinct group. Perhaps some moved south into Mexico; others may have joined nomadic groups to the west. Apparently, the resources that had supported at least a small human population for some nine thousand years became inadequate in the eyes of residents—and have largely been seen that way ever since.

The land along the middle Río Grande from the Big Bend to present-day El Paso served as a home in the late prehistoric period to a people called the Jumanos (probably from the Spanish word for "human"), one of the least known groups of early Texans. The origins of their language are unclear, and they did not share a common ethnic background or a tightly unified culture. They may have been related to the Puebloan civilization of New Mexico or simply descended from prehistoric ancestors in that particular region. In any case, it seems reasonably clear that the Jumanos grew corn, beans, squash, and sunflowers in the valleys near the Río Grande that had enough moisture to produce crops as a result of runoff or occasional stream rises. The Jumanos also hunted buffalo on the plains to the north where they killed the animals with bows and arrows and brought home hides and dried meat. Early Spanish explorers reported that the Jumanos were especially active as traders, carrying out the exchange of food, pottery and blankets, and salt between groups as far apart as the Caddos of East Texas and the Pueblos of New Mexico.

The Jumanos who lived along the Río Grande did not build multiroomed, several-storied dwellings typical of the Puebloan people but instead lived in separate houses clustered together. Rectangular in shape and about twenty-eight to thirty feet in size, most of the houses were sunken half below ground level, with the half above ground constructed of adobe bricks. Saplings and brush covered with adobe made the roofs. Inside walls were plastered and painted in places. Such buildings were adapted perfectly to the environment, offering cool quarters during the summer and suffering little damage from the region's light rainfall.

Jumanos used hard gourds very effectively in a form of cooking known as stone-boiling. Cooks began by filling a gourd with water and building a fire to heat stones. They then placed the stones in the gourd to bring the water to a boil, after which the food to be cooked was added. Cooling stones were replaced with hot ones until the meal was ready.

Physically, the Jumanos resembled the Karankawas, being impressively tall and muscular. Men wore a minimum of clothing, but women had ponchos and skirts of deerskin. Little is known of their social or political organization, but personal conflict and warfare between groups seems to have been minimal. Their culture flourished from approximately 1000 to the early 1700s and then declined rapidly, probably due to the increasingly arid climate, which ruined their crops and drove away the buffalo, and disease brought by Europeans.

During the years of Jumano domination in the Trans-Pecos, another group, one destined to be of far greater importance in the early history of

Texas, appeared in the Panhandle-Plains region. Called Apaches, they spoke Athapaskan, a language common to Indians in Alaska and Canada. Attracted by the wealth of the Puebloans of New Mexico, they broke away from their northern brethren and moved south along the eastern side of the Rocky Mountains in the twelfth or thirteenth century until they reached the Southwest. They warred with Indians already in the region—their name probably came from the Zuñi word for "enemy"—and after about 1300 established themselves in Texas as the primary residents of the present-day Panhandle and the plains area from the headwaters of the Brazos River westward into New Mexico. The easternmost group, those destined to play the most important role in Texas, became known as Lipan Apaches. Mescalero Apaches occupied the region west of the Pecos River.

During the late prehistoric period, Apaches—or more specifically, Apache women—practiced some agriculture, growing corn, beans, squash, and pumpkins. Also, like other Indians in western Texas they gathered the bulbs of the sotol and century plants. Even then, however, most drew their subsistence primarily from the buffalo. Hunts took place in the spring and fall when huge herds appeared on the South Plains. Hunters surrounded the animals and moved in for the kill with bows and arrows. In the off-season when buffalo were less plentiful, individual hunters waited in ambush at watering places. When an Apache killed a buffalo, very little went to waste. The hunter first opened the body and ate the liver raw. Intestines were cleaned and roasted. Likewise, heads and leg bones were roasted, and the latter were cracked open for marrow. All the meat not consumed on the spot was smoked or sun dried. Hides provided clothing, tent covers, and shields. Sinews were used as bow strings and thongs. Stomachs served as portable water containers. The hunters were successful and efficient enough to produce a surplus of meat and hides that they traded with Pueblo groups in New Mexico for cotton blankets and pottery.

Apache bands in Texas lived part of the time near the crops that they cultivated, but they also moved regularly in pursuit of the buffalo. Women loaded tipi covers and other belongings on travois that were dragged by large shaggy dogs. Historical observers expressed surprise at how well trained the dogs were, but eventually of course they would be replaced as a beast of burden by the horse.

Families served as the basic social unit in Apache life. Quite the opposite of the Karankawa practice, marriage among the Apaches meant that the man, in addition to providing numerous gifts to his bride's family, took up residence with them. Thus, families consisted of parents, unmarried sons, daughters, and sons-in-law. When sons married, they moved away, leaving the sons-in-law to provide for the family. Even if a married daughter died, the son-in-law had a responsibility to her family and could not leave. The family usually provided another wife, if possible a sister or cousin of the deceased.

Several extended families lived together and joined other similar units to form bands for purposes of defense and offense. Each band had a leader chosen for his bravery and wisdom, but the position was not necessarily hereditary. Younger men, seeking to demonstrate their courage and thus become leaders, tended to ignore older chiefs. This approach to leadership made it difficult for Europeans to deal with the Texas Apaches—an agreement with one band did not always bind all its members, let alone any other group.

Apaches believed in harmony in their world and society. Disharmony among their people, created by lying or theft, for example, led to disturbances in nature such as extreme weather, sickness, and death. Death brought ghosts who acted as threats to the harmony of the living. To avoid ghosts, the dead were buried quickly and all their possessions were destroyed. In order to confuse ghosts that might be in pursuit, burial parties returned to camp by a different route than the one taken to the grave site. The family of the deceased moved its tipi and avoided contact with others for a time in case of contamination by ghosts. To avoid provoking the ghost, the name of the deceased was not spoken again. Apparently, this practice so depleted the list of Apache names that they began to use Spanish names.

There is no indication that the Apaches fought earlier inhabitants for land in Texas, as they had in New Mexico and Arizona, but successful warriors always had places of honor in Apache society. A man who could "count coup" by touching a living enemy in battle or take captives to become slaves was assured of respect.

Three groups to be considered last among the Indians of prehistoric Texas occupied the northern Panhandle and the prairies of north-central Texas at about the same time that the Apaches approached the Panhandle and plains region from the west. These groups had a lifestyle that differed notably from the Apaches, however, and all disappeared before the arrival of Europeans, leaving only a fascinating archeological record from about 1200 to 1500. None of these groups has a historical name, so they are known by cultural designations assigned by archeologists. The first, the Antelope Creek phase, includes Indians who lived in villages extending across the northern Panhandle along the Canadian River; the second, the Henrietta focus, includes those who occupied sites in north-central Texas on the upper Brazos River and its tributaries; the third, the Wylie focus, includes residents of the area in and around the cross timbers on the upper reaches of the Trinity River.

All three groups of these late prehistoric Indians depended on hunting, gathering, and agriculture. Buffalo were, of course, the preferred animal, but they also killed deer, antelope, and smaller animals. They collected local plant products such as hackberries and grew corn, squash, and beans in fields near the streams. All used the bow and arrow in hunting, and they had a wide array of stone and bone tools. One especially interesting adaptation was the use of the scapula (the large flat "shoulder blade") of buffalo as a hoe for cultivating crops. Their ceramics appear to have come primarily through trade with the Caddos to the east and the Pueblos to the west.

Indians who shaped the Antelope Creek phase differed dramatically from all their neighbors in one respect—the architecture of their homes. Borrowing, it seems, from the Puebloan people of New Mexico, they built villages that consisted of large rectangular buildings divided into a number of adjoining rooms. Foundations consisted of stone slabs, and walls were of masonry or adobe. Four interior posts situated around a central hearth in the main room supported the roof, which was either flat or hipped with grass thatch. The larger main room had benches in a work area; some of the smaller auxiliary rooms had storage pits. Located on high ground overlooking the Canadian River, these pueblo-style structures undoubtedly provided comfortable homes, and yet the culture their residents built lasted only a relatively short time.

By 1500 the Antelope Creek phase and the Henrietta and Wylie focuses in the northern Panhandle and north-central Texas had disappeared—destroyed, it seems, by drought and other Indians. The peoples who created these cultures cannot be connected with certainty to historical Indian groups. Many archeologists, however, believe that the Wichita Indians descended in part from peoples of the Henrietta Focus.

Humans occupied Texas for more than ten thousand years before the arrival of Europeans early in the sixteenth century. These first Texans proved remarkably adaptive in finding ways to survive as climatic changes altered plant and animal life in the region. Much of Texas, as its weather slowly became drier and hotter, presented ever-increasing challenges to survival, but from the early big game hunters to the late prehistoric Indians, those challenges were met. Some of the first Texans, most notably the Caddos, eventually built advanced cultures and lived in considerable comfort; others led extremely difficult lives. All, however, exhibited inventiveness and a tenacious will to live.

Chapter 2

EXPLORATION AND ADVENTURE, 1519–1689

The first Europeans to reach Texas came from Spain, a development that was anything but accidental. Having spent nearly eight hundred years reconquering their own country, the Spanish were uniquely qualified to conquer new frontiers. Muslims from North Africa called Moors occupied virtually all of Spain in 711–718, and the fight to drive the invaders out continued intermittently until the fall of Granada in 1492. This war of reconquest brought unity to Spain and inextricably linked the Roman Catholic Church with the government. When Ferdinand of Aragon and Isabella of Castile, who married in 1469, took over the thrones of their respective kingdoms ten years later, Spain had the unity necessary not only to defeat the Moors but to expand into other lands as well. Centuries of fighting Muslim invaders intensified Spanish Catholicism, providing a spiritual motivation for further conquests. Once Ferdinand and Isabella neared their goal—"one nation, one monarchy, one faith"—at home, they were well prepared to look outward for new worlds to conquer.

In addition to building political unity and religious motivation, the reconquest prepared Spain for exploration and conquest in one other way as well. It elevated the profession of soldier to equal that of priest or lawyer in Spanish society. War brought excitement and glory and placed a premium on individual courage and pride. After the defeat of the Moors, young men, especially those from proud but poor families, needed new opportunities to realize their ambitions and serve their faith. The accidental discovery of America by Columbus in 1492 was an answer to their dreams. As one conqueror later said when asked his reasons for going to Mexico: "We came to serve God and get rich." Perhaps he misstated his priorities, but the two objectives did go hand in hand. Would-be conquistadors believed many fantastic legends about the New World—stories, for example, about giants, amazons, and headless people with eyes in their navels—but above all they expected to find incredible riches. As it turned out, the Americas provided enough gold and silver to cause general inflation in Europe, but men who sought mountains

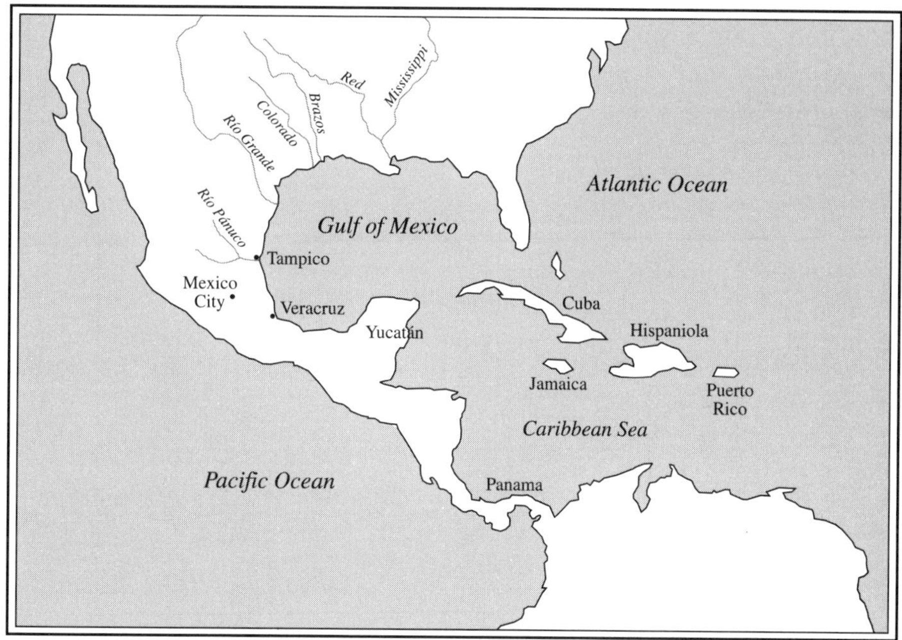

The Caribbean Sea and Gulf of Mexico

of silver and gold so plentiful that Indians tipped arrows with them would be sorely disappointed in Texas.

The First Spanish Explorers in Texas

Columbus's first voyage of discovery quickly led to the creation of a Spanish empire in America, based first on islands in the Caribbean Sea. The Spanish had no doubts concerning their right to these lands because Pope Alexander VI's Line of Demarcation in 1493 coupled with the Treaty of Tordesillas the following year gave them title to all of the Americas except Brazil. In 1493, Columbus himself settled a permanent colony on Hispaniola, later called Santo Domingo, and other explorers soon took over Puerto Rico (1508), Jamaica (1509), and Cuba (1511). (See map: The Caribbean Sea and Gulf of Mexico.) Indians on these islands resisted, but the Spanish had far too many advantages over the natives. First, and most important, weapons made of steel and the use of gunpowder overmatched anything the Indians could offer in a fight and terrified them as well. Second, the Spanish had the ships to cover long distances of open sea and carry supplies. Third, their horses provided mobility and speed that the Indians could not match on land. Fourth, the Spanish brought Old World diseases such as smallpox, measles, and cholera that eventually would decimate the Indians. Bringing God and the search for gold to the Caribbean proved relatively easy.

Building on their base of island colonies, the Spanish next entered the Gulf of Mexico and began to explore the coast of North America. Juan Ponce de León reached Florida in 1513, and Vasco Núñez de Balboa crossed the Isthmus of Panama the same year. Four years later exploration of the coast of Mexico began, opening the way for the famed conquest of the Aztec Empire by Hernando Cortés in 1519–1521.

By 1519, Spanish explorers had sailed the Gulf of Mexico along the western coast of Florida and the coast of Mexico from Yucatán north to the site of present-day Tampico. The possibility remained, however, that between Florida and Mexico there existed a water route to Asia. With this in mind, Francisco de Garay, the governor of Jamaica, financed an exploration of the northern Gulf. Garay was a lucky man. He and a partner on Hispaniola found a huge gold nugget worth 36,000 pesos, which he parlayed into a livestock venture and then a governorship. Perhaps his luck would hold, and he would find a southerly version of the famed "northwest passage."

Garay outfitted an expedition of four ships and 270 men and put it under the command of Alonso Alvarez de Pineda. Leaving Jamaica early in 1519, the explorers sailed to Florida and then westward along the Gulf coast to Villa Rica de la Veracruz (near present-day Veracruz) in Mexico. On July 2, Pineda noted a tremendous discharge of fresh water into the Gulf from a river that he called the Río del Espíritu Santo because of the feast day on which it was discovered. Eventually, this river would become known by its Indian name, Mississippi, meaning "Big River." Soon after passing the Mississippi, Pineda and his men became the first Europeans to see and chart the coast of Texas. He described "very good land" and fine looking rivers and ports. After reaching Veracruz, Pineda sailed back north again as far as the Río Pánuco, entered it and spent forty days repairing his ships, and then returned to Jamaica.

Some historians have insisted that the Pineda expedition actually entered the Río Grande rather than the Pánuco and thus became the first Europeans to set foot in Texas. This claim apparently received support from the discovery in 1974 at Boca Chica near Brownsville of a clay tablet inscribed with a description of Pineda's supposed stop there. The "Pineda Stone," however, incorrectly spells the captain's name with a tilde over the n and uses a slash on the number 7, a practice that did not begin until the nineteenth century. Most scholars believe that it is a fake. The whole issue serves best as an example of what might be called "Texas Nationalism," the desire to enlarge the significance of every aspect of the state's past. If the first European to see and chart the coast of Texas actually landed on the Río Grande, then it makes Texas that much more important.

The careers of the men first responsible for European contact with Texas did not come to a happy end. In 1520 Governor Garay attempted to follow up on Pineda's discoveries by sending the explorer back to plant a colony on the Pánuco. However, Indians in the area killed Pineda and most of his soldiers. Garay himself then went to the Pánuco in 1523 only to find that Cortés had moved north from central Mexico and conquered that region as well and by royal decree had been given control of all of New Spain. Accepting the situation, Garay visited Cortés in Mexico City, where he fell violently ill and died after dining with the conqueror following a Christmas Eve mass.

Somewhat ironically, Cortés, who was at least partly responsible for the death of Garay and his claims, had a hand in creating the next Spanish contact with Texas. The chain of events unfolded as follows: Cortés's sponsor for the expedition to Mexico in 1519, Governor Diego de Velázquez of Cuba, quickly discovered that the man he had chosen as commander was far too independent. Governor Velázquez therefore sent an army under the command of Panfilo de Narváez to Mexico in 1520 to arrest Cortés and take over the expedition. Cortés, however, defeated the force sent after him, and in the battle Narváez took a spear thrust that gouged out his right eye. Disgraced, Narváez eventually returned to Spain where he complained bitterly to royal officials about his treatment by the conqueror. Compensation finally came to the "one eyed casualty" in November 1526 in the form of a royal contract permitting him to settle a colony in Florida, at that time meaning the entire Gulf coast from present-day Florida to the Río Pánuco. In 1528 Narváez and some of his men would unintentionally reach Texas while trying to sail from Florida to Mexico. Thus, a spear thrust by one of Cortés's soldiers in 1520 led Spaniards to the shores of Texas eight years later.

Narváez raised an expedition of six hundred men and five ships that left Spain for the Caribbean in June 1527. His second in command and treasurer, a man destined to become far more famous than the commander, had the strange name, Alvar Núñez Cabeza de Vaca. Translated "Cow's Head," this family name carried considerable prestige because it had been won by an ancestor during the Reconquest when he contributed to a great victory over the Moors by marking an unguarded mountain pass with the skull of a cow. The name actually descended from Cabeza de Vaca's mother rather than his father, another indication that it was a point of pride. Nearly forty at the time, Cabeza de Vaca received the appointment because of his record as a soldier and faithful servant of Emperor Charles V. A better man could not have been chosen.

The Narváez expedition spent the winter of 1527–1528 in the Caribbean, stopping at Hispaniola and Cuba. Ill-fated practically from the beginning, it lost 140 men to desertion in Hispaniola and suffered through a devastating hurricane on Cuba. After refitting, five ships and four hundred men sailed from Cuba to the western coast of Florida in April 1528. Narváez then decided to take three hundred men and go inland to find gold and a site for settlement, while sending the ships ahead to meet them at another point on the coast. Cabeza de Vaca objected strongly but then accompanied his commander. The men who went inland soon became hopelessly separated from the ships. After reaching northwestern Florida in mid-June, they camped for three months and then, facing food shortages and unfriendly Indians, returned to the coast. Using great ingenuity, Narváez and his men built five boats of rough-sawn timber caulked with pine resin and made sails from their own clothes. Food came from slaughtering their horses, whose hides covered the boats and hair made rigging for the sails.

Leaving Florida in late September 1528, about 250 men in the five boats attempted to sail along the coast westward to Mexico. All went well for a month, but then water and food supplies ran short and storms separated the crude small craft. Two, including the one carrying Cabeza de Vaca, were swept toward the upper Texas coast. As Cabeza de Vaca's boat approached land, a great wave, in his words, lifted it "out of the water as far as a horseshoe can be tossed." He and the others who were able to walk scrambled overboard and struggled to shore through the surf. The date was November 6, 1528, and the weather was bitterly cold. On the previous day, another boat had landed nearby with about forty-eight survivors. The first European immigrants in Texas thus arrived involuntarily under anything but auspicious circumstances. They landed most likely on San Luis, a small island just west of Galveston Island, but their name for it, "Isla de Malhado," the island of misfortune, best expressed their feelings.

Karankawa Indians soon found the Spaniards, who in spite of being terribly frightened made no effort to fight because, in the words of Cabeza de Vaca, "there were scarcely six men who could even get up from the ground." The Karankawas were not hostile, however, and the next day brought food to the castaways. Strengthened by food and water, Cabeza de Vaca's group attempted to launch their boat again, but it capsized, drowning three of the men and casting the remainder up on the same beach. The survivors, he wrote, "were as naked as the day they were born." Indeed, naked and miserably cold, they presented such a sad spectacle that the Karankawas sat down with them and cried for half an hour. Seeing themselves the objects of pity by such "brutes" caused the Spanish to feel even worse, a foretaste of many things that would test their belief in inherent Christian superiority.

Once the two groups of survivors on Malhado joined, they chose four of the strongest and sent them westward along the coast in the hope that they could reach Pánuco and bring help. No rescuers came, of course, and by the spring of 1529 only fifteen of the Spaniards remained alive. The rest died of exposure, hunger, and dysentery. Some who survived did so by cannibalizing the bodies of those who died; an act that shocked the Indians who, although they practiced ritualistic cannibalism, could not imagine eating one of their own.

Two more of the Narváez expedition's boats made landfall farther west along the Texas coast. One wrecked at the mouth of the San Bernard River, and one carrying Narváez reached shore safely somewhere on Matagorda Island. The crews united and continued down the coast, some on land and others sailing close to the shore, but then a nighttime norther caused the boat to pull its anchor and drift out to sea. Narváez, bad-tempered as always, had argued with one of his lieutenants and was sleeping on the boat, so he disappeared with it. The other men soon met the same fate as most of those who had landed on Malhado.

Cabeza de Vaca survived the winter of 1528–1529, but near the beginning of spring, he traveled to the Texas mainland and became seriously ill there. Believing him dead, all but two of those still alive left Malhado to travel along the coast toward the Pánuco. After their departure, Cabeza de Vaca recovered and returned to Malhado, which he used as a home base for nearly four more years.

During the years he spent in the Galveston area, Cabeza de Vaca was at various times a doctor, a slave, and a merchant. The Karankawas demanded that he treat their ill, "without testing or asking for any degrees," he wrote. His ministrations, which consisted of reciting prayers, making the sign of the cross, and breathing on patients, apparently satisfied the Karankawas. For nearly a year, however, he was forced to live with other Indians who treated him almost like a slave. Later, he escaped and lived the life of a trader, taking coastal products such as seashells and sea snails into the interior and bringing back hides, red ocher, and flint for arrowheads and weapons.

Cabeza de Vaca remained near Malhado for such a long time in part because he did not want to leave the two Spaniards who stayed behind when the others departed in 1529. Finally, late in 1532, after one of the men died, he convinced the other to go with him. Traveling westward along the coast they met Indians who told of three other men like them who were being held captive and badly mistreated by another group of natives. To illustrate the plight of the other Spaniards, the Indians slapped and beat Cabeza de Vaca and his companion, so frightening the latter that he turned back toward Malhado and disappeared from history. Cabeza de Vaca, obviously much less faint of heart, continued on, and several days later in the area of the Guadalupe River met Alonso Castillo Maldonado, Andrés Dorantes de Carranza, and Estevanico, a slave who belonged to Dorantes. (Estevanico, a nonwhite native of Azamor on the Atlantic coast of Morocco was the first of many enslaved people of African descent who would come to Texas.) The "Four Ragged Castaways," as they became known, would continue their adventure together for about four years.

Cabeza de Vaca joined Dorantes, Estevanico, and Maldonado as a slave to groups of Coahuiltecan Indians. They immediately began to plan an escape, but for one reason or another, especially because they belonged to different groups and spent much of the time apart, nearly two years passed before a good opportunity presented itself. Finally, in September 1534 the four escaped and headed south. Exactly where they went during the next two years is subject to much debate among historians, but the best evidence indicates that their route took them in a southerly direction across the Río Grande to the area of present-day Monterrey, Mexico, then to the northwest back into Texas at present-day Presidio, and finally in a western direction across the Río Grande south of El Paso and through northern Mexico to the outpost of Culiacán near the Pacific Ocean. (See map: Routes of Exploration: Cabeza de Vaca, Coronado, and Moscoso.) Some have posited routes that have Cabeza de Vaca and his companions never leaving Texas until they headed west from near El Paso, but these claims probably should be filed with the "Pineda Stone" under the heading of Texas Nationalism.

The Four Ragged Castaways reached Culiacán early in 1536, having traveled about two thousand miles by foot in less than two years. In 1542 Cabeza

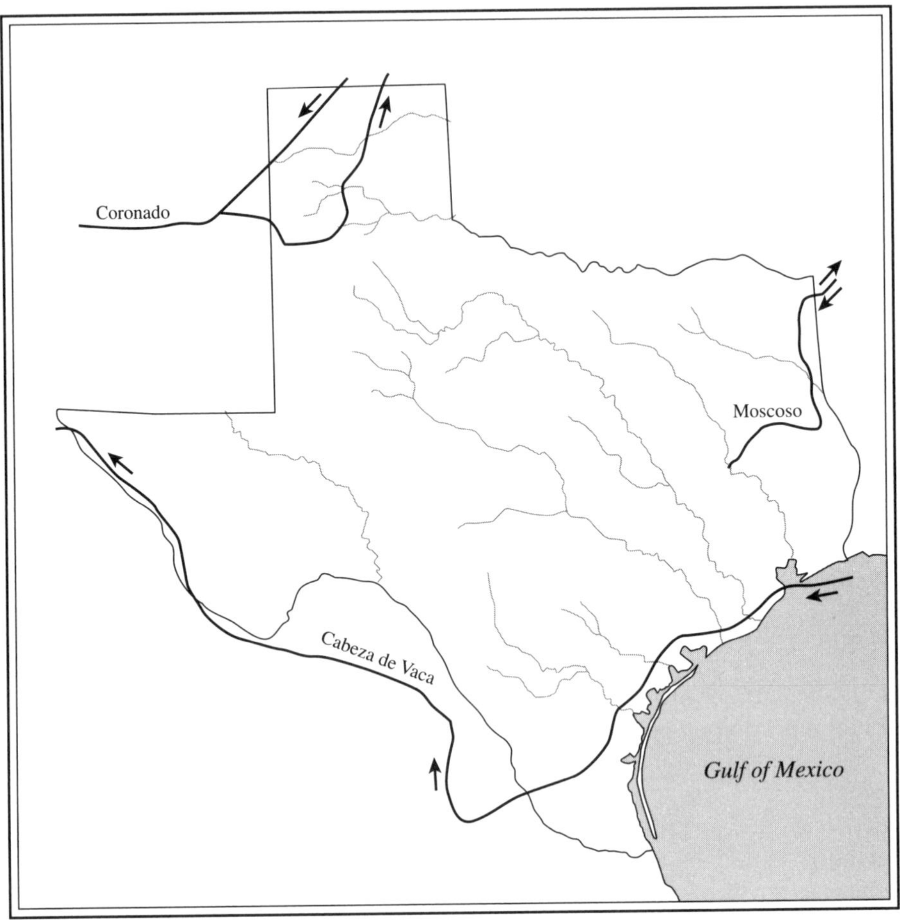

Routes of Exploration: Cabeza de Vaca, Coronado, and Moscoso

de Vaca published an account of his adventures that has the distinction of being the first book relating to Texas. Best known as the *Relación*, this book is especially important for the observations of Indian life that made Cabeza de Vaca the first ethnologist of Texas. He offered accounts of Karankawa and Coahuiltecan cultural practices in often chilling detail. Consider, for example, his description of how several Coahuiltecan groups treated female infants: "When their daughters are born they cast them to the dogs, which eat them. The reason for doing this, according to them, is that all the people of that land are their enemies with whom they are constantly at war, and if their enemies were to marry their daughters, they would multiply so much that they would conquer them and take them as slaves. For this reason they preferred to kill their daughters rather than have them bear offspring who would be their enemies. We asked them why they did not marry their daughters to their own men and they replied that they considered it an unseemly thing to marry them to their relatives and that it was better to kill them than to give them to their relatives or their enemies. . . . When they want to get married, they buy wives from their enemies, each one paying the price of the best bow he has and two arrows. . . . They kill their own children and buy the children of strangers."

Cabeza de Vaca described the Jumanos of the Trans-Pecos region as "Cow People" because they hunted buffalo once a year. Actually, he was probably the first European to see bison, having come in contact with them while enslaved by the Coahuiltecans. These "cows," he wrote, "have two small horns, like Moorish cattle, and very long hair, like a fine blanket made from the wool of merino sheep. Some are brownish and others black. It seems to me that they have more and better meat than cattle here in Spain. From the small ones the Indians make blankets to cover themselves, and from the large ones they make shoes and shields."

Cabeza de Vaca also continued to act as a physician while on the trek to the west. In northern Mexico he removed an arrowhead from the chest of an Indian, thus performing the first surgery by a European in the American Southwest. Describing how he closed the Indian's chest after the operation, he wrote: "With a deer bone, I practiced my trade as a physician and gave him two stitches. After I had stitched, he was losing a lot of blood. I stopped the bleeding with hair scraped from an animal skin. . . . The following day I cut the stitches and the Indian was healed." More than four hundred years later, his feat was the subject of an article in the prestigious *New England Journal of Medicine,* and the insignia of the Texas Surgical Society to this day features the skull of a cow and an arrow. Somewhat ironically, considering Cabeza de Vaca's role as a healer, he and other members of the Narváez expedition probably introduced some of the diseases that would eventually decimate the Indians of Texas, reducing the populations of some groups by as much as 90 percent.

The Spaniards who met Cabeza de Vaca and his Spanish companions near Culiacán barely recognized them as coming from Europe. For that matter, Indians in the area had the same difficulty, although for different reasons. They were confused by the differences between the Four Ragged Castaways and the Spanish, who were engaged in capturing slaves. You, they said to Cabeza de Vaca, "healed the sick and they killed the healthy." You "gave away everything that was given to [you] and kept none of it, while the sole purpose of the others was to steal everything they found. . . ."

Reaching Mexico City in July 1536, the castaways found a highly motivated listener to their stories of adventure in the person of Antonio de Mendoza, Viceroy of New Spain. Mendoza especially liked Cabeza de Vaca's claim that he had seen "undeniable indications of gold" in northwestern Mexico and that Indians had told him of a great city to the north. These stories revived a belief in the legendary Seven Cities of Cíbola, fabulously rich cities supposedly settled by seven Portuguese bishops fleeing Muslim invaders in the eighth century, and led to the first authorized expedition into the borderlands of New Spain.

In the spring of 1539 Viceroy Mendoza sent Fray Marcos de Niza, a priest with experience in the conquest of Central and South America, to explore northern Mexico. Estevanico, who served as a guide, probably because Mendoza had bought him from Dorantes, tired of the party's slow pace and convinced Niza to permit him to scout ahead. He was to communicate by sending crosses back to the main party; the larger the cross, the greater the amount of wealth he had found. Could there have been a more perfect combination of God and gold? In any case, Estevanico sent back progressively larger and larger crosses but, apparently carried away by his independence, he began to enter Indian towns and make excessive demands on his own. As a result, Zuñi Indians in Háwikuh, a village in what is now western New Mexico, killed him. Fray de Niza, frightened and frustrated, returned to Mendoza and reported that Estevanico had lost his life in a city larger than Mexico City. He claimed to have seen it himself from a distance and predicted that Cíbola, as Háwikuh and the other pueblos north of it became known, would yield more gold and silver than any previous Spanish conquest.

Viceroy Mendoza, now more interested than ever in conquering Cíbola before some other adventurer arrived, organized an army of 370 Spaniards and 1,000 Indians under the command of Francisco Vázquez de Coronado and sent it north early in 1540. Coronado, the second son of a family that gave its entire estate to the firstborn son, was a classic, if inexperienced, conquistador. He had come to Mexico with Mendoza in 1535 and rose quickly under the viceroy's patronage. His borderlands expedition would not bring the riches that he sought, but it would enshrine his name in the history of Texas.

Guided by Fray Niza, Coronado reached Cíbola in July 1540, but instead of cities of gold, he found only shabby pueblos inhabited by hostile Indians. Coronado sent scouting parties to the west where they found Hopi towns and viewed the Grand Canyon, but, again, found no riches. In the meantime, encouraged by Indians from the east who spoke of towns and "cattle" beyond the mountains, he sent a small force to explore in that direction. This party reached the country of the Tiguex Indians on the Río Grande just north of present-day Albuquerque and moved on to Pecos, a point east of present-day Santa Fe where pueblo and plains Indians met to trade. At Pecos the Spanish acquired the services of two plains Indians as guides. Ysopete and the Turk, as the Spanish called them, led the explorers down the Pecos River and then eastward along the headwaters of the Canadian River. Near the Texas Panhandle, they encountered bison so numerous that one Spaniard compared them to "fish in the sea." The thrill of seeing and killing buffalo quickly paled, however, when the Turk began to tell about Quivira, a land of great riches on the plains to the north, a place where "golden jingle bells" hung from a tree. This exciting lie caused the scouting party to rush back to the main army on the Río Grande.

Coronado's army, now some 1,800 strong thanks to Pueblo captives forced into service as porters, left the Tiguex region in April 1541 and moved eastward, retracing the route to Pecos taken by the small exploring party the previous year. The expedition's exact route from that point on will never be known, but a "Coronado Corridor," as one scholar has termed it, may be traced with reasonable certainty. A few weeks' travel in a southeasterly direction from Pecos brought the army within sight of a giant mesa that would be called the Llano Estacado, literally the "stockaded plain," because the rimrock that marked its edge looked like the walls of a stockade or palisade. Perhaps the reconnoitering force had seen the Llano Estacado in 1540, but if so they had made no effort to describe this tableland topped by thirty thousand square miles of virtually flat grassland. Everyone had to see and describe it for himself. In the words of Coronado, the plains had "no more landmarks than as if we had been swallowed up in the sea, . . . because there was not a stone, nor a bit of rising ground, nor a tree, nor a shrub, nor anything to go by."

In mid-May 1541, the Spaniards, at the direction of the Turk, climbed onto the Llano a little southeast of present-day Tucumcari, New Mexico, and made their way forward on the sea of grass. They encountered groups of eastern Apaches who lived primarily by hunting the countless buffalo that virtually were never out of sight. The Querechos, as the Spanish called them, knew nothing, however, of Quivira as the Turk described it. After several weeks of following their guide's vague directions and changing their course to avoid huge buffalo herds, Coronado's army became lost. They were probably somewhere on the virtually flat, featureless plain between present-day Lubbock and Plainview. Coronado still wanted to believe the Turk about the riches of Quivira, but he no longer trusted him as a guide on the Llano. Using scouting parties and sea compasses, the commander moved his army in a northeasterly direction until it reached the canyon country on tributaries of the Red River, probably in present-day Briscoe County.

Coronado's men doubtless breathed a sigh of relief upon descending into Tule Canyon. There really was an end to the seemingly illimitable Llano. Almost immediately, however, a massive afternoon thunderstorm gave the Spaniards another lesson in the harsh West Texas environment. Strong winds and heavy rain were accompanied by torrents of hailstones "as big as bowls and larger." Hail dented helmets, knocked holes in tents, broke crockery, and stampeded the horses. As they surveyed the damage, the Spanish had to be thankful that at least the storm had not caught them on the open plain.

Indians whom the Spanish called the Teyas lived at the edge of the Llano Estacado and in the canyon country. Some scholars believe that the Teyas were Apaches; others have suggested that they were related to the Caddos to the east; still others argue for an origin among the Pueblos to the west. Curiously, in spite of being unable to agree on an identification of the Teyas, a few scholars have suggested that the word "Texas" came from Teyas, which the Spanish translated as "fierce warriors." This is almost certainly incorrect, but if Texas really were named for the Teyas, then the state motto would have to be changed from "Friendship" to "Don't Mess With Texans."

The Teyas provided guides to the region and helped with the gathering of food but did not offer any encouraging information on Quivira. Refusing to give up, Coronado decided to take a party of thirty mounted men and push ahead. The rest of his army would return to the Tiguex country and wait. Coronado's party, guided now by Ysopete because the Spanish had lost faith in the Turk, left the canyon country and traveled north by northeast through the Texas Panhandle, across the Oklahoma Panhandle, and into present-day Kansas. After crossing the Arkansas River they came to Quivira near the modern town of Lindsborg, Kansas. Instead of cities of gold and silver, however, they found only the grass huts and cornfields of the Wichita Indians. The Wichitas spoke a Caddoan language and shared the sedentary, agricultural lifestyle of the East Texas Caddos. Coronado ordered the execution of the Turk who had been held in chains since misleading the army on the Llano, and his party returned to the Río Grande by a route that took them across the northwestern part of the Texas Panhandle near modern Dalhart. After wintering in the Tiguex country, during which time Coronado suffered a riding injury that discouraged further explorations, the expedition returned to Mexico in 1542.

Coronado's expedition, in addition to being a great adventure story, provided information on the land, resources, and Indians of the Panhandle. His leadership, especially in crossing the Llano Estacado, was admirable. And yet, he and his superiors considered the expedition a failure. It found no riches, only people who, in his words, "do not plant anything and do not have any houses except of skins and sticks [and] wander around with the cows." Coronado lived another dozen years in Mexico, but he never commanded another venture of any sort.

While Coronado explored the western reaches of Texas in 1541, another Spanish expedition approached the region from the east. Hernando de Soto, like Coronado the second son of a prosperous family who came to America to make a fortune, served with Francisco Pizarro in the conquest of Peru and became rich. Returning to Spain, he parlayed his experience and fortune into a grant in 1537 that gave him permission to explore and settle a huge colony somewhere within the expanse then known as Florida. De Soto landed with six hundred men in May 1539 and spent the next three years moving about the region from present-day Florida to Louisiana. His frankly avowed purpose of stealing anything he found of value meant constant trouble with the Indians but no riches. Finally, while camped on the Mississippi River in Louisiana, he died of an illness marked by a high fever. De Soto's men sank his body in the river to protect it from the Indians.

Upon De Soto's death, Luis de Moscoso Alvarado took command of the army and moved to the west, intending to travel overland to Mexico. His exact route, like those of Cabeza de Vaca and Coronado, is a matter of debate, but the best evidence is that in August 1542 his party entered Texas east of Atlanta in modern Cass County. Turning south, Moscoso traveled through Harrison County and on to the vicinity of San Augustine where he took a westward course across the Neches River and possibly beyond the Trinity River in Houston County.

While in East Texas, Moscoso's army encountered an Indian woman who may have set records for adventure and bad luck, even in an age of explorations frequently marked by misfortune. She had been a prisoner of one of

Coronado's captains, escaped while in the canyon country of the Panhandle in 1541, and made her way to East Texas where she wound up a captive of Moscoso in 1542. He, however, refused to believe her story about other white men to the west and retraced his route to the Mississippi. Had Moscoso taken her word, his army might have succeeded in marching overland to Mexico. As it was, they built boats, floated down the Mississippi, and made their way along the coast to their objective in 1543. They were forced ashore by a storm at one point, possibly at the mouth of the Sabine River, and used the opportunity to caulk their leaky boats with crude petroleum that surfaced naturally in the region. (Some 350 years later the Spindletop gusher would be brought in a few miles to the north.)

Moscoso had explored the land and made the first recorded contact with the Caddo Indians of East Texas, but he, like Cabeza de Vaca and Coronado, had found no riches. All of these great explorers and many of their companions wrote reports on the lands and peoples that they visited, and all concluded that Texas was a gigantic expanse populated by generally inhospitable savages who had no gold or silver. They saw little purpose in further explorations and no reason to occupy the region. Thus, for fifty years following the explorations of the 1530s–1540s, the Spanish gave virtually no attention to Texas. And the equivalent of "GTT" did not appear on doors in New Spain in any truly significant way for more than a century.

Spanish Colonization of Northern Mexico and New Mexico

In 1546, only a few years after the return of Coronado and Moscoso, the Spanish found new sources of riches much closer to Mexico City than to faraway Texas when an exploring party discovered a mountain of silver ore at Zacatecas in the north-central plateau region. (See map: The Northern Frontier of New Spain, 1550–1710.) The resulting mining boom required roads to connect Zacatecas with Mexico City and moved the frontier north. Settlement of the region led to warfare with the Chichimeca Indians; a conflict that was unlike any previously experienced by the Spanish in Mexico and led to the development of new institutions of conquest and colonization. Eventually, those new institutions, the presidio and the mission, would be vital to the settlement of Texas.

The Chichimecas, a diverse group of northern tribes described by the Aztecs and Spanish alike as "barbarians," did not live a sedentary, agricultural life. Instead, they were nomads who subsisted as hunter-gatherers and had awe-inspiring skills with the bow and arrow. Chichimeca bowmen could hit an orange thrown in the air and kill rabbits on the run. And their arrows struck with enough force to go through the neck of a horse and penetrate the armored breastplate of its rider. They prepared for battle with peyote and alcohol and entered the fight totally nude, "for the effect," the Spanish said.

War with the Chichimecas began in 1550 and continued for the remainder of the century. Finding that they could not defeat these Indians as they had others by destroying their crops and villages, the Spanish waged a "guerra

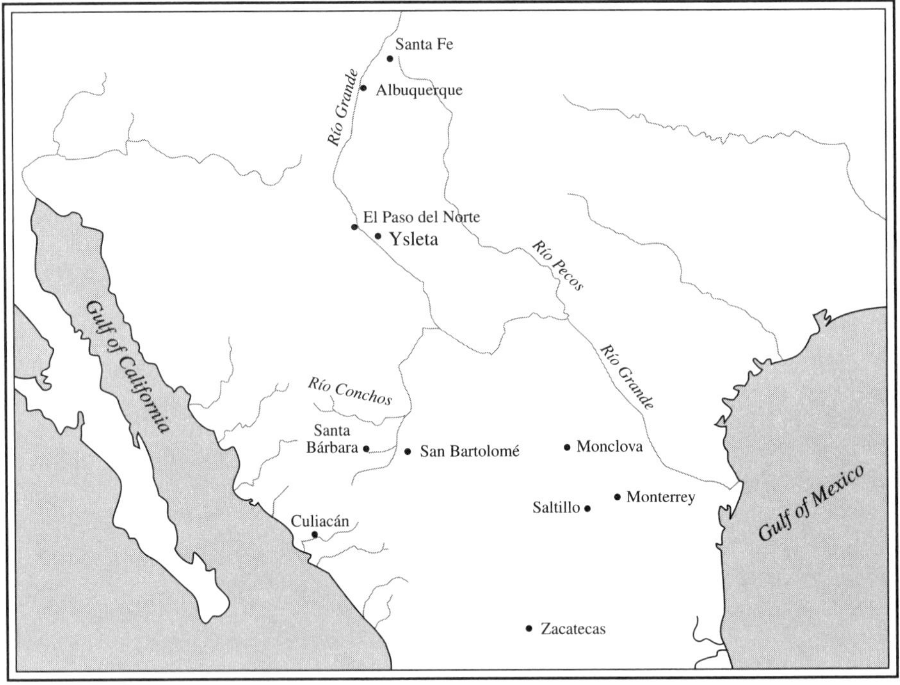

The Northern Frontier of New Spain, 1550–1710

a fuego y a sangre," but even a war of fire and blood did not pacify the frontier. Institutions that worked well to control sedentary Indians—for example, the *encomienda,* which gave control of the labor and spiritual lives of all the natives in a particular town or area to a wealthy miner or rancher—were of no use in dealing with nomads. Thus, out of necessity the Spanish developed the presidio and mission system.

Presidios were walled fortresses with garrisons of soldiers responsible for the security of a particular point or area. Built first along the road from Zacatecas to Mexico City, presidios probably angered the Chichimecas rather than pacifying them. Stationary fortresses rarely defeat mobile enemies. Nevertheless, presidios maintained a military presence on the frontier and offered protection to Spaniards in the immediate vicinity.

Missions were religious establishments staffed by Franciscan padres, members of the Roman Catholic order established by St. Francis of Assisi in 1206. Franciscan missions had three purposes: to bring the Indians to a settled life and Christianize them; to make the Indians into civilized, tax-paying subjects of the King of Spain; and to uphold Spanish claims against any other nation attempting to enter the area. Missionaries were chosen by the Franciscan college that trained them, but they were paid by the Crown. In contrast, then, to the conquistadors who came for "God and gold," the Franciscans worked for "God and country."

Presidios and missions, which were generally established near each other, did not defeat the Chichimecas, but by 1600 the Spanish had worn down or bought off the Indians. In the meantime, the mining and ranching frontier pushed farther and farther north in Mexico. One leader in this expansion, Luis de Carvajal, may have actually reached Texas as early as 1573. Operating under a commission from Viceroy Martín Enríquez, Carvajal explored northeastern Mexico and went to the mouth of the Río Grande to punish Indians for their treatment of shipwrecked Spanish sailors. One of the soldiers with this expedition testified that they crossed the river, which, if true, made them the first Spaniards to enter Texas from that direction on the lower Río Grande. Later, Carvajal went to Spain and in 1579 petitioned successfully for a huge grant that stretched from the Río Pánuco northward beyond the site of modern San Antonio, Texas. Returning to Mexico, he created a small settlement at modern-day Monclova and supposedly reconnoitered his land in Texas, although there are no records of such an exploration. Eventually Carvajal ran afoul of laws against enslaving Indians and died in prison, one of the first promoters to see grandiose plans involving Texas come to little or nothing.

Farther west in the 1560s and 1570s, miners and ranchers founded Santa Bárbara and San Bartolomé on tributaries of the Río Conchos, a river that flowed north to the Río Grande. These settlements soon became gateways for new explorations of New Mexico that also led into Texas. The first came in 1581 when three Franciscans led by Fray Agustín Rodríguez and a small escort of soldiers commanded by Francisco Sánchez Chamuscado left San Bartolomé to investigate the Pueblo country that had not been visited by Spaniards since Coronado's expedition. Descending the Río Conchos to the Río Grande, the Rodríguez party made contact with the Jumanos and then traveled upriver to El Paso and on to the Tiguex country north of present-day Albuquerque. They explored the region and did not return for nearly a year. Two of the Franciscans insisted on remaining in New Mexico in spite of the fact that the third, who had left the main party near Santa Fe, was killed by Indians.

The next year (1582) Spanish authorities, concerned for the safety of the friars who had remained in the Pueblo country, authorized another mission to the area. Led by Antonio de Espejo, two Franciscans and fifteen soldiers left the upper Río Conchos in November and retraced the route of the Rodríguez party to Albuquerque only to find both friars also had been martyred by Indians. Their return route took them eastward to the Pecos River, which they followed to the site of modern Pecos, Texas, where they left the river and headed directly for the Río Grande, passing near present-day Fort Davis and Marfa on the way. Espejo and his companions were the first Europeans to see the Trans-Pecos region; none would return for a century.

Renewed explorations of New Mexico led the Spanish government to authorize pacification of the Pueblo country by a private individual. Finding the right person took time, but finally in 1595 the contract was given to Juan de Oñate, a wealthy descendant of a discoverer of the silver mines at Zacatecas. In the meantime, a "wildcat" venture in colonizing New Mexico led to an interesting contact with Texas. Gaspar Castaño de Sosa, the lieutenant governor of Nuevo León, attempted in 1590 to make a settlement in New Mexico regardless of the fact that he had no authorization from the crown. Thinking, apparently, that success would cause officials to overlook illegal actions, Castaño de Sosa led a party of 170 men, women, and children across the Río Grande at the site of today's Del Rio and then up the Pecos all the way to the Pecos Pueblo east of modern Santa Fe. They fought their way into Pecos and then moved west to the Río Grande. Unfortunately for Castaño de Sosa, Spanish soldiers arrived in 1591 and sent him back to Mexico in chains for invading "lands of peaceable Indians." His expedition had pioneered a new route across Texas to New Mexico and a means of transportation as well, the use of two-wheeled carts on the plains.

Oñate acted on his contract, which obviously made it legal for him to occupy the lands of peaceable Indians, and colonized New Mexico in 1598. Three years later, still dreaming of riches in Quivira, he led an expedition to Kansas that crossed the Texas Panhandle on a route that followed the Canadian River. He confirmed Coronado's experience with Quivira and returned to New Mexico by the same route. Oñate resigned as governor in 1607, and two years later his successor, Pedro de Peralta, established Santa Fe as the capital of New Mexico, making it the third-oldest permanent European settlement in the present-day continental United States. Only St. Augustine, Florida (1565), and Jamestown, Virginia (1607), were older.

The move to occupy New Mexico thus brought some Spanish contact with the western reaches of Texas during the second half of the sixteenth century, but government officials still saw little reason to move into the interior. Religious leaders busied themselves with missionary work in New Mexico and gave little thought to Texas either—until a truly strange occurrence in 1629. In July of that year, a group of Jumanos from the Trans-Pecos area arrived at the Franciscan convent near modern Albuquerque, having come, they said, on the advice of a beautiful young woman who had mysteriously appeared to them in Texas. From her they claimed to have gained basic knowledge of Christianity, especially the sign of the cross. Moreover, the "Lady in Blue," as she became known because she wore a blue cloak with her brown and white habit, had urged the Indians to go to New Mexico to find religious teachers.

The arrival of the Jumanos, which would have excited the Franciscans under any circumstances, was doubly amazing because of a letter they had just received from the archbishop of New Spain concerning the claims of a young nun in Spain. María de Jesús de Agreda, a member of the Poor Clares Order of Franciscan nuns, had fallen into deep trances on hundreds of occasions during the 1620s and dreamed of visiting Indians on the northern frontier of New Spain. These experiences led her to claim miraculous bilocation, the feat of appearing physically in Texas and New Mexico without ever leaving her convent in Spain. María de Jesús told her confessor of the bilocations, and he in turn informed the archbishop of New Spain. The latter then wrote a letter of inquiry to the New Mexico Franciscans, the one that arrived just before the visit by the Junamos.

Excited by the combination of events, the Franciscans sent two of their number, Fathers Juan de Salas and Diego López, back to Texas with the Jumanos. The padres visited with large numbers of Indians who expressed a friendly interest in Christianity and talked of the "Lady in Blue" who had come to them as a "light at sunset." Upon their return, Father Alonso de Benavides went to Mexico City to report on these developments and then in 1630 continued to Spain to meet María de Jesús in person at her convent in Agreda. The nun claimed to recognize Father Benavides from her visits to New Mexico and described other persons with whom he was familiar there. She also gave him a written account of "what happened in the provinces of New Mexico, Quivira, and Jumanas, and the other nations . . . to whom I was carried by the will of God, and by the hand and the assistance of the Angels. . . ."

The Franciscans in New Mexico sent two priests on another visit to the Jumanos in 1632, but no permanent mission was established. María de Jesús later admitted that some of her claims may have been "exaggerated or misunderstood," and that "either it was all the work of my imagination or that God showed me those things by means of abstract images. . . . Neither then nor now was, or am, I capable of knowing the way it happened." Historian David J. Weber has suggested that María de Jesús, who often fasted for days in her extreme desire for spiritual perfection, may have had visions as the result of a form of anorexia. Others insist to this day that she actually experienced miraculous bilocation and deserves sainthood. Belief in miracles is an individual matter, of course, but legends associated with the "Lady in Blue" likely will live forever. One of the best came from the Indians who said that on the morning after her last visit they awoke to find the fields covered with flowers of a deep blue color like her cloak—the first Texas bluebonnets.

Early Spanish Influence in West Texas

Well into the second half of the seventeenth century, more than 150 years after the first explorations of Texas, colonizing efforts on New Spain's northern frontier focused only on New Mexico and the area south of the Río Grande around Monterrey and Saltillo. Settlement near El Paso, a key point on the route to New Mexico, began in the 1650s at modern Ciduad Juárez across the river from Texas. Several expeditions crossed the lower Río Grande during the 1660s and 1670s, either in pursuit of marauding Indians or with the thought of establishing missions to the Indians, but nothing came of them. Even without settling in Texas, however, the Spanish, simply by this presence in New Mexico and along the Río Grande, had an important impact on life in Texas between 1600 and 1680. For one thing, European manufactures such as metal and cloth began to filter eastward from New Mexico. Far more important, however, was the introduction of the horse.

Horses were, in the words of one historian, "the perfect animal for the Indians of Texas." They extended the range and effectiveness of hunters. Imagine, for example, the advantages of hunting buffalo from horseback as opposed to on foot. They provided a means of moving a camp faster and farther. They changed the face of warfare on the plains, making warriors into cavalrymen who could raid and fight far more effectively than foot soldiers. They were even a food source if necessary. It is not surprising that horses became a valued commodity and status symbol among the first Texans.

Oñate's settlement of New Mexico in the 1590s provided the first opportunity for Texas Indians to acquire horses in significant numbers. The Spanish forced the Pueblos, whom they had conquered, to take care of their livestock. Soon, however, the prisoners began to escape, taking with them horses that they sold or traded to Indians in Texas. In the 1650s mounted Apache warriors began to raid the Spanish settlements in New Mexico, carrying off hundreds of additional horses. By the end of the century, the horse spread from the plains of West Texas far to the east into the woodlands home of the Caddos.

Generally called *mesteños* (mustangs), the Spanish horses acquired by Indians in Texas had a mixed ancestry but were perfectly suited to the plains country. Most had Arabian blood and had proved their fitness by surviving the trip from Spain, a voyage that took a toll of about one in every three horses that began it. Although not large (fourteen hands high and weighing seven hundred pounds on the average) or well formed, they proved to have tremendous endurance, toughness, and speed. Texas Indians had only the crudest forms of bridles and saddles, but they became, in the words of one scholar, "incomparably magnificent horsemen." Thus, the Spanish made an important difference in the lives of Texans long before they came to Texas to stay.

In 1680, the Spanish in New Mexico suffered a disaster that soon led to a lasting settlement in Texas. By that date, approximately 2,800 Spaniards—missionaries, traders, and ranchers—lived in the Pueblo country on the Río Grande. They had infuriated the Indians in numerous ways, especially by attempting to suppress their religion, and discredited themselves by constant squabbling between governors and religious leaders over the region's limited resources. As a result the Pueblos organized a revolt that killed four hundred Spaniards and drove the survivors and many friendly Indians down the Río Grande to El Paso. The refugees located at first on the Mexico side of the river and expected to return quickly to the Pueblo country. However, unsuccessful efforts to reconquer New Mexico in 1681–1682 led to the recognition that their stay would be longer. Among the refugees were a sizable number of Indians from the Tiguex Pueblo, and to separate them from the Spanish, the mission and pueblo of Corpus Christi de la Isleta was established in 1682. Located a few miles east of El Paso at the site of modern-day Ysleta, it was the first permanent European settlement in Texas.

Developments by the early 1680s suggest that in time, had nothing interfered, Spanish migrants from Mexico would have settled Texas by a gradual movement from the west and southwest across the state. A "logical" progression of this sort from settled to unsettled lands likely would have built the defense system, transportation network, and economic base necessary to support colonists in numbers large enough to control the frontier as it advanced. Perhaps the harsh climate and unrewarding land of western Texas made it impossible for settlement to begin there; nevertheless, it seems certain that, but for special circumstances, the Spanish would have attempted to move in from the southwest. Whatever might have happened, however, changed dramatically in the late 1680s, thanks to a Frenchman named René Robert Cavelier, Sieur de La Salle.

The French Threat and Spain's "Wilderness Manhunt"

Born the son of a wealthy merchant in Rouen in 1643, La Salle went to Canada in 1667 and became a fur trader and explorer. He explored west from Canada in 1669 but is generally not credited with any significant discoveries. Père Jacques Marquette and Louis Joliet reached the Mississippi River ahead of him in 1673. Returning to France in 1674 and 1677, La Salle received a trade concession to western Canada and developed plans to build a string of posts across the Illinois country and down the Mississippi to the Gulf of Mexico. In the winter of 1682, he traveled down the frozen Illinois River by sled and then, after the spring thaw, canoed down the Mississippi to the eastern passes of its delta's mouth on the Gulf. Arriving in April, he claimed all the lands drained by the Mississippi—merely one-half of the continental United States—for France and named the region Louisiana in honor of Louis XIV.

La Salle, even this early in his career, demonstrated an ability to accomplish great things in spite of having the sort of personality and behavior that led many to question his mental stability. Always suspicious, secretive, and willing to heed no man's opinion except his own, his moods swung wildly from exhilaration during extreme effort to deep depression when an adventure ended in failure. He showed no concern for those who served with him and reacted in paranoid fashion to criticism. There were good men who served him faithfully, but he always had more enemies than friends, a fact testified to by four plots or attempts to kill him before 1682. Historian Robert S. Weddle has speculated that La Salle, like many great achievers, was a manic-depressive whose faulty body chemistry could have been corrected by medications available in more modern times. This is likely true, but a question still remains: Would La Salle on medication have had the drive and determination to pursue the adventures that he undertook? The only thing known for certain is that La Salle's accomplishments came in spite of serious deficiencies in leadership qualities.

Once La Salle's exploration proved that the Mississippi emptied into the Gulf of Mexico rather than the Gulf of California as earlier adventurers had hoped, an effort by the French to colonize near the mouth of the river made sense for several reasons. First, the Spanish already had colonies in Florida and Mexico. If they were to close the gap between, the French would have no access to the Gulf from Canada. Second, a French colony would increase their influence over the Indians and the rich fur trade and bring them closer to the Spanish silver mines in northern Mexico. La Salle therefore went to France in 1683 and persuaded the king to support his plan for entering the Mississippi from the Gulf and planting a French colony "a secure distance" up the river. Louis XIV subsequently provided La Salle with ships and generous amounts of supplies and munitions.

Knowing that the Spanish had become aware of some sort of French designs on northern New Spain, La Salle outfitted his expedition of some three hundred colonists and soldiers, including more than a dozen women and children, and left France under the utmost secrecy. Even the naval commander, Sieur de Beaujeu, was uncertain of the precise destination when his ships sailed from La Rochelle on August 1, 1684. Ill fortune plagued the expedition from the beginning. Beaujeu's ship, the thirty-six-gun man-of-war *Le Joly*, could easily outsail the three slower, equipment-laden vessels, and eventually left one so far behind that it fell prey to Spanish privateers. Upon reaching Hispaniola, the western portion of which the French had claimed and were turning into a colony called Ste. Domingue, La Salle suffered a near-fatal illness, giving time for some of his sailors to desert and join local pirate ships and other members of the expedition to contract venereal diseases. Finally, in November 1684, La Salle recovered, and the three remaining ships ventured into the Gulf of Mexico in search of the mouth of the Mississippi River.

La Salle overshot the mouth of the Mississippi by some four hundred miles and landed at Matagorda Bay on the coast of Texas in February 1685. (See map: La Salle in Texas.) Some historians, finding such a mistake in navigation incredible, have argued that the Frenchman deliberately sought to place his colony closer to the silver mines of Mexico, but in all likelihood he simply miscalculated very badly. Existing maps, showing the continent's greatest river flowing straight south into a large bay at its mouth, were grossly inaccurate. La Salle, having approached the mouth of the Mississippi from the north and explored only the eastern passes (rather than the entire delta), assumed the existence of a solid land mass to the west. Therefore, a stream called the "Río Escondido" (the present-day Nueces River), which flows into Corpus Christi Bay, appeared on the maps most like his understanding of the Mississippi. Having no reliable readings of the latitude of the mouth of the Mississippi, he set course for the "Escondido" and struck the coast of Texas. Even then, he remained convinced that he had made landfall near the great river.

Carefully exploring the coast, La Salle discovered Aransas Pass, which opens into Corpus Christi Bay, but decided that the Mississippi was behind him. So, he landed a party of soldiers who marched back along Matagorda Island until they came to Pass Cavallo, the entry to Matagorda Bay. One ship, the *Belle*, successfully marked the channel through the pass, and preparations were made for landing the colonists at a temporary camp on Matagorda Island. Then, on February 20, 1685, a second vessel, the *Aimable*, carrying most of the settlers and supplies, attempted to sail through the narrow, shallow channel and grounded on a mud bar. Beaujeu had advised against the attempt, but La Salle ordered it—and provided wine to fortify the nerve, if not the judgment, of *Aimable*'s captain and pilot. La Salle, of course, blamed the

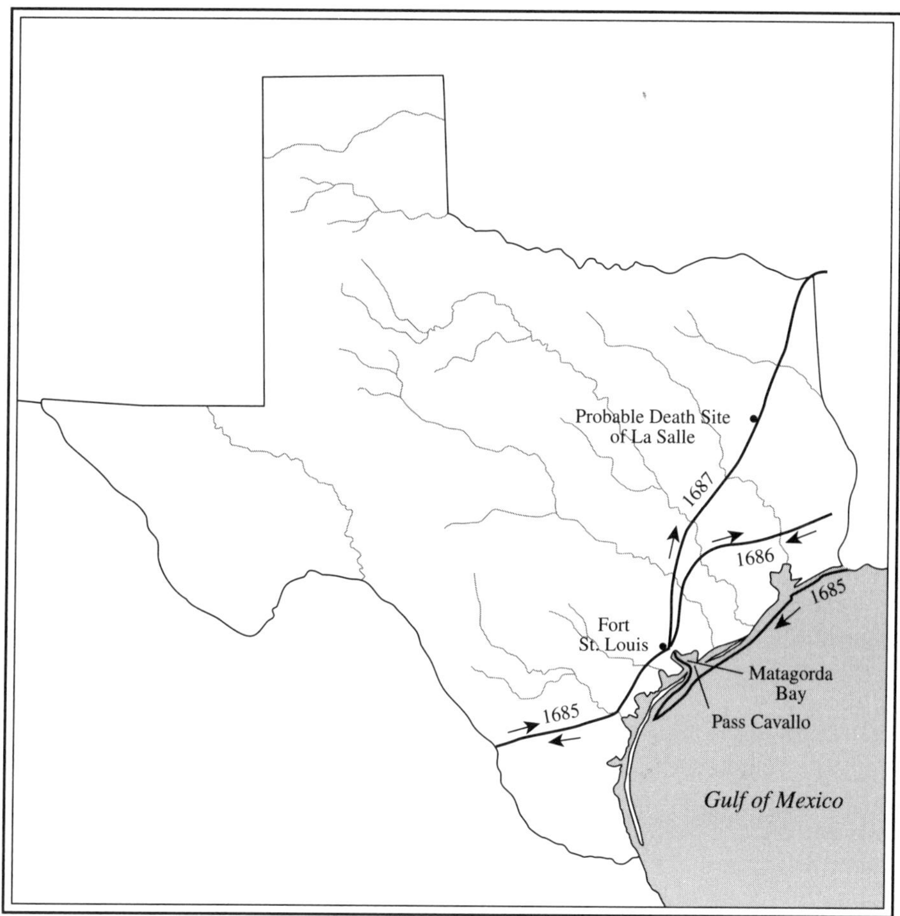

La Salle in Texas

captain. In any case, although a great deal of the ship's cargo was salvaged and piled on the beach, its loss dealt a serious blow to the expedition.

As if the would-be colonists did not have enough problems, they immediately ran into difficulties with Karankawa Indians. Groups of Karankawas helped themselves to supplies on the beach, and when the French went to retrieve the goods or get canoes in exchange, violence broke out. Two Frenchmen were killed, establishing a hostile relationship that plagued the colony to the end.

Captain Beaujeu, standing safely offshore on board the *Joly*, offered to do additional exploring of the coast or to sail to Martinique in the Caribbean for supplies, but La Salle declined. The *Joly* then sailed for France on March 12, 1685, leaving the approximately two hundred colonists who remained in circumstances best described by historian Robert S. Weddle: "Huddled in their temporary camp on the windswept beach, they watched their last link with France and civilization disappear on the Gulf horizon." La Salle finally admitted that he had missed the main mouth of the Mississippi but insisted that he was on a small western channel of the river and would continue his venture there.

After the departure of *Joly,* La Salle explored northward across Matagorda Bay to the head of Lavaca Bay in search of a more suitable temporary site for his colony until he could transplant it to the Mississippi's main channel. The French outpost, he decided, would be built on elevated ground near Garcitas Creek about five miles from its mouth on Lavaca Bay. (La Salle's biographer, Robert S. Weddle, has pointed out that, contrary to popular usage that developed later, La Salle never called his settlement "Fort Saint-Louis.") The settlers began to transport building materials and supplies from the mouth of the bar to the new camp, using the *Belle* as far as possible and canoes for the last eighteen miles. La Salle worked his men mercilessly and then became infuriated at delays due to illness and death as disease, poisonous fruits, snake bite, and Indian attacks wore away at the colony. Finally, in October 1685, with the post still incomplete, he decided to make an extended exploration of the region, still intending to "go up the Mississippi again and carry out the rest of the enterprise." To the undoubted dismay of the settlers, he had the *Belle* reloaded with supplies that had just been carried to the fort with great difficulty.

La Salle's actions over the next few months remain largely a mystery. After exploring Lavaca Bay for some time, in January 1686 he took a small party of men and headed west, a strange direction to go in looking for the Mississippi River. He returned in late March, claiming to have reached the Mississippi, when in fact his party had walked all the way to the Río Grande, possibly to its confluence with the Pecos River, and back. Only a few of those who left with La Salle lived through the adventure, and then to add to the colony's woes, it was discovered that the *Belle* had run aground and was lost. (More than three hundred years later, archeologists from the Texas Historical Commission discovered and salvaged the wreck of the *Belle,* finding more than a million artifacts from the ill-fated ship and sparking renewed interest in La Salle's venture.)

Having lost all their ships, the only means of escape left to the French colonists on the Texas coast was to go overland thousands of miles to Canada. La Salle led an exploring party in that direction in April 1686, going as far as the region inhabited by the Hasinai group of Caddo Indians between the Trinity and Sabine Rivers. The Hasinais received the French in a friendly manner and traded food and horses for metal goods such as axes. Indeed, so hospitable were the Indians that four of the Frenchmen deserted to live with them. Shortly afterward, La Salle became ill and broke off the exploration. Only eight of twenty men who left Fort Saint-Louis in April returned in August. While crossing the Brazos River, La Salle's personal servant met an especially grisly fate, being pulled off a raft by an alligator.

By January 1687, only about forty-one of two hundred settlers who had stayed in Texas when *Joly* left in March 1685 remained alive, and four of those had deserted to live with Indians. La Salle then took seventeen of the most fit and again headed toward Canada, leaving only "missionaries, women and children, and the disabled" behind at the fort on Garcitas Creek. His party crossed the Trinity in March, but then a dispute among a small group sent out to hunt led to the murder of three of its members. Two days later, as La Salle came to investigate why the hunters had not returned, he was shot from ambush and killed instantly. Eventually, seven of the Frenchmen with La Salle, whom the murderers had no reason to harm, moved on toward Canada. Five survived the trip to report on La Salle's fate; the others, as did the earlier deserters, remained in East Texas with the Hasinais.

The colonists on Garcitas Creek survived for almost two years after the death of La Salle. However, around Christmas 1688 the Karankawas attacked and killed everyone except five children. Karankawa women took the children and a woman with a three-month-old infant, the first European baby born in Texas, to their camp, but once the warriors returned, they killed the woman and smashed the baby's brains out against a tree. The children, four of whom were from the Talon family, were adopted into the tribe.

La Salle's venture thus ended horribly, and the whole affair might have amounted to little more than a tragic footnote in the story of Texas had it not been for Spain's reaction. When they learned of the French intrusion, the Spanish mounted a frantic effort to locate and destroy La Salle's colony. And this "wilderness manhunt" led in turn to the creation of settlements in East Texas well ahead of the time that they would otherwise have been attempted. So, La Salle unintentionally acted as a painful thorn in the side of Spanish complacency about the northern Gulf coast and Texas.

Spanish officials learned of La Salle's plans from some of the sailors who had deserted in Santo Domingo and joined pirates who preyed on settlements along the coast of Mexico. In September 1685, following a raid on the Yucatán peninsula, one of the pirate ships and its 120-man crew was captured by a Spanish warship. The Spanish executed the pirates, but not before a thorough interrogation elicited information from the French deserters about La Salle's intention to settle on a river called the "Micipipi." Although they did not know the exact location of either the river or the colony, Spanish officials quickly concluded that a French colony anywhere in the area was a threat to their shipping in the Gulf and their control of northern New Spain. It had to be found and destroyed.

From 1686 to 1689, the Spanish dispatched five sea and six land expeditions in their hunt for La Salle and his colony. The first search by sea discovered nothing, but the second, which left Veracruz in December 1686 was more successful. This expedition located Pass Cavallo in April 1687 and, upon entering Matagorda Bay, found the wreck of the *Belle* and pieces of *Aimable.* The Spanish searched Matagorda Bay but did not go into Lavaca Bay, a step that might well have led them to the fort on Garcitas Creek. More than likely by that time the few survivors there would have welcomed a Spanish prison. Three more searches by sea in 1687–1688 added new knowledge of the Texas coast and its rivers—the fifth actually sailed one hundred miles up the Río Grande—but it did not find anything more of significance concerning the French outpost.

The land searches for La Salle's colony had far greater importance for the future of Texas than did those made by sea. Spanish authorities in Mexico City gave responsibility for overland expeditions to the governor of Nuevo León, the Marqués de San Miguel de Aguayo, who in turn selected an experienced forty-six-year-old explorer, Alonso de León, to lead the first one. De León, the son of a man by the same name who had participated in dozens of campaigns of discovery in northeastern Mexico, had been educated in Spain and then returned to take up a career similar to his father's. He would eventually find the site of La Salle's colony and in the process make key contributions to the colonization of Texas.

De León's first expedition moved north from Nuevo León in the summer of 1686, reached the Río Grande, and followed it to the coast. Of course, he found nothing of the French. Not satisfied, the Marqués de Aguayo sent de León north again early in 1687. This second expedition crossed the Río Grande near present-day Roma, moved down the Texas side to the Gulf of Mexico, and then went northeast along the coast to the area of modern Kingsville before returning to Mexico empty-handed again. Fortunately for de León, these failures to find evidence of La Salle's colony did not harm his career. Instead, in July 1687 he received an appointment as governor of Coahuila, a position that assured him a continuing role in the "wilderness manhunt."

Just as de León became governor, Father Damián Massanet, the resident priest at Mission Caldera in Coahuila, informed him of stories about a white man who lived with the Indians some distance across the Río Grande. An Indian contact attempted to bring the white man to Mexico, but when that failed, de León took a small party of soldiers in May 1688 and went to Texas to find him. In modern Kinney County, the governor found a Frenchman named Jean Jarry living among a group of Coahuiltecan Indians who apparently venerated him as a king. Naked, tattooed, and mentally confused, Jarry, although almost certainly a survivor of La Salle's colony, proved at first a very poor source of information. However, his very presence concerned Spanish authorities, and they authorized a fourth expedition in 1689.

With a force of 114 men, including Father Massanet, de León forded the Río Grande in April and moved toward Matagorda Bay. Much of his route would become part of the Camino Real, the King's Highway, that eventually extended from Mexico City northward through Coahuila across Texas to beyond the Louisiana border. He crossed the Nueces and Guadalupe Rivers, naming them in the process, and on April 22, 1689, with Jarry as a guide, marched down Garcitas Creek and found the remains of the French colony. There were, he recorded, "six houses, not very large, built with poles plastered with mud, and roofed with buffalo hides, another house where pigs were fattened and a wooden fort made from the hulk of a wrecked vessel."

Three bodies, one with the remains of a dress on its bones, lay among the ruins as did eight cannon. Massanet presided over a burial mass for the French victims. De León buried the cannon and explored the Bay region where he saw the remains of the *Aimable.*

Even before finding the post, de León learned from the Indians that four Frenchmen, recent visitors in the area, lived with the Hasinai branch of the Caddos in East Texas. He immediately sent a letter inviting the Frenchmen to join him and return to civilization. Two agreed, and a party of soldiers went to meet them on the Colorado River in the area of modern La Grange. The Frenchmen provided details on the fate of La Salle's outpost and explained that they and several others had buried most of the victims. Doubtless de León and Massanet listened to their two prisoners with fascination, but they were at least as interested in meeting the Indians who accompanied the Frenchmen, a chieftain and eight others from the Hasinais.

The Spanish had heard great things of the Caddos for years and hoped to, in the words of Father Massanet, reap a rich harvest "among the many souls in those lands who know not God." The Indians, on the other hand, knew of the search for La Salle and were seeking to make contact with the Spanish for the purpose of obtaining goods and possibly forming a military alliance. Both sides were pleased with the meeting. De León and Massanet presented numerous presents, including both of the priest's horses, to the Hasinai chieftain, and he in turn promised to visit the Spanish in Coahuila and to welcome Catholic missionaries to East Texas.

De León's 1689 expedition completed the work begun by sea searches in 1687 in finding La Salle's colony, and Spanish authorities naturally found the result a satisfying relief. To the viceroy of New Spain, the fate of the French colonists was a sign of God's "divine aid and favor." To Father Damián Massanet, a man of an even more religious turn of mind, the attempt by La Salle was a sign of God's desire for missionary work among the Caddos. Before leaving them in 1689, he promised that he would bring priests to their land "in the following year, at the time of sowing corn." De León supported Massanet's call for Christianization of the Indians and offered a highly positive account of the climate, soil, and people of East Texas. Massanet kept his promise in 1690, and Spain began a new approach to settling Texas, one that attempted to jump from northern Mexico to the eastern woodlands with little regard for the huge expanse between the Río Grande and the Neches River.

The 170 years between Pineda's voyage in 1519 and de León's fourth expedition in 1689 marked many Spanish contacts with Texas and increasing knowledge of the region's geography. Overall, however, Texas did not have the riches necessary to hold the attention of the crown or officials in New Spain, and religious leaders in Mexico had missionary work enough to occupy them close to home. There simply was no reason to see "Gone To Texas" on doors south of the Río Grande. Indeed, the only permanent Spanish settlement in Texas during this whole period, that near El Paso in 1682, came accidentally as a result of the Pueblo Revolt in New Mexico.

Then, from 1685 to 1689, La Salle's miscalculation in attempting to create a French colony in Louisiana and landing instead at Matagorda Bay dramatically changed the history of Texas. The government of Spain finally became interested in Texas because another nation wanted it. The Caddo Indians encouraged that interest by appearing willing, for their own reasons, to accept Franciscan missionaries. No doubt some attention was better than none, but even at that Texas would remain largely the poor stepchild of Spain's North American empire.

Chapter 3

SPANISH TEXAS, 1690–1779

On April 2, 1690, an expedition of 110 Spanish soldiers and four Franciscan priests crossed the Río Grande and headed toward the site of La Salle's tragic attempt at colonization on Garcitas Creek. The leaders, Governor Alonso de León of Coahuila and Father Damián Massanet, had no difficulty finding the settlement, having located its ruins the previous year. But their purpose in 1690 was far more ambitious than simply plucking what historian Robert S. Weddle called the "French Thorn" from the northern Gulf coast of New Spain. This time the Spanish came to establish a settlement of their own in East Texas; one that would bring Christianity to the Indians and prevent any future incursions by the French.

De León and Massanet had agreed, following their meeting with the Hasinais (whom they called Tejas) in 1689, that missions should be established immediately in East Texas. The enthusiasm of their reports coupled with the French threat encouraged the viceroy and his advisors in Mexico City to move with what amounted to lightning-like speed for the bureaucracy of that day. In a matter of months Massanet received approval of his suggestions for missionary work among the Hasinais. At the same time, the viceroy's advisors asked Governor de León for his ideas about how best to carry out the project. He responded with a plan that the governing officials and Father Massanet both found unacceptable, although for different reasons. Taken together, however, their objections foreshadowed many of the problems that would plague Spanish Texas for the next ninety years.

De León, a practical man with years of experience in dealing with Indians, did not believe that the Hasinais (or any group for that matter) would accept missionary efforts to change their religious practices and way of life unless the Spanish also maintained a military presence in the area. He also knew that only the threat of force would discourage the French. Therefore, he proposed that a line of presidios be constructed to support the new Spanish commitment in Texas—one each on the Río Grande, the Frío River, and the Guadalupe River, and one near the missions to be established among the Hasinais. These four presidios would amount to a fortified supply line, and the soldiers in each would pacify and defend the area nearby.

Authorities in Mexico City ignored de León's proposals, primarily because of the expense involved, thus setting a precedent for the "peso-pinching" policy that consistently hampered Spanish attempts to settle or develop Texas. Massanet on the other hand disliked the governor's ideas because they involved too much of a military presence. The Indians, the father insisted, would be conquered by persuasion and Christian love rather than by soldiers in battle. Governing officials tended to agree with Massanet, at least in part because his argument saved them money. Their immediate concern about the French threat, however, led them to approve sending 110 soldiers with the 1690 expedition, a decision that Massanet disliked and blamed on de León. The governor could not win. His long-range plans came to nothing, and his short-range leadership drew criticism from a respected religious leader.

The expedition reached La Salle's settlement on April 26 and found it undisturbed since the past year. "I myself set fire to the fort," Massanet wrote later, "and as there was a high wind . . . in half an hour the fort was in ashes." The Spanish then continued northeastward to the Colorado River, where they encountered Indians who had with them two young Frenchmen, survivors of the last party led east by La Salle before his death in 1687. These youths, by now tattooed like the Indians, directed de León's expedition on to the first major town of the Hasinais near the Neches River. The governor's initial contact with this westernmost group of the Caddo impressed him greatly. They have, he wrote, "very clean houses and high beds in which to sleep," and their fields are bounteous. The village chieftain brought out "a bench on which to seat me and . . . [gave] me a luncheon of corn tamales and atole, all very clean."

De León and Massanet quickly chose a spot and established Mission San Francisco de los Tejas. (See map: Spanish Missions and Presidios, 1682–1722.) After overseeing the building of a mission church and a residence for the padres, the governor gave possession to the Franciscans, who celebrated their first mass there on June 1, 1690. The establishment of this mission marked the first step in building Spanish Texas—the 1682 creation of the Isleta mission near El Paso notwithstanding. Isleta was more a product of developments in the New Mexico settlements than of any intention to expand to the east. San Francisco de los Tejas, on the other hand, reflected a genuine Spanish interest in Texas—an interest likely to wane, however, if the French no longer appeared to be a threat.

For the moment at least, the de León expedition found new evidence concerning French activity among the Caddos. The person involved, although the Spanish could not know it, was Henri de Tonti, an associate of La Salle's from Illinois. Tonti had traveled to the mouth of the Mississippi searching for La Salle in 1686 and in the process created a trading post near the mouth of the Arkansas River. Then, in 1689, inspired by survivors of La Salle's colony who told him about the colony but did not divulge news of the leader's death, he undertook another search that carried him into the country of the Caddos in early 1690. Tonti got along well with the Natchitoches and the Kadohadacho groups but had less success with the Hasinais, in part because he suspected

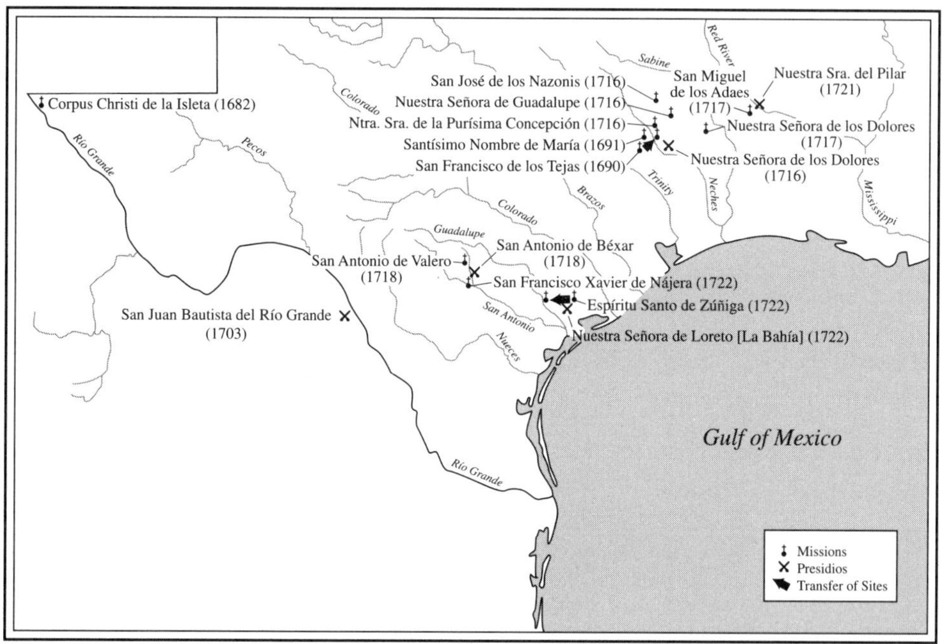

Spanish Missions and Presidios, 1682–1722

them of killing several Frenchmen who had actually been killed by others of their own party. The Hasinais told de León of Tonti's visit, but he was not overly alarmed, especially since the new mission could warn Spanish authorities if the French appeared again.

As de León and Massanet prepared to leave East Texas in early June 1690, their differences led to serious disagreement. The governor wanted to leave fifty soldiers to secure the mission, whereas the Franciscan father insisted that the three priests who would remain needed only a like number of soldiers as protectors. Massanet exacted a promise from the local Hasinai chief that no harm would come to the friars, and de León reluctantly agreed to leave just three soldiers. On the trip back to Mexico, de León ransomed three of the French children whom the Karankawas had taken at La Salle's fort, but not before what he thought to be excessive demands by the captors led to violence and the deaths of four Karankawas. Massanet claimed that de León's troops had caused the trouble and that the loss of life was avoidable. By this time the conflict between the governor and the Franciscan resembled the classic difference between military men and missionaries in regard to the treatment of Indians.

Back in Mexico, de León and Massanet wrote reports and made recommendations for future actions in Texas. The governor called for making settlements on the Guadalupe and Matagorda Bay to provide a lifeline to the mission field in East Texas, a compromise on his original proposal for four presidios from the Río Grande to the Neches. Father Massanet agreed with the idea of a Spanish settlement on the Guadalupe, but most of all he wanted to found eight new missions in Texas. And he opposed creating presidios or sending soldiers into Hasinai country. Authorities in Mexico City generally sided with the Franciscan, especially since his proposals were less expensive. Also, they seemed to accept Massanet's attacks on De León for his handling of the Indians and criticized him themselves for not investigating the Frenchman Tonti's incursion into Caddo country. De León died in March 1691 while yet another expedition was in the planning stages, but it was clear that he would not have been allowed to lead it. A highly capable commander, Alonso de León deserved better than to be discredited by men who could not or would not recognize that his realistic approach to settling Texas offered a better chance of success than any other.

On January 23, 1691, the viceroy in Mexico City indicated the increasing importance of Texas by giving the province its own governor. (Incidentally, the viceroy did not delineate specific boundaries for Texas. Throughout the province's history as a part of New Spain, it began somewhere north of the Río Grande, but in such an unsettled region no exact line was necessary.) The first Governor, Domingo Terán de los Ríos, seemingly had perfect credentials for the job, having already held the same position in two other provinces of northern Mexico. Unfortunately, Governor Terán was an arrogant man who considered dealing with Texas beneath his abilities. And to make matters worse from his point of view, he had to work with Father Massanet, who had full authority on all matters relating to the missions there.

Terán's expedition of fifty soldiers and ten priests left Coahuila in May 1691, driving more than a thousand horses plus herds of cattle, sheep, and goats to resupply Mission San Francisco de los Tejas and support the eight new missions to be created. Arrangements were made also for supply ships to meet the governor at Matagorda Bay. Terán's expedition moved slowly into Texas along the route pioneered by De León, passing the future site of San Antonio and moving on to the vicinity of modern Austin by late June. From there, Terán sent a smaller party to meet the supply ships at Matagorda Bay. His men found no ships, waited five days, and left; not knowing that the ships would arrive later that same day. Terán, when informed that the supplies had not arrived, wanted to wait for them. Massanet, however, argued furiously against further delay and in effect forced the governor to move on toward the Neches. Even then, the priests soon became so angry over the expedition's slow pace that they left without permission and hastened, unescorted, to San Francisco de los Tejas.

Upon their arrival, the Franciscans found the missionary effort that had seemed so promising the year before in near-total disarray. The basic problem was simple: the Hasinais wanted Spanish goods (especially weapons) and protection but had no reason to accept changes in their religion and customs, whereas the Spanish refused to provide weapons and sought to impose acceptance of their ways on the Indians. One incident related by a priest perfectly encapsulated the attitude of the Spanish. As a medicine man performed a burial ceremony, the priest put his hand over the Indian's mouth and ordered him to be quiet, saying that his words were "of no use and that what I was going to say to God would alone be useful to the dead man." Small wonder that tension grew and then became worse when the death of a priest was followed by an epidemic of disease in which three to four hundred Indians died. The Hasinais discussed killing the two remaining Franciscans, but reconsidered when a seriously ill medicine man recovered after allowing himself to be baptized. The mission survived, but just barely.

As Terán inched toward the Neches, he became increasingly disenchanted with what he found. Heat and drought caused deaths among his livestock, while ticks and chiggers made life miserable for the men. Finally arriving at the mission, he left the animals, distributed gifts, and quickly headed back to the supply ships, which he expected to be waiting at Matagorda Bay. Once he left, the Hasinais killed the cattle that he had brought and stole some of the horses. When Terán reached the coast in September 1691, he found the ships patiently waiting with supplies and, to his dismay, new instructions calling for extensive explorations that would keep him in Texas for the rest of the year. The drought broke as he returned to the mission, forcing his party to march through torrents of rain that turned the dust to mud.

Terán's expedition then became a nightmare in the fall of 1691 as he explored to the northeast from the Neches, crossed the Sabine River, and finally reached the Red River in Arkansas. By that time, the Spaniards had endured three days of freezing rain followed by a foot of snow. Even Father Massanet became discouraged. The return march brought flooded streams and more rain and snow before the group reached the missions at the end of the year. After a brief rest, Terán again headed for Matagorda Bay through rain so heavy that his men could not build fires to cook food or warm themselves. Most of his horses and mules had long since worn out in the miserable weather. Terán finally reached the coast and departed Texas by ship in late March 1692, leaving his men and six priests who had left East Texas with them to walk back to Mexico. Instead of founding eight new missions, he left only three priests, including Father Massanet, and nine soldiers at the one mission already existing. Of the countryside, the governor wrote, "no rational person has ever seen a worse one."

Mission San Francisco de los Tejas survived only another year and a half. The Hasinais' crops failed in 1692, and a second epidemic of disease broke out. Moreover, the priests had no success in eliminating what they called the Indians' "witchcraft, frauds, and superstitions of the devil." By the time new supplies arrived in the summer of 1693, Massanet had become so disillusioned that he advocated building a presidio and forcing the natives to live together in order to improve the chance of conversion. Surprised at this proposal, which he was unwilling to fund when there was no apparent French threat to East Texas, the viceroy in Mexico City sent a force to bring the priests home. Before the escort arrived, however, the Hasinais became so threatening that the Spaniards buried the bells and cannon, burned the mission, and fled. Leaving on October 25, they spent forty days wandering through East Texas before hitting the coast and finding their way to Coahuila in February 1694.

Thus, the first attempt at a permanent Spanish settlement in the interior of Texas came to an inglorious close. At least it had provided geographical knowledge and demonstrated that missions could not succeed without presidios and supporting settlements.

Permanent Spanish Occupation of Central and East Texas

For twenty years after the retreat from Mission San Francisco de los Tejas in 1693, Spain did not engage in any important activity in Texas. Settlement of northern Mexico continued to advance, however, building the base necessary for future advances across the Río Grande. Most important, in 1703 the government constructed Presidio San Juan Bautista del Río Grande on the south side of the river about thirty miles below present-day Eagle Pass. This fortress and the adjacent missions would become the gateway to Spanish Texas in the eighteenth century.

As the new century opened, the Spanish and French continued to maneuver for control of lands bordering the northern coast of the Gulf of Mexico. Spain solidified its hold on Florida in 1698 by establishing a settlement at Pensacola, the site of one of the best harbors in the region. The French, in order to secure Louisiana as their colony, created posts at Biloxi (1699) and Mobile (1702) and established the future city of New Orleans in 1718. And they began to pursue trade with Indians on the Mississippi and its tributaries, a policy that meant building a relationship with the Caddos. Once again, a French threat would draw Spain's attention to Texas.

The French received encouragement in expanding their contacts with the Caddos from a very unlikely source, Francisco Hidalgo, a Spanish Franciscan priest. Father Hidalgo had served at Mission San Francisco de los Tejas in 1691–1693 and in spite of that failure had become an enthusiast about missionary work in East Texas. He helped found a mission at San Juan Bautista on the Río Grande in 1700 and continually sought to convince authorities in New Spain to create new missions among the Hasinais. Finally, after a decade of failure, the priest hit upon a way to achieve his goal, conveniently disregarding the fact that what he would propose bordered on treason. Hidalgo's plan involved inviting the French to begin missionary work in East Texas in the hopes that his own government, seeing a new threat from France, would then agree to help accomplish his original objective. Thus, in 1711, he sent a letter to the governor of Louisiana, Antoine Laumet, Sieur de Cadillac, proposing that the French establish missions for the Caddos. When the letter finally reached him in 1713, Governor Cadillac immediately saw an opportunity to serve God and himself. The French had no intention of trying to occupy Texas, but participation in mission activity there would give them an opening to introduce their trade goods to the Indians.

Governor Cadillac needed an experienced explorer, trader, and diplomat to pursue the possibilities opened by Hidalgo's letter, and he quickly found just the man—Louis Juchereau de Saint-Denis. Born in Canada but educated in Paris, Saint-Denis knew the Caddos, having made contact with them shortly after 1700 and visited their homes periodically thereafter. Cadillac provided him with trade goods such as guns and cloth as well as instructions to travel to the land of the Caddos and open trade with the Indians. Also, in the event that Father Hidalgo had begun missionary activity in East Texas during the two years that had elapsed since his 1711 letter, Cadillac instructed Saint-Denis to assist in that effort as well. (The governor did not know, of course, that Hidalgo had no hope of creating missions in East Texas unless the Spanish became alarmed by the French presence there.) In late 1713, Saint-Denis began to store goods at the site of Natchitoches on the Red River among the easternmost group of the Caddos and started to use that post for trade with all three major Caddo groups, including the Hasinais in East Texas.

Saint-Denis knew that any hope of convincing the Spanish to tolerate a French presence in East Texas depended on developing a joint effort to save souls, and yet by mid-1714 there were no missionaries in the area. In short, Saint-Denis needed priests as a "cover" for French commercial activity. The Frenchman therefore persuaded the Hasinais, who apparently were willing to forget the bad experiences of 1690–1693, to ask for a return of Spanish Franciscan missionaries to their villages. Moreover, the Indians were to travel to Mexico and deliver the petition in person, accompanied by Saint-Denis.

On July 19, 1714, four Indians and four Frenchmen led by Saint-Denis rode into Presidio San Juan Bautista and presented themselves to Commandant Diego Ramón. Saint-Denis explained the religious purpose of his visit and asked for Father Hidalgo. He also indicated that he wanted to begin trading in Texas. Commandant Ramón, having no idea what to do with his French visitors, placed them under house arrest while he sought advice from Mexico City. Saint-Denis enjoyed his time at San Juan Bautista, especially in courting Manuela Sánchez, step-granddaughter of the commandant. Then, he and Father Hidalgo were called to Mexico City where they emphasized how badly the Hasinais wanted religious instruction and Saint-Denis explained that he knew of no prohibition against trade between Spanish and French colonies. The government agreed to attempt missionary work again in East Texas and permitted Saint-Denis to participate in the project. Spanish officials, however, did not completely trust the Frenchman and his plans for Texas. They once again had reason to be alarmed about their nation's hold on the region, and the result this time was a truly substantial effort to establish permanent occupation of East Texas.

In the spring of 1716 an expedition commanded by Captain Domingo Ramón, son of the commandant of Presidio San Juan Bautista, left the Río Grande for the Hasinai country. Saint-Denis, having married Manuela Sánchez and declared himself a Spanish subject, served in effect as second in command. Exactly what he was up to will always be a puzzle. His actions made it clear that Texas belonged to Spain, and that hardly pleased his French superiors. Yet, they never condemned him and continued to communicate with him while he served Spain. More than likely, the French did not really care about owning Texas so long as they had the opportunity to profit from trade there, and they recognized that Saint-Denis's cooperation with the Spanish brought them closer to Louisiana and thus furthered the possibility of commercial ties. (After traveling to East Texas with Ramón, Saint-Denis returned to Mexico and his bride in 1717, taking with him a large supply of trade goods. The Spanish still considered him a French subject, however, and seized the goods. Eventually, he made his way back to Natchitoches, his wife was allowed to join him, and he served as commandant of the French post there until his death in 1744. He and his descendants had great influence over Texas Indians throughout the eighteenth century.)

The Ramón expedition included twenty-six soldiers, nine priests (including Father Hidalgo), three lay brothers, and several dozen settlers. Seven of the soldiers were accompanied by their wives, the first recorded Spanish women in Texas. Reaching the land of the Hasinais in June 1716 to an enthusiastic reception from the Indians, the expedition soon established four missions. One was near the original site of San Francisco de los Tejas, and another (Nuestra Señora de Guadalupe) was located at modern Nacogdoches. Early the next year, two more missions—one near present-day San Augustine (Nuestra Señora de los Dolores) and one named San Miguel de los Adaes in Louisiana, to the east of the Sabine River and only fifteen miles from Natchitoches—brought the total to six. The missions were protected by soldiers in a centrally located presidio (also called Nuestra Señora de los Dolores).

Although far better supported than the first mission in 1690, those established by Ramón faced many similar problems. They were four hundred miles from the Río Grande without any presidios or settlements along the route. The Caddos, after their initial enthusiasm, were no more inclined than ever to accept the Catholic faith, and once again a serious outbreak of disease occurred. Fortunately for these missions, however, a new viceroy, the Marqués de Valero, who had taken over in Mexico City in 1716, made support for the Franciscan missions one of his primary objectives. In 1717 Valero made Martín de Alarcón, a veteran of much service in northern Mexico, governor of Texas and directed him to lead an expedition to create a mission, presidio, and civilian settlement on the San Antonio River as a halfway post to East Texas. Alarcón, accompanied by Father Antonio de Buenaventura y Olivares who was to be responsible for the mission, crossed the Río Grande in April 1718 at the head of seventy-two persons, including soldiers, missionaries, and ten families recruited in northern Mexico. On May 1, he founded a mission—San Antonio de Valero—that would become famous as the Alamo more than a century later. In the beginning it amounted to a structure of mud, straw, and brush with a few Coahuiltecan Indians living nearby. A few days later Presidio San Antonio de Bexár was established a mile west of the mission. The civilians, who included an engineer, a stonemason, and a blacksmith, built their homes around the presidio and called their settlement Villa de Bexár.

Alarcón traveled on to East Texas, then returned to Mexico and resigned late in 1718, having accomplished at least one thing of importance to the future of Texas—the founding of San Antonio. He disappointed the priests among the Hasinais, however, by not bringing more soldiers or settlers to that region. Their missions continued to struggle, and then in 1719 a brief war between Spain and France threatened to destroy them completely. The war, which originated solely from European issues, led the French in June 1719 to send seven soldiers from Natchitoches to capture the new Spanish mission fifteen miles away at Los Adaes. Finding only a single soldier and one lay brother defending the mission, the French easily accomplished their objective. They then busied themselves raiding the mission's henhouse and in the process caused such a commotion that they lost sight of the lay brother and allowed him to escape. He fled westward to the presidio and other missions in East Texas with word that the French were coming, and the soldiers and priests there, believing that the Indians would probably side with the invaders, decided to abandon the area. They reached San Antonio in the early fall.

The abandonment of East Texas could have meant failure for a second time in efforts to occupy the region, but circumstances in 1719 were not the same as in 1693. For one thing, the refugees did not have to cross the Río Grande; they could stop at San Antonio. For another, a threat from France caused the problem, so the Spanish government was motivated to respond quickly. Even before word reached Spain of developments in East Texas, the king and his advisors had directed officials in New Spain to strengthen the missions created by Ramón in 1716–1717, to send new missionaries to San Antonio, and to build a presidio at the spot of La Salle's abortive colony near Matagorda Bay. These directives seconded plans already being made by the viceroy, the Marqués de Valero, and led in 1721 to the largest expedition ever to enter Texas from New Spain.

To command this expedition, the viceroy chose the Marqués de San Miguel de Aguayo, a wealthy nobleman from Coahuila who offered to spend his own funds to meet the French threat in Texas. Aguayo became governor of Coahuila and Texas in 1719 (placing control of both provinces in the hands of one man) and spent nearly a year organizing his expedition. In the meantime, Father Antonio Margil de Jesús, leader of the missionaries who had fled East Texas, sought and won the governor's permission to found a second mission near San Antonio. He argued, reasonably enough, that all the exiles in the area put too much strain on local religious resources. Named San José y San Miguel de Aguayo for the governor—a tactful move that may have helped overcome the opposition of Father Olivares who led the existing San Antonio mission—the new establishment became in the words of historian Donald E. Chipman, "the most successful and beautiful mission in Spanish Texas."

Aguayo's expedition left the Río Grande in March 1721 with 500 men, 2,800 horses, 4,800 head of cattle, and 6,400 sheep and goats. Passing through San Antonio, the expedition moved on to East Texas where the Hasinais gave their usual emotionally enthusiastic welcome as the Spanish showered them with gifts. Aguayo reestablished the six missions and the fort created by Ramón and built a new presidio at Los Adaes, which he staffed with one hundred soldiers. Saint-Denis, now the French commandant at Natchitoches, did not want the Spanish to return to Los Adaes, but the size of Aguayo's force convinced him to accept a truce and not interfere. Los Adaes became the capital of Spanish Texas and remained so until 1772. The Río Hondo, a small

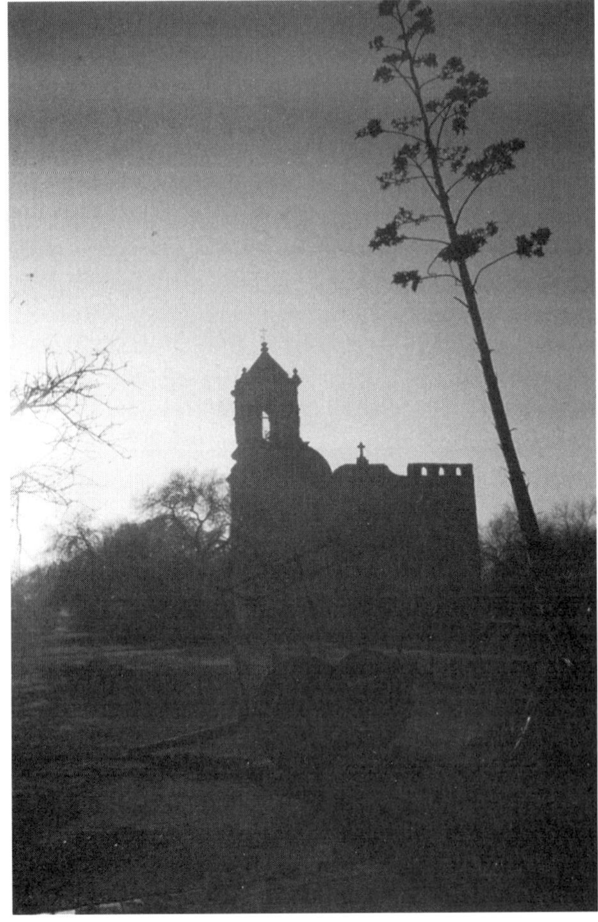

Mission San José y San Miguel de Aguayo, founded in 1720 in San Antonio. This photograph was taken in 1979. Credit: Bob Parvin/TxDOT.

stream between it and Natchitoches, served as the boundary with French Louisiana.

Aguayo returned to San Antonio in January 1722 and relocated the presidio there before moving on in the spring to supervise building a new fort at the site of La Salle's colony. The presidio, along with a mission Aguayo established for the Karankawas and other local Indians, came to be known as La Bahía from the Spanish name for Matagorda Bay. This settlement would be moved several times before eventually being located at the site of present-day Goliad, where it became one of the few towns in early Texas.

Having done more than any other individual to shape Spanish Texas and assure its survival, Aguayo left Texas later in 1722 and retired. The system of missions and presidios that he left behind, however, sounded far better in the-

Rose window in Mission San José y San Miguel de Aguayo, founded in 1720 in San Antonio. This window is generally regarded as a masterpiece of decorative art. This photograph was taken in 1979. Credit: Bob Parvin/TxDOT.

ory than it functioned in practice. Presidios were commanded not by professional soldiers but rather by men who had established themselves as merchants or ranchers and expected military service to help their careers as well as their country. The soldiers who staffed presidios were not professionals either. Instead, they were citizen soldiers who had the responsibility of settling the land as well as protecting local missions and other colonists. Their meager salaries had to pay for all necessary equipment and support their families. Often times captains acted as storekeepers for their presidios and charged their own soldiers exorbitant prices. Soldiers even had to work land belonging to the captains.

Missions in East Texas had virtually no success in convincing the Hasinais to give up their beliefs and accept the Catholic faith and lifestyle. In the

San Antonio area, however, there was some success with the Coahuiltecans, who led such miserable lives that missions had something to offer them—although it seems to have been more material than spiritual. As one Franciscan wrote: "They are more concerned about having food in abundance than with any fear of life eternal." In any case, thousands of these Indians eventually came in to receive religious instruction, be baptized, and learn new vocations. The Franciscans taught converts in their own language at first and then introduced them to Spanish. Mission Indians had to attend daily mass and lessons in the faith as well as perform assigned tasks. Absence from an assembly and other forms of unacceptable behavior often were punished by whippings, ordered by the friars but administered by an Indian assistant. Mission San José at San Antonio became the most successful, having hundreds of resident Indians who learned skills such as cloth making and carpentry and cultivated fenced, irrigated fields that produced enough food to help feed other missions in the area.

Perhaps the greatest long-range contribution of the missions at San Antonio and La Bahía was the establishment of ranching. Early expeditions such as Governor Terán's in 1691 brought large numbers of livestock to Texas, but the thousands of head that crossed the Río Grande with Aguayo in 1721 stocked the first mission herds. Within thirty years, pastures along the San Antonio and Guadalupe Rivers in the region from San Antonio to present-day Goliad teemed with literally thousands of horses, cattle, goats, and sheep managed by Indian *vaqueros* and shepherds.

During the years from 1690 to 1722, while the Spanish attempted with only limited success to convert the Indians to mission life, the French pursued a commercial-minded policy that met with greater approval on the part of the first Texans. Spanish missionaries provided gifts of cloth and tools, for example, to potential converts, but they did not offer weapons of any sort. Moreover, the Spanish did not permit their citizens to trade with the Indians, let alone sell them firearms. The French, on the other hand, sought trade with all groups and willingly provided them with weapons in return for furs, horses, and slaves. Given the role of firearms as an essential in hunting and fighting, this sort of trade changed the lives of the Indians.

Saint-Denis opened commercial exchange with the Caddos from Natchitoches in 1713, and six years later another agent, Bérnard de La Harpe, established a trading post just south of the Red River in present-day northeastern Texas. At that point, all of the Caddo confederacies had easy access to French goods, which proved something of a mixed blessing to the Indians. They gained weapons to defend themselves, but they also discovered the benefits of going on the offensive to capture enemies for sale as slaves. Trade with the French militarized the lives of the Caddos.

French traders also made contact at this time with groups of Wichita Indians, Caddoan-speaking agriculturalists who had been driven from their homes in present-day Kansas by disease and enemies such as the better-armed Osages. By 1719, a lesser-known Wichita group, the Kichais, had settled south of the Red River in northeast Texas, and two other Wichita groups, the

Tawakonis and Taovayas, were living in present-day Oklahoma while, in effect, on their way to Texas, where their presence would be felt for many years. La Harpe opened trade with all these Wichita groups, bringing them under the influence of European goods and weapons. As in the case of the Caddos, the change was not entirely for the better, a fact that the Indians would never have acknowledged. "For no Indian of the North," a French trader wrote later, "is there any jewel more precious than firearms."

Retrenchment and Arrival of the Comanches in Texas

By the mid-1720s, with Spain and France again at peace in Europe and America, Spanish budget cutters began to look longingly at expensive frontier presidios in distant places such as Texas. Viceroy Juan de Acuña in Mexico City accommodated the desire for "economy" in 1724 by appointing Pedro de Rivera y Villalón to make a tour of inspection of all presidios on the northern frontier of New Spain from California to Louisiana and report on their condition and possible savings to be effected at each. Rivera traveled 7,500 miles by horseback, finally reaching Texas in the summer of 1727 and examining the presidios at San Antonio, La Bahía (which had relocated in 1726 to the Guadalupe River near modern Victoria), in East Texas, and at Los Adaes. He found three of the four reasonably well run, but described the one in East Texas as a "collection of huts poorly constructed of sticks and fodder [that does] not merit the honorable name of Presidio de los Tejas." Missions in that area, he noted dryly, "minister to the Indians when they want to be christians."

Rivera returned to Mexico in 1728 and wrote a report that recommended closing the East Texas presidio and reducing the garrisons in each of the others. In 1729 the viceroy accepted these recommendations, but made even deeper cuts than Rivera had proposed. Closing the East Texas presidio left the three missions in the immediate area without protection, so the resident priests reacted by moving them to San Antonio in 1731. East Texas was not entirely abandoned in that missions still existed near Nacogdoches and San Augustine and the presidio and mission at Los Adaes remained operative. Los Adaes also remained the official capital of Texas. Nevertheless, this reduction of commitment in the late 1720s discouraged the increase in population so essential if the Spanish ever intended to govern the region effectively.

By contrast, San Antonio's population grew significantly from several sources during the late 1720s and early 1730s. First, most of the soldiers who were discharged as a result of Rivera's recommendations remained in the community as permanent settlers. They established an important precedent in that presidial soldiers, either by retiring or marrying into local families, would be a key component of San Antonio's population for years to come. Second, the three missions from East Texas relocated along the San Antonio River in 1731, bringing the total in the immediate area to five and increasing the number of Indians and support personnel associated with mission work. A third major addition to the population came that same year with the arrival of fifty-five settlers from the Canary Islands. The idea of recruiting these colonists had been promoted some twelve years earlier by the Marqués de Aguayo who thought that civilian settlers would protect their own land (and Texas) at less expense than presidios. Years of bureaucratic foot dragging slowed implementation of Aguayo's suggestion, and the whole venture proved so expensive that the government refused to continue it after 1731, which in some ways may have been just as well. The Isleños, as these new colonists became known, had great difficulty adjusting to Texas and getting along with other residents of San Antonio. For example, after establishing the villa of San Fernando de Béxar, the first municipal government in Texas, the Isleños insisted that only they could live in it. They also quarreled constantly with older settlers over crops and livestock. One frustrated official in Mexico City, after pointing out that the Isleños complained about the missions, the Indians, the presidio, and the other families, concluded, "It seems that they desire to be left alone in undisputed possession. Perhaps even then they may not find enough room in the vast area of the entire province."

Regardless of such problems, San Antonio grew into the most important settlement in Texas after 1730. Beginning in 1735 governors of the province generally lived there rather than in the official capital at Los Adaes. Population growth also had a negative effect, however, in that it made San Antonio the focal point of a new problem in Texas—Indian warfare. Conflicts between the Spanish and Indians occurred from the earliest European arrivals onward, of course, but incidents happened sporadically and involved relatively few people. In the 1720s and 1730s, however, warfare of a much more sustained nature developed between settlers in San Antonio and the Lipan Apaches.

Conflict between the Spanish and the Apaches developed from several causes. First, Apaches and Caddos had a long-standing hatred for each other rising from cultural differences and competition for buffalo hunting grounds in north Texas. Thus, in the eyes of the Apaches, Spanish mission activity among the Hasinais amounted to consorting with the enemy and justified raids on San Antonio soon after its founding on the edge of Apache country in 1718. The most destructive early raid came in 1723 when the Apaches stole eighty horses from the presidio's herd. In retaliation, Captain Nicolás Flores y Valdez led a force of soldiers and mission Indians that killed thirty Apache warriors, captured twenty women and children, and took 120 horses. Depredations then ceased for a time, leading Pedro de Rivera when he inspected San Antonio in 1727 to propose a reduction in the size of the garrison there because the "only enemies in the area are a few Apaches . . . who know from experience how efficiently the soldiers perform their duties." However, shortly after his proposal was accepted Apache hostilities resumed and continued until the late 1740s.

This resumption of raids in 1731 reflected a second cause for trouble with the Apaches—the arrival of Comanche Indians in Texas. The Comanches, a branch of the Northern Shoshones, came from the Great Basin region of the west. During the late seventeenth century, they acquired horses and adapted to a nomadic way of life dependent on buffalo hunting on the Great Plains.

Warriors to the core, Comanches probably received their name from a Ute word meaning "anyone who wants to fight me all the time." Hunting and fighting from horseback so occupied the Comanches that they appeared more at home riding than on foot. The artist George Catlin observed: "In their movements they are heavy and ungraceful; and on their feet one of the most unattractive and slovenly races of Indians I have ever seen; but the moment they mount their horses, they seem at once metamorphosed, and surprise the spectator with the ease and grace of their movements." Mounted Comanche warriors were the most fearsome enemy ever faced by other Indians and Europeans alike in Texas.

Comanche hunting parties killed buffalo by surrounding a herd and tightening the circle until men could ride within a few feet of the right side of an animal and shoot an arrow behind the ribs into the heart. Hunters preferred this method even after they acquired firearms. Kills were butchered on the spot so that the meat could be wrapped in hides and packed to camp. Most of the Comanches' food, clothing, and shelter depended on these hunts, although they also collected wild fruits and nuts and engaged in some trade for manufactured items. To acquire guns and ammunition from French traders, for example, they offered buffalo hides and horses or even captives.

Comanches generally lived in kinship bands with very limited political organization. Each camp had a peace chief, an older leader agreed to by common consent, whose primary job was to mediate among the others. Important decisions about matters other than war were reached in council and reflected a consensus among members of the band. Leadership in warfare, however, was a matter of individual initiative. Any man could lead a raid or attack, providing that he could convince others to join him. Warriors who had been successful in the past or had an especially compelling vision of their proposed foray obviously had the best chance of persuading others to participate. The war party held a dance the night before their raid and left before dawn. Usually they attacked by surprise, killed and looted, and withdrew. If pursued, they scattered into smaller groups or even fled alone. Pursuing enemies could not use the same tactic of breaking up to follow one or two Comanches for fear of being attacked by suddenly reunited warriors.

Warfare was a way of life but not, as some have said, a game to the Comanches. Warriors did go to extremes to demonstrate their bravery—making a "coup" by touching a living enemy, for example—because of the status to be gained from such acts. Basically, however, they fought because they had to. In the words of one scholar: "To gain a foothold on the teeming buffalo plains the Comanches had to be willing to fight and fight hard, and once they had won their land they had to fight with equal vigor to defend themselves against a varied assortment of white and Indian enemies." Small wonder that virtually every aspect of their lives related in one way or another to war.

The Comanches appeared in New Mexico shortly after 1700 and probably reached Texas by the 1720s, although there is no record of actual contact with the Spanish until the early 1750s. Eventually, Comanche country, or the Comanchería, would extend from the Panhandle eastward to the Cross Timbers in North Texas and then south across the center of the province to the Edwards Plateau northwest of San Antonio. The arrival of the Comanches immediately put pressure on the Apaches, who in turn renewed their attacks on the Spanish settlement. Horses remained their main objective, as was the case in a raid in September 1731 that cost the presidio's herd sixty head, but the Indians also stole other livestock and guns and ammunition. Retaliatory expeditions by the Spanish had little effect, and efforts by missionaries to negotiate peace were equally unsuccessful. Off and on warfare continued through the 1730s and into the next decade.

New Efforts to Expand Spanish Texas, 1740s–1760s

By the mid-1740s Spanish Texas generally showed the signs of some twenty years of retrenchment and neglect. The missions in East Texas and at Los Adaes continued to operate, but they had not a single Indian convert in residence, an indication that the natives, in the words of Governor Tomás Winthuysen in 1744, were "irreducible to civilization and to subjection to the missions." La Bahía, consisting of a mission and presidio, had been moved from the site of La Salle's colony to the Guadalupe River near present-day Victoria, but at least it still existed. San Antonio represented the only success story of the past two decades.

In spite of this less than overwhelming progress, however, viceregal authorities in Mexico City during the late 1740s approved plans for four initiatives to spread the gospel and improve Spain's hold on Texas. Three of the four failed, demonstrating once again from the Spanish point of view just how difficult it was to colonize a harsh land filled with dangerous inhabitants. The Indians had no single point of view, of course, given the amount of time that they spent fighting each other and trying in the process to manipulate the Spanish to their own advantage, but certainly one group of natives or another saw every Spanish failure as a success for themselves.

The first new Spanish initiative involved an effort to expand mission activities into the interior 130 miles northeast of San Antonio by creating new establishments on the San Gabriel River in present-day Milam County. (See map: Expansion of Spanish Missions, Presidios, and Settlements, 1746–1779.) Missionaries became interested in that region after the Ramón and Aguayo expeditions both explored it, and their interest turned to action in the 1740s when Indians from the region requested the establishment of a mission. In their enthusiasm, the priests overlooked or discounted the fact that the Indians to whom they would minister—primarily Cocos, Deadose, and Tonkawas—were a truly disparate lot. The Cocos were a Karankawan group who ranged north from the Gulf coast, and the Deadose were Atakapans who had moved west from around Galveston Bay. They were joined by the Tonkawas, relatively recent migrants from the plains forced into central Texas by the Apaches. Their name meant "they all stay together," and their language had no relationship to those of other Indian groups of the area. Exactly why these Indians asked missionaries to live among them is not clear, but their motives probably included protection from other groups.

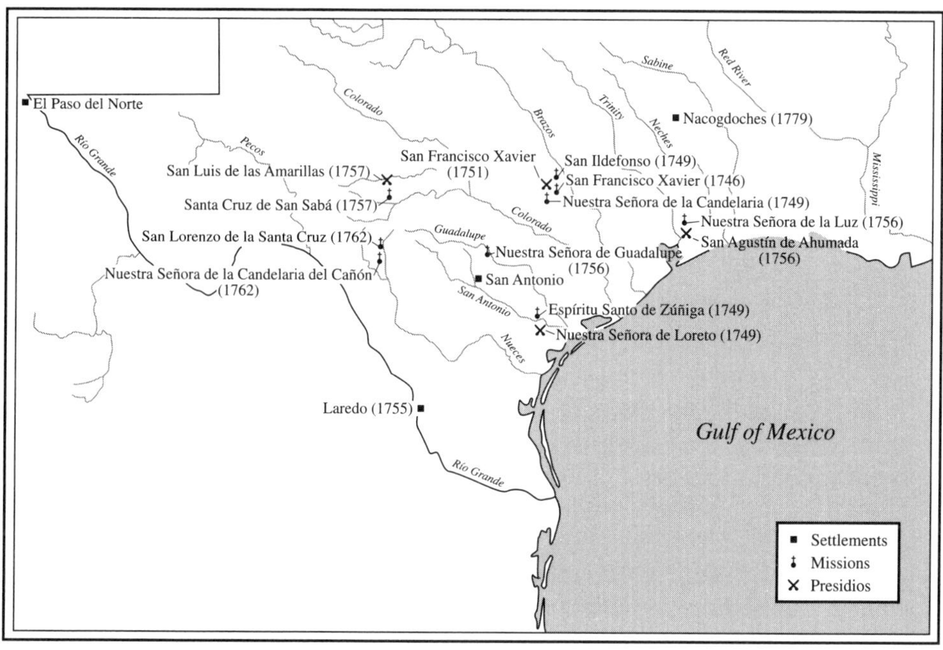

Expansion of Spanish Missions, Settlements, and Presidios, 1746–1779

Father Mariano Francisco de los Dolores y Viana began the creation of the San Gabriel missions in 1746 by choosing a site for the first, San Francisco Xavier de Nájera, and with the aid of Indians from San Antonio and a few soldiers clearing fields and beginning the construction of a chapel. The project ran into numerous delays in winning final approval from authorities in Mexico City and Madrid, but by July 1749 three missions stood ready to work with the Indians—sensibly enough, one to focus on the Tonkawas, one for the Cocos, and one for the Deadose and related groups. The first two soon attracted several hundred Indian residents.

These missions on the San Gabriel needed a presidio to protect them, particularly from raiding Apaches, but it took the priests several years to convince the viceroy to spend the money necessary for a military establishment. Finally, in 1751 he authorized the creation of Presidio San Francisco Xavier de Gigedo with a garrison of fifty soldiers who were to be accompanied by their families and other settlers. The priests were delighted, but had they known much about the man chosen to command the fort, Captain Felipe de Rábago y Terán, they would have shed tears of despair rather than joy.

Captain Rábago, a handsome man known best for his constant and successful pursuit of women, scandalized the missionaries and destroyed morale among his soldiers before even reaching the San Gabriel. En route, he seduced the wife of a civilian tailor in his command, Juan José Ceballos. The husband objected, so Rábago had him arrested and, upon reaching the San Gabriel, confined to a cell. Rábago found the missions in miserable condition. One had no Indian coverts; the others had 109 and 25 respectively. He reported to the viceroy that the entire enterprise should be abandoned, and while waiting for a response consoled himself with Ceballos's wife. The priests sought to end the affair by ordering the woman back to San Antonio, to which Rábago responded by having Ceballos tied up, placing a cot in the cell, and having sexual relations with the wife in front of her husband. On Christmas Eve 1751, Ceballos escaped and took refuge in the mission church, only to have Rábago ride his horse into the chapel on Christmas Day and return the poor man to his cell. Father Miguel Pinilla, the chaplain of the presidio, complained angrily, and Rábago responded to the extent of freeing Ceballos.

With their captain as a role model, the presidial soldiers outdid themselves in illicit relations with Indian women at the missions. Father Pinilla finally lost all patience in February 1752 and excommunicated Rábago and his entire command, an action that caused them to beg forgiveness (which they quickly received) but not necessarily to change their ways. As would be expected, both the priests and Rábago complained about each other to authorities in Mexico City; however, before any action could be taken, the situation ended in tragedy. On May 11, Ceballos and one of the priests in the mission where he had taken refuge earlier were murdered. Rábago blamed Coco Indians for the deaths, but almost certainly soldiers from the presidio committed the murders.

The murders of Ceballos and the priest caused the other missionaries and all the resident Indians to flee and for all practical purposes ended the attempt to create a mission field on the San Gabriel. Removed from command, Rábago spent the next eight years at a presidio in Coahuila while authorities investigated his role in the murders. No complicity on his part was ever proven. The missions remained alive, although just barely so, for three more years and then in 1755 were transferred to the San Marcos River, a site much closer to San Antonio. Success for the missions on the San Gabriel was unlikely under any circumstances, as Rábago pointed out upon his arrival there in 1751. Had he been a capable and decent commander the attempt probably would have lasted longer; his conduct, however, amounted to an early coup de grace.

The second important initiative undertaken in the late 1740s focused on building a mission for the Lipan Apaches on the San Saba River northwest of San Antonio. Franciscan leaders, believing that bringing understanding and religious instruction to the Lipans in their own country was the best means of ending the warfare that plagued San Antonio, had long wanted to missionize the Apaches. As it happened, by the late 1740s the Apaches had a reason to accept overtures from the Spanish, a pressing reason called the Comanches. The Lipans planned to turn the whites into an ally against their more dangerous Indian enemy. As a first step, four chiefs went to San Antonio in August 1749 and signed a treaty renouncing war, which religious leaders took as an indication of willingness to accept Christian conversion as well as peace.

Enthusiastic reports about possible mineral riches in the San Saba country, brought back by several exploring expeditions in the early 1750s, coupled with the arguments of religious leaders eventually led the viceroy in 1756 to appoint Colonel Diego Ortiz Parrilla to lead an effort to provide missions for the Apaches. The priests involved were led by Father Alonso Giraldo de Terreros, who received the position primarily because he had a wealthy cousin who agreed to pay all the expenses of the mission for three years. Colonel Ortiz Parrilla had considerable experience as an Indian fighter and administrator, but he was instructed, probably as a result of the Rábago fiasco, to be very respectful of the wishes of Father Terreros and the other priests.

In the spring of 1757, Colonel Ortiz Parrilla transferred the properties of the abortive presidio and missions on the San Gabriel, which had been relocated to the San Marcos in 1755, to a new site on the San Saba near present-day Menard. The colonel, already doubting the sincerity of the Apaches because a group who had visited San Antonio early that year seemed more interested in gifts and help against the Comanches than in religious instruction, had his suspicions confirmed when the Spanish arrived to find not a single Lipan ready to join the mission. Ortiz Parrilla suggested an immediate move back to San Antonio, but Father Terreros insisted on remaining. The Spanish then built a mission (Santa Cruz de San Sabá) and a presidio (San Luis de las Amarillas), placing the two establishments more than three miles apart in order to assure the priests that soldiers would not interfere with Indian converts.

The San Sabá mission failed to attract a single convert during its first year. At the same time, Apache war parties raided Comanche camps and left items of Spanish clothing and shoes to indicate how friendly they were with the Europeans. Apaches also visited the mission regularly but only to keep up the hopes of the priests until the anger of the Comanches boiled over. In early March scouts from the presidio reported that the Apaches were rapidly moving southward while hundreds of Comanches, Tonkawas, Hasinais, and Wichitas—groups that the Spanish called Norteños because they generally lived north of San Antonio—were converging on the San Saba. Colonel Ortiz Parrilla had to protect his command, which included 237 women and children in the fort, and could send only a few soldiers to the mission. He urged the three priests to move to the safety of the presidio, but they refused.

Shortly after sunrise on March 16, 1758, in the words of one of the priests, Father Miguel de Molina, "a furious outburst of yells and war cries was heard outside the gate of the enclosure." The Indians, in spite of their threatening appearance, claimed to have only peaceful intentions and persuaded the two soldiers at the mission to open the gate. Pouring in, "armed with guns and arrayed in the most horrible attire," the Indians began to steal horses and loot the kitchen. One Hasinai chief proposed to take the personal mount of Father Terreros, and when the priest objected, "took up his musket and aimed it at the horse." Father Terreros and a soldier then offered to go with the Indians to the presidio, but as they rode toward the gate, shooting began, fatally wounding the two Spaniards. A general melee ensued in which another priest and five others were killed and the mission set afire. Father Molina survived and made his way to the presidio two days later to tell the story. In the meantime the Indians tried to lure the presidio's soldiers out into the open, but that failing, left. Colonel Ortiz Parrilla then visited the mission and found only charred ruins and mutilated bodies. Even the mission's cats had been killed.

Mission Santa Cruz, the only religious establishment in Spanish Texas destroyed by outright Indian attack, was never rebuilt. However, the Spanish refused to run away from their failure on the San Saba and planned instead a retaliatory expedition to be commanded by Colonel Ortiz Parrilla. Organizing this force proved so difficult and slow that no action had been taken by March 1759 when the Norteños appeared again, this time raiding the presidio's livestock herd and killing twenty soldiers in the process. All of the deaths resulted from bullet wounds rather than arrows, and the firearms could have come only from the French. Thus, when Colonel Ortiz Parrilla finally led a force of more than five hundred men, including 130 Lipan Apaches, north from the San Saba in the late summer of 1759, he hoped to punish the Indians and the French.

Ortiz Parrilla's expedition moved northward across the Brazos River and successfully fought several minor engagements with Wichita warriors. Then, in early October as his forces pursued a small group of Indians through a wooded area, they came into an opening near the Red River and, to their amazement, saw warriors waiting for them in defensive positions on the south side of the river and a massive fort of twelve-foot high posts on the north bank. Within the fort's walls flew the flag of France. The Spanish had come face to face with the most impressive fort ever constructed by the Taovaya Wichitas. (Ironically, the site opposite the fort in present-day Montague County eventually became known to Anglo-Americans as Spanish Fort.)

Ortiz Parrilla's forces engaged the Wichitas in battle on the south side of the river, using two cannons dragged with his expedition all the way from San Sabá. By one account, however, every shot fired by a cannon was followed by the sound of Indians laughing, whereas the Spanish were met with concentrated fire that stopped their attack. Mounted Wichitas then counterattacked under the leadership of a chief dressed in white doeskin and forced the Spanish to retreat to the cover of nearby woods. The next day Ortiz Parrilla retreated toward San Sabá, having suffered fifty-two casualties, the worst defeat for Spanish arms in Texas.

The Spanish maintained the San Sabá presidio for another ten years, but no attempt was made to reestablish the mission. In an interesting turn of events, Ortiz Parrilla was removed from command in 1760 and replaced by none other than Felipe de Rábago y Terán, the licentious captain who had gained infamy on the San Gabriel eight years earlier. A new viceroy who arrived in Mexico City in 1760 cleared Rábago of all charges and then, on the grounds that the captain had merely been suspended as commander of the presidio on the San Gabriel before its relocation to the San Saba in 1757, restored him to that position. Franciscan fathers with long memories were appalled, but Rábago's conduct at San Sabá disproved the old saying about a leopard and his spots. Finding the presidio in terrible condition, he spent his own money to clothe, feed, and equip the garrison and rebuilt the wooden fort with quarried stone. Almost singlehandedly, he kept the presidio on the

San Saba alive and even made a new effort to expand mission activity in the region.

Somewhat ironically, in 1761–1762 Rábago allowed himself to be misled by people even more skilled than he in deceit—the Lipan Apaches. The Indians told the captain that they would congregate in a mission if only it had a suitable location, one not so close as San Sabá had been to their Comanche enemies. Persuaded, Rábago brought in missionaries from Mexico and set up two new missions on the upper reaches of the Nueces River in present-day Real County. He did not have the approval of the Franciscans in San Antonio, who knew him by his reputation, or the consent of authorities in Mexico City. The Apaches then used the same trick that they had played on the San Sabá mission—raiding the Norteños and leaving evidence of their close ties to the Spanish. The Norteños in turn harassed the new missions and besieged the presidio on the San Saba for months at a time. Rábago's trust in the Apaches doomed his efforts to redeem the fiasco on the San Gabriel.

The third attempt at settling a new area during these years came almost solely from that most typical of reasons in the story of Spanish Texas—responding to a threat from France. Although they had crossed the Trinity River many times on the way to East Texas, the Spanish found no reason to settle its lower basin until word came in 1754 that Frenchmen had set up a post near the mouth of the river and were trading with a local Atakapan group known as the Orcoquizas. Spanish officials responded immediately by sending soldiers to arrest the French interlopers and confiscate their goods, which they did to the considerable aggravation of the Indians. The captives were sent to Mexico City for questioning, and more than a year later, officials there ordered the establishment of a presidio and mission on the lower Trinity near the present town of Anahuac. Built during the summer of 1756, El Orcoquisac, as the two structures are often called, never flourished. Few Indians joined the mission, storms and floods occurred often, and undrinkable water, flies, and mosquitoes made life miserable. Thus, the effort to settle the lower Trinity led to no spectacle of any kind, as did those on the San Gabriel and the San Saba; it just quietly came to nothing.

The fourth initiative in expanding the northern frontier of New Spain during the 1740s and 1750s succeeded, probably because of the ways that it differed notably from the three failed attempts. For one thing, this attempt focused on the coastal region stretching from Tampico in the south to Matagorda Bay in the north and was therefore much closer to support bases in Mexico. For another, because it did not have the primary purpose of establishing missions for the Indians, there was no conflict between soldiers and priests. And finally, this initiative had truly outstanding leadership in the person of José de Escandón y Elguera.

José de Escandón came to Mexico at the age of fifteen from his birthplace in Spain and established himself as a military man who dealt effectively but fairly with Europeans and Indians alike. Thus, when the need arose to explore and pacify the coast of northern Mexico and southern Texas, the viceroy chose Escandón to serve as the colonizer and governor of a new province to be called Nuevo Santander. This name, which was given in honor of Escandón's birthplace, would eventually be changed to Tamaulipas. Receiving the appointment in September 1746, Escandón did a rapid but thorough job of planning and sent seven expeditions into Nuevo Santander in 1747, two of which explored portions of present-day Texas.

A force of forty soldiers and twenty-five mission Indians led by Miguel de la Garza Falcón crossed the Río Grande near San Juan Bautista and marched down the north bank to the Gulf. Although many expeditions had headed into Texas from the point that Falcón crossed the river, none had explored in the direction that he took, which he soon discovered to be just as well. Finding the land rough and water short, Falcón's force struggled down the river, missed a scheduled rendezvous with other groups sent out by Escandón, and went back to Coahuila on their own.

The second expedition, which included twenty-five soldiers who marched all the way from Los Adaes to participate, set out from the presidio at La Bahía in January 1747 under the command of Captain Joaquín Orobio Bastera. Orobio first located yet another site for the La Bahía presidio and mission—a place that became known as Goliad. Two years later Escandón approved moving La Bahía to this new location. Orobio next marched to the Nueces River and determined that it flowed into Corpus Christi Bay. Continuing southward along the coast through country rarely seen by Europeans since Cabeza de Vaca, Orobio's force finally reached the Río Grande. The commander found little to encourage settlement of the land from the Nueces to Mexico.

Escandón's seven expeditions completed their assignments within three months with no loss of life among the 765 men involved, a truly impressive accomplishment. Then, over the next eight years, he oversaw the establishment of twenty-three towns and eighteen missions. Only two of these, however, were in Texas, and only one had any significance for the future. In 1754, Tomás Sánchez of Nuevo León proposed to create and defend a settlement at a crossing of the Río Grande called Paso de Jacinto. Escandón authorized a colonizing venture but ordered that it be located on the Nueces. Unable to find a suitable spot there, Sánchez threatened to abandon the project unless he could settle the original location on the Río Grande. Escandón relented, and in May 1755 Sánchez established Villa Laredo, which eventually became one of the major border towns of Texas.

While Escandón explored and established missions and towns, a few Mexican ranchers moved their livestock into pastures north of the Río Grande and thereby instituted ranching in South Texas. For example, in 1750 Don José Vázquez Borrego obtained from Escandón the rights to approximately 329,000 acres in present-day Webb and Zapata Counties downstream from the site of Laredo and created a *hacienda* called Nuestra Señora de los Dolores. By 1757, the *hacienda* of Dolores had thirty families who worked as servants, herdsmen, and guards. And its livestock herd included 3,000 cattle, 3,400 horses, and 2,650 mules and donkeys. Tomás Sánchez, the founder of Laredo, joined Vázquez Borrego as a large rancher on the north side of the Río Grande during the early 1750s. Ranching and trade with Mexico would be the keys to the economy of South Texas for many years.

Retrenchment Again

In the early 1760s, Spanish Texas still had essentially the shape given to it by the Ramón and Aguayo expeditions forty years earlier. San Antonio had developed into a truly viable community with successful missions and a population capable of supporting and defending itself with limited help from Mexico City. Even there, however, the number of Spanish-speaking settlers amounted to only about one thousand. The East Texas settlements around Nacogdoches, San Augustine, and Los Adaes taken together probably had fewer than five hundred residents and had made no progress in converting the Indians. La Bahía, the one important post in the coastal region, also had a population of fewer than five hundred Spanish speakers. The only remnants of the efforts at expansion into the interior during the 1740s and 1750s were El Orcoquisac on the Trinity, a presidio on the San Saba, and Rábago's new missions on the upper Nueces, all of which were moribund. Escandón's brilliantly successful work along the Gulf coast had created only Laredo and a few large ranches on the north side of the Río Grande. Overall, Spanish Texas in the early 1760s remained a sparsely settled province regarded primarily by the mother country as a buffer zone against France and as a field for missionary work, not as a colony of value in its own right. And then, in 1762, the usefulness of Texas as a buffer suddenly disappeared.

This change in the value of Texas to Spain resulted from a war that had nothing to do with the land from Los Adaes to Laredo or for that matter with the whole of New Spain. From 1754 until 1763 England and France fought what historians now call the Great War for Empire, a contest with theaters in Europe, North America, and India. Spain had no role in this war until early 1762 when links between members of the Bourbon family that ruled both countries brought it in on the side of France. Entering the war so late, the Spanish could not help the French recover from defeats already suffered and to boot lost their own colony, Cuba, to the English within less than a year. When preliminary peace negotiations were held in late 1762, Spain regained Cuba only by ceding Florida to England. France, partly to compensate Spain and partly to hurry an end to the war, then gave Louisiana to Spain. The Spanish knew that France had spent a fortune trying to control and defend Louisiana but never earned a penny in return, an experience very similar to their own on the northern frontier of New Spain. However, to reject the French offer would make Englishmen their neighbors along the Texas border, a spot too close for comfort to the mines in Mexico. The Treaty of Paris in 1763 formally ended the war and finalized the territorial arrangements agreed on the previous year.

Spain did not take actual control of Louisiana until 1766, thanks to opposition by men of French ancestry in New Orleans. Nevertheless, ownership of Louisiana meant that Texas no longer constituted the first line of defense against foreign incursions into New Spain and permitted revisions, ideally ones that would save money, in frontier policy. The first step toward change, an obvious and sensible one, was to commission an inspector to examine and report on conditions along the frontier from California to Louisiana. Accordingly, in 1765 King Charles III appointed the Marqués de Rubí to visit all presidios on the northern frontier, the first such visitation since Rivera's approximately forty years earlier.

Reaching Texas in 1767, Rubí first visited the presidio on the San Saba commanded by Felipe de Rábago and found it the worst in all of New Spain. It was, he said, as effective in protecting the region as a ship anchored in the middle of the Atlantic Ocean would be at preventing foreign trade with America. From San Sabá the inspector moved on to San Antonio, where he found a pleasant contrast in the form of a sound presidio, flourishing villa, and five "rich" missions. He recommended an increase in troop strength there to protect against Indian raids.

Rubí next visited the missions in East Texas and the presidio at Los Adaes and found them all in appalling condition. The missions still had no converts, and the presidio had sixty-one soldiers, twenty-five horses, and two functional muskets. Most of the soldiers were clothed in rags, largely because they could not afford goods sold by the commandant, Governor Angel de Martos, who demanded a 1,000 percent profit from his store. One detachment of soldiers spent their time as cowhands on the governor's ranch. Rubí found that Martos had just been removed and sent to Mexico City to face charges concerning his administration, but that did not give him any hope for the establishment at Los Adaes. He would recommend that it be closed.

The situation encountered by Rubí at El Orcoquisac on the lower Trinity was worse than anything that he had seen to that point. Three years earlier Governor Martos had attempted to replace the commander of the presidio there, only to meet resistance on the grounds that the officer had received his appointment directly from the viceroy. Martos sent soldiers to remove the defiant commander, who responded by barricading himself in the presidio. At that point, the soldiers could think of nothing to do but set fire to the fort. The commander escaped, but when Rubí arrived, only charred ruins remained. Priests at the mission had a single convert to show for their work among the Indians. His report would describe the entire establishment as "useless."

La Bahía at Goliad was the last presidio visited by Rubí. He found it more satisfactory, in spite of the fact that many of the people there suffered from malaria. The two local missions had nearly two hundred Indian converts in residence. The inspector left Texas by way of Laredo, which had about sixty huts on both sides of the Río Grande.

In 1769 Rubí prepared a brutally direct report on his inspection tour, pointing out that in most cases presidio and mission activities in Texas amounted to a waste of money. He recommended sweeping changes that would leave fifteen presidios in a line extending from the Gulf of California to the lower Guadalupe River, only two of which—San Antonio de Bexár and La Bahía—

would be in Texas. The presidios and satellite missions at San Sabá, El Orcoquisac, and Los Adaes would be abandoned as would the missions near Nacogdoches and San Augustine in East Texas. Rubí also suggested a new policy for dealing with the Apaches, one totally in opposition to that favored by religious leaders. Since the Lipans often asked for missions and then refused to enter them, he said, while at the same time using the presence of missions to irritate the Comanches and other northern Indians, the Spanish should wage a war of extermination on the Apaches. At the same time, Rubí argued, his government should adopt the French policy and trade with all except the Apaches. That approach, he concluded, would remove one especially bothersome group of Indians and promote friendship and peace with their enemies.

The Spanish bureaucracy acted with its usual glacial speed on Rubi's report, and in the meantime several of his proposals became reality unofficially. Heavy attacks by the Norteños on the San Sabá presidio, combined with the removal of Rábago in 1768, led to the closing of all establishments in that area in 1771. El Orcoquisac in effect closed that same year when the soldiers in its presidio were called to San Antonio to bolster the garrison there and the missionaries followed. Finally in 1772 the Spanish Crown acted on Rubí's report by issuing an order known as the "New Regulations for Presidios," which accepted all of his major proposals. Implementation of these new rules fell to Governor Juan María de Ripperdá, who had taken over in 1769 and set up his residence in San Antonio, the first governor of Texas to do so officially.

Governor Ripperdá's most difficult task involving enforcement of the New Regulations came from the requirement that he remove all Spanish settlers from East Texas and relocate them in San Antonio. The population of the eastern region, which was concentrated near Nacogdoches, had grown from two to five hundred since Rubí's inspection. Most had homes, crops, and livestock to care for when the governor arrived in the summer of 1773 and gave them a week to pack and be ready to leave for San Antonio. Moving westward in the summer heat created terrible hardships on the East Texans. Once at San Antonio, finding an alien environment and no good land on which to live, they reacted by petitioning Governor Ripperdá for permission to return home. Allowed to take their request to Mexico City in person, two leaders, Gil Antonio Ybarbo and Gil Flores, made the long trek southward. They were accompanied by a Hasinai leader, Texita, who also pleaded for the Spanish to return to East Texas. Ybarbo, a wealthy rancher and trader who enjoyed high regard among Spanish officials, and Flores, with the aid of Texita, impressed the viceroy, Antonio María de Bucareli y Ursúa, and won his approval to move to a "suitable place" in East Texas, provided that it was at least three hundred miles from Natchitoches.

Ybarbo chose a spot on the Trinity River near the crossing of the Camino Real (now Highway 21) and established a town in 1774, which the East Texans diplomatically called Bucareli. It grew rapidly for three years, having 347 people by 1777, but marauding Comanches and flooding during the next two years caused the settlers to abandon the site and, without authorization, move back to Nacogdoches. The Spanish government allowed this action to stand and eventually in 1795 sent troops to defend the town. Nacogdoches thus became the center of permanent settlement in East Texas from 1779 onward.

The New Regulations of 1772 also called for a major change in Indian policy provoked primarily by two considerations. For one thing, the mission system simply had not worked with most Texas Indians. For another, along with Louisiana the Spanish had acquired what might be called the "French policy" for dealing with Indians. The French, rather than trying to settle the natives around missions and Christianize them, sent out traders to buy their good will through annual gifts from the king and to arrange profitable commercial relationships with each group. When the Spanish took over Louisiana, they did not alter this French policy there but instead began to think about implementing it in a modified form in Texas as well. Without dropping their religious commitment to the Indians in San Antonio, they would cultivate trade with those whom they favored and punish others, such as the Apaches, by withholding goods from them.

Spain's implementation of the French policy in Texas drew on the experience and talent of its new citizens of French descent in Louisiana, especially a man named Athanase de Mézières. Born in Paris in 1719, de Mézières had endured misfortune that would have destroyed many people. His father died when he was fifteen, and his mother quickly remarried a wealthy nobleman and acquired a position at the court of Louis XIV. Bothered by her children, especially since they gave away her age, de Mézières's mother placed her daughter in a convent and had the boy exiled to Louisiana by royal decree in 1738. He moved upriver to Canada and lived with Indians there for four years, submitting to the tattooing of his entire body as a condition for staying with them. In 1742 de Mézières joined the army and was posted at Natchitoches where he met and married one of the daughters of Louis Juchereau de Saint-Denis, commandant of the post. His first wife died in 1748, and he took another a few years later, all the while building himself into one of the richest men in the area. A census in 1766 showed him as the owner of thirty-five slaves and ten thousand pounds of tobacco.

When Spain took over Louisiana in 1769, de Mézières was called to New Orleans and made lieutenant governor of Natchitoches with responsibility for keeping the peace and arranging trade with Indians on the Louisiana-Texas border. The Frenchman worked faithfully for the next ten years as a diplomat and commercial agent for Spain, maintaining good relations with the Caddos (both the Hasinais in East Texas and the Kadohadachos on the Red River), Tonkawas, and Wichitas. In keeping with Spain's developing policy of hostility toward the Apaches, he had no dealings with that group, but sought, generally without success, to improve relations with the Comanches. De Mézières went to San Antonio in 1778 and proposed to Teodoro de Croix, the first commandant general of a new administrative unit for defending the northern frontier called the Interior Provinces, that an alliance be created between the Spanish and the Comanches and other Indians of the north to destroy the Apaches. Croix agreed, but de Mézières, in his travels to forge this alliance in

1779, suffered an injury when thrown from his horse and never fully recovered. The Frenchman turned down an offer of the governorship of Texas and died in November 1779. His proposed alliance died with him, but the concept of working with the Comanches and other Norteños to destroy the Apaches lived on into the next decade.

Commandant General Croix of the Interior Provinces of New Spain wrote the following utterly unflattering description of Texas and its capital in the late 1770s: "A villa without order, two presidios, seven missions, and an errant population of scarcely 4,000 persons of both sexes and all ages that occupies an immense desert country, stretching from the abandoned presidio of Los Adaes to San Antonio, . . . [that] does not deserve the name of the province of Texas . . . nor the concern entailed in its preservation." In spite of some exaggeration, Croix's statement accurately reflected the attitude of most Spanish officials toward the province. They saw it as an inhospitable backwater, more trouble than it was worth. Even as Croix wrote, however, the Americas and Europe were moving into an age of revolutions that would leave no part of the Spanish empire untouched, not even the remote, thinly populated, and impoverished province of Texas.

Chapter 4

SPANISH TEXAS IN THE AGE OF REVOLUTIONS, 1779–1821

The Treaty of Paris in 1763, which officially ended the Great War for Empire, required dramatic revisions in maps showing the possessions of European nations in North America. (See map: North America before and after the Treaty of Paris, 1763.) France lost virtually all its colonies, ceding Louisiana to Spain and giving Canada and all French claims east of the Mississippi to England. Spain gave Florida to England but at least acquired Louisiana. As befitted the victor, England took control of a vast area stretching from the Gulf of Mexico to Hudson Bay and the Atlantic Ocean to the Mississippi. The thirteen English colonies along the seaboard from Georgia to New England, so insecure before the war, now appeared to have a great future as part of the world's most powerful empire.

Ironically, however, the war proved too successful for the good of Britain's relationship with her mainland North American colonies. Issues such as taxation and enforcement of trade regulations developed almost immediately to upset the long-standing working relationship between English colonials and their mother country. Moreover, removal of the French threat made the colonials less dependent on British military power and therefore more willing to take strong stands against actions that they saw as threats to their interests and rights as Englishmen. The result was conflict that turned into war in 1775 and brought a Declaration of Independence in 1776. The age of revolutions thus began in America.

France soon came to the aid of the thirteen American colonies to get even with the British for earlier defeats, but the government of Spain did not embrace the revolt nearly so eagerly. After all, an independence movement on the Atlantic seaboard set a bad example for its own colonial possessions to the south. Spain therefore followed France's lead in providing assistance to the colonies only to a point. Soon after the outbreak of war, the government at Madrid began to aid the revolutionaries with subsidies, loans, guns, and ammunition, but it drew the line at an actual military alliance and refused to become a party to the agreement signed between the French and Americans

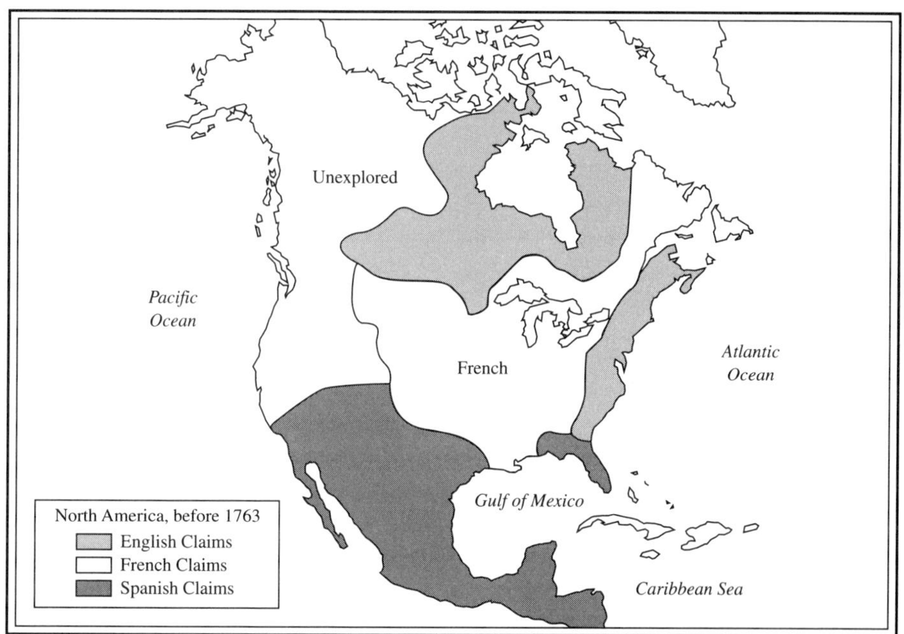

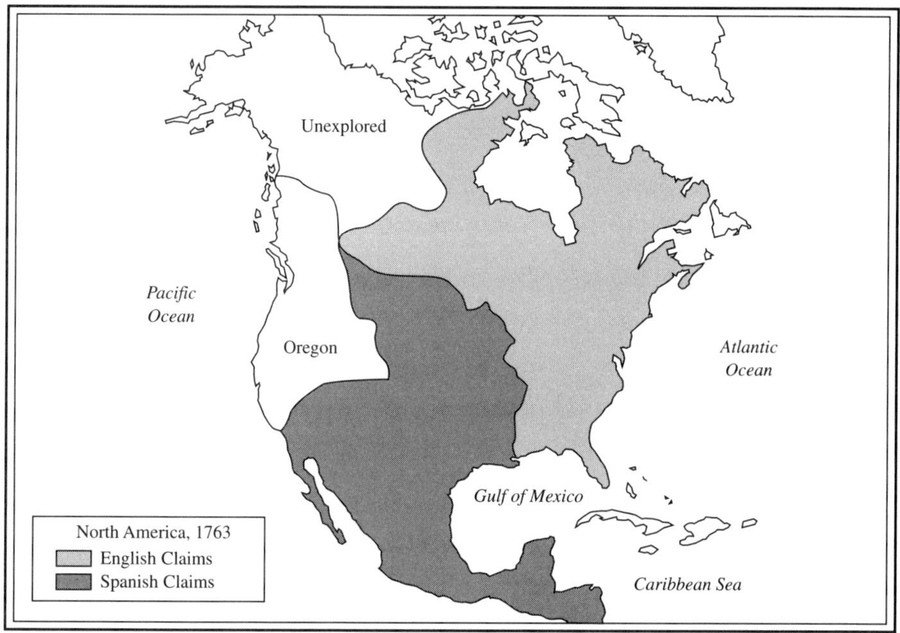

North America before and after the Treaty of Paris, 1763

in 1778. When Spain finally entered the war against England in June 1779, it acted only as an ally of France and made no commitment to the thirteen colonies.

Spain, in spite of its reluctance, contributed more to the success of the colonies in the War of the American Revolution than is generally recognized. In 1779–1781, armies commanded by the governor of Louisiana, Bernardo de Gálvez, drove the English from the region known as West Florida by taking Baton Rouge, Natchez, Mobile, and Pensacola. The Spanish also kept the Mississippi River open to the colonies as a lifeline for supplies throughout the war. After the Treaty of Paris confirmed the independence of the United States in 1783, the American Congress adopted an official expression of gratitude to Governor Gálvez. Spain's contributions to the war were rewarded more substantially, too, in that it regained Florida, which had been taken by England twenty years earlier. At that point the far northern frontier of New Spain appeared thoroughly protected by the ownership of Louisiana and the entire northern coast of the Gulf of Mexico. Certainly, Mexico and Texas seemed secure.

Texas at the Time of the American Revolution

Texas assisted Spanish forces in the War of the American Revolution in only one way. During the summer of 1779, Governor Gálvez bought two thousand head of cattle from the ranches of missions and individuals in the region of San Antonio and La Bahía and had the beeves herded to Louisiana to feed Spanish troops, thus beginning a famed Texas tradition—the cattle drive. Over the next three years ten to fifteen thousand head of cattle were driven along a trail that ran from La Bahía to Nacogdoches, across the Sabine River to Natchitoches, and then on to Opelousas, Louisiana. Texas *vaqueros* herded the cattle, and soldiers from several presidios served as escorts.

Beef was about the only contribution that could have been expected from Texas when Spain declared war on England in 1779. In the first place, a great majority of the province's people were Indians who had little interest in wars between Europeans and were themselves, in many cases, a threat to Spanish settlements north of the Río Grande. No one can say with certainty how many Indians lived in Texas in the late 1770s. Some groups such as the Karankawas, Caddos, and Wichitas had suffered sharp losses of population, especially as a result of smallpox epidemics during the 1770s. The number of Karankawas decreased from around eight thousand in the late 1600s to about three thousand by 1780, and some groups of Caddos virtually ceased to exist. The Taovaya Wichitas on the Red River lost one thousand people from a total population of three thousand over a six-year period. Regardless of these losses, however, approximately twenty thousand Indians still lived in the province at the end of the 1770s, far outnumbering the residents of Spanish settlements. Moreover, the Comanches, the most fearsome Indians in Texas where Europeans were concerned, apparently did not suffer a major epidemic at this time. Athanase de Mézières reported in 1770 that those West Texans were "a people so numerous and so haughty that when asked their number, they make no difficulty in comparing it to the stars."

By contrast the first census of Spanish settlements, taken in 1777, enumerated a total population of only 3,103, and even that number is misleading in that it included residents of the missions, priests and Indian converts alike. Approximately half of these people were considered Spaniards (most of them born in America); Indians (mostly Coahuiltecans) constituted a quarter of the total; and those of mixed race such as mestizos (of Spanish and Indian parentage) and mulattoes (of Spanish and African parentage) amounted to nearly another quarter. There were only twenty slaves, mostly of African descent. More than half of the population (55 percent) were males, but even at that, Texas obviously had few men available to fight a war.

Texans could provide cattle for the armies in 1779–1782 because available resources and frontier conditions had dictated that ranching would be the first truly important step in the province's economic development. Farming proved extremely difficult, even with irrigation, in the San Antonio area where most Spanish settlers lived, and agriculture remained largely at the subsistence level. The sparse population limited opportunities for merchants, craftsmen, and laborers. Thus, ranching became the one way to earn significant wealth in all parts of Spanish Texas. Missions, beginning with the Aguayo expedition in 1721 that stocked herds at religious establishments near San Antonio and La Bahía, began livestock production in Texas, but by the 1750s private ranches developed also. Soldiers, usually officers, from the presidios near those missions began to acquire land, cattle, and horses and set themselves up as ranchers. Building herds was inexpensive because so much livestock was there for the taking. Most of the major exploring expeditions had brought cattle, horses, sheep, and goats, and left them free to roam and reproduce. Alonso de León, for example, deliberately left male and female animals at each river crossing from the Río Grande to the Neches. Private ranching began in South Texas in the 1750s in connection with the explorations and settlements made by José de Escandón. By the 1770s Texas had three ranching centers. Stockmen around Nacogdoches concentrated on raising horses, while those in the San Antonio/La Bahía region and the lower Río Grande valley raised both horses and cattle.

Spanish authorities granted generous amounts of land, most commonly a square league of 4,428 acres, for stock raising to individuals who applied and paid a fee. Texas had no huge *haciendas* except at the very beginning of private ranching in South Texas; instead, large stock farms called *ranchos* became the rule. *Ranchos* acted as distinct civil institutions in settling Texas and developing all facets of the cattle industry. Breeding and selling livestock led to improvements in the saddle and lariat and to the roundup or "rodeo" and the cattle drive. Even before taking herds to Louisiana during the American Revolution, stock raisers in Texas drove horses and cattle to Coahuila and Nuevo León in Mexico. Ranchers tended to see themselves as rulers of their domains, but they had to accept some regulation from the government. For example, Teodoro de Croix, the first commandant general of the Interior

Provinces, issued an order in 1778 that all cattle had to be branded or become the property of the king. His order led to the registration of marks and brands, a practice still required in Texas counties.

Transportation and communication in such a thinly populated frontier region can best be described as "primitive." Two long roads crossed Texas from west to east—the Camino Real or King's Highway, which ran from San Juan Bautista on the Río Grande to San Antonio and on nearly to Natchitoches, and another that ran from Laredo to La Bahía and then northeastward to connect with the Camino Real at the Trinity River. A branch of the Camino Real connected San Antonio and La Bahía. Texans traveled these main roads and the even more crude trails that linked scattered ranches and homes on foot or riding horses or mules or in wagons drawn by horses, mules, or oxen. The province had no organized means of communication until 1779 when Teodoro de Croix set up post offices at Bucareli, San Antonio, and La Bahía. Presidial soldiers carried mail to and from these settlements and to Coahuila as well.

Obviously, the daily lives of most men and women in late eighteenth-century Texas revolved around the requirements of survival. Marriage was the norm, and married couples worked together to provide food, shelter, and clothing for themselves and their children. If men had to leave to fight in defense of their settlements, women assumed full responsibility for their homes and children. Women did not have equal status with men, but Spanish laws and traditions growing out of the reconquest from the Moors gave them rights not generally accorded women in other societies. For example, Spanish law included the concepts of separate and community property, meaning that unmarried women who owned property maintained title to that property even after marriage and that married women shared equally in the ownership of property acquired after entering into the bonds of matrimony. Community property could not be sold without the consent of both husband and wife.

Most Spanish Texans were illiterate, and neither they nor their children had an opportunity for education. Still, they were remarkably well informed of their rights under the law. The case of a poor mulatto woman in San Antonio during the 1740s provides a good example. Antonia Lusgardia Hernández had worked for years in the home of Miguel Núñez Morillo. During that time, she had given birth to a son whom her employer's wife liked and had baptized as a godchild. After some time, the servant, finding herself unpaid and mistreated, took her child and left the Morillo home, whereupon her former employer entered her new home and took the boy. Hernández, with the aid of someone who could write, petitioned the governor as the chief judicial officer of the province for the return of the boy, calling herself "a poor, helpless woman whose only protection is a good administration and a good judicial system." After hearing Morillo's response to this petition, the governor ordered the return of the boy to his birth mother. It seems that even the poorest women in Spanish Texas knew their rights and could expect a fair hearing when an issue arose.

Texas Indians during the Age of Revolutions

Thus, as the age of revolution opened in the late 1770s, Texas showed signs of economic and social progress such as the development of productive ranching and the use of Spanish laws that protected the rights of both men and women. Overall, however, the province remained a poor backwater on New Spain's far northern frontier. Life was hard under the best of circumstances, and continuing Indian raids and warfare made it even more difficult. The Apaches, the first group to give serious trouble to Spanish settlers in Texas, were so hard pressed by the Comanches and other Norteños that some of their bands moved south of the Río Grande into Coahuila during the 1770s, only to come under attack by Spanish forces there. Pressured by both the Comanches and the Spanish, Apache leaders came to San Antonio and arranged a peace settlement in 1780. Promises by the Lipans did not end their raiding, however, which continued during the next decade.

Even coastal regions were not secure enough to avoid Indian depredations, as witnessed by an incident involving the Karankawas in 1778. A ship sent by Governor Gálvez of Louisiana to explore and map the coast from the mouth of the Mississippi to Matagorda Bay ran short of supplies near the Texas bay and sent five men ashore to find provisions. Karankawas murdered the five, and then two Indian leaders approached the ship, professing ignorance of the Spaniards' fate. The captain allowed the two to board and talk him into sending three more sailors to help secure fresh meat. Once out of sight, the Karankawas murdered those three as well. Then, they returned with meat, claiming that the three sailors had remained with the kill. While the famished Spaniards busied themselves with cooking and eating, more Indians slipped aboard and killed the remainder of the crew. They took guns and ammunition and burned the ship. When Governor Domingo Cabello y Robles, who had just recently taken office, learned of these murders in 1779, he planned to wage a war of extermination on the Karankawas, but Spain's involvement in the War of the American Revolution and problems with the Comanches prevented any action.

The western Comanches suffered a major defeat by Spanish forces in New Mexico during the summer of 1779, which caused them to turn even more attention to the weaker province of Texas. Within a year, Governor Cabello wrote from San Antonio: "There is not an instant by day or night when reports do not arrive from all these ranches of barbarities and disorders falling on us. Totally unprotected as we are, they will result in the absolute destruction and loss of this province." The Indians had stolen so many horses, he reported, that he did not have mounts for a retaliatory campaign. Ironically, the Apaches took advantage of Comanche pressure on the Spanish to raid in the San Antonio area as well.

Teodoro de Croix, commandant general of the Interior Provinces, sympathized with Cabello but could offer no military help. He advised the governor to try gifts and diplomacy, an approach that finally paid dividends in

1785 when Pedro Vial, a French-born trader and blacksmith who had won favor with the Wichitas by repairing their broken weapons, was sent north to meet with Comanche leaders. Supported by several Wichita chiefs, Vial rewarded the Comanches with gifts such as tobacco and knives and gave a long speech reminding them of all the harm that came with war as opposed to the benefits of peace. Continuing warfare, the emissary pointed out, means that you cannot get trade goods—"you do not have a knife to cut meat, a pot with which to cook, nor a grain of powder with which to kill deer and buffalo for your sustenance." Peace will bring all that and more, he promised. Speaking for Governor Cabello, Vial asked the Comanches to come to San Antonio and talk "like friends, as also they would be to the other nations who are my friends, except the Lipans and Apaches, with whom I do not want anyone to be friends, but to make continual war against them." Clearly, Cabello's approach to Texas Indians was the French policy adopted more than a decade earlier.

The Comanches spent a day and a night considering what Vial had said and, encouraged by the Wichitas, responded with a pledge to "forget the deaths of our fathers, sons, and brothers caused by the Spaniards . . . and from now on the war with our brothers the Spaniards is finished, we will not kill, nor make any raids, nor rob." Three "little captains" returned to San Antonio with Vial and in October 1785 signed a treaty ending all hostilities with the Spanish. The agreement also gave the Spanish sole trading rights with the Comanches and provided for annual gifts to the Indians. Lipan Apaches remained the enemies of both signatories.

This 1785 treaty proved a blessing for Spanish Texas by preserving relatively peaceful relations with the Comanches for more than forty years. Moreover, the alliance against the Apaches soon put an end to trouble with that group as well. In 1790 a Spanish army from Coahuila marched into Texas, where it was joined by soldiers and civilians from San Antonio and by Comanches in an attack on a large force of Apaches at Soledad Creek in present-day Duval County. The defeat inflicted on the Apaches in this battle destroyed their ability to raid the frontier for many years to come.

Peace with the Comanches and defeat of the Apaches left the Karankawas as the only Indians in Texas who were consistently hostile to Spanish settlers. Rather than try to negotiate with or destroy the Karankawas, however, authorities sought to "civilize" them through the mission system. This approach was already discredited by repeated failures, but the Spanish could not resist a request from the Karankawas for a mission close to the coast in their own territory. Therefore, a mission called Nuestra Señora del Refugio was established at the junction of the San Antonio and Guadalupe Rivers in 1791, moved several times, and finally located in 1794 at the site of present-day Refugio. The Karankawas never settled at this mission in large numbers, but it provided a reasonably successful bridge between the Spanish and the Indians.

This attempt to missionize the Karankawas in the 1790s marked the last gasp of a dying system. Missions had succeeded among the Coahuiltecans in the San Antonio area, failed badly in East Texas and with the Apaches, and not even been considered for the Comanches and Wichitas. By the 1770s, the Franciscans, seeing their limited success in Texas and believing that they had more fertile fields elsewhere, began to work toward ending their involvement across the province. This meant secularizing the missions, a process by which the government took over all mission properties and managed their affairs, while secular clergy (that is, priests who did not belong to an order such as the Franciscans) took charge of religious services. Christianized Indians generally received parcels of land that had belonged to the mission and thus became taxpaying citizens of New Spain. Secularization would free the Franciscans of providing clergy to missions in Texas and end the government's financial responsibility to them as well. San Antonio de Valero (the Alamo) was secularized in 1793, and two other San Antonio missions were closed completely the next year. The governor of Texas, however, argued against secularizing La Bahía and several others because he did not believe their Indian converts ready for full citizenship, so a few missions struggled on with little or no success. Evaluation of the mission system in Texas is not a simple matter. From one point of view, it is a story of heroic sacrifice to bring civilization and salvation to the Indians. From another, it is a matter of arrogant Europeans interfering with and destroying native cultures. The "truth" is a matter of individual choice.

Spanish Texas and the United States

During the 1780s, Spanish officials kept a wary eye on the United States, the new nation born in the first revolt in an age of revolutions. Some feared that they had helped create a monster that threatened Louisiana, Florida, and Mexico. "This federal republic is born a pigmy," wrote the Count of Aranda, Spain's minister to France during the Revolution, but "the day will come when it will be a giant, even a colossus. . . . In a few years we will watch with grief the tyrannical existence of this same colossus." Juan Gassiot, a senior member of the staff of the commandant general of the Interior Provinces, echoed this concern, albeit with less exaggeration, in 1783. Anglo-Americans, he wrote, are "active, industrious, and aggressive," and far more unified and determined to expand than are the Spanish. Vicente Manuel de Zéspedes, the first governor of Florida after it was reacquired, described Anglo frontiersmen as "nomadic like Arabs and . . . distinguished from savages only in their color, language, and the superiority of their depraved cunning and untrustworthiness." Such people, the governor thought, had an appetite for land that could never be satisfied.

The dynamic growth of the United States during its first decade as an independent nation only added to these fears on the part of the Spanish. By 1790 the United States had about 3.7 million people, nearly a million of whom were black slaves. New Spain had a population of 4.8 million, but more than half of those were Indians. Even more to the point, Anglo-Americans poured over the Appalachian Mountains during the 1780s, bringing the "western" population of the United States to 277,000 in 1790. By contrast, Texas had only

3,169 Spanish-speaking inhabitants at that time, and even ten years later Louisiana's non-Indian population stood at about 50,000, more of whom were English, French, German, or American than Spanish. In addition to outstripping Spain's colonies in population growth, the United States advanced much more rapidly in economic growth as well. Free of any regulations or traditions that held down entrepreneurial activity, Anglo-Americans built an economy that by 1800 was twice as productive as that of New Spain.

Spain attempted to deal with the threat posed by the United States to its border colonies such as Louisiana by regulating commerce and promoting immigration. Commercial regulation depended on the fact that Spain controlled the mouth of the Mississippi River. Once Americans crossed the mountains, their complete dependence on the Mississippi and its tributaries for transportation earned them the nickname, "Men of the Western Waters." During the 1780s, the Spanish government permitted Americans who paid fees to use the river as well as unload and store goods at New Orleans, but the possibility of closing the river remained a trump card that could be played to wean settlers away from loyalty to the United States. The other policy, promotion of immigration, made sense but had a paradoxical result. Spanish officials knew that, in the words of Governor Zéspedes of Florida, "[t]he best fortification would be a living wall of industrious citizens." But they could not convince colonists from Spain or New Spain to move where they were needed and therefore, beginning in the 1780s, turned to citizens of the United States and began to encourage immigration to Louisiana with land grants and access to the Mississippi. Bringing in Americans to build a wall against Americans seemed a curious policy to some at the time, but it was the best that Spain could do, especially as developments associated with the French Revolution took the attention of the Spanish government.

In 1789, due in part to financial strains resulting from giving aid to the colonies in the American Revolution, a far greater and more radical upheaval erupted in France. By early 1793, the French overthrew the monarchy, made their nation a republic, executed the king and queen, and declared "war against all kings." Other monarchs in western Europe, not wishing to suffer the fate of Louis XVI, went to war against France. Spain, its throne occupied since 1788 by the ineffectual Charles IV but its government effectively in the hands of Manuel Godoy, the queen's twenty-five-year-old lover, soon joined England and Prussia in the war. Within three years French troops crossed the Pyrenees into Spain's northern provinces and forced Godoy to ask for peace and a renewal of the traditional alliance between the two nations. Poor Spain: growing ever weaker militarily, it could not successfully fight the French and would soon find that an alliance with its revolutionary neighbor would not bring protection either.

Spain's situation in the mid-1790s became even more difficult because peace with France almost inevitably meant war with England. Fearing that the English might encourage the United States to join them in an Anglo-American alliance and attack Louisiana, Godoy decided to go farther than ever in giving Americans access to the Mississippi as a way of maintaining their friendship. In 1795 the Treaty of San Lorenzo (called Pinckney's Treaty in the United States for Thomas Pinckney who handled negotiations in Madrid) guaranteed Americans duty-free navigation of the Mississippi and the right to deposit goods at New Orleans. Spanish officials knew that the treaty would allow Louisiana to become even more heavily Americanized, but most believed that they were only facing economic and demographic reality. Americans would push in one way or another; Spain's only hope was to encourage loyalty to it as a generous host.

Similar Spanish policies welcoming immigrants during the 1790s did not apply to Texas, however. Concerned that traders from the United States would build relationships with Indians along the Red River, the Crown in 1795 ordered Governor Manuel Muñoz of Texas to take "the utmost care to prevent the passage to this kingdom of persons from the United States of America. The king has been informed on good authority," the order continued, "that the United States has ordered emissaries to move here and work to subvert the population. . . . For this reason you are to exercise the utmost diligence and care to avoid the entry of any foreigner or any suspected person." Enforcement of this order proved difficult, of course, but not impossible, as is demonstrated by the story of Philip Nolan, the first well-known intruder from the United States into Texas.

Philip Nolan (who should not be confused with the fictional character of the same name in Edward Everett Hale's 1863 story, *The Man Without a Country*) was a native of Ireland who migrated to America and wound up in New Orleans in the late 1780s. Learning of trading opportunities in Texas, in 1791 Nolan obtained a passport from Governor Esteban Miró for a commercial expedition into the province. Spanish authorities seized his goods, and after two years he returned to Louisiana with only fifty Texas mustangs (wild horses) to show for his trouble. Undeterred, Nolan got a passport from the new governor, the Barón de Carondelet, and made another visit to Texas in 1794–1795. He went to San Antonio on this second trip, convinced Governor Muñoz to help him obtain a permit to catch mustangs, and took 250 head back to Louisiana. A third venture into Texas in 1797, again on a passport issued by Carondelet, was even more successful in that Nolan spent two years there and returned with 1,200 horses. By 1799, however, his activities had aroused Spanish suspicions about Anglo-American efforts to take control of the province. Pedro de Nava, Commandant General of the Interior Provinces, instructed the governor of Texas in 1800 to arrest Nolan if he entered again.

Ignoring the threatening attitude of authorities and his inability to obtain another passport, Nolan entered Texas again in October 1800 with a party totaling eighteen armed men. They passed north of Nacogdoches, crossed the Trinity, and set up camp on a tributary of the Brazos River in present-day McLennan or Hill County (the exact site is unknown). After spending the winter catching mustangs, Nolan's party awoke before dawn on March 22, 1801, to find their camp surrounded by Spanish troops from Nacogdoches. "As day broke," one of the Americans, Peter Ellis Bean, wrote later, "without speaking a word, they commenced their fire. After about ten minutes, our gallant leader Nolan was slain by a musket-ball which hit him in the head." The others fought on for most of the day before surrendering, according to Bean, with a promise that they would be allowed to return to Louisiana. They were taken to Nacogdoches, then sent to Mexico, where Spanish authorities decided that one of nine remaining prisoners would be executed for having fired on the king's soldiers. The nine cast dice to determine who would be hanged, and Ephraim Blackburn unluckily threw the low number. Bean and the others were held for years in a succession of Mexican prisons.

Philip Nolan probably intended to do nothing more than catch mustangs and possibly trade with the Caddos and Wichitas. After all, any design to take Texas for the United States while Louisiana remained in Spanish hands would have faced serious logistical problems. How much success could Americans have had crossing Spanish Louisiana to take and hold Spanish Texas? His attempts to trade with Texas Indians indicated that Anglo-Americans might replace the French as suppliers of weapons and other goods and undermine Spanish interests in that sense. But Spain's ownership of Texas could not be threatened seriously by citizens of the United States until their country acquired Louisiana. That change of possession, however, happened sooner than anyone expected.

In 1795 Manuel Godoy, chief adviser to Charles IV, offered to trade Louisiana to France in return for Haiti, the French-held part of Hispaniola. Godoy hoped to escape the costs of administering Louisiana and place France in the position of a protective buffer between the United States and Mexico. The French refused the asking price, but after Napoleon Bonaparte took over the revolutionary government in 1799, they acquired Louisiana at virtually no cost. On October 1, 1800, in return for Napoleon's promise to place the brother of the queen of Spain on the throne of an Italian kingdom, the Spanish signed the Retrocession of San Ildefenso, returning Louisiana to France. Napoleon, who planned at that time to use Louisiana as the "breadbasket" of an American empire based in the Caribbean, promised never to allow the colony to fall into the hands of another country. Three years later, however, after seeing an army sent to put down a slave rebellion in Haiti destroyed by the rebels and yellow fever, he broke his word and sold Louisiana to the United States. Sparsely settled and poorly defended Texas now stood as Spain's frontier with the United States, an aggressive young country that had just doubled its size.

American and Spanish leaders had very different ideas as to exactly what the United States had bought. President Thomas Jefferson, accepting wholeheartedly the famed response by Talleyrand, the French foreign minister, when asked about the boundaries of Louisiana—"You have made a noble bargain for yourselves, and I suppose you will make the most of it"—claimed that the province extended to the Río Grande. This meant that it included all of modern Texas and the eastern half of New Mexico as well. The Spanish countered with the argument that the Red River constituted the western boundary.

Jefferson sought to make good American claims by placing United States soldiers at Natchitoches and sending exploring parties into the Red River region. The first expedition, commanded by William Dunbar and John Hunter, left Natchez in 1804 with orders to follow the Red to its source and explore the headwaters of the Arkansas River as well. Dunbar and Hunter soon learned, however, that Spain intended to prevent their exploration and therefore never left the modern state of Louisiana. A second expedition in 1806 led by Thomas Freeman and Peter Custis traveled six hundred miles up the Red River by boat, but shortly after reaching what is now the boundary between Texas and Arkansas, was intercepted and forced back by several hundred Spanish soldiers.

In addition to blocking American explorations, Spain responded to the U.S. occupation of Natchitoches by placing soldiers only fifteen miles away at Los Adaes, the old capital, and increasing the number of troops at Nacogdoches. War seemed imminent in the fall of 1806, but General James Wilkinson, commander of American forces in Louisiana, and Lieutenant Simón de Herrera, his counterpart in Texas, reached an agreement by which United States troops would stay east of the Arroyo Hondo (a small stream betweeen Natchitoches and Los Adaes) and Spanish soldiers would stay west of the Sabine. (see map: The Neutral Ground Agreement.) This so-called Neutral Ground Agreement preserved peace and provided an unpoliced haven for every criminal in the region—"the refuse of both Texas and Louisiana," as one historian has called them.

As tensions eased on the lower Red River, yet another American exploring expedition sought its upper reaches. Lieutenant Zebulon M. Pike left St. Louis in July 1806 with orders to explore the Arkansas and Red Rivers to their sources. Pike reached the Arkansas at its Great Bend in Kansas, followed the river to its source in Colorado, and then turned south in a vain search for the headwaters of the Red. In the spring of 1807, his party moved into northern New Mexico and camped on the upper Río Grande where they were found and arrested by Spanish soldiers. Taken to Texas by way of Santa Fe, El Paso, and northern Mexico, Pike's group received a reasonably cordial welcome in San Antonio. The Spanish confiscated notes and maps but did not punish the Americans in any other way. Instead, they escorted the explorers on to Natchitoches in July 1807. Pike's report, which emphasized the fertile soil and teeming wildlife of Texas, added to the land hunger among Americans, who needed very little encouragement in that respect.

Texas and the Origins of the Mexican Independence Movement

Texas's return in 1803 to the position of buffer province on the northern frontier of New Spain meant that the Spanish government had to pay more attention to its long-range defense. The crown planned in 1804 to send thousands of new settlers to Texas and to create a new military command for the northeastern frontier based in San Antonio, but because of circumstances in Europe neither project came to anything. Defending Texas thus fell to officials in America led by Nemesio Salcedo, Commandant General of the Inte-

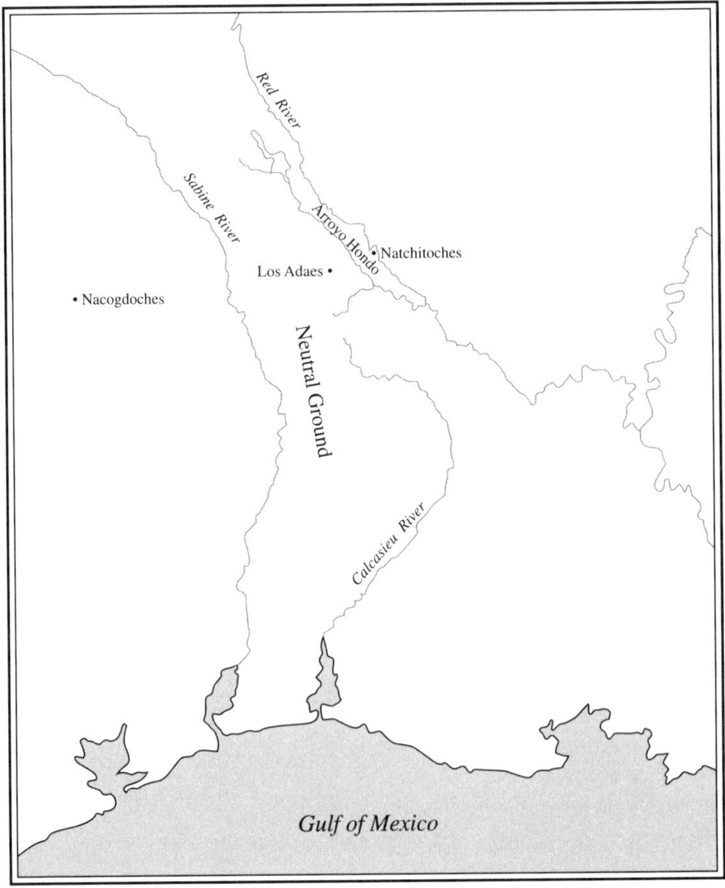

The Neutral Ground Agreement

rior Provinces from 1803 to 1813. Salcedo welcomed Indians from the United States in the hope that they would help keep Americans out and arranged for William Barr and Peter Samuel Davenport to operate a Nacogdoches-based trading company that made goods and gifts readily available to them. Barr, an Irishman who had served in the U.S. Army and then taken an oath of loyalty to Spain, and Davenport, an American, took advantage of this opportunity to become independently wealthy by 1810. Moreover, their dealings with the Indians may have worked exactly in reverse of Salcedo's intentions, moving them toward dependence on goods from the United States rather than loyalty to Spain. Salcedo also promoted immigration into Texas, even agreeing to permit Anglo-Americans who had been Spanish subjects in Louisiana to enter, but he absolutely disagreed with subordinates who would allow Americans to enter freely. Such immigrants, he wrote in 1809, "are not and will not be anything but crows to pick out our eyes." In the words of another

Spanish official, however, no one could "put doors on an open country." Americans continued to come into Texas to catch mustangs and trade with the Indians.

Any hope the Spanish may have had of protecting Texas against infiltration by citizens of the United States disappeared in 1808 when Napoleon, on the pretext of protecting Spain's coasts against the English, sent 100,000 troops over the Pyrenees and forced Charles IV and his son, Ferdinand VII, to renounce the throne in favor of Joseph Bonaparte. French occupation led to a bloody war of resistance by the Spanish, an effort coordinated by a Central Junta of Seville acting in the name of Ferdinand VII.

Events in Spain in 1808 provoked mixed reactions among citizens of New Spain. Those called *peninsulares,* natives of Spain who generally held the most powerful offices, insisted that the colonial government should remain unchanged—out of loyalty to Ferdinand VII. By contrast, *criollos,* those of Spanish blood born in America, argued that a junta, a small council of political leaders, should take over. Since *criollos* outnumbered *peninsulares* ten to one, almost certainly they would control such a revolutionary junta—in the name of Ferdinand VII. Given these circumstances, Viceroy José de Iturrigaray, an ambitious schemer, decided to play to the *criollos* in the hope of making himself the ruler of an independent Mexico. Iturrigaray convened a junta for New Spain, but a group of *peninsulares* quickly responded by arresting the viceroy on September 15, 1808, and sending him back to Spain. The "rebels" then appointed a senile old man as viceregent and began to arrest disloyal *criollos.* All went well at first, but the *peninsulares* had angered the more-numerous *criollos* and created a dangerous precedent by overthrowing a representative of the crown.

In 1809–1810, *criollos* in Querétaro north of Mexico City planned an uprising against the *peninsulares.* The plotters included a parish priest, Miguel Hidalgo y Costilla, a well-educated *criollo* who took a decidedly nontraditional approach to his position. Hidalgo kept a mistress and fathered three children, read books on the Index of Forbidden Literature, and questioned the infallibility of the pope and the virgin birth of Christ. An obvious target for the Spanish Inquisition, he was questioned in 1800 but somehow escaped prosecution and continued to minister to his Indian parishioners. His unorthodox views also made him a likely revolutionary, and he became involved in the plot that called for an uprising against the *peninsulares* in December 1810. Unfortunately for the conspirators, so many people were involved that security could not be maintained. Those in control in Mexico City learned of the plot and immediately informed the new viceroy, Francisco Javier de Venegas, when he arrived in August 1810. Venegas issued orders to arrest the leaders of the conspiracy. However, his security was no better than that among the *criollos,* so Hidalgo and the others received a warning. Forced to act ahead of schedule, Hidalgo on the morning of September 16, 1810, delivered an address known as the "Grito de Dolores" to his parishioners. This "Cry," which came to mark independence day in Mexico, was actually a call for good government and reform, not an outright call for separation from Spain. Soon, however, it developed into a struggle between royalists who remained loyal to Ferdinand VII and rebels who wanted self-government in Mexico.

Responsibility for making the revolt more radical than anything the *criollos* had planned or wanted rested first with the conspirators themselves. Forced to act in a hurry, they recruited thousands of Indians and mestizos to help defeat the *peninsulares* and then discovered to their horror that people of the lower classes did not make careful distinctions when it came to dealing with wealthier rulers. Hidalgo provided leadership for the Indians and mestizos, but he either could not or would not try to control their anger at the upper class. In late September, his army overwhelmed royalist forces in the town of Guanajuato north of Mexico City and engaged in an orgy of plunder and murder, making no distinctions between the property and lives of *peninsulares* and *criollos.* The rebel army then moved on to the capital, defeated its defenders, and seemed poised to ravage the city. At that moment, however, Hidalgo refused to occupy his prize, perhaps because he did not want to subject it to the fate of Guanajuato. This decision alienated the Indians and mestizos in his army, and many simply went home. Royalist forces then went on the offensive and in January 1811 decisively defeated a makeshift army put together by Hidalgo. The priest and other insurgent leaders retreated north toward Texas.

Hidalgo's revolt in central Mexico increased the importance of Texas because of its location as a corridor to the United States. If the Anglo-American republic provided military assistance—supplies or men—to either side, Texas was almost certain to be involved. Recognizing this, Governor Manuel María de Salcedo, the nephew of Commandant General Salcedo and a thorough royalist, took action to improve security in the province as soon as news of the revolt arrived. He sent an agent to Louisiana to buy arms and ammunition, closed the border to foreigners, and restricted the movements of residents. Even at that, however, the governor could not prevent a revolt fired by the disaffection of poorer soldiers and citizens and the ambitions of would-be leaders. Revolution broke out in San Antonio on January 21, 1811, when a retired militia captain from Nuevo Santander, Juan Bautista de las Casas, and a small group of conspirators arrested Governor Salcedo and his staff. The prisoners were sent to Coahuila to await the result of Hidalgo's revolt (which unknown to them had just suffered a crushing defeat). Las Casas then proclaimed himself head of a revolutionary government, arrested local royalists and confiscated their property, and sent agents to spread the revolt to other Texas communities. Nacogdoches and other towns across the province quickly fell into line, and it appeared that Hidalgo would have a stronghold on the northern frontier.

Las Casas, however, had made several mistakes that spelled an end to his revolt almost as quickly as it had succeeded. For one thing, his arbitrary rule angered many, but more important, he had not paid enough attention to the older army officers and old-line families. Within a month, a counterrevolutionary movement developed under the leadership of a local deacon, Juan Manuel Zambrano. The royalists created a junta with Zambrano as president, pledged fidelity to Ferdinand VII, and proceeded to topple Las Casas only thirty-nine days after he had overthrown Governor Salcedo. When messengers reached Coahuila with word of the counterrevolution in San Antonio, the men guarding Salcedo switched loyalties and freed him. The governor then had the satisfaction of setting a trap and capturing Hidalgo and his officers as they rode north toward Texas. He escorted the rebels to Chihuahua, headquarters of his uncle's command, where they were tried and executed in the summer of 1811. Las Casas met a similar fate. Tried by royalists in Coahuila, he was shot in the back as a traitor, decapitated, and his head returned to San Antonio for display in the military plaza. Governor Salcedo resumed control of the government from the junta late in 1811, believing that the brief storm of revolution in Texas had passed. In fact, the worst was yet to come.

Hidalgo's execution did not end the revolt in central Mexico because a new leader, a mestizo priest named José María Morelos, quickly emerged to carry on the fight. And even in the north some rebels escaped royalist retribution. One such man, Bernardo Gutiérrez de Lara, a blacksmith and merchant from Revilla just south of the Río Grande, came into Texas late in 1811 and made his way to Washington, D.C., where Secretary of State James Monroe received him in a friendly and encouraging manner. Although Monroe rejected the pleas of Gutiérrez for aid against royalists in Mexico, he did provide a letter of introduction to the U.S. Governor of the Orleans Territory. Gutiérrez traveled to the Crescent City and then on to Natchitoches, where he began to recruit an army to invade Texas in the name of the Mexican revolution. He had no difficulty recruiting volunteers, especially when Augustus William Magee, a graduate of the United States Military Academy, resigned as an officer in the army at Natchitoches and joined the invasion force as commander of its American contingent.

The Republican Army of the North, as Gutiérrez styled his 130-man force, crossed the Sabine in early August 1812 and took Nacogdoches without a fight. Civilians in the area refused to come to the aid of the royalist commander, and all but ten of his soldiers deserted to the invaders. The army grew to about three hundred and continued across Texas to La Bahía, which offered no resistance in November 1812 as the would-be defenders all fled. Shortly thereafter, a royalist army of about fifteen hundred men under the command of Governor Salcedo and Colonel Simón de Herrera moved to dislodge Gutiérrez's force. Fighting went on sporadically until February 19, 1813, when the royalists, having suffered heavy losses due to deaths and desertions, lifted the siege and moved back toward San Antonio. The invading army, deprived of its military leader by the death of Magee a few weeks before, followed the retreating royalists and on March 28 engaged them in a major battle at the juncture of Salado Creek and the San Antonio River. In only twenty minutes, the Republican Army, strengthened to about 800 men by Indians and more volunteers from Louisiana, routed Herrera's force of 1,500 regulars and 1,000 militiamen, killing 330 soldiers and losing only six of its own. Samuel Kemper, a native of Virginia who replaced Magee as military commander, led the charge that broke the royalists' line. Victory in the Battle of Salado (also called the Battle of Rosalis or Rosillo) allowed Gutiérrez to enter San Antonio in triumph on April 1, 1813, and establish a revolutionary governing junta.

Governor Salcedo, Colonel Herrera, and a dozen officers surrendered to Gutiérrez, who immediately had the junta try them for treason against Hidalgo. To charge royalists with treason against a rebel who had no recognized government was flimsy at best. Nevertheless, the fourteen men were found guilty and sentenced to death. Kemper and other Anglo-American leaders protested such treatment of soldiers defeated in battle, so Gutiérrez promised to imprison the royalists somewhere outside San Antonio. On April 3, Captain Antonio Delgado and sixty Mexican soldiers rode out of Béxar with the prisoners. At the site of the battle on Salado Creek, the military escort stopped, threw the governor and officers off their horses, and set upon the bound and defenseless men with knives. Leaving the mutilated bodies on the field, Delgado's party returned to San Antonio and bragged about what they had done. These murders so upset the Anglo-Americans that one hundred of them, including Kemper, left the army and returned to Louisiana.

Undeterred by desertions, Gutiérrez proclaimed the independence of Texas on April 6, 1813, and issued a constitution creating a centralized form of government with himself as "President Protector of the State of Texas." He remained in power less than three months, however, largely because of actions taken by William Shaler, an American agent who accompanied the Republican Army into Texas. Shaler, having been appointed by the Madison Administration to express the good will of the United States toward the developing revolution in Mexico, considered Gutiérrez's actions an appalling threat to republicanism and liberty. So, he began an effort to replace the "President Protector" with a Cuban-born revolutionary, José Alvarez de Toledo, who had helped plan the original expedition. Part of their strategy involved printing the first newspaper in Texas, the *Gaceta de Tejas,* to carry propaganda in favor of a change in leadership. Type for the paper was set by Shaler and Toledo in Nacogdoches, but before it could be printed Gutiérrez became aware of their scheme, which forced them to take the press back to safety in Natchitoches. The two-page paper dated May 25, 1813, appeared in mid-June; a second number bearing the title *El Mexicano* was published on June 19. Both numbers criticized Gutiérrez, but the second described him as "despicable" and called for his removal. Once riders carried copies of the second number to San Antonio, the power of the press asserted itself. The remaining Anglo-Americans threatened to abandon the revolution unless Gutiérrez resigned and left Texas. Seeing no alternative, the "President Protector" departed San Antonio on August 6, unaware that being forced out of his command probably amounted to a piece of life-saving good luck.

José Alvarez de Toledo rode into Béxar in early August and took over command of the Republican Army of the North just in time to face a two thousand-man royalist force led by Joaquín de Arredondo, a former governor of Nuevo Santander who had come on a mission of revenge. Wearing his gold-braid general's uniform, Toledo led 1,400 men, who amounted to more of an undiscipled mob than an army, into a battle at the Medina River on August 18, 1813. According to Arredondo's report of the battle, Toledo's forces, coming into contact with a small party of royalist cavalry first, blindly pursued it until they "found themselves confronted by the main body of our army formed in line for attack, with the artillery placed on the flanks of our cavalry." Surprised, the "rabble" tried to retreat, but four hours of hard fighting destroyed them, leaving about one thousand dead on the field. The Battle of the Medina proved to be the bloodiest in the history of Texas. Toledo escaped after the battle, but Arredondo remained in Texas for some time to give the population a fearsome lesson in the price of rebellion. His troops executed 327 soldiers from the republican army who surrendered or were captured after the battle. In San Antonio forty men suspected of supporting Gutiérrez and/or Toledo paid with their lives, and eight women and children from their families died of suffocation while packed into prison compounds. A detachment of the conquering army advanced toward Nacogdoches, executing seventy-one more accused rebels along the way. One of Arredondo's junior officers, a young man named Antonio López de Santa Anna, looked on and learned.

The Last Years of Spanish Texas

The events of 1811–1813 in Texas ruined the province for years to come. Its Hispanic population, which had reached about four thousand by 1803, fell to fewer than three thousand in 1821. And conditions in the settled areas, in the words of Antonio Martínez, who became governor in 1817, amounted to "chaos and misery," thanks to royalist soldiers who had "drained the resources of the country, and laid their hands on everything that could sustain human life." Even then, the men in charge at San Antonio still faced threats associated with the Mexican independence movement. It appeared that the revolt in central Mexico had been suppressed with the capture and execution of Morelos in 1815, but revolutionary groups continued to operate on the fringes of New Spain, and that meant continuing trouble in Texas. Developments on Galveston Island in 1816–1817 provide a good example.

In the summer of 1816, Louis Michel Aury, a one-time associate of Simón Bolívar, the future Liberator of South America, occupied Galveston Island. Claiming to act under the authority of a revolutionary government of Mexico, Aury actually presided over a pirate fleet that attacked ships of all nations in the Gulf of Mexico and smuggled the prize goods into Louisiana from Galveston. He was soon joined by Henry Perry, a participant in the Gutiérrez/Magee expedition who had escaped death at the Battle of the Medina and returned to Louisiana to raise a small force with the intention of capturing La Bahía. In November 1816, the situation at Galveston became even more complicated with the arrival of Francisco Xavier Mina, a Spanish-born revolutionary, who planned to use his small 140-man army to invade Mexico. Aury's ships carried the combined forces of Mina and Perry to the town of Soto La Marina on the coast of Tamaulipas in April 1817. After taking the town, Mina headed inland, but Perry, thinking that the Spaniard would ultimately fail, took forty-three men and headed northeast along the coast toward his original objective, La Bahía. Mina won a few victories, but he had the misfortune to draw the attention of Joaquín Arredondo, who defeated the rebels and sent their leaders to Mexico City for trial and execution. Perry reached La Bahía in June, only to be surrounded by a royalist army. With most of his men killed or wounded, Perry, also wounded, committed suicide. Aury sailed back to Galveston Island, only to find that in his absence the Lafitte brothers, Jean and Pierre, had taken control of pirate activities there.

The Aury/Mina/Perry affair amounted to little, except to show the continuing effect of revolutionary unrest on the far northern frontier of New Spain. Only two years later, however, another invading army with Anglo-Americans in its ranks would come with a very different motive. Caring little or nothing about Mexico's revolt against Spain, its leader, James Long, would seek the independence of Texas, probably as a preliminary to making it part of the United States.

In a roundabout way, events in Florida in 1815–1818 produced Long's Anglo-American invasion of Texas in 1819. Spain owned Florida, but like Texas it was thinly settled and barely governed. For several years following the War of 1812, bands of Indians and runaway slaves living in northern Florida raided into Georgia and, when pursued by United States troops, fled across the border for safe haven in Spanish territory. In March 1818, General Andrew Jackson, dealt with this situation in his typically decisive manner by using an order approving "hot pursuit" of the Indians as the basis for an invasion of Florida. He in effect conquered the province by occupying Pensacola and St. Marks and putting American army officers in control of those towns. Spain protested furiously, and the United States returned the territory. At the same time, Secretary of State John Quincy Adams told the Spanish Minister in Washington, Luis de Onís, that the whole affair had resulted from Spain's failure to control Florida and suggested that the best solution was to give the province to a country that could govern it, that is, the United States. Adams did not have to point out the obvious lesson of Jackson's action—the United States could take Florida anytime it chose to.

Under these circumstances, the government in Madrid agreed to a treaty that gave Florida to the United States and settled the boundary between Louisiana and Texas, which had been in dispute since the Louisiana Purchase. The boundary, as drawn by the Adams-Onís Treaty (now often called the Transcontinental Treaty) in 1819, followed the Sabine River north from its mouth on the Gulf of Mexico to the 32nd parallel, due north to the Red River, up the Red to the 100th meridian, due north to the Arkansas River, up the Arkansas to its source, due north to the 42nd parallel, and along that parallel to the Pacific Ocean. (See map: The Adams-Onís Treaty Boundary Line.) Spain hoped that ceding Florida and establishing a boundary between Spanish and American claims from the Gulf to the Pacific would ease Anglo pressure on Texas, especially since the treaty gave up American claims to territory west of the Sabine River. For other reasons, however, that had nothing

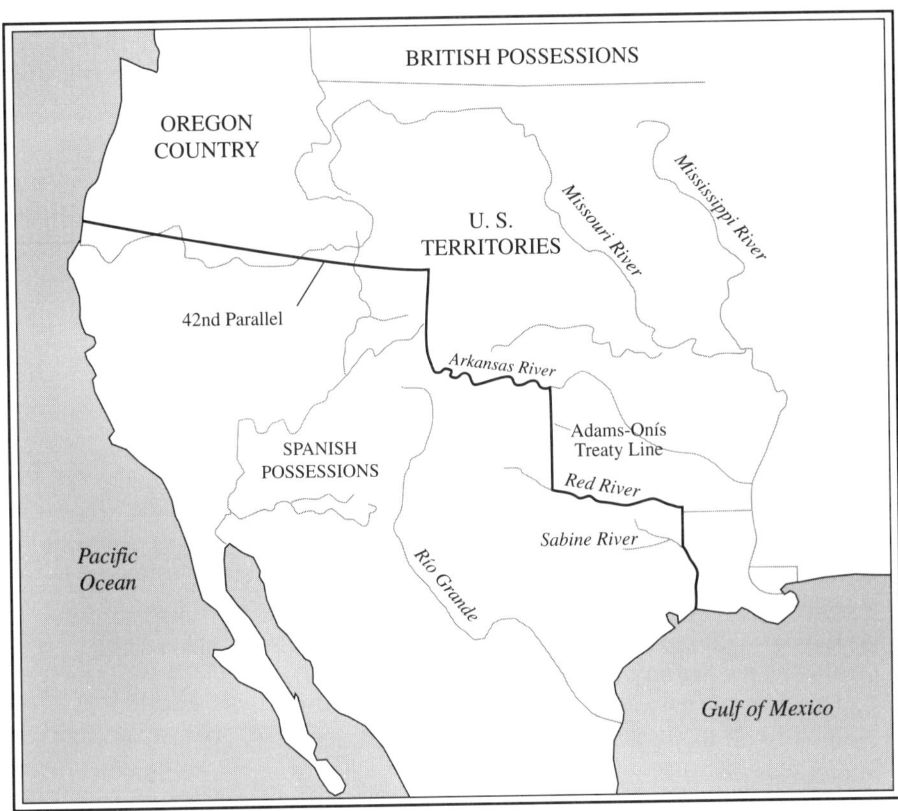

The Adams–Onís Treaty Boundary Line

to do with Texas, the Spanish delayed ratification of the treaty for two years after it was negotiated in February 1819. Finally, in February 1821, the two nations exchanged ratifications and put the agreement into effect.

The Adams-Onís Treaty established a completely reasonable boundary between Louisiana and Texas. After all, when the French owned Louisiana, Los Adaes, the first capital of Texas, was east of the Sabine River, indicating that the province extended at least to that river. And when the Spanish acquired Louisiana in 1762 they governed it separately from Texas, a clear indication that the two provinces remained distinct. Nevertheless, some Americans insisted that Texas was part of Louisiana and that Secretary of State Adams had given it away. And one, James Long, decided to do something about this unwarranted "surrender of Texas."

In the summer of 1819, Long, a Natchez merchant, developed plans for a filibustering expedition (that is, an invasion by an unauthorized or irregular military force) into Texas. He gained the support of local merchants and of Bernardo Gutiérrez, leader of the disastrous invasion in 1812–1813, raised an army of about three hundred men, and moved across the Sabine to occupy Nacogdoches. After setting up an independent republican government and authorizing a land policy that would provide a league (4,428 acres) for every soldier, Long traveled south to Galveston Island in an effort to gain the support of Jean Lafitte, the pirate. He failed, and in his absence Spanish troops sent by Governor Martínez from San Antonio drove the filibustering force out of East Texas in the fall of 1819. Long managed to escape to New Orleans where he soon raised another "army," one of about fifty men this time, and returned to Texas. He set up headquarters at Point Bolivar opposite Galveston at the entrance to Galveston Bay and planned another invasion. After more than a year of uncertainty, in September 1821 Long and fifty-two men sailed down the coast to attack La Bahía. They captured the town easily, but a few days later troops from San Antonio forced them to surrender. He was imprisoned in Mexico City and about six months later shot and killed by a guard, perhaps by accident or possibly on the orders of Mexican leaders whom he had angered.

James Long's wife, Jane, and their daughter had joined him at Point Bolivar in 1820 and remained behind when he sailed for La Bahía in 1821. The few other filibusters' families there soon left, but Jane stayed on through the winter of 1821–1822, stubbornly waiting for word from her husband. On December 21, alone except for her daughter and a young slave girl named Kian or Kiamata, she gave birth to another child, Mary James Long. This girl is generally believed to be the first Anglo-American born in Texas, leading some to call Jane Long "the mother of Texas," a preposterously incorrect title of honor in light of all the infants born earlier to Indian, French, Spanish, and mixed-blood women.

The fate of James Long's filibustering activities shows that Spanish loyalists still had a reasonably firm grip on Texas in 1819–1821. At the same time, however, revolutionary unrest came to a climax in Spain and New Spain. Stability could have returned to the government of Spain, and perhaps its colonial possessions as well, at the close of the Napoleonic Wars but for the person of Ferdinand VII. From 1808 until 1814, while he was kept from the throne by French invaders, Ferdinand served as a unifying symbol to the Spanish. The Central Junta at Seville governed in his name, but in 1812 it called a *cortes* (parliament), which met in Cádiz and wrote a constitution that reduced the king's previously nearly absolute power. In the new constitutional monarchy, for example, adult householders would vote for representatives in the *cortes* and there would be freedom of the press except on matters relating to religion. Ferdinand, however, upon his restoration to the throne in 1814 quickly proved himself, in the words of one historian, "cowardly, selfish, grasping, suspicious, and vengeful." He dismissed the *cortes,* threw out the Constitution of 1812, and set out to destroy liberalism in Spain and America. Ferdinand's attempt to restore absolutism drew opposition at home and in Mexico that finally bore fruit in 1820–1821. A revolt led by the Spanish army in 1820 forced him to reinstate the Constitution of 1812 and reconvene the *cortes.*

The creation of constitutional monarchy in Spain encouraged *criollos* in Mexico to move in the same direction, thinking that a similar move would assure their control without unleashing radical revolution. Accordingly, the leading royalist military commander, Agustín de Iturbide, proposed to Vicente Guerrero, leader of the main rebel force, the signing of an agreement to make Mexico an independent constitutional monarchy with full protection for the Catholic Church and equal treatment for *peninsulares* and *criollos*. This Plan de Iguala gained widespread support across Mexico, and the viceroy, seeing that opposition was hopeless, accepted it by signing the Treaty of Córdoba on August 24, 1821. At that point Spanish Texas became Mexican Texas.

Spain's Legacy in Texas

Centuries of rule by Spain had done little to develop Texas; nevertheless, the Spanish left a lasting imprint on the province's cultural heritage. First, the Spanish legacy is obvious in the names of geographical and political features across the state. For example, every major river except the Red has a name derived from Spanish, and forty-two of modern Texas's 254 counties have Hispanic names. Second, cattle ranching developed most of the practices for which it is famous—herding from horseback, roping, branding, the roundup, etc.—in the eighteenth century, well before Anglo-Americans entered Texas. Incidentally, Spanish livestock may have contributed to a major change in the landscape as well as the economy of Texas. Mesquite, it seems, originally grew only along streams in coastal areas, and mesquite beans, when carried through the digestive tracts of animals into grazing areas, could not reach the soil to germinate due to the tall, thick grass. However, cattle grazed the grass short enough to allow the mesquite a foothold and thus helped this water-hungry tree to spread across millions of Texas acres.

A third, extremely important legacy of Spain in Texas is found in the law. Spanish civil law, unlike the English common law, gave separate and community property rights to women. Even after Texas became part of the United States, property belonging to women at the time they married remained theirs after marriage. Husbands managed separate property, but they could not dispose of it without the approval of the wife. Also, a wife who thought that her husband was misusing her property could take legal action to have its management put in her hands. Community property laws assured women that half of all property acquired after marriage would be theirs if the union ended because of divorce or death.

Spanish law also had a role in the creation of a nineteenth-century homestead law that gave Texas debtors strong protection for their principal residence and the necessities of life and earning a living. Finally, Texas water law developed on the basis of precedents established by early Hispanic residents. Under Spanish practice water belonged to all inhabitants, and Texas reserves title to water in all perennial streams and beds "in trust for the whole people."

First Immigrants from the United States

During the last years of Spanish rule in Texas, in spite of the chaos created by the independence movement in Mexico, the province began to attract its first true immigrants from the United States, people who came not for adventure and immediate economic gain as was the case with the Republican Army of the North, but to settle and stay. Beginning around 1815, Anglo-Americans started to drift from Louisiana through the Neutral Ground, across the Sabine, and into the area around San Augustine east of Nacogdoches. Often entire families, they established homesteads and even set up commercial enterprises such as sawmills. Other settlers from the United States arrived on the south side of the Red River in northern Texas at about the same time. Those who came first established trading posts at Pecan Point in 1815 in modern-day Red River County, where they were joined the next year by farmers such as Claiborne Wright from Tennessee. By 1818, five Indian traders and twelve families lived at Pecan Point. Two years later, when the legislature of the United States Territory of Arkansas created Miller County, it included not only southwestern Arkansas but southeastern Oklahoma and northeastern Texas as well. This bold move did not hold up, but it recognized that Anglo settlers on the Red River considered themselves there to stay.

These people who came to Texas from the United States beginning around 1815 began the Anglo-American phase of "Gone to Texas." Their numbers cannot be determined, especially since they were squatters with no legal right to be in the province. Spanish officials tended not to mind the newcomers so long as they simply settled and stayed out of politics. Those who established trading posts tended to undermine Spanish influence with Indians such as the Caddos and Wichitas, but that was not an immediate threat.

During the last years of Spanish control, Texas also became a home for significant numbers of non-Anglo immigrants from the United States. The Alabama and Coushatta Indians, groups that left their central Alabama homeland after the English took control there in the 1760s, began to move from Louisiana into the Big Thicket region south of Nacogdoches as early as the 1780s. Adapting to life in a jungle-like wilderness, they depended on hunting, gathering, and growing small crops. Outsiders generally left them alone, although eventually the trails that they created through the thicket would allow Anglo-Americans to enter. By 1809, approximately 1,650 Alabamas and Coushattas lived within seventy miles of Nacogdoches.

A group of Cherokees, probably the best known of all southeastern Indians, also migrated to East Texas during the waning of Spanish rule. The principal occupants of western North Carolina, eastern Tennessee, and northern Georgia during the late eighteenth century, the Cherokees began to face pressure on their lands from Anglo pioneers soon after the close of the American Revolution. Hoping to preserve their traditional culture, small groups voluntarily moved west of the Mississippi River between 1790 and 1820 and settled in present-day Arkansas and Oklahoma. During the winter of 1820–1821, about sixty Cherokee families led by Chief Bowl, also known as Duwali, settled near the three forks of the Trinity River in the vicinity of modern Dallas. Finding the nearby Taovaya Wichitas dangerously hostile over hunting rights, these Cherokees soon moved eastward and settled north of Nacogdoches in present-day Rusk County on land once used by the Caddos. By 1822, at least three hundred Cherokees lived in Texas.

Three other groups of Indians—the Delawares, Shawnees, and Kickapoos—ended long-range migrations by coming to Texas around 1820. The Delawares and Shawnees, both Algonkian-speaking peoples whose homelands lay in the east, had been pushed first into the Ohio Valley and then Missouri by white expansion. After the Louisiana Purchase, Anglo-American settlers pushed them farther west, and groups began to move into Texas. By the early 1820s, at least a few hundred Delawares lived in what had been Caddo country along the Red and Sabine Rivers, and a large band of Shawnees, with approximately 270 warriors, had settled near Pecan Point. The Kickapoos, also an Algonkian-speaking group, lived originally in the central Great Lakes region before being pushed southwestward. Some eight hundred members of this group settled in the area between the upper Sabine and Trinity Rivers after 1820.

Thus, by the early 1820s the lure of Texas had brought a truly diverse population to its eastern woodlands. The Nacogdoches area had Hispanic ranchers and farmers, and the town proper had merchants of varied national origins. Anglo-Americans lived in small settlements and on isolated farms scattered from the Red River southward to the Neches. Finally, Indians, particularly the Alabamas, Coushattas, Caddos, Cherokees, Delawares, Shawnees, and Kickapoos, likely outnumbered settlers of European origin.

Most residents of Texas in August 1821 probably cared little that they had just become citizens of an independent nation rather than subjects in a colonial empire. Hispanic Texans and those who lived in the main Spanish settlements—San Antonio, La Bahía, Nacogdoches, and Laredo—undoubtedly were glad to be rid of revolutionary unrest. Their communities remained small, however, and had not overcome the losses associated with the independence movement. Recent Anglo-American immigrants in East Texas probably hoped only to be left alone, especially since they had no legal right to be there. Indians, those who had long resided in Texas and the new arrivals alike, doubtless thought in terms of protecting themselves against each other and using rivalries among Europeans to their advantage, especially when it came to maintaining access to trade goods and weapons.

Nothing indicated in 1821 that the new government in Mexico City, with all the difficulties it faced in stabilizing affairs there, could take any action that would drastically affect conditions on its far northern frontier. How could anyone guess that as the age of revolutions closed Texas stood on the threshold of changes far more revolutionary than anything that had happened in the province during the past forty years?

Chapter 5

MEXICAN TEXAS, 1821–1835

"To govern is to populate." If this aphorism from Juan Bautista Alberdi, a mid-nineteenth-century Argentine political theorist, is true, then Spain never governed Texas, and Mexico as an independent republic in 1821 inherited the results of that failure. Independence in itself was not likely to convince more people from the interior of Mexico to move to Texas. So Mexican leaders faced a problem: How could an infant nation populate its far northern frontier province when a great colonial power had failed for so many years to accomplish that objective? An obvious answer lay with the Anglo-Americans who were already beginning to settle around San Augustine in East Texas and on the south side of the Red River. Mexico needed only to open Texas to immigrants from the United States, with certain stipulations, sit back, and watch the population grow.

Anglo-American immigration, of course, held the potential to create a new problem. Suppose the new settlers, and the influx of relatives and friends certain to follow them, did not become loyal citizens of Mexico. What would happen then? Would Mexico learn that Alberdi's aphorism about governmental responsibility—"To govern is to populate"—should carry with it a corollary warning: "But take care to populate with the 'right' people"?

The Origins of Austin's Colony

The first steps toward allowing Anglo-Americans to populate Texas actually were taken during the last days of Spanish rule. Interestingly, however, citizens of the United States already in the province, the "squatters" who had begun to move into East Texas around 1815, had virtually nothing to do with shaping new policies favorable to their countrymen. Poor and concerned mostly with subsistence, these early settlers lacked the experience, the connections, and the financial drive necessary to formulate and promote immigration schemes. Instead, the initiative came primarily from adventuresome Anglo-Americans who were men of wealth, or at least who had experienced wealth, and of broad ambition—men such as Moses Austin.

Born in Connecticut in 1761, Moses Austin established himself as a merchant and lead smelter in Virginia and then moved to Missouri, where, as a resident of Upper Louisiana, he became a Spanish citizen in 1798. He amassed a fortune in lead mining and smelting there, but eventually ran into financial difficulty during the War of 1812 and faced complete ruin when the economy of the United States collapsed in 1819. Called the Panic of 1819, this collapse began with the failure of banks that could not collect on loans made during the boom times after the war and deepened into a depression that lasted into the 1820s. Moses Austin had been interested in Texas for many years—he wrote in 1813 that "an adventure to that Country would be both safe and advantageous"—so he turned there in 1819 to rebuild his finances. At first he hoped that James Long's filibusterers would pave his way. I am planning to visit "St. Antonio," he wrote a friend, which "I have but little doubt is now in the hands of the Americans." Long's failures made it clear that Austin would not be able to move into a Texas already controlled by his countrymen, but adventuresome and optimistic entrepreneurs are not easily discouraged, especially if they are seeking to rebuild their fortunes. If Americans could not go to Texas on the heels of filibusterers, perhaps they could enter as "useful citizens."

In November 1820, Moses Austin and a slave named Richmond rode across the Sabine River and headed toward San Antonio. Arriving at the capital on December 23, Austin immediately presented himself to Governor Antonio Martínez. The governor, however, instinctively distrusting foreigners and upset over James Long's intrusion, told him to leave the province and not return. Good fortune then intervened for Austin. Walking through the square, he encountered Philip Hendrik Nering Bögel, a man of Dutch ancestry who after various adventures had wound up in San Antonio living as a poor but respected member of the community under his invented title, the Baron de Bastrop. Bastrop knew Austin from a meeting in New Orleans twenty years earlier, so he persuaded Governor Martínez to allow the American visitor to stay for a while. On the day after Christmas, the two men placed a proposal before the governor calling for Austin to settle three hundred Catholic American families from Louisiana in Texas and create a town at the mouth of the Colorado River. The promoter apparently expected to receive fees from settlers for his services and to set up a mercantile business to sell them supplies. Martínez, frustrated with his inability to settle and develop the frontier, accepted this proposal as "the only one which is bound to provide for the increase and prosperity of this province." He forwarded it with an endorsement to his superiors in Monterrey where it was endorsed on January 17, 1821. In what appears a supreme irony, Austin's proposal was approved by Commandant General of the Eastern Interior Provinces, Joaquín de Arredondo, the officer who had given Texas such a fearsome lesson in the price of rebellion in 1813. Arredondo would soon leave Mexico and live out his years until 1837 in Cuba. His reactions to the ultimate results of the proposal that he approved are not known.

Having completed the critical first step in bringing Anglo-Americans into Texas legally, Moses Austin left San Antonio in late December 1820. The return trip through East Texas proved harrowing after a traveling companion stole his and Richmond's mounts. Although he finally reached Missouri in March 1821, his health never recovered. He died in June, leaving a deathbed request that his son, Stephen F. Austin, take up his Texas venture. In fact, the younger Austin, in response to pressure from his father and encouragement from several close friends, had already decided to participate. Anglo Texas had its founding father.

Stephen Fuller Austin was born in Virginia on November 3, 1793, and moved with his father to Missouri seven years later. He studied two years at Transylvania University in Lexington, Kentucky, entered the family business, and served nearly five years in the territorial legislature of Missouri, being elected first when he was only twenty-one-years old. When the Panic of 1819 ruined the Austin family financially, he lived briefly in Arkansas before moving on to New Orleans in December 1820. He made arrangements to live with a friend, Joseph Hawkins, and planned to study law. The next year, somewhat reluctantly at first, he took up his father's Texas project.

Personally, Stephen F. Austin had energy and patience coupled with intelligence, but he also carried a considerable psychological burden. The eldest son of a domineering father, he had been reared to achieve "greatness in life." In his youth that goal seemed within reach, but then Moses Austin had led the family to financial ruin and seemingly destroyed his son's chance for greatness. The father's last project, however, in the words of biographer Gregg Cantrell, provided a "golden opportunity to recover the family's lost fortune, pay his own massive debts, and restore the house of Austin to its former status." Texas offered Stephen F. Austin a cause, a "chance for personal redemption," and a way to escape his father's shadow. In this sense, he represented the many men to whom "Gone to Texas" meant entering a land of new beginnings.

In June 1821 Austin traveled to Natchitoches where he learned from a group of San Antonio residents led by Erasmo Seguín, the head of a politically important family, that authorities in Monterrey had approved his father's proposal. He set out for Texas with Seguín's party but was soon overtaken by the news of Moses Austin's death. Returning to Natchitoches, he learned from Spain's agent there that he probably would be allowed to take up the project in the place of his father and so once more headed back toward the Sabine River, crossing it into Texas on July 16, 1821.

Arriving in San Antonio just as news came of Mexico's independence, Austin received a friendly welcome from Governor Martínez, who accomplished a completely peaceful transfer from Spanish to Mexican rule. The governor agreed that Austin could take up his father's project and asked him to submit a detailed plan for distributing land to settlers. With the aid of the Baron de Bastrop's services as an interpreter, Austin proposed to give each family 320 acres of land fronting a river and 640 acres off the river for grazing. Each family head would also receive 200 acres for his wife, 100 for each

Stephen F. Austin, the "Father of Texas" (1793–1836). Portrait painted in New Orleans in 1836. Credit: Texas State Library and Archive Commission.

child, and 50 for each slave; the acreage equally divided between farming and grazing land. Martínez approved this plan, contingent, of course, on its acceptance by higher officials. He also told Austin that until colonists came under the control of civil authorities, "they must be governed by and be subordinate to you."

The new empresario (colonization agent) spent more than a month exploring the region south of San Antonio as well as his proposed colony on the lower Brazos and Colorado Rivers. After mapping out an area extending from near the coast into the interior beyond present-day Brenham and La Grange, he returned to Louisiana in October 1821. In the meantime he wrote Joel Silbey, a leading citizen of Natchitoches, about his venture, counting on the latter to spread the word. The response surprised even Austin. Nearly a hundred letters from would-be settlers awaited him at Natchitoches, and he knew that there would be more at New Orleans. "I am convinced," he wrote Governor Martínez, "that I could take on fifteen hundred families as easy as three hundred if permitted to do so." It appeared that Anglo-American settlement in Texas needed only a facilitator, not a promoter.

Austin spoke little and wrote less about the financial rewards he expected to reap from his colony, but they had to be significant to rescue the family from debt. He proposed to Governor Martínez that he be allowed to collect twelve and a half cents per acre from the colonists, a fee that would provide a gross revenue of $48,000 from three hundred families composed of a husband, wife, and two children. Larger families and slaveholders obviously would pay more. If all went well, even after paying the costs of surveying and issuing titles, the empresario would net a sizable profit.

After resting in Natchitoches, Austin traveled to New Orleans where he borrowed money and purchased a small schooner, the *Lively,* to take the first colonists to Texas. The ship, carrying fourteen men and tools, seed, and supplies, sailed in late November 1821 for the mouth of the Colorado River, the intended site of the first settlement. Austin entered Texas again by land in December and went to the Colorado where he waited in vain for the *Lively.* The ship had gotten off course and landed at the mouth of the Brazos, a setback that portended others to come but in itself did not threaten the colony. A few settlers arrived on the Colorado before the empresario, and others came soon after. Austin later told the Mexican congress that by March 1822 one hundred men were on the Colorado and fifty on the Brazos. That same month, a friend wrote from East Texas about "people Crowding on their way to the brassos and Collorado and are all coming for your Claim."

Anglo-Americans poured into Austin's colony for a simple reason—cheap land. In the United States after 1820, public lands sold for $1.25 an acre in cash, purchasable in lots no smaller than eighty acres. Few farmers could afford $100 up front, and credit was not available, thanks to the Panic of 1819. Austin offered thousands of acres of the best farmland in Texas for a fraction of the price in the American states, payable sometime after settlement. Frontiersmen could not resist the lure.

The Shaping of Mexican Texas

Suddenly in the spring of 1822, political changes that came with Mexican independence threatened to destroy the promising beginnings made by Moses and Stephen F. Austin. Their project, which to that point had the approval only of officials appointed by Spain, did not meet with favor when the specific plans for land distribution came before new Mexican authorities. Governor Martínez (whose own position was in jeopardy) had to inform Austin that he could not go forward with his colony until the supreme government in Mexico City gave its permission. In the meantime all settlement would be provisional. The empresario, declaring that he "would rather die than not effect what I had promised to the Settlers," decided on the advice of Martínez to present his case personally in Mexico City. Leaving Josiah H. Bell in charge on the Brazos, Austin and two companions set out in mid-March on the nearly one thousand mile journey by horseback to the capital city. At least the month and a half spent traveling gave him an opportunity to work on his Spanish.

Austin arrived in Mexico City at the end of April 1822 but could accomplish nothing immediately because the political situation was so unsettled. The people of Mexico did not share a consensus concerning the form of their government. Some favored monarchy, some wanted to establish a republic, and others wanted to give control to Agustín de Iturbide, the military leader of the independence movement. They did not agree either on whether to have a completely centralized government or to create a federal system with separate states. Three weeks after Austin's arrival, Iturbide's supporters forced the provisional congress to declare him Emperor Agustín I. The empresario now had a government to deal with, but obtaining approval for his grant still would take time. While he waited, he cultivated friendships with key Mexican leaders such as General Anastacio Bustamante, the new commandant general of the Interior Provinces, and Lorenzo de Zavala, a young liberal politician from Yucatán.

Fortunately for Austin, a commission headed by Juan Francisco de Azcárate had studied the question of immigration in 1821 and prepared a report ready for use by the Iturbide government. Colonization is essential to frontier defense, the report concluded, and it recommended encouraging Europeans and Anglo-Americans to settle the far northern provinces. Unless Texas is populated quickly, the commission warned, hordes of North Americans will one day descend on the province "just as the Goths, Ostrogoths, Alans, and other tribes devastated the Roman Empire." This report did not address the potential difficulties inherent in employing Anglo-Americans to protect against Anglo-Americans, probably because the commissioners saw no alternative.

Congress worked on a colonization bill through the summer of 1822 but had not completed the process in October, when Iturbide dissolved it and appointed a hand-picked junta as Mexico's legislative body. Finally, in mid-January 1823, the junta passed an Imperial Colonization Law that confirmed Austin's grant. Under its terms each family in his colony would receive a league *(sitio)* of land (4,428 acres) if they were stock raisers or a *labor* (177 acres) if they planned to farm. The land had to be occupied within two years. Settlers were to be Catholics. Provisions on slavery were somewhat unclear, but the law's provision that slave children were to be free at age fourteen implied that settlers could bring bondsmen with them. Austin would receive for his services as empresario twenty-two leagues (97,416 acres) from the government and a fee from each family of colonists of $60 plus twelve and a half cents per acre for each league granted.

Austin faced one final scare before he could return to Texas. Iturbide was overthrown in March 1823, which called into question all recent actions such as the colonization act. In April, the new government voided the law but, thanks to the contacts Austin had cultivated, left his grant in effect. He left Mexico City after a year's residence, the possessor of the first empresario contract for Texas (and the only one granted under the Imperial Colonization Law of 1823).

Austin's success was mirrored by a failure on the part of the Cherokees to obtain a land grant in Texas. In February 1822, Richard Fields, a one-eighth Cherokee who served as their chief diplomatic representative, sought a meeting with Governor Martínez in San Antonio. "What is to be done with us poor Indians?" he asked. Fields and five other Cherokees then traveled to Mexico City, arriving in early 1823 while Austin remained in the city, but they failed to obtain a meeting with Emperor Iturbide before he was removed from office and then were put off by the new Mexican government with promises that a soon-to-be-enacted general colonization law would protect their interests. Fields and the other Cherokees headed back to Texas in June 1823 without a grant. Perhaps they were less adept than Austin at playing politics in Mexico City, but arriving before Iturbide's rule weakened would have helped also.

While Austin was away, Anglo-Americans continued to move into his colony. Upon returning in the summer of 1823, he and the Baron de Bastrop, who served as land commissioner, gave land titles to settlers, explained to them their responsibilities, and urged unity. Austin governed from a new town on the Brazos River called San Felipe de Austin, a name given in the empresario's honor by Luciano García, the Mexican political chief in San Antonio. In January 1824, he issued a set of Civil and Criminal Regulations that served as a code of laws for the next four years. Most of this code represented a practical mix of Spanish and American legal concepts; the only exception being the regulations concerning slavery. Those were imported directly from codes in the American South. By late 1824 Austin had essentially fulfilled his contract in that the colony had the number of families called for in the original proposal. These "Old Three Hundred" became Anglo Texas's version of the "First Families of Virginia" or "Mayflower Descendants."

During 1824, as Austin's colony took shape, the constituent congress in Mexico took three actions of great importance to the future of Texas. First, on May 7 an act united Texas with Coahuila as a single state in the new nation's federal system. It did not, however, specify a boundary between the two, leaving the matter of Texas's southwestern limits still undefined. This act passed in spite of strong opposition from José Erasmo Seguín, the best-known political figure in San Antonio and Texas's representative in the constituent congress. Seguín, like most Texans of Spanish descent, wanted the province to have separate statehood, but politicians from more populous Coahuila overwhelmed him on that issue. Second, on August 18, congress passed a federal colonization law, which left details largely up to the states with the exception of a requirement that foreigners not be allowed to settle within thirty miles of the coast or sixty miles of a national boundary. Third, on October 4, congress promulgated a Federal Constitution of the United States of Mexico. This Constitution of 1824, with its emphasis on giving power to the individual states rather than the central government, had strong appeal to most Anglo-Americans in Texas.

Mexico's federal system obviously enhanced the importance of the government of Coahuila y Texas with its capital in Saltillo. The state legislature, which had only one representative from thinly populated Texas and ten from Coahuila, operated as a legislative as well as constituent body while it wrote a state constitution and, in the former capacity, passed a vitally important Colonization Law on March 25, 1825. This act, following the outlines of Iturbide's law in 1823, offered settlers a league and a *labor* of land for less than $100 in fees. Moreover, the fees could be paid over six years with nothing due for the first four. Empresario contracts were to run for six years and became void if one hundred families had not been settled in a colony by that time. Successful empresarios were to receive five leagues of grazing land and five *labors* of farm land for each one hundred families brought in. Settlers agreed to become Mexican citizens and Catholics. These generous provisions immediately furthered the Texas land rush. As one settler later wrote: "What the discovery of gold was to California, the Colonization Act of 1825 was to Texas."

Another act passed by the state legislature in 1825 separated Texas from the rest of Coahuila for administrative purposes and called for the state governor in Saltillo to appoint a political chief (in effect, a lieutenant governor) to reside in San Antonio and take primary responsibility for the government there. This act also designated the Nueces River as the line dividing the Department of Texas from Coahuila. After more than a century of being understood as a distinct province, Texas had a specific southwestern boundary; significantly however, it was not the Río Grande.

Finally, the legislature completed the writing of a constitution for the state of Coahuila y Texas in 1827 and promulgated it in 1828. Local government, which had critical importance in a decentralized system controlling a huge territory, depended on the municipality, a political unit that could cover anything from one town to a thousand square miles. In 1828, four municipalities—Béxar, Goliad (La Bahía renamed with an anagram of Hidalgo), San Felipe de Austin, and Nacogdoches—encompassed all of Texas. Each municipality was governed by a four-man council called an *ayuntamiento,* which, much like a modern county commissioners court, had responsibility for local roads, public buildings, public safety, taxes, and charity. An official called the *alcalde,* a combination of mayor, sheriff, and judge in Anglo local government practice, presided over the *ayuntamiento.* Adult male citizens elected the *alcalde* and other members of the *ayuntamiento.*

While Mexican Texas took shape constitutionally and politically during the mid-1820s, Stephen F. Austin and other empresarios, most of them Anglo-Americans, brought in thousands of colonists. Austin received four additional contracts—in 1825, 1827, 1828, and 1831—calling for a total of 1,700 more families and extending his colony into central Texas beyond present-day Austin and Waco. Although never fulfilling any of these contracts to the letter, Austin brought in about 1,500 more families. He worked on these additional ventures in spite of never attaining the wealth that he had expected. Settlers were slow to pay fees, and, so long as land was virtually free, his own holdings were worth little. "My labors in this country altho arduous and in every way perplexing," he wrote his sister in 1825, "will not yield me anything for some years and then not the fortune which some had supposed. I shall benefit others much more than myself in proportion." Austin's tendency to emphasize his sacrifices with just a tinge of self-pity is understandable if not wholly admirable; at least he earned the psychological rewards of acting as the father of his colony.

Texas's second empresario, Martín de León, the only Mexican-born promoter to create a colony in the province, actually received his grant before passage of the Colonization Law of 1825. Born in 1765 to a wealthy creole family in Nuevo Santander, de León established himself as a merchant and soldier before settling on a ranch in present-day San Patricio County in 1805. He survived the revolutionary events of 1812–1813 in spite of siding with the republicans. Then in 1824, he received permission from provisional governing authorities in San Antonio to settle forty-one Mexican families on the lower Guadalupe River and found a town to be named for Guadalupe Victoria, a hero of the independence movement. De León brought in the forty-one families from Mexico in 1824–1825, and sixteen Anglo and Irish families also settled in his colony. Each family received a league and a *labor* of land, and the colonists were exempt from most fees and duties for at least seven years. De León himself received five leagues for his services and continued to welcome additional families to his colony until his death in 1833.

The first empresarios other than Austin to receive grants under the 1825 law—Green DeWitt, Haden Edwards, Frost Thorn, and Robert Leftwich—all had their contracts approved in April of that year. Thorn and Leftwich played no role of significance in bringing settlers to Texas, but DeWitt and Edwards did, and became engulfed in controversy in the process. DeWitt, a native of Kentucky who had been inspired by accounts of Moses Austin's success, received a grant to settle "four hundred industrious Catholic families" in a colony adjacent to and southwest of Austin's first grant. Unfortunately, its poorly defined boundaries included the whole of de León's colony on the Guadalupe. DeWitt attempted to settle first at Gonzales, a site far enough north on the Guadalupe to avoid conflict with de León, but several considerations, especially attacks by Comanche raiders, led him to move southward toward Victoria. This caused a bitter dispute during which the Mexican empresario threatened at one point to kill his Anglo counterpart. Austin helped mediate the dispute, and it ended late in 1828 when DeWitt moved his base back to Gonzales. By 1831, he had issued 144 land titles to immigrant families.

While de León and DeWitt argued, threateningly at times, Haden Edwards created a much more serious problem for both Mexicans and Anglo-Americans in Texas. Edwards, like Stephen F. Austin a Virginian by birth but some twenty-two years older, was the son of a wealthy land speculator who became a United States Senator from Kentucky. Also inspired by Moses Austin, he sought a colonization grant in Mexico City in 1823 and two years later received an empresario contract allowing him to settle eight hundred families in East Texas around Nacogdoches. He agreed to respect all preexisting grants made by Spanish and Mexican officials, a promise likely to make trouble in light of the many long-time settlers in that region.

Edwards arrived in Nacogdoches in September 1825 and immediately issued a decree ordering all residents to produce titles to their grants and announcing high land fees. Old settlers protested, but the empresario ignored their complaints and then made matters worse in December by certifying the election of his son-in-law as *alcalde* of Nacogdoches. The young man represented newly arrived colonists who did not yet own land, and old settlers cried fraud. They appealed to José Antonio Saucedo, the political chief in San Antonio, who reacted in March 1826 by nullifying the election result and placing the old settlers' candidate in office. Even worse for Edwards, when word of his conduct reached Mexico City, President Guadalupe Victoria nullified his contract. Edwards's friends and new settlers then resorted to violence. In November thirty-six armed men from east of Nacogdoches rode in and arrested the *alcalde,* the commander of the town's small Mexican garrison, and other officials. To disguise their true intent, they also arrested Edwards. A court then tried the prisoners for oppression and corruption, convicted all except the empresario, and removed them from office.

When word of this "coup" reached San Antonio in December, Saucedo sent the principal military commander in Texas to Nacogdoches with 110 infantrymen and 20 dragoons. Stephen F. Austin, from the vantage point of his colony, expressed complete dismay at what the Anglo-Americans had done. "It appears," he wrote the rebel leaders, "as tho. the people in your quarter have run mad or worse—they are distroying themselves, building up the credit of their enemies with the Govt. and jeopardising the prospects of hundreds of innocent families who wish to live in peace and quietness in the country." He urged them to humble themselves immediately before Mexican officials. Edwards and his supporters, however, ignored these warnings and decided to make their movement into a full-fledged revolution. On December 21, Haden Edwards, his brother Benjamin, and others signed a declaration of independence creating the Republic of Fredonia, which stretched from the Sabine River to the Río Grande.

In an effort to increase their numbers, the rebels signed a treaty with Richard Fields, the local Cherokee diplomat, promising to divide Fredonia along an east-west line and give the northern half to the Indians. The Cherokees had failed to take advantage of the State Colonization Law of 1825, partly because they did not understand its workings and partly because they had received no help from Mexican officials. Fields convinced them that uniting with the Fredonians would solve the problem of land ownership.

Government troops reached San Felipe de Austin on their way to Nacogdoches on January 3, 1827, and found the town's namesake working hard to rally his colony against the Fredonians. Austin referred to the rebels as a "small party of infatuated madmen" and pointed out that they had made an "unnatural and bloody alliance with the Indians." When the Mexican force finally moved on toward Nacogdoches in late January, Austin and a company of volunteers accompanied them. Fortunately for all concerned, the Fredonian revolt fell apart before they arrived. The rebels had never gained the support of all Anglos in the area, let alone non-Anglos. Although they successfully defended themselves in the town's Old Stone Fort when attacked by local loyalists on January 4, their movement disintegrated due to internal bickering and the threat of overwhelming force. Most of the rebels fled to Louisiana on

January 28, well before the arrival of the Mexican army supported by Austin and his men. Angry Cherokees executed Fields for involving them in the rebellion, but otherwise reprisals were mild, in no small part because Austin recommended leniency and conciliation. The Fredonian rebellion had the immediate effect of a public relations triumph with the Mexican government for Austin and other Anglo-Americans such as Green DeWitt who opposed the rebels, but in the long run, raising the specter of revolution did not work to the advantage of empresarios bringing settlers from the United States into Texas.

Texas Becomes an Anglo Province

By 1830, the approximately ten thousand Anglo-Americans in Texas began to give the province an indelible imprint of the southern United States. Most of these colonists were natives of the American South. At first they came from the states closest to Texas—Louisiana, Arkansas, Mississippi, and Missouri—but increasingly they arrived from older states such as Georgia and Virginia as well. New arrivals from the upper South tended to move into northern Texas and those from the lower South into southern areas of the province, thus establishing a pattern that held throughout the next century.

Southern-born colonists were intensely Protestant and therefore generally unwilling to comply with the requirement that they practice only the Catholic religion. Fortunately for them, Mexico did not have the means to enforce its rules in Texas. There were no priests in Texas to minister to non-Mexican settlers until 1831. The one who came then, Michael Muldoon, proved so lenient, providing that his fees were paid, that those who accepted his faith in order to secure their land became known as "Muldoon Catholics." In the meantime, Baptist, Methodist, and Cumberland Presbyterian missionaries traveled and worked freely in the province, regardless of the illegality of their activities. And Anglo settlers remained overwhelmingly southern Protestants at heart.

Most immigrants lived on land acquired through empresarios, although a good many, especially in northeast Texas along the Red River and in East Texas around San Augustine, had come strictly on their own. Regardless of how they came, the great majority were family people lured by cheap land and/or driven by financial failures associated with the Panic of 1819. Some were criminals escaping justice—the results of an illness, some joked, that caused the United States to "vomit the dregs of the land" on Texas—but most were not fugitives or adventurers seeking to get rich quick. The great majority supported themselves as subsistence farmers, planting gardens and corn and raising hogs or a few cattle. Their isolated homesteads centered on one- or two-room log cabins that often had a packed-earth floor and no windows. Although subsistence remained the first priority, a trend toward cash-crop agriculture also developed almost immediately. Farmers in Austin's colony produced six hundred bales of cotton in 1827, and other colonists followed suit as quickly as they could.

Cotton production depended on slavery, which in turn provided the strongest link of all between Texas and the American South. Slavery had existed in New Spain but never become truly important anywhere outside Veracruz, certainly not on the northern frontier. A census in 1809, for example, showed only thirty-three slaves in Nacogdoches, and San Antonio and La Bahía together had only nine persons of "African origin" in 1819. Anglo-Americans made slavery an institution of significance in Texas beginning in the 1820s because they saw it an economic necessity. No one man could clear enough land or provide enough labor to move beyond subsistence agriculture, and free labor could not be hired where land was so inexpensive. Who would work another man's land any longer than it took to acquire his own? Thus, the only means of advancing to the production of cash crops was slave labor, workers who could be owned and therefore controlled. Most Texas immigrants had generations of experience with slavery and held racist views that allowed them to see nothing wrong with the practice of whites owning blacks in order to profit from their labor. Any moral qualms that may have remained were mitigated by a belief in the Christianizing and civilizing benefits of the institution.

Some of the first settlers in Austin's colony, including the empresario himself from time to time, were slaveowners. For example, Jared E. Groce, who arrived in January 1822 from Georgia, brought ninety slaves and established a plantation called "Bernardo" near present-day Hempstead on the Brazos River. Slave craftsmen built a plantation home for their master and cabins for themselves, and slave field hands immediately began to produce cotton crops that were sold to neighbors and even in the interior of Mexico. Legend has it that Groce's slaves transported the cotton by mule train. In the fall of 1825, a census enumerated 443 slaves (25 percent) in a total population of 1,800 in Austin's colony, and the empresario's Civil and Criminal Regulations provided the laws necessary to protect slavery.

Regardless of its economic potential, however, the "peculiar institution," as southerners called it, faced opposition in Mexico dating to the revolutionary idealism of Hidalgo and Morelos. The latter declared in 1813 that "slavery is forbidden forever," a sentiment that had little or no practical result then, given the few slaves in the colony, but that could make a great deal of difference if honored once Mexico attained independence. Actions taken while the national and state governments passed through the formative process between 1821 and 1827 neither confirmed Morelos's idealism by outlawing slavery nor rejected it by guaranteeing the institution's existence. Mexican leaders considered slavery an evil but recognized the rights of property and the need for growth, so they took a stand on the institution negative enough to alarm Anglos but too weak to prevent its growth. For example, Iturbide's Colonization Law of 1823, which applied only to Austin's first colony, permitted slavery but called for emancipation at the age of fourteen of slave children born in Texas. In 1824, the national constituent congress prohibited the importation of slaves into Mexico as merchandise, but the colonization law and constitution it adopted that same year said nothing about slavery.

Under Mexico's federal system, the ambiguity of the national government's position on slavery would have made little difference had the state of Coahuila y Texas chosen to act decisively. The Colonization Act of 1825 said nothing important about slavery, but Article 13 of the 1827 state constitution seemed crystal clear. It read: "From and after the promulgation of the Constitution in the capital of each district, no one shall be born a slave in the state, and after six months the introduction of slaves under any pretext shall not be permitted." In September 1827 the legislature enacted a law to put this article into effect, calling for a census of slaves in each municipality and requiring *ayuntamientos* to keep records of slave births and deaths. At that point, with only a few months left during which slaves could be brought in and all children promised freedom at birth, the peculiar institution appeared to be on the road to extinction in Texas.

These actions in 1827 confirmed the worst fears of many Anglo-American immigrants and the most important empresario, Stephen F. Austin. From the beginning, although many had brought in bondsmen and enjoyed protection for that special kind of property, they had worried about Mexican attitudes toward slavery. An 1825 letter to Austin from a prospective immigrant in Mississippi spoke for many: "Nothing appears at present to prevent a portion of our wealthy planters from emigrating immediately to the province of Texas but the uncertainty now prevailing with regard to the subject of slavery." On a philosophical level, Austin, like many American leaders of his generation, thought slavery a "curse of curses," but as a practical matter he considered it "of greatest importance" to Texas. Without slavery, he explained to the governor of Coahuila y Texas in 1825, Texas could not attract the people to make it a land of rich plantations but would instead be populated by shepherds and the poor. On a few occasions when it seemed that Mexican authorities genuinely intended to destroy slavery, Austin made statements critical of the institution and turned his thoughts to developing Texas with free labor; overall, however, from 1822 until 1835 he worked to ensure immigrants the opportunity to bring slaves into the province and keep them for life.

Austin unsuccessfully opposed Article 13 of the 1827 state constitution, but early in 1828 settlers found a way around its restrictions. Slaves would be "freed," then brought into Texas and held indefinitely as indentured servants working to pay their former masters for freedom. The *ayuntamiento* of San Felipe de Austin suggested adoption of this policy to the state legislature in March, saying that it would relieve "the paralized state of immigration to this Jurisdiction from the U.S. arising from the difficulties encountered by Imigrants in bringing hirelings and servants with them." Austin endorsed the proposal, and José Antonio Navarro, one of Texas's representatives, introduced it in the state legislature. That body, noting the "deficiency" of agricultural laborers in the state, adopted it on May 5, 1828, in a brief law that guaranteed the validity in Texas of labor contracts made in foreign countries. This act undid Article 13 and assured the continued growth of slavery in Texas.

Complying with the indentured servant requirement involved a simple procedure. Before leaving the United States, slaveholders took their bondsmen before a notary public and drew up a contract whereby the latter agreed to accompany his master to Texas. The slave technically would be free in

Texas, but he owed his value plus the cost of emigrating to his master. This debt would be paid by very low annual wages, less the cost of maintenance. Slave children would emigrate with their parents, and once they reached the age of eighteen serve on the same terms. Those born to indentured servants in Texas would serve without pay until they were twenty-five and then be indentured like their parents. Soon slaveholders created numerous variants on this contract. One, for example, bound male slaves for ninety years to learn "the art and mystery of farming and planting" and female slaves for the same period to learn "the art and mystery of cooking and housekeeping." In practice, once in Texas, these supposedly indentured servants were treated like slave property—that is, they were bought and sold, hired out, and bequeathed in wills.

Anglo-Americans were delighted with the subterfuge of indentured servitude, but in 1829 a new threat appeared, as one historian put it, like "a bolt from the blue." On September 15, in honor of Mexican independence day on the 16th, President Vicente Guerrero issued a decree emancipating all slaves in the republic. Interestingly, the political chief at San Antonio, Ramón Múzquiz, took steps to thwart this attack on slavery before Anglo immigrants even heard of it. He appealed to the governor at Saltillo to have Texas exempted from the decree because it threatened the development of the province, which depended on "the aid of the robust and almost indefatigable arms of that race of the human species which is called negroes, and who, to their misfortune, suffer slavery." The governor accepted this argument and passed it on to the president, adding another consideration—the possibility of violent reactions in Texas if slaves were freed. President Guerrero, for reasons that are not clear, responded to these appeals by issuing another decree on December 2, exempting Texas from general emancipation.

At the close of 1829, Austin expressed optimism that the slavery issue finally had been settled in the interests of Anglo immigrants. "All our difficulties as to Slaves . . . are removed," he wrote his brother-in-law. In a few years, he added, Texas will be a "Slave State" and then grow into "the best State in the Mexican Union." The San Felipe de Austin *Texas Gazette,* the first true newspaper in the province, pointed out in January 1830 that Mexican authorities had granted "all we could wish for, as colonists—the SECURITY of our PERSONS and PROPERTY." There is no thorough census for all of Texas at this time, but it is clear that the province's approximately ten thousand Anglo settlers owned more than one thousand slaves.

As Anglo-Americans, coming primarily from the southern United States and often bringing slaves with them, populated and began to shape eastern Texas and the region along the lower Brazos and Colorado Rivers, older Texans found themselves in danger of being overwhelmed by the sheer numbers and aggressiveness of the new arrivals. In many respects, Texas in the 1820s and 1830s became a battlefield of conflicting cultures.

In 1830, the province had about four thousand people of Mexican descent—Tejanos, as they became known from this time onward. Most of the Tejanos lived in San Antonio, Goliad, and Victoria or on ranches in the vicinity of those towns. Nacogdoches in East Texas also had a sizable Mexican population as did Laredo on the Río Grande, although technically it was part of Coahuila rather than Texas. Mexico had no more success than Spain in persuading settlers to move to the northern frontier, so population growth continued to come primarily from presidio soldiers who remained in Texas after being discharged or retiring. They often married locally, and many became leaders in civilian life.

Ranching continued as the key economic activity of Tejanos—in the Nacogdoches area, along the San Antonio River from Béxar to Goliad, and in South Texas from the Río Grande northward nearly to the Nueces River. Wealthy ranchers constituted the elite of Tejano society, living in the words of one observer "in the grandee style with many servants and retainers." These *ricos,* in cooperation with government officeholders and would-be businessmen, largely controlled their society. The several thousand poor Tejanos who lived in or near the towns of San Antonio, Goliad, and Victoria and worked as herders, cartmen, and day laborers had little voice in what happened to them or the province. At least all Tejanos, regardless of class, shared two cultural characteristics. All carried on Catholic religious practices as best they could, given the lack of interest in the frontier on the part of religious leaders in Mexico. And virtually all were mestizos, racial mixtures of Spanish and Mexican Indian blood.

Many of the Tejano elite dreamed of a dynamic, capitalistic northern Mexico that would build an expanding economy based on trade with the United States and the growth of cotton. Their leaders such as Erasmo Seguín agreed with Austin's view of the role Anglo-Americans would play in Texas's future, and politicians, including José Antonio Navarro, worked in the state legislature to find ways that Anglo-Americans could bring slaves into the province. At the same time, they were very concerned with maintaining control of their province. They did not wish to have a central government in Mexico City or even a state government in Saltillo control their province and prevent its development. On the other hand, they did not wish to lose control to recent immigrants from the United States, who had no respect for their traditions or interests and thought of themselves as racially superior to boot. The arrival of Anglo-Americans truly trapped the Tejanos between two nations.

Indians, perhaps twenty thousand in all, far outnumbered Anglo immigrants and Tejanos in Texas at the beginning of the 1820s. They were far from unified, however, and responded to Mexican independence and the influx of Anglo-Americans in different ways. Recent immigrants such as the Cherokees, Delawares, Shawnees, and Kickapoos sought to win approval of Mexican officials and obtain land grants. To do this they were willing to aid in the fight against Indians who were hostile to Tejano and Anglo settlements. Otherwise, they lived quietly and prospered. Older tribes such as the Comanches, Apaches, and Caddos responded positively at first to offers from the Mexican government to enter into peace treaties and trade arrangements. The Wichitas, however, did not believe that Mexico could provide enough trade goods and continued their practice of raiding old Spanish settlements. Other

Indians such as the Karankawas and Tonkawas continued to live on the lower Brazos and Colorado Rivers and avoided conflict before Anglo immigrants entered the picture. However, when Stephen F. Austin's first colony brought settlers to their homelands, violent confrontations soon followed.

Austin set the tone for relations with the Karankawas immediately upon encountering them for the first time while on his survey of Texas in 1821. "These Indians . . ." he recorded in his journal, "may be called universal enemies to man." They are killers, and cannibals as well, he wrote, and the arrival of "an American population will be the signal of their extermination for their [*sic*] will be no way of subduing them but extermination." The empresario's prediction came true in a conflict that erupted within two years of the arrival of Austin's first colonists on lands usually occupied by the Karankawas. Settlers accused the Indians of theft and murder, and a general war developed in 1824. Austin led an armed force of about ninety men, thirty of whom were slaves belonging to Jared Groce, against the Karankawas and forced them to take refuge at the Goliad mission. As a price for peace, the Indians promised to abandon the lower Brazos and Colorado and remain west of the Guadalupe River. Bands of Karankawas broke this agreement, however, primarily because they could not support themselves in competition with other Indians who already lived beyond the Guadalupe. Those who returned to their homes in 1825–1826 became fair game for Austin's colonists who continued to attack them on sight until a second peace settlement was arranged in 1827. At that point the surviving Karankawas had to live along the Gulf Coast west of the Guadalupe River, an unfamiliar location that brought them into conflict with Tejano ranchers. Their numbers continued to decline.

(Incidentally, these early Indian conflicts brought the first appearance of the famed Texas Rangers. Following the unofficial mustering of a ten-man force in 1823 by a settler named Moses Morrison, Austin considered calling out similar units to "act as rangers for the common defence." He did not carry through on this idea, but "rangers" became part of Texas language and lore from that time forward. For the next fifty years, volunteers who mobilized for temporary duty, regardless of their official title, were commonly known as Rangers. In 1874, when the need for volunteer citizen soldiers had largely disappeared, the Rangers took on a different role as a permanent law-enforcement agency of the State of Texas.)

The Tonkawa Indians who lived a little further inland than the Karankawas on the Brazos and Colorado had a very different experience with Anglo-American settlers. Pressured from the north by Comanches and Wichitas and cut off from trade to Louisiana by immigrant Indians such as Cherokees, the Tonkawas welcomed the Anglos as possible military allies and trading partners. Austin and Green DeWitt, recognizing the value of the Tonkawas as guides and fighters against other Indians, treated them fairly. Thus, the Tonkawas allied themselves with the newest Texans.

Where the Wichitas were concerned, Austin and DeWitt inadvertently guaranteed trouble by placing their colonies squarely between the Indians' major villages in the region around present-day Waco and their favorite raiding targets at San Antonio and Goliad. Wichita raiding parties stole Anglo livestock for several years and then in 1823 began to kill settlers, touching off a conflict that continued for more than ten years. Gradually, in spite of periodic successes in attacking San Antonio, Gonzales, Goliad, and other smaller settlements, the Wichitas lost this "war." Their defeat came in no small part because of the Cherokees who still hoped to win favor with Mexico by fighting Indians regarded as hostile to Tejano and Anglo interests. In 1829, for example, Cherokees made a surprise attack at dawn on a Wichita village near Waco and killed fifty-five of its residents before help arrived from another Wichita village nearby. The next year more than one hundred Cherokees, accompanied by a few Tonkawas, attacked a village of the Tawakoni Wichitas. They set fire to the grass houses and shot men, women, and children as they sought to escape and then left with most of the village's horse herd. Under this kind of pressure from Cherokees and an equal amount from Anglos and Mexican army forces, the Wichitas retreated from their villages in central Texas. By 1835, many had left Texas, and those who remained lived on the upper reaches of the Trinity and Brazos Rivers. The Wichitas thus joined the Karankawas in providing an example of the fate of Texas Indians in an increasingly Anglo province.

Early Clashes between Anglo Settlers and the Mexican Government

As Anglo influence in Texas steadily increased during the 1820s, the fears of Mexican leaders who had never trusted American intentions in the province intensified. Two men in particular, Manuel de Mier y Terán and Lucas Alamán, both of whom served as cabinet members in the government of President Guadalupe Victoria, worried that the nation's federal system would allow frontier regions to wind up in the hands of foreigners. The British chargé d'affaires in Mexico City during the 1820s, Henry G. Ward, never missed an opportunity to play on these fears, out of jealousy for his own nation's interests rather than any concern for Mexico. Ward began in 1825 to call for an inspection of conditions in Texas, and two years later, in the aftermath of the Fredonian Rebellion, the government acted. In November 1827, Mier y Terán left Mexico City in a splendid silver-inlaid coach, ostensibly to survey his nation's boundary with the United States but in fact to report on the state of affairs in Texas and make recommendations on how the government could save that province from the Anglo-Americans.

Mier y Terán, born in Mexico City in 1789, possessed one of the finest intellects and best educations among Mexico's independence-era leaders. He graduated from the College of Mines, excelling in mathematics and engineering, and fought in the war against Spanish rule before holding a variety of positions in the new government during the 1820s. A truly dedicated patriot, Terán was an excellent choice to make the inspection, a man who would look at the situation carefully and not flinch from what he saw. Traveling slowly, he reached San Antonio on March 1, 1828, San Felipe on April 27, and

Nacogdoches on June 3. Illness and bad weather detained him in East Texas so long that he did not begin his return to Mexico City until January 1829.

At every stage of his trip, Mier y Terán found evidence of Mexico's increasingly precarious hold on Texas. Tejanos in San Antonio expected a revolt by the Anglos at any time, he said. Worse yet, he found that Mexican influence steadily declined from San Antonio eastward, partly because Anglos heavily outnumbered Mexicans (the margin was ten to one in Nacogdoches) and partly because the Mexicans in East Texas were "very poor and very ignorant." Foreigners have a negative view of us, he said, because most "know of no other Mexicans than the inhabitants about here." This situation, he argued, will create such antagonisms that unless "timely measures" are taken "Texas could throw the whole nation into revolution." He also pointed out that both Anglos and Tejanos, in spite of their usual dislike for each other, wanted a separate state government for Texas because of the distance to Saltillo. That, he considered a "radical step" to be prevented. Upon returning to Mexico, Mier y Terán prepared a formal report on his inspection. A single sentence in an 1829 letter to a friend perfectly summarized his overall conclusion: "If the colonization contracts in Texas by North Americans are not suspended, and if the conditions of the establishments are not watched, it is necessary to say that the province is already definitely delivered to the foreigners."

Mier y Terán's report did not result in quick action. In August 1829 Spain disrupted Mexican affairs by attempting an invasion at Tampico, and continuing political instability in the national government also caused delay. President Manuel Gómez Pedraza, a conservative centralist elected in 1828, was overthrown in April 1829 by supporters of Vicente Guerrero, the liberal federalist who previously had served as vice president. Then, in December, another coup removed Guerrero and replaced him with Vice President Anastacio Bustamante. Bustamante, a far more conservative leader than Guerrero, sought to weaken the states and strengthen the central government, a policy likely to bring conflict with Anglo-Americans in Texas.

Less than a week after Bustamante became president, Mier y Terán prepared a formal set of recommendations for the government's consideration. He proposed colonizing Texas with Mexican citizens and Germans, increasing coastal trade between the province and Mexico to foster commercial ties, and placing more Mexican soldiers in the province. He did not go so far as to suggest ending immigration from the United States, but Lucas Alamán, a member of Bustamante's cabinet, eagerly endorsed that step. On April 6, 1830, congress prohibited all immigration from the United States, ended all empresario contracts not already fulfilled, outlawed bringing in slaves under any guise, and called for the collection of customs duties on imports and exports. (Settlers of Texas had been exempted from duties for seven years by an act of September 29, 1823.) This Law of April 6, 1830, angered most of the Anglo-Americans in Texas. To Mexican officials, it was essential to meet the threat of losing their province, but to Anglo colonists it was an insult with potentially disastrous consequences. Most Tejanos also disagreed with the government in Mexico City and did not approve ending immigration from the United States. Instead, still intent on controlling and developing their province, they worked to have the law repealed. Thus, the Law of April 6, 1830, while it turned many Anglos against the Mexican national government, did not cause serious problems in their relations with Tejanos.

Stephen F. Austin, demonstrating that he would have been a fine lawyer had he joined the bar in New Orleans rather than coming to Texas, found a loophole in Article 10 of the law, which said that there would be no change to "colonies already established." He argued that all of his contracts, which numbered four by that time, constituted only one "colony," so his fulfilling of the first grant met the requirements of the law in spite of the fact that three others had not been fulfilled. Somehow, perhaps because they liked Austin personally, Mexican officials including Mier y Terán accepted his inspired reasoning. Immigrants continued for at least another year to enter Austin's colony legally. DeWitt's colony, the only other empresario grant that had brought in significant numbers of colonists, also benefited from this loophole. Of course, some Anglos simply violated the law; how many cannot be determined.

Anglo-American colonists did not immediately protest the Law of April 6, 1830. Austin helped by using the *Texas Gazette* to put the best face possible on the act, all the while planning to work for its repeal. The empresario toyed with the idea of acquiescing in Mexican opposition to slavery as a means of persuading the government to reopen immigration, but settlers, even some from northern states, rejected that thought instantly. "Do you believe," asked one Pennsylvania native, "that cane and cotton can be grown to advantage by a sparce white population? . . . we must either abandon the finest portion of Texas to its original uselessness or submit to the acknowledged, but lesser evil of Slavery—." Austin recognized that he would have to convince Mexican officials to permit the immigration of slaves as well as American citizens.

Those like Austin who hoped that patience and flexibility would change Mexican policy in due time were disappointed by developments in 1831–1832. Mexico sent additional troops to San Antonio, Goliad, and Nacogdoches and built a series of new forts at strategic points in the province. The most important were Velasco, at the mouth of the Brazos River, and Anahuac, near the mouth of the Trinity River on Galveston Bay. (See map: Mexican Texas in 1832.) Mexico also established customs houses at Anahuac and at Matagorda, a town at the mouth of the Colorado River begun in 1827 as an entry point for settlers in Austin's colony. Trouble began at Anahuac in January 1831 as a dispute between Colonel Juan Davis Bradburn, a Kentuckian who had been in the service of Mexico for many years, and José Francisco Madero, a land commissioner sent by the government of Coahuila y Texas to issue titles to settlers on the lower Trinity who had arrived before 1828. Bradburn, arguing that restrictions in the Law of April 6 on foreigners' settling near the coast annulled any previous grant, arrested Madero. State authorities intervened, freeing Madero and allowing him to issue more than fifty titles and also to organize an *ayuntamiento* on the Trinity called Liberty. Anglos in the area, who generally disliked Bradburn as a countryman in the service of foreigners, enjoyed the colonel's defeat.

Mexican Texas in 1832

More trouble at Anahuac came in November 1831 with the arrival of George Fisher, another former citizen of the United States, to act as customs collector. Fisher announced that all ships then on the Brazos River or Galveston Bay would have to pay duties and that, until an assistant collector reached Velasco, ships leaving the Brazos had to pay duties at Anahuac. This meant that captains intending to clear from Velasco had to travel overland to Anahuac, a 140-mile round-trip, to pay duties on their cargoes. Mexican officials soon placed a collector at Velasco, but in the meantime some captains ignored the rules, exchanging rifle fire with Mexican soldiers at the mouth of the Brazos as they left.

The next problem at Anahuac, which developed in the spring of 1832, involved several runaway slaves from Louisiana, Colonel Bradburn, and hotheaded Anglo newcomers led by William Barret Travis and Patrick Jack. The runaways escaped across the Sabine to Anahuac, whereupon Bradburn added them to his garrison, a step that in effect assured their freedom. A Louisiana slave catcher then hired Travis and Jack, who were law partners, to help him reclaim the runaways. Unable to accomplish anything legally, Travis attempted to bluff Bradburn into releasing the slaves by creating a rumor that a large force of armed Louisianans was approaching Anahuac. The colonel reacted by arresting Travis and Jack for giving false information and holding them in a brick kiln without trial. Outraged, a group of 150 to 200 Anglos from as far away as Austin's colony, marched on Anahuac. They also sent men to Brazoria for cannon to use against the fort if necessary. The Anglo force captured Bradburn's nineteen-man cavalry, whom they released in exchange for Travis and Jack, only to have Bradburn argue that they had not met all conditions of the agreement and refuse to give up the two Anglo-Americans. At that point, the Anglos retired to Turtle Bayou, about six miles north of Anahuac, to await the arrival of the cannon.

This disturbance at Anahuac smacked of revolution and could have brought the penalty for treason down on the Anglos involved. Fortune smiled on the troublemakers, however, in the form of renewed political instability in Mexico. In 1832, General Antonio López de Santa Anna began a revolt against the centralist-leaning Bustamante government, promising to maintain the federalist Constitution of 1824. Santa Anna, a career soldier born in 1794, served in Arredondo's royalist army that destroyed the uprising in Texas in 1813 but then supported Iturbide's independence movement. He remained active in politics during the next decade, participating in the overthrow of Iturbide in 1823 and Gómez Pedraza in 1829, and then became a national hero by commanding the force that turned back Spanish invaders at Tampico in 1829. At the time Stephen F. Austin described Santa Anna as a "sort of Mad Cap difficult to class" politically. Soon it became clear that the only thing consistent about Santa Anna was his devotion to himself, but when the uprising against Bustamante began, the general had a record of support for federalism as embodied in the 1824 constitution. And federalism obviously would benefit Anglo Texans by providing a greater degree of control at the state level. Thus, when the men gathered near Anahuac in early June 1832 learned of a significant victory for the anti-Bustamante revolt, they claimed that their actions against Bradburn, rather than rebellion against Mexico, constituted support for the liberal Santa Anna. To some extent, which cannot be measured, they were telling the truth.

The "rebels" at Anahuac offered an official explanation of their position by adopting the Turtle Bayou Resolutions on June 13, 1832. Four in number, these resolutions expressed opposition to the Bustamante administration because of its violations of the Constitution of 1824 and called on all Texans to support the patriot opposition led by Santa Anna. A few days later Colonel José de las Piedras, commander of the fort at Nacogdoches, arrived with troops and ended the crisis. Thinking that he was outnumbered and convinced by the Anglos' arguments, Colonel Piedras removed Bradburn from command and freed Travis and Jack. Bradburn returned to Mexico, and shortly thereafter the Mexican soldiers at Anahuac declared support for Santa Anna and

Antonio López de Santa Anna (1794–1876). This lithograph presents a highly romanticized view of the Mexican leader around the time of the Texas Revolution. Credit: The San Jacinto Museum of History, Houston.

also sailed for home. The post had no garrison for the next three years, and commerce continued without the collection of customs duties.

Fortunately then, the disturbances at Anahuac ended without bloodshed; unfortunately, there was a very different result on the Brazos on June 26, 1832. The men sent to bring cannon to Anahuac decided to move them by water down the Brazos, east to Galveston Bay, and then up to the Trinity, but Domingo de Ugartechea, commander of the post at Velasco, refused to let them pass. A battle ensued in which ten Texans and five Mexicans were killed before Ugartechea, outnumbered and short of ammunition, surrendered. He and his soldiers were allowed to sail for Mexico on a ship provided by the colonists. The Battle of Velasco can be considered the first instance of bloodshed between Anglos and Mexicans as Texas moved toward revolution.

A bloody confrontation also occurred at Nacogdoches shortly after Colonel Piedras returned there from Anahuac in the summer of 1832. The Mexican commander, fearing a local version of the conflict he had just ended, ordered all men in the area to turn in their weapons to him. The *ayuntamiento* of Nacogdoches organized resistance to Piedras, demanding that he rescind the order and declare for Santa Anna and the federalists. When he refused, Anglos attacked Mexican forces in Nacogdoches on August 2 and forced them to evacuate the town. The next day a running battle continued for some time as Anglos pursued the Mexicans, who were retreating toward San Antonio, and ended with Piedras's men turning against him and surrendering. Forty-seven Mexican soldiers and four Anglos died in the Battle of Nacogdoches. Piedras was allowed to return to Mexico, and his soldiers were sent to San Antonio.

Thus by midsummer 1832, Anglo-Americans acting in the name of Santa Anna's federalist revolt had cleared all of Texas except San Antonio and Goliad of Mexican troops. Their actions, however, resulted from local grievances and a desire to maintain local control rather than from any genuine move for independence. At this time, most Texans, especially the older settlers, saw revolution as a last resort at best. Their stance certainly proved advantageous when a four hundred man army led by a federalist general, José Antonio Mexía, arrived on the Brazos on July 16, 1832. Accompanying Mexía from Matamoros was Stephen F. Austin, who was returning from a meeting of the state legislature in Saltillo. The empresario spent hours en route explaining how Anglos in Texas had no intention of a break with Mexico and were in full agreement with Mexican liberals in upholding the Constitution of 1824. Then, colonists at Brazoria supported his words by greeting Mexía with a cannon salute and a lavish dinner and ball. The general could hardly punish people who gave him a warm welcome and expressed such loyalty to Santa Anna, so he returned to Mexico and reported that all was well in Texas.

A Request for Separate Statehood

Anglo Texans, not realizing the sheer good luck involved in the way their "disturbances" during the summer of 1832 coincided with Santa Anna's attack on Bustamante, decided to push for reforms to solidify control of their own state. In August, the *ayuntamiento* of San Felipe called a convention, which assembled there on October 1. Fifty-eight delegates representing every municipality in Texas except San Antonio, but including only one Tejano, Rafael Antonio Manchola, met for six days with Austin presiding and prepared a petition to the state and national governments. They asked that Texas be exempted from customs duties for another three years and that the ban on immigration from the United States in the Law of April 6, 1830, be lifted. Most important, they requested the separation of Texas from Coahuila. William H. Wharton, the son-in-law of Jared Groce and an outspoken advocate of Anglo interests, and Manchola were chosen to carry the petitions to Mexico City. Before adjourning, the convention set up a central committee to call future meetings if necessary and established committees of correspondence in each municipality. In spite of the convention's professions of loyalty to Mexico and the Constitution of 1824, these committees sounded suspiciously like agencies created in England's colonies before the American Revolution.

Nothing came of the Convention of 1832, primarily because Ramón Múzquiz, the political chief at San Antonio, pointed out that it had convened illegally. Under Mexican law, petitions could come only from *ayuntamientos,* not from conventions, so they were not delivered. Stephen F. Austin, also aware from the beginning that the convention was illegal and likely to cause trouble, breathed a sigh of relief when it did not, but then, knowing that the Anglos likely would not give up, went to work to gain the support of Tejanos and make the petitions properly. He persuaded his friends in San Antonio to draft a pro-reform petition to the state legislature. The work of younger Tejanos such as Juan Nepomuceno Seguín, the son of Erasmo Seguín, the petition criticized interference by the national government in state colonization. It attacked in particular the Law of April 6, 1830, for the way it excluded useful "capitalists" from Texas. The San Antonio petition was endorsed by meetings in Goliad, San Felipe, and Nacogdoches. However, before Austin's approach of going through proper channels and enlisting Tejano support could be tested further, new developments in Mexico City allowed more impatient Anglos to push their point again.

On January 3, 1833, Santa Anna took over the national government from Bustamante, and three months later the Mexican states elected him president. This turn of events seemingly favored Anglo Texans' desire for separate statehood in that the general had long stood for federalism, and his notably liberal vice president, Valentín Gómez Farías, was totally committed to that position. Rather than wait for the wheels of government to turn, however, the central committee set up in 1832 called for another convention at San Felipe on April 1, 1833. This second convention was controlled not by Austin and older, moderate settlers but by men like William Wharton, who were more recent arrivals willing to take stronger stances against Mexico. Wharton, whom Austin had defeated for the presidency of the 1832 convention, presided this time. A new resident of the province, Sam Houston, represented Nacogdoches, the first act in his role as an Anglo founding father of Texas second only to Austin.

Sam Houston supported Wharton and the more aggressive colonists at the Convention of 1833 and seemed ready to live up to his reputation as a man of extremes and erratic behavior. Born in Virginia in 1793, Houston, after moving at an early age with his family to Tennessee, ran away from home at the age of sixteen and lived with the Cherokee Indians for several years. Following his years as a runaway, he joined the United States Army as a teenager during the War of 1812. At the Battle of Horseshoe Bend against the Creek Indians, he demonstrated foolhardy courage and suffered near-fatal wounds but also became a favorite of Andrew Jackson. He studied law and then, as a protégé of Jackson, was elected Governor of Tennessee only to resign in disgrace in 1829 after the breakup (for reasons that will never be

Sam Houston (1793–1863). This 1848 lithograph captures Houston's strength and pride far better than do earlier portraits. Credit: Center for American History, UT-Austin.

known) of his marriage to Eliza Allen. After three aimless years with the Cherokees, during which he gave in completely to his weakness for alcohol—the "flowing bowl," he called it—and earned the nickname "Big Drunk," he went to Texas. Anyone would have been justified in expecting Sam Houston to behave like an irresponsible radical when he rode across the Red River in 1832, but fortunately for Anglo Texans, caution and practicality dominated his thinking once he took on the responsibilities of leadership.

Some have claimed that President Andrew Jackson sent Houston to create a revolution in Texas, but that is untrue. Officially, Houston entered the province for the purpose of negotiating with the Comanches concerning hunting grounds for Indians being moved from the southeastern United States to present-day Oklahoma. He carried out that mission, but he had a personal purpose as well. Like so many Americans who came to Texas, Sam Houston's fortunes had played out at home. He crossed the Red River not as an agent of revolution but as another immigrant in search of new beginnings.

The Convention of 1833 met for two weeks and again asked for a repeal of the immigration restrictions in the Law of April 6, 1830, and for separate statehood for Texas. It went one step beyond the 1832 convention, however, by drafting a proposed constitution for the state of Texas, patterning it on the

Tennessee state constitution of 1796 and the Louisiana constitution of 1812. Austin, Erasmo Seguín, and James B. Miller, a Kentucky-born doctor who had come to Texas in 1829, were chosen to deliver the convention's petition and proposed constitution to the government in Mexico City. Seguín and Miller could not make the trip, however, so it fell to Austin alone. Initially, the empresario had doubted the wisdom of the conventions, but by the close of the second one, he had made up his mind to support its demands. He had grown tired of waiting for more Tejanos to accept separate statehood, and his position as a leader of the Anglos depended on taking a stand. One of the oldest settlers put it succinctly: "He [Austin] is closely watched and his future prospects depend greatly upon his Conduct in this matter. If he succeeds he will do well for himself and if for the want of proper Exertion on his part the application should fail Col. Austin will be a Ruined man in Texas."

Austin once more made the long trip to Mexico City, arriving on July 13, 1833. He found that Santa Anna, after winning the presidency earlier that year, largely left the government in the hands of Vice President Valentín Gómez Farías, a liberal federalist who gave Austin a "kind and friendly" reception. The empresario seemingly made progress at first, but then his proposals for reform bogged down in the Mexican congress, and a cholera epidemic paralyzed the capital city. Austin himself barely survived an attack of the disease. Finally, in early October, frustrated and depressed by news that cholera was taking a toll in Texas as well, Austin made an uncharacteristic mistake. He wrote to the *ayuntamiento* of San Antonio recommending that it unite the people of Texas in "a measure to organize a local government independent of Coahuila, even though the general government withholds its consent." Rather than the standard Mexican closing, *dios y libertad* (God and Liberty), he ended with *Dios y Tejas*. The usually cautious Austin seemed to be recommending revolution.

Later in the fall, congress approved removing the restriction on immigration from the United States, and Santa Anna, having resumed the presidency for a brief time, accepted the repeal with a proviso that it would become effective in six months. Neither congress nor the president would act on the separate statehood proposal, although it seemed likely that they soon would make other reforms that Anglo Texans wanted. Austin decided that he had accomplished as much as possible and left for home on December 10, 1833. "Texas matters are all right," he wrote his partner, Samuel May Williams, just before he departed, "nothing is wanted there but *quiet*." "Matters," however, were not all right for the empresario himself.

When Austin reached Saltillo on the way to Texas, he was arrested by Mexican authorities on January 3, 1834. The problem, of course, was his letter to the *ayuntamiento* of San Antonio recommending action on separate statehood without the approval of the national government. Upset at what they termed this "exceedingly rash" proposal, the *ayuntamiento* sent the letter to the state government, and that, in turn, led to the arrest. The acting governor of Coahuila y Texas told Benjamin Lundy, the American abolitionist who happened to be visiting Saltillo at the time, that the "treasonable letter" led him to think that Austin "must be partially insane." An armed guard escorted the empresario back to Mexico City where he was imprisoned in February 1834.

Austin spent three months in a sixteen-by-thirteen foot cell with a small skylight that allowed him to see to read only from 10 A.M. to 3 P.M. At first he was visited only by a lawyer and Father Michael Muldoon, the priest who had ministered to Anglo-Americans in Texas. In April Santa Anna again resumed the presidency briefly and ended Austin's solitary confinement, but months passed without an indictment or a decision as to what law had been violated, let alone a trial. Eventually Patrick Jack and another Texas lawyer, Peter Grayson, came to help with the case. Thanks to their efforts and numerous appeals from *ayuntamientos* in Texas, Austin was allowed to post bond and leave prison on Christmas Day, 1834. He had spent nearly a year in jail, and another eight months would pass before he could obtain amnesty and return home. During his long absence, however, developments had generally favored Texas.

When first arrested, Austin urged Anglo Texans to stay calm and "discountenance all revolutionary measures or men," a request that, fortunately for him, was honored. Meanwhile, Santa Anna in his brief return to control during the spring of 1834 proved friendly not only to the empresario but to Texas as well. On his recommendation, the state legislature of Coahuila y Texas passed several important reforms. A liberal land law allowed Anglos to buy directly from the state on generous terms. English became an official language in the state, and its citizens received the right to trial by a jury, a practice unique in all of Mexico. The legislature also divided Texas into three departments—Béxar, Brazos, and Nacogdoches—and accordingly increased its representation from one to three.

These reforms did not mean, however, that Mexico's national government forgot about the Conventions of 1832 and 1833 or Austin's inflammatory letter. Concern over conditions in Texas led in 1834 to yet another investigative mission, this one led by Colonel Juan Nepomuceno Almonte, the illegitimate son of the revolutionary hero Morelos. Educated in the United States, Almonte undertook his mission with an open mind. He spent several months in Texas during the summer of 1834 and prepared a detailed report. The province, he estimated, had a population of 21,000 non-Indians—4,000 in the Department of Béxar, 8,000 in Brazos, and 9,000 in Nacogdoches. Béxar had no slaves, but the other two departments had one thousand each. Although his statistics demonstrated the ever-increasing control of Anglos, Almonte found the political situation generally quiet and suggested that stability in the government of Mexico would maintain calm in Texas. Austin, still on bond in Mexico City but much encouraged by the reforms in 1834, agreed and decided that separate statehood could wait. Few observers if any considered revolution imminent in Texas at the beginning of 1835, but then few Mexicans or Anglos understood the ambitions of President Santa Anna.

For most of his first two years as president Santa Anna left the government in the hands of Vice President Gómez Farías, using him as a "stalking horse" in determining how to govern Mexico. He permitted Gómez Farías to introduce liberal reforms such as abolishing special courts for members of the army and mandatory tithing to the church in order to judge the reaction. Finding that powerful military and religious leaders hated liberal reform, Santa Anna decided that he could become a centralist, win their support, and gain absolute power. Accordingly, in April 1835 he took charge from Gómez Farías for the final time, and soon replaced the existing congress with a new body controlled by centralists and subject to his will. He then proceeded to abolish the Constitution of 1824 (which he had previously championed) and to abolish the states and replace them with departments run by officials whom he appointed. When the state of Zacatecas rebelled, he suppressed it militarily and allowed his soldiers to brutalize the city's citizens, killing thousands of them. In short, by October 1835 Santa Anna made himself nearly all-powerful in the government of Mexico.

Like many other citizens of Mexico, Anglo Texans did not know at first what to think of Santa Anna's actions. For years they had seen him as a federalist and friend, a champion of the Constitution of 1824. Also, the state government of Coahuila y Texas had just discredited itself in the eyes of many Texans by granting huge expanses of Texas land to its own members and other favored individuals. Perhaps, Texans reasoned, leaders of the state government were worried about Santa Anna's centralist policies only because he threatened their own selfish interests. Gradually, however, residents of the province came to see that the Mexican president had indeed turned his back on federalism and become a serious threat to them. The Texas Revolution developed before the end of the year.

In less than fifteen years, Mexico populated Texas between the San Antonio and Sabine Rivers, an accomplishment that had eluded Spain for more than a century. The process, however, created an Anglo-American province that threatened the interests of its Tejano and Indian inhabitants and stood on the verge of revolt against Mexico in 1835. Manuel de Mier y Terán, the Mexican patriot who first sounded the alarm about Anglos in Texas, despaired of the future as early as 1832. No one knew better than he that immigrants from the United States had too little respect for Mexico and the opportunities it provided; nevertheless, he criticized his own government for the problem. "A great and respectable Mexican nation," he wrote his friend Lucas Alamán, "a nation of which we have dreamed and for which we have labored so long, can never emerge from the many disasters which have overtaken it. How could we expect to hold Texas when we do not even agree among ourselves? It is a gloomy state of affairs. If we could work together, we would advance. As it is, we are lost. . . . Texas is lost. . . . What will become of Texas? Whatever God wills." The next day, while on his morning walk wearing full dress uniform, Mier y Terán drew his sword, braced it against a stone, and drove the blade through his heart.

Chapter 6

THE TEXAS REVOLUTION, 1835–1836

The seeds of revolution in Texas, planted by the arrival of Anglo-Americans during the 1820s, germinated in 1835 when President Santa Anna centralized the government of Mexico. Perhaps the concentration of so many Texians, as immigrants from the United States called themselves, in a single province situated in close proximity to their homeland made revolution inevitable—some day. However, the train of events that led to war in 1835 and independence in 1836 might easily have taken other directions at that time.

Texians presented anything but a united front in the summer of 1835. Uncertain of Santa Anna's intentions, concerned that Stephen F. Austin remained a prisoner in Mexico City, confused by the political games of state officials in Coahuila, and divided by personal jealousies, the majority had no stomach for the risky business of revolution. Many Tejanos also felt threatened by Mexico's move toward centralism, but for them rebellion could mean a war against their own people. Thus, when trouble broke out in June, Texans—Anglos and Tejanos alike—had no commitment to any particular plan of action.

The Outbreak of War

Anahuac, the scene of the 1832 disturbances, became the focal point for renewed difficulties in 1835 when Captain Antonio Tenorio arrived with a small detachment of troops and orders to reestablish the customshouse at that site. Local residents accused Tenorio of collecting higher duties than was the practice at Velasco on the Brazos River and responded by smuggling and refusing to provide supplies for Mexican soldiers. The captain reacted by warning his superior in Mexico, General Martín Perfecto de Cos, commander of the Eastern Internal Provinces, that the Anglos were on the verge of revolt. Cos, however, could not send additional troops at that time because of the federalist rebellion in Zacatecas.

Tension between Tenorio and Anahuac residents reached a climax in June when Andrew Briscoe, a local merchant, tested the captain's patience by loading bricks in a suspicious manner that gave the appearance of smuggling. Unamused, Tenorio arrested Briscoe. When news of the arrest reached San Felipe, William B. Travis, a leader in the original Anahuac disturbances, raised a party of armed volunteers, variously estimated at twenty-five to fifty in number, who went to Anahuac and forced Tenorio to surrender. The articles of capitulation, signed on June 30, called for the Mexicans to evacuate Anahuac and turn over their arms to the Anglos in return for safe passage to San Antonio.

Travis's action drew applause from the "War Party," the relatively small group who had favored a strong stand since 1832, but the majority of Texians disapproved. Across the province, meeting after meeting passed resolutions condemning the attack on Anahuac. The citizens of Brazoria honored Tenorio and his men at a July 4 barbecue. Even Travis felt the need to make a public apology for his rash actions. By July 25, a "Peace Party" leader in San Felipe proclaimed, "[A]ll here is in a train for peace, the war and [speculating] parties are entirely put down."

Texians who wanted peace also appealed directly to General Cos, protesting their loyalty to Mexico. Cos, however, disregarded all such appeals and planned to send additional troops to Texas. Back in the spring he had reacted to Tenorio's reports on problems at Anahuac by concluding that the time had come "to let those ungrateful strangers know that the Govno. has sufficient power to repress them" and that they should "march from the country if they do not want to submit themselves to its laws." The general's "get tough" attitude was then reinforced by Colonel Domingo de Ugartechea, the commander at San Antonio, who also informed him regularly that disloyal Anglos stood on the verge of revolt. "Nothing is heard [here]," the latter wrote on June 20, "but God damn Santa Anna, God damn Ugartechea." Thus, the refusal by Cos, who was Santa Anna's brother-in-law and a committed centralist, to listen to Anglo appeals following the attack on Anahuac is understandable. It also brought on war.

Cos believed that only military occupation could bring Texas under control, but he also knew that Texians were likely to resist. Ugartechea had warned that the Anglos would arm "even the children" to keep Mexican troops out. Cos and Ugartechea, therefore, announced in early August that the additional occupying forces would respect law-abiding citizens, but they asked Texas officials to demonstrate their loyalty by arresting some of the leading troublemakers. In particular, the Mexican commanders called for the arrest of Travis and other leaders at Anahuac; Samuel May Williams, Austin's partner and a leading land speculator; and Lorenzo de Zavala, a liberal federalist from Yucatán who had fled to Texas in July. These men were to be tried by the Mexican military rather than a jury. Texians had no intention of turning over their own, or Zavala either, for that matter, to such a fate. No arrests were made.

News of the impending military occupation and the request for arrests led Texians, even many of those previously committed to peace, to change their strategy. Leaders and local committees began to call for a convention or

"Consultation" of representatives from across the province to be held at Washington-on-the-Brazos on October 15, 1835. One committee stated its purpose succinctly: "The only instructions which we would recommend be given to our representatives is to secure peace if it is to be obtained on constitutional terms, and to prepare for war—if war is inevitable." The reaction to military occupation delighted War Party men. "The people," wrote William B. Travis at the end of August, "are becoming united, more and more every day & I think in a month more, there will be no divisions at all."

The likelihood of unified action by Texians increased in early September when Stephen F. Austin arrived home after his long stay, much of it as a prisoner, in Mexico City. Although never a radical, Austin had concluded that Santa Anna's switch to centralism and brutal suppression of Zacatecas left no choice—Texas had to become independent of Mexico. Buoyed by a warm reception at Brazoria on September 8, he blamed Mexico for the threat to peace and quiet in Texas and endorsed the Consultation called for October 15. Most Texians followed his lead and couched their protest in conservative terms, picturing Mexico as the aggressor in the conflict.

General Cos, determined to arrest Travis, Williams, Zavala, and other troublemakers and to bring Texas under control, left Matamoros with five hundred soldiers on September 17. He traveled by water to Copano Bay on the coast north of modern Corpus Christi, landing there on the 20th, and marched inland toward San Antonio. There, he would take command of the garrison commanded by Colonel Ugartechea. Austin reacted to reports of Cos's movements by pronouncing efforts at conciliation "hopeless." "WAR is our only resource," he wrote. Events bore out his words—even before Cos reached San Antonio.

Fighting began in early October 1835 in a way loosely reminiscent of how the War of the American Revolution started at Lexington and Concord in 1775. The little town of Gonzales, located on the Guadalupe River about seventy miles east of San Antonio, had a cannon, loaned to them by the Mexican army in 1831 for Indian defense. Because of the growing tension with Texians, Colonel Ugartechea sent out a small detachment of soldiers to reclaim the cannon. Texians at Gonzales refused to hand over the weapon, so Ugartechea dispatched Lieutenant Francisco Castañeda at the head of one hundred dragoons to take it. (See map: Texas Revolution in 1835.) When the Mexicans arrived on September 29, they found the rain-swollen Guadalupe too high to ford and the ferry and all available boats tied up at the town on the east side. Shouting across the torrent, Castañeda informed the Anglos of his mission. He then made camp and waited. Local residents took advantage of the delay to ask other settlements for assistance, and by October 1, enough volunteers converged on Gonzales to create an "army" of about 150 Texians. They elected John H. Moore as their colonel, put the cannon on wheels, loaded it with scraps of metal, and fashioned a white banner with an image of the cannon and the words "COME AND TAKE IT." Crossing the river late on October 1, they attacked the Mexicans shortly after dawn on October 2. The Texians fired their cannon once and then charged wildly, but they never closed with their

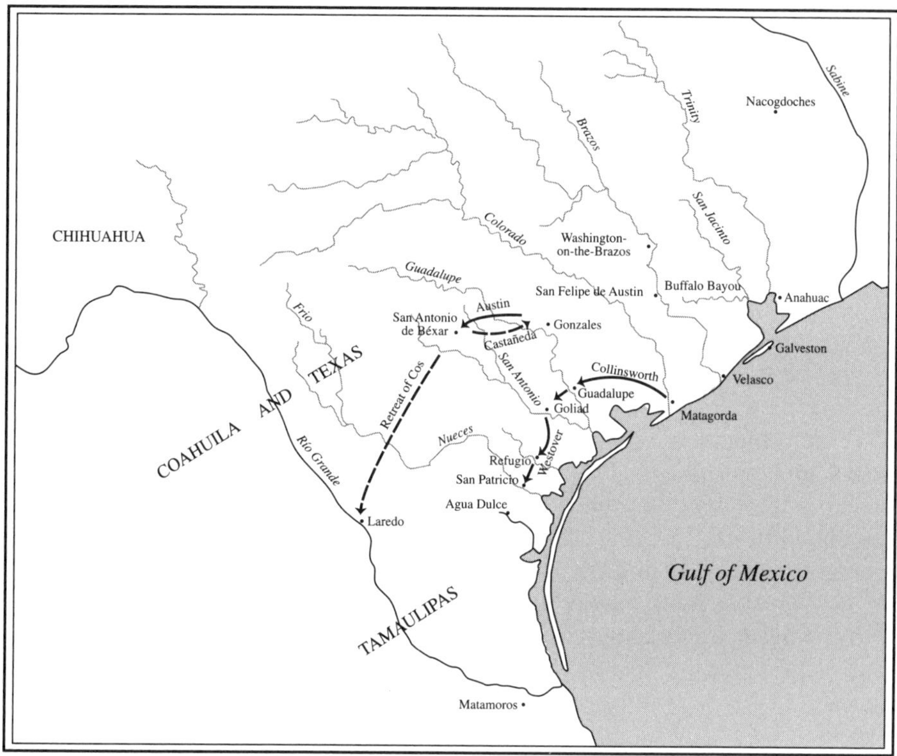

Texas Revolution in 1835

foe because Castañeda, outnumbered and without orders to engage in battle, withdrew. He lost one or two men; one Texian suffered a bloody nose when thrown from his horse.

Although barely a skirmish, the fight at Gonzales marked a point of no return. Virtually all Texians, and the sizable number of Tejanos who soon joined them, knew that they could not turn back. Either they would, in the words of Stephen F. Austin, "drive the military out of Texas and organize a government for this country," or they would be crushed and have to flee the province or lose their lives.

Causes of the Texas Revolution

Why had affairs in Texas come to this point? What caused the revolution? Contemporaries and historians offer varying explanations. American and British abolitionists, for example, insisted that slaveowners created the revolt in Texas because of their concern for protecting the South's Peculiar Institution there. A few historians have blamed a conspiracy hatched in the United States, arguing that President Andrew Jackson sent Sam Houston to Texas to stir up a revolution that would lead to annexation. Patriotic Americans explain the conflict in terms of a democratic, freedom-loving people rising up against Mexican oppression. Those seeking a more comprehensive interpretation emphasize ethnic and cultural conflict between peoples of Mexican and Anglo-Celtic descent.

The Jackson-Houston conspiracy theory manages to hang on in some popular accounts and movies, but it should be laid to rest. It is true that Jackson wanted Texas and that he encouraged Houston to go there in 1832. However, other than these circumstances, there is no evidence of a conspiracy. After his initial involvement in the convention of 1833, Houston lived quietly in Nacogdoches and played no role in the events that led to war in 1835. In fact, when War Party men visited him in August of that year, he urged them to calm down. He supported the idea of a Consultation only after Stephen F. Austin endorsed it. If Sam Houston wanted a revolution, he thoroughly hid that desire.

The protection-of-slavery interpretation seems plausible, especially since Mexican governments had regularly threatened the institution in Texas, whereas the revolution made it secure there. This argument, however, is undermined by the fact that slavery was not a major issue in any of the developments from 1830 to 1835. It played no important part in the disturbances of 1832 or the events that led to fighting in 1835, and Mexico took no action threatening it immediately or directly during those years. This is not to say that slavery had no role in bringing on the Texas Revolution. It was one of the differences separating Mexicans and Texians, but it was not THE cause of rebellion.

In a similar fashion, the "American freedom and democracy versus Mexican oppression" argument is an oversimplification. Mexico offered considerable self-government at the local level—Texians, for example, served as *alcaldes* and on the *ayuntamientos* in their towns. Also, during the early 1830s Anglos in Texas received important concessions such as trial by jury and use of the English language. Santa Anna's turn to centralism alarmed Texians about a likely loss of self-government in the future and thus contributed to the revolt, but it alone is not an explanation.

Interpreting the revolution in terms of ethnic and cultural conflict is a more encompassing and therefore more satisfying approach, but even it requires qualification. Most Anglos definitely thought themselves inherently superior to Mexicans. David G. Burnet, a New Jersey–born leader of the revolution, expressed this view perfectly in an 1836 letter describing its causes: "One general fact may account for all; the utter dissimilarity of character between the two people, the Texians and the Mexicans. The first are principally Anglo Americans; the others a mongrel race of degenerate Spaniards and Indians more depraved than they." Some Mexicans had equally negative views of the Texians. They are a "lazy people of vicious character," wrote José María Sánchez in 1828 while accompanying Mier y Téran's tour of Texas. To meet one who is kind or courteous is "a very rare thing among individuals of his nationality." Culturally, Texians and Mexicans differed in language and religion. Moreover, most Anglos at least accepted slavery, whereas Mexican officials threatened to destroy the institution. Immigrants from the United States traditionally favored subordinating military to civil authority and had no respect for unstable governments such as the one in Mexico City.

Even these ethnic and cultural differences, important as they were, do not completely account for the revolution. Texians, concentrated in East Texas and along the lower Brazos and Colorado Rivers, had only limited contact with Mexicans. Differences in religion or language were not major irritants. Moreover, it is clear that when they did associate before 1835, Texians and Tejanos generally cooperated in a friendly fashion. The fact that a sizable minority of Tejanos fought alongside the Anglos in 1835–1836 indicates that ethnocultural conflict alone cannot explain the revolution.

Frontier conditions contributed one final element to the mix that led to revolt. As frontiersmen, the people of Texas—both Anglos and Mexicans—had interests that drew them together and often placed them in conflict with policies adopted in Mexico City. For example, Anglo and Tejano merchants, although rivals to an extent, cooperated in important ways. Anglos gave their Hispanic counterparts contacts with suppliers in the United States and, in turn, received assistance in dealing with Mexican officials and regulations. Anglo and Tejano land speculators also had a common interest in populating and expanding their province as rapidly as possible and therefore opposed anti-immigration laws and tariffs and supported slavery. Overall, Texian and Tejano leaders tended to unite in the belief that politicians at the capital simply did not understand the economic interests of Texas. Settlers in other Mexican frontier provinces such as New Mexico and California had similar difficulties with the government in Mexico City during the 1830s and 1840s.

So, in the final analysis, the Texas Revolution resulted from a special complex of combustible conditions and a spark that ignited them. The first, and essential, combustible was put in place when Anglo-Americans populated a Mexican province. Concentrated in a limited area close to their homeland, they maintained a distinct ethnic and cultural identity and had little or no loyalty to Mexico. A second combustible was added when leaders of the province, Texians and Tejanos alike, came to believe that the central government did not recognize or support their interests. The spark that touched off these combustibles came in the form of Santa Anna's move to centralism and the demand by General Cos that the people of Texas subject themselves to the new system in Mexico and accept military occupation. Facing a reduction of local control, Texians, with the support of significant numbers of Tejanos, rebelled.

The War in 1835

Once word of the fight at Gonzales on October 2 spread, volunteers from other Texian settlements rushed to join the men who had defended the cannon. At the same time, a force of volunteers from Matagorda commanded by George M. Collinsworth moved to attack Goliad. General Cos had marched past the old presidio there on his way from Copano Bay to San Antonio but had not reinforced its garrison significantly. Thus, when the Texians attacked in the early morning darkness on October 10, Mexican soldiers offered little resistance. They opened fire from their barracks, wounding Samuel McCulloch, a black volunteer who had once been Collinsworth's slave, but quickly surrendered when threatened with "massacre." The taking of Goliad left Mexican forces in San Antonio cut off from the Gulf of Mexico. Supplies or reinforcements would have to move across the deserts of northern Mexico.

Most of the men who took Goliad immediately marched toward Gonzales to join the larger force of Texians gathering there. Upon arriving, they found that Stephen F. Austin, at the urging of several leaders, had joined the volunteers on October 11 and been elected their commander. The next day, raising the cry "On to Béxar," the Texians marched toward San Antonio, gathering additional men as they went. Dressed in "uniforms" of every description, armed with rifles and shotguns (or in too many cases without arms at all), completely untrained, and led by a general who had extremely limited military experience, this first Texian army presented a truly ragtag appearance as it went on the offensive. By October 20, some four hundred strong, it reached Salado Creek five miles east of San Antonio.

Taking the city presented a formidable challenge because General Cos, after arriving on October 9, had used his time well. He had more than six hundred men in defensive positions supported by twelve cannon. Austin decided against a frontal assault, a decision that was reinforced by reports from two groups of Tejano horsemen who joined his army at this time. Plácido Benavides, the *alcalde* of Victoria, arrived on October 15 with thirty mounted rancheros, and Juan N. Seguín came out from San Antonio on October 22 with a like number of mounted men. These Tejanos acted as guides and scouts, giving the Texians "eyes" they could not have had otherwise.

One week after reaching the outskirts of San Antonio, Austin decided to move his base of operations closer to the city and dispatched a force of nearly one hundred men to probe the area near Mission Concepción. He gave command to forty-year-old Jim Bowie, the famed knife fighter who had come to Texas in 1828 and married into a wealthy Béxar family. When Bowie's wife died in 1833 he drowned the loss in alcohol, but even at that, his reputation and physical presence commanded respect. The best-known officer accompanying Bowie was thirty-one-year-old James W. Fannin, a Georgian who had attended West Point for two years in the 1820s before dropping out. Fannin brought his family to Texas in 1834 and soon involved himself in an illegal African slave-trading venture. He was one of the few men in the province with any formal military training, so Texians looked to him for leadership in spite of the fact that he was largely a ne'er-do-well who had no experience in actual command.

Bowie and Fannin had orders from Austin to return as quickly as possible so that the whole army could move to the new forward position. However, after taking an entire day to locate a suitable spot, a tree-lined horseshoe bend in the San Antonio River near the old mission, the officers decided to camp there rather than return to the main army. The decision to disregard orders nearly proved disastrous, because General Cos learned of the detachment's presence and attacked it at dawn on October 28 with three hundred cavalry and a hundred infantrymen. The Texians used the steep, tree-lined

Juan N. Seguín (1806–1890). A Tejano leader who supported the Texas Revolution and fought at San Jacinto, Seguín, shown here in an 1838 portrait, left the Republic in 1842 after his loyalty was questioned and did not return until 1848. Credit: Texas State Library and Archive Commission.

river bank as a breastwork and obeyed Bowie's order to "be cool and deliberate and to waste no powder and balls, but to shoot to hit." Their long rifles took a toll on the attackers at distances up to two hundred yards, whereas the Mexicans' muskets were ineffective at any range greater than seventy yards. The Mexicans brought cannon into play, but the grapeshot they fired ripped harmlessly through the trees above the Texians, knocking down showers of ripe pecans to be eaten by the combatants.

Facing devastating fire that prevented closing to an effective range, Mexican troops became demoralized and began to retreat. They abandoned the field completely when Bowie led a charge against the cannon. A short time later, the main army arrived with a cavalry unit commanded by William B. Travis in the vanguard. Travis had orders to wait for the main army before making any attack, but, matching Bowie and Fannin in disregarding directives from Austin, he ordered a charge against the retreating Mexicans. Austin allowed himself to be carried away momentarily by the victory and called for an immediate attack on the city, but Bowie and Fannin persuaded him to stop.

He then reprimanded Travis so severely that the hot-headed South Carolinian resigned his command and returned to San Felipe, where he served as a recruiting officer.

The battle at Concepción cost the Mexicans about seventy-six casualties while the Texians lost only a single man. Bowie and Fannin had been more lucky than good in that Cos chose to attack frontally and allowed them to stay under cover of the trees and river bank and use their rifles effectively. Had the Mexicans flanked the Texians by moving into and along the tree-lined banks on either prong of the horseshoe, the battle might have ended differently. Cos did not enter the trees, however, because that sort of fighting was largely alien to the Mexican army. The Texians, most of whom grew up east of the Mississippi, were accustomed to wooded terrain and fought well in it. By contrast, Mexicans were familiar only with open country and therefore relied on cavalry.

Only a few days after Concepción a smaller skirmish near San Patricio on the Nueces River again demonstrated the advantage enjoyed by Texians if they could fight from cover. A force of about sixty men commanded by Ira Westover marched from Goliad to San Patricio and on November 3 forced the surrender of the small Mexican earthworks there called Fort Lipantitlán. The fort surrendered because most of its garrison, knowing of Westover's approach, had ridden out hoping to intercept him. As the Texians crossed the Nueces River the next day on their way back to Goliad, they encountered the main Mexican force. The battle that followed replicated Concepción in that the rebels fired from the tree-lined river bank at Mexicans advancing across open ground. In about thirty minutes, the Texians inflicted twenty-eight casualties at the cost of one man wounded. We "flogged them like hell," one rifleman wrote.

Thus, by early November 1835, the rebellion had defeated Mexican forces everywhere except in San Antonio, and Austin's army expected to force Cos to surrender soon. Texians were confident—overconfident, as it turned out—of military success, but they had not yet agreed on their goal. Were they fighting for independence? If so, they proved very reluctant to say so.

The Consultation

Politically, the revolution moved haltingly and with great confusion in 1835. The Consultation, originally scheduled for mid-October, was expected to determine a course of action and set up a government, but the outbreak of fighting delayed its meeting until November. In the interval, Stephen F. Austin attempted to create a temporary government by asking each district to send representatives to a "Permanent Council" at San Felipe. This first governing body turned out to be wonderfully misnamed in that it lasted only three weeks—from October 9 to November 1. A handful of men representing only seven districts, the Permanent Council issued appeals to stir up support across Texas and in the United States. Other than generating propaganda, its most important action was to close land offices in the province. This step came at the request of volunteers in the army who feared that speculators would take advantage of the situation to grab the best land, but it irritated many prospective landowners.

The Permanent Council passed away quietly when the Consultation assembled at San Felipe on November 1. Although its fifty-eight delegates did not represent all of Texas—none came from the war-zone districts such as Béxar, Goliad, Victoria, and San Patricio—those present generally came from the established Anglo leadership of the province. One faction led by John A. Wharton disliked Stephen F. Austin and favored immediate independence, but another group led by Don Carlos Barrett supported Austin and advocated a more cautious approach. Branch T. Archer, a Virginian who served as chair, and Sam Houston tended to favor Wharton's faction but indicated a willingness to compromise in the interest of unity. After a week of debate the delegates adopted a highly ambiguous declaration of their position. Santa Anna's actions, it said, have given the people of Texas the right to create "an independent government . . . but [they] will continue faithful to the Mexican government, as long as that nation is governed by the Constitution [of 1824]." Why did the Consultation claim a right to independence and then declare loyalty to a government that no longer existed? Politics, explained Austin, from his position with the army. "This declaration secures to Texas *everything*," he wrote, because it appeals to Santa Anna's federalist enemies in Mexico and shows everyone else that the people of Texas are not impulsive or extreme. By this time, most Texian leaders had independence as their ultimate goal, but they saw the need to build strength before making an actual declaration.

Having wisely played for time in explaining the rebel cause, the Consultation then badly mishandled the creation of a provisional Texas government. The Organic Law adopted on November 13 provided for a governor, lieutenant governor, and a General Council made up of representatives from each district. Unfortunately, the governor's powers were not thoroughly defined, and he had to govern jointly with the General Council. This failure to separate executive and legislative power was a serious mistake, especially when coupled with equally bad judgment in the selection of a provisional governor. Henry Smith, the man chosen by a 30–22 vote over Stephen F. Austin, was a Kentuckian identified with the Wharton faction. Known best for his bad temper and prejudice toward all Mexicans, Smith soon became embroiled in a no-compromise conflict with the General Council that paralyzed the government.

The Consultation also made a serious mistake in its efforts to organize Texas's military forces. It created a regular army composed of two-year volunteers and chose Sam Houston as commander in chief. However, the volunteers already in the field, many of whom saw Houston as an overly ambitious and conniving newcomer, were not brought into the new army. Thus, when Major General and Commander in Chief Houston set up headquarters in San Felipe in November 1835, he had no army to command. Texas's only army of any size remained at Béxar, recognizing the authority (when it suited) only of elected officers and debating if, when, and where to fight.

Thus, the Consultation, meeting at a critical juncture in the development of the revolution, structured a government and an army that could easily degenerate into anarchy. It also removed a key force for stability by sending Stephen F. Austin to seek support in the United States. Austin had enemies—one of whom, William H. Wharton, accompanied him on this mission—but he also had the respect of many. His presence might well have been a steadying influence in the months following adjournment of the Consultation on November 14, 1835.

Victory at Béxar and an Abortive Matamoros Expedition

During the first weeks of November, Austin's army found the siege of San Antonio far less exciting than the fight at Concepción. Volunteers relieved their boredom by getting drunk, roaring through camp, and firing their rifles. Austin's orders had no effect, to the despair of more sober observers. "No good will be atchieved *[sic]* by this army," William H. Wharton complained, "except by the merest accident under heaven." Under these circumstances Austin might have welcomed the news on November 18 that the Consultation wanted him to go to the United States. He believed, however, that his immediate departure would cause a total collapse, so he remained in command and ordered an attack on the city at dawn on the 23rd. To his dismay, most of the volunteers refused to obey. The next day Austin paraded the troops and found that about four hundred would continue the siege if they could choose their new commander. Tactful to the end, he thanked the soldiers for their "obedience and good conduct" and rode toward San Felipe. The "Father of Texas" would not add the luster of military glory to his reputation.

The volunteers elected Edward Burleson, a veteran Indian fighter from North Carolina, as their new commanding officer, but his rough-and-ready approach was no more successful than Austin's more gentlemanly manner in bringing discipline. On November 26, the Texian scout, Erastus "Deaf" Smith, rode in and reported an enemy column approaching the city. A rumor quickly spread among the volunteers that the horsemen were escorting the payroll for soldiers in Béxar. Burleson ordered one hundred mounted men commanded by Jim Bowie to reconnoiter the column, but soon after they left camp, most of the other soldiers, determined to win a share of the treasure, raced after them. As soon as he encountered the column about a mile south of the city, Bowie attacked. The fight went back and forth as General Cos twice sent reinforcements onto the field, but in the end the Mexicans retreated into San Antonio, suffering an unknown number of casualties. Only two Texians were wounded in taking the "treasure train," which, to the considerable dismay of the victors, turned out to be bags of freshly cut grass. The Mexicans were gathering forage for their horses rather than escorting a payroll.

The "grass fight" did nothing to improve the Texians' chance of taking Béxar. Volunteers, short of food and without winter clothing, increasingly drifted away, and when Burleson ordered an attack on December 3 the majority responded as they had to a similar command by Austin—they refused.

Burleson reacted by announcing the next day that the army would lift the siege and go into winter quarters at Goliad. Then, one man made a dramatic difference. As the demoralized men prepared to break camp, forty-seven-year-old Benjamin Rush Milam returned from a scouting expedition. Milam, a native of Kentucky, had come to Texas by 1818, participated in James Long's filibustering expedition, engaged in mining and land speculation during the 1820s, and gotten into trouble in Mexico in 1835 because of his association with federalists in Coahuila. He escaped to Texas in time to join the force that took Goliad in October and then joined the volunteers at Béxar. Disgusted at Burleson's decision to lift the siege, Milam convinced the general to allow him to ask for volunteers to take the city. "Who will follow old Ben Milam into San Antonio?" he asked. Of the five hundred men still in camp, about three hundred answered, "I will."

The attack began at dawn on December 5 with a cannon shot aimed at the Alamo to divert the defenders' attention while Texians, joined by the Tejanos led by Benavides and Seguín, entered the town from the south. Milam's attacking force moved to within two hundred yards of the central square before Cos's troops discovered them and opened fire. At that point, the Texians took refuge in houses along the narrow streets, and the Tejanos, finding that there was no place for cavalry in such a fight, joined them. Houses in San Antonio were built to withstand Indian attacks so each was like a small fort, having thick adobe walls, oak doors, and few windows. The attackers found that they had to fight from one of these houses to the next and, in some cases, from room to room within a single house. Climbing onto rooftops and knocking holes through which they could fire into the rooms below or tearing holes in the walls of adjoining rooms for the same purpose, Milam's attackers slowly gained control of the town. They inflicted about 150 casualties on Cos's army but not without suffering losses themselves. Milam fell on the third day, shot through the head by a sniper armed with a far better rifle than the muskets carried by most Mexican soldiers. By early morning on December 9, the rebel force reached the central square, leaving Cos the choice of making a final stand in the Alamo or surrendering. He authorized Lieutenant Colonel José Juan Sánchez-Navarro to seek a cease fire and negotiate the best terms possible.

Colonel Sánchez-Navarro went to meet Burleson under a flag of truce, and the fighting ended. Then, as he later described it, "surrounded with crude bumpkins, proud and overbearing," he and the Texian leaders negotiated surrender terms. Soldiers in the Mexican army kept their personal arms and ten rounds of ammunition. They were given six days to recover from the battle and then allowed to leave San Antonio on the promise that they would cross the Río Grande and in no way "oppose the re-establishment of the Federal Constitution of 1824." A few volunteers complained about giving such generous terms, but Burleson's action made sense in light of the size of Cos's army and the fact that its removal would leave Texas free of all Mexican troops.

The taking of San Antonio created unreasonable optimism in Texas that the war had been won. A few hundred soldiers, mostly volunteers from the United States who craved more action, remained at the Alamo under the command of Colonel James C. Neill, but many Texian soldiers, including General Burleson, simply went home. Sam Houston, as commander in chief of the nonexistent "regular army," recognized the folly of such overconfidence and on December 12 called for the creation of a trained army of five thousand men by March 1, 1836. The General Council, however, did nothing other than appoint a few field officers. Texian leaders thus wasted the opportunity to organize and train an army, all the while remaining unaware that Santa Anna had begun to gather an invasion force of more than six thousand men in northern Mexico.

To make matters worse, some of the volunteer leaders, most notably Dr. James Grant and Francis W. Johnson, called for using the few men still in the army to attack the Mexican city of Matamoros on the lower Río Grande. An attack there, they argued would bring rich spoils of war and gain the support of Mexican federalists who opposed Santa Anna. In reality, Grant, a Scotsman, hoped to regain large landholdings in Coahuila that he owned before 1835, and Johnson, a Virginian by birth, was carried away by revolutionary enthusiasm. "Our first attack will be upon Matamoros," he proclaimed; "our next, if Heaven decrees, wherever tyranny shall raise its malignant form." Sam Houston opposed any offensive operation, as did Governor Henry Smith, but in late December the General Council authorized a Matamoros expedition under the joint command of Johnson and James W. Fannin. Johnson and Grant immediately stripped Béxar of all but about one hundred men and most military supplies and marched to join Fannin at Goliad, the staging point for their offensive.

Houston, seeing the Matamoros expedition as a recipe for disaster, attempted to deal with the situation by going to Goliad himself. Arriving on January 14, 1836, he found Fannin, Johnson, and Grant all busy elsewhere and took advantage of the opportunity to address the soldiers gathered there. He warned them that an attack into Mexico with the intention of taking spoils would be piracy rather than war and would never gain the support of Mexican federalists, no matter how much they opposed Santa Anna. Texas, he argued, should declare independence and defend it at home.

As Houston spoke, a courier arrived from San Antonio with a report that part of Santa Anna's army had crossed the Río Grande. If true, this meant that Neill's small force at Béxar, which for defensive purposes he had concentrated in the Alamo, was in serious danger. Jim Bowie, who had joined the proposed Matamoros expedition, immediately convinced about thirty volunteers to go with him back to San Antonio. As Bowie left, Houston sent orders to Colonel Neill to remove all military equipment, destroy the Alamo, and retreat to Gonzales. Bowie, however, expressed the belief that the Alamo could not be taken, so Houston in effect revised his order and placed the final decision in Neill's hands.

After Bowie left, the army marched south from Goliad to Refugio where Grant, the "acting commander in chief" waited. In Refugio, Johnson appeared with the news that he and Fannin had command of the expedition, although Fannin was still in Goliad. Obviously, chaos ruled the expedition, and Houston, who had ridden with the army to Refugio, again pointed out to the volunteers that they had little chance of success and would be treated as mercenaries when they failed. His speech planted seeds of doubt that flourished after he left to return to San Felipe. Some two hundred of the volunteers decided to march back to Goliad and join Fannin, who, after all, was one of their commanders. Only about sixty or seventy men remained with Grant and Johnson, who moved to San Patricio to wait and see what would happen next. Some criticize Houston for undoing the Matamoros expedition, but in reality it had amounted to an unwise, doomed venture from the outset.

While Texian military operations degenerated into factionalized foolishness between late 1835 and early 1836, civilian government deteriorated into near anarchy. Governor Smith and the General Council disagreed angrily over key issues such as whether or not to create a regular army and what they were trying to accomplish—was it independence or restoring the Constitution of 1824? In January 1836, Smith suspended the council, and it responded by removing him from office. The governor, however, refused to surrender his title, and the council, which after January 18 did not have enough members present to constitute a quorum, could not work with his supposed replacement, Lieutenant Governor James W. Robinson. At that point Texas in effect had no government. The only hope lay in a new convention called by the General Council back in December 1835 to assemble on March 1, 1836, at Washington-on-the-Brazos.

Fall of The Alamo

At the beginning of February 1836, Texian military forces consisted of nearly one hundred men in the Alamo, a little more than four hundred under the command of Fannin at Goliad, and sixty or seventy with Johnson and Grant at San Patricio. Overconfident because of successes in 1835, they had no idea of what was about to hit them. The Mexican army, although poorly funded and lacking in transportation and medical support, was formidable. Its infantry, even if composed mostly of untrained recruits armed with muskets ineffective at more than seventy yards, could overwhelm the rebels by sheer numbers, and its highly disciplined cavalry—armed with sabers, lances, and rifles—could devastate any Texian force caught in the open. Santa Anna's army suffered terribly from cold and snow as it moved through northern Mexico in early February 1836, but at the very least he had two thousand men and twenty-one artillery pieces when he crossed the Río Grande on the 16th. Moreover, the next day a force of 550 cavalry commanded by General José Urrea, an exceptionally capable officer, left Matamoros to sweep into Texas along the Gulf coast. (See map: Texas Revolution in 1836.)

Santa Anna's first objective, the Alamo, would have been abandoned long before he arrived had Houston's January 17 "order" to evacuate the old mission been followed. That directive, however, left the final decision to Neill, and he had already decided to stay. Impressed by Neill's having moved nineteen of the cannon captured from Cos into the Alamo and bolstered its de-

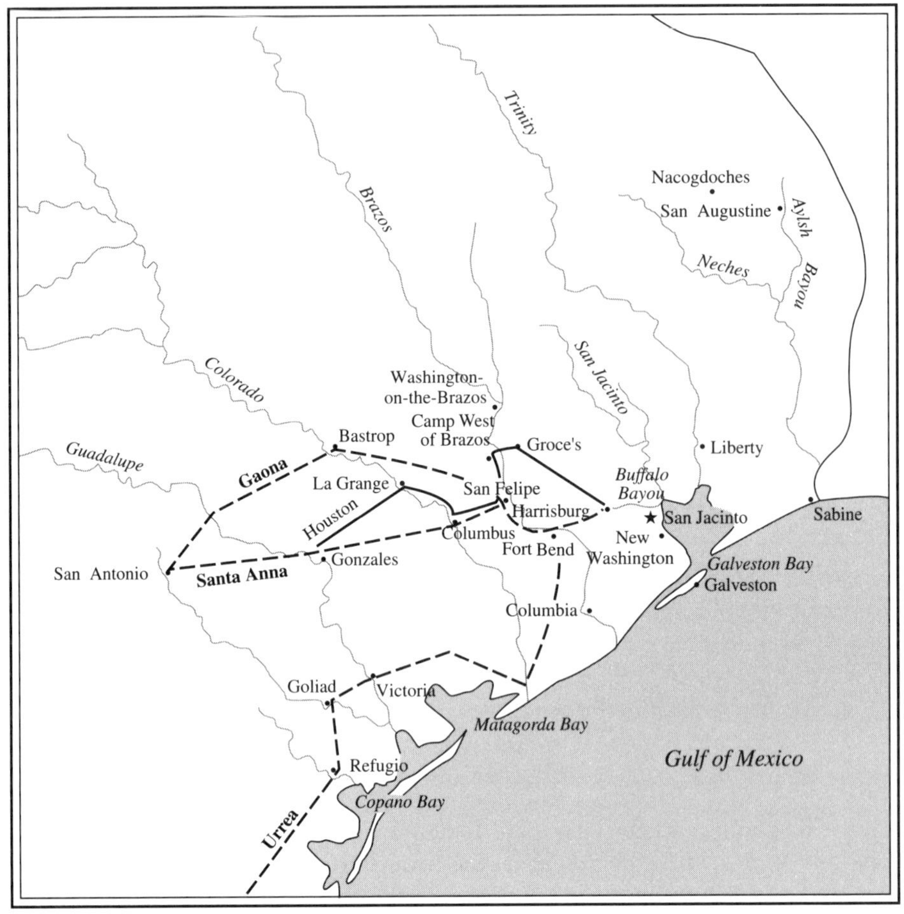

Texas Revolution in 1836

fenses, Bowie agreed that it should be held. We will "die in these ditches rather than surrender," he wrote Governor Smith. Smith responded by ordering William Barret Travis, a recruiting officer in San Felipe at the time, to raise a company and reinforce the Alamo. Reluctantly, because he feared that the fort did not have enough men or supplies, Travis raised twenty-nine volunteers and headed for Béxar, arriving on February 3. Five days later a small group of volunteers from Tennessee entered the Alamo under the leadership of forty-nine-year-old David Crockett.

Few western frontiersmen could best David Crockett as a hunter and teller of tall tales or in terms of personal charisma. Gaining recognition first for killing bears and fighting Indians, Crockett had served two terms in the Tennessee legislature and three in the U.S. House of Representatives. He loved to parade his humble origins and lack of formal education and even proposed abolishing the United States Military Academy because only the sons of the "rich and influential" attended it. Crockett's political career ended in the mid-1830s, however, when a candidate supported by Andrew Jackson took away his seat in Congress. So, he told his constituents that they could "go to Hell" while he "would go to Texas" and joined the long list of men who crossed the Red or Sabine in search of new beginnings. "I had rather be in my present situation," he wrote his children, "than to be elected to a seat in Congress for life. I am in hopes of making a fortune yet. . . ."

Colonel Neill left the Alamo on February 11 due to illness in his family and turned over command to Travis, who held a commission from the General Council. Many of the men, however, preferred Bowie. The two leaders avoided trouble by agreeing to act as joint commanders, an arrangement that held until Bowie became ill and turned over full control to Travis on the 24th. By that time, the Alamo was under siege. Somehow, in spite of reports by Seguín's scouts, the Texians did not expect Santa Anna's army before mid-March, but on February 20 residents of San Antonio began to leave the city and Tejano soldiers began to terminate their service as defenders. The first Mexican troops arrived on the 23rd, prompting Travis to send a courier to Gonzales with a hastily written message: "The enemy in large force is in sight. We want men and provisions. Send them to us. We have 150 men and are determined to defend the Alamo to the last."

The Alamo's twelve-foot-high, two-foot-thick walls offered considerable protection to defenders, providing that there were enough soldiers to man a defensive perimeter nearly a quarter of a mile long. (See Diagram of the Alamo.) But Travis's 150 men simply could not defend such a large fort. Riflemen were spread too thinly along the wall, and the cannon were manned by too few men to fire them rapidly. Moreover, no matter how strong the walls, they could not withstand the pounding of Mexican artillery indefinitely. Officers on both sides knew that the Alamo would fall unless reinforcements came to the aid of the Texians. Travis and Bowie were not suicidal; they expected relief to come. Santa Anna kept cavalry units constantly in the field to intercept any Texians who might attempt to lift the siege.

As Santa Anna's soldiers poured into San Antonio, he ordered the raising atop the San Fernando Church of a red flag signifying no quarter and then asked the Texians to surrender unconditionally. Travis replied with a single shot from the largest cannon in the Alamo, an eighteen pounder. Mexican artillerymen then began to break down the walls of the fort, a slow process because their heavy siege guns had not arrived. It also proved very dangerous in that lighter cannon were effective only at distances within range of the Texians' rifles. To protect their artillerymen, the Mexicans dug trenches and gun emplacements under cover of darkness, thus moving closer to the walls each night.

On the second day of the siege, Travis sent Captain Albert Martin to Gonzales with his most famous plea for help. "To the People of Texas and All Americans in the World," he wrote, "The enemy has demanded a surrender at discretion. . . . *I shall never surrender or retreat*. . . . I call on you . . . to come to our aid with all dispatch. . . . If this call is neglected, I am determined to

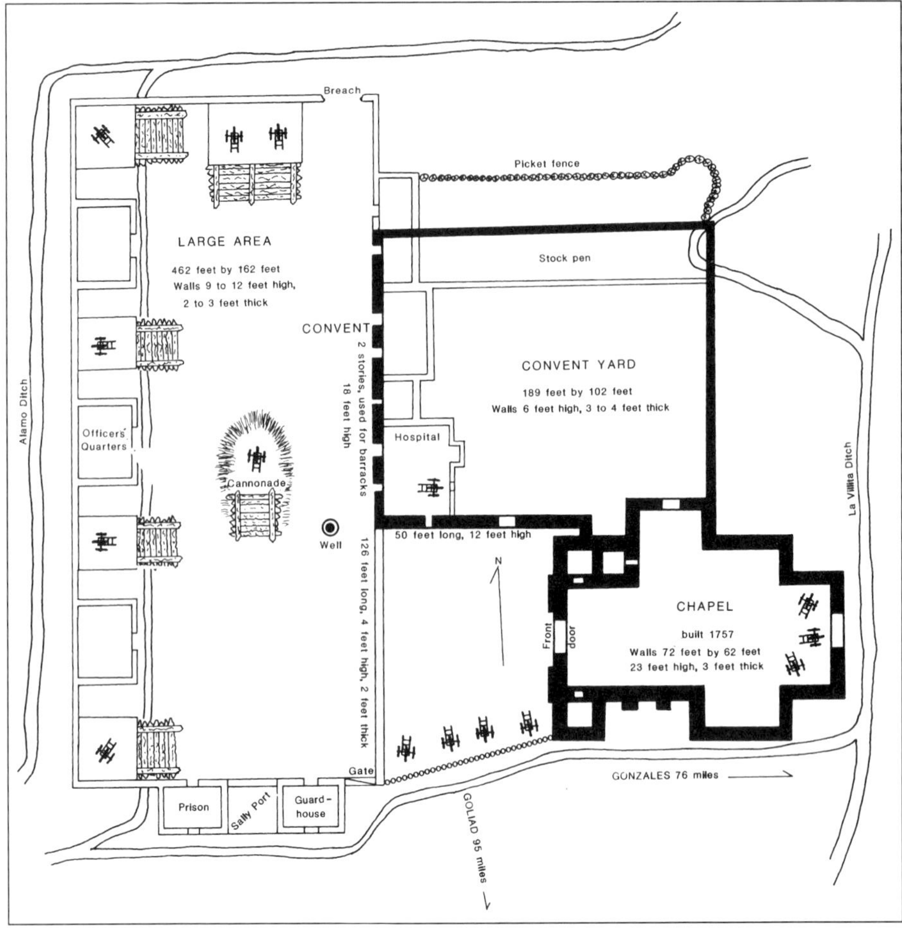

Diagram of The Alamo in 1836. The Convent Yard and Chapel constitute the present-day tourist attraction in San Antonio. Credit: © 1988 University of Oklahoma Press

sustain myself as long as possible & die like a soldier who never forgets what is due his own honor & that of his country. VICTORY or DEATH."

In response to this plea, thirty-three men from Gonzales made their way into the Alamo under cover of early morning darkness on March 1. Two days later, young James Butler Bonham daringly rode in during broad daylight. Bonham, who as a lawyer in South Carolina had been jailed for contempt of court when he caned opposing counsel for insulting his female client, was just the sort of man who would ride into rather than away from a death trap. He brought the worst news possible—the four hundred or so men at Goliad, the only sizable force in Texas, would not be coming to the relief of the Alamo. Fannin had actually marched his army toward San Antonio on February 28, but when an oxcart broke down and the weather turned bad, he went back to Goliad. In fairness to Fannin, he was short of supplies and knew that General Urrea's cavalry had begun their advance along the coast. His force at Goliad, he reasoned, might impede their movement into more settled areas of Texas.

On March 5, as hopes of relief faded, Travis called together the defenders. Years later, a Texian named William Zuber claimed that the commander, after summarizing the situation, drew a line in the dirt and asked all those willing to stay and die with him to step across. All but one, a Frenchman named Louis Rose, joined him. This great story, like so many told about the last days at the Alamo, may be a fabrication; no one can say for sure. At the least it seems that Travis told the soldiers to stay or go as they chose, whereupon Rose left and became Zuber's source for the line-in-the-dirt story. (Rose lived until 1851 and always had the same explanation of his action: "By God, I wasn't ready to die.")

Clearly the men in the Alamo stood ready to fight to the death if attacked, but still they were not suicidal. The memoirs of several Mexican officers indicate that as late as March 5 Travis would have surrendered had Santa Anna been willing to guarantee the lives of the defenders. The Mexican commander, however, replied that there could be no guarantees for traitors and decided to attack the fort on March 6. He acted over the objections of most of his officers, who thought that the defenders could be starved out, or driven out by the siege guns that would arrive in a day or two, at much less cost. Apparently the "Napoleon of the West" wanted a victory immediately, regardless of the cost.

Santa Anna ordered the attack to begin just before dawn at four different points on the walls. By the time Texians became aware of the Mexican advance their troops were within musket range; nevertheless, the attackers paid a huge price. Texian artillery pieces, loaded with cut-up horseshoes, bits of chain, and all sorts of scrap metal that turned them into giant shotguns, knocked down dozens of infantrymen with a single discharge. Rifle fire cut into the advancing columns as well. Still, the attack continued, and the Texians began to lose men as well. Travis was one of the first to die, shot in the forehead after exposing himself above the wall to fire at the Mexican infantry. The attackers reached the walls and huddled under them in confusion until a few climbed over the north wall and opened a door that permitted free access to the interior. Once the walls had been penetrated, Texians withdrew to the chapel and barracks on the east side of the fort, but the outcome was not in doubt. The Mexicans used the defenders' cannon to blast their way into the barracks and chapel, and the fighting became hand-to-hand, saber and lance against bowie knife. Bonham died beside his cannon at the rear of the church; Bowie, too sick to stand, was killed in his bed.

As the fight ended, seven men, possibly including Crockett, were captured by General Manuel Fernández Castrillón. Santa Anna, however, expressed indignation that any of the defenders remained alive and ordered their execution. Several officers disagreed with the murder of helpless men, but members of the commander's staff hacked them to pieces. Mexican soldiers then piled and burned the bodies of the 182 or 183 dead Texians. A few women, children, and Travis's slave, Joe, survived. They were allowed to go to Gonzales and tell what had happened. Their versions of the battle, stories told by Tejanos from Béxar, the memoirs of Mexican officers, and fanciful accounts created by various Texians eventually encrusted the Alamo in so many legends that no one can be certain of the details. Only one fact is indisputable—a small group of Texians commanded by William B. Travis all died in defending the Alamo against a much larger Mexican army commanded by Santa Anna.

Perhaps neither side should have fought the Battle of the Alamo. Santa Anna had no strategic need to take the fort. Located nearly 150 miles from the Gulf coast, San Antonio did not control an indispensable land or water route into Texas. Supplies for the Mexican army could come by water or along the coast from Matamoros. The Napoleon of the West did, however, have emotional and psychological reasons for the attack. Destruction of the Alamo would avenge the defeat of General Cos and renew Mexican control of the capital of Texas. Moreover, it would show Texians that as a price for rebellion they would be swept from the state, leaving no pockets of resistance behind. Thus, Santa Anna had valid reasons for insisting on taking the Alamo. His real mistake lay in ordering an assault rather than waiting a few more days for the siege guns that could have reduced the fort with much smaller losses. The general's ego and impatience cost his army about six hundred of its best soldiers dead or wounded and weakened it for the rest of the Texas campaign. As one of his officers put it, "With another such victory, we will all go to the devil."

The defenders had no good strategic reason for their sacrifice either and did not really claim that they did. Neill and Bowie made the original decision to hold the Alamo simply because they thought that they could. Then, once they were trapped, basic beliefs took over. When it became clear that other Texians would not ride to their rescue and that surrender was not an option, they had the choice of trying to escape or fighting to the end. Imbued with a romantic concept of honor and unwilling to betray their comrades, their response was, "I'll die before I'll run." In the final analysis then, the Alamo's defenders, like Santa Anna, fought not out of strategic necessity but for reasons perfectly understandable to themselves.

The defenders of the Alamo did not, contrary to an often-heard argument, give Sam Houston time to raise and train an army. That did not happen during the thirteen days of the siege. But their sacrifice benefited the Texas cause in several ways. First, the destruction of the Alamo woke up Texians—especially older settlers who did not strongly support the revolution—to the fact that their survival in Texas hung in the balance. Second, the story of fighting to the last man stirred imaginations and increased support for Texas in the United States. Third, the battle weakened Santa Anna's army and provided a rallying cry for Texians for the rest of the war. Finally, by delaying the Mexican invasion for more than two weeks, the Alamo defenders gave the convention that met on March 1 an opportunity to declare independence and organize a temporary government for Texas. At last, leaders clarified the purpose of the revolution and brought a little order out of political chaos.

Creation of the Republic of Texas

When the General Council called a convention to meet at Washington-on-the-Brazos on March 1, 1836, it scheduled the election of delegates to take place one month before that date. Voters on February 1 tended to reject men associated with the Consultation and General Council and send younger, more recent arrivals who favored decisive action. Nearly half of the fifty-nine delegates had lived in Texas less than two years; more than 40 percent had fought Mexican troops. Only two—José Antonio Navarro and José Francisco Ruiz—were native Texans.

Even a popular leader such as Sam Houston—the "people's man," in the words of one observer at the convention—had difficulty winning a place as a delegate, probably because he had been a leader in the Consultation. Voters in Nacogdoches, his home district, rejected his candidacy, but Refugio, which he had only visited briefly once, elected him. He then spent most of February 1836 carrying out a mission to the Cherokee Indians assigned to him by Governor Smith. Seeking to keep the Cherokees and other sedentary tribes such as the Delawares and Shawnees neutral, Houston signed a treaty with Chief Bowl and several other Cherokee leaders that declared a "a firm and lasting peace forever" and guaranteed the Indians' claims to lands in northeast Texas. A long-time friend of the Cherokees, Houston gave the chief a ceremonial sword and probably did not consider how difficult it might be to gain ratification of this treaty by the new government of Texas.

Houston arrived at Washington-on-the-Brazos on February 27 just as news of Santa Anna's siege of the Alamo reached the delegates assembling there and threatened to disrupt the convention. Some wanted to march to Béxar, but Houston argued persuasively that they should meet on schedule and take care of the business at hand. On March 2, the convention without debate adopted a declaration of independence. Written by George C. Childress, a Tennessean who had been in Texas less than eight months, and patterned on the American Declaration of Independence, this document argued that Mexican violations of the Constitution of 1824 had caused the revolt and necessitated separation as a matter of "self-preservation." Texas, it concluded, is a "free sovereign, and independent republic."

Having declared independence, the convention turned to creating an army and a government for their republic. On March 4, with only one negative vote, the delegates named Sam Houston commander in chief of the entire Texas army, volunteers and regulars alike. Houston did not leave immediately, which proved fortunate two days later when another message arrived from Travis at the doomed Alamo. Following the reading of yet another plea for help, Robert Potter, a hothead from Nacogdoches, proposed that the delegates march to San Antonio. Houston responded with an hour-long speech urging the convention to remain in session and complete its work. He promised to go immediately to Gonzales and lead the small force of Texians gathering there to relieve the Alamo, if that was possible, and to defend Texas. Then, without waiting for a vote, he left the convention. The delegates took his advice rather than follow Potter into the waiting arms of General Santa Anna. Again, as in the case of the proposed Matamoros expedition, Houston spoke for calm and practicality, an approach that he would take again and again as a leader of Texas during the next twenty-five years.

The convention remained in session until March 17 and wrote a constitution for the Republic of Texas. Modeled on the Constitution of the United States, it included a Declaration of Rights and varied from the 1787 document mainly in restricting the power of the government. For example, representatives served one-year terms; senators and the president for three years. Presidents could not succeed themselves. Also, the constitution contained an absolute prohibition on imprisonment for debt. Section 9 of the General Provisions, which undoubtedly confirmed the suspicions of abolitionists, prohibited the importation of slaves from outside the United States, but otherwise guaranteed that people held as slaves in Texas would remain in servitude and that future emigrants to the republic could bring slaves with them. Furthermore, no free black could live in Texas without the approval of congress, and any slave freed without the approval of congress had to leave the republic. Most of the leaders of the Texas Revolution were southerners, and the new republic would protect their Peculiar Institution.

As a last step before adjourning, the convention chose leaders of an interim government to operate until regular elections could be held. David G. Burnet became the first president, and Lorenzo de Zavala, the noted federalist refugee from Yucatán, was elected vice president. Although honest and intelligent, Burnet had an unsavory reputation as a land speculator and proved quarrelsome as a leader. Five cabinet members were also appointed, including Houston's friend, Thomas Jefferson Rusk, as secretary of war. The convention adjourned on March 17, leaving the interim government in control at Washington-on-the-Brazos. Of course, the future of the Republic of Texas actually rested in the hands of Sam Houston as commander in chief. Revolutions that fail militarily are not long in need of governments.

The Road to San Jacinto

Houston began the 150-mile ride to Gonzales on March 6 not knowing that the Alamo had fallen that very morning or that the remnants of the Matamoros expedition had met an equally grim fate even earlier. General Urrea's cavalry, advancing along the Gulf coast, attacked thirty-four Texians under Colonel Frank Johnson at San Patricio on February 27. Surprised and outmanned, the rebels put up a fight, but only six, including Johnson, escaped. Urrea then set a trap for James Grant and twenty-six other men who were on a horse-catching expedition south of San Patricio. Near Agua Dulce Creek, Grant, Plácido Benavides, and a man named Reuben Brown were riding ahead of the main party when Mexican cavalry suddenly surrounded the larger group. Grant, ordering Benavides to ride to Goliad and warn Fannin, raced back with Brown to the fight. Mexican lancers rode them down and killed Grant; Brown became a prisoner and survived to tell the story. Thus, as Houston rode westward, Fannin's command of about 400 men at Goliad and a force of 374 volunteers gathered under the leadership of Edward Burleson at Gonzales were the only Texian military forces left in the field.

Hampered by bad weather and high rivers, Houston did not reach Gonzales until March 11. News of the Alamo's fate came later the same day, setting off a wave of grief among the widows and children of the men who had answered Travis's call for help. Houston took command of the volunteers and then, recognizing that the loss of Béxar left Goliad open to attack by Santa Anna's army to its north and Urrea's cavalry to its south, sent orders to Fannin to fall back to Victoria. He hoped that if both Texian armies took defensive positions on the Guadalupe, at Gonzales about seventy miles east of San Antonio and at Victoria some sixty miles to the southeast of Gonzales, they could support each other successfully and prevent a Mexican invasion of Anglo Texas. Fannin received Houston's orders on the 14th, but as usual he found reasons to delay.

Houston remained in Gonzales for two days, but then Henry Karnes and Deaf Smith came in with the news that the Mexican army, estimated at as many as five thousand men, was advancing on the town. Actually, although Houston could not know it, Santa Anna had devised a three-pronged movement across Texas. An army commanded by General Antonio Gaona was to swing north and proceed to Nacogdoches by the upper crossing of the Trinity River; General Urrea's cavalry was to continue its advance along the coast toward Galveston; and the main force under General Vicente Filisola was to move directly into the Anglo settlements. Santa Anna would accompany the main army until about April 1, at which time he would be picked up by a ship at Matagorda. He expected no more serious resistance, but nevertheless intended, as Houston wrote later, to unleash "three rolling streams of fire" to "cover the land with devastation." Having learned from a master, Joaquín de Arredondo, Santa Anna meant to give Texas a lesson in the price of rebellion equal to the one administered by his mentor in 1813.

Faced by overwhelming numbers and convinced by the experience of the Alamo that attempting to defend fixed positions was a mistake, Houston saw no real choice except to retreat. "By falling back," he explained to James Collinsworth, chairman of the military committee at the convention, "Texas can rally, and defeat any force that can come against her." His army left Gonzales late on the thirteenth, burning the town as they departed, and headed eastward toward the Colorado River. Immediately, some men began to grumble that they had volunteered to fight rather than run, a complaint that steadily increased in magnitude over the next month.

The army reached Burnham's Crossing on the Colorado on March 17 and found their task complicated by the civilian population. Word of the Alamo's fall caused such panic among Texians that they hurriedly threw what belongings they could onto any available means of conveyance and headed east. Fearful of the Mexican army, Comanche raiders, and rebellious slaves; made miserable by traveling in rain and mud; throwing away possessions as they went; refugees clogged the roads and fought for places on ferries at the rivers. Texans called this flight the "Runaway Scrape."

At Burnham's Crossing, Houston had the army aid the refugees in crossing the Colorado, then move over to the east side itself and remain for two days while the civilians moved on toward the Brazos River. At that point the commander marched his troops about twenty-five miles down the river to Beason's Ferry at present-day Columbus. By that time volunteers arriving from the east had increased his army to more than six hundred men, and he hoped to make a stand on the Colorado. However, should further retreat become necessary, he could use the Cushatti Trace, a better road on high ground, to reach San Felipe on the Brazos. Houston always tried to keep open as many options as possible.

The Texians reached Beason's Ferry on the east side of the Colorado on March 20, two days before an advance unit of the Mexican army commanded by General Joaquín Ramírez y Sesma arrived on the west bank. Having about 750 men under his command, Ramírez y Sesma seemingly gave Houston an opportunity to attack an enemy force of about equal size. Texian hotheads, led now by Lt. Colonel Sidney Sherman, a recent arrival with a group of volunteers from Kentucky, insisted on attacking, but Houston very wisely refused. He did not have the manpower or firepower to mount an offensive requiring the crossing of a flooded river under the guns of an entrenched enemy. Within a few days, he received two dispatches with news that made him even more hesitant to risk an attack. First, he learned that the provisional government, frightened by the advancing Mexican armies, had fled from Washington-on-the-Brazos to Harrisburg on Buffalo Bayou. This retreat, he wrote Rusk, will demoralize the troops, "and I am half provoked at it myself." Second, and far worse, Houston learned that Fannin's army had been captured outside Goliad, leaving his the only Texas force in the field.

Fannin, after receiving Houston's order to fall back to Victoria, had delayed, waiting for the return of several detachments that he had sent out to evacuate Texian settlers near Refugio. After several days, he learned that Urrea's cavalry, aided by loyalist Tejanos, had killed or dispersed these detachments, but even then he took another day readying for the retreat. Finally, Fannin's army moved out of Goliad on the morning of March 19. Moving at a slow pace because the commander insisted on using wagons drawn by oxen to haul nine cannon and hundreds of muskets, it covered only six miles before halting to rest in the middle of a prairie. Some of Fannin's men, aware of what the Mexican cavalry could do to them in the open, begged him to move on to the cover of trees along Coleto Creek, which was five miles farther on, but he would not listen. Shortly after noon, the army moved forward again, but it was too late. Urrea's dragoons surrounded them, forcing Fannin to form his men into a hollow square. The Mexican cavalry could not break this defensive formation, but sharpshooters killed Fannin's artillerymen and the oxen that could move his heavy weapons and equipment. Enemy infantry moved close enough in the tall prairie grass to fire into the Texians' square as well. By nightfall, the Mexicans had taken more casualties than had Fannin's army (nearly two hundred to only sixty), but the Texians were short of food, water, and ammunition. They could not run nor hide.

At dawn the next day, Fannin saw that Urrea had brought up reinforcements during the night, leaving the rebels no choice but to ask for terms. Urrea offered only "surrender at discretion," but Fannin told his men that their lives would be spared. Perhaps he misunderstood the terms, or maybe he wanted to convince the soldiers to quit, hoping that somehow they would be allowed to live. In any case, the volunteers put down their arms and were marched back to Goliad as prisoners. Urrea moved on to occupy Victoria.

News of Fannin's defeat hit Sam Houston hard. "You know I am not easily depressed," he wrote Rusk, "but before my God, since we parted, I have found the darkest hours of my past life." He knew that an attack across the Colorado, even if successful, would leave his bloodied army on the west side of the flooded river and easy prey to enveloping movements by Gaona to the north and Urrea to the south. Therefore, on March 26, he ordered a retreat to San Felipe on the Brazos, intending to keep his army intact and wait for Santa Anna to make a mistake. Hotheads, however, raged against retreat, and several hundred volunteers left, some to look after their families but others simply in disgust.

By the time the army reached San Felipe on the 28th, many critics of the commander in chief felt free to advise him on his next step. Captains Moseley Baker and Wylie Martin were especially open in their criticism, and talk of choosing a new leader began to circulate. "On my arrival on the Brazos," Houston wrote Rusk, "had I consulted the wishes of all, I should have been like the ass between two stacks of hay. Many wished me to go below [downriver], others above. I consulted none—I held no councils of war. If I err the blame is mine." Sam Houston had long ago proven his physical bravery; now he showed his moral courage as well. After one day at San Felipe, he decided to move northward about twenty miles along the west bank of the Brazos to the plantation of Jared Groce. He knew that he could use the steamboat *Yellow Stone,* which was at Groce's, to cross the flooded river and be in a position to continue retreating to the east or to move toward Harrisburg, the location of the provisional government. Baker and Martin refused to obey the order to leave the central town in Anglo Texas, so Houston left the former to defend the crossing at San Felipe and sent the latter down river to do the same at Fort Bend. Juan N. Seguín's cavalry, which had helped cover the retreat from Gonzales, remained with Baker at San Felipe.

Two days of marching over terrible roads through heavy rains brought the Texian army to Groce's and a camp on high ground suitable for drill and training. The men's spirits improved to some extent, but then word came concerning the fate of Fannin's men at Goliad. Imprisoned after surrendering, they had been joined by several smaller groups of rebel soldiers captured by Urrea's cavalry, bringing the total to more than 350. Santa Anna had ordered the execution of all prisoners, and Urrea, after an unsuccessful appeal to the commander in chief, had to comply. On Palm Sunday, March 27, the prisoners were separated into four groups, told that they were being sent to Matamoros, and marched out of town. The Mexicans then halted the columns and opened fire. Most of those who were not killed by musket fire were ridden down by lancers. Nearly 350 men died; only twenty-eight escaped and took word of the massacre east to the Brazos. Fannin, who had been wounded at Coleto Creek and was too weak to march, was executed in the fort. He asked that his watch be sent to his family and that he be shot in the chest and given a proper burial. The officer in charge took the watch and had him shot in the face and his body burned in the pyre with the other murdered soldiers. Houston used news of the massacre to inflame his soldiers. "The day of just retribution ought not to be deferred," he wrote Rusk.

While Houston rested and trained his army at Groce's, interim President David G. Burnet could no longer contain his anger at the commander's tactics and sent Rusk with a message. "The enemy are laughing you to scorn," Burnet wrote Houston. "You must fight them. You must retreat no further. The country expects you to fight. The salvation of the country depends on you doing so." Houston's reply was succinct: "I have kept the army together under most discouraging circumstances, and I hope a just and wise God, in whom I have always believed, will yet save Texas." When a second complaint from Burnet arrived a few days later, Houston responded that he was sick of "taunts and suggestions . . . gratuitously tendered to me" and concluded: "I beg leave to assure you that I will omit no opportunity to serve the country."

Santa Anna reached San Felipe on April 7 and learned that Houston was to the north at Groce's while the government was to the southeast at Harrisburg. A Texian prisoner told the Mexican commander that Houston had only eight hundred men and would retreat toward Nacogdoches, so he decided to pursue the government and deal with the army later. Needing to cross the Brazos but bothered by the small force of rebels under Baker guarding the crossing at San Felipe, Santa Anna led most of his force down the river toward Fort Bend. A few miles north of the town, the Mexicans captured a ferry and used it to cross the Brazos unopposed. At that point, Baker's force was outflanked and had to retreat to rejoin the main Texian army. Moseley's detachment guarding the main crossing at Fort Bend found itself in the same situation.

When Houston learned that Santa Anna had moved south and probably intended to cross the Brazos, he saw that unless he crossed also his army could be trapped between enemy forces on both sides of the river. So, on the twelfth, he had the *Yellow Stone* ferry his troops to the east bank where they found a very welcome surprise waiting them—two six-pound cannon donated by the citizens of Cincinnati. These "Twin Sisters" constituted only a very small artillery unit, but they improved morale as the army prepared to march south. On April 16, word came that a Mexican force of fewer than one thousand men had crossed the Brazos and headed toward Harrisburg. This news puzzled Houston, but he immediately set out to take advantage of an opportunity for a battle in which numbers would be relatively equal. The Texas army covered fifty-five miles in two-and-one-half days through continuing rain that turned the road into a quagmire. At one point as it moved south, the army came to a crossroads where it could have turned east to Nacogdoches or continued on to Harrisburg. Houston's detractors, then and to this day, claim that against his will the men decided to continue southward to meet the enemy. Evidence for this charge, however, comes from men who hated Houston from personal spite or jealousy or who insisted that his earlier retreats resulted from cowardice. Moreover, if Houston actually gave in to the judgment of others at the crossroads, it was the first time that had happened during the campaign. In any case, the army reached Harrisburg on the eighteenth with Sam Houston still firmly in command.

The Mexican army unit led by Santa Anna had reached Harrisburg three days earlier but failed to catch the government leaders there. (See map: Movements of the Mexican and Texian Armies Just Prior to Battle of San Jacinto.) Learning that Burnet and the others had fled to New Washington on Galveston Bay, Santa Anna sent a party of cavalry commanded by Colonel Juan N. Almonte in pursuit. He also learned that Houston had left Groce's but still assumed that the Texian army was heading for Nacogdoches and would be slowed by high water and civilian refugees. Therefore, the Mexican commander had Harrisburg burned and hurried on to New Washington, hoping that Almonte had captured the government leaders. After dealing with them, he planned to turn north, cross the San Jacinto River near Lynchburg above Galveston Bay, and catch Houston's fleeing army before it crossed the Sabine River. From that point, however, nothing went as the Napoleon of the West intended.

First, Almonte's dragoons did not capture the government, reaching the coast of Galveston Bay just as the leaders pulled away from the shore in rowboats. Although Burnet and others were within range, Almonte ordered his men not to fire because women were in the boats. Second, and far more important, Houston, rather than running for Nacogdoches, had begun to stalk the Mexican force. Shortly after the Texians reached Harrisburg, Karnes and Smith captured three Mexican couriers (one of whom carried a pouch inscribed "W. B. Travis") who carried messages showing that Santa Anna was with the force that had passed through Harrisburg and that all other Mexican soldiers were west of the Brazos. Presented with exactly the opportunity he hoped for, Houston acted quickly. He left behind about 250 men who were too sick to travel (most had measles) and crossed Buffalo Bayou, intending to move along its south bank and put his army in front of Santa Anna's when it turned back north from New Washington. He gathered his men and told them that a battle was near. "Some of us may be killed and must be killed,"

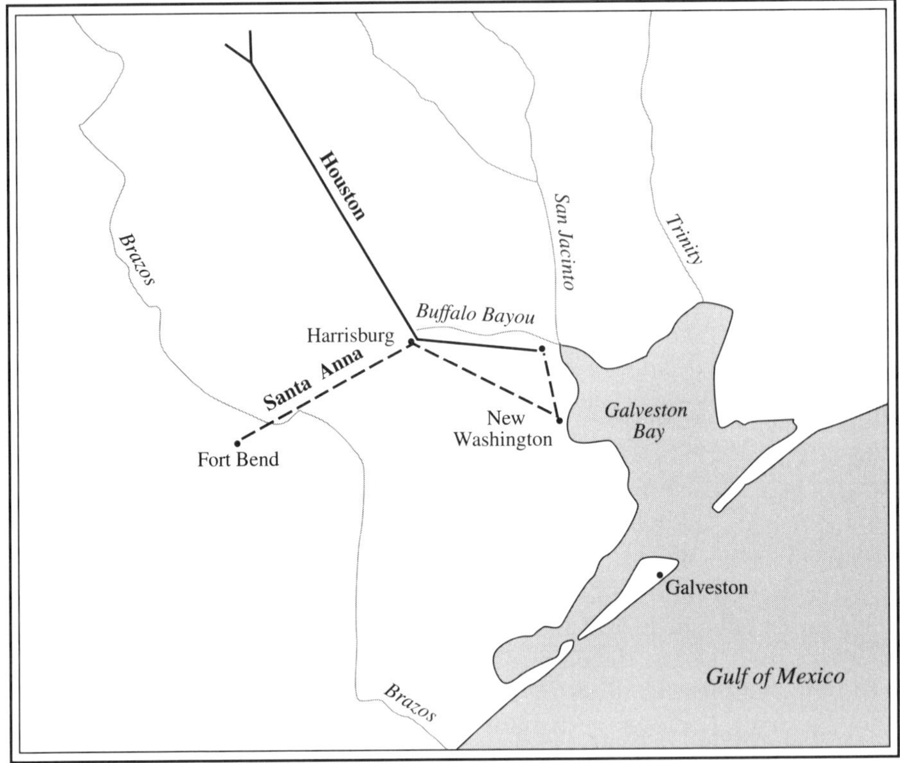

Movements of Mexican and Texian Armies Just Prior to Battle of San Jacinto

he shouted, "but soldiers remember the Alamo! the Alamo! the Alamo!" This battle cry, Houston remembered later, "was caught up by every man in the army."

Pushing his men to the limit during the night of April 19–20, Houston reached Lynch's Ferry on the San Jacinto River in the morning before the Mexicans, who had burned New Washington and turned north, arrived. The rebel army made camp in the trees lining Buffalo Bayou and placed the "Twin Sisters" in full view. To reach the ferry on the San Jacinto or to attack, Santa Anna's army would have to cross an open prairie in front of the guns and Houston's men sheltered in the timber. The Texians now had a chance to fight, as Houston put it, on "our own ground."

At two o'clock in the afternoon of April 20, Mexican scouts saw the two cannon and determined the location of the rebel army. Santa Anna ordered a probe against the enemy camp, but fire from the "Twin Sisters" stopped it short. The Mexicans then brought up their single cannon and initiated a brief artillery duel that, although drawing blood on both sides, did not change the situation. At that point, Santa Anna withdrew to the south about three-quarters of a mile from the Texians' position and made camp. Some of Houston's men, seeing the withdrawal and believing that they could turn it into a rout, demanded an immediate attack. To mollify these hotheads, Houston approved a request by their leader, Sidney Sherman, that a party of sixty-one mounted riflemen go out to reconnoiter the field. He gave strict orders, however, not to go within range of the Mexicans' guns or to provoke an attack.

Sherman then proceeded to do what so many officers did during the revolution—disobey orders. He drew fire from the Mexican infantry and charged their cavalry. The Texians, who had to dismount to reload their rifles, soon found themselves in danger of being overrun by Mexican lancers. Sherman called for infantry support, and in spite of Houston's opposition, one regiment began to move from the cover of the timber. Fortunately, the mounted Texians managed to withdraw with only minor casualties, thanks especially to the heroism of a recently arrived volunteer from Georgia named Mirabeau Bonaparte Lamar. Lamar rode to the rescue of both Secretary of War Rusk, who was surrounded at one point by Mexicans, and a young soldier who had been severely wounded. Houston gave Sherman a verbal dressing down that would never be forgotten and rewarded Lamar with the rank of colonel and command of the cavalry.

The morning of April 21 dawned clear and bright. Sam Houston later remembered thinking it was an omen favoring the battle that he had decided to fight that day. He did not attack immediately, however, and at mid-morning, General Cos arrived with about 550 reinforcements, bringing Mexican strength to nearly 1,350 men compared to approximately 900 in the Texas army. Houston's soldiers began to complain anew about the delay, and his detractors, then and today, insist that he feared a fight and was forced into it by his own men. The commander in chief called a council of war with six field officers and Rusk at noon, and the accounts of those present disagree diametrically as to whether he wanted to attack or not. Such conflicting stories, told by those who hated Houston and those who defended him, can never be reconciled. Again, however, as in the case of the decision-at-the-crossroads story, the fact is that the army did attack and Houston commanded it.

After the council of war, Houston sent Deaf Smith and a few other men to destroy the bridge over Vince's Bayou, a stream that crossed the road about eight miles to the west of the Texas army's position. Destruction of this bridge blocked any easy route for more reinforcements to reach the Mexican army from Fort Bend, and it also cut off the only line of retreat for the Texas army. At three o'clock in the afternoon, Houston ordered his troops into a battle formation that stretched across the prairie. An infantry regiment commanded by Edward Burleson occupied the center, with smaller infantry units under Sidney Sherman and Henry Millard to its left and right respectively. Lamar's cavalry was on the far right, and the "Twin Sisters" were placed in an advanced position just to the right of Burleson. (See Diagram of Battle of San Jacinto.) Nineteen Tejanos led by Juan N. Seguín also joined the Texas line. Fearing for their safety because of the hatred for Mexicans aroused by the Alamo and Goliad, Houston had ordered them to guard the army's baggage at Harrisburg.

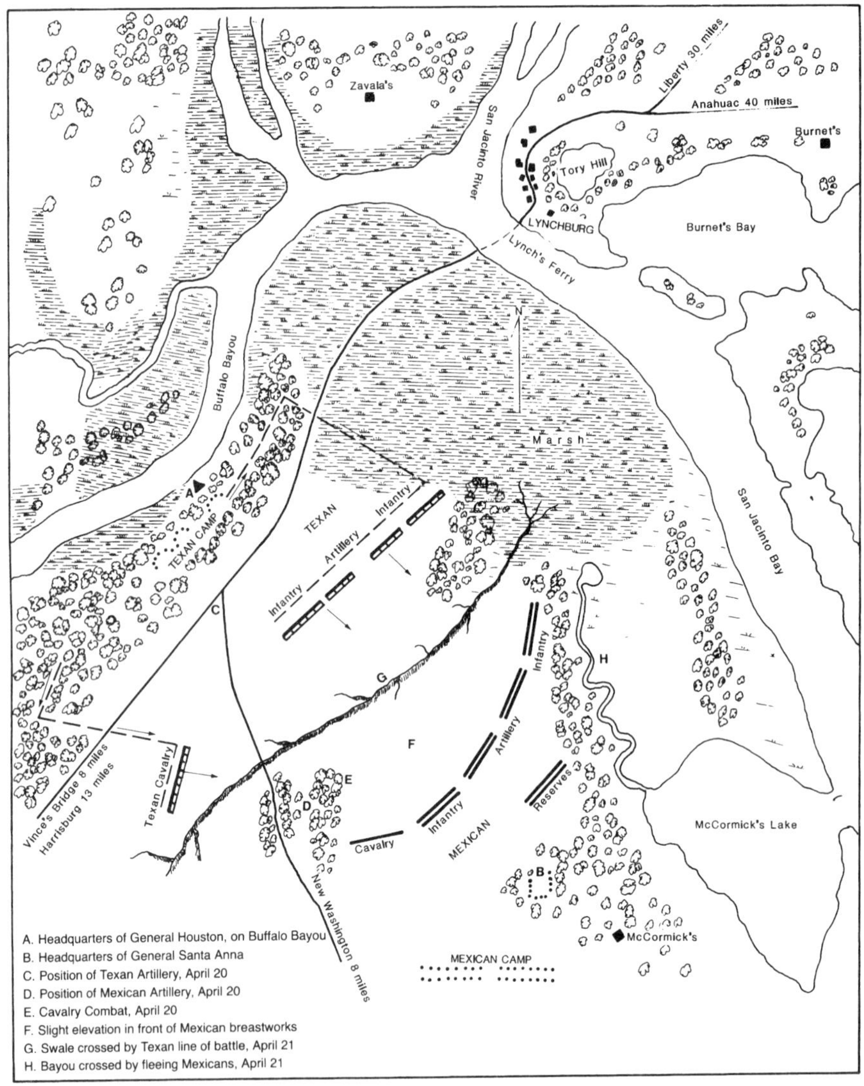

Diagram of the Battle of San Jacinto, April 21, 1836. Credit: © 1988 University of Oklahoma Press

Seguín, however, had angrily disagreed and persuaded the commander to allow his men to fight. They went into the battle with distinctive pieces of cardboard in their hats to identify them from the enemy.

At three-thirty the Texas army began to advance across the prairie toward the Mexican camp. Houston led, mounted on a huge stallion named Saracen. The artillerymen hurried their cannon forward to within two hundred yards, and the rest of the line advanced with as little noise as possible, having been ordered to hold their fire until they reached point-blank range. Meanwhile, Santa Anna's camp was quiet. He and his force had worked hard during the night erecting a breastworks of equipment, and Cos's men were tired after their march from Fort Bend. Many of them, including the commander, were asleep when Mexican sentries detected the attack and opened fire. Soon their twelve-pounder also came into play, but it fired over the heads of the Texans who were advancing through a depression in the prairie at that point. The "Twin Sisters" responded by blasting the enemy breastworks with grapeshot and pieces of horseshoes. All the while, the Texas infantry, crouching low in the grass, moved forward without firing.

When the Texans came within sixty yards of the breastworks, the Mexicans fired a concerted volley, most of which also went over the heads of the assailants. Houston, mounted and in the lead, was not so lucky. A musket ball shattered the front part of the tibia bone about an inch above his left ankle, and at least five struck his mount in the chest. The horse kept moving forward, however, and Houston led his men to within twenty yards of the Mexican line, where they delivered one organized volley and then charged. Screaming "Remember the Alamo, Remember Goliad," they clubbed with their muskets and killed with pistols and knives as well. Lamar's cavalry charged the left flank of the Mexicans' position, and soon the battle lost all form. After eighteen minutes, the Texans had control of Santa Anna's camp, but the killing went on until twilight as Mexican soldiers sought to flee to the south and west. Houston tried to stop the slaughter, but his order to take prisoners was often ignored. As one captain supposedly told his men: "Boys, you know how to take prisoners, take them with the butt of yor guns, club guns & remember the Alamo, remember Labaher [Goliad], & club gun right & left, and nock there brains out!"

Houston rode about the battlefield attempting to end the killing until his horse finally fell dead. The commander then discovered that he could not stand on his wounded leg and mounted another horse to ride back to the camp on Buffalo Bayou. His troops, as he put it later, had accomplished "almost a miracle." They killed 630 Mexican soldiers and captured 730 at a cost of two killed and six fatally wounded. Even this great victory, however, left the Texas army and its cause far from secure because they had defeated only a small part of the Mexican army. A much larger force under Generals Filisola and Urrea waited at Fort Bend. Houston, lying wounded on a blanket under an oak tree, knew that if Santa Anna managed to escape to the Brazos and resume command of the main army, he might still destroy the rebellion. Then, on April 22, a search party brought in a prisoner whom other Mexicans saluted as "El Presidente." The Texians had captured General Santa Anna, commander in chief of the army and president of Mexico.

Santa Anna presented himself to Houston with typically vainglorious words: "That man may consider himself born to no common destiny who has conquered the Napoleon of the West; and it now remains for him to be generous to the vanquished." "You should have remembered that at the Alamo,"

Houston answered. Some of the Texians wanted to execute Santa Anna immediately, but Houston, in spite of his anger, knew that the president was worth a great deal alive and nothing dead. He protected the Mexican leader and forced him to sign an armistice calling for an end to fighting and the retreat of Filisola to San Antonio and Urrea to Victoria. Deaf Smith took Santa Anna's order to Filisola, who decided, over the protests of Urrea and other officers, to withdraw across the Río Grande.

The Battle of San Jacinto, although obviously a great victory for the Texians and their Tejano allies, left the Republic of Texas far from secure in any way. Certainly, no one at the time could have imagined the battle's tremendous impact on the future. With the advantage of a century of hindsight, however, the inscription on the base of the monument at the battlefield said it well, with some pardonable exaggeration: "Measured by its results, San Jacinto was one of the decisive battles of the world. The freedom of Texas from Mexico won here led to annexation and to the Mexican War, resulting in the acquisition by the United States of the states of Texas, New Mexico, Arizona, Nevada, California, Utah, and parts of Colorado, Wyoming, Kansas, and Oklahoma. Almost one-third of the present area of the American nation, nearly a million square miles, changed sovereignty."

Chapter 7

THE REPUBLIC OF TEXAS, 1836–1846

The Republic of Texas had a difficult birth and rarely enjoyed a calm moment during its ten years of life. Plagued by factional politics and chaotic finances, unable to win annexation to the United States or recognition of its independence by Mexico, the Republic never developed a national identity and struggled constantly just to survive. Yet Texas attracted more immigrants than ever before. No amount of political turmoil or diplomatic uncertainty could discourage those who saw opportunity in the cheap lands of the new republic. Indeed, these were the years in which "G.T.T." became legendary in the southern United States and even began to appear, figuratively at least, on doors in Germany.

Population statistics for the Republic of Texas are estimates only, drawn from contemporary accounts and tax rolls, but they give a reasonable indication of the spectacular growth from 1836 to 1846. Shortly after the revolution, the Republic had an estimated population of 30,000 Anglos, 5,000 black slaves, 3,470 Mexicans, and 14,500 Indians. An incomplete state census taken in 1847 counted 102,961 whites—some 12,000–14,000 of whom were of Mexican ancestry, at least 8,000 of German descent, and the rest primarily Anglo or Celtic in origin. There were also 38,753 slaves and 295 free blacks. No estimate of the Indian population exists, although their numbers probably declined due to warfare and disease. Thus, the population, excluding Indians, increased 269 percent during the ten years of the Republic, an amazing testimonial to the lure of Texas in spite of its insecure present and uncertain future.

The Interim Government in 1836

The personal quarrels that had threatened the success of the revolution continued in at least equally disruptive form after the Battle of San Jacinto. In spite of his wound, Sam Houston remained near the battlefield for two weeks after April 21, protecting Santa Anna and waiting for the government leaders to arrive. Interim President Burnet and some cabinet members finally reached San Jacinto on May 4 and, apparently out of contempt for the way

Houston had waged the campaign and jealousy of his success, immediately began to treat him as anything but a hero. They were especially furious that he had distributed the contents of Santa Anna's money chest to the soldiers. When Houston, his inflamed wound requiring treatment, asked to travel on the *Yellow Stone* with the government officials as they returned to Galveston with Santa Anna, Burnet refused, telling him to remain with the army. The boat's captain refused to transport anyone unless Houston went as well, so Burnet relented. But upon reaching Galveston, he would not allow a ship belonging to the Republic to take Houston to New Orleans for medical treatment. The hero of San Jacinto took passage on an American trading ship and reached New Orleans on May 22. He would not recover sufficiently to return to Texas until late June. In the meantime, disorder ruled.

Burnet at least agreed with Houston that, in his words, "Santa Anna *dead* is no more than Tom, Dick, or Harry *dead,* but living he may avail Texas much." So the government took the Mexican commander to Velasco at the mouth of the Brazos and offered him freedom in return for his signature on two treaties, one public and the other private. The public Treaty of Velasco, signed on May 14, brought an end to the war and provided that all Mexican armies would move south of the Río Grande. In the secret treaty, Santa Anna promised to use his influence to have the government of Mexico accept the public agreement and also to recognize the independence of Texas with a boundary at the Río Grande. These treaties originated Texas's claim that the Río Grande was its southern border, although the province had never previously extended beyond the Nueces.

Burnet's way of dealing with Santa Anna made sense, but Mirabeau B. Lamar, who had become secretary of war when Rusk took over the army from Houston, and Robert Potter, secretary of the navy, disagreed. They wanted to hold the Mexican commander and perhaps make him pay for the Alamo and Goliad. Lamar and Potter drew support from hotheads who had just arrived from the United States as volunteers in the Texas army. Finding no Mexicans to fight and rations short, these new arrivals threatened to overwhelm the government they had come to support. In early June—after Santa Anna, Almonte, and other officers had been put on board a ship at Velasco for the trip to Mexico—General Thomas Jefferson Green, a very recent arrival in Texas, led other volunteers in forcing Burnet to remove the Mexicans from aboard the ship and return them to prison. Burnet managed to protect Santa Anna from mob violence, partly by moving the prisoners and the government to Columbia about twenty miles up the Brazos from Velasco, but problems with the army increased through the summer of 1836.

While the interim government struggled unsuccessfully with the army, it had equally bad fortune in attempting to gain diplomatic recognition by the United States. Stephen F. Austin, William H. Wharton, and Branch T. Archer, sent east by the Consultation late in 1835, spent the months of the revolution attempting to gain aid for the Texas army and managed to get loans of $75,000 from private sources. However, when the subject of official recognition arose after the victory at San Jacinto, President Andrew Jackson pointed out that the leaders of Texas had done nothing to show that they headed a truly de facto government. There was not even an official report of the battle, let alone letters showing that Texas had declared independence and created a functioning government.

The interim government was scheduled to operate until December 1836, but Burnet, desperate to bring order to the Republic, decided to hold elections and institute regular government earlier than planned. On July 23, he issued a proclamation setting September 5 as the date Texans would vote on accepting the constitution written by the convention in March, elect officials under that constitution, and express their opinions on annexation to the United States. Everyone expected the constitution and annexation to win overwhelming approval, so the only real contests involved the election of officials such as president and vice president.

Texas had no political parties in 1836. The prerevolutionary "War Party" and "Peace Party" largely disappeared during the war, and the Democratic and Whig Parties, which were relatively new in the United States at the time, did not develop immediately in the new republic. Instead, the elections hinged on personal popularity. Henry Smith, governor of the provisional government set up by the Consultation, announced early as a candidate. Apparently he wanted vindication for the treatment accorded him by the General Council. The second candidate was Stephen F. Austin, just back from his diplomatic mission to the United States. Austin had obvious qualifications and wanted to work for annexation. However, now that the revolution had succeeded, many thought that he had been too slow to favor a break with Mexico. Moreover, because he had accepted the diplomatic mission in 1835, he had missed all the major battles and a chance to win military glory.

Smith and Austin were the only candidates until less than two weeks before the election; then Sam Houston entered the race. Houston had won undying fame at San Jacinto—"Old Sam Jacinto," some called him—and his military reputation led inevitably to requests that he run for the presidency. In mid-August, mass meetings across East Texas passed nominating resolutions, and eleven days before the election he accepted. "You will learn," he wrote a friend, "that I have yielded to the wishes of my friends in allowing my name to be run for president. The crisis requires it or I would not have yielded." Apparently by "crisis" Houston meant the problems facing the Republic and the bitter division between Smith and Austin that threatened ongoing conflict regardless of which man won. Running as the hero who could bring unity, he received 5,119 votes to 743 for Smith (who announced his withdrawal once Houston entered the contest) and only 587 for Austin. Mirabeau B. Lamar, a courageous soldier during the revolution but no friend of Houston's, easily won the vice presidency. Voters at this September 5 election also chose the first congress of the Republic, unanimously endorsed the constitution written back in March, and overwhelmingly (3,277–91) supported annexation to the United States. Thus, Texans, even as they established a government for their Republic, indicated a willingness to give up independence in order to return to the nation in which most had been born.

Sam Houston as the Republic's First President, 1836–1838

Burnet convened the first congress at Columbia on the lower Brazos River in early October, and once it organized, he and Zavala resigned so that Houston and Lamar could be inaugurated. The new president's cabinet appointments demonstrated his desire for unity. He brought both of his defeated opponents into the government—Austin as secretary of state and Smith as secretary of the treasury. His friend Thomas Jefferson Rusk, who had earned popular support as interim secretary of war before San Jacinto and commander of the army after Houston was wounded, became secretary of war. Houston even tried to conciliate Burnet by offering the position of attorney general to one of his supporters, James Collinsworth. That olive branch, however, was refused, and James Pinckney Henderson took the position.

Houston's inaugural address emphasized the problems facing the republic and the need for unity in dealing with them. "I am perfectly aware," he said, "of the difficulties that surround me. . . ." He called for vigilance in dealing with Mexico and a policy of fairness and peace toward the Indians. Reminding his listeners of the recently expressed mandate that Texas join the United States, he asked "Will our friends disregard it?" Given the situation of the republic at that time, annexation certainly appeared its best hope. The war had caused much of the population to flee temporarily, disrupted the planting of crops, and destroyed towns such as Gonzales and San Felipe. Mexico threatened to attack again at any time, and Indians, especially the Comanches, raided frontier settlements. The government was $1.25 million in debt, and the treasury empty. At Columbia the congress met in an unfinished shack, and the president worked in a one-room office. He did not have a good copy of the constitution or an official seal or even a pen to sign commissions.

Obtaining diplomatic recognition from the United States, the first step toward eventual annexation, should have been easy for Texas. After all, President Andrew Jackson and most Americans had strongly supported the revolution, and the United States had a tradition of quickly recognizing new nations in Latin America. In the case of Texas, however, two roadblocks stood in the way. First, Mexico did not accept the independence of its rebellious province, so recognition by the United States would almost certainly mean trouble between the governments in Washington and Mexico City. Second, antislavery spokesmen, especially Benjamin Lundy and Congressman John Quincy Adams of Massachusetts, insisted that the revolution had resulted from a conspiracy to add more slave territory to the Union. Jackson's vice president, Martin Van Buren, who was a candidate in 1836 to succeed Old Hickory in the White House, did not want to agitate the slavery issue during his campaign. Texas had to wait.

President Houston and Secretary of State Austin decided that perhaps Santa Anna, who was still held as a prisoner, could help with the Republic's diplomatic problems. The Mexican commander had been a useful hostage in having his armies moved south of the Río Grande, but after that he provided an inviting target for vengeful Texans. Thus, when Santa Anna offered to argue for the recognition of Texas's independence with President Jackson, Houston and Austin jumped at the chance to send him to Washington. Even if nothing came of his meeting with Jackson, he would be safely out of Texas and the Republic would not be disgraced by killing another nation's leader. On November 25, Santa Anna, escorted by three Texas officers, left Columbia for Washington. The Texans also carried a confidential letter from Houston to his old friend Jackson, explaining that the Republic intended to send William H. Wharton as an official diplomatic representative to Washington and expressing the "great desire . . . that our country Texas shall be annexed to the United States."

Santa Anna had a friendly meeting with Jackson and then sailed home on a U.S. Navy vessel. Once safely back in Mexico, although having lost control of the government after his defeat in Texas, he agreed with other Mexican leaders in repudiating all the promises made in the Treaties of Velasco. (Mexico had never recognized the treaties anyhow.) Within a few years, he would return to control of the government and again become a threat to Texas. Nevertheless, Houston and Austin acted in the best interests of the Republic in freeing him in 1836.

After sending Santa Anna away, Houston urged congress to pass an act establishing the boundaries of Texas. This, he believed, would also improve chances of receiving recognition. Congress responded on December 19, 1836, with an act that based the southwestern boundary on the Río Grande. The line followed the river from the Gulf of Mexico to its source and thence due north to the 42nd parallel, the boundary established between American and Spanish claims by the Adams-Onís Treaty of 1821. (See map: The Republic of Texas, 1836.) Since Texas had never extended beyond the Nueces River during the Spanish or Mexican periods, this definition, which claimed half of modern New Mexico and lands stretching northward to present-day Wyoming, was brash indeed.

Recognition by the United States was painfully slow in spite of the efforts of Houston and Austin in Texas and Wharton in Washington. President Jackson's annual message on December 22, 1836, dismayed Texans by questioning the Republic's ability to survive and calling immediate recognition "impolitic." Five days later the Republic suffered another blow to its standing in the eyes of other nations when Secretary of State Stephen F. Austin—the "Father of Texas"—died of pneumonia at the age of forty-three. Houston sought to overcome Jackson's attitude and the loss of Austin by appointing James Pinckney Henderson to act as secretary of state and sending Memucan Hunt, a recent arrival from Mississippi, to join Wharton in representing Texas in Washington.

Wharton responded aggressively to Jackson's annual message, telling Old Hickory that his stance denied Texas the opportunity to establish credit and secure itself financially. The Mexicans, Wharton said, will have your words "printed on satin and circulated throughout all the country." In reply Jackson indicated that he would act favorably as soon as Congress recommended recognition. Wharton and Hunt then began to lobby Jacksonian legislators,

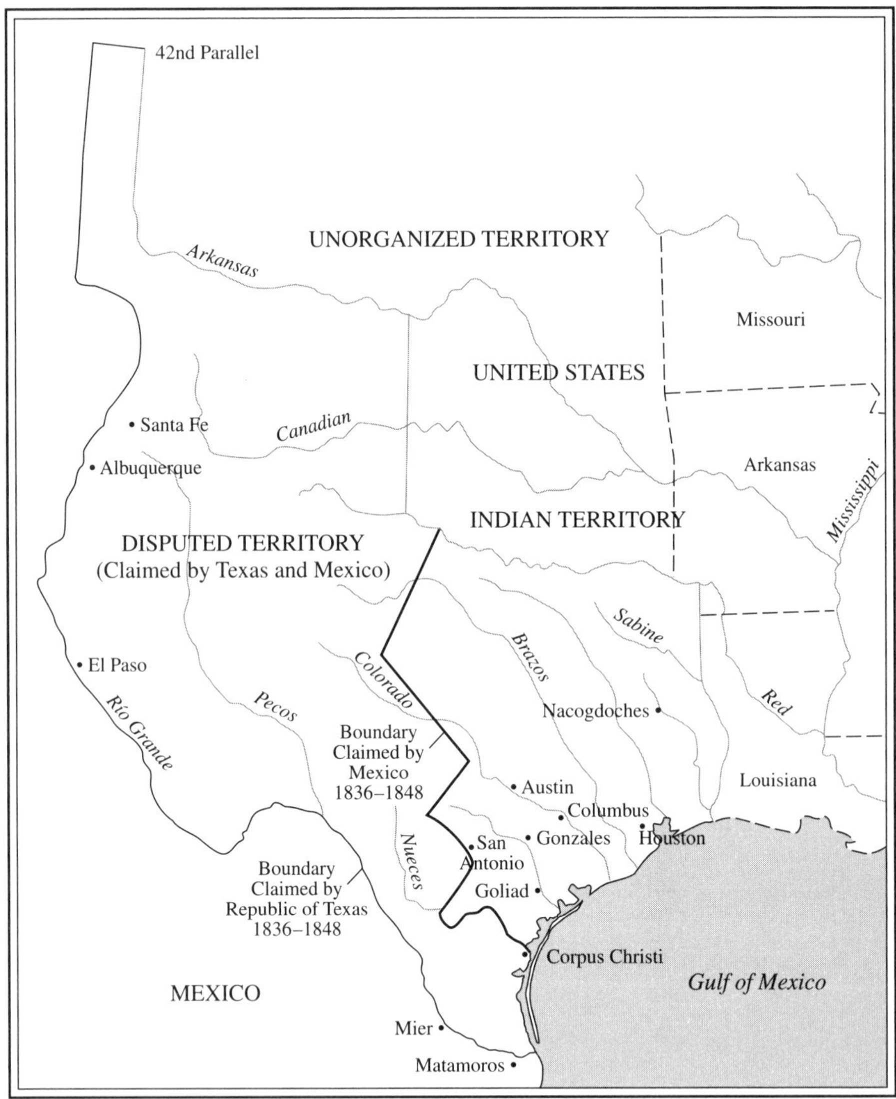

The Republic of Texas, 1836

seeking to overcome opposition from those who believed that Texas would cause conflict over slavery between the North and South. Their efforts paid off when the appropriations bill passed at the end of February 1837 contained funds to pay a diplomatic agent to Texas. On March 3, just one day before his term ended, Jackson called in Wharton and Hunt and announced that he had nominated Alcée La Branche of Louisiana to be chargé d'affaires to Texas. The Texans accepted the president's request that they join him in "the pleasure of a glass of wine."

Texans celebrated Jackson's action, but realists knew that diplomatic recognition did not cure the Republic's weaknesses. "All persons are disappointed," one observer wrote. "Texas independent and compelled to fight her own battles and pay her own debts, will necessarily have to impose heavy burdens [on] her citizens." President Houston, of course, had no intention of stopping the pursuit of annexation. When congress assembled for its second session in April 1837, he spoke hopefully of action by the United States in the near future. Little had changed, however, to support his optimism. The Republic had moved its capital from Columbia to the new "city" of Houston about five miles north of the ruined town of Harrisburg, but that was hardly an indication of increasing stability or prosperity. Although Houston's founders, John K. and Augustus C. Allen, described it as "handsome and beautifully elevated, salubrious and well watered," one congressman probably exaggerated less when he called it "the most miserable place in the world." A young lawyer, impressed with the town's opportunities for gambling, described it as "the greatest sink of dissipation and vice that modern times have known." The president's mansion was a log cabin of two rooms separated by a covered breezeway or "dog trot."

In August 1837 Memucan Hunt formally proposed the annexation of Texas to the administration of Martin Van Buren. Secretary of State John Forsyth quickly rejected the offer on the grounds that it would involve the United States in a war with Mexico and that the annexation of an independent foreign nation would be unconstitutional. Van Buren did not need trouble abroad or at home, especially since a serious financial panic had hit the United States in 1837. Houston did not respond immediately, but in May 1838 he instructed Hunt to withdraw the annexation request. Texas would go its own way—at least for a while.

An independent Texas badly needed friendly relations with the great powers of Europe, so in 1837 Houston appointed James Pinckney Henderson minister to Great Britain and France with the task of gaining recognition, negotiating commercial treaties, and securing financial aid. Henderson found the British friendly but unwilling to act, probably because they did not wish to antagonize Mexico, opposed slavery, and thought that Texas would soon join the United States. The French government, which was on the verge of war with Mexico, was even friendlier than the British, but it made no commitment either. Thus from 1836 into 1838, the Republic of Texas had only one diplomatic success—recognition by the United States—and even that did not come easily.

Texas's early foreign policy failures came primarily from external considerations beyond the control of the Houston Administration, especially the fact that other nations did not want trouble with Mexico, but a look at the infant Republic's domestic problems also would have given pause to any government considering recognition. First, the army remained full of recently arrived volunteers who wanted to mount an offensive against Mexico rather than simply defend the independence of Texas. In October 1836 when Houston appointed Rusk secretary of war, he made General Felix Huston, a

Kentucky-born adventurer who had arrived after San Jacinto, commander in chief of the army. To Houston's disgust, Huston began to advocate an attack on Matamoros, so in January 1837 the president replaced him at the head of the army with Albert Sidney Johnston, a West Point-trained officer of great ability. Huston, however, saw this as an insult to his honor and challenged Johnston to a duel. Neither man was much of a marksman, but finally, on the sixth exchange of pistol fire, Huston seriously wounded Johnston in the hip.

Having won the duel, Huston remained in command until May 1837, when he left the army of some two thousand men at San Antonio and went to the capital with the intention of persuading congress to support his scheme for an attack on Matamoros. His promises of glory for Texas and spoils to pay the Republic's debts received a favorable hearing, but while the commander was away from his army, President Houston had the secretary of war go to San Antonio and give thirty-day furloughs to all but six hundred of the soldiers there. When Huston returned to find most of the army gone, he retired from command. The government then rebuilt its armed force with fewer hotheads and adventurers.

Ironically, while many in the Texan army thought only in terms of fighting Mexico, Indians constituted an equal if not greater threat. Comanches and their allies, the Kiowas, had complete control of the Republic's western reaches and regularly raided frontier settlements. In May 1836, for example, more than five hundred warriors attacked Parker's Fort in present-day Limestone County, killing the defenders and taking women and children as prisoners. One of the prisoners, nine-year-old Cynthia Ann Parker, eventually married Chief Peta Nocona and gave birth to Quanah Parker, the last famous chief of the Comanches. The Wichitas and Caddos also spent the summer of 1836 raiding Anglo settlements in central and north Texas. Even the Cherokee leader, Chief Bowl, who had signed a treaty with the revolutionaries in February, indicated in August that he would join the Mexicans if they continued the war.

In responding to these threats, President Houston had the opportunity to lead Texas for the first time in shaping an Indian policy of its own. Having lived for years with the Cherokees, he believed that the Republic should demonstrate friendship with all Indians by negotiating treaties that established trade and promised evenhanded justice. In November 1836 he sent the Comanches, Wichitas, and Caddos an invitation to a council in North Texas, but his agents did not establish contact with these groups. Off-and-on hostilities continued with them in 1837 and 1838. In an attempt to live up to his word and win over the Cherokees, Houston submitted the treaty that he had negotiated with them during the revolution to the Texas Senate in December 1836, calling it "just and equitable." The senate, however, delayed for nearly a year and then, at the urging of Vice President Lamar, rejected it on the false grounds that the Cherokees had aided Mexico and therefore not kept their part of the bargain.

Houston's hopes for peace based on fair treatment of the Indians suffered another serious blow during the summer of 1838 when several tribes were implicated in an abortive rebellion against the Republic. In February of that year, General Vicente Filisola, the military commander at Matamoros, contacted Vicente Córdova, a Tejano from Nacogdoches who opposed Texas independence and resented the treatment of fellow Tejanos in East Texas since 1836. Filisola urged Córdova to raise a force of Tejanos and encourage the Indians of East Texas to join in an uprising against Anglo settlers. The Indians' reward would be clear title to the land on which they lived. In July, following the arrival of a small supply party sent by Filisola, Córdova went to Chief Bowl's village and attempted to convince the Cherokees, Kickapoos, Shawnees, and Delawares to rise against the Republic. He also sent an agent to meet with the Caddos and Wichitas. All of the Indians professed sympathy for Córdova's cause, and some of the more militant warriors from each tribe joined. Most of the chiefs, however, would not formally commit to the insurrection until they saw proof of more support by Mexican soldiers.

By early August, Córdova gathered a force estimated at three to six hundred Tejanos, Mexicans, and Indians on the Angelina River near Nacogdoches, and isolated attacks on Anglo settlers began. Learning of this threat, President Houston issued a proclamation against unlawful assemblies, whereupon Córdova and eighteen others issued a counterstatement to the effect that they had taken up arms in response to usurpation of their rights. Thomas J. Rusk then called out a militia unit and in mid-August forced Córdova's forces to break up without a fight. Some Tejanos from the Nacogdoches area went home; others slipped away to the north. In mid-October, however, the Tejano rebels, joined by several hundred Indian allies, began attacks on frontier settlements along the upper Trinity in the lands claimed by Cherokees. This time the militia led by Rusk found Córdova's main force at the Kickapoos' village and killed eleven Indians and Tejanos at a cost of eleven of their own men. This battle, although not really a major defeat for the rebels, ended the insurrection.

Córdova soon left for Mexico. President Houston insisted that Tejano families not involved in the rebellion should be protected in their persons and property, but most males were arrested or harassed. All were eventually freed, but many suffered financially from the costs of defending themselves. Where the Indians were concerned, Houston gave a blanket pardon—to the Cherokees and other groups alike—for any involvement they may have had with Córdova. This action was in keeping with the words he had written to Chief Bowl in August: "My brother, Be at peace and tell my red brothers to do so." He had been unable, however, to bring a genuine peace between the Republic and any of its Indian inhabitants. In fact, during his last months in office, Texans commanded by Rusk continued an offensive against Caddos implicated in the Córdova Rebellion and forced them to move out of Texas. Some went to northern Louisiana; others, north of the Red River into the Indian Territory.

Land policy also bedeviled the Houston administration. Texas's millions of acres constituted its primary resource for attracting settlers, rewarding soldiers, and raising money. The Constitution of 1836 honored all valid land grants made by Spain and Mexico and promised every head of family in Texas at that time a league (4,428.4 acres) and a *labor* (177 acres) and every single man one-third of a league. The interim government extended these grant privileges to men who arrived during the revolution (before August 1, 1836) and those who fought in the army and were honorably discharged. Beginning in the fall of 1836, Congress also provided land to those who had served in the revolution, especially veterans of the siege of Béxar and the Battle of San Jacinto. Statistics on the exact amount of land granted by the Republic are always open to question, but one estimate places the total at nearly 10 million acres. In addition, the Republic also accepted the validity of Spanish and Mexican grants totaling approximately 26,280,000 acres. Huge expanses of land, made available at low prices by grantees and the government, pulled immigrants into Texas in ever-increasing numbers.

The Republic's land policy meant that a huge number of claims and surveys had to be recorded, so congress in December 1836 created a General Land Office "to superintend, execute, and perform all acts touching or respecting the public lands of Texas." President Houston vetoed the act on the grounds that it did not establish clear rules for determining what land was already held by valid title and what was vacant—thereby inviting numerous legal actions—and that it would create a speculative mania as Texans, old and new, rushed to make claims. Congress passed the act over his veto, but he delayed as long as he could before appointing a commissioner and opening the General Land Office in October 1837. Then, as the president predicted, overlapping claims and fraud led to constant litigation and, in some cases, even violence.

Finally, the Republic faced seemingly insurmountable problems in financial policy. The Houston administration inherited a debt of $1.25 million from the revolution and no effective way to raise money. Texans were generally too cash-poor to pay taxes, and tariff duties, levied for the first time in December 1836, brought in only a little revenue. Land sales were not a viable source of income because so much land was being given away. The government attempted to borrow by passing a bill in the spring of 1837 that authorized the issuance of $5 million in bonds, but creditors in the United States, upset by the financial Panic of 1837, did not buy them. So, by early June 1837, President Houston informed congress that the government could not support the army or even pay its own officials and turned to the final resort—paper money. Congress responded by authorizing the issuance of $500,000 in paper money, redeemable in specie one year after the issue and bearing interest at 10 percent. These notes, although not legal tender, were backed by the "full faith and credit of the government" and could be used to pay debts to the Republic, so they did not depreciate immediately. However, when the government's financial status did not improve and additional issues pushed the amount of paper in circulation to more than $810,000, its value began to decline. Texas paper money fell by late 1838 to about 65 cents on the American dollar. As it turned out, this was only the beginning of the Republic's paper-money debacle.

The constitution limited the term of the first president of the Republic to two years, December 1836 to December 1838, and made him ineligible for reelection. Sam Houston, therefore, could not run again, a circumstance that may have been best for his reputation. After all, his administration could boast of success only in obtaining recognition by the United States. It had not gained annexation nor recognition by other nations, and its handling of the army, Indians, land policy, and financial matters had met with limited success at best. Moreover, the president's weakness for alcohol and his unsettled personal life provided additional ammunition for his enemies. Vice President Lamar announced as a candidate early in 1838 and indicated that he would run primarily against Houston's record. Houston and his friends attempted unsuccessfully to convince Thomas J. Rusk to run, and then turned to Peter W. Grayson, the attorney general. Grayson, however, committed suicide in a fit of depression while on a trip to Tennessee in July. The Houston faction quickly gave their support to James Collinsworth, the chief justice of the Texas Supreme Court, only to have him also commit suicide by leaping from a steamboat into Galveston Bay. Collinsworth, some said, had been drunk for a week when he took his life. At this point, Houston's group turned to Robert Wilson, a little-known senator who had no chance of winning. On election day in October 1838, Lamar defeated Wilson 6,995 to 252, and David G. Burnet easily won the vice presidency. Texas's voters thus turned the government over to men who hated Sam Houston and promised to stabilize and strengthen the Republic by reversing his policies.

The Lamar Administration, 1838–1841

Mirabeau B. Lamar took office as the second president of the Republic of Texas on December 10, 1838, but Sam Houston ruined the occasion for him. Seizing on this one last chance to defend his administration against Lamar and other critics, Houston appeared in knee breeches with silver buckles, a silk coat, and a powdered wig—an outfit best suited to the era of George Washington—and proceeded to make a "Farewell Address" that continued for three hours. Indulging in every oratorical trick imaginable, he regaled the audience with a wildly exaggerated account of how successful his presidency had been. When he finally turned the stage over to Lamar, who had spent much time preparing what he considered a literary masterpiece among inaugural addresses, the new president was so upset that he could not deliver his speech. Instead, his private secretary read it. Lamar's only consolation was that he had the presidency.

Lamar wasted no time in taking an aggressive stance toward the Indians of Texas. In his first message to congress, the new president announced that the time had come for "the prosecution of an exterminating war on [Texas Indian] warriors; which will admit no compromise and have no termination except in their total extinction or total expulsion." The Cherokees in particular, he said, have no legitimate land titles from Mexico or the Republic and can either accept Texas law, which will open their lands to settlers, or move, or be destroyed. Congress responded to Lamar's bellicose words by passing several acts intended to strengthen the Republic's armed forces. To some extent these improvements were on paper only, but the administration did raise three companies of militia and get them ready for service.

Cherokee leaders such as Bowl adopted an ingratiating policy toward Lamar's government, but in the spring of 1839 the president found the excuse that he needed to justify an attack. In May a small party of Mexican rangers and Cherokees led by Manuel Flores, a Mexican loyalist who had participated in the Córdova Rebellion, traveled from Matamoros toward East Texas with the intention of uniting Indians there in attacking Anglo settlers. A party of Texas Rangers discovered Flores's party at a crossing on the San Gabriel River twenty-five miles north of present-day Austin. In the fight that followed, the Texans killed Flores and found on his body a packet of letters outlining the plot involving the Indians. Obviously, since Flores had not reached East Texas, the Cherokee leaders had not agreed to help him. To Lamar, Secretary of War Albert Sidney Johnston, and others in the administration, however, the Cherokees were guilty of plotting insurrection.

The president immediately sent Texas troops to occupy land within the Cherokees' claim. Bowl protested, and in response received an ultimatum delivered by representatives of Lamar—either agree to eventual removal from the Republic and be left alone temporarily or face immediate destruction in war. "You are between two fires [Texans on one hand and Mexicans on the other]," General Rusk told Bowl and the other leaders in July 1839. "If you remain you will be destroyed." Days of negotiations produced no treaty for removal of the Indians, so the Texas leaders sent word to Bowl that they would march on his village unless he and the others signed an agreement. The Cherokees left their town but were attacked at dusk on July 15 as they moved north. This first fight ended indecisively, but the next day's battle on the headwaters of the Neches River in modern Van Zandt County destroyed the Cherokees and their allies, the Delawares, Shawnees, and Kickapoos. Short of arms and ammunition, the five hundred or so warriors were overrun by Texans commanded by Rusk and Edward Burleson. As the Battle of the Neches drew to a close, the eighty-three-year-old Bowl stood alone on the field. Texans shot the chief in the head, scalped him, and took his hat and the ceremonial sword given him by Sam Houston.

The Battle of the Neches forced most Cherokees to move from Texas into the Indian Territory of the United States. A few remained and joined remnants of the Delawares and Shawnees in trying to establish a home on the upper Brazos River. Some of the Caddos returned from the United States to the Republic in 1839, but they, too, lived on the Brazos in north-central Texas. In effect, then, the Lamar Administration eliminated Indians as a significant presence in East Texas. Only the Alabamas and Coushattas, who had aided Texans fleeing Santa Anna during the revolution, remained unmolested and eventually received land on the lower Trinity. Most Anglo Texans approved of this aggressive policy, especially since it was successful, but Sam Houston denounced it so angrily that, in the words of one newspaper, he "excited the grief and shame of his friends, and just reproach and scorn of his enemies." Burleson responded to Houston's attack by sending him the hat taken from Bowl's body at the Battle of the Neches, and a soldier named Samuel Jordan attempted to assassinate the hero of San Jacinto at Bullock's Hotel in Austin in December 1840. Jordan, using an axe, fell short of his goal and was not arrested for the attempt, an indication perhaps of public sentiment. Force had destroyed the Cherokees in Texas and not even Sam Houston could help them.

The Lamar administration dealt with the Comanches, who continued in the late 1830s to raid all along the Republic's western frontier, in an equally bloody but somewhat less successful fashion. Once Lamar became president, Texas volunteers regularly mounted punitive expeditions against the Comanches, especially in the region to the west of San Antonio, but could not stop the raiding. Then, in January 1840, three Penateka Comanche chiefs came into San Antonio and offered to negotiate a peace treaty. Motivated apparently by threats from Cheyenne and Arapaho warriors to the north, losses of life from a recent smallpox epidemic, and retaliatory raids by Texans, the Comanches agreed to meet with negotiators under a flag of truce at the Council House in San Antonio. The Texans insisted that the Indians bring with them all the white captives in their possession. If the Comanches did not comply, Colonel Henry W. Karnes, who arranged the meeting, planned to violate the truce and hold the chiefs hostage to gain the release of the prisoners. Lamar and Secretary of War Johnston approved this plan, and three companies of Texas troops were sent to support it.

On March 19, thirty-three Penateka chiefs and warriors and thirty-two others, mostly women and children, came into San Antonio. The main peace chief Muk-wah-ruh and about a dozen of the lesser chiefs entered the Council House to negotiate with two Texas commissioners, William G. Cooke and Hugh McLeod, while the other Indians and Texas troops remained outside. Trouble developed immediately because the Indians brought with them as prisoners only several Mexican children and one Anglo girl, sixteen-year-old Matilda Lockhart. She told stories of sexual and physical abuse that were borne out by her appearance. Her nose had been burned off by Indians who amused themselves by waking her when she fell asleep by touching her nose with embers from the fire. The furious Texans asked about other prisoners only to be told by Muk-wah-ruh that any remaining captives belonged to groups beyond his control. The commissioners then brought Texas troops into the Council House and told the chiefs that they would be held as hostages until other prisoners were brought in. A young chief reacted by stabbing the commander of Texas troops, and a general fight developed that quickly spread to those outside. In the end thirty-five Comanches were killed and twenty-seven captured. Seven Texans died. One of the women prisoners was sent to the main Comanche camp to arrange an exchange of prisoners for captives, but she never returned. According to one story, the Indians tortured most of the whites to death in retaliation for what they regarded as a treacherous attack on peace negotiators.

The Council House Fight led to the greatest Comanche raid in the history of the Southwest. In August 1840 a band of approximately five hundred warriors and another five hundred members of their families swept into the Guadalupe Valley south of Gonzales. Led by Chief Buffalo Hump, they raided Victoria and Linnville, killing settlers and stealing livestock and merchandise as they went. The raiders could not take Victoria, but they sacked Linnville completely. Residents of the town survived only by escaping in boats on Lavaca Bay where they sat and watched the Comanches loot and burn. As the raiders moved back west, slowed by the goods and horses they had stolen (one chief wore a high-top silk hat, leather boots and gloves, an elegant broadcloth coat with brass buttons, and carried an umbrella), they were intercepted at Plum Creek north of present-day Lockhart by a two-hundred-man force of Texan volunteers led by Edward Burleson, Felix Huston, and Ben McCulloch. A running battle ensued, covering twelve to fifteen miles and costing the Comanches about one hundred lives. Further retaliation came in October when a Texan force commanded by John H. Moore moved into Comanche country and attacked a large village near present-day Ballinger. The Texans, aided by friendly Lipan Apaches and Tonkawas, killed 130 Comanches and took back much of the loot from the raid on Victoria and Linnville.

In 1841 the Lamar Administration mounted an important offensive against the Wichita Indians in North Texas. A force commanded by General Edward Tarrant destroyed several Wichita towns on the West Fork of the Trinity in present-day Tarrant County and forced the Indians to ask for peace the next year. Overall, Lamar's approach, although it inflicted severe losses on the western Indians such as the Comanches, did not bring lasting peace to the frontier.

President Lamar proved equally aggressive in relocating the capital of Texas. In January 1839 congress passed an act creating a five-man commission to locate a site "at some point between the rivers Trinity and Colorado and above the old San Antonio road." This provision meant moving the government out of the namesake city of Lamar's leading critic, Sam Houston, and away from East Texas. The commissioners quickly recommended a hamlet on the Colorado River called Waterloo as the future site of Austin (the name of the new capital already chosen by congress). Houston's supporters pointed out that the site was remote from the homes of most Texans and that Mexicans and Indians could easily attack it, but Lamar seized on the recommendation. During the summer, Edwin Waller constructed the necessary buildings, and the government arrived from Houston on October 17, 1839. Lamar and his cabinet members arrived first, followed by forty wagon loads of furniture and records. That night, residents of the Republic's new capital held a ball at one of the town's two hotels.

Lamar's Indian policies and the relocation of the capital put pressure on the Republic's finances and added tremendously to the debt that he had inherited from Houston. The second president had no more success than the first in borrowing money, and sources of revenue such as taxes and tariffs remained woefully inadequate. Lamar therefore turned to the expedient of paper money. During his three-year administration, the Republic's public debt rose from two to seven million dollars, and the purchasing power of Texas paper fell to fifteen cents on the United States dollar. Financial chaos seemed imminent.

President Lamar had no interest in annexation, preferring to think of Texas as a "future empire," so he concentrated on gaining recognition of the Republic by European nations and establishing peace with Mexico. When he took office, James Pinckney Henderson already represented Texas in France, having been sent there by Houston. Circumstances favored gaining recognition in Paris because France was on the verge of war with Mexico over unpaid debts due French citizens. Moreover, the secretary of the French legation in Washington, D.C., came to Houston as Lamar took office and reported that the Republic had the capability to maintain its independence. The French government finally took action in September 1839, signing a treaty of friendship and commerce that made it the first European nation to grant recognition to Texas. A year later, a new agent from Texas, James Hamilton, negotiated similar agreements with both Holland and Great Britain. To obtain the treaty with Britain, Hamilton also had to sign two other agreements—one provided for suppressing the African slave trade and the other allowed Britain to mediate a settlement between Texas and Mexico. Before returning home, Hamilton also began negotiations with Belgium that bore fruit in the form of recognition from that nation in 1841. Hamilton believed that European bankers would make loans to Texas once it became clear that the Republic could win recognition from major powers and would not join the United States, but he was wrong. No loans were forthcoming.

Diplomatic successes in Europe were important, but clearly the Republic of Texas could not attain security as a new nation unless it reached an agreement with Mexico on peace and independence. The attitude of most Mexican leaders, however, made this virtually impossible. As one Veracruz newspaper stated it in 1839: the supreme government "is not aware of the existence of a nation called the republic of Texas, but only a horde of adventurers in rebellion against the laws of the government of the republic." Not surprisingly then, all of Lamar's diplomatic efforts in Mexico failed. First, in the spring of 1839 Secretary of State Barnard Bee attempted to negotiate the recognition of an independent Texas with its boundary on the Río Grande but found the Mexican government unwilling even to talk to him. Second, a British-born adventurer named James Treat, who had spent some time in Mexico, convinced Lamar that he could arrange a peace settlement with the aid of his old friend Santa Anna (and a little bribe money). Treat spent nearly a year in 1839–1840 as an agent of Texas working on this scheme, but nothing came of it. Finally, in March 1841, Lamar sent then-Secretary of State James Webb to Mexico, only to have authorities at Veracruz refuse to allow him to land.

Lamar always tended toward belligerence—witness his Indian policy—so, as his administration neared an end in 1841 and all attempts at negotiation failed, he became more aggressive toward Mexico. One of his weapons was the Texas Navy—technically, the second of the Republic of Texas's two navies. The General Council created a four-ship navy in 1835, but it lasted only until the middle of 1837 by which time all four were lost to Mexican warships or the elements. The Republic commissioned a second navy early in 1839, and its six ships under the command of Edwin Ward Moore were ready for action in the spring of 1840. That summer three Texas ships sailed to Yucatán where a revolt against the central government of Mexico had developed. Commodore Moore initiated friendly relations with the Yucatán rebels, beginning a relationship that culminated in September 1841 in a treaty between a would-be independent state government there and the Republic of Texas. One provision pledged the cooperation of the Texas Navy in preventing an invasion of Yucatán by the central government of Mexico in return for the payment of $8,000 a month by the rebels. To uphold this part of the agreement, Commodore Moore left Galveston with three ships on December 13, 1841, just as Lamar's term ended.

The other, more aggressive, step toward Mexico taken by Lamar in 1841 involved sending an expedition to Santa Fe. Located just east of the northern Río Grande, Santa Fe was within the boundaries of Texas claimed by the new Republic in 1836 and served as the center of a rich trade with the United States via the Santa Fe Trail from Missouri. Lamar believed that an expedition from Texas might persuade the people of Santa Fe to break their ties with Mexico, which was wracked by near-constant warfare between centralists and federalists, and join his Republic. Even if it failed in that objective, he reasoned, a mission would show how merchandise for the Santa Fe trade could be brought overland from Houston more profitably than from St. Louis. The president could not persuade congress to enact a law authorizing an expedition to Santa Fe, but each house passed a bill of some sort on the subject, so he announced that he had approval and in April 1841 issued a call for volunteers.

The Santa Fe Expedition left Brushy Creek just north of Austin on June 18, 1841, under the command of General Hugh McLeod, a West Point graduate who had served capably in the Cherokee War. McLeod had his hands full from the beginning with an assortment of 321 soldiers, merchants, and adventurers. Lamar also named four commissioners, including José Antonio Navarro of San Antonio, to accompany the expedition and express Texas's sympathy for local residents. So confident was he of a sympathetic reception that he actually addressed a proclamation to the people of Santa Fe announcing that the expedition was on its way.

The expedition soon turned into a disaster. First, it had a miserable time crossing the largely unknown terrain between Austin and Santa Fe. Traveling north to the Brazos River and following it to a point just west of present-day Wichita Falls, McLeod's party then turned toward Santa Fe. They faced the devastating summertime heat of that region and ran short of food as well. When they finally reached New Mexico, they found the governor, having had time after receiving Lamar's proclamation to ask for instructions from Mexico City, ready to arrest them. The main party surrendered without resistance on October 5, 1841, after being promised that their lives would be spared. Immediately, however, Mexican officers sent them on a forced march to Mexico

City. Many died on the way, and the survivors were imprisoned. Navarro received a sentence of life in prison, but eventually managed to escape and return home. Overall, the Santa Fe Expedition ruined all hope of establishing trade relations with New Mexico and boosted the morale of Mexicans badly in need of any victory over Texas. Lamar's administration, which began with great promise and had some positive accomplishments to its credit, thus came to an inglorious end.

The Second Houston Administration

Actually, the Republic elected a new president in September 1841 before the full extent of the Santa Fe debacle became known. Lamar could not succeed himself, and it became obvious well in advance of the election that his hated foe, Sam Houston, intended to run. Houston, after leaving the presidency in December 1838, had remained out of the Republic's political life only briefly. In the summer of 1839 while he was on a trip to the United States, voters in San Augustine elected him as their representative in the Fourth Congress, which met in December of that year. Houston quickly established himself as the leading critic of the administration in congress and completed the process of dividing politically active Texans into pro and anti-Houston parties. He attacked Lamar's moving the capital to Austin, partly out of hurt pride that his namesake city had been abandoned by the government and partly because its location on the frontier exposed it to attacks by Comanches and Mexicans. His irritation at the relocation of the capital was nothing, however, compared to his fury at Lamar's policy toward the Cherokees. In speech after speech he charged the administration with duplicity and fraud in unjustifiably driving the Indians from their homes and land. His position was far from popular, but it did not cost him reelection to the Fifth Congress in 1840 or ruin his chances for returning to the presidency in 1841.

The anti-Houston forces attempted unsuccessfully to persuade Rusk or Albert Sidney Johnston to run and had to settle on Vice President David G. Burnet, former interim president of the Republic and a confirmed Houston-hater. Houston and Burnet could have debated the many issues facing the Republic—public finance, Indian policy, and ways of dealing with Mexico, for example—but as was so typical of politics in the Jacksonian era, the contest became personal. Burnet ridiculed Houston as a drunken half-Indian, notable only for his cowardice at San Jacinto. Houston called Burnet a land swindler and hog thief. Enraged, the vice president challenged Houston to a duel, only to be laughed off on several grounds, including a claim that he "never fought downhill." The two also exchanged personal insults in the newspapers—Burnet charging Houston with "beastly intemperance and other vices degrading to humanity" and being called in return a "canting hypocrite, whom the waters of Jordan could never cleanse from your political and moral leprosy."

Houston's popularity, especially in more populous East Texas, and his ability to trade insults proved more than Burnet could handle. The former president gained political and personal vindication, defeating his opponent

7,508 to 2,574. As one observer put it, "Old Sam H. with all his faults appears to be the only man for Texas—He is still unsteady, intemperate, but drunk in the ditch is worth a thousand of Lamar and Burnet." Actually, where alcohol was concerned, Houston's new wife, Margaret Lea of Alabama, whom he had married in May 1840, had him on the road to abstinence and membership in the Baptist Church. His victory celebration was, in the words of one observer, "a cold water *doins*." He and his vice president Edward Burleson, who had defeated Memucan Hunt for that office, took office on December 13, 1841.

In his first annual message to congress, Houston outlined policy changes intended to reverse what he saw as Lamar's mistakes. Finance presented the greatest difficulties. "We have no money," he told congress, "we cannot redeem our liabilities." In this situation, he recommended suspending all payments of interest and principal on the public debt, limiting use of paper money to a new issue of $350,000 that could be used at par to pay all debts to the government, and borrowing $300,000 that would be backed by designated public lands. Turning to Indian policy, the new president urged a drastic change—from war to peace—by signing treaties that would establish boundaries between Texan settlements and Indian lands and by licensing everyone who traded with the tribes. Where Mexico was concerned, Houston pointed out that diplomatic relations had not improved since 1836 and recommended leaving the situation alone. Civil unrest will weaken Mexico, he argued, while emigration from the United States will give Texas the power to withstand aggression.

Congress enthusiastically embraced the president's proposals for tightening the republic's purse strings, in some cases advancing stringency even beyond his recommendations. Payments on the public debt were suspended, and no effort was made to borrow more money. The government issued only $200,000 in paper money, a new type of "exchequer bill" that could be used to pay taxes and custom duties. Salaries paid to public officials were reduced; the president, for example, saw his pay cut from $10,000 to $5,000. Military expenditures were greatly reduced as well. Houston's second administration cost approximately $500,000, whereas Lamar had spent nearly $5 million, and the Republic operated with an almost balanced budget by 1844. Nevertheless, its paper money continued to circulate at depreciated rates, and the public debt, with no interest or principal being paid, grew to $12 million by 1846.

Congress also generally supported Houston's proposals for pacifying the Indians through negotiations and the licensing of trade. In 1842, trading posts were authorized along the frontier at points such as San Marcos and Waco, and the next year saw the creation of the Bureau of Indian Affairs to regulate those commercial operations. Negotiations with the Caddos, Shawnees, and Delawares during 1843 resulted in several treaties, most notably an agreement signed at Bird's Fort on the upper Trinity in September, calling for peace and trade between the Indians and the Republic. The Wichitas and Comanches, however, did not participate in the 1843 treaties, so trouble with those tribes continued. For example, in June 1844, a fourteen-man company of Texas Rangers commanded by Captain John Coffee "Jack" Hays engaged seventy Comanches in a notable battle near Walker Creek to the north of San Antonio. Fighting from horseback against a foe whose ability with the bow and arrow while mounted usually gave him an advantage, the Rangers used a new weapon, a five-shot revolving-cylinder pistol invented by Samuel Colt. Using their new-found firepower, the Rangers killed twenty Comanches at a cost of one dead among their own. Finally, in October 1844, Houston took the initiative to meet personally with representatives of all the major groups, including the Penateka Comanches and Wichitas, in a council at Tehuacana Creek near present-day Waco and signed another treaty providing for peace and commerce. Although incidents still occurred, Houston's policy ended major white-Indian conflict in the republic. There would, of course, be no lasting peace until Anglos controlled all of Texas, but for the moment an end to most of the fighting saved lives and money.

Houston had no great difficulty in obtaining congressional cooperation on financial and Indian policy, but gaining support for his cautious approach to relations with Mexico proved quite another matter. Many Texans welcomed any excuse for conflict with Mexicans, and the fate of Lamar's Santa Fe Expedition, which became known in Austin just as Houston began his second administration, gave the belligerent element an excellent opportunity to demand action. The president prevented a declaration of war against Mexico, but the legislature passed a ridiculous bill redefining the republic's boundaries to include all of the land south of the forty-second parallel and west of Texas to the Pacific Ocean plus the northern two-thirds of Mexico. It would have made Texas larger than the United States at that time. Houston called this bill a "legislative jest" and vetoed it, only to have congress override his veto in February 1842. Nothing came of these wild boundary claims, but the Santa Fe Expedition and its aftermath helped undermine the president's efforts to avoid trouble with Mexico.

The Texas Navy created additional difficulties in relations with the Mexican government. Pursuant to the agreement signed with the rebel government in Yucatán while Lamar was president, Commodore Edwin W. Moore left Galveston for southern Mexico on inauguration day in December 1841. Houston sent recall orders immediately, but Moore managed to stay ahead of the messenger until March 1842 and then obeyed slowly. The government of Mexico could hardly be blamed for irritation at the interference of the Texas Navy in what amounted to a domestic conflict.

Congress adjourned on February 5, 1842, but many Texans, still enraged over the treatment of the Santa Fe Expedition prisoners, demanded an attack on Mexico. Houston explained the difficulties of attacking Mexico City, the probability that an attempt to rescue the prisoners would lead to their execution, and the futility of angry threats. "The true interest of Texas," he wrote a group of Galveston citizens on March 3, "is to maintain peace with all nations and to cultivate her soil." Within a few days, however, Mexico invaded Texas for the first time since 1836, and Houston faced even greater difficulty in attempting to avoid war.

The Mexican government, again under the control of Santa Anna, needed no excuse to attack, but the invasion was at least partially in response to the Santa Fe Expedition and the actions of the Texas navy. General Rafael Vázquez crossed the Río Grande on March 5 with 1,400 men and quickly took San Antonio. He withdrew two days later, taking one hundred prisoners back to Mexico. In response, Vice President Edward Burleson organized three companies of mounted volunteers and led them to San Antonio, apparently with the intention of pursuing Vázquez. Houston issued a general call to arms, but he meant to keep Texan forces under the command of regularly chosen officers and avoid an offensive war. He ordered General Alexander Somervell, commander of the Republic's forces on the frontier, to take charge of all troops arriving at San Antonio. Many of the volunteers under Burleson would not accept Somervell as their commanding officer, but the vice president did not want to go against Houston's orders. While Burleson hesitated, Vázquez's army crossed the Río Grande, and many of the volunteers became disgusted and went home.

The invasion in March 1842 greatly complicated Houston's policy toward Mexico because, in addition to facing new pressures for an offensive war, he had to prepare to defend the Republic against another attack. Taking a strong stand and preparing for defensive war, without at the same time encouraging those who wanted to invade Mexico, proved difficult. Houston began by calling a special session of congress to meet in the city of Houston on June 27. Texans from western counties grumbled that this amounted to a de facto relocation of the capital, but a quorum was present to hear his message on the opening day. After reviewing recent problems with Mexico, the president raised the question of "aggressive warfare" and pointed out that the decision rested with congress. But then he quickly added that if the lawmakers thought it "unwise or impracticable to invade Mexico," they could, at much less expense, allow the president to raise and maintain a force to defend the frontier. Houston hoped to ease war fever and yet build Texas's defenses.

Congress quickly destroyed Houston's hope that it might join him in easing the agitation for war. Instead, hotheaded legislators passed a bill declaring war on Mexico and authorizing the president to draft one-third of the adult male population, sell ten million acres of land to raise funds, and personally lead the army across the Río Grande. When Houston hesitated to sign the bill and reminded congress that nothing had been done to stabilize finances or protect the frontier, outraged Texans threatened his life. He waited until July 22, the day before congress was scheduled to adjourn, and sent in a veto message. His reasoning was simple—Texas did not have the means to put the necessary army into the field and support it. "Resources are one thing," he wrote, "means are another." The veto momentarily increased the furor among extremists who wanted war at any cost, but congress adjourned without voting to override, and the crisis gradually passed.

Having gained a little breathing space in dealing with Mexico, Houston again turned his attention to the issue of relocating the capital. His namesake city had not been popular as a site for the recent special session, and after a new congress was elected on September 5, 1842, he offered a compromise. Leaders in Washington-on-the-Brazos had earlier proposed their town for capital of the Republic. Now, in early September, Houston accepted and ordered the government to move there for the fall meeting of congress. Relocation would not be complete, however, until the Republic's archives had been moved to the capital, and the citizens of Austin were ready to fight rather than part with the government's papers. One frontiersman dared Houston to complete moving the capital. "Truth is," he wrote, "that you are afeard you Dam old drunk Cherokee. We . . . would shoot you and every dam waggoner that you could start with the papers."

Houston always insisted that Austin was not secure against attack from Mexico, and on September 11, 1842, one day after he ordered the government to Washington-on-the-Brazos, a Mexican army under General Adrián Woll swept into Texas and captured San Antonio. Any satisfaction the president may have gained from another demonstration of Austin's vulnerability, however, quickly faded in the face of renewed demands for an offensive war against Mexico. Volunteers and a small force of rangers commanded by Captain John C. "Jack" Hays rushed to San Antonio and lured the Mexican army into a battle on Salado Creek just to the east of the city. The Texans defeated Woll but allowed him to retreat into the city and then to head back to Mexico on September 18. Houston ordered three companies of militia to San Antonio and once again gave command to General Alexander Somervell, authorizing him to pursue Woll's army to the Río Grande and, if there was "a prospect of success," to invade Mexico. Texans at last had their offensive war, although Houston did not give the order until more than two weeks after the Mexicans left San Antonio and probably hoped that delay would allow this crisis to pass also.

If the president wanted delay, Somervell was the perfect commander. His eight hundred man army did not leave San Antonio until November 25 and took more than two weeks to travel the 150 miles to Laredo. Finding no Mexican troops there, Somervell moved his army, already reduced by about two hundred men who went home when he forced them to return property they stole from the people of Laredo, down the Río Grande to a spot opposite the town of Guerrero. (See map: The Somervell and Mier Expeditions, 1842.) Many of the Texans wanted to cross into Mexico and conduct an offensive war while living off the land, but on December 19 Somervell ordered a retreat. However, about three hundred men refused to obey, chose Colonel William S. Fisher as their commander, and decided to continue the campaign.

Fisher and his men moved on down the north side of the Río Grande about ten miles, then crossed the river and entered the town of Mier. They demanded supplies and money, took the *alcalde* hostage to ensure delivery, and went back across the river to wait. Almost immediately, General Pedro de Ampudia occupied Mier with an army of more than nine hundred men. When Fisher learned of the arrival of Mexican troops, he decided to attack without first ascertaining how large a force he faced. The battle began on Christmas Day and continued into the 26th before the Texans, running short of ammunition and supplies, surrendered. Fisher and his men were marched toward Mexico City. South of Saltillo in February 1843, they escaped their guards, only to be recaptured as they headed northward through the Mexi-

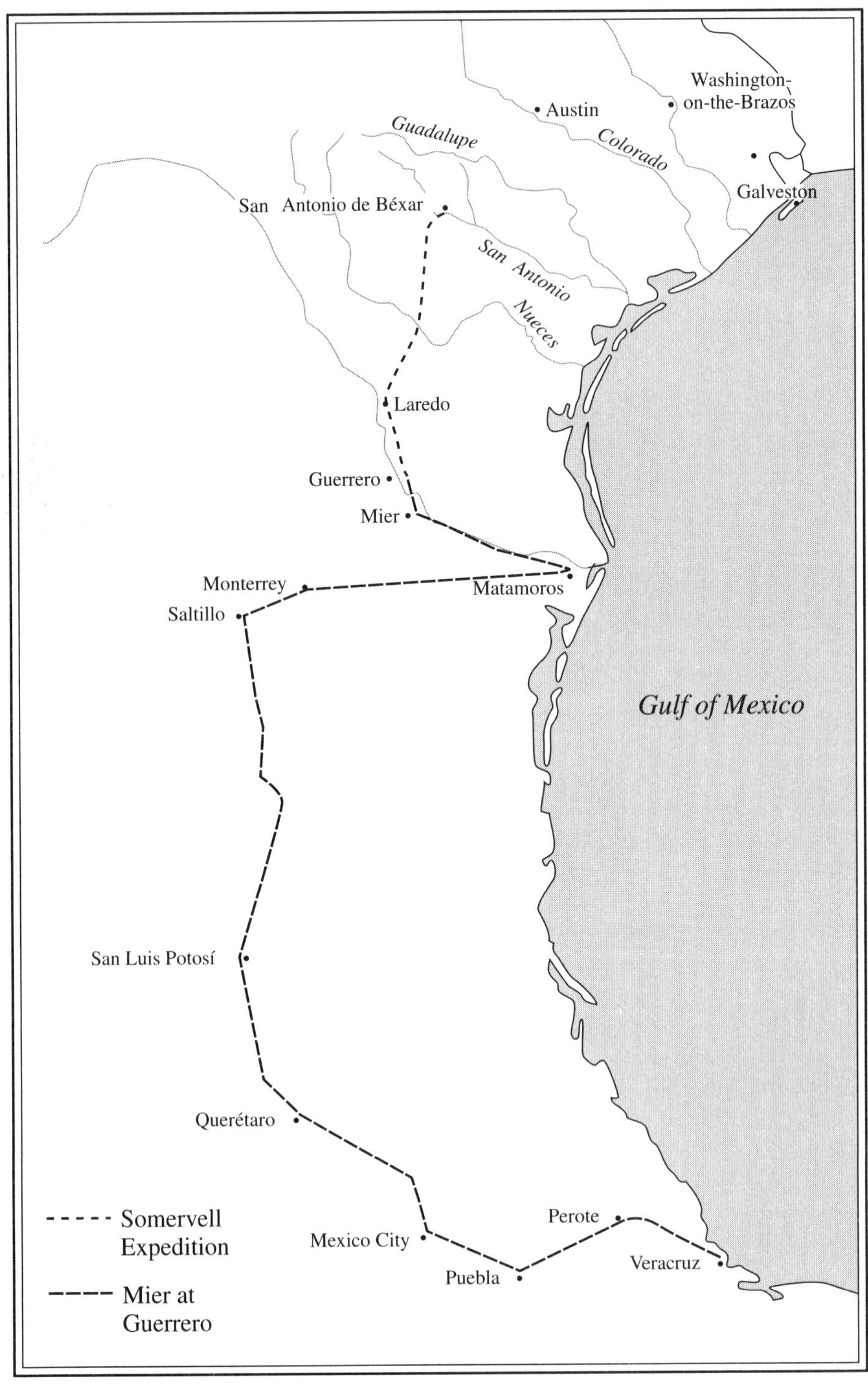

The Somervell and Mier Expeditions, 1842

can desert. As retribution for the deaths of five Mexican soldiers killed in the escape attempt, Santa Anna ordered the execution of one in every ten of the 176 men still alive. The Mexicans put 159 white beans and 17 black beans into a pot and forced the Texans to draw. The seventeen who drew black beans were shot on March 25, 1843, and the survivors continued the march to Perote Prison about 160 miles inland from Veracruz.

As news of the fate of the so-called Mier Expedition filtered back into Texas, Houston once again came under pressure to attack Mexico. He responded by pointing out that Fisher had not been given authority to cross the Río Grande and that anything but a defensive war was foolish. Houston did what he could for the Mier prisoners by appealing to the British to intercede on their behalf and continued to seek an end to hostilities with Mexico that would bring freedom to all captive Texans. He succeeded to the point of signing an armistice on June 15, 1843, ending all fighting, but further negotiations failed to produce a satisfactory treaty. A few of the Mier prisoners were released from time to time at the request of the United States or foreign governments, and Santa Anna finally freed the remaining survivors in September 1844.

Houston faced numerous other problems while the Mier disaster unfolded. The most embarrassing was to some extent a difficulty of his own making—the location of the capital. He had sought to compromise with westerners who favored Austin by moving the government from Houston to Washington-on-the-Brazos, but many members of the Seventh Congress showed their displeasure by not showing up until December 1842 for a session called to meet in October. Undeterred, Houston sent a "confidential" force to Austin to bring the republic's archives back to Washington. The president's men loaded the papers on December 30, 1842, and were preparing to leave when Angelina Eberly, the manager of the Bullock Hotel, sounded an alarm and rushed out on Congress Avenue where a small cannon was kept loaded in the event of an Indian attack. She fired it in the general direction of the government buildings, doing some minor damage to the General Land Office, and a party of Austinites left in pursuit of the archives. The chase was slow, since the papers were in three ox-drawn wagons and the pursuers pulled their cannon with them. On the morning of the 31st, however, the men from Austin surrounded the camp of their quarry and forced a surrender. Both parties returned to Austin for a New Year's Eve party.

The Texas Navy also continued to cause trouble. Commodore Moore finally obeyed the recall order issued by the new president shortly after his inauguration and came home to Galveston in May 1842. Securing a promise from Houston that congress would provide funds for refurbishing the navy, Moore took four ships to New Orleans (the other two were unseaworthy and remained in Galveston) and began repairs. That summer, congress authorized spending $100,000 to support the navy, but Houston, again demonstrating his commitment to financial retrenchment, gave Moore only the power to borrow money to meet his expenses in New Orleans. No financier was willing to extend credit to the Republic of Texas, so Moore's navy was in effect stranded. The commodore sought a solution by sending one of his ships to Yucatán to negotiate a new agreement with federalist rebels there, but it was lost at sea. In January 1843, Houston convinced congress to sell the navy as an unnecessary expense. Moore finally headed back to Galveston but changed his mind en route and decided to take his remaining three ships to Yucatán to help the rebels against Santa Anna's central government, leading Houston to issue a proclamation calling the commodore a pirate. Although the Texas ships fought and won several engagements with Mexican vessels, their efforts were pointless without support at home. The navy returned to Galveston in July 1843 where Houston had Moore discharged from the service and sold the two remaining ships that had any value.

Finally, 1842 also marked the outbreak of serious civil disorder in an area of East Texas centering on Shelby County. Trouble began in 1839 when Charles W. Jackson decided to expose the land commissioners of Shelby County for issuing fraudulent land titles. Jackson had been an unsuccessful candidate for congress and blamed the commissioners and their friends for his defeat. Soon, Joseph Goodbread, a land speculator, argued with Jackson over the sale of a slave for an invalid land certificate, and Jackson killed Goodbread. The murderer and his friends then prevented a trial by the threat of violence and formed an organization called the "Regulators," supposedly to maintain order and prevent fraud. An opposing group, styling themselves the "Moderators," appeared, and the two sides began a struggle that bordered on open warfare by 1842. Houston had no armed force to handle the situation and knew that a call for volunteers would likely attract men who would take sides in the contest, so he contented himself until late in his administration with appeals to local law enforcement officials to do their jobs and for law-abiding citizens to help. Eventually, in 1844, he stationed a company of volunteers in Shelby County and brought the lawlessness to an end.

Annexation to the United States

During the first two years of his administration, although Houston spoke optimistically about the Republic, he knew that it had not built the internal strength necessary to survive as an independent nation. It was simply too thinly populated (in spite of recent growth), too financially unstable, and too weak militarily. Therefore, even as the president bragged about Texas's progress, he opened discussions about the future of his Republic with representatives of the governments in Washington, London, and Paris.

On January 24, 1843, Houston wrote Charles Elliot, England's chargé d'affaires in Galveston, a friendly letter in which he commented that nine-tenths of Texans who talked with him favored annexation to the United States. Leaders in Washington, regardless of their sectional loyalties, also favor annexation, he told Elliot, and both parties will advocate the policy in upcoming elections. In fact of course, Texas had much less support in the United States than Houston claimed. Northern Whigs and abolitionists screamed so loudly in rage at the mention of Texas—"All who sympathize with that pseudo-Republic hate liberty and would de-throne God," wrote William Lloyd Garrison—that those such as President John Tyler who favored annexation hesitated to open the subject. Therefore, having spoken of American "interest" in Texas to spur the British, Houston next used British "ambitions" to stir the government in Washington. On January 30, 1843, Washington D. Miller, a close personal friend and advisor of the president, wrote to Tyler, expressing alarm over the success of Captain Elliot in building British influence in Texas. Most Texans, including President Houston, favored annexation, Miller wrote, but the British might overcome that sentiment by forcing Mexico to recognize the republic's independence. He urged Tyler to seize the opportunity at hand, concluding: "Let it be done before peace with Mexico is obtained. That is important." The words were Miller's, but the policy behind them was Houston's.

The Tyler administration did not respond positively to this prodding; indeed, in April Secretary of State Daniel Webster told Texas's minister to Washington, Isaac Van Zandt, that the republic's unsettled affairs made it impossible to act. Houston, furious, poured his anger into a letter to Captain Elliot on May 13. The United States thinks that Texas is merely its "appendage," he wrote, and refuses to recognize that "we now form two nations." Once, he told Elliot, the only question facing the United States was: shall Texas be annexed? Now, he continued, "there are two: First, Is Texas *willing* to be annexed: Second, in that case, shall it be annexed?" He concluded by reiterating his belief that recognition by Mexico would lead Texas to remain independent and at least as friendly with Britain as with the United States. Elliot forwarded Houston's letter to London, where undoubtedly it proved encouraging, especially since British representatives in Mexico were helping to arrange an armistice between that nation and Texas. Houston announced the armistice on June 15 in a proclamation that recognized Britain's role in bringing peace. Some of his enemies in Texas said that he had sold out Texas to England, and the New Orleans *Picayune* accused him of agreeing to end slavery in the Republic as a price for aid from London. Such charges seem to have been just what Houston wanted leaders in Washington to read.

It was not especially difficult to prompt John Tyler, a Virginian and former Democrat, to support annexation. He had succeeded to the presidency on the death of William Henry Harrison in 1841 and then quickly broken with the Whig Party over issues such as rechartering a bank of the United States. The Texas question offered a president without a party an opportunity to gain favor with Democrats and southerners and perhaps rebuild his political fortunes. When Secretary of State Daniel Webster resigned in May 1843, Tyler replaced him with Abel P. Upshur of Virginia. By the end of that summer, Texas's diplomats in Washington became the recipients of positive inquiries concerning annexation.

In October 1843, Upshur approached Van Zandt about a treaty of annexation, assuring the Texan that President Tyler stood ready to support it. Van Zandt relayed this offer to Houston, who delayed for a while and then sent word to Upshur that such negotiations could be dangerous to Texas. Britain would drop her support, he feared, and Mexico would not sign a treaty granting independence. He did not want to risk these consequences unless the Tyler administration could assure protection for Texas in the event of a Mexican attack while negotiations were underway and guarantee passage of the completed treaty by the United States Senate. Tyler and Upshur could give no full guarantees, but the president announced that he planned to send United States naval vessels on a "friendly" cruise in the Gulf of Mexico.

Houston remained coy through the closing months of 1843, probably with the intention of improving his negotiating position, but the Texas congress, meeting in December, threatened to force his hand when nine-tenths of its members signed a memorial advocating immediate annexation. He responded on January 20, 1844, by sending congress a secret message explaining his policy to that date. An unsuccessful effort by Texas to win annexation, he pointed out, would cost the republic support from Britain and France. "Hence," he argued, "the utmost caution and secrecy on our part as to the true motives of our policy should be carefully observed." Even if annexation fails, he continued, the United States might offer to negotiate a defensive alliance with Texas. Houston concluded by reminding congress that Texas had to wait calmly for action by the United States. "If we evince too much anxiety," he said, "it will be regarded as importunity, and the voice of supplication seldom commands, in such cases, great respect."

Houston's efforts to spur annexation by playing on the dislike of England in the United States soon succeeded. "All things really prove now the *very great* desire of the U.S. to annex us," James Pinckney Henderson, who had joined Van Zandt in representing Texas in Washington, wrote Thomas Jefferson Rusk in mid-February 1844. "You would be amused to see their jealousy of England. Houston has played it off well & that is the secret of success if we do succeed." Annexation negotiations suffered a temporary setback on February 28, 1844, when Secretary of State Upshur died in the explosion of a new gun being demonstrated on the USS *Princeton*. However, President Tyler soon appointed John C. Calhoun to replace Upshur and continue the effort to bring Texas into the Union. Calhoun completed negotiations with Van Zandt and Henderson, gave assurances that Texas would be protected from attack by Mexico, and signed a treaty of annexation on April 12, 1844. By its terms, Texas would become a territory of the United States. The government in Washington would acquire the public lands and property of Texas, but it would also assume the Republic's public debt up to ten million dollars. The United States and Mexico would settle the southwestern boundary of Texas.

When Houston received a copy of the treaty on April 28, he expressed satisfaction with the terms but concern that the guarantees of Texas's security extended only to the period of negotiations. If annexation failed, the Republic would be left without protection from an angry Mexican nation. Soon, developments in the United States showed that Houston had good reason for the pessimism that usually crept into even his most hopeful letters. As expected, the treaty of annexation drew bitter opposition from abolitionists and antislavery spokesmen such as Representative John Quincy Adams of Massachusetts. Secretary of State Calhoun's letter to the British Minister, Richard Packenham, explaining that annexation was necessary to protect slavery in Texas only made matters worse. The treaty's chances for approval were destroyed, however, when it became an issue in the presidential election. The probable major party nominees, Henry Clay (Whig) and Martin Van Buren (Democrat) both came out on April 27 with statements opposing immediate annexation on the grounds that it would mean war with Mexico. Apparently the two had agreed in advance that this stance would remove Texas as an issue, placate antislavery opinion, and avoid problems with Mexico. Their strategy worked well for Clay who received the Whig nomination in early May, but the Democratic Party rejected Van Buren and nominated James K. Polk of Tennessee on an avowedly expansionist platform. This development made the annexation of Texas a campaign issue and cost the treaty the support of many southern Whigs who otherwise would have voted for the addition of a new slave state. On June 8, 1844, the United States Senate defeated the annexation treaty by a vote of 35 to 16.

Texans reacted bitterly, but Houston did not substantially alter his annexation policy. He announced publicly that the Republic was "free from all involvements and pledges" and should pursue its own national interests. And he again approached the British and French concerning guarantees of Texas independence. However, his public announcement also said that in the event of a new offer from the United States that was unequivocal in character and removed all impediments to annexation, "it might be well for Texas to accept the invitation."

Houston had little time left to negotiate because his second term was to end on December 2, 1844, and the constitution prohibited successive terms for the president. He called a general election for September 2 and once again pro- and anti-Houston political divisions came into play. Former president Lamar and others who disliked Houston supported Vice President Edward Burleson. The other candidate, Secretary of State Anson Jones, received Houston's endorsement and was immediately attacked by Burleson's friends for being nothing more than the president's puppet. In return, Jones's friends did their best to associate Burleson with all of Lamar's discredited policies. Amidst all the mudslinging, annexation was barely mentioned. In any case, the election resulted in an easy victory for Jones. " 'Old Sam,' wrote James Morgan, "can beat the D——l himself when he trys, and make anyone President."

Before Houston left office, James K. Polk, the expansionist Democrat, won the presidential election in the United States. President Tyler, who had continued to work toward annexation even after the defeat of the treaty in June, took Polk's victory as a mandate to add Texas to the Union. He sent Congress a message in December 1844, recommending annexation by a joint resolution that would require only majority approval in both houses. The House of Representatives responded by passing an annexation resolution in late January 1845 by a vote of 120 to 98, and, following minor amendments, the Senate concurred on the night of February 27 by the narrow margin of 27 to 25. The joint resolution differed from the defeated annexation treaty in that it called for Texas to enter the Union as a state rather than a territory. The new state would differ from all others by retaining its public lands and its public debt. However, all public buildings, weapons, and military establishments belonging to the republic were to be turned over to the United States without any recognition that the costs of those properties had contributed heavily to Texas's public debt. The United States would settle all boundary disputes, and if Texas approved, it could be subdivided to create as many as four additional states. President Tyler sent the resolution to Texas on March 3, 1845, urging acceptance without reservations by the January 1, 1846, deadline set by Congress.

As events moved toward annexation, President Jones agreed to a proposal by representatives of Britain and France that their nations make one last attempt to persuade Mexico to recognize Texas's independence. Jones promised to delay annexation for ninety days, thus providing time for this final effort to keep his Republic from joining the United States. Texans, however, were ready for annexation. News of the congressional joint resolution spread across the Republic during the spring, touching off a spontaneous outpouring of support for joining the United States. Residents of virtually every county held mass meetings to endorse annexation. President Jones, who was playing for time to see if the British and French could persuade Mexico to guarantee independence, responded to public pressure by calling a special session of the Texas Congress to meet on June 16 and a convention to meet in Austin on July 4 to consider propositions concerning the "nationality of the republic." In late May, British diplomats brought a promise from Mexico that rejection of annexation would bring a treaty recognizing the independence of Texas. Jones hoped to use this Mexican promise to convince congress that there was time to negotiate more favorable terms with the United States. However, the Texas Senate unanimously rejected the proposal from Mexico, and both houses of the legislature unanimously accepted the annexation resolution of the U.S. Congress.

The convention met in Austin (thus returning the capital to Lamar's city, where it remained) on July 4 and immediately, with only one negative vote, adopted an ordinance approving annexation. (Richard Bache, who cast the one "no" vote, allegedly did so on the grounds that he had left the United States to escape his ex-wife and did not wish to be in the same country with her again.) The delegates then proceeded to write a state constitution patterned on that of the other southern states and including protection for slavery. On October 13, 1845, Texans approved annexation by a 4,254 to 267 margin and the constitution by a vote of 4,174 to 312. The United States Congress accepted the state constitution in December, and President James K. Polk signed the Texas Admission Act on December 29, 1845. All that remained was to establish a state government to take the place of that of the republic.

Texans went to the polls on December 15 and elected a governor (James Pinckney Henderson), other executive officials, and a state legislature. On February 19, 1846, members of the state's new government met with the leaders of the Republic in front of the capitol in Austin for a ceremony marking the completion of annexation. Anson Jones delivered his last oration as president, concluding: "The final act in this great drama is now performed. The Republic of Texas is no more." As the flag of the Republic was lowered, Sam Houston stepped forward from the crowd and caught it in his arms. The stars and stripes rose in its place.

Chapter 8

FRONTIER TEXAS, 1846–1861

Annexation brought greater security and stability than white Texans ever experienced under the Republic, thanks above all to the presence of the United States Army. Also, statehood meant that Americans who joined the continuing stream of immigrants going to Texas could do so without leaving their home country. The new state's population, excluding Indians, increased by more than seventy thousand during its first five years in the Union. In spite of greater security and rapid growth, however, Texas's position on the frontier guaranteed continuing conflict and disorder for many of its people. In fact, the state had two frontiers—one with Mexico in the south and another with Indian-controlled lands in the west—and both presented threats to peace. Disagreement over the boundary with Mexico soon led to a major war that had a decisive impact on the future of all Texans, especially those of Mexican descent in South Texas. Conflict on the Indian frontier showed that ultimately the Comanches and their allies would be outnumbered and outgunned but proved indecisive during the early years of statehood.

The Mexican War

The Republic of Texas, citing the Treaties of Velasco and the Boundary Act of 1836 for support, consistently claimed that the Río Grande marked its boundary with Mexico. Mexican officials, who never accepted the legitimacy of the treaties or recognized the independence of Texas anyhow, insisted that the province stopped at the Nueces River, as it had while part of Mexico. This left the land between the two rivers, the so-called "Nueces Strip," as a disputed area. Ultimately, of course, accepting the Nueces as its boundary would greatly restrict the size of Texas, whereas successfully insisting on the Río Grande would give the new state claims to half of present-day New Mexico and territory reaching northward across Colorado into Wyoming.

Even before the formal completion of annexation, the United States strongly indicated that it intended to support the boundary claims made by Texas. In June 1845, President James K. Polk ordered General Zachary Taylor to move to a position "on or near" the Río Grande and stand ready to defend Texas and U.S. interests there. The Republic, although still technically an independent nation, agreed to bringing in soldiers from the United States because of fear that Mexico would attack before annexation could be completed. Taylor prudently set up a camp for his nearly four thousand soldiers on the south side of the Nueces River near Corpus Christi and remained there, just inside the disputed territory, for the rest of 1845. In the meantime, Mexico, which had broken diplomatic relations with the United States immediately upon learning of the annexation invitation, kept its troops at their traditional post south of the Río Grande at Matamoros.

The Texas boundary was the most basic diplomatic issue between the United States and Mexico in 1845, but other matters complicated the situation. President Polk also wanted to acquire California for the United States and to settle financial claims American citizens had against Mexico. To this end, he sent John Slidell of Louisiana on a special mission to Mexico late in 1845, empowering the envoy to make several offers where California and the claims were concerned but to make no deal that did not include the Río Grande as the boundary of Texas. Then, apparently thinking that a little saber rattling might encourage the Mexicans to make a generous deal with Slidell, he ordered Taylor in January 1846 to move his army from the Nueces to the Río Grande opposite Matamoros. Taylor, after several months of delay because of heavy rain, reached the site of present-day Brownsville in late March and built a fortification. General Pedro de Ampudia, commander of Mexican troops across the river, declared that Taylor had occupied Mexican territory, thus in effect creating a state of war, and demanded that he immediately withdraw to the Nueces. In response, Taylor trained his guns on Matamoros and cut off Mexican use of the Río Grande.

Slidell's mission failed to produce any agreement, and Polk decided in early May 1846 to ask for a declaration of war even though Mexico had committed no act of aggression. However, just as he was planning his war message to Congress, news came to Washington that fighting had begun on the Río Grande. In late April, six hundred Mexican soldiers crossed the river above Taylor's position and a detachment of sixty-three United States cavalry sent out to spy on the larger force rode into a trap. Sixteen were killed or wounded and the rest captured. This incident permitted Polk to claim that Mexico had "shed American blood on American soil" and get a declaration of war on May 13.

Fighting began in earnest on the Texas side of the Río Grande even before the United States Congress formally declared war. On the afternoon of May 8, a Mexican army of nearly 3,500 troops commanded by General Mariano Arista attacked Taylor's 2,200 men at Palo Alto north of Brownsville. Fought largely as an artillery duel, the battle proved indecisive. During the night Arista retreated to a stronger defensive position at Resaca de la Palma opposite Matamoros, but Taylor's cavalry and light infantry overran the Mexicans the next afternoon and forced them to move across the Río Grande. Regular U.S. Army troops fought these early battles, and the only Texans to participate in beginning the war were small units of scouts led by Samuel Walker, a captain in the Texas Rangers who fought the Comanches alongside Jack Hays. Walker's exploits in dodging, or fighting his way through, Mexican patrols while carrying messages from Port Isabel on the coast to Taylor at Brownsville captured the imagination of the nation and made him the first hero of the Mexican War.

No fighting took place in Texas after early May, but many Texans—in all, some five to seven thousand men—volunteered during the summer of 1846 for service in Taylor's army as it prepared to invade Mexico. Governor James Pinckney Henderson took a leave of absence from his duties to command a division of Texan volunteers that included a regiment led by Jack Hays, the Ranger captain already well known for his fights with the Comanches. Texas soldiers played key roles in Taylor's army as it took control of northern Mexico by defeating Mexican forces at Monterrey in September 1846 and holding its own against vastly superior numbers at Buena Vista in February 1847. Captain Ben McCulloch's company of Rangers served so effectively as scouts and spies that Taylor attached them to his headquarters rather than to Henderson's command. The Rangers under Hays's leadership fought brilliantly, although their appearance and behavior often appalled officers in the regular army. "A more reckless, devil-may-care looking set, it would be impossible to find this side of the Infernal Regions," one cavalryman wrote. "Take them altogether, with their uncouth costumes, bearded faces, lean and brawny forms, fierce wild eyes and swaggering manners, they were fit representatives of the outlaws which made up the population of the Lone Star State." Indeed, the Rangers were almost too rough and ready for "Old Rough and Ready," General Taylor himself. "Them Texas troops are the damndest troops in the world," he reportedly said. "We can't do without them in a fight, and we can't do anything with them out of a fight." Later in 1847 Hays formed another Ranger unit and joined the army commanded by General Winfield Scott that landed at Veracruz and moved inland to occupy Mexico City and end the war. Hays's Rangers kept communications and supply lines open for Scott's army, and in the process meted out such ruthless and deadly treatment to Mexican guerillas that the civilian population referred to them as *"los Tejanos diablos."*

The Treaty of Guadalupe-Hidalgo, which ended the Mexican War in February 1848, established beyond debate the Río Grande as the boundary between Texas and Mexico. This clarification of the border defined the size and shape of the South Texas frontier, but the sort of society that would grow there remained to be seen. Occupied primarily by citizens of Mexican rather than Anglo ancestry, South Texas during the 1840s and 1850s attracted a notable influx of Anglo merchants, ranchers, and lawyer/ politicians. The region became a frontier for the meeting of a Mexican majority and Anglo minority as well as for settlement and economic development.

The South Texas Frontier

South Texas stretched south and southwest from the San Antonio River to the Río Grande. In some ways the Nueces River subdivided this region—the land above being fairly well settled and dominated by the city of San Antonio and the land below, the Nueces Strip, being largely unsettled for most of the antebellum years. Except for a thin line of settlements along the north side of the Río Grande and a few gigantic ranches, the strip belonged to outlaws and Indians. Regardless of this division at the Nueces, however, the land below the San Antonio River had enough economic and cultural unity to constitute a distinct South Texas, a region that belonged to the United States but closely resembled Mexico. As one Civil War–era observer put it: "[T]he political border was at the Río Grande, but Military Plaza [in San Antonio] was the commercial and social border between the countries."

Always thinly populated, South Texas had fewer than twenty thousand people in 1850, and even after that number more than doubled by 1860, it still had less than 10 percent of the entire state's population. Texans of Mexican descent—old Tejanos and a sizable number of immigrants who crossed the Río Grande to escape political disorder in their native land—dominated most of the region. However, a steady influx of Anglos and Germans into the San Antonio area overwhelmed Tejanos there by 1861.

South Texans of Mexican descent lived in a three-tiered society during the antebellum years. At the top stood the landed elite, the owners of huge ranches, many of which originated as haciendas in the Spanish colonial period. The elite based their economic lives on cattle raising. They sold some cattle in Mexico and Louisiana and exported hides and tallow, but access to major urban markets outside the region was so limited that South Texas ranchers did not develop highly commercial operations during the antebellum years. This apparently suited most very well anyhow in that they viewed their ranches primarily as a way of life rather than a business investment and therefore focused on keeping their property intact as well as turning a profit.

Families in the landed elite lived in spacious, flat-roofed houses that often, especially in the cases of ranches located in the Nueces Strip, had to serve as forts as well as homes. The furnishings for these homes were imported from Mexico or through the new cities of Brownsville and Corpus Christi. Hand-carved beds with canopies and silk drapes, marble-topped tables, and other pieces of fine furniture indicated the wealth and style of the residents. Kitchens generally stood apart from the main house, and dishes of beef, goat, corn, and flour were prepared at large fireplaces there or in dome-shaped ovens located outside.

The elite broke the isolation of ranch life in numerous ways. Much like the Anglos, Mexican men came together for horse races, cockfights, and gambling. Men and women gathered simply to visit or for dances, the great social events of the year. Dances began in the early evening hours and concluded at a midnight dinner replete with fine wines.

Small landowners occupied the second rung of the South Texas economic and social ladder. These *rancheros,* as they were called, lived in one-room adobe houses and spent most of their time caring for their small herds of horses and cattle. Although a smaller part of the population, they can be compared, it seems, to the plain folk Anglos of East Texas. That is, they differed from the elite only in the extent of their property, not in their dependence on the land or the way they tried to live.

Finally, South Texas had a lower class composed primarily of *peóns, vaqueros,* and cartmen. *Peóns* had a status above that of the slaves in antebellum Texas but below that of genuinely free men. They owned no property, could not travel or call in a doctor without the permission of the estate owner (the *patrón*), and needed his approval for marriages. When a *peón* was accused of an offense, the *patrón* acted as judge and jury. On the other hand, *peóns* were not property and therefore could not be bought and sold or treated as personal chattels in any way. Somewhere in an ill-defined place between that of slaves and free men, they served as "faithful servants" to the upper class.

Peóns worked at the direction of the *patróns*—planting and harvesting crops, herding goats, digging wells, and doing any sort of manual labor necessary. In return they received wages or credits at the estate's store in amounts so small that they were constantly in debt. They lived in tiny one-room *jacales,* huts with walls of mud or any other material available and thatched roofs. The one room served for both living and sleeping; cooking and eating took place in a separate enclosure made of grass or corn stalks.

The poor, landless class also included *vaqueros,* the men who herded and took care of cattle. Ranch owners and mission priests generally considered it beneath their dignity to do such work and thought of these first Texas cowboys simply as laborers riding horses. No one involved could have imagined that millions of Americans would one day see working cattle as an ultimately romantic and heroic part of Texas's past. At least *vaqueros,* as befitted their future image, had more independence than *peóns.* They were not bound to the land and could even expect to acquire property of their own someday.

Cartmen lived in San Antonio or along the route from that city to Indianola and earned their living by transporting food and merchandise from the coast to the interior. Using oxcarts, they virtually monopolized this particular freight route by moving goods quickly and cheaply. Anglo competitors appeared by the 1850s but were unable to match the rates charged by the Mexicans. Carting appears to have been the most lucrative business open to poorer Tejanos during these years.

Mexicans and Anglos in South Texas

The arrival of increasing numbers of Anglos during the twenty-five years or so before 1860 put great pressure on the Mexican population of South Texas. Around San Antonio and along the river toward the coast, Tejano landholders found themselves threatened with violence and at times actually assaulted because they stood in the way of ambitious Anglos. Under these circumstances, hundreds of the old elite sold their lands—more than a million acres changed hands, largely from Mexican to Anglo, between 1837 and 1842—and left. Even Juan N. Seguín, the famed Tejano veteran of San Jacinto, became a victim. Elected mayor of San Antonio in 1840, he tried to help Mexicans who felt threatened, but his efforts brought accusations against his loyalty. When

General Vázquez's army occupied the city in March 1842, threats of violence against Seguín and his family forced him to flee Texas and remain in Mexico for six years. He commanded a frontier defense unit that fought against the United States during the Mexican War and then returned to the San Antonio area after 1848. Old Tejano families around Victoria and Goliad faced similar pressure, sometimes with the same results. For example, the family of Martín de León, the founder of Victoria, had to leave the area in 1836 and could not return for ten years. The family eventually regained much of its land, but its home and goods were lost. By contrast, Carlos de la Garza, the owner of a large ranch on the San Antonio River near Refugio, kept his land and possessions, possibly because he had intervened to save some of his Irish neighbors from the massacre at Goliad.

Even poorer Tejanos in the San Antonio area ran afoul of Anglo ambitions and prejudice. In 1857 Anglo teamsters, frustrated by their inability to break the near-monopoly of Mexican cartmen, began a campaign of terror, destroying carts, stealing freight, and in many cases killing drivers. Local authorities did little, but soon the "Cart War" raised the cost of transporting merchandise, and San Antonio businessmen began to worry. Mexico's minister to the United States complained to the government in Washington, which led in turn to an appeal to Texas, and the state legislature approved funds to provide armed escorts for the cartmen. The Cart War ended, but the Tejanos' hold on trade to the coast was weakened.

Below the Nueces River, Anglos were far less numerous; nevertheless, the Mexican elite there had to accommodate the rise of newcomer merchants, soldiers, and lawyers to positions of dominance in the region's economy and government. Men such as Charles Stillman, Mifflin Kenedy, and Richard King ran business enterprises, built towns, acquired huge estates, and gradually transformed South Texas into a land of profit-oriented ranching and commerce. Stillman, a native of Connecticut, moved to Matamoros in 1828 to manage the Mexican end of his family's shipping business. He engaged in the cotton trade, real estate, mining, transporting passengers and goods on the lower Río Grande, and carrying merchandise into the Mexican interior. During the war with Mexico in 1846–1848, Stillman ferried and supplied United States soldiers on the Río Grande. Once the war ended, he bought a massive grant north of the river and established a town at Fort Brown opposite Matamoros. The land on which Brownsville, as he called it, grew originally belonged to Matamoros as community property that under Spanish and Mexican law could not be sold, but annexation allowed Stillman to overlook that technicality. He also bought all the surplus ferries and river boats from the United States, creating a monopoly on transportation in the area. Stillman's successes in the late 1840s put him on the road to becoming one of the wealthiest men in the United States within the next twenty years.

Mifflin Kenedy, a Pennsylvania-born Quaker, and Richard King, the son of poor Irish parents in New York City, both came to Texas to serve the United States Army as pilots of steamboats transporting men and supplies on the Río Grande during the Mexican War. The two met while serving as pilots on

Florida riverboats during the Seminole War and then moved on to Texas. Following the war, Kenedy and King continued in the steamship business—with Charles Stillman as one of their partners—and soon became ranchers as well. Both acquired huge estates, but King began building a ranch that would outstrip all others. Supposedly having been advised by Lt. Colonel Robert E. Lee to "buy land and never sell," King began to make one purchase after another, the most important being the 53,000 acre Santa Gertrudis de la Garza grant, which he bought in 1854. Eventually the King Ranch would total nearly 1,250,000 acres. As it grew, Anglo lawyers such as Stephen Powers, a native of Maine who first came to the Río Grande Valley with General Zachary Taylor's army in 1847, cleared titles to the land. Kenedy, King, and others like them used capital generated by commercial enterprises such as steamboating to enter ranching, but they did so with the intention of making a profit from that business as well. And, thanks to the Mexican longhorn, they would—although not in a major way until after the Civil War.

This new Anglo elite and the old Mexican elite reached an accommodation that proved reasonably satisfactory to both as South Texas became a part of the United States. Intermarriage often brought the two classes together. For example, in 1852 Mifflin Kenedy married Petra Vela de Vidal, the daughter of Gregorio Vela, who served as a provincial governor under Spain, and the widow of Luis Vidal. She had six children with her first husband and six more with Kenedy. Henry Clay Davis, a soldier mustered out of the U.S. Army during the Mexican War, married Maria Hilaria de la Garza, the daughter of a landed family, and set up a ranch and mercantile operation north of the Río Grande at the site that became Río Grande City. Mexican elite families whose daughters married Anglos were acting largely on the defensive to protect their landed estates, but others sought to maintain their position by cooperating with new arrivals and engaging in commercial enterprises themselves. Perhaps the most successful was Santos Benavides, the great-great-grandson of the founder of Laredo. Known as the "merchant prince of the Río Grande," he conducted business on both sides of the river and served as mayor of Laredo and chief justice (county judge) of Webb County.

Regardless, however, of a generally successful accommodation among the elite below the Nueces, incidents of ethnic conflict also occurred in that part of South Texas. The best known involved Juan N. Cortina, the son of an aristocratic mother whose family held title to a huge land grant near Brownsville. Following the Mexican War, in which he fought against the United States, Cortina developed a hatred for Anglos, whom he accused of stealing land from Tejanos in the lower Río Grande Valley. His anger apparently boiled over in Brownsville in July 1859 when he saw a city marshal use unnecessary force in the arrest of a Mexican ranch hand. He shot the lawman, took the prisoner, and crossed the river into Mexico. Two months later Cortina returned to Brownsville at the head of forty to eighty armed men, who rode through the streets shouting "death to the gringos" and killed at least three men as they took control of the town. Mexican authorities persuaded him to give up Brownsville, whereupon he retreated to his mother's ranch west of

Santa Rita in Cameron County and issued a proclamation denouncing the presence of Anglos in South Texas. Cortina's "army" increased to four hundred men as Tejano volunteers joined his cause, and all efforts to drive him from the ranch failed, until a combined force of United States Army regulars and Texas Rangers forced him to retreat and then inflicted a sound defeat at Río Grande City on December 27, 1859. Cortina escaped into Mexico. Colonel Robert E. Lee, commander of the U.S. Eighth Military District, then arrived and restored peace that held until the outbreak of the Civil War gave Cortina an opportunity to begin another attack on Anglos in South Texas.

Clearly, then, from the 1830s to the 1860s the South Texas frontier constituted a unique part of the state. Anglo arrivals there served notice that they intended to dominate the region—through their commercial strength, their control of the law and politics, and in some cases through intimidation and violence. Tejanos sought to hold their own, using everything from intermarriage to becoming more commercial-minded themselves to—in the case of the "Cortina War"—force. People of Mexican descent maintained numerical supremacy, and Mexican culture still ruled most of the region. Nevertheless, the process by which most of the Mexican elite in South Texas would lose their lands and social position to Anglos by the end of the nineteenth century was well underway by 1861.

Exploration and Occupation of the Indian Frontier

At the time of annexation and the Mexican War, Indians were the only Texans who had any real knowledge of the land west of a line running roughly north to south through Gainesville, Dallas, Waco, Austin, and San Antonio to Laredo on the Río Grande (the route of present-day Interstate Highway 35). Soon, however, Anglo explorers opened travel routes across this uncharted region, and settlers began to push the line of frontier homesteads farther west. Their rapid progress came to a large extent because Texas, rather than having to rely solely on its own resources, could depend on the United States Army for assistance. In 1848 the army designated Texas as its Eighth Military Department and ordered nearly fifteen hundred troops to the state under the command of General William J. Worth. Their presence proved vital to the exploration and defense of the frontier and the overall development of the state.

In 1848, a group of San Antonio merchants took an important first step in exploring western Texas by hiring Colonel "Jack" Hays of Mexican War fame to locate a wagon route from their city to El Paso. Settlement had existed on the south side of the Río Grande at El Paso for centuries, of course, but the Texas town by that name originated during the late 1840s from the creation of several stores and ranches on the U.S. side of the river. The men who hired Hays saw this new settlement as an ideal spot from which to open trade with the silver mining region of Chihuahua. Hays, his Indian guides, and thirty-five Texas Rangers traveled westward from San Antonio during the late summer of 1848, but they lost their way, nearly starved, and turned back far short of El Paso. In spite of this failure, however, Hays brought back

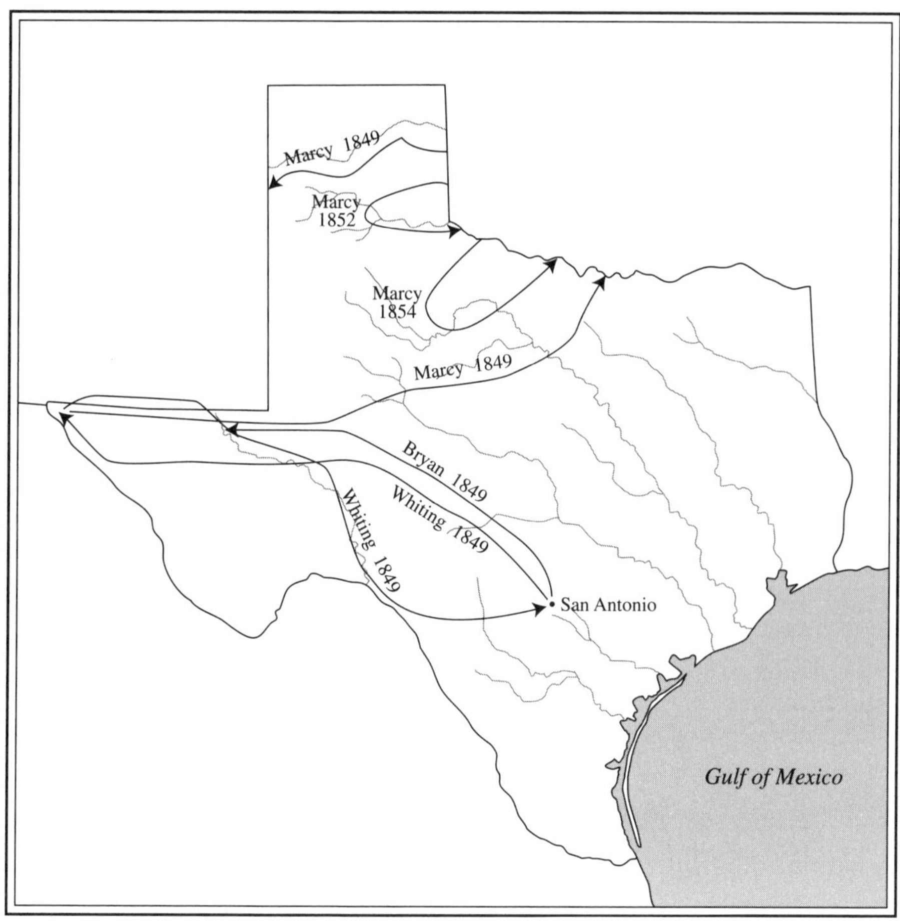

Army Explorations in Texas, 1846–1861

information on West Texas just as the United States Army, working through its Corps of Engineers and Corps of Topographical Engineers, took up the job of exploring, mapping, and establishing trails across the region.

Early in 1849 General Worth ordered a twenty-four-year-old engineer, Lt. William H. C. Whiting, to explore a route from the Gulf of Mexico at Corpus Christi through San Antonio to El Paso. Whiting's fifteen-man party left San Antonio in mid-February, following a route that ran essentially due west and took them to El Paso by early April. Their return route went east to the Pecos River, southward along its course nearly to the Río Grande, and then again east to San Antonio, which they reached in late May. (See map: Army Explorations in Texas, 1846–1861.) That summer engineers built a wagon road along this route, which became known as the "lower" El Paso road and received heavy traffic from the army, mail stages, cattle drovers, and settlers on their way west.

Shortly after the Whiting expedition began its return from El Paso, a second group of explorers arrived, following orders from General Worth to locate a more northerly route to the west. Commanded by a Texas Ranger, Major Robert S. Neighbors, this small party also included "Rip" Ford of Mexican War fame and relied on Comanche guides. They went north from San Antonio to the Waco area and then traveled westward to El Paso, reaching the settlement on May 2 and then returning by a route that ran through the Guadalupe Mountains and required only twenty-one days to reach San Antonio. Later in 1849, an expedition commanded by Lt. Francis T. Bryan retraced the route taken by Neighbors, and the establishment of a wagon road soon followed. This "upper" El Paso road became a key route for travelers from the South who came into central Texas on their way to California.

Although the army focused on establishing the new roads to El Paso, it also began in 1849 to explore the West Texas frontier lying north of those routes. Capt. Randolph B. Marcy, a Massachusetts-born West Point graduate, was by far the most active explorer in that part of the state. From June to August 1849, he commanded the escort for a group of "Forty-Niners" who traveled from Fort Smith, Arkansas, to Santa Fe along a route that followed the Canadian River across the Texas Panhandle. Marcy returned by going southeast to the site of present-day Pecos, Texas, and thence northeastward over the prairies and through the Cross Timbers of North Texas to Preston on the Red River near the modern city of Sherman. Three years later, Marcy and a seventy-man party that included his future son-in-law Lt. George B. McClellan explored the headwaters of the Red River in the Panhandle. Finally, he twice (1854 and 1856) led parties to the upper reaches of the Brazos and Big Wichita Rivers. Marcy's elaborate reports on these explorations often read like adventure tales while describing the land and its resources, wildlife, and Indian inhabitants.

Explorers faced dangers such as severe weather, water shortages, and uncertain relations with Indians, but the problems involved in occupying and pacifying the frontier, albeit less threatening immediately, proved even more difficult to overcome. First, there was simply the matter of distance. As one historian has pointed out, Napoleon's supply line from Poland to Moscow in 1812 was a little shorter than that from the Gulf coast to El Paso. Then, there was the great mobility of the enemy. Comanche war parties, for example, could move far more rapidly than the U.S. forces sent against them. The army attempted to counter these problems by building strings of forts along the frontier just ahead of the settlement line. There really was no other alternative, except a campaign to kill all the Indians or drive them from the state. A good many Texas frontiersmen might well have favored the latter approach, but the army had to try to pacify the frontier by methods short of all-out war.

The building of a first line of frontier forts began in 1848 under the direction of General Worth and was completed by General George M. Brooke, who took command after Worth died of cholera in 1849. To secure the lower Río Grande border with Mexico, three forts were established upriver from the existing post at Brownsville. Fort Ringgold (often called Ringgold Barracks),

Fort McIntosh, and Fort Duncan stood near towns or settlements above Brownsville—respectively Río Grande City, Laredo, and Eagle Pass—and guarded much-used crossings on the river. Troops were also ordered to El Paso in 1848, but the post there was closed in 1851. To protect the line of settlements pressing west, a line of seven forts stretched north from Fort Duncan at Eagle Pass to Fort Worth on the upper reaches of the Trinity River in North Texas. (See map: U.S. Army Forts in Texas, 1848–1850.)

These forts consisted of buildings grouped in a square without any enclosing walls and therefore bore little resemblance to the stockades usually shown in western movies. Located at considerable distances from each other and manned primarily by infantry, the posts and their soldiers were, in the words of one newsman, "as much out of place as a sawmill upon the ocean." They had little success in dealing with Indian raiders, and settlers who were pushing the frontier westward an average of ten miles per year complained bitterly. Under these circumstances, General Brooke's successor, General Persifor F. Smith, decided in 1851 to construct a new string of forts 150 miles west of the first line. This second chain of seven posts, which was completed in 1852, extended from Fort Clark near Brackettville, the southern anchor much as Fort Duncan anchored the first line, north to Fort Belknap near the Salt Fork of the Brazos River. In 1854, the army added to the list of major posts in Texas by building Fort Davis on the road from San Antonio to El Paso and reactivating the post at El Paso, which became known as Fort Bliss. (See map: Additional U.S. Army Forts in Texas, 1851–1858.)

General Smith devised a plan of defense that called for placing infantry in the outer line of forts and cavalry in the inner (older) posts. The infantry had the job of spotting raiders and somehow reporting their presence to the cavalry, who would pursue the enemy while troops in the outer line cut off retreat. Texas frontiersmen readily saw the flaws in this plan and pointed out that only cavalry could locate highly mobile raiders and attack before they reached settlements between the first and second lines of forts. The United States attempted to remedy this problem in 1855 by assigning the Second U.S. Cavalry to Texas. An elite outfit, riding the best mounts and equipped with the newest arms and commanded by outstanding officers such as Albert Sidney Johnston and Robert E. Lee, the Second Cavalry greatly strengthened the army's presence on the frontier. The regiment established headquarters at Fort Mason and focused its efforts on central Texas and the Mexican frontier. The creation of more forts in that area, such as Forts Lancaster (1855) and Stockton (1859), also strengthened security there. On the northwestern frontier, however, the Second Cavalry manned only one new fort—Camp Cooper, built in 1856. The system of forts gradually improved control of the Mexican border, but it would never provide the sort of protection demanded by settlers, especially in the region from central Texas to the Red River.

Explorations by the U.S. Army and the establishment of forts brought important developments in transportation and communication that further opened the frontier. In 1851, Henry Skillman began mail and passenger service by stagecoach between San Antonio and El Paso. Six years later George

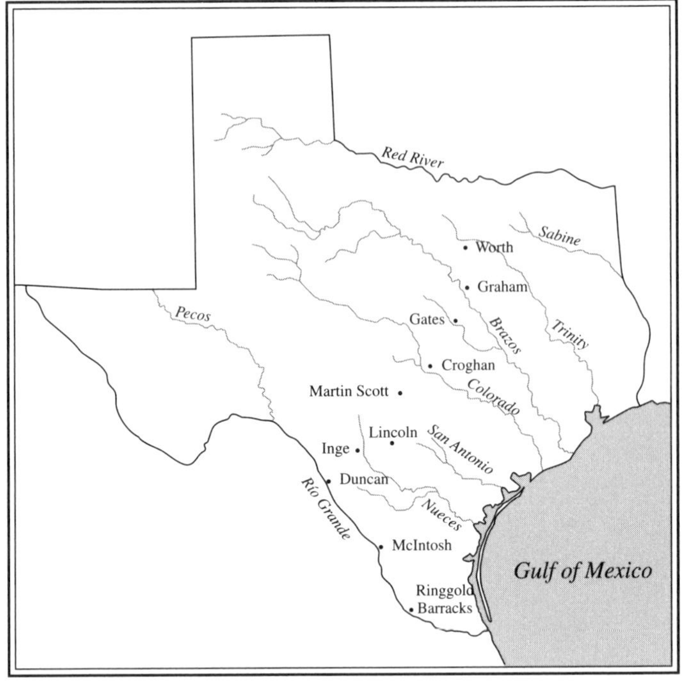

U.S. Army Forts in Texas, 1848–1850

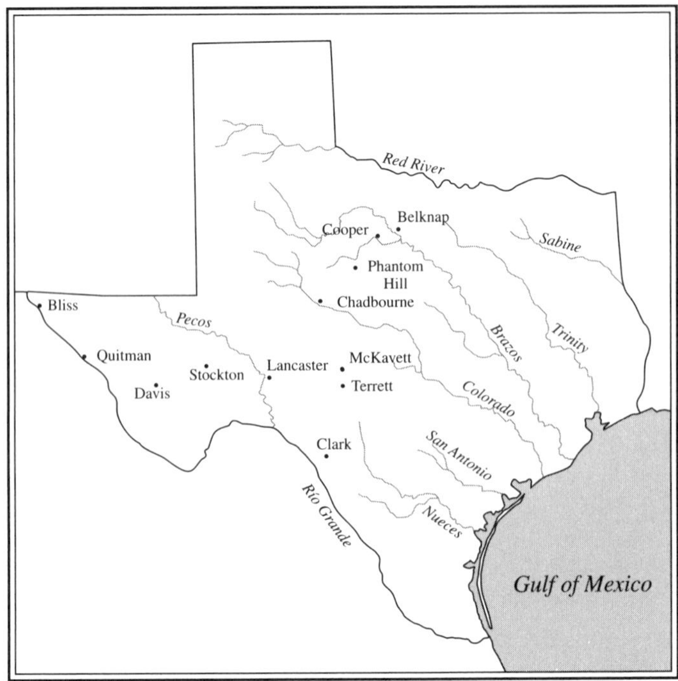

Additional U.S. Army Forts in Texas, 1851–1858

H. Giddings offered similar service by stage from San Antonio to San Diego, California, a distance of 1,476 miles. Early trips took nearly seven weeks, but eventually the coaches reached the Pacific in slightly less than a month at a cost of $200. Another stage route across Texas to California began operating in 1858 as the Butterfield Overland Mail, which ran from St. Louis and Memphis to Los Angeles and San Francisco. Crossing into Texas near Preston on Red River, this line's stages took eight days to cover the 645 miles to El Paso, much of the route following the trail explored by Marcy in 1849. Travel on these stage lines was not for the impatient or those demanding comfort—"The severest ordeal I have ever experienced of this kind," wrote one officer after a trip from El Paso to Sherman. Passengers also had to be concerned about attacks on the stages by Indians and bandits, although the army did everything possible to prevent depredations.

Stage lines carried mail to major points along their routes, but the army played a key role in creating a reasonably efficient postal system all along the frontier. During the 1840s and 1850s, mail to and from Texas to the Mississippi Valley and East Coast largely went through New Orleans. With this in mind, the army in western Texas established a system that depended on water transport to New Orleans and overland express riders in the state's interior. For example, a mail sloop ran weekly from Corpus Christi to Indianola, which in turn had weekly steamer service to New Orleans. At the same time riders made weekly trips from Corpus Christi to San Antonio and back, delivering mail from the outside and returning with mail brought to San Antonio from all the posts scattered across West and North Texas. Express riders, generally extra-duty soldiers and a few civilians, earned good money, but their job was tiring and dangerous. By the mid-1850s, this mail system worked to the satisfaction of men in the army and provided personal and business communication service to civilians, too.

During these years the army also engaged in an imaginative but ultimately unsuccessful experiment in using camels as beasts of burden on the frontier. Jefferson Davis, secretary of war in the Pierce administration from 1853 to 1857, and other important Americans subscribed to the view that western Texas was part of the "Great American Desert" and therefore a fitting place to use camels for transportation. In 1855, funded by a congressional appropriation, the army purchased thirty-three camels in Africa, which were landed at Indianola in April 1856 and taken inland to Camp Verde a little northwest of San Antonio. Within a year, another forty-one camels were imported and quartered at Camp Verde. The army used these camels successfully in exploring the Big Bend area and on expeditions across New Mexico and Arizona to California. They carried loads of as much as six hundred pounds over long distances, required little water, and ate almost anything available. The use of camels did not flourish, however, and came to an end after the Civil War, not because the animals failed as beasts of burden but because of other problems. Camels smelled awful, caused horses to spook, and were despised by American handlers used to dealing with mules. Most of those that survived by 1866 were sold to civilians, and some wound up roaming free in the west.

Overall, the United States Army after the Mexican War successfully explored most of West Texas and devoted a large part of its limited manpower and money to building forts intended to control the Indian frontier as well as the border with Mexico. In the process this military presence contributed vitally to the development of all of the state west of a line from Gainesville to Corpus Christi. Not only did the army open essential lines of transportation and communication, thereby facilitating commercial growth, it provided a financial boon of incalculable value. Texans sold the army land for forts, horses for mounts, mules to pull wagons, forage for the animals, beef and grain for food, and wood to use in cooking and heating. And every one of the millions of dollars spent by the military had a multiplier effect in the economy. Older towns such as San Antonio, which had always depended on the army in many ways, grew under the impetus of serving as command and supply centers, and new towns sprang up near the forts constructed along the frontier. The story of this military/commercial complex provides an ironic counterpoint to the mythological view of a frontier that was won by the guns and guts of self-reliant individualists. It is true that Texas frontiersmen depended on themselves and faced their own problems, but it is also true that federal troops and dollars played an indispensable role in their success.

Conflict on the Indian Frontier

Conditions on the western Texas frontier during the late 1840s and 1850s amounted to a recipe for disaster, especially for the fragmented peoples lumped under the heading "Indians." The Comanches, the largest group, had several subdivisions, and then, to offer only a partial list, there were Kiowas, Wichitas, Lipan Apaches, Tonkawas, and Caddos. Pressured by settlers from the east, the agriculturalists were unable to stay in one place and grow crops and the hunters saw buffalo herds begin to decline in size. Bovine diseases and the number of hunters began the process of decimating the herds, but the Indians' own practice of killing primarily breeding age cows for their tender meat and easy-to-work hides also contributed. Under these circumstances, the Indians' world disintegrated more rapidly perhaps than ever before. "For all," one historian has written, "unfamiliar hunting territories, competition with outlaws, settlers, soldiers, and travelers for declining game, and exposure to violence and disease encouraged raiding and shattered traditional cultures. The entire area from well below the Río Grande to the Arkansas River, along and west of the line of settlement, became a haven for lawlessness centered around the stealing of captives and horses." Even Indians who did not raid and steal could not escape blame and retribution. To Texas frontiersmen and the army, virtually every Indian was "hostile"; so, not knowing who had committed a particular raid, they simply attacked the first group that they found.

The United States government, which took over responsibility for Indian policy from the Republic of Texas in 1846, attempted at first to implement its traditional policy of negotiating peace treaties that regulated trade and land claims. In May 1846, agents of the United States met with the Penateka Comanches, Caddos, Lipan Apaches, Tonkawas, and Wichitas at Council Springs on Tehuacana Creek near Waco and signed a treaty that called for the Indians to remain peaceful, surrender stolen property and captives, and deal only with licensed traders. The federal government promised to protect the Indians and to keep white trespassers off the lands occupied by the signatory tribes.

Treaties such as this agreement at Council Springs had limited success at best on the American frontier, but they had no chance to work in Texas because of the special terms of annexation in 1845. Texas, unlike all other states, retained ownership of its public lands. Thus, the land on which Indians lived belonged to the state rather than the federal government, and the latter's laws could not apply there. Moreover, unlike the United States, which recognized Indian land claims until they were given up by treaty, the State of Texas insisted that Indians had no right to any land anywhere in the state. The United States Senate, recognizing the limits created by ownership, removed the article promising to keep trespassers off lands occupied by Indians before approving the treaty in 1847. When Robert S. Neighbors, a one-time Indian commissioner for the Republic and newly appointed special agent for the United States, explained this amendment to the Penateka Comanches, a chief named Buffalo Hump eloquently voiced the Indians' protest: "I cannot agree that the third article in the treaty be stricken out, for that article was put in at my request. For a long time a great many people have been passing through my country; they kill all the game and burn the country, and trouble me very much. The commissioners of our great father promised to keep these people out of our country. I believe that our white brothers do not wish to run a line between us, because they wish to settle in this country. I object to any more settlements. I want this country to hunt in."

Buffalo Hump's Comanches not only hunted in Texas; they also raided into Mexico, an activity that the United States promised to stop in the Treaty of Guadalupe Hidalgo in 1848. Other Comanche and Kiowa bands, angered by the pressure of new settlers, attacked white frontiersmen. The more sedentary Caddos and Wichitas, most of whom lived on the Brazos some 150 miles above Waco, also had violent confrontations with settlers. The whites' insistence on moving onto Indian lands, in the words of Special Agent Neighbors in March 1848, "regardless of the consequences . . . must necessarily and inevitably lead to serious difficulty." A bloody clash came a month later when a company of Texas Rangers investigating the rumored murder of a settler met a party of Wichitas on the Llano River. The Indians attempted to flee, but the Rangers drove them into the river and killed twenty-five. Seeking revenge, the Wichitas killed and scalped three surveyors who were running lines for the Peters Colony grant. A few days later another Ranger company, after supervising the burial of the three surveyors, killed a Caddo boy who ran rather than obey their orders to stop. Agent Neighbors managed to stop further bloodshed, but these clashes and the situation all along the frontier convinced him that the "Indian question" called for bold steps and a final resolution. Accordingly, in March 1849 he proposed the creation of a system of reservations for the Indians, each with its own agent and nearby military post to enforce all laws and treaties. Neighbors also suggested that the government offer education and vocational instruction and supply the seeds and equipment necessary to help the Indians become self-supporting.

Unfortunately for Neighbors, who was a Democrat, his proposal coincided with the advent of Zachary Taylor's Whig administration in Washington, and he lost his job as Indian agent. His removal from office, plus the Texas legislature's insistence that Indians had no right to any land in the state, meant that, although the federal government gave approval to the idea in 1849, nothing came of the call for a reservation system for the next four years. Indian raids continued, and the army and Texans took what amounted to a "no prisoners" response. The Indians were further weakened by disease and privation. For example, a cholera epidemic in 1849 reportedly killed half of the Kiowas and, in the words of one historian, "literally destroyed the Penatekas [Comanches] as a tribe." Groups such as the Tonkawas, having lost familiar hunting grounds, lived on the edge of starvation. Apparently their condition was so pitiful that even the army at times suspended its "no prisoner" policy for them. One observer wrote of a band who came to beg at Fort Mason in 1853, "a more squalid, half-starved looking race I have never seen."

Neighbors regained his position in 1853, following the election of Franklin Pierce, a Democrat, and resumed his quest for a reservation system. Finally, in February 1854, the Texas legislature authorized the federal government to take control of twelve leagues of vacant land "for the use and benefit of the several tribes of Indians residing within the limits of Texas." The law required the removal of all Indians not native to Texas and stipulated that ownership of the land would revert to Texas when reservations were no longer needed. Neighbors then directed the creation of two reservations on the upper reaches of the Brazos River. The first, at the mouth of the Clear Fork, was for the Penateka Comanches; the second, on the main fork, was for the remnants of the Caddos, Tonkawas, Delawares, Shawnees, and some of the Wichitas. The more sedentary, agricultural groups had little difficulty in adjusting to reservation life. By late summer 1856, nearly one thousand had settled on the Brazos Reservation. According to one historian, "They resided in family-oriented villages; built cabins and used wagons; wore clothing similar to the Texans of that day; planted crops of corn, beans, and squash; raised herds of horses and cattle; and sometimes went hunting for buffalo or deer on the plains." The Penatekas found it more difficult to give up their migratory life based on hunting, but under the supervision of Neighbors, more than five hundred lived peacefully on the Clear Fork Reservation in 1856.

In spite of these successes, however, the reservation system did not provide an answer to the "Indian question" in Texas. For one thing, thousands of Indians—the Penatekas led by Buffalo Hump and other bands of Comanches, Kiowas, Lipan Apaches, and some bands of Wichitas and Tonkawas—continued to roam and raid in the region stretching from Mexico across western Texas to Kansas. White Texans may well not have tolerated Indians even if all had become peaceful residents of reservations, but the continuation of raiding fueled continuing rage against all "savages." A second problem appeared as soon as the line of settlement reached the reservations and frontiersmen wanted the land. Settlers pressed the borders of the Indians' land, and some even set up farms within reservation boundaries. Neighbors and U.S. troops removed these illegal occupants, but that only created more anger among white settlers. As would be expected, they began to scapegoat the residents of reservations, blaming them for every incident of violence or thievery perpetrated by non-reservation Indians.

The reservation experiment came to an end in 1858–1859 amidst threats and violence orchestrated primarily by John R. Baylor, a recently fired agent at the Clear Fork Reservation. Baylor obviously hated Indians, even though he worked briefly as an agent, and his dismissal created a fury that he took out by demanding that Neighbors be removed and the reservation Indians punished for their supposed role in depredations against whites. In late December 1858, six white settlers killed seven Caddos, three of them women, who were hunting outside the Brazos Reservation. An investigation led to nothing because the grand jury would not indict settlers for murdering Indians. Then, in May 1859, Baylor led 250 mounted settlers into the same reservation with the intent of driving out its residents. U.S. Army troops forced Baylor to back down, but not before two elderly Indians were killed. By this time the reservation Indians were so fearful for their lives that they could not tend their crops or livestock. Governor Hardin R. Runnels appointed peace commissioners to investigate, and their report, although indicating that few reservation Indians were to blame for the problems, called for an end to the reservations. "We believe it impracticable," they wrote, "if not impossible, for tribes of American Indians, scarcely advanced one step in civilization, cooped up on a small reservation and surrounded by white settlers, to live in harmony for any length of time."

Neighbors, his own life often threatened because of his opposition to the claims of whites, recognized that he had no choice but to remove the reservation Indians across the Red River to the Indian Territory. During the summer of 1859, with the approval of the federal government, Neighbors supervised the removal. United States troops provided an escort as the reservation Indians, leaving behind their homes, crops, and livestock, experienced a limited version of the Cherokees' infamous "Trail of Tears." "I have this day [August 8, 1859]," Neighbors wrote his wife, "crossed all the Indians out of the heathen land of 'Texas' and am now 'out of the land of Philistines.'" Unfortunately, Neighbors soon returned to Texas, where, at Fort Belknap on September 14, 1859, he was murdered by a man whom he did not even know. In a sense, he literally gave his life in protecting those of the reservation Indians.

In 1857–1859, as the reservation experiment came to an end, warfare with the Comanches and Kiowas reached a new level of intensity on the northwestern Texas frontier. Conflict focused in this area because the U.S. Army's presence on the Río Grande reduced the ease of raiding into Mexico and the increasing number of farms and ranches around the reservations provided inviting targets. When the situation worsened, Texans became more critical than ever of the army's efforts to defend the frontier from widely scattered forts, and the state government called out mounted volunteers who could equal the Indians in mobility and carry out "active and offensive operations" against them. In January 1858 Governor Runnels appointed John S. "Rip" Ford to take command of all state troops and attack the Indian raiders. Ford's force of slightly more than one hundred Rangers, supported by 110 Indians from the Brazos Reservation who wanted to prove their loyalty, crossed the Red River into present-day Oklahoma and attacked the Comanche village of Chief Iron Jacket in May 1858. In the battle that followed, the Texans killed seventy-six Comanches, including Iron Jacket, who was shot by the Tonkawa chief Placido, and captured eighteen at a cost of only two dead and two captured. Prisoners told Ford that Buffalo Hump had a village only twelve miles away, but the victors were too tired to risk another fight. They returned to Texas, not having brought an end to raiding, but having demonstrated that raiders could no longer find haven outside the state.

Recognizing that the nature of the conflict had changed, Buffalo Hump and other Comanche elders discussed peace with federal agents in the Indian Territory and moved their camp to a spot near Fort Arbuckle where they expected to be safe. Unfortunately for them, General David E. Twiggs, who had taken over command of the army in Texas the year before, decided that he would emulate Ford and also take the war to the Indians. In mid-September 1858, four cavalry companies and an infantry detachment under the command of Major Earl Van Dorn moved into the Indian Territory. Van Dorn's force also had the support of 135 Indians from the Brazos Reservation, commanded in this case by nineteen-year-old Lawrence Sullivan "Sul" Ross, the son of the subagent on the reservation. The troops and their allies attacked Buffalo Hump's village at dawn on October 1, killing men, women, and children in their lodges. When the battle ended, fifty-six Comanches were dead at a cost of five soldiers killed and ten wounded, but Buffalo Hump and two-thirds of his warriors escaped. Sul Ross's reservation Indians played a key part in the fight by capturing three hundred horses, but Ross himself barely survived his first battle, as he suffered two serious wounds while trying to recapture a white girl found with the Indians. Texas nearly lost a future governor and university president to the gun and knife of a Comanche warrior whom he had known since childhood.

Buffalo Hump's Comanches fled northward into Kansas, and Van Dorn pursued them there in the spring of 1859. The fight that followed was indecisive, except that the Comanches were driven even farther north. Eventually, they straggled back to the Indian Territory where they met the fugitives from the Clear Fork Reservation brought there in August 1859 by Neighbors.

Surprisingly, all the punishment dealt out by the army brought little relief to settlers living on the northwestern frontier. Offensives such as those mounted by Van Dorn tended to kill the weak or drive them to reservations but left the younger warriors enraged and looking for revenge. Reports of raids increased throughout 1859 and into 1860. Frontiersmen still accused the federal government of "a cold blooded indifference to our condition," and the

Cynthia Ann Parker (ca. 1825–ca. 1871). This daguerreotype was made soon after Parker's rescue/capture at the Battle of the Pease River in 1860. She cut her hair short in the belief that her husband, Peta Nocona, had been killed. She is shown nursing her daughter, Prairie Flower. Credit: The Texas Collection, Baylor University, Waco, Texas.

state legislature endorsed this criticism in early 1860 by authorizing the newly elected governor, Sam Houston, to raise a regiment of mounted Rangers to protect settlers. One of the captains appointed by Houston to raise a company of volunteers was Sul Ross, the young man who had nearly been killed at Buffalo Hump's village in 1858. In November 1860 when a Comanche band led by the war chief Peta Nocona raided settlements as far east as Parker and Jack Counties, leaving behind a trail of theft, rape, murder, and mutilation, Ross pursued them northwestward into the Panhandle. His force of about forty Rangers and twenty-one soldiers provided by the U.S. Second Cavalry surprised a party of Comanches on December 19 as they were breaking camp near the Pease River, killing some and scattering the rest. Among the prisoners was a blue-eyed woman soon identified as Cynthia Ann Parker, one of the children taken captive at Parker's Fort in 1836. She had become thoroughly Comanche, married Peta Nocona, and given birth to three children, including Quanah Parker, who was destined to become the last leader of his tribe. Anglo Texans were delighted at her return—the state legislature even voted her an annual grant of $100 a year for five years—but she never adjusted to living in a white society. She tried several times unsuccessfully to return to the Comanches before her death in the early 1870s.

Like other successes by Rangers and the army, the Battle of Pease River did not end Comanche raids on the frontier, especially since it came on the eve of Texas's secession from the Union. Disunion and the war that soon followed diverted men and money from the frontier, enabling raiders actually to roll back the line of settlement during the early 1860s. Warfare continued on the northwestern frontier until 1875 when Quanah Parker's band finally entered a reservation in the Indian territory.

Both of Texas's frontiers during the 1840s and 1850s—the Mexican frontier in the south and the Indian frontier in the west—left lasting imprints on the state. Some historians have seen the stories of these frontiers as the triumphant march of white civilization; others view them as matters of raw exploitation by Anglos and the decimation of earlier arrivals. Certainly elements of both views were present, allowing every reader to place his or her interpretation on the meaning of these frontiers. However, the more basic story of Texas during these years did not play out in the south or the west. Instead, the key to Texas then—and in many respects ever since—lay in its development as an essentially southern state, a part of the South.

Chapter 9

EMPIRE STATE OF THE SOUTH, 1846–1861

The earliest Anglo migrants in the 1820s began making Texas southern, and those who arrived during the years of the Republic accelerated the process. Coming primarily from the southern United States and bringing with them the institution of slavery, they created a predominantly agricultural, slaveholding economy and society. By 1845–1846, when it joined the Union, Texas was essentially a part of the Old South, and during the next fifteen years, bolstered by a continuing flow of southern-born immigrants, it marched toward secession only a few steps behind the most extreme slave states such as South Carolina and Mississippi. Given its size and importance to the region's future, Texas could properly be called, in the words of one observer in 1858, the "Empire State of the South."

The total population of Texas, excluding Indians, grew from approximately 142,000 in 1847 to 212,295 in 1850 and 604,215 in 1860, an increase of 325 percent in less than fifteen years. By the 1850s, three-quarters of the state's families were headed by natives of the South, and approximately 25 percent of those families owned at least one slave. The slaves themselves constituted about 30 percent of the total population, numbering 38,753 in 1847, 58,161 in 1850, and 182,566 by 1860. Texas did not match older southern states such as Virginia in sheer numbers of slaveholders and slaves, but it was closely comparable in the proportions of masters and bondsmen in its total population. Virtually all of these southern-born slaveholders and slaves lived east of a line extending from the Red River at the ninety-eigth meridian southward to the mouth of the Nueces River. Thus the eastern two-fifths of the state, an area as large as Alabama and Mississippi combined, may properly be called "antebellum Texas"—that is, the part of the state that would propel Texas into the Civil War. (See map: Antebellum Texas.)

Texas differed from most other states of the Old South in notable ways. It had a large concentration of immigrants from Europe, primarily Germans, who arrived during the 1840s and 1850s. By 1860 at least twenty thousand residents of German birth, pulled from their native country by the lure of

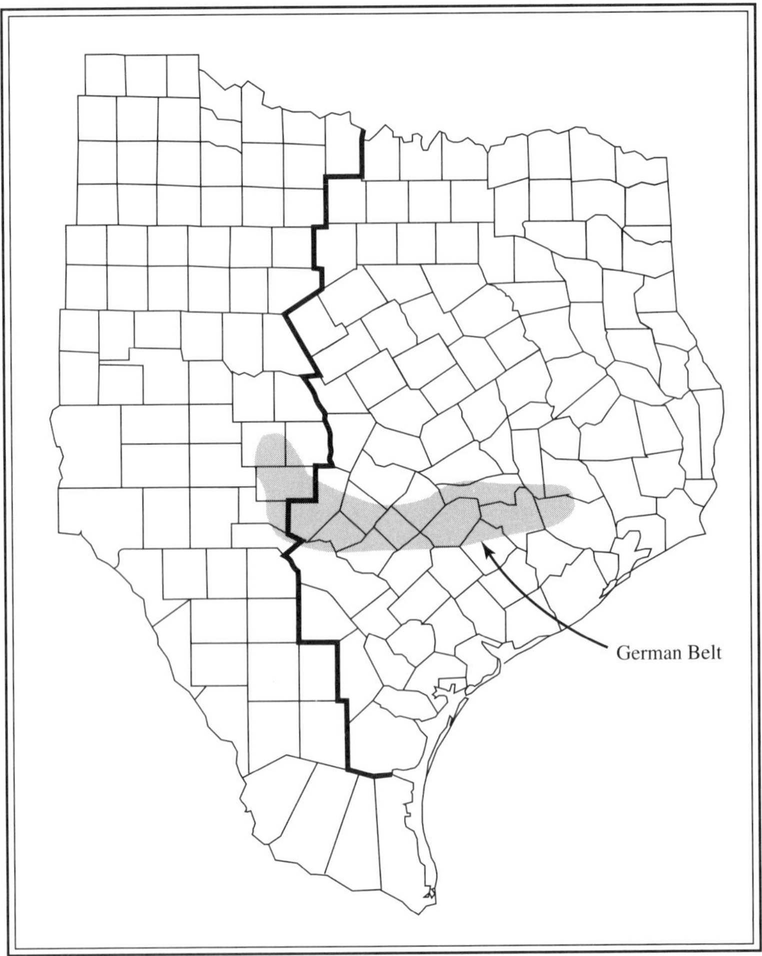

Antebellum Texas

cheap, rich land and pushed by political repression and revolution, lived in a belt stretching across the south-central part of the state from Galveston and Houston to Kerrville and Mason in the Hill Country. Along this "German Belt," especially in and around towns such as New Braunfels, there were islands of non-southern social and cultural institutions that could not be found in other slave states, except perhaps in large cities such as New Orleans. Some of these German residents disliked slavery, and most supported the Union. Nevertheless, they did not alter the essentially southern nature of the population, economy, and society of antebellum Texas.

Texas differed from the rest of the South, too, in having a southern frontier occupied primarily by citizens of Mexican rather than Anglo ancestry and a western frontier populated by Indians still strong enough to resist encroachments on their lands. These frontiers made Texas different; however, they did not have the voters or economic interests to control the state's government. Texans east of the ninety-eigth meridian—the region dominated by southerners and southern interests—determined what happened to the state during this era.

The Economy of Antebellum Texas

Antebellum Texas had the overwhelmingly agricultural economy typical of the Old South. Three-quarters of all families drew their livelihood from farming the state's plentiful land, which as late as 1860 generally sold for only five or six dollars per acre. And this was rich, virgin soil, capable of producing bountiful crops with only a minimum of effort. As one settler exclaimed, with perhaps a little of the famed Texas tendency toward exaggeration, "If you put ten-penny nails in the ground you will have a crop of iron bolts."

About two-thirds of the farmers in antebellum Texas, including an even greater percentage of the Germans, owned no slaves and practiced a subsistence or "safety-first" type of agriculture. That is, they focused on feeding their families before turning their energies to the production of a cash crop. Many of these farmers owned enough land to permit the cultivation of a market crop such as cotton—their farms averaged more than two hundred acres in size—but they did not have the labor to feed themselves and produce for the market as well. So, they grew corn and depended for meat on hogs that ranged free. There were some regional variations—for example, farmers in north-central Texas produced wheat—but the staple crops for nonslaveholding farmers statewide were corn and pork. Most also cultivated garden vegetables such as sweet potatoes and cabbage, kept a milk cow or two, and supplemented their food supply by hunting and fishing and the gathering of berries and edible plants. As the 1850s progressed, more and more of the nonslaveholding farmers, including the Germans, grew cotton to earn cash, but they did so on a small scale.

The one-third of antebellum Texas's farmers who owned slaves produced food for the people on their places and cultivated sizable cash crops as well. In addition to growing corn and vegetables and having hogs and at least a few milk cows and cattle, these farmers—nearly all of whom were Anglos—planted cotton and participated in the market economy. Farms owned by slaveholders were notably larger than those of their nonslaveholding counterparts, averaging about one thousand acres in size statewide, but their ability to produce a crop for sale depended on labor rather than land. Planting and cultivating cotton during the months from late winter to early summer took a good deal of manpower, but the greatest demand for workers came at picking time in the late summer and through the fall. With hard work and good luck, a nonslaveholder might produce a good crop, but without slaves he had very little chance of picking all of it. For this reason above all, farmers and planters who owned slaves produced 90 percent of all the cotton grown in antebellum Texas.

Texas soils typically produced one bale of cotton (weighing from 450 to 500 pounds) per acre, so as the increasing population of farmers and slaves brought more and more land into cultivation, the total crop skyrocketed. From an 1849 output of 58,072 bales, production rose to 431,463 bales in 1859, an increase of 643 percent in ten years. Even if allowances are made for the possibility that 1849 was a bad year and 1859 a good one, this was a spectacular growth in productivity. Texas rose from ninth to fifth among cotton-producing states during the 1850s.

Most of the planters and farmers who produced cotton with slave labor profited from their investments. One obvious piece of evidence supporting this claim is the way that they continued to pour money into slaves and land. Few people can afford to invest year after year in unprofitable ventures. Also, calculations using census data to match the expenses of producing cash crops, such as the costs of land and labor, against the returns, such as the proceeds from the sale of cotton and the value of the natural increase of slaves (their children), show returns of more than 6 percent in 1850 and 1860. Slaveholding farmers and planters in Texas were earning returns comparable to those that they would have received for putting their money into business loans in a northeastern city. When spokesmen of the Old South said "Cotton is King," Texans could only nod in assent.

Texas's slaveholding farmers also produced sugar, but only a handful of the state's counties along the lower Brazos and Colorado Rivers had the warm, wet weather and long growing season needed by that particular crop. Sugar production was further limited in Texas by the fact that it required sizable outlays of capital for processing cane into the final product. For example, Brazoria County, the center of sugar growing in Texas, had twenty-nine planters in 1852 who owned "sugar houses," the buildings that contained the boilers and steam kettles necessary to process sugarcane. The median value of these houses was $15,000, a significant investment when added to the costs of land and slaves on those plantations. Thus, Texas's climate and the fact that most Texas farmers could not afford the necessary capital outlay restricted the state's sugar industry to a handful of wealthy planters in a relatively small area.

A few Anglo migrants, especially among those living on the Gulf coastal prairies, focused on cattle raising rather than more traditional agricultural pursuits. James Taylor White of Liberty County in the southeastern corner of the state provides a good example. A native of Louisiana who came to Texas in 1828, he owned more than four thousand acres of land and nearly two thousand head of cattle in 1840 and remained a large herdsman until his death in 1852. His cattle roamed unimproved, unfenced land and fed on natural vegetation. Once a year White and other cattlemen in the region rounded up their livestock and branded the calves. Also, on an annual basis they met with buyers from New Orleans, their primary market, and made contracts to deliver cattle there. Then, following a practice developed by Tejanos in the eighteenth century, these Anglo cattlemen formed a trail herd and drove it eastward from Texas across southern Louisiana to the Crescent City.

Thus, the great majority of antebellum Texans drew their livelihood in one way or another directly from the land. Only about one-quarter of the state's families did not live on farms and depended on nonagricultural pursuits such as commerce, the professions, trades, and unskilled labor. Every county had at least one small town, usually the seat of local government, that was home to merchants and grocers; doctors, lawyers, and teachers; blacksmiths, carpenters, and gunsmiths; and wagoners and day laborers. These people largely served the farmers and planters of the surrounding countryside, so their well-being also depended heavily on crops and livestock, albeit indirectly. Antebellum Texas had a few towns—Galveston, Houston, and San Antonio being good examples—that were large enough to generate demand on their own for the services of merchants, professionals, and artisans, but they represented only the tiniest steps toward the building of cities that could forge links with other urban centers and generate economic momentum on their own. At least these larger towns provided employment in commerce and the trades to many foreign-born immigrants, especially the Germans.

The economy of antebellum Texas, like that of many states in the Old South, grew and developed during the 1840s and 1850s—but in only one way. Clearly, where agriculture was concerned, expansion occurred. Texans, older settlers and new arrivals alike, brought more land under cultivation and produced larger and more valuable crops nearly every year. Between 1850 and 1860, the amount of improved acreage in the state rose 305 percent, the corn crop 187 percent, and the cotton crop 643 percent (from 58,072 to 431,463 bales). However, this productive success of Texas agriculture was not matched by comparable advances in any other aspect of economic development. Like the rest of the South, the state lagged far behind in transportation, manufacturing, and urbanization.

Texas's great distances presented tremendous challenges to transportation before the Civil War. Most roads were little more than tracks through the woods and across the prairies, likely to be ankle-deep in dust in the summer and even deeper in mud during the spring and fall. Stagecoaches carried passengers, mail, and light freight along these roads, but such travel was generally uncomfortable and expensive. By 1861, Texas had thirty-one stage lines, including the famous Butterfield Overland Mail that crossed the state in a southwesterly direction from the Red River in Grayson County to El Paso on its way from St. Louis to San Francisco. Eight of the twenty-five days required for the entire trip from Missouri to California were spent bumping along in Texas at a cost of ten cents per mile. Heavy freight and cotton had to be shipped by wagons or oxcarts that moved even more slowly than stagecoaches and were just as costly.

Texas rivers from the Red to the Río Grande offered a somewhat better means of transporting people and goods than did the state's roads and were used for that purpose from the 1820s onward. By the 1840s shallow-draft steamboats ran on all major rivers, at times with amazing success. A boat called the *Kate Ward,* which could carry six hundred bales of cotton in three feet of water, ascended the Colorado to Austin in 1845. Another, the *Branch T. Archer,* traveled 350 miles up the Trinity. River transportation, however, was highly unreliable due to periodic low water, rafts of logs and brush, and sand bars. Steamboatmen might brag, like one on the Brazos, that he could "tap a keg of beer and run the boat four miles on the suds," but Texas rivers could never provide the transportation necessary to build an advanced economy. That would depend on the railroad.

Texans saw the need for railroads as early as 1836 when the First Congress of the Republic chartered a company to build tracks "from and to any such points . . . as selected." Promoters found it far easier, however, to obtain charters than to overcome the financial, organizational, and engineering problems involved in actually constructing a railroad. The Republic of Texas never had a mile of track, and statehood brought only limited success. Texas's first operational railroad, the Buffalo Bayou, Brazos, and Colorado Railway Company, received a charter from the legislature in 1850 to build a line from Harrisburg near Houston to Alleyton, a town eighty miles to the west on the Colorado River. Financed by a coalition of Texans and Bostonians, it began operating twenty miles of track to Stafford's Point in 1853, reached Richmond on the Brazos River in 1856, and began service to Alleyton by late 1860. The BBB&C, the first railroad in Texas and the second west of the Mississippi, eventually was absorbed by the Southern Pacific system and remains in use today as part of the Union Pacific.

As would be expected, railroad promoters, in the tradition of public assistance for private enterprise, looked to the state government for subsidies—and obtained them. The Texas Legislature in 1854 authorized granting sixteen sections of land (10,240 acres) for each mile of railroad completed, providing that at least twenty-five miles of track were built. Two years later it authorized loans of $6,000 per mile once twenty-five miles had been constructed. Encouraged by these incentives, dozens of railroads received charters in the 1850s, but for every company that actually operated, six came to nothing. By 1860, Texas had granted many thousands of acres and loaned nearly $2 million but had only about four hundred miles of railroad tracks, almost all radiating out from Houston. Only the San Antonio and Mexican Gulf Railroad, which ran from Port Lavaca to Victoria, and the Southern Pacific Railroad, which operated solely in Harrison County and is not be confused with the later system of that name, did not connect in some way with Houston. None of these railroads crossed into an adjoining state to provide land transportation to the larger world outside. They only ran from the interior to ports on or near the state's borders.

While the development of a transportation system lagged during the 1840s and 1850s, manufacturing remained virtually nonexistent. Only 1 percent of antebellum Texan families earned their livelihood from any form of industry, and most of them did not engage in anything close to large-scale production. Manufacturers of cotton gins, furniture, and wagons and carriages, for example, produced only for local markets, and the state had nothing like the textile, shoe, and iron industries of the Northeast. Antebellum Texans, surrounded by cotton fields and forests, imported cotton cloth and paper.

Texas's cities during these years amounted to little more than large towns by national standards. In 1860, San Antonio, which stood on the border between antebellum and South Texas, was the largest in the state with a population of 8,235, followed by Galveston with 7,307 residents, Houston with 4,800, and Austin with 3,500. The heads of more than half of the families in these four towns were Mexican or foreign-born. Marshall was the metropolis of East Texas with a population of about 2,000, and Dallas, the future giant of North Texas, had fewer than 500 people. By contrast, Milwaukee, Wisconsin, the major city in a state that entered the Union slightly later than Texas, reported a population of 45,246 in 1860. Antebellum Texans, especially the Anglos, simply were not urban dwellers.

Reasons for the lack of diversified economic development in antebellum Texas are complex and debatable, but first and foremost there is geography. Texas's natural resources, especially its land and climate, gave agriculture an advantage and at the same time retarded other forms of economic activity. Its rivers, for example, deposited rich alluvial soils to grow crops, but they did not fall steeply enough (like those in New England by contrast) to provide water power for industries. What other source of power available at that time could would-be Texas manufacturers have exploited? Perhaps steam engines fired by wood could have been successful for a while, but their large-scale use would have soon threatened even the extensive forests of East Texas. The state's geography, particularly its sheer size and lack of dependably navigable rivers, also made transportation difficult, and that in turn discouraged the rise of manufacturing and urbanization.

Slavery was second only to geography in making and keeping antebellum Texas an overwhelmingly agricultural economy and society. In the first place, the profitability of producing cotton and sugar with slave labor meant that the planters, the state's richest and most enterprising businessmen, had no reason to look for other types of investment. Why would a man who earned acceptable returns from agriculture put his money into a risky venture such as, for example, cotton textile manufacturing? Planters did not have their capital "tied up," as some like to say, in slaves. Slave property could be liquidated easily. But planters had no economic or financial reason to do so. Moreover, the agrarian lifestyle, which was so much a part of their culture, discouraged any thought of diversification. Many Texas planters involved themselves to some extent in developing railroads, and a few invested in manufacturing enterprises, but even for those men such ventures remained peripheral to planting. Texas's leading capitalists maintained a firm commitment to agriculture, slavery, and southern agrarian values.

Slavery also contributed to the state's limited economic diversity by drastically limiting the number of free consumers in the population. Obviously, businesses and industries thrive only where there are large numbers of people with enough money to buy what is produced and sold. However, nearly one-third of antebellum Texans, the slaves, through no choice of their own, had virtually nothing to spend and no ability to use transportation facilities. This circumstance compounded the problems of developing manufacturing and building railroads in an agricultural economy.

Finally, a long-standing political bias against banking in particular and corporations in general retarded commercial and industrial development in Texas. Most early Texans were Democrats who remembered Andrew Jackson's fight with that "hydra of corruption," the Second Bank of the United States. Moreover, many blamed losses suffered in the Panic of 1837 on the various state banks. The Constitution of 1845 prohibited banking in Texas and required every corporation to obtain a charter from the legislature, thereby creating a serious deterrent to economic expansion in the new state.

The Social Structure of Antebellum Texas

The booming agricultural economy of antebellum Texas created considerable social mobility among whites, particularly in the sense of families improving their standing in the community; nevertheless; the region's free population had a class structure with a distinctly southern look. At the apex stood the slaveholding planters, the owners of a disproportionately large share of the state's slaves and land. The usual definition of "planter" in the Old South required the ownership of twenty or more slaves, but in Texas as late as 1860 only 3 percent of families met that standard. Another 5 percent, however, were small planters who owned from ten to nineteen bondsmen and often were expanding their holdings rapidly. Therefore, in the case of antebellum Texas it is reasonable to include small planters with larger planters in the upper class. The further inclusion of wealthy merchants and professionals, virtually all of whom owned a few slaves but whose status rested on commercial or urban property, completes the list of the richest people in antebellum Texas. Defined here as those worth at least $10,000 in 1860, this wealthiest 15 percent of all families owned almost 75 percent of all the slaves and other forms of property in their part of the state.

Members of the upper-income class, even the few very large slaveholders, did not live like South Carolina nabobs or Natchez-area aristocrats, but generally they had the best homes and highest standard of living in antebellum Texas. Immediately upon arriving in the state, planter families generally constructed log cabins of only one or two rooms with a loft sleeping space, and some smaller planters could always be found living in such homes. Most, however, as soon as they established themselves and began to prosper, moved to more substantial homes or built onto or around the original log cabin. Jared Groce, the first large slaveholder in Texas, demonstrated that even a log structure could be impressive. His Brazos River home, "Bernardo," was built with hewn cottonwood logs, but his slave craftsmen gave it a fine appearance by making the logs perfectly square and as smooth as glass. Across its front, which extended fifty-five feet, ran a broad porch supported by six polished walnut posts. Groce's son-in-law, William H. Wharton, built one of the first frame houses in Texas at "Eagle Island" and hired a Scottish gardener to tend a garden filled with more than five hundred imported plants. By the 1840s, wealthier planters began to construct their homes of brick. For example, John J. Webster, who owned eighty slaves and a plantation northeast of Marshall in Harrison County, had his craftsmen fire brick and in 1844 build a Greek Revival mansion called "Mimosa Hall." With its large windows, high ceilings, and column-lined veranda, Webster's home still stands, as does the nearby C.

"Mimosa Hall," Plantation Home of the John J. Webster Family in Harrison County. Built in 1844 by slaves, this house still stands in the countryside northeast of Marshall, Texas. Credit: From the Collections of the Harrison Country Historical Museum, Marshall, Texas.

K. Andrews house built by the same slaves in 1845. (During the early twentieth century, Claudia Alta Taylor, who became famous as Lady Bird Johnson, grew up in the Andrews house.)

Well-to-do merchants and professionals in Texas's towns matched planters in building fine homes. For example, Michael B. Menard, one of Galveston's first businessmen, had a two-story frame home with high ceilings, large doors, windows that came nearly to the floor, wide stairways, and broad verandas. This construction was typical of the Queen City because it provided the greatest possible enjoyment of the cooling breezes off the Gulf of Mexico. The San Augustine home of James Pinckney Henderson, a leading lawyer and politician, was modeled on a Virginia mansion with upper and lower galleries supported by large columns. James H. Raymond, state treasurer and an Austin businessman, built a two-story Greek Revival home in Austin during the 1850s. Designed and constructed by Abner Cook, the architect of the Texas Governor's Mansion, the Raymond House had a portico across its entire front supported by six Ionic columns.

All major rooms in Texas homes were heated by fireplaces, which gave architects and builders an opportunity to display their decorative abilities by creating marble hearths and ornate mantels. Fortunately, since fireplaces are always a more decorative than efficient means of heating, Texas had a generally mild climate. Even then some Texans forsook the fireplace for a more effective free-standing Franklin stove.

Many planters and well-to-do merchants, even in the 1830s and 1840s, had fine furniture, drapes, silver, and china, which they either brought with them as they migrated from the Old South or imported after arriving in Texas. Tastes in furniture inclined toward heavy, elegant pieces made of mahogany, walnut, and rosewood. Parlors, lighted by brass chandeliers, had sofas, huge ornate mirrors, and often a grand piano. The sale of twenty-three grand pianos in Galveston alone in 1858 is an indication of that particular instrument's popularity. Dining rooms were furnished with long tables to accommodate large families and numerous guests as well as marble-topped sideboards from which to serve meals. Bedrooms usually had four-poster, canopy-topped beds and smaller trundle beds that could be pushed under the larger ones when not in use by children. Each bedroom also had a washstand with a bowl and pitcher on top and a chamber pot in the bottom compartment. Virtually no Texas home had an indoor bathroom, a circumstance that probably did not bother residents much since they tended to believe that daily bathing weakened the body. However, for those too fastidious to get by with sponge baths, there were tin bathtubs that could be placed near a fireplace and filled with heated water. Outdoor toilets or privies were located near, but not attached to, the main house.

Kitchens in upper-class Texan homes, whether part of the main house or a separate building, had large fireplaces in which all the cooking was done. Cooks used pots that hung on iron cranes and swung over the fire, skillets and pots that sat on trivets above hot coals, and a variety of pots that could be set among the coals to prepare foods typical of the South in that age. Above all, they prepared meat. "These Texans," wrote future president Rutherford B. Hayes after a visit to the Brazos River Valley in 1848, "are essentially carnivorous. Pork ribs, pigs' feet, veal beef (grand), chickens, venison and dried meat frequently seen on the table at once." Undoubtedly, he saw wild turkey, fish, and oysters as well. Corn provided bread in many forms, whereas wheat flour was an expensive delicacy, even for wealthy planter families. Sweet potatoes and black-eyed peas were the basic vegetables, and many enjoyed grapes, figs, and peaches in season. Families drank milk fresh because refrigeration was lacking, and consumed huge quantities of strong black coffee, as many as fifteen to twenty cups a day.

Where clothing was concerned, members of upper-class families were far more likely than other Texans to have ready-to-wear garments purchased at stores or ordered from merchants in a city such as New Orleans. Everyday wear had to be practical, but visits to town and special social occasions provided the best opportunities to show off sartorial splendor. For example, a fashionable young woman might appear on the street in a black silk dress that reached to her ankles, a white cape embroidered with lace, and a pink satin bonnet. On her feet she wore black slippers. Men wore black frock coats, elaborately adorned waistcoats, shirts with ruffled fronts, and black string cravats. They favored hats with low crowns and wide, floppy brims and military or Wellington-style boots. A special occasion, such as the San Jacinto ball in Houston, would bring out planters' wives in velvet and silk gowns and the husbands in frock coats or military uniforms and white dancing slippers. Sam Houston, although a lawyer and political leader rather than a planter, matched their style in 1837 by attending the ball in a gold-corded black velvet suit with ruffled shirt and crimson waistcoat. Gentlemen, of course, carried a pistol, either a revolver or smaller derringer, and a knife, probably worn in a leather sheath, as accessories.

The great majority of antebellum Texans, of course, did not have the housing, food, and clothing enjoyed by the upper class. Instead, some two-thirds of the free population, mostly southern-born Anglos but including many German immigrants as well, formed a less well-to-do middle class. Often called the yeoman class or the plain folk (a term usually applied only to southern Anglos), these people owned a relatively small share of land and other forms of property. Most were farmers, but skilled tradesmen such as blacksmiths and carpenters fell into this class as did teachers, clerks, and other assorted town dwellers. A handful held small numbers of slaves, but most owned none. To give precise statistics, in 1860, the middle class, defined as families owning from $500 to $10,000 worth of property, amounted to 60 percent of the total and owned only 26 percent of all wealth.

The first houses in Texas for Anglo plain folk and German yeomen alike were cabins built of rough-hewn logs with the spaces between the logs chinked with any available material. Split pieces of wood or boards held in place by rocks or heavy poles laid across them and secured with pegs made a roof. Packed earth served as a floor unless the builder had time to construct one of puncheons—split logs with the flat sides up. Fireplaces provided heat and a place to cook, but their chimneys, often built of sticks and mud, were a constant fire hazard. Although some cabins had only one room and a lean-to for additional space, the most common type had two rooms connected by a covered breezeway or "dog trot" that allowed ventilation. Internal furnishings generally consisted of homemade tables and chairs and beds that were built in corners and attached to the wall so that they needed only one leg on the floor.

Some Anglo plain folk eventually improved their log cabins by weatherboarding them on the outside, adding wings or second stories, and building stone chimneys. Germans, however, tended to replace their log cabins with more substantial structures as soon as possible. In the eastern end of the German Belt centering on Austin County, they built frame houses and turned the original cabins into barns or chicken houses. Farther west in the Hill Country, German Texans constructed small houses of stone and also used the half-timbering *(Fachwerk)* method found in their homeland. Middle-class town dwellers followed the same pattern as the Germans, living at first in log cabins but then erecting frame homes. Visitors to Galveston in the 1850s, for example, commented on the town's numerous clapboard houses kept white with lime whitewash or oil paint. Other towns from Marshall in the northeast to Indianola on the Gulf coast similarly passed beyond the log cabin stage, except on the outskirts where new arrivals built whatever they could afford.

The diet of Anglo plain folk depended on pork, beef, wild game, corn bread, sweet potatoes, and coffee, differing notably from wealthier Texans only in having fewer fruits. Germans ate essentially the same foods, although they added white potatoes when possible. Some observers claimed that the Germans paid more attention to gardening than did Anglos and should be credited with introducing vegetable gardens to Texas, but this is an exaggeration. The great majority of middle-class Texans, whatever their ethnic background, grew and consumed vegetables.

Plain folk families generally dressed in clothing made of homespun cotton and wool. Women and girls carded, spun, and wove fibers into cloth, which they dyed with the juices of berries and nuts and sewed into dresses, pants, shirts, and coats. Heavy blankets served as overcoats. Even shoes of deer or cow hides were made at home. This clothing was serviceable, but probably the first thing that plain folk spent money on as their finances improved was "store-boughten" shoes and manufactured cloth from which to make Sunday dresses. Throughout the antebellum years, however, only a rare person in the middle class—probably one living in a larger town—dressed daily in ready-to-wear clothing.

Some observers found the homes and food of antebellum Texas's Anglo plain folk appalling. The most famous of these critics, Frederick Law Olmsted, a travel writer who is best known as the designer of Central Park in New York City, visited Texas in 1853–1854. He entered the state at Gaines's Ferry on the Sabine River, crossed East Texas to San Antonio, made that city the base for side trips to the Gulf coast and Mexico, and then left by way of Houston and Beaumont. Olmsted's account of this trip, published in 1857 as *A Journey Through Texas,* described attempting to sleep in cabins with roofs that had holes through which he could see the stars and walls with openings between the logs large enough for him to place both of his hands, one on the other. East Texans' diets, he wrote, consisted invariably of fried pork or beef, corn bread, and coffee, which he called the "black decoction of the South . . . than which it is often difficult to imagine any beverage more revolting." Even when he reached Austin, his hotel was "exceedingly dirty," had a latchless door that could not be closed when it blew open during a norther, and offered meals that were "a succession of burnt flesh of swine and bulls, decaying vegetables, and sour and mouldy farinaceous glues, all pervaded with rancid butter." To some extent Olmsted's strong antislavery views influenced his observations—he found the Germans, whom he identified as opponents of slavery, just as attractive as he found the proslavery white southerners appalling—but it is probable that many of the plain folk had the kind of housing and food that he described. Yet they flourished, and thousands more like them came to Texas every year in the 1840s and 1850s.

The bottom rung of the free population's social ladder was occupied by poor whites, a highly mobile class of people that in any one year included a notable proportion of antebellum Texans. In 1860, for example, the poorest 25 percent of families, those with total wealth of less than $500, owned only 1 percent of all property. Most of these poor whites were farmers who had not yet acquired land of their own and worked someone else's on a rent or share arrangement. Others earned their livelihood as overseers, day laborers, and clerks. Some were young members of middle-class families just striking off on their own who, therefore, only appeared to have little or no stake in society. In any case, poor whites tended either to move up the economic ladder where they were or move on in search of opportunity elsewhere. Those who lived out their years in poverty—a smaller group than could be found in this class at any particular time—constituted antebellum Texas's version of the degraded "poor white trash" so often mentioned in accounts of the Old South. They played no major role in the state's settlement or development.

Finally, the free population of antebellum Texas included a small group of African Americans who were not slaves. Too few to constitute a class—the census listed fewer than four hundred in the state in both 1850 and 1860—these free blacks had importance beyond their numbers. First, in the eyes of most whites, their presence threatened slavery by demonstrating that blacks were capable of freedom and thus encouraging unrest among those who were enslaved. Consequently, harsh constitutional and statutory restrictions on free blacks existed throughout the antebellum years. After 1836 no "free person of color" (defined until 1858 as having one-fourth or more African blood and thereafter as having one-eighth African blood) could live in Texas without the permission of the legislature. A few gained such approval during the 1830s and 1840s; virtually none after 1850. Those free blacks permitted to stay in Texas were often subjected to the same laws as slaves. For example, all the crimes such as rebellion or rape of a white female that were capital offenses if committed by slaves were to be punished in the same way if a free black was the offender.

Health and Medical Care

Antebellum Texans loved to boast about the healthfulness of their region, but in reality virtually all, regardless of social class, suffered from diseases common to the southern United States. Most newcomers contracted malaria during their first spring or summer in Texas and endured its chills and fever intermittently for years thereafter. Devastating epidemics of yellow fever also broke out in warm weather, especially in the seaport towns. For example, an outbreak in Galveston in 1844 killed four hundred people, and another in 1853 took 535 lives. William Pitt Ballinger, a leading attorney, had four children die of the fever, and Ferdinand Flake, the German newspaper editor, lost five in various epidemics. Pneumonia attacked during the cold season, and dysentery was always present. Influenza appeared for the first time in 1845, and whooping cough began to take its toll the next year.

Texans, like other Americans of that time, had only a limited understanding at best of the causes of these diseases. Malaria, for example, was attributed to everything from "miasma" rising out of the swamps to becoming overly excited during political campaigns, and only a few noted the apparent advantages of avoiding mosquito bites. The government of Galveston, the town hardest hit by yellow fever, did virtually nothing to drain stagnant pools of water or enforce sanitary regulations concerning the outhouses that stood behind every home. Quarantines, which would have reduced the spread of contagions, also generally went unenforced.

Doctors were numerous in antebellum Texas and also expensive, charging three to five dollars for a house call. Some had attended the best medical schools available and applied their knowledge and skills with some success under the most difficult of circumstances. For example, Ashbel Smith, who studied at Yale and in Paris and served as surgeon-general of the Texan army, performed successful breast surgery on Mrs. Margaret Lea Houston in 1847. He offered her whiskey as an anesthetic, but she, as a teetotaler who was working to reform her hard-drinking husband, refused and bit on a silver coin during the operation. Overall, however, the state of medical science meant that even the best-educated doctors often were powerless against serious diseases. Indeed, in many cases the care of a physician was at least as dangerous as the illness itself. For example, doctors commonly treated malaria by the "puke, purge, and bleed" technique, an approach that provided no cure but could either kill the patient outright or so weaken him that he died of some other disease. "My indisposition was of short duration," wrote a Galveston-area resident in 1841, "but the d——d Doctor came near Physicking me to death. He poured it into me at *both ends* for 24 hours without cessation—making an apothecary shop of my abdomen." In the late 1840s some doctors made a major advance in medical practice by adopting the use of quinine as a treatment for malaria, but in general their efforts remained largely ineffective. Child mortality was especially high, running at about 50 percent in coastal areas.

Given the suffering associated with disease and the relative inability of even the best doctors to effect cures, it is not surprising that antebellum Texans were receptive to medical quacks and patent medicines. Totally uneducated men became "doctors" simply by claiming that they had medical training and took advantage of the sick by selling cures of every sort imaginable. "These pseudo 'M.Ds' or 'Drs,'" said one Houston newspaper, "are, we sincerely believe more dangerous than the hostile Indians; and not considerably less numerous." Educated practitioners made efforts from time to time to form associations and establish standards for physicians, but even the Texas Medical Association, created in 1853, had little importance before the Civil War. Texans continued to patronize quacks and, of course, to buy the numerous patent medicines advertised in the state's newspapers. They ate buckets of pills and drank gallons of tonics such as Sanford's Family Blood Purifying Pills, Hostetter's Stomach Bitters, and Dr. Larzetti's Juno Cordial or Procreative Elixir (possibly a precursor of Viagra).

Slaves in Antebellum Texas

In another wonderful historical irony, while southern whites and Germans poured into antebellum Texas of their own accord, the most rapidly increasing group of people in the region—slaves of African descent—had no voice in the decision to migrate. Most came with their masters as they moved from the Old South. Others, although not a majority, entered Texas as merchandise sold through the interstate slave trade. The state's newspapers during the 1840s and 1850s regularly carried advertisements placed by slave traders in New Orleans and Shreveport as well as those in Galveston and Houston. For example, McMurry and Winstead of Galveston informed would-be customers that "we have made arrangements for fresh supplies during the season and will always have on hand a good assortment of field hands, house servants and mechanics." Whether brought by their owners or sold from older slave states, these forced migrants generally knew the meaning of "GTT." Most had no desire to be uprooted from their homes and moved, but they simply had to make the best of their situation. By 1860, they amounted to one-third of all antebellum Texans, constituting a "mudsill class" at the bottom of the social ladder that provided the labor on which much of the state's growth rested. (See map: Distribution of Slaves in Texas, 1860.)

A majority of Texas slaves belonged to farmers who owned at least ten bondsmen, so their daily working lives can be discussed in terms of agricultural labor. This meant, in the words of one, "Us ain't never idle." The work necessary to grow cotton, corn, lesser crops, and gardens; take care of livestock; build fences and dig ditches; and clear new ground left little leisure time. Most slaves, male and female alike, labored at both the cultivation of crops and the myriad everyday chores. Men generally did the heaviest work, such as cutting trees and plowing, but women sowed corn and cotton seed and worked as hoe hands. Virtually all were pressed into service as cotton pickers during the height of the season. Children worked from the age of ten or twelve—gathering firewood, carrying water, and knocking down old cotton stalks.

Working hours extended, as one slave put it, "from can see to can't see," meaning days of about twelve hours in the summer and ten in the winter. The work week extended until at least noon on Saturday. Some owners made it a practice to give their slaves Saturday afternoons off, but others did not. Nearly all, however, gave Sunday as a day of rest, except during cotton picking season.

A minority of the slaves on farms and plantations, perhaps 10 to 20 percent, spent their time at tasks other than field labor. Generally, these bondsmen had special training or skills. Men worked as blacksmiths, carpenters, brickmasons, and tanners; women as cooks, laundresses, spinners, and weavers. Some male and female slaves also worked in and around the household as servants. These non-field workers had in one sense, at least, an easier daily routine than the others. They did not work outdoors all day under the summer sun or in the winter cold, and their jobs were generally less burdensome physically. However, their hours were equally long, and they were likely to be under closer supervision by whites.

A small minority—5 percent or less—of Texas slaves lived in towns. Most of the women were domestic servants, and the men worked primarily as day laborers. Enough of the men became skilled mechanics that white workers in

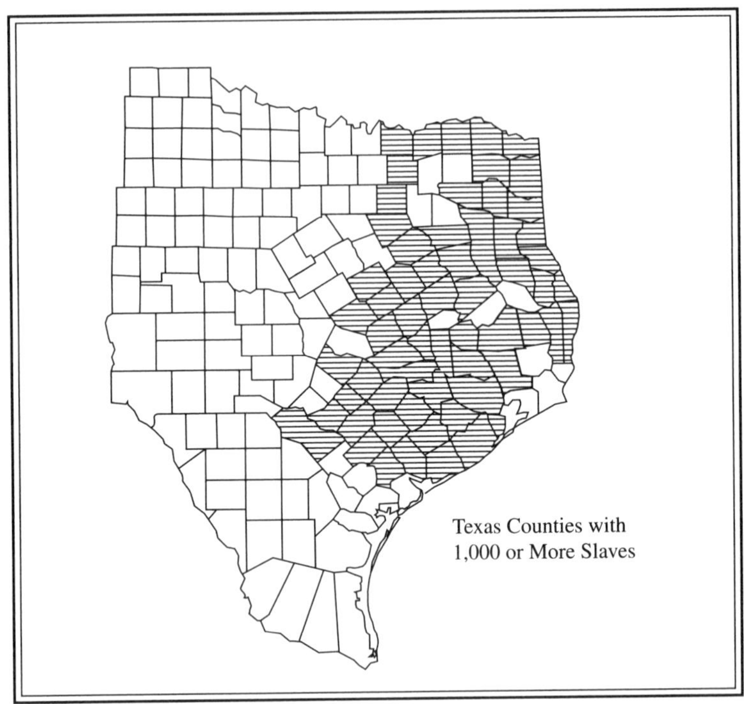

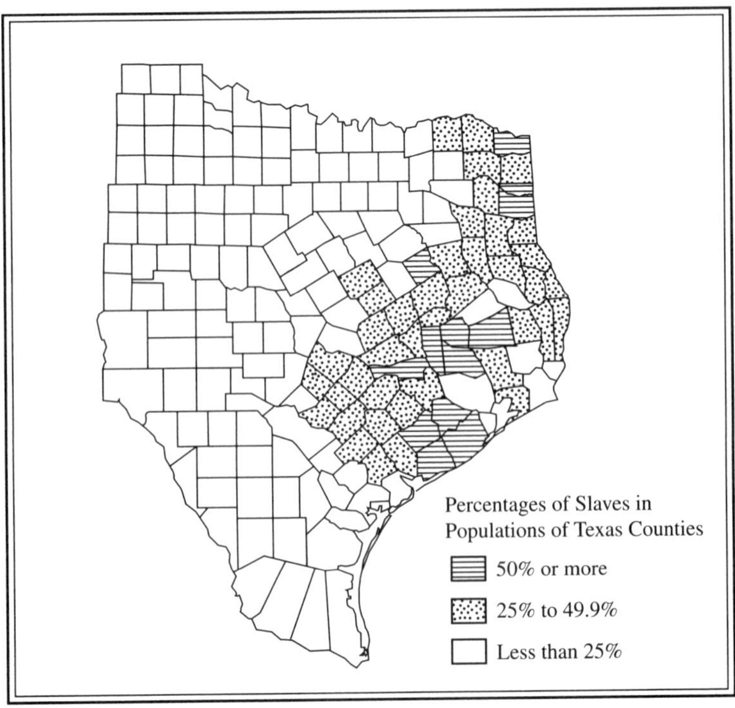

Distribution of Slaves in Texas, 1860

both Houston and Marshall during the 1850s organized to demand that they not take work away from free mechanics. These "urban" slaves generally enjoyed better working conditions than their farm counterparts and were able to associate among themselves with a good deal of freedom. Few would have willingly changed places with a plantation slave.

In return for their labor, slaves generally received food, housing, clothing, and medical care at, or only a little above, subsistence levels. Owners obviously had an interest in maintaining the health and strength of bondsmen who represented by far their greatest investment, but at the same time most sought to keep costs at a minimum. Slaves therefore could expect to have the basics of life, but not much more.

Slaves, like poorer whites, ate primarily corn and pork, both of which were high in energy-producing calories. A few planters had common kitchens to prepare food for all their slaves, but most gave out weekly rations of corn and pork and permitted slave families to fix their own meals as they saw fit. Some Texas slaves suffered from not having enough to eat or from nutritional deficiencies due to the way foods were preserved and prepared, but most supplemented their diets with sweet potatoes, which were grown in large quantities on Texas farms, and with garden vegetables and wild game, which they supplied themselves. In general slaves ate as well or better than did poor whites.

Slave housing usually consisted of a log cabin for each family. On the average, five people lived in a single twenty-by-twenty square foot room. Having dirt floors, a window with shutters rather than glass, a fireplace for heating and cooking, and little in the way of furniture except beds attached to the walls, these small houses afforded some protection against the elements but little comfort. They were likely to be crowded, ill-furnished, and cold or hot depending on the season.

The clothing worn by slaves was less satisfactory to them than their housing. Owners generally had their slave seamstresses make new clothes to be distributed twice a year. In the spring men received two pairs of pants, two shirts, a hat, and a pair of shoes, and women were given two dresses, two chemises, and a pair of shoes. Children up to the age of ten to twelve wore only long shirts and received no shoes until they began to work in the field. Clothing for the winter was the same, except that men and women who worked outdoors were given jackets or coats. Men received hats, but women did not. Some owners provided handkerchiefs, but none gave underwear or socks. Summer clothing made of cotton was reasonably comfortable, but winter outfits made of coarse woolen cloth or wool-cotton blends rubbed and scratched. "Negro shoes," made without specific sizing from notoriously stiff leather and worn without socks, did nearly as much damage to feet from the inside as they protected against from the outside.

When Texas slaves suffered the great variety of illnesses that afflicted residents of the state in the nineteenth century—fevers and pneumonia, for example—and the numerous accidental injuries to be expected among farm workers, their owners generally brought in doctors to provide medical attention. To repeat, any rational master would want to protect the health of such valuable property. Doctors of that time, however, had so little knowledge that they were powerless in dealing with many diseases and injuries. Inadequate medical science obviously took a toll on whites as well as blacks, but the slaves generally worked at harder and more dangerous jobs and therefore suffered more illnesses and injuries.

In addition to constant work and subsistence-level material conditions, Texas slaves had to live daily with the possibility of physical punishment. State law permitted masters to demand "obedience and submission" from their slaves and to inflict punishments, most commonly whippings, necessary to that end. Slaves received whippings for many reasons, including running away, fighting, insolence, and unsatisfactory work. Some escaped such punishment because their masters did not believe in it; others had the misfortune to belong to owners who, in the words of one, "had to beat somebody every day." In any case, all slaves lived with the frightening knowledge that they could be whipped anytime at the whim of their masters. As one woman runaway told her owner after she was caught and asked if she had not been afraid of wild animals in the woods where she hid: "I'm more scared of you than the animals, they don't whip."

Some slaves suffered whippings and other punishments that went beyond discipline and became cruelty and even murder. For example, in 1861 William Wilson of Harris County killed one of his slaves by inflicting six hundred lashes with a "gutta percha strap." Laws protected bondsmen from such extremes, but juries virtually never convicted whites of serious offenses against blacks. Charged with murder and with cruel and unusual punishment, Wilson escaped conviction on the first count and paid a $2,000 fine when convicted on the second. In the final analysis, as Justice James H. Bell of the Texas Supreme Court put it, punishment of slaves was "left to the master's judgment, discretion, and humanity." Every slave in antebellum Texas knew that owners varied greatly in the degree to which they possessed those qualities.

Faced with a lifetime of manual labor under subsistence-level material conditions and subject to harsh punishments at the whim of their masters, slaves had to reach out to each other as well as within themselves to find the psychological strength to endure. Most had the good fortune to live on farms or plantations with ten or more other slaves and therefore were in a position to take advantage of the old adage about strength in numbers. They used their families, religious beliefs, and music to build a "culture" that helped them survive the mental and emotional assault of slavery.

Slaves had no legal rights of marriage and the family, but most were reared and lived a large part of their lives in a family setting. Owners had an interest in encouraging the formation of families, in that marriage promoted the production of valuable slave children in a socially acceptable way—deliberate "breeding" being too inhumane for most. Moreover, people with family ties were more easily controlled than those who had none. So masters generally encouraged marriages, and slaves were happy to comply. Sometimes the ceremony consisted of nothing more than jumping over a broomstick together (the first one over would "rule" the family); on other occasions ministers officiated and the whole community attended. Even then, of course, the marriage had no legal standing.

Families gave slaves others on whom they depended and who depended on them, creating an identity and a sense of worth very important to survival. Yet the family also could bring almost unbearable pain when it was disrupted by sales, gifts, and migrations. Some masters took care not to separate family members, but others showed no concern at all when they decided to sell bondsmen or wrote wills distributing property to their heirs. Husbands, wives, and children faced the heartrending experience of permanent separation from each other. They cried, in the words of one slave, "like they at the funeral when they am parted, they has to drag them away." Some—like a woman in San Patricio County who stopped the sale of her daughter by promising to cut her throat unless the child was taken off the block—went so far as to threaten suicide in order to prevent the disruption of their families. When slaves' families were broken up, fathers, mothers, and children did the best they could to stay in contact and visit each other.

Many, and perhaps most, slave families were disrupted; certainly every slave lived with the knowledge that his or her family could be broken up at the whim or need of their owner. And yet this basic part of their lives survived, providing much of the love and support necessary to endure slavery.

Slaves found religion second only to their families as a source of strength in surviving the psychological assault of enslavement. This was true, however, only after bondsmen sorted through the spiritual messages that they received. Masters generally wanted their slaves to learn that, as one traveler put it, "a good christian is not a bad servant." So thousands were permitted to join, or at least attend the services at, the familiar Protestant denominations such as Methodist and Baptist, where white ministers told them to be "obedient, industrious, trusty, and faithful," in order to win eternal salvation. But Christianity carried another message—the promise of equality before God in the next life and possibly even deliverance in this one—and slaves could glean that from the sermons they heard. This was especially true when they attended services conducted by slave preachers, whom the Methodists and Baptists in particular allowed to take the pulpit. "Emancipation wouldn't have come," a former slave insisted years later, "if it hadn't been for the prayers of my mother and grandmother."

Finally, slaves used music as a way of adjusting to servitude. They sang to set a pace for their work and as a means of communication. Hands at work on their own, for example, often placed a lookout who sang a particular song to warn that they were about to receive a visit from the overseer. Above all, it seems, slaves used music to protest against bondage and express their hopes for freedom. "We hummed our religious songs in the field while we was working," one slave remembered. "It was our way of praying for freedom, but the white folks didn't know it."

Slaves adopted a variety of behavior patterns in response to their circumstances as human property. Obviously, behavior was an individual matter, but most bondsmen fell into one of three general categories. A minority behaved as loyal servants who identified with their masters and were obedient and faithful. As one old man put it when asked why slaves had not done more to help the North win the Civil War: "We couldn't help [but] stick to our masters. We could no more shoot them than we could fly." Of course, the extent to which such slaves internalized the behavior patterns of the loyal servant as opposed to engaging in deliberate accommodation for the purpose of getting along will never be known.

Other bondsmen hated their masters and rebelled in numerous ways, large and small. An East Texas slave spoke for these people: "If there is a Hell; old Master sure went there for the way he used the innocent Negroes." Some acted on their hatred simply by day-to-day troublemaking. They worked grudgingly, broke equipment, mistreated livestock, and constantly misbehaved. For example, the administrator of an estate in Washington County told the probate court that Kate, one of the slaves at his disposal, was "so vicious and unmanageable that when hired out no person to whom she was hired would keep her." Kate and many others like her were anything but loyal servants.

Other slaves took their resistance to the point of running away. Some runaways headed back to the homes and families they had left when removed to Texas; some attempted just to hide out in the neighborhood; but thousands headed for Mexico. Mexico would not extradite slaves, making the land across the Río Grande, in the words of a San Antonio newspaper, a "Paradise for happiness" among Texas bondsmen. By 1844, thirty fugitives, including two who had belonged to Sam Houston, were reported living at Matamoros. Slaves did not run away in numbers large enough to threaten the existence of the Peculiar Institution in Texas, but that form of resistance constantly worried the state's slaveowners.

Slaves' ultimate expression of hatred and rebellion, of course, was organized insurrection aimed at freeing large numbers of bondsmen and killing their masters. The whole period of slavery in Texas, however, saw only one attempted uprising—in Colorado County during October 1835—and one or two plots that were exaggerated by slaveholders eager to blame "abolitionists" for causing trouble. Of course, insurrection or even plotting an insurrection meant certain death for those involved if they failed.

Most Texas slaves adopted a behavior pattern that involved being neither a loyal servant nor a rebel of any sort. This meant taking a clear-eyed view of owners and seeing that no one who held human property deserved great respect or loyalty. A slave named Josephine Howard put this view well. "I reckon old [Master] Tim," she said, "wasn't no worse than other white folks that owned slaves." At the same time, this behavior pattern meant recognizing that open resistance generally brought heavy punishment and that some degree of accommodation was necessary. In the words of Mollie Dawson : "It hurt us sometimes to be treated the way some of us was treated, but we couldn't help ourselves and had to do the best we could which nearly all of us done."

Finally, regardless of how they behaved from day to day, most slaves lived daily with a desire for freedom. Even those who belonged to benign owners such as Mrs. Isaac Van Zandt, a woman so generous that other whites referred to her slaves as "Van Zandt's free negroes," dreamed of emancipation. "All of the Van Zandt negroes wanted to be free," one said later. Mary Gaffney spoke for the majority. The only thing we thought about, she said, was "not being a slave because slavery time was hell." Keeping alive the dream of freedom amidst the "hell" of slavery was the ultimate testimonial to the human spirit of the enslaved blacks and their ability to build and maintain the mental and emotional strength to endure servitude.

Social Institutions and Life in Antebellum Texas

Given the overwhelmingly southern character of the population, economy, and social structure of antebellum Texas, it is hardly surprising that the region's religious and educational institutions and cultural practices in general mirrored those of the Old South. Most of the ministers and teachers who migrated to Texas beginning in the 1830s had received their spiritual and academic training in the older slave states. When they crossed the Sabine or Red River or landed at Galveston, they arrived with and among their own kind of people.

Formal religion in the shape of organized church congregations had a difficult time taking root in Texas because of the distances separating people of the same spiritual persuasion, a scarcity of missionaries, and inability or unwillingness of busy frontiersmen to observe the Sabbath. Gradually, however, churches in the evangelical tradition of the Old South emerged. Methodist missionaries began to work during the late 1830s with a tenacity that amused at least one observer. "The backwoodsman has gone into the forest," he wrote, "and the panther is scarcely more keen scented for his blood than the Methodist preacher for his soul." By 1860, these ministers' success in bringing the "Methodist excitement"—a highly emotional brand of religion—to Texas earned their denomination more than thirty thousand members, far outnumbering all others. The Baptist Church, whose missionaries also went to work after the revolution, stood second among denominations in 1860, followed by Presbyterians of the Cumberland and "Old School" varieties. The Cumberland Presbyterians, who broke away from the main church as a result of frontier revivalism during the 1820s, accepted uneducated ministers whereas the "Old School" churches insisted on an educated ministry. The Episcopal Church, which appealed primarily to the planter elite and town dwellers, had relatively few congregations in antebellum Texas. Recently created denominations such as the Disciples of Christ existed but gave little indication before 1860 of the strong position that they would eventually attain in the state.

Although in the words of one young woman, "the theologians of the different schools pronounced a sufficient variety of dogmas to daunt the souls and bewilder the minds of ordinary mortals," the teachings of the various denominations had little if any basic difference. They emphasized salvation by faith and taught Christian morality based on the Ten Commandments and the Golden Rule. Emotionalism played a large role in the services of some denominations, especially the Methodists and Cumberland Presbyterians when they held camp-meeting revivals. Sermons, hymns, and prayers emphasizing the torments of eternal damnation that awaited those who did not accept their Savior whipped worshipers into a frenzy. Men cried; women fainted; young people became hysterical. One critical observer wrote of a Methodist meeting: "No pen or tongue can give you an adequate description of these riotous scenes—a person must see & hear in order to be convinced of their mad extravagancies & I fancy most will distrust the evidence of their senses. They call it a revival."

Church services and camp meetings, of course, met a need for social contact as much as for spiritual/emotional fulfillment. Churches sponsored dinners and weeknight meetings that meant regular social interaction. Protracted revivals brought people away from their isolated farmsteads and into close contact for days at a time. Some observers criticized the social as opposed to spiritual nature of these events. "I thought," one wrote, "if some people would take as much trouble and pain to get to *heaven* as they do to get to *preaching*—that they certainly would succeed."

Some religious denominations also affected life in antebellum Texas by placing emphasis on education and certain reforms such as the temperance movement. "Old School" Presbyterians, for example, extended their belief in an educated ministry to support for education in general. Ministers of all denominations often taught school during the week. Methodists and Cumberland Presbyterians became noted for their role in the temperance movement, a reform aimed at reducing or even eliminating the sale and consumption of alcoholic beverages. Indeed, temperance—"religion's handmaid," in the words of one minister—was the only reform of the many sweeping the United States during the antebellum years to receive support in Texas. The reason, incidentally, was slavery. Southerners, including Texans, came to identify reform with abolitionism and therefore steered clear of all proposals for change.

Antebellum Texans talked a great deal about what one newspaper called "that rock on which the whole structure of freedom rests—the education of the whole people," but they did very little in the way of actually establishing public schools. The Congress of the Republic granted four leagues (17,712 acres) to each county to support public schools and provided for a school board to administer these lands and the schools that they paid for, but virtually nothing came of this legislation. A provision in the Constitution of 1845 stipulating that at least one-tenth of all state revenue be set aside in a "General Education Fund" to support public schools also failed to produce any action. Finally in 1854, the legislature set aside $2 million of the bonds received from the United States in payment for the settling of Texas's western boundary in 1850 (a part of the Compromise of 1850 that will be discussed in detail below) as a "Special School Fund." Interest from this fund was to be allocated annually to the counties on a per student (defined as children aged six to sixteen) basis. The law required commissioners courts to divide their counties into school districts and oversee the election of trustees for each. The trustees would hire teachers, whose salaries would be paid by money from the special fund, and provide for school buildings to be paid for by the parents of school children in each district. Nothing came of this fairly elaborate plan either, primarily because the fund did not generate enough money and citizens were unwilling to pay taxes to supplement it. For example, the fund produced $.62 per student in 1854 and $1.50 in 1855, hardly enough to pay a school teacher a living even if he or she attempted the impossible task of teaching every student in a particular county.

Because public education remained only a much-talked-about dream in Texas before the Civil War, formal schooling was essentially a matter of private enterprise. At the most basic level, would-be teachers established common schools and offered primary and elementary education to children whose parents could pay tuition. Academies, which nearly every town of any size could claim by 1850, offered courses of a more advanced nature. For example, students at the Marshall Grove Academy in Harrison County could take Latin, Greek, Hebrew, Higher Mathematics, Natural Philosophy, Metaphysics, Declamation, and Composition. All such schools generally admitted boys and girls, although some separated them into male and female departments. If, however, parents wanted their girls to attend a school for females only, those were widely available, too. The courses of instruction in female institutes included "ornamental courses" such as music and art, but the basic curriculum differed little from that of the boys' academies. Girls also took ancient languages, higher mathematics, and philosophy.

Higher education took place in dozens of state-chartered colleges and universities, many of which offered a good deal less than their names suggested. The University of San Augustine (1842) and Marshall University (1842), for example, both had primary departments that taught reading, writing, and arithmetic. Rutersville College, the first to bear that name in Texas when it opened in 1840, had so few students capable of collegiate work that one German observer referred to it as "an American elementary school." Even the religious-affiliated institutions that began in the antebellum period and still exist today—Baylor University (founded by Baptists at Independence in 1845), Austin College (founded by Presbyterians at Huntsville in 1849), and St. Mary's University (founded by Catholics at San Antonio in 1852)—offered little or no work at the college level during their early years. Most Texans who aspired to and could afford true higher education sent their children to schools in the East. For example, Guy M. Bryan, a son of planter James F. Perry's wife by her first husband, attended Kenyon College in Ohio where he was a classmate of future president Rutherford B. Hayes. Mirabeau B. Lamar sent his daughter to school in Georgia until her death at an early age in 1843.

The level of academic achievement in all these schools is difficult to measure. Generally, there was no established progression of study over a period of years culminating in a particular degree or diploma. Teachers could be only so demanding when their students were customers who paid them directly.

Moreover, discipline was a constant problem. One Harrison County school hired a teacher on the basis of his reputation for "thrashing" boys large and small, and a Washington County academy that promised an end to corporal punishment for boys over twelve years of age had to close when the students got out of hand. Under such circumstances, schools tended to cover their shortcomings and bolster their academic reputations by holding elaborate public examinations at the end of each session. Parents and local newspaper editors loved these events and generally overlooked the fact that these "examinations" were more on the order of recitations of prepared and rehearsed materials. E. H. Cushing of the *Houston Telegraph* called such public displays "humbuggery."

Regardless of its quality, private school education lay beyond the means of most antebellum Texas families. A five-month session typically cost from $15 per student in the primary department up to $30 for senior-level instruction. "Ornamental" courses such as instrumental music bore an additional cost. Books and supplies were an additional expense, and students who boarded had to pay for a room and food. Considering that in most parts of antebellum Texas an acre of land cost less than $10 and a bale of cotton brought less than $50, it is clear that relatively few families could afford education for their children.

Limited educational opportunities notwithstanding, most adults in antebellum Texas apparently could at least read and write. Census enumerators reported a high degree of literacy in 1850 and 1860, and the huge number of newspapers published in the state demonstrates the presence of a market for reading matter. In 1860 Texas editors published three dailies, three triweeklies, and sixty-five weekly papers. Most consisted of only four pages, but they reported international, national, and local news, carried literary matter and advertisements, and editorialized about state and local issues. What these newspapers lacked in newsgathering facilities, they made up for with colorful editors and political partisanship.

Antebellum Texans enjoyed a great variety of amusements and entertainments. Large towns such as Houston and Galveston had theaters that attracted professional actors who performed plays fresh from the stages of New Orleans and even New York. Smaller towns had amateur theatrical groups and debating societies to provide cultural and intellectual stimulation. Any community with a sizable German population had a brass band that entertained regularly. Many other amusements, however, were notably less genteel. Texans of all backgrounds loved gambling, horse racing, and drinking, and anyone interested had access to card games (usually in hotels or saloons), racetracks, and a staggering variety of alcoholic drinks. A Houston newspaper described the card games played there in 1840 according to the diversity of the population: "The Texians play at *rounders*; the Frenchmen at *vingt-et-un*; the Mexican at *monte*; the Kentuckian, Mississippian and Tennessean at *poker*; the Dutch [Germans] at *euchre*; the sons of Erin at *forty-fives*; and the negroes at *old sledge*." Racetracks operated at all sizable towns and even in those as small as Boston and Texana. Texans imported whiskey, brandy, cognac, gin, champagne, claret, and port by the boatload and served up those beverages in establishments ranging from fancy barrooms to cheap "grogshops." Some of the mixed drinks offered at Galveston bars—"moral suasion," "vox populi," "deacon," "heater," and "smasher"—are likely to defy the imaginations of even modern-day tipplers.

Gambling, horse racing, and drinking often sparked violent confrontations among antebellum Texans, many of whom needed very little provocation before reaching for their pistols and knives. Personal disputes among individuals who saw themselves as gentlemen frequently led to duels during the early years of the Republic. For example, in 1837 General Felix Huston seriously wounded Albert Sidney Johnston in a duel fought over which man should command the Texian army. Later that year Dr. Chauncey Goodrich, a surgeon in the army, accused Levi Laurens, reporter of the house of representatives, of stealing from him, thus forcing Laurens to issue a challenge over the insult to his honor. The two fought with rifles at twenty yards, and Goodrich shot the younger man through both thighs, wounds that proved fatal. Dueling largely ended after congress passed a strong law against the practice in 1840 and the Constitution of 1845 outlawed it as well, but violence continued in a more spontaneous and less stylized form. Killings, most of which seem to have gone unpunished, occurred regularly. For example, in Harrison County, which had a free population of fewer than seven thousand, at least four men were killed within two years in 1852–1854. "They have not forgot how to fight in Harrison County yet," an observer wrote. "They have a fight in Marshall every week or two." In Hempstead during June 1860, a man looking out on the street from a second-floor hotel room window spotted another man with whom he had a long-standing quarrel. Firing three times from his vantage point, he hit the other in the neck, side, and thigh. As the shooter came down and prepared to ride away, a crowd gathered around the dying victim. "By God, a good shot that," one said.

As a largely rural society marked by underdeveloped cultural institutions, crude amusements, and violence, antebellum Texas was very much a man's world. The region, it has been said, was heaven for men and dogs and hell for women and oxen. In reality, however, Texas women lived in a complex world of restrictions and rights that, although far from ideal, gave them considerable room to grow and assert themselves. A "true woman," as set out in the prescriptive literature of that day, was a pious and pure homemaker and mother, who was strong and hard working and yet docile and submissive. She had no political rights and suffered serious disabilities under the law such as being barred from serving on a jury or witnessing a will. On the other hand, girls whose families could afford it studied the same subjects as boys, and women had truly significant property rights arising from the state's Spanish origins. Married women had the right to separate property (that is, they kept title to property owned before marriage), community property rights to everything acquired while living with their husbands, and full title to property that came into their hands following divorce or the deaths of husbands. Women had the right to sue for divorce, and even with all-male judges, lawyers, and juries, won as often as they lost—generally winning fair property settlements and child-custody arrangements in the process. These rights allowed women in antebellum Texas to own farms and plantations, head families, and direct their lives in ways that were anything but docile and submissive.

Political Life in Antebellum Texas

By mid-nineteenth-century standards, the political institutions of antebellum Texas provided for a democratic system. The Constitution of 1845 permitted all adult white males to vote and hold state or local office without having to meet any taxpaying or property-holding qualifications. Adult males of Mexican descent were considered "white" and generally accorded the same privileges, leaving women and "Indians not taxed, Africans, and descendants of Africans" as disfranchised groups. These provisions, although obviously undemocratic to Americans a century and a half later, represented advanced political liberalism during the 1850s.

When antebellum Texas voters went to the polls, they generally elected members of the slaveholding elite to run state and local government. In 1860, for example, when slaveholders headed a little more than one-quarter of all households, they held more than two-thirds of all state and local offices across antebellum Texas. These officeholders were more than four times as wealthy on the average as the typical family head. This domination of officeholding by slaveholders in no way violated the precepts of democracy. In much the same way that voters across the United States generally defer to their economic superiors, poorer nonslaveholders freely elected their richer neighbors and supported their policies. Nevertheless, leadership by a minority whose status depended on the ownership of slaves introduced an element of aristocracy and guaranteed a pro-southern cast to antebellum Texas politics.

Leadership by slaveholders meant that politics during the early statehood years operated within what should be called a southern consensus. No one could criticize slavery or slave-based agriculture and expect to receive support at the polls; indeed, to be accused of holding antislavery views was a political death sentence. The story of Lorenzo Sherwood, a New York-born lawyer and state legislator from Galveston, provides a good case in point. In the mid-1850s, Sherwood proposed a plan to have the state build a railroad system for Texas rather than give aid to private promoters. His opponents, frightened by the support given the "State Plan," attacked his willingness to let the U.S. Congress decide the issue of slavery in the territories and warned that no Texan should listen to a man who did not take "a southern tone on the subject of slavery." Soon, opposition to the "wiseacre and nigger lover" reached a point that the threat of mob violence prevented his making public speeches in Galveston and in effect forced him to resign from the legislature.

The southern consensus in Texas played a key role in creating the state's tradition of one-party politics that appeared immediately after annexation. "We are all Democrats," wrote Guy M. Bryan in 1845, "since the glorious victory of that party, who fearlessly espoused our cause and nailed the 'Lone

Star' to the topmast of their noble ship." The Democratic Party's willingness to support annexation, of course, reflected its tendency, which emerged in the 1830s, to take pro-southern positions on matters relating to slavery. Adding a new slave state in 1845 and supporting the Mexican War in 1846–1848 are perfect examples. By contrast the Whig Party, although it had strong support in many southern states, had tended to oppose annexation, criticize the war, and listen to vocally antislavery leaders in the North. Sam Houston, a longtime admirer of Andrew Jackson, summarized the dominance of Old Hickory's party in 1848 while poking fun at the opposition. "There are but six men belonging to the Whig Party in Texas," Houston told a Pennsylvania audience, " one of whom [is] a horsethief—another a black-leg—a third a land grabber, and the other three were the mere tools and understrappers of the first three, ready to do their bidding at all times for a glass of grog or an occasional suit of old clothes." Houston exaggerated, of course; Texas Whigs actually organized for the presidential elections of 1848 and 1852 and won more than a quarter of the vote each time. The dominance was real, however, as Democrats won every presidential and gubernatorial election from 1845 to 1860.

The southern consensus and one-party politics did not eliminate political conflict in antebellum Texas. Significant differences of opinion and policy existed—within the consensus. Politicians did not question the morality of slavery or the importance of securing its future, but they disagreed on the best means of protecting their Peculiar Institution. Above all, there was the issue of secession. Should Texans prepare themselves to leave the Union if the federal government came under the control of politicians who thought slavery wrong and intended to stop its spread, or should they think primarily in terms of protecting the institution by remaining part of the United States? This question led to bitter disagreement among Texans, much of it centering on the towering figure of Senator Sam Houston.

Houston staked out his position on slavery and related issues in 1847. He had to because a year earlier Congressman David Wilmot of Pennsylvania had injected antislavery into national politics in a new way by proposing that the South's Peculiar Institution be prohibited in any territory that might be taken in the Mexican War. Many northerners who would never have supported radical abolitionism agreed with this so-called Wilmot Proviso because it promised only to stop the spread of slavery. By contrast, most southerners saw the proviso's implicit condemnation of slavery (if the institution was too wrong to spread, how right was it anywhere?), and hotheads soon raised the specter of secession. The proviso passed in the House of Representatives, where the North's population advantage could come into play, but not in the Senate, which reflected the nearly equal number of free and slave states at the time.

Houston took a stand in support of the Union that never varied for the remainder of the antebellum period. "Let not the name of Texas, his home, the last to be incorporated into the Union," he told the Senate, "ever be blasphemed by the word 'disunion.' Let not the Union be severed." The question of slavery's future, he said, should be postponed. "It [is] an evil which ought not to be invited; but when it shall come, let it be managed with the judgment of reasonable men, and not by passionate excitement." Houston, a slaveholder all his life, thus took no stand against slavery as a moral wrong and clearly had no wish to see it eliminated any time soon. Even this stand, however, which does him little credit from a modern point of view, drew angry responses from other Texas Democrats who agreed with the famed South Carolina senator John C. Calhoun that slavery could afford no criticism and should be welcome in all territories of the United States. Moreover, according to Calhoun and his followers, the election of an administration dedicated to restricting the spread of slavery would provide justification for immediate secession.

The question of extending slavery became an urgent issue in Texas politics early in 1848, when the Treaty of Guadalupe-Hidalgo assured the Río Grande as the boundary between the United States and Mexico. This appeared to be a great victory for Texas, which had claimed the Río Grande boundary since 1836 and thereby extended its western border to include half of modern-day New Mexico. However, problems quickly arose because citizens of Santa Fe, the main town in that thinly settled region, insisted that the Río Grande was the boundary only to El Paso and that the rest of the Texas–New Mexico border was well to the east of the river from that point on. The United States Army, which had occupied Santa Fe during the war, agreed with local citizens and, disregarding Texas's claims, organized a civilian government there. Texans reacted angrily, not only in response to losing their claim to the land but also because their state permitted slavery, whereas New Mexico would almost certainly be free. The western boundary of Texas thus became a point of dispute with implications for the future of slavery.

The Texas legislature acted quickly to assert its control over the area by passing an act in March 1848 that designated the eastern half of New Mexico as Santa Fe County. Governor George T. Wood, a Trinity River planter who had succeeded James Pinckney Henderson as governor in 1847, appointed Spruce M. Baird to serve as county judge in Santa Fe and set up a county government there according to Texas law. Baird arrived in November, but after half a year of attempting unsuccessfully to do his job in the face of opposition from local citizens and the U.S. Army, gave up and returned home in July 1849. In the meantime, the Whig Zachary Taylor took over the presidency and invited residents of the Santa Fe area to write a constitution and enter the Union as a state. Taylor's proposal, by putting the decision into the hands of those who lived in and around Santa Fe, amounted to a virtual guarantee that New Mexico would not have slavery and a rejection of Texas's claims to the Río Grande boundary as well. Most Texans were outraged, and some seemed inclined to agree with extremists from other southern states that unless Congress agreed to permit slavery in all the territory taken from Mexico, passed a stronger fugitive slave law, and stopped abolitionist agitation, the South should secede from the Union.

Governor Wood announced in November 1849 that Texas would assert its boundary claims "with the whole power and resources of the state," but the matter was out of his hands in that he had already been defeated for reelection by a candidate who advocated an even more aggressive stance on the issue. The new governor, Virginia-born Peter Hansborough Bell, endorsed Calhoun's position that slavery had a right to enter all federal territories and asked the legislature for additional support in making good Texas's claims to New Mexico. On December 31, 1849, the legislature responded with an act redefining the boundaries of Santa Fe County and creating three additional counties in the disputed areas. Governor Bell then sent Robert S. Neighbors, the Indian agent, to organize Texas civil governments in those counties. Neighbors accomplished his objective in El Paso County, but, like McCoy, failed in New Mexico.

Texans greeted news of Neighbors's failure by holding indignation meetings across the state, and Governor Bell called a special session of the legislature to meet in August 1850. In the meantime, a national crisis developed over a variety of sectional issues such as the admission of California to the Union as a free state, slavery in the District of Columbia, and the South's call for a stronger fugitive slave law. The southern states elected representatives to a meeting at Nashville, Tennessee, to consider "mutual action on the subject of slavery and Southern rights," and talk of secession flourished. Meeting in June, the Nashville Convention (former governor James Pinckney Henderson represented Texas) did not endorse disunion, but it supported Texas's claims to New Mexico and urged the entire South to take a similar stand. Governor Bell, in his address to the August special legislative session, told Texans to defend their state's claims "at all hazards and to the last extremity." At that point, however, with the nation seemingly on the verge of violence, the spirit of compromise, which had begun to build when Senator Henry Clay proposed a settlement back in January, overcame extremism and ended the crisis.

The Compromise of 1850 dealt with all the major sectional issues of the day, but obviously the part of immediate importance to Texas was a bill passed in September that offered a solution to the disputed boundary with New Mexico. The bill proposed to fix the western and northern boundaries of the state where they stand today. The western boundary followed the Río Grande to the thirty-second parallel just north of El Paso and then ran east along that parallel to the 103rd meridian, due north to the parallel 36° 30′, and east again to the 100th meridian. (At that point it met the boundary established by the Transcontinental Treaty of 1821.) In return for accepting this limit on its western claims, Texas would receive $10 million in United States bonds to pay public debt left from the Republic era.

Texas's congressional delegation supported this bill, with Sam Houston delivering an emotional speech begging his listeners to reject extremism and accept compromise. Anticipating Abraham Lincoln's famed biblical reference by eight years, Houston concluded: "For a nation divided against itself cannot stand. I wish, that if their Union must be dissolved, that its ruins may be the monument of my grave, and the graves of my family. I wish no epitaph to be written to tell that I survive the ruin of this glorious Union." Pro-southern extremists back home raged at Houston and the "Infamous Texas Bribery Bill," but voters statewide accepted the proposal by a two-to-one margin. Most Texans apparently recognized that the compromise represented all that their state could reasonably expect, but their acceptance in no way lessened the Lone Star State's commitment to the South. Governor Bell, who had spoken of going to "the last extremity" during the crisis, easily won reelection in 1851, and most voters apparently agreed with an East Texan who said: "Texas having so recently come into the Union, should not be the foremost to dissolve it, but I trust she will not waver, when the crisis shall come."

Internal matters such as railroads and education took the attention of Texans away from sectional issues for the next few years, as evidenced in 1853 by the election of Elisha M. Pease to the governorship. Pease, although a longtime, slaveholding resident of Texas, was a Connecticut-born unionist whose views on sectional issues were not acceptable to a majority. Fortunately, he was not called on to take a stand in 1854 when Congress destroyed the spirit of compromise between the North and South by passing a measure that called for the organization of territorial governments in Kansas and Nebraska, two territories that would cover the remainder of the Louisiana Purchase north of the parallel 36° 30′. The 1820 Missouri Compromise had prohibited slavery in that area while it remained unorganized, but the Kansas-Nebraska Act replaced the restriction with an idea known as "popular sovereignty," which meant letting the first legislature elected in each territory decide whether or not to have slavery there. This repealed a thirty-four-year-old limitation on the spread of slavery—a step that outraged antislavery northerners. Southerners, on the other hand, saw the act as an overdue recognition of their rights and found northern opposition infuriating.

Pro-southern Texans had a special focus for their anger—Sam Houston, who alone among Democratic senators from the South spoke and voted against the Kansas-Nebraska Act. "Stir not up agitation," Houston begged his colleagues. "Give us peace!" But they would not listen, and neither did Texans when he sought to explain how the act would unleash sectional forces that could not be controlled as they led to secession and war. The result, he warned, will be an "unequal contest" in which the South will "go down . . . in a sea of blood and smoking ruin." Few predictions have proven so tragically correct.

Somewhat ironically, since it intensified sectional feelings, the Kansas-Nebraska Act also introduced a nonsectional political movement into Texas. The flood of immigrants into the United States had prompted the rise in the Northeast of a secret nativist organization known as the American or Know-Nothing Party (because members were to say "I know nothing" when asked about it). Opposing foreigners and Catholics and supporting the Union, the Know-Nothings grew rapidly when the Kansas-Nebraska Act destroyed the Whig Party by splitting it along sectional lines. It appealed to Texans who disliked Mexicans or Germans and drew some support from the state's unionists and former Whigs. Even Sam Houston, believing that Democrats were deserting the principles of Jackson, flirted with the new party. In 1855, the Know-Nothings nominated David C. Dickson, the lieutenant governor, to challenge Pease's bid for reelection and mounted enough of a threat to force the Democrats to organize and campaign as they never had before. The new party had some success in state legislative races, electing about twenty representatives and five senators, but Pease defeated Dickson easily and within a year or so the movement faded away. It lost strength in the North as the Republican Party rose to replace the Whig Party and declined in the South because the threat of a party opposed to the spread of slavery forced more voters than ever to commit to the Democrats. As the Know-Nothings declined, Texas became more of a one-party state than ever, although the Democrats still had pro- and anti-Houston factions.

Determined to show Houston where he stood, on November 26, 1855, a joint session of the legislature passed by a vote of 77 to 3 a resolution saying that it "approves the course of Thomas J. Rusk in voting for the Kansas-Nebraska Act and disapproves the course of Sam Houston in voting against it." Several months later the Democratic State Convention passed similar resolutions. Houston's Senate term, provided he completed it, would not end until March 1859, but several newspapers called on him to resign at the halfway point. Rather than give in, however, even to the point of simply remaining quiet and waiting for the storm to pass, Houston went on the attack. In May 1857, following the nomination of Hardin R. Runnels, a Calhoun-style ultra-southerner as the Democratic Party's candidate for governor, Houston announced himself as an independent candidate for the same office. "The people want excitement," he wrote Rusk, "and I had as well give it as anyone."

Houston proved true to his word. Riding in a crimson buggy furnished by a plow salesman, he traveled across the state and made at least sixty speeches during a little more than sixty Texas summer days. It was a punishing pace for a sixty-four-year-old man. Democratic speakers such as the pro-southern "fire eater" Louis T. Wigfall followed Houston on the campaign, hammering at his voting record in Congress and claiming that he was betraying the South in an effort to gain a presidential nomination with northern antislavery support. The senator made a mistake by defending his unionist stance, rather than focusing on state-level issues, and thus allowing the charge that he did not uphold southern interests to become central to the campaign. Moreover, his flirtation with Know-Nothingism hurt him with German and Mexican voters. He lost to Runnels by a vote of 32,552 to 28, 678, the only defeat ever suffered by "Old Sam Jacinto" after 1836.

In November 1857 Democrats in the Texas legislature, having elected James Pinckney Henderson to take the U. S. Senate seat of Rusk, who had committed suicide in July, went ahead and chose John Hemphill, a judge on the Texas Supreme Court, as a successor to Houston. Ignoring this additional pressure to resign before his term ended in 1859, Houston returned to Washington. "I cherish every manly sentiment for the South," he told critics who accused him of being antislavery, "and I am determined that . . . none of the fraternal bonds which bind it to this Union shall be broken." He came home in March 1859 and soon embarked on a second campaign against Runnels for the governorship. Unlike the 1857 contest, which focused on his national record, Houston in 1859 took advantage of voter discontent with problems in Texas, such as lawlessness on the frontier, that could be blamed on Runnels. His campaigners also turned the tables by pointing to the governor's position on outside issues—support for reopening the African slave trade, for example—that even most pro-southern Texans found too extreme. Fire-eating Democratic candidates for other offices furthered his cause as well by their extremism. For example, Thomas N. Waul, a pro-slavery enthusiast who ran for Congress against the Unionist Andrew Jackson Hamilton, frightened many with his pledge to "drink all the blood" that would be shed as a result of secession. When the votes were counted, Houston gained revenge for 1857, defeating Runnels 33,375 to 27,500.

Houston's inauguration in December 1859 made him the only man to this day who served as the governor of two states (Tennessee as well as Texas) and brought expressions of bitter anger from ultra-southerners. The new governor's "Demagogical Union saving doctrines," Runnels wrote, will "inflict an irreparable blow upon Southern interests at this time." In fact, however, the state legislature remained under the control of men who disagreed with Houston's unionism, a fact demonstrated by the election of the fire-eating secessionist Louis T. Wigfall to the U. S. Senate in November 1859. "Texas will maintain the Constitution and stand by the Union," Houston told the legislature early in 1860, but his words rang somewhat hollow. True, Texas had fewer hair-trigger secessionists than did, for example, South Carolina; nevertheless, any threat to slavery by the United States government might well provoke a majority of Texans to join their fellow southerners in a movement to leave the Union and form a new nation.

Chapter 10

THE CIVIL WAR, 1861–1865

Southern Democrats, including most Texas politicians, entered the presidential campaign of 1860 in a "rule or ruin" mood. Either their party's convention would write a platform guaranteeing protection of slavery in all the territories of the United States, or they would walk out and prevent the nomination of a candidate. And they proved true to their word. When the convention, which assembled in Charleston, South Carolina, in April 1860, refused to include the plank protecting slavery, delegates from seven Deep South states walked out, breaking up the meeting. The Texas delegation under the leadership of former governor Runnels, Guy M. Bryan (a nephew of Stephen F. Austin), and Francis R. Lubbock joined in the withdrawal. Eventually, after another failed national convention in Baltimore, Texas delegates participated in a meeting in Richmond, Virginia, that nominated John C. Breckinridge of Kentucky and wrote the platform desired by southerners. The remnant of the Democratic Party (primarily northerners, of course) nominated Stephen A. Douglas and endorsed his version of popular sovereignty, which by that time was unacceptable to ultra-southerners.

Once the Democrats split along sectional lines, they virtually assured victory for the Republican candidate, Abraham Lincoln of Illinois. Lincoln had a record of consistent opposition to the spread of slavery into new territory and at the same time refusal to support immediate abolition. Radical abolitionists despised Lincoln's caution; indeed, Wendell Phillips called him "the slave hound of Illinois." His stance, however, had great political appeal in the North because opposition to slavery's expansion offered moral condemnation of the institution without the radicalism that might bring war. It appealed to all gradations of antislavery opinion except the most radical abolitionists. Those who genuinely believed slavery morally wrong and wished to stop its spread could support Lincoln, as could those who cared nothing about slaves but simply did not want to compete with slaveholders.

Soon, the campaign turned into a four-way contest with the appearance of a new political organization calling itself the Constitutional Union Party. Appealing to men of conservative temperament, primarily in the border states of the upper South, this party said that its only principles were the Constitution and the Union. It offered no specific plan for dealing with issues such as the spread of slavery. The Constitutional Union Party, of course, represented exactly the position that Sam Houston had taken throughout the building sectional crisis, and many thought that he should be its candidate. Houston did not seek the nomination, but four conservative Unionists from Texas who attended the party's convention put his name into consideration. He ran second to John Bell of Tennessee, a former Whig senator, on the first ballot, but then, on a second ballot, shifts of support among other potential nominees gave the nomination to Bell.

Only the nomination of Sam Houston could have created the slightest doubt as to the outcome of the election of 1860 in Texas. The state had no Republican Party and hence no Republican presidential electors for whom anyone wishing to support Lincoln could have voted. Douglas may have had a few supporters, but the remnants of the national Democratic Party were not organized in Texas either. Adherents of the Constitutional Union Party created enough of an organization to choose a slate of electors and campaign, but without a well-known and appealing candidate, they had no chance. That left Breckinridge, with the only question being his margin of victory.

In July 1860, to make matters even more hopeless for conservatives, a wave of panic about an abolitionist-inspired slave rebellion swept the state. The "Texas Troubles," as this scare became known, began with a series of fires in Dallas and other North Texas towns. These fires probably resulted from the spontaneous ignition of a new type of phosphorous match, but several slaves were forced to confess to arson. Then Charles R. Pryor, the ultra-Southern editor of the *Dallas Herald,* took the lead in spreading the fear of a plot by white abolitionists to begin with the fires and culminate in a general servile insurrection. The plotters, Pryor wrote, have even selected "certain ladies . . . as the victims of these misguided monsters." Reprisals against the supposed rebellious slaves and abolitionist plotters began immediately, of course, and included numerous whippings and lynchings. A citizen of Fort Worth perfectly summarized the mood of the day while explaining the hanging of a man accused of "tampering" with slaves. "It is better for us," he wrote, "to hang ninety-nine innocent (suspicious) men than to let one guilty one pass."

The "Texas Troubles" subsided in August and September, but they played a part in destroying what little hope Unionists had of a strong showing in the election. Indeed, Sam Houston and other conservatives believed that the whole affair had been built up for political effect. The governor knew from the outset, of course, that Breckinridge would carry Texas regardless of what happened during the campaign, and he also recognized that Lincoln was the likely winner nationally. Therefore, he devoted his energies during the summer and fall of 1860 to speaking for the Union and begging Texans to see that Lincoln's election would not be a reason for secession. On September 22 in Austin, he used the picturesque term *whipsters and demagogues* to describe the men who would bring what he called the "calamitous curse of disunion" on Texas.

On November 6, 1860, Texas voters rendered the decision that everyone expected and some feared. Breckinridge received 47,561 votes, 75 percent of the total, and carried every county in the state except for three on the sparsely populated frontier. Only 15,402 Texans voted for the Constitutional Union candidate John Bell. Breckinridge won all seven Deep South states, but Lincoln received virtually all of the free states' electoral votes and won the presidency. Almost immediately leaders in the states carried by Breckinridge began to call for secession.

Secession

Lincoln's election led to a spontaneous grassroots movement for disunion in Texas. Community after community held mass meetings and adopted resolutions condemning Lincoln as a dangerously radical "Black Republican" and calling for the election of a state convention to consider secession. And local leaders admitted that war was likely to follow disunion. "I deprecate war," said John B. Webster, a planter who chaired Harrison County's meeting, "but bad as war is . . . there is something worse; and the people who will not rise in defense of their rights and their honor, will soon be fit for servitude and for chains." There is irony, or at least curiosity, today in the reference of a slaveholder to the horrors of servitude, but Webster and others saw themselves in the tradition of American revolutionaries who had opposed Great Britain's efforts to reduce them to slavery. In the words of one East Texas newspaperman: "It takes us back to the days of the revolution, when men forgot everything in their patriotic devotion to their country."

An impressive group of leaders in Austin, including Supreme Court Justice Oran M. Roberts, Attorney General George M. Flournoy, Democratic Party leader Guy M. Bryan, and the famed Ranger John S. "Rip" Ford, eagerly took up the cry for secession raised first at the local level. However, they encountered opposition from equally well-known men. Congressman A. J. Hamilton, German newspaper editor Ferdinand Flake and lawyer William Pitt Ballinger of Galveston, state senator James W. Throckmorton of Collin County, and lawyer-editor George W. Paschal sought to prevent disunion. These Unionists were at a huge disadvantage in that the public generally stood ready to secede, but they did have one major weapon on their side—Sam Houston in the governor's office. Under Texas law, the convention sought by the secessionists could be called only by the state legislature, which was not scheduled to meet until the next year. To issue the call immediately would require a special session of the legislature, but only the governor could call legislators to Austin for that purpose. Houston had no intention of issuing such a call.

Sam Houston fought secession the same way that he had conducted the San Jacinto campaign in 1836; that is, he delayed, retreated when necessary, and looked for an opportunity to strike the blow that might win his objective. On November 20, he urged a group of Texans who had sought his opinion on the situation to wait and see if Lincoln would violate the Constitution.

"Passion is rash," he warned them, "wisdom considers well her way." Two weeks later, he issued an "Address to the People of Texas," making the same argument and pointing out that he had suggested a meeting of a Southern convention to consider ways to deal with the crisis. The secessionists, however, ignored the governor's arguments and on December 3 issued a call for a convention to be elected on January 8, 1861, and to assemble in Austin on January 28. They brushed aside questions of legality with the argument that the urgency of the situation—"the insults, threats, and aggressions" from the North—justified acting without the approval of the governor or legislature.

Houston reacted to the secessionists' planned convention by issuing a proclamation calling the legislature to meet in special session on January 21, 1861. The legislature, he explained, would allow the "whole people" of Texas to find a way for the state to maintain its rights in the Union. Obviously, the governor hoped to use the legislature to head off the convention. His task became even more difficult, however, on December 20, when South Carolina became the first Southern state to secede from the Union. South Carolina's action touched off celebrations among secessionists across Texas and whipped up additional enthusiasm for disunion.

When the legislature assembled on January 21, Houston sought to have it reject the convention scheduled to meet one week later. He urged legislators to call a new meeting of "delegates fresh from the people" so that voters could speak in a "legitimate manner." Furthermore, the governor said, any action taken by that convention should be submitted to the people for their approval. He closed by asking the legislature to reject those who wished to "plunge madly into revolution." These pleas largely fell on deaf ears. The legislature passed a joint resolution approving the meeting of the convention on January 28 and allowing it to assemble in the chambers of the house of representatives. Houston's only success came in the form of a requirement that any action taken by the convention be submitted to the voters for approval.

The 177 delegates who assembled on January 28 were overwhelmingly southern in background and interests—91 percent were born in slave states and 72 percent owned slaves. They organized by electing Judge Oran M. Roberts as president and made their intent clear on January 29 by adopting a sense-of-the-convention resolution that "Texas should separately secede from the Union." A committee quickly drafted an ordinance of secession that repealed the annexation ordinance of 1845 and returned Texas to its status as a sovereign state. If the state's voters approved in a referendum scheduled for February 23, the ordinance would take effect on March 2, 1861, the twenty-fifth anniversary of the Declaration of Independence of the Republic of Texas. Over the years many have argued that the U.S. Constitution, properly interpreted as a compact among sovereign states, sanctioned secession as a legal action, but certainly the symbolism of disunion in Texas shows that leaders in the movement understood it as an act of revolution.

A vote on the ordinance of secession came on February 1 in front of packed galleries and in the presence of Governor Houston and other officials. Although the final result held no suspense, the roll call generated several dramatic moments. Senator Throckmorton could not resist making a statement as he voted. "Mr. President," he said, "in view of the responsibility, in the presence of God and my country—and unawed by the wild spirit of revolution around me, I vote 'no.'" Many in the galleries hissed, leading Throckmorton to retort, "Mr. President, when the rabble hiss, well may patriots tremble." The ordinance passed by a vote of 166 to 8, and the audience broke into cheers as a group of women moved into the chamber and presented a Lone Star flag to the convention. Governor Houston spoke briefly to Roberts and left the room.

The convention remained in session until February 4 and completed the process of leaving the Union. It arranged the referendum to be held on February 23 and prepared a public "Declaration of the Causes which Impel the State of Texas to Secede from the Federal Union." Also, operating on the assumption that voters would approve its action, the convention chose seven delegates to join those from six other seceding states at a meeting already underway in Montgomery, Alabama, for the purpose of creating the Confederate States of America. The meeting at Montgomery created a provisional government for the Confederacy on February 9, and the Texas delegation, led by U.S. Senators John Hemphill and Louis T. Wigfall and Congressman John H. Reagan, stood ready to participate in its affairs just as soon as voters approved secession and the convention passed an ordinance joining their state to the new government.

Finally, the Texas convention created a fifteen-man Committee on Public Safety and authorized it to take control of all property in the state belonging to the national government. The committee sent three commissioners to San Antonio to negotiate with General David E. Twiggs, the seventy-year-old Georgia-born commander of the Department of Texas. Having no instructions from Washington and largely sympathetic to the Texans, Twiggs agreed to surrender federal property and supplies once voters approved secession. He asked only that he and his troops be allowed an honorable withdrawal from the state. Problems developed, however, when the general refused to put this agreement in writing, and the commissioners, impatient with the delay anyhow, learned that Twiggs was to be replaced as commander by a strong Unionist. Accordingly, they ordered Ben McCulloch, who had raised a force of about four hundred men at Seguin, to move on San Antonio. Before dawn on February 16, McCulloch's troops, supported by six hundred additional volunteers, took control of the city and forced the commander to surrender federal property there and order all other post commanders in Texas to do the same. Twiggs, who was humiliated to the point of tears by McCulloch's show of force, thus turned over more than $3 million worth of property to Texas and arranged the removal of more than two thousand U.S. soldiers from the state.

The referendum on February 23 bore out the confidence shown by the secessionists in sending a delegation to Montgomery and taking over federal property even before the voters spoke. Although Unionists worked hard—for example, twenty-four legislators and members of the convention signed an "Address to the People" that urged Texans to remain in the Union on several grounds, including the likelihood that disunion would destroy rather than preserve slavery—they had no chance. The secessionists, who circulated thousands of copies of their declaration of the causes of disunion in German and Spanish as well as English, carried the popular vote 46,154 to 14,747 and won 104 of the state's 122 organized counties. (See map: Referendum on Secession in Texas, February 23, 1861.) Every East Texas county except lightly populated Angelina, which had relatively few slaves and an influential local unionist leader, voted in the affirmative. Successful opposition appeared only in two clusters of counties, one in central Texas and another in the north. Ten counties in the area around and west of Austin rejected disunion, partly because the Central Texas frontier benefitted from the presence of the U.S. Army and partly due to voters of German descent who tended to support the Union. In the region north of Dallas and Fort Worth, seven counties voted no and six others approved by only narrow margins. The people of these counties generally came from the upper South or Midwest and were nonslaveholding small farmers. Also, many lived in an exposed position on the Comanche frontier and feared the loss of army protection.

Once the voters approved secession, the convention reassembled and on March 5 adopted an ordinance making Texas part of the Confederate States of America. At that, Governor Houston balked. In spite of his unionism, Houston probably would have accepted secession provided that Texas became an independent republic again. He had said as much back in January. However, he believed that joining the Confederacy would involve Texas in a war that the South could not win, so he told the convention that it had exceeded its powers. The delegates replied on March 14 with a resolution requiring all state officers to take an oath of loyalty to the Confederate States of America and, when the governor refused to do so, ordered him to appear at the capitol at noon on March 16. Houston spent much of the night of the 15th pacing in an upstairs bedroom at the executive mansion before finally coming down and saying to his wife, "Margaret, I will never do it." He went to the capitol at the appointed time, but when the secretary of the convention called his name three times, he sat in the basement whittling on a piece of soft pine. The convention declared the governor's office vacant and elevated Lieutenant Governor Edward Clark to that post on March 18. Houston issued a public statement and sent a message to the legislature, which met that same day, protesting the legality of everything done by the convention after it approved the ordinance of secession and sent it to the voters. But he also indicated that he would make no effort to hold his office by force because of the possibility that civil conflict would result. I am not willing, he told a group of men who offered their help on March 19, "to deluge the capital of Texas with the blood of Texans, merely to keep one poor old man in a position a few days longer, in a position that belongs to the people." And he stuck to that position even though President Lincoln twice offered military assistance to help him hold Texas in the Union. As the Houston family's coach, followed by wagons carrying their possessions, left Austin in late March, the flag of the Confederacy flew over the state capitol.

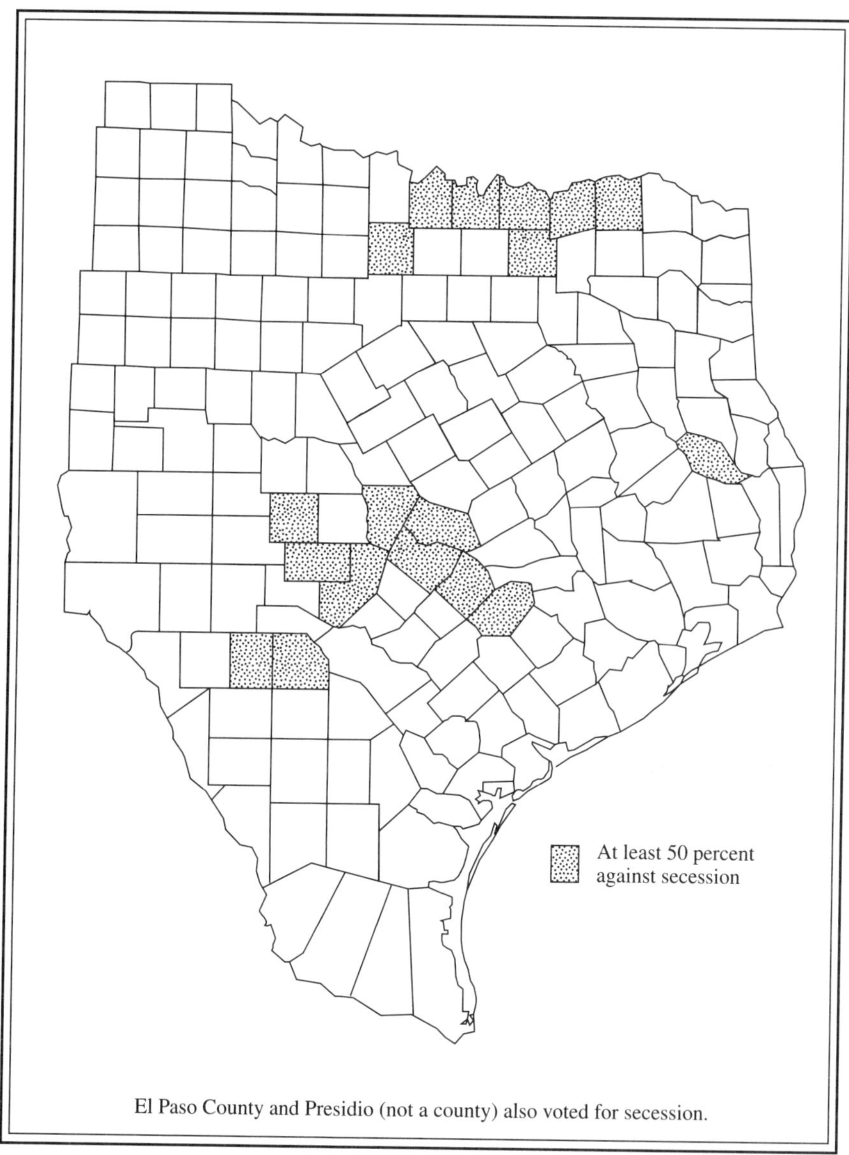
At least 50 percent against secession
El Paso County and Presidio (not a county) also voted for secession.

Referendum on Secession in Texas, February 23, 1861

Why did Texans made the fateful decision to leave the Union and cast their lot with the Confederate States of America? Explanations abound, the most popular perhaps being the claim that the United States threatened states' rights. In reality, however, states' rights is largely an abstract constitutional principle usually appealed to by minorities who believe that an opposing majority in control of the national government threatens their interests. For Texans, slavery was that interest, and the secession convention itself said so very directly in its "Declaration of the Causes." Texas, the declaration said, had joined the Union while "holding, maintaining, and protecting the institution known as negro slavery . . . which her people intended should continue to exist in all future time." The controlling majority in the federal government, however, had sought to exclude slavery from the territories—and to make matters worse, a "great sectional party" had been formed in the North based upon hostility to the Southern states' "beneficent and patriarchal system of African slavery." This party, the declaration continued, proclaimed "the debasing doctrine of the equality of all men, irrespective of race or color, a doctrine at war with nature, in opposition to the experience of mankind, and in violation of the plainest revelations of Divine law." Our own view, the declaration concluded, is that the "servitude of the African race . . . is mutually beneficial to both bond and free . . . and the destruction of the existing relations between the two races, as advocated by our sectional enemies, would bring inevitable calamities upon both and desolation upon the fifteen slave-holding states." Accordingly, Texas dissolved its connections with the United States. Thus, according to the secession convention, the defense of slavery played the key role in disunion. Why look for another explanation?

Early Months of the Civil War

Every realistic Texan expected secession to lead to the war that began with the Confederate bombardment of Fort Sumter on April 12, 1861. However, the first military activity in Texas came not in preparation for conflict with the United States but because the removal of all federal troops from the state left the Mexican and Indian frontiers undefended. The Committee on Public Safety authorized the recruitment of volunteers in March, and a month later at San Antonio the First Texas Mounted Rifles became the first unit from the state to be mustered into Confederate service. Commanded by Colonel Henry E. McCulloch, Ben McCulloch's younger brother, its troops occupied the line of federal posts from Fort Mason in Central Texas north to the Red River and took up the job of defending settlers against Comanche raiders. In May the Second Texas Mounted Rifles entered Confederate service with Colonel John S. "Rip" Ford in command. Ford occupied Fort Brown on the lower Río Grande, and his troops took control of key positions up the river to El Paso.

After the firing on Fort Sumter, President Jefferson Davis of the Confederacy asked for volunteers and young Texans responded enthusiastically. By the end of 1861 some 25,000 men entered the service, more than two-thirds of them in cavalry regiments. Raising infantry units proved difficult because, in the words of a British observer, "no Texan walks a yard if he can help it." These volunteers generally equipped themselves, resulting in an incredible array of clothing and weaponry. Most "uniforms" had some shade of gray, but similarities ended there. Firearms included everything from squirrel guns, bear guns, shotguns, and Colt pistols to ancient fowling pieces, flintlocks, and silver-plated handguns. Some companies actually carried lances. Eventually, some degree of standardization developed as inmates at the state penitentiary at Huntsville manufactured thousands of yards of cloth for uniforms and ordnance works across the state produced rifles, ammunition, and powder. Texans in the Confederate service, however, rarely, if ever, appeared in beautifully turned out and equipped units.

Texas Soldiers East of the Mississippi River

Most of the Texas soldiers recruited into the Confederate Army did not see service east of the Mississippi River. Those who did, however, participated in much of the heaviest fighting of the war, proved themselves worthy as soldiers, and paid a terrible price for their valor. Only three units from the Lone Star state—the First, Fourth, and Fifth Texas infantry regiments—fought in the eastern theater as part of the Army of Northern Virginia. Arriving in the east too late to play a role in the Confederate victory at Manassas (Bull Run), the war's first major battle on July 21, 1861, these three regiments were organized in October into the Texas Brigade under the command of Brig.Gen. Louis T. Wigfall. This unit became known as Hood's Texas Brigade in March 1862, when Wigfall resigned and John Bell Hood, a Kentucky-born West Point graduate who had once served with the U.S. Second Cavalry in Texas, took command. Even when Hood won promotion to major general and gave up command, the brigade continued to be identified with his name. Joined for a time by the Eighteenth Georgia Infantry and then by the Third Arkansas Infantry for the duration of the war, it fought in thirty-eight battles and skirmishes between 1862 and 1865.

At Gaines' Mill on June 27, 1862, a bayonet charge by Hood's Texas Brigade turned the tide in a key battle that stopped the Federals' attempt to take Richmond. The unit then saw heavy fighting at the Second Battle of Manassas in August and a month later, as part of General Robert E. Lee's first invasion of the North, took the brunt of the first Union assault in the bloodiest day of fighting during the war. At the Battle of Sharpsburg (Antietam) on September 17, 1862, the First Texas had 82 percent of its 226 men killed, wounded, or captured—the highest percentage of casualties suffered by any Confederate regiment during any single day in the war. The Fourth and Fifth Texas infantries had approximately 50 percent casualties. Following a respite from fighting during the first half of 1863, Hood's Texas Brigade participated in Lee's invasion of Pennsylvania that ended in defeat at Gettysburg on July 1–3, 1863. Then, almost immediately they were detached as part of General James Longstreet's corps and sent to aid Confederate forces fighting to control East Tennessee. The Texans helped win a great victory at Chickamauga Creek on September 18–19, 1863, but their army did not follow up its advantage and lost any opportunity it had to drive the Federals from the area. Returned to Lee's army in the spring of 1864, Hood's Brigade fought in every major battle, including the gruesome struggle at the Wilderness, as the Confederates sought to stop General Ulysses S. Grant's determined offensive against Richmond. When Richmond finally fell in April 1865, the Texas troops formed the rear guard for Lee's retreating army. The brigade surrendered at Appomattox on April 12, its three Texas regiments having sustained a casualty rate of 61 percent in a little more than three years of fighting.

Far more Texas soldiers fought in the western theater, the region stretching from the Allegheny Mountains to the Mississippi, than in the east. Four regiments of Texans went to western Kentucky in 1861 under the command of General Albert Sidney Johnston, the West Pointer who had been secretary of war in the Republic of Texas and fought brilliantly in the Mexican War. Johnston, however, did not have the manpower or equipment to defend such a huge region, especially in the face of an aggressive attacker such as Brig. Gen. U. S. Grant. In February 1862 Grant saw that the Tennessee and Cumberland Rivers provided the gateways to breaking Johnston's defenses and mounted offensives up both waterways. The Seventh Texas Infantry commanded by Col. John M. Gregg wound up trapped in Fort Donelson on the Cumberland. Forced to surrender, they and thousands of other Confederate soldiers captured with them and at Fort Henry on the Tennessee were imprisoned at Camp Douglas in Illinois. Johnston then concentrated his forces, which included the Second Texas Infantry just arrived from Houston and the Eighth Texas Cavalry regiment, at Corinth in northern Mississippi. In early April, he launched a massive attack on Grant's army near a country church named Shiloh. The ensuing two-day battle, the bloodiest in U.S. history to that time, cost the Texas units heavy casualties—one of those near-fatally wounded was Sam Houston Jr., of the Second Texas Infantry—and took the life of the army's commander. On the afternoon of the first day, a stray bullet hit General Johnston in the leg, severing an artery and causing him to bleed to death in fifteen minutes. The Confederates, commanded then by Gen. Pierre G. T. Beauregard, continued the attack, but Grant received reinforcements during the night and changed the momentum of battle on the second day. Many Confederates believed that only Johnston's death prevented a great victory at Shiloh; indeed, Texans later demonstrated their veneration by moving his body to the Texas State Cemetery in Austin.

Following the defeat at Shiloh, Confederate forces under Gen. Beauregard fell back to Corinth, where they were joined by Gen. Earl Van Dorn's army, which included four Texas cavalry regiments (the Third, Sixth, Ninth, and Twenty-seventh). Soon, however, General Henry Halleck forced the Confederates from Corinth and took control of northern Mississippi. In the early fall of 1862, the Texans participated in a thrust aimed at regaining the region, but they were defeated in battles at Iuka and Corinth. Grant then prepared to move on Vicksburg, the key to the Mississippi River, in 1863.

Elsewhere in the western theater in 1862 the war went a little better for Texas soldiers fighting for the Confederacy but wound up equally unpromising by the end of the year. Gen. Edmund Kirby Smith led an army from Knoxville, Tennessee, into eastern Kentucky in September, defeated Union forces at Richmond, and occupied Lexington and Frankfort. Four regiments of Texas dismounted cavalry played a key role in breaking the Federal line at Richmond. (Increasingly, Texas cavalry units were designated as "dismounted," maintaining their favored designation even if they did not have horses.) In the meantime, an army commanded by Gen. Braxton Bragg moved across central Kentucky toward Louisville. The Ninth Texas Infantry commanded by twenty-four-year-old William H. Young of Grayson County served with Bragg's invading army, and a cavalry brigade that included the Eighth Texas Cavalry protected its right flank. Better known as Terry's Texas Rangers for their first colonel, Benjamin F. Terry, who had been killed in December 1861 while they served with Johnston's army in Kentucky, the Eighth Texas had also fought at Shiloh. Before the war ended, it would fight under the command of the the famed General Nathan Bedford Forrest and earn a reputation for valor among Texas units second only to Hood's Texas Brigade. Smith and Bragg's invasion looked promising, but the Confederates soon ran into a Federal army three times their number at Perryville, Kentucky. After a bloody day of fighting on October 8, Bragg's army held the field. Then, however, recognizing that numbers were against them, he and Smith withdrew to Tennessee.

During the first half of 1863, most of the Texas soldiers in the western theater fought in the defense of Vicksburg. The four cavalry regiments that had come to northern Mississippi with Van Dorn's army in 1862 participated in harassing Gen. Grant's supply lines as Federal forces moved in position to besiege the key riverport city. The Seventh Texas Infantry, which had been captured at Fort Donelson but released in an exchange of prisoners of war, also fought in the region east of Vicksburg. Two Texas units, the Second Infantry and a force of infantry known as Waul's Texas Legion (for its commander, the fire-eating secessionist Thomas N. Waul) had the misfortune to be among the thirty thousand Confederates in Vicksburg when the city surrendered on July 4, 1863. They were released on parole pending a prisoner of war exchange; that is, they gave their word not to return to the army until the Confederacy released a matching number of captured Union soldiers.

Having split the Confederacy and taken control of western Tennessee and northern Mississippi during the first half of 1863, United States armies in the western theater then focused on eastern Tennessee and occupied the key railroad center at Chattanooga on September 9. At that point Gen. Braxton Bragg lured Union forces into pursuing his Army of Tennessee southward into northern Georgia, where he mounted a sudden attack on September 19. Some four thousand Texans fought in the ensuing two-day Battle of Chickamauga, leading one to write, "Nearly all of the Texans east of the river are concentrated here, and they will give a good account of the 'Lone Star State.'" Major units from Texas in the battle included the Ninth Infantry and Terry's Texas Rangers, both of which had been in Bragg's army since 1862; three dismounted cavalry regiments (the Tenth, Fourteenth, and Thirty-second) in the brigade commanded by Matthew D. Ector, a Rusk County lawyer-planter who enlisted as a private when the war began; the Seventh Infantry; and even the three infantry regiments from Lee's army just ordered to Tennessee with Longstreet's Corps. The Confederates paid a terrible price for their victory at

Chickamauga—eighteen to twenty thousand casualties—and did not follow it up by attacking Chattanooga, which was soon reinforced by Grant's army from Vicksburg.

In the spring of 1864, a Federal army commanded by Gen. William T. Sherman moved from East Tennessee toward Atlanta, taking the war into the heart of Georgia and pushing the Confederacy to the verge of final defeat in the western theater. Several thousand Texans fought in the Army of Tennessee as it sought to defend Atlanta. In addition to Terry's Rangers, four regiments in Ector's Brigade, and several smaller detachments, Texas units included a recently formed brigade of four infantry regiments (including the Seventh Infantry) and four dismounted cavalry regiments commanded by Gen. Hiram Granbury of Waco and a brigade of four cavalry regiments under the command of twenty-six-year-old Sul Ross, hero of the Comanche wars in Texas. Overmatched by Sherman's army, the Confederates under Gen. Joseph E. Johnston, who had replaced Bragg after the failure at Chattanooga, essentially fought defensively until mid-July 1864, when Gen. John Bell Hood was given command. Hood's courage was unquestioned—he had suffered a wound at Gettysburg that permanently disabled one arm and a thigh wound at Chickamauga that forced the amputation of a leg—but his judgment was questionable. Joe Johnston, said one Texas soldier, "has more military sense in one day than Hood ever did or ever will have." Hood threw his men into massive assaults that cost thousands of casualties—many of them Texans; nevertheless, Sherman occupied Atlanta in early September.

After losing Atlanta, Hood attempted to force Sherman out of Georgia by moving north to cut Union supply lines into Tennessee. Sherman, however, had enough troops to send one army to deal with Hood and lead his main force across Georgia to the coast at Savannah. The Confederate invasion of Tennessee turned into a disaster. On November 30, Hood's army attacked entrenched Federals at Franklin in an uncoordinated assault that cost seven thousand casualties, including Gen. Hiram Granbury who was shot in the face and killed. The defenders then pulled back to Nashville, and Hood's battered army followed with the intent of taking up siege positions and waiting for help from west of the Mississippi. Unfortunately for the Confederates, Union forces, having received reinforcements, attacked in overwhelming numbers on December 15. Hood's troops held their lines for a day but then broke and retreated toward Mississippi. By December 31, Granbury's Brigade had fewer than 350 men, and Ector's had fewer than 575. As they retreated, the Confederates sang, to the tune of "The Yellow Rose of Texas," "You can talk about your Beauregard and sing of General Lee, but the Gallant Hood of Texas played Hell in Tennessee." Gen. Joe Johnston resumed command of the Army of Tennessee, but for all practical purposes it no longer existed.

By January 1865 the Confederacy clearly had lost the war in the western theater, but Texas units held on with the army until the end in April. Ector's Brigade and Ross's Brigade were detached from the Army of Tennessee and completed their service in Alabama and Mississippi respectively in April. Three Texas regiments, including Terry's Rangers and the remnants of

Granbury's Brigade, remained with Johnston's army as it sought hopelessly to oppose Sherman in the Carolinas and surrendered in late April. Actually, a good many of the men in Terry's regiment did not formally surrender; they simply broke up and drifted home individually and in small groups.

Texas Soldiers in the Trans-Mississippi

Obviously, Texans, while interested in the fate of Confederate armies in the east, had more concern with the war west of the Mississippi River, and most Texas soldiers spent the war in the Trans-Mississippi region. (See map: The Trans-Mississippi Theater, 1861–1865.) Fortunately for them and their homes, most of the battles they fought took place outside Texas. To some extent, particularly in 1861–1862, this resulted from the application of an old adage: "the best defense is a good offense."

In May 1861 Col. William C. Young of Cooke County in North Texas raised a mounted regiment and acted to secure the state's boundary with the Indian Territory. Taking his unit, which soon went into Confederate service as the Eleventh Texas Cavalry, across the Red River, Young took control of Forts Washita, Arbuckle, and Cobb and negotiated treaties with several of the Indian groups in the area. Union forces were not strong in the Indian Territory—the forts were abandoned before Young's cavalry arrived—nevertheless, his action eliminated any potential threat of invasion from that direction.

Texans also went on the offensive in New Mexico in 1861. In July Lt. Col. John R. Baylor, the noted Indian-hater who had played a key role in destroying the Texas reservations, led several companies of the Second Texas Mounted Rifles northward from El Paso to occupy Mesilla on the Río Grande near present-day Las Cruces. He then created the Confederate Territory of Arizona,

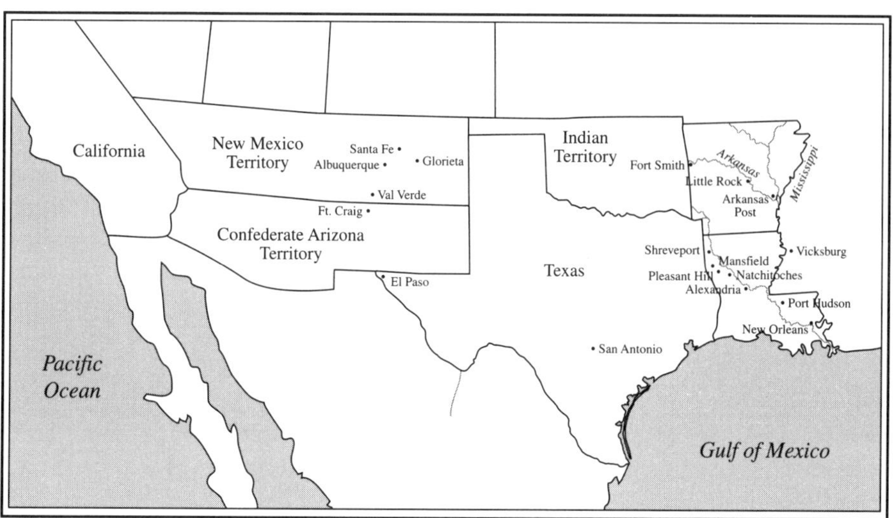

The Trans-Mississippi Theater, 1861–1865

which included the Southern half of New Mexico and Arizona. In the meantime, President Jefferson Davis authorized Gen. Henry H. Sibley, a Louisiana-born West Point graduate with an outstanding military record, to conquer all of New Mexico and then attack Colorado and possibly even California. Sibley traveled to San Antonio, organized three regiments of Texas cavalry into the "Army of New Mexico," and took up the conquest begun by Baylor. From Mesilla, Sibley moved north along the Río Grande toward Fort Craig, which was held by Union troops. Finding the fort too strong to attack from the south, Sibley decided to bypass it on the east side of the river. When his army sought to cross back to the west at Valverde ford about five miles above the fort on February 21, 1862, Union troops blocked their way. The Texans led by Tom Green and William R. Scurry won the battle at Valverde, but they did not pursue their advantage and take the fort. Sibley's army pushed on to occupy Albuquerque and Santa Fe, although the men increasingly lost confidence in Sibley who appeared to be a drunk and a coward. In March, Confederate units moving into the mountains east of Santa Fe on their way to attack Fort Union near present-day Las Vegas were met by Federal troops at Glorieta Pass. Texans under the command of Scurry won the battle, but while it raged, a Union force moved in behind the Confederates and destroyed a wagon train carrying essential food, ammunition, and medicine. Gen. Sibley, facing problems of supply and hearing of Union reinforcements, decided to return to Texas, effectively ending all Confederate presence there. In New Mexico, the battle of Glorieta Pass is called the "Gettysburg of the West."

Confederate Texans also went on the offensive in Missouri during the summer of 1861 when Ben McCulloch, the veteran of many fights in Texas and Mexico, led a brigade that included the Third Texas Cavalry to the support of Gen. Sterling Price's army of pro-south Missourians. On August 10, troops commanded by Price and McCulloch defeated a Union army at Oak Hill (Wilson's Creek) in southern Missouri. The Confederates followed up their advantage by occupying Springfield but then went into winter quarters in northern Arkansas. Early the next spring, Gen. Earl Van Dorn, a Mississippian appointed to command of the combined forces of McCulloch and Price, planned an invasion of Missouri aimed at capturing St. Louis and threatening Illinois. Van Dorn opened his campaign with an attack on a Union army in northwestern Arkansas that turned into the two-day battle of Pea Ridge (Elkhorn Tavern) on March 7–8, 1862. On the afternoon of the first day, McCulloch suffered a fatal wound; his successor in command, Arkansas Col. James McIntosh, died a few minutes later leading a charge; and the third commander, Col. Louis Hebert of Louisiana, was captured. These losses crippled and immobilized about half of the Confederate force. Col. Elkanah Greer of the Third Texas Cavalry assumed command of the division. Fighting continued the next morning, but at noon Van Dorn broke off the engagement and retreated. Some of the Texans criticized the decision bitterly—"I was never so astonished in my life," said one—but regardless of blame, the defeat at Pea Ridge ended Confederate hopes of taking Missouri from the Union.

During the summer and fall of 1862, the focus of Texan efforts in the Trans-Mississippi turned from taking the offensive in the Indian Territory, New Mexico, and Missouri to defending the Lone Star State. The four hundred miles of coastline stretching from the Sabine River to the Río Grande offered numerous opportunities for an invasion, but the United States, although it began a bothersome naval blockade in July 1861, made no serious attempt to land on Texas's shores until more than a year later. Most expected the first attack to come at Galveston, but in mid-August 1862, a five-ship Union flotilla attempted to capture Corpus Christi. Confederate defenders under the leadership of Maj. Alfred M. Hobby beat back several landing parties and even captured the Union commander. A month later Union warships entered Sabine Pass at the mouth of the river separating Texas and Louisiana, destroyed Confederate defensive positions there, and threatened Beaumont. The Federals' real target, however, was Galveston, the state's most important port city.

Galveston had no defense against Union occupation because of decisions made by Gen. Paul O. Hebert, commander of the District of Texas since September 1861. Hebert, the top student in his 1840 graduating class at West Point, was the classic example of a textbook soldier utterly lacking in common sense. Believing it impossible to prevent a landing at Galveston, he had ordered all the island's heavy weapons removed to the mainland. Thus, when Union Commander William B. Renshaw brought four warships into Galveston Bay on October 4, 1862, the Confederates could only ask for a four-day truce to permit civilians to evacuate and then surrender. Local attorney William Pitt Ballinger, although a Unionist, called it "a bleak day in our history" as 150 U.S. troops occupied the city.

In November, Gen. John B. Magruder took command of the District of Texas and immediately began to plan to retake Galveston. "Prince John," as his friends called him because of his love of fancy dress uniforms, fine food, and the theater, organized a coordinated attack by land and water. (See map: The Battle of Galveston, January 1, 1863.) After midnight on January 1, 1863, a force of nearly two thousand Texas troops, many of them participants in the New Mexico campaign, crossed the railroad bridge from the mainland to the island and moved to a position in town from which their artillery could shell the 260 Union troops barracked on the bayside wharf. They opened fire at 4 A.M. and attempted a charge with five hundred men but were driven back by the Federals, who had supporting fire from the six Union gunboats in the harbor. Just then, as the land attack appeared on the verge of failure, the other half of Magruder's plan came into play. Two Confederate gunboats, each carrying more than one hundred soldiers protected behind cotton bales, steamed into the harbor from the upper part of Galveston Bay. Not having heavy firepower equal to the Union gunboats, the Confederates hoped to have their "marines" use rifles to clear the decks of the enemy warships until they could be approached close enough to board. The Federals' heavy guns had the better of the fight at first, nearly disabling both Confederate vessels. But the sharpshooters forced sailors on the nearest Union gunboat, the *Harriet Lane*,

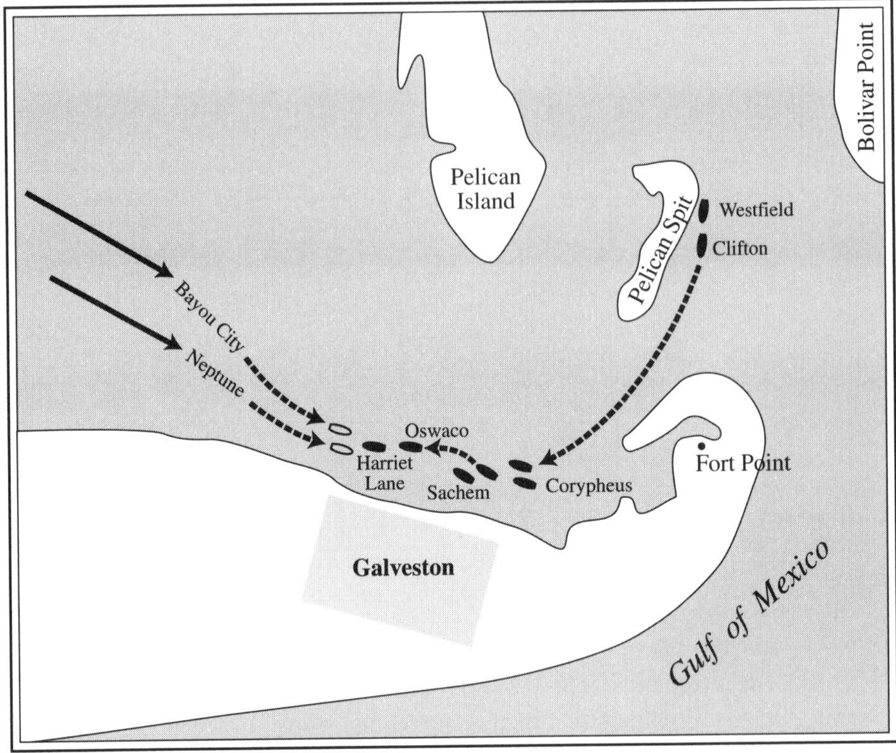

The Battle of Galveston, January 1, 1863

belowdecks until one of the attacking gunboats could ram it and lock the two together. The Texans then leaped to the deck of the *Lane* and forced its surrender. One of the Federal officers killed, Lt. Commander Edward Lea, was the son of Lt. Col. Albert M. Lea, an officer on Magruder's staff. The next day the Confederate father presided over the funeral of his Union son. In this terrible instance, the Civil War, rather than a "war among brothers," was a fight between father and son.

The capture of the *Harriet Lane* created confusion among the other Union gunboats, and then William Renshaw, commander of the flotilla, ran his ship aground near the mouth of the harbor. Renshaw refused Confederate demands that he surrender, planning instead to scuttle his ship, but the improvised explosive charge used for that purpose blew up as he was climbing down a ladder into a small boat and killed him. At that, the next ranking officer ordered the Union gunboats to leave the harbor and head for New Orleans. The Union troops on the wharf, seeing the gunboats leave, had no choice but surrender. Magruder and the Confederates had retaken Galveston, much to the joy of Texans and the chagrin of Union authorities. "Prince John" then strengthened the city's defenses with heavy guns to the extent that the United States did not attack it again.

During the summer and fall of 1862 Texas soldiers in the Trans-Mississippi also fought in the defense of Arkansas and Louisiana, campaigns that obviously involved the security of their home state in the future. Five Texas cavalry regiments aided in the successful defense of Little Rock and central Arkansas throughout 1862, but disaster came early in 1863. By January of that year Confederate commanders had ordered nearly five thousand troops, including two infantry regiments and five dismounted cavalry regiments from Texas, into Fort Hindman, an earthenworks post on the Arkansas River about twenty-five miles from its mouth on the Mississippi. One of the Texans commented that the fort, which was also known as Arkansas Post, looked like "Fort Donaldson *[sic]* No 2," and events soon proved him correct. In early January a Union force of thirty thousand men supported by gunboats arrived and quickly forced a Confederate surrender. The enlisted men wound up as prisoners of war at Camp Douglas, and officers were sent to Camp Chase in Ohio, where conditions were a little better. Union forces did not follow up their advantage immediately, but by September they took Little Rock and forced the Confederates into southwestern Arkansas.

In 1863 Texas troops in Louisiana, most importantly a division commanded by Gen. John G. Walker, sought to ease the pressure being placed on Vicksburg by Grant's Union army. Walker's Texas Division, often called the "Greyhound Division" for its ability to cover long distances in a short time, was the only such unit of men from a single state to serve in either army. It consisted of three brigades, each with several regiments of infantry and dismounted cavalry and an artillery battery, and at times had a fourth brigade as well. Walker attacked several Union positions on the Mississippi, and several thousand other Texas troops under the command of Gen. Richard Taylor campaigned against Federal forces in the bayou country of south Louisiana, but nothing they did could prevent the fall of Vicksburg in July 1863 and the surrender of Port Hudson at the mouth of the Red River a few days later.

Once the United States cut the Confederacy in two at the Mississippi and gained control of much of Arkansas and Louisiana, Texas appeared open to invasion from many directions. Union armies could move up the Red River to attack northeast Texas, an especially inviting target because Gen. Edmund Kirby Smith, commander of the Trans-Mississippi Department after February 1863, had located his entire base of operations in that region. Also, they could attack at many points along the Gulf coast or possibly even move through the bayou country toward southeastern Texas.

The first Federal attack on Texas in 1863 came in September at Sabine Pass. Gen. Nathaniel P. Banks, knowing that Union troops had landed at the pass in 1862 and destroyed the fort there, believed that it would be lightly defended. Moreover, once the Federals secured Sabine Pass, they could easily capture Beaumont and use rail connections from there to Houston to break out into the entire region. In September 1863 Banks sent five thousand troops on transports escorted by four gunboats to take Fort Griffin, a recently constructed post just north of the one destroyed a year earlier. The fort, which had six guns covering the waterway, was commanded by Lt. Richard "Dick"

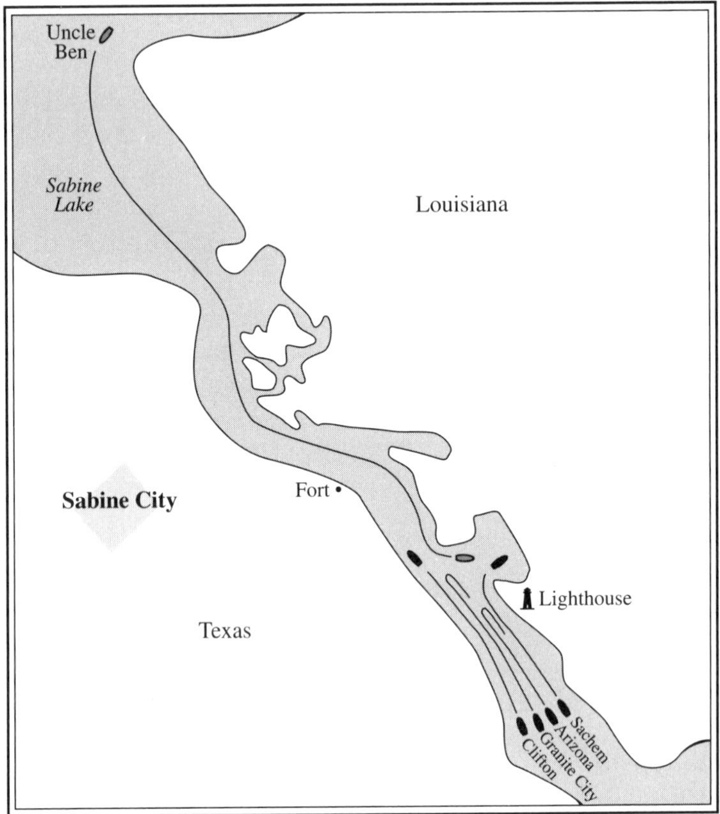

Battle of Sabine Pass, September 8, 1863

Dowling, an Irishman who had become an artilleryman during the war. Prior to the conflict most of his experience involved running a variety of saloons.

Three of the Union gunboats opened the action by moving up the pass to attack the fort while the fourth covered the landing of troops from transport vessels. (See map: The Battle of Sabine Pass, September 8, 1863.) When the warships came within twelve hundred yards, however, Dowling's gunners, who had practiced sighting their weapons at that distance, poured devastatingly accurate fire on them. In less than an hour the forty-two Confederates commanded by Dowling disabled and captured two of the gunboats and caused the other two and the transports to withdraw, killed or captured 350 Federals, and forced the entire Union expedition to withdraw. Jefferson Davis called the defense of Sabine Pass "one of the most brilliant and heroic achievements in the history of this war." As was the case with Galveston, Gen. Magruder then strengthened defenses along the pass so that the Union did not attack there again.

General Banks sought to recover from the embarrassment of Sabine Pass by launching two new offensives against Texas in the fall of 1863. First, he sent an expedition from New Orleans across southern Louisiana to Bayou Teche where it could turn north toward Alexandria on the Red River with the intention of following that waterway into northeast Texas or moving directly west toward Houston. This so-called "Texas Overland Expedition" came to nothing in November, when units from Walker's Texas Division and a cavalry brigade commanded by Tom Green, a veteran of the New Mexico expedition and the retaking of Galveston, defeated the Federals near Opelousas at Bayou Bourbeau.

Union troops had more success on the lower Texas coast in November, landing at Brazos Santiago off the mouth of the Río Grande and moving inland to occupy Brownsville. Gen. Hamilton P. Bee, who had replaced "Rip" Ford as commander in the area, saw that he had no chance to defeat seven thousand Federals, so he evacuated the city and ordered the burning of all supplies that could not be moved. The occupying force then moved north along the coast—taking Corpus Christi and Matagorda Island by the end of December 1863—and up the Río Grande as far as Roma. South Texas appeared lost at the beginning of 1864, and General Magruder, fearing an attack on the coast somewhere between the Sabine and Brazos Rivers, concentrated more than five thousand Texas troops in that area. This did not mean, however, that he conceded control of South Texas. Instead, in March 1864 he ordered Col. "Rip" Ford, commander of the forces that occupied Brownsville at the beginning of the war and later head of recruitment in Texas, to raise an army and drive the Federals from the lower Río Grande. Ford's cavalry force left San Antonio for Brownsville in mid-March, but while en route, he learned that Union troops had attempted to take Laredo. A small group of defenders commanded by Col. Santos Benavides, a local rancher-merchant who became the highest-ranking Mexican American in the Confederate Army, had repulsed the attack; nevertheless, Ford decided to see to Laredo's defense before moving on Brownsville. Reaching that point on April 15, he then began a cautious move down the Río Grande. Fortunately for Ford's eighteen hundred soldiers, the Union had withdrawn most of its six thousand troops from the area for use in Louisiana. On July 30, the Confederates rode unopposed into Brownsville, all Union troops except for twelve hundred on Brazos Island off the mouth of the Río Grande having been evacuated. A similar evacuation had taken place in the vicinity of Corpus Christi.

The United States all but eliminated its military presence in South Texas during the first half of 1864 because its leaders decided to focus on an invasion of northern Louisiana and eastern Texas via the Red River. A successful campaign up the Red River, Union commanders reasoned, would disrupt the Trans-Mississippi's command center and capture an estimated 150,000 bales of cotton, which could be sold by the government to supply-hungry New England manufacturers. General Banks began his advance up river in March with thirty thousand troops supported by the largest flotilla of gunboats to participate in any inland waters expedition during the war. To oppose the invaders, Gen. Richard Taylor had some seven thousand Confederates, including Walker's Texas Division and another division under Gen. Alfred Mouton of Louisiana. One of the brigades in Mouton's division consisted of Texans under the command of a French aristocrat, Camille Armand Jules Marie, Prince de Polignac, who had volunteered to fight for the Confederacy. The Texas soldiers, admiring Polignac's fighting ability but having limited experience with French, called him "polecat." In early April two more Texas units, Tom Green's cavalry division and a new cavalry brigade commanded by Hamilton P. Bee, joined Taylor's army.

For nearly a month, Taylor's army retreated up the Red River in the face of overwhelming numbers, but then on April 8, some forty miles south of Shreveport, the Confederates took a stand and fought. The resulting Battle of Mansfield (Sabine Crossroads) shattered Banks's offensive against Texas. His army suffered 2,200 casualties among the 12,000 soldiers involved and lost huge numbers of animals and supplies as well. Taylor, although his forces lost 1,000 of the 8,800 men who fought, pursued the retreating Federals and attacked them again on April 9 at Pleasant Hill. This second battle also cost both armies heavy casualties and ended inconclusively. Banks continued his retreat down the river, and the Confederates were too bloodied to do more than harass the invaders, especially since Walker's "greyhounds" were sent north where they helped stop a Federal invasion of southern Arkansas.

Ironically, the Red River campaign brought thousands of Union soldiers to Texas as prisoners of war rather than conquerors. Most of the several thousand prisoners taken at Mansfield and Pleasant Hill were marched to Camp Ford, a prison compound near Tyler. Camp Ford, which was originally established as a training center, became a military prison in August 1863. Until the spring of 1864 it had only a few prisoners taken in Arkansas and Louisiana and in fights on the Texas coast, but then the number rose to more than 4,500, making Camp Ford the largest military prison in the Trans-Mississippi Department. Living conditions in the crowded camp deteriorated from a lack of shelter, food, and clothing, and 286 prisoners, 5 percent of the total, died. This death rate drew criticism, as it should have, but was far lower than the 12 percent rate for Confederates in Union prisons such as Camp Douglas. In 1864 some of the prisoners were moved to Camp Groce near Hempstead, where living conditions were somewhat worse and the death rate slightly higher.

During the second half of 1864 and the early months of 1865, while the Confederacy's last hopes died in the war east of the Mississippi, the Trans-Mississippi saw little heavy fighting. Texas had no Union troops on its soil, except for a small force at Brazos Santiago, when word came in April 1865 that Lee and Johnston had surrendered, so the reaction among leaders tended to be one of defiance. Gens. Kirby Smith and Magruder appealed to their troops to stand firm, and newspaper editors urged no surrender. When on May 8 the Union commander at St. Louis proposed a surrender on terms similar to those granted at Appomattox, Kirby Smith and the governors of the Trans-Mississippi states met and rejected the offer, proposing instead that the war simply end without a formal surrender. Increasingly, however, Texas soldiers, recognizing that the war was lost, voted for peace with their feet. That is, they simply went home.

While the surrender of Texas remained in doubt, Confederate and Union troops fought the last battle of the Civil War on May 13, 1865, at Palmito Ranch near Brownsville. Confederates under Col. "Rip" Ford routed a unit of Federal soldiers that crossed from Brazos Island to the mainland and moved upriver, but even a fighter such as Ford had to admit that the war was over. Several days after the battle, he met with Union officers in Brownsville and arranged to stop the fighting. Ford's soldiers went home while he and his wife crossed into Mexico.

The second half of May 1865 became known in Texas as the "break up." Gen. Kirby Smith had ordered troops to concentrate at Houston and await his arrival, but increasing numbers ignored their commander and headed home. Many of the soldiers who left looted government supplies of clothing and food and in some cases stole from civilians as well. Arsenals and munitions factories were left open for pillage. One young man described the situation at a powder mill near Marshall: "Boys and men helped themselves—no guards, no precautions—bags were torn, kegs shattered and powder covered the floor." Thomas Affleck, a pro-Confederate Washington County planter, wrote, "[T]he army has entirely disbanded, & are sacking as they go. . . . We have no Govt. or country. God help us." The end was at hand for Texans—not only for the soldiers but also for those who had endured the war at home.

The Home Front

Texas escaped any major invasion of its interior by Union armies during the war; therefore, Texans at home did not pay quite the price exacted from many other Southerners between 1861 and 1865. There were material privations and hardship, of course, but few suffered seriously from shortages of the necessities of life. Instead, the greatest burdens for those at home came from the heartbreaking loss of life in the army, the brutal disputes resulting from internal dissent, and continuing conflict on the Indian frontier.

With no invasion to disrupt its agricultural economy, Texas continued throughout the war to produce food and raise livestock in quantities that fed the army and the population at home. Shortages of salt caused problems, but the state never had bread riots such as those in Richmond, Mobile, and Atlanta. Nonessentials such as coffee and liquor were in short supply at times, but even those often became available thanks to the Texas home front's economic "ace in the hole"—the cotton trade. War did not dampen the world's demand for cotton, and Texas producers, because of their state's border with Mexico, were perfectly situated to get around the Union blockade and sell their staple crop. Almost immediately after the firing on Ft. Sumter, Texans began to organize wagon trains that carried cotton to Matamoros, the Mexican town opposite Brownsville on the Río Grande. Producers generally moved their cotton to either Alleyton in Colorado County or San Antonio; then, teamsters followed a route that ran through the King Ranch and on to Matamoros. Small steamboats then took the cotton down the Río Grande to a coastal town called Bagdad, where it was transshipped to oceangoing vessels. When Union troops occupied Brownsville in late 1863, Texans took the cotton across upriver at Laredo and then down the Mexican side to Bagdad. Before the war ended, Texas exported 320,000 bales of cotton and used the proceeds to import military supplies, medicines, dry goods, liquors, and coffee. Some cotton was carried out and goods brought in by fast steam and sailing ships that ran the Union blockade outside Gulf ports such as Galveston and Corpus Christi, but this activity amounted to little compared to the Río Grande trade.

Texas agriculture remained so productive during the war in large part because the conflict did not disturb slavery in any major way. Even when thousands of white men left for the army, slaves continued to produce food and cotton. Bondsmen knew that a Union victory probably would bring freedom. One remembered a white minister asking slaves at a worship service to raise their hands if they wished to pray for a Confederate victory. "We all raised our hands because we was scared not to," he said, "but we sure didn't want the South to win." Texas slaves, however, did not rebel or run away in larger numbers during the war, and only a handful served in the Union army—forty-seven in a total of 98,594 black Union soldiers recruited in the Confederate states. Texas slaveholders saw this, of course, as "commendable loyalty" on the part of the bondsmen, but in fact it was a matter of opportunity. Federal troops never penetrated the interior of the state and provided encouragement to runaways; moreover, security measures such as slave patrols were strengthened. Bondsmen in Texas had little choice but to work and wait.

Indeed, slavery remained so secure in Texas during the war that thousands of bondsmen were brought in for safekeeping as Federal forces overran other regions of the Confederacy. "Refugeeing," as this Civil War version of "Gone to Texas" became known, began in 1862 and continued through most of 1864. A Texas soldier in southern Arkansas in December 1863 described refugees "bound for Texas; with hundreds and I might truthfully say thousands of slaves." The total number of refugeed slaves probably reached more than thirty thousand. Most of the refugee masters and slaves lived along the middle Trinity and Brazos Rivers in the interior of East Texas. The presence of so many new arrivals alarmed some Texans, but Governor Francis Lubbock offered assurances in November 1863 that the state had enough land, food, and work "to keep these negroes beneficially and constantly employed."

The most important disruption of slavery during the war came from the use of slave labor to build fortifications and supply other manpower needs of the Confederacy. In November 1861, General Paul O. Hebert asked slaveholders to loan their bondsmen to construct coastal defenses but found them generally reluctant to risk valuable property in such unhealthy and dangerous work. This attitude, in other states as well as Texas, led the Confederate Congress in March 1863 to authorize the impressment of slaves for sixty days of public service at a rate of fifteen dollars a month. In July of that year, Gen. Magruder established a Labor Bureau that impressed slaves to construct fortifications, drive cotton wagons to the Río Grande, and build a stockade to hold Federal prisoners at Camp Ford near Tyler. He proposed mass impressment when Federal forces under General Banks threatened to move inland from the Gulf coast in December 1863 but then relented. Ironically, impressment united master and slave in that both opposed it for nearly the same reason—absence from home and the risk of injury or disease.

The greatest suffering for many and perhaps most Texans at home during the war came not from material privation but from the terrible toll taken by disease and battle on men in the army. It is impossible to determine exactly how many soldiers from Texas entered military service or the number who lost their lives to illness or in battle or suffered crippling wounds. Volunteers rushed to join in 1861, but by April 1862 their numbers slowed in Texas and across the South to the point that the Confederate Congress passed a conscription act making all able-bodied white males between the ages of eighteen and thirty-five eligible to be drafted for three years of military service. This act also extended the service of volunteers already in the army to a total of three years. The upper age limit was raised to forty-five in September 1862 and to fifty in February 1864 at the same time that the lower limit was reduced to seventeen. Ultimately then, all white males who were aged thirteen to forty-six in 1860, and therefore seventeen to fifty by 1864, were liable for the draft. To be drafted, however, generally was considered a disgrace, so these laws acted to encourage volunteering rather than to fill the ranks with draftees. As one East Texas newspaper editor put it when the first act passed, "There will be no conscripts in Texas for everyone between the ages of 18 and 35 is volunteering."

Although estimates have ranged as high as ninety thousand the most reasonable approximation of the number of Texans who served between 1861 and 1865, either in the Confederate Army or in state troop units, is sixty to seventy thousand, a little more than half of its military-age population in 1860. These men came from all ranks of society, with the wealthiest slaveholders and their sons often being among the first to volunteer. Some critics then and since, noting such things as the provision in the 1862 conscription act that provided exemptions for anyone charged with the supervision of twenty or more slaves, have argued that the conflict was "a rich man's war and a poor man's fight." In-depth studies of Texas units in the Confederate Army show a very different picture, however. For Texans, the war, while it was indeed a "rich man's war" brought on by slavery, was also a "rich man's fight" and to a somewhat lesser extent a "poor man's fight" as well.

Approximately 20 to 25 percent of Texas soldiers died while in the army. More than half of these deaths resulted from a variety of illnesses. Putting thousands of men who had built up relatively few immunities while growing up on scattered farms and in small towns into camps with virtually no sanitation facilities guaranteed devastating outbreaks of infectious diseases. Deaths in battle and Union prisoner-of-war camps accounted for the other lives lost. The final death toll can be estimated at between twelve and fifteen thousand men, most of them in their twenties and thirties. (To appreciate the magnitude of such a loss, consider the following: If Texas had entered a war in 2001 with its population as reported in the 2000 census and had 50 percent of its males aged thirteen to forty-six in the census enter military service and

20 percent of those who served die, total deaths would have been more than 540,000 men.) These statistics, of course, tell nothing of the losses in human terms. Most deaths brought heartbreak to fathers, mothers, brothers and sisters, wives, and children. In a scene repeated literally thousands of times across the state, the Harrison County family of Josiah D. Perry learned in the fall of 1862 that one son had been killed and another wounded at Sharpsburg. Perry's brother, Dr. Harwood P. Perry, also lost one son and had another barely survive his wounds in the same battle. "I am so sorry for them all," wrote the wife of a family member. "They are in great distress." One of the wounded boys recovered, only to rejoin his unit in Hood's Texas Brigade and be killed at the Battle of the Wilderness in 1864.

Many Texas soldiers survived the war but came home weakened by wounds, disease, and imprisonment. The stories of only two exemplify those of thousands. Twenty-seven-year-old James C. Bates of the Ninth Texas Cavalry suffered a gunshot wound in the mouth during an engagement near the Etowah River in northern Georgia on May 19, 1864. The minié ball split Bates's tongue, broke his jaw, and exited below and behind his left ear, carrying with it most of the teeth from the left side of his mouth. The wound caused his mouth and tongue to swell so that he could not eat or drink, requiring him to push a tube down his throat as the only way to ingest water. Somehow Bates survived. After the war he became a doctor, but he never fully recovered from his years of service and died in 1891 at the relatively young age of fifty-four. Josiah Perry Alford of the Seventh Texas Infantry entered the war at the age of nineteen in 1861. He suffered a wound to his left thigh at Chickamauga in 1863 and endured an amputation on the battlefield without benefit of anesthetic. After the war Alford served as county clerk of Harrison County, but he died at the age of fifty-three in 1897. His wife, in applying for a Confederate pension many years later, said that he "suffered from [the amputation] as long as he lived."

Texas women, with perhaps one or two exceptions, did not serve in Confederate or state military units, but certainly they joined men in paying a high price for the war. Women settlers on the frontier faced even greater dangers from Indian raiders than they had before the war. Those who lived in more settled areas were not in immediate danger, but few if any escaped hardship from 1861 to 1865. First, there was simply the pain of separation when sons, husbands, and brothers left home. Undoubtedly thousands shared the sentiments expressed by one East Texas wife to her husband in 1862: "I frequently wake up at night and feel as though my heart would break, tears are my greatest relief. I do not sleep at all. I often get up and sit by the window for some time and would give worlds, if I had them, if you could be with me."

Often, while adjusting to the loneliness of separation, women also faced the pressure of managing farms and plantations and supervising slaves. For some widows and unmarried women, this was not a new experience, and others apparently shouldered the new responsibility with little difficulty. Rebecca Adams, for example, the daughter of one of Texas's largest slaveholders, took over the family plantation near Fairfield when her husband and oldest son

Josiah Perry Alford (1843–1897). This 1860 photograph shows the legendary fighting pride of young Texans. Alford served in the Seventh Texas Infantry until the Battle of Chickamauga where, on September 18, 1863, he suffered a wound in his left leg and endured an amputation on the battlefield. Credit: From the Collections of the Harrison Country Historical Museum, Marshall, Texas.

entered the army. She successfully supervised fifty slaves in doing all necessary farm work while taking care of nine children. Sara Armour Munson of Brazoria County also ran a plantation while her husband was in military service. Under her direction, slaves produced cotton and food crops, raised livestock, and made shoes and hats. Some women, of course, found the demands placed on them overwhelming. Lizzie Scott Neblett of Grimes County regularly complained to her husband about problems with their slaves. "I am awfully tired of them," she wrote in 1864. "Ten thousand times I have wished you had listened to me—sold them all but what we wanted to wait on us, years ago. I don't say much about them [!], but they are a great trouble to me—a perfect vexation." Yet, when an overseer whipped some of the slaves, Neblett stepped in to stop it. Eventually the frustrations and anxieties she faced led her to begin abusing her five children.

Finally, women had to live every day during the war with the fear that a husband or other family member would die in the army. How could anyone not pity Harriet Person Perry of Harrison County whose husband Theophilus was an officer in Walker's Texas Division? Two of her husband's cousins were killed at Sharpsburg in 1862. "I don't know what is to become of us," Harriet wrote her sister. "We are sorely scourged if any people were." A year later she learned of the deaths of two of her brothers serving in North Carolina units. "Now sorrow is added to sorrow," she wrote her mother. "Truly misfortunes come not singly." Earlier, thinking of her husband, she had written her sister, "I want to stay as near to him as I can while he lives for I have no idea he will ever return to stay. War makes its widows by the thousands." The Battle of Pleasant Hill in April 1864 made her one of those widows.

In spite of the hardships and terrible loss of life, most Texans continued throughout the war to support the Confederacy as they had supported secession in the first place. Voters demonstrated their stance by choosing governors on the basis of their commitment to the cause. Edward Clark, who succeeded Sam Houston as governor in March 1861, worked closely with Confederate authorities to provide men and supplies for the army. However, when Clark ran for full term that fall, he lost very narrowly to Francis R. Lubbock, a South Carolina–born Democrat known for his ultra-Southern views. Lubbock strongly supported the Confederacy during his two-year term, working especially hard to uphold the conscription law. In 1863, Lubbock entered the army rather than run for a second term, opening the way for a gubernatorial contest between Pendleton Murrah and Thomas Jefferson Chambers. Although much better known, Chambers lost, primarily it seems because of his outspoken hostility toward Jefferson Davis's Confederate government. Murrah became involved in disputes with Magruder and Kirby Smith over conscription and the cotton trade—arguing that men enrolled in state service in frontier counties were not eligible for the draft and that the state rather than the Confederate military should control the selling of Texas cotton—but he remained loyal to the end. When Kirby Smith surrendered the state in 1865, the governor left for Mexico, where he died later that year.

The minority of Texans who opposed secession varied widely in their reactions to the Confederacy. Some accepted the decision to the point of serving in political office or in the army during the war. The best known of these "Unionist Confederates" was James W. Throckmorton of Collin County, who voted against disunion but then commanded a regiment in the Confederate Army and later became a brigadier general of state troops. Others such as former governor Elisha M. Pease never supported the Confederacy but simply remained quietly at home throughout the war. Some of the more vocal Unionists had to leave Texas. James P. Newcomb, editor of the *San Antonio Alamo Express,* fled to New Mexico after a mob attacked his press, and federal judge Thomas DuVal of Austin moved to New Orleans. William Marsh Rice, one of the wealthiest merchants in Houston, moved his business to Matamoros during the war and never returned to Texas. Eventually, of course, his fortune endowed the educational institution that became Rice University.

Some Texans carried their opposition to disunion and the Confederacy to the point of joining the United States Army. Edmund J. Davis, a native of

Florida who came to Texas in 1848 and served as a district judge in the region from Corpus Christi to Brownsville, became the best known of these Unionists. He left the state in 1862 and, after receiving a colonel's commission from the government in Washington, raised a regiment of loyalists like himself. The First Texas Cavalry (Union) served in the Texas Overland Campaign in 1863 and participated in the Federal occupation of the lower Río Grande Valley at the end of that year. Once Brownsville was occupied, Unionists under the command of Virginia-born John L. Haynes formed the Second Texas Cavalry (Union). In July 1864 these two regiments, by then united as a brigade commanded by Davis, left Texas for Louisiana where they served out the war. A little more than two thousand Texans, including 958 Tejanos, served in these units.

Finally, small groups of Unionists living in regions that voted against secession organized internal opposition to the Confederacy. Authorities in Texas took such organizations as dangerously subversive, and predictably grim events followed. One serious incident came when Germans in the Hill Country northwest of San Antonio formed a Union Loyal League with its own military companies, supposedly for purposes of frontier protection but also to help restore Federal authority if possible. In the spring of 1862 Confederate officials sent Texas troops into the region to disband the military companies and enforce the conscription law, whereupon sixty-one of the Unionists, mostly Germans led by Frederick "Fritz" Tegener, decided to go to Mexico and from there join the United States Army. They headed for the Río Grande but were overtaken by a detachment of ninety-one Texas Partisan Rangers commanded by Lt. Colin D. McRae, while camped on the Nueces River. Attacking before dawn on August 10, 1862, the Confederates killed nineteen of the Germans and captured nine who were badly wounded. The remaining Unionists, including Tegener, who was wounded, escaped. McRae and seventeen of his men were wounded; two were killed. After the battle, state troops executed the nine wounded Germans, and nine of those who escaped were caught and killed before they reached Mexico. In 1866, loyalists gathered the remains of those who died in the fight and buried them under a monument at Comfort in Kendall County.

An even more notorious incident involving internal dissent occurred during October 1862 in Cooke County, which is located in the area of North Texas that had voted against secession. There, the passage of conscription led to the formation of a secret Peace Party that opposed the draft and supported the Union. Rumors that the Peace Party planned to seize local militia arsenals and foment a general uprising led to the arrest on October 1 of more than 150 suspected insurrectionists by state troops. Col. William C. Young of the Eleventh Texas Cavalry, who was home on sick leave, and Col. James G. Bourland of the state troops supervised the selection of an extralegal "Citizen's Court" that found seven leading Unionists guilty of treason and sentenced them to death. At that point, a mob, panicked by rumors of the plot, lynched fourteen more of the prisoners and killed two who tried to escape. Matters became even worse a few days later when unknown assassins killed Col. Young from ambush while he was hunting. The jury then sentenced another nineteen men to hang, bringing the total number of victims to forty-two. Texas authorities condoned this "Great Hanging at Gainesville," but it embarrassed the Confederacy by lending credence to charges about rebel barbarism.

The Indian frontier, which saw few calm times during the late 1850s, remained a troubling aspect of the home front from 1861 to 1865. Confederate authorities in Richmond considered Indian raids in Texas "merely predatory," in the words of one official, and left frontier defense to the state. The First and Second Texas Mounted Rifles took over that task in the spring of 1861, but those units soon entered Confederate service and focused their efforts elsewhere. To fill the void, the state legislature in December 1861 created a unit called the Frontier Regiment. This regiment of about one thousand men established sixteen camps just west of the line of settlements and used a system of patrols between the various camps to locate Indian raiders. The frontier remained relatively quiet in 1862, but by early 1863 Comanches and Kiowas from the Indian Territory recognized the routine nature of patrols and began to make more frequent and daring raids, particularly in northwestern counties such as Montague and Wise. Confederate authorities responded by allowing Col. James Bourland, who had recently gained notoriety for his role in the Great Hanging, to raise a so-called Border Regiment of cavalry. Bourland's command operated on both sides of the Red River until the close of the war. The last important change in protecting the frontier came in March 1864 when the Frontier Regiment was transferred to Confederate service and replaced with the Frontier Organization. Operating on the idea that those who lived on the frontier had primary responsibility for defending it, the Frontier Organization enrolled all men liable for military service who lived in the fifty-nine frontier counties of Texas. It had nearly four thousand men in service when it became operative and remained in effect until mid-1865.

These units would have had enough difficulties defending the frontier if they could have focused on Indian raiders alone. However, from 1863 to 1865, deserters and draft dodgers added immensely to their problems. Nearly five thousand Texans deserted from Confederate and state service, and an unknown number avoided conscription. They hid in isolated areas throughout the state—for example, the Big Thicket in Hardin County and the swamp bottoms of northeast Texas—but the largest groups were found in the northwestern frontier counties. Living by hunting and, in many cases, stealing from settlers in the region, these "brush men," as they were sometimes called, created a serious threat to property and morale. Units of the Frontier Organization and Bourland's Border Regiment had to give at least as much time to arresting deserters and draft dodgers as they devoted to dealing with the Indians.

It is commonly said that Indian raiders rolled back the frontier fifty miles or more during the Civil War. And there is no question that settlers suffered a great deal, having perhaps four hundred men, women, and children killed, wounded, or carried off. Isolated homesteads made inviting targets for small parties of raiders, and at times the Indians launched major attacks. For example, in October 1864 several hundred Comanches and Kiowas raided the Elm Creek Valley in Young County, killing seven settlers and carrying off seven women and children along with livestock and other possessions. A company of the Border Regiment pursued the raiders but rode into an ambush and had five of its men killed. Such attacks and losses, however, had occurred before the war and would continue afterward and should not be blamed on the inadequacy of efforts from 1861 to 1865. As a leading historian of the subject has written, "Frontier defense in Texas during the Civil War, for all its difficulties and apparent failures, was equal to that of antebellum days and superior to that of the immediate post-war years."

Close of the War, June 1865

Gen. Kirby Smith reached Houston on May 27, having ordered all Texas troops to concentrate there, but he found no army to command and had to accept the inevitable. On June 2 he and Gen. Magruder boarded a Union warship at Galveston and signed articles of surrender by which Confederate troops were paroled and allowed to return home. All Confederate property was turned over to the United States. Some Texans—Governors Edward Clark and Pendleton Murrah among them—fled to Mexico rather than face occupation by victorious Union troops, and a few migrated to Brazil. Most, however, remained at home and braced for the arrival of occupying forces. Texans had paid a terrible price for the war; now the question was: What would they pay for defeat?

Chapter 11

RECONSTRUCTION, 1865–1876

Wars, even decisive ones such as the American Civil War, often raise as many questions as they settle. In the spring of 1865, victory by the United States made it clear that states could not successfully claim a constitutional right to secede from the Union. None have tried in the century and a half since. Also, the defeat of the Confederacy sealed the fate of slavery. President Abraham Lincoln had fought the war primarily to save the Union rather than to destroy slavery, but in the fall of 1862, seeing the importance of linking his cause and freedom for the enslaved, he had announced his intention of freeing all bondsmen behind Confederate lines as of January 1, 1863. The Emancipation Proclamation freed virtually no slaves on the day that Lincoln issued it, but as Union troops advanced so did freedom. Winning the war and freeing the slaves, however, raised two new issues. First, how and on whose terms would the defeated states be returned to full membership in the Union? Second, what would be the place of former slaves, now freedmen, in southern society? Did freedom bring full citizenship, including the right to vote and hold office? Would the former slaves be given any economic assistance in establishing themselves as freedmen? These questions—restoration to the Union and the status of freedmen—dominated the years of Reconstruction from 1865 to 1876 and left an indelible stamp on Texas to this day.

Reconstruction in Texas began in mid-June 1865 with the arrival of occupation troops at Galveston on the coast and Marshall in the northeastern part of the state. Federal troops reached Marshall on June 17, hurrying there because that town had been a center of Gen. Kirby Smith's Trans-Mississippi command. However, a force that reached Galveston two days later under the command of General Gordon Granger had broad responsibility for beginning Reconstruction statewide. Granger immediately began paroling Confederate soldiers and announced the Emancipation Proclamation, making June 19, or "Juneteenth" as it became known, forever a day of celebration for Texas blacks. "All slaves are free," Granger's proclamation read in part, and the connection between former masters and slaves "becomes that between employer and hired labor." He advised freedmen "to remain quietly at their present homes and work for wages" and told them not to gather at military posts or expect to "be supported in idleness either there or elsewhere." A careful reading of Granger's words suggested that freedmen could expect only limited assistance from the government.

It took time for Gen. Granger's order to become known and be obeyed across the state. Given the size of Texas, the relatively poor communication system, and the bitter hatred of many owners for the idea of emancipation, it is not surprising that some slaves remained in bondage for months after Juneteenth. Nevertheless, the great majority obtained their freedom before the end of the year. In most cases, their owners called them together and read the Emancipation Proclamation; in others, freedom came only with the arrival of Federal troops in their neighborhood.

Most slaves greeted freedom with the joy that would be expected of people receiving the answer to a lifelong prayer. One remembered: "Everyone was singing. We was all walking on golden clouds. Hallelujah!" Another recalled a woman calling out "Free, free my lord. Oh! Free, free, my Lord. Free, free, free oh my Lord." In some cases, however, whites did not permit such celebrations. One slave reported that in Crockett the slave patrol whipped one hundred celebrants. Another described how he, when told of his freedom, leaped into the air to express his delight, whereupon his master pulled a pistol and fired several shots between his feet. Jump again, he said, and I will shoot you between the eyes.

Even those slaves left free to celebrate soon found their joy constrained by the realization that, as one put it, "freedom could make folks proud but it didn't make them rich." Another remembered his owner saying, "How are you going to eat and get clothes and such?" What were they to do with their freedom, and how were they to live as freedmen? Most accepted Gen. Granger's advice, at least immediately after freedom, that they stay where they were and work for wages, because they had nowhere else to go. A sizable minority, however, (maybe one-quarter) left their masters immediately. Some did so simply to assert their freedom. They showed that at least they had control of their own bodies and could come and go as they pleased. Others moved in search of family members from whom they had been separated during slavery or to find a master for whom they would rather work.

How the great majority of slaves wanted to live as freedmen is fairly clear and simple. For one thing, most had no desire to "get even" with whites or former owners. Revenge was not part of their agenda. As one freedman put it, "We could no more shoot them [masters] than we could fly." Instead, most hoped to live in peace with whites and concentrate on supporting themselves and their families in the ways that they knew—primarily small-scale farming. Freedmen tended to have a peasant mentality, meaning that they wanted to acquire small parcels of land on which they could support themselves. The one way perhaps that they did not think like peasants was a very strong desire to obtain education for their children. Essentially, then, the freedmen

Texas freedmen, probably dressed for a celebration of "Juneteenth" (June 19, 1865, the day Federal troops arrived at Galveston and announced the Emancipation Proclamation in Texas) Credit: PICA 05476, Austin History Center, Austin Public Library.

wanted only an opportunity to become good Americans—working for themselves, becoming property owners, and improving the lives of their children.

Presidential Reconstruction, 1865–1867

Reconstruction began according to a plan established by Abraham Lincoln in 1863 and continued by his successor, Andrew Johnson, in 1865. Lincoln insisted that the southern states, having no right to secede and failing in their attempt to do so, had never actually left the Union. Since he as commander in chief had led in putting down their revolution, he would direct the process of bringing the southern states back into a proper relationship to the Union. Reconstruction, which was to be carried out as quickly as possible, would be handled largely by civilians appointed by the president and working with the support of the military. Lincoln made virtually no place for the freedmen in his original plan for Reconstruction. They received freedom and nothing more. His successor, Andrew Johnson, a Democrat from Tennessee whom the Republicans made vice president in 1865 solely because of his unionism, cared even less about what happened to African Americans. Thus, when Reconstruction began in Texas, the situation was not particularly threatening for whites who could swallow defeat, accept the end of slavery, and renew their allegiance to the United States. Blacks faced a less promising future.

The civilian most responsible for initiating Reconstruction in Texas arrived at Galveston on July 21 in the person of Andrew Jackson Hamilton, President Andrew Johnson's appointee as provisional governor. A. J. Hamilton was a native of Alabama who had come to Texas in 1846, served two terms in the state legislature during the early 1850s, and been elected to the United States House of Representatives in 1859. A committed Unionist of the Sam Houston school, Hamilton refused to support the Confederacy and left Texas in July 1862. In 1863, after meeting President Lincoln and receiving an appointment as military governor of Texas, he accompanied the Federal force that briefly occupied the Brownsville region, but then spent most of the rest of the war in New Orleans. His wife Mary Jane Hamilton and their six children remained in Austin until Confederate sympathizers burned their home in 1864, forcing them into exile as well.

When A. J. Hamilton returned as an agent of Presidential Reconstruction, his primary responsibility was to direct the restoration of a state government that would bring Texas back to its proper constitutional relationship in the Union. This meant registering eligible voters—defined as those who could take the oath of amnesty promising future loyalty to the United States—and supervising the election of a convention to revise the state constitution. One key revision would be the elimination of all references to slavery. Once the constitutional convention completed its work, voters would again go to the polls to approve the new fundamental law and elect state and local officials under its terms. At the same election, voters would choose United States Representatives, and the new state legislature, once it assembled, would select United States Senators. When the president approved these steps and Congress indicated its approval by seating the new representatives and senators, Presidential Reconstruction in Texas would be complete.

During the summer of 1865, Governor Hamilton appointed interim state officials, such as a secretary of state and attorney general, and named judges to reopen the state's district courts. Also, to restore local government on an interim basis in the more than one hundred counties created in Texas by that time, the governor appointed key officials such as county judges (usually called the Chief Justice), sheriffs, and county commissioners. In all cases, of course, he sought to appoint men of known loyalty to the United States, a task that proved difficult in a state with so few true Unionists. Most of the appointments were satisfactory to ex-Confederates. On August 19, 1865, while in the midst of appointing interim officials, the governor issued a proclamation ordering the registration of voters preparatory to electing a constitutional convention.

Federal authority arrived at Galveston in yet another form on September 5, 1865, when Gen. Edgar M. Gregory reached his headquarters as the state's first Assistant Commissioner of the Bureau of Refugees, Freedmen, and Abandoned Lands. Established by Congress under the Department of War, the Freedmen's Bureau, as it was generally called, had the primary responsibility of helping blacks adjust to freedom. Providing relief for the destitute was a relatively minor problem, but the bureau's efforts in supervising labor contracts, establishing schools, and protecting freedmen against violence drew opposition from many whites. "There is no organized resistance to the General Government," Governor Hamilton wrote shortly after the bureau began operations, "but there is in many portions of the State a sullen dissatisfaction, growing out of the loss of slaves, which defies moral suasion and manifesting itself mainly in a total disregard of the rights of freedmen and the policy of the government toward them." Nevertheless, by January 1866 Gregory had twenty-one sub-assistant commissioners, generally called Freedmen's Bureau agents, in the field in towns such as Marshall, Waco, and Columbus, and the bureau was on its way to becoming a major factor during Reconstruction in Texas. By July 1867, the bureau would have seventy agents working in localities across the state.

In mid-November 1865, Governor Hamilton called for an election on January 8, 1866, to choose delegates to the constitutional convention. Registration for this election had begun in August as officials appointed by the governor for each county administered the general amnesty oath to prospective voters. Hamilton recognized that many who swore the oath, although technically loyal, did not intend to cooperate with the federal government, and he knew that high-ranking ex-Confederate leaders and individuals worth more than $20,000 needed a special presidential pardon once they took the oath. However, he could not deny the oath to anyone willing to swear it, and everyone expected President Johnson to pardon all former leaders who asked. This allowed former secessionists to win far more seats than did supporters of Hamilton. As one voter put it, we elected the same men "who engineered us *out*" to "engineer us *back*." The balance of power, however, was held by conservative Unionists who had opposed disunion but generally supported the Confederacy during the war.

The convention met in Austin from February 7 until April 2 and completed what amounted to a new fundamental law for the state—the Constitution of 1866. Delegates declared the secession ordinance null and void (without any reference to whether or not it had ever been a valid act), repudiated public debt incurred during the war, and recognized (but did not ratify) the Thirteenth Amendment by removing slavery from the constitution. The convention also promised basic rights of person and property to freedmen but denied them the right to vote, hold office, serve on juries, testify in court against whites, or attend public schools. All of these provisions would become operative only when the state legislature passed laws to make them effective. Nevertheless, it was clear that where freedmen were concerned, the convention had followed the wishes of Oran M. Roberts, the chairman of the secession convention and former Confederate colonel who served as a delegate even though he did not yet have a presidential pardon. We must form, Roberts said, "a white man's Gov[ernmen]t" that will "keep Sambo from the polls."

During the convention and the period between its adjournment on April 2, 1866, and the election on June 25 to approve the new constitution and elect officials under its terms, a significant division developed among those who hoped to lead in reconstructing the state. One faction, generally termed Radical Unionists and including Governor Hamilton, favored a total condemnation of secession and took a moderate stance toward the freedmen. Their candidate for governor, Elisha M. Pease, a native of Connecticut who had held that office from 1853 to 1857, favored granting the franchise to literate blacks. The other faction led by gubernatorial candidate James W. Throckmorton, the noted prewar Unionist who later served as a Confederate officer, became known as Conservative Unionists because of their desire to restore the Union with as little change as possible and their refusal to consider enfranchising the freedmen. Former secessionists, although well represented in the convention, were not yet in a position to run a candidate for governor, but their obvious choice was Throckmorton. Conservative Unionists tended to accuse their opponents of "radicalism" and a willingness to cooperate with northern Republicans in punishing the South and elevating the former slaves. Radical Unionists retaliated with charges that the conservatives were disloyal and intended to punish true loyalists in Texas.

Conservative Unionists easily won the gubernatorial election on June 25, 1866, because they appealed to ex-secessionists as well as to those who had opposed disunion but had no intention of extending equal rights to blacks or making radical changes. Throckmorton received 48,631 votes to 12,051 for Pease, and conservatives, defined at this point as Unionists like the new governor and former secessionists, gained total control of the new state legislature. Voters also approved the new constitution. The Eleventh Legislature assembled on August 6, Throckmorton took office three days later, and President Johnson issued a proclamation on the 20th declaring that the rebellion had ended in Texas and returning control of the state to civil authorities. During the late summer and early fall, the state district courts and county government offices also were taken over by men elected on June 25, most of whom had supported secession and the war. Conservatives celebrated their victory over men who "openly proclaimed social and political equality with the negro," while Radical Unionists cursed having to "give way to rebels" and prewar Unionists who had chosen to run with "the dogs of treason."

The new legislature immediately indicated that it intended, so far as possible, to restore prewar conditions in Texas. First, it elected Oran M. Roberts and David G. Burnet to the United States Senate. Roberts, of course, was well known as the foremost secessionist in the state. Burnet, who was much older, had not endorsed disunion or served in the army, but he had supported the Confederacy and was bitterly critical of the Radical Unionists. The legislature also refused to ratify the Thirteenth and Fourteenth Amendments. Rejecting the former amounted to only symbolic defiance because three-quarters of the states had approved the constitutional abolition of slavery by December 1865. However, refusing to ratify the Fourteenth Amendment, which Congress sent to the states in June 1866, had real meaning. This proposed amendment defined U.S. citizenship to include blacks and prohibited state action that denied equal protection of the laws to any citizen. Also, the amendment carried a provision to the effect that any man who had taken an oath to support the

Constitution of the United States and subsequently engaged in rebellion could not hold public office again without the approval of two-thirds of both houses of Congress. This provision obviously would keep virtually all of Texas's prewar leaders out of office and dramatically reduce the control that they were establishing over Reconstruction. Small wonder that the legislature rejected it.

Finally, the legislature passed laws—similar to the "black codes" adopted by other southern states at the time—to codify the state constitution's denial of equality to African Americans. Freedmen were given the right to acquire and sell property, to make and enforce contracts, and to sue and be sued in court. However, blacks could not serve on juries, testify against whites, vote, or hold office. Also, blacks were denied a share of the public school fund and restricted from intermarrying with whites. Railroad companies had to provide separate accommodations for whites and blacks. Finally, the legislature passed elaborate contract, vagrancy, and apprentice laws designed to assure control over black workers without restoring slavery or even mentioning race. The contract law, for example, required a written agreement between employer and worker for all work arrangements that lasted more than a month. Workers were given a lien on the crop to assure payment of wages, but employers had the power to deduct wages for infractions such as disobedience, "impudence," and wasting time. The vagrancy law allowed local authorities to arrest people who were "idle," fine them, and hire them out as a means of paying the fine.

As Reconstruction went forward in 1866 and the early months of 1867, those who objected to conservative control faced intimidation and terror. Unionists, blacks, and Freedmen's Bureau agents may have exaggerated in order to build a case against their opponents, but the evidence of threats and violence across much of the state is overwhelming. Black laborers complained of being cheated or driven off the land they worked without pay. The bureau's attempts at establishing schools often met violent resistance. "My house on last Monday evening was the target of an enraged rebel mob," wrote a Harrison County bureau teacher in January 1867, "the windows were smashed and fired into to such an extent that bullets were found on the floor the next morning." Unionists insisted that the local justice system afforded no relief. "What chance do they [Unionists] stand," asked a McLennan County man, "with rebel judges, rebel lawyers, sheriff, & jury? No show at all." Governor Throckmorton generally responded to such complaints by calling for an investigation, but he did not take them seriously. "As a matter of course, I do not believe one word of this," he told an East Texas county judge. Instead, the governor criticized the bureau for interfering with civilian affairs and urged the army to give all its attention to the frontier.

Congressional Reconstruction, 1867–1870

Thus, from 1865 to 1867 Presidential Reconstruction in Texas created state and local governments controlled by a conservative combination of prewar Unionists and former secessionists, with the latter holding the upper hand. The story was essentially the same in the other ex-Confederate states. In the meantime, however, Congress under the leadership of Radical Republicans was moving successfully to take Reconstruction away from the president. Disgusted at the lack of penance among white southerners, the mistreatment of Unionists in the South, and the refusal to accord freedmen any semblance of equal rights, Republicans in Congress during late 1865 refused to seat the representatives and senators sent to Washington by states reconstructed under President Johnson's direction. Texas, although it did not complete Presidential Reconstruction until mid-1866, acted in essentially the same way as the other southern states and provided additional ammunition for the Radicals. For example, the election of the pro-Confederate Roberts and Burnet as U. S. Senators, passage of a black code, and reports that many black Texans suffered violence showed that most of the state's whites were just as nonrepentant and unwilling to accept change as those elsewhere in the Old South. Roberts and Burnet, of course, met the same reception as other senators elected in the reconstructed states—the Senate refused to seat them.

In the fall of 1866, Republicans, using the attitudes of southerners and conditions for blacks and Unionists in the old Confederacy as their primary weapon, swept the midterm congressional elections and took two-thirds control of both houses. In March 1867 Congress passed the first of four Reconstruction Acts that in effect began the process anew in the former Confederate states, this time under the direction of the United States Army. Texas would have to register eligible voters (black as well as white this time), elect a convention to write a new state constitution, establish state and local governments under that constitution, ratify the Fourteenth Amendment, and elect new United States Representatives and Senators. Then, if Congress approved, it could return to a full relationship in the Union.

Congressional Reconstruction called for dividing the South into five military districts and placing each under the command of a general in the army. Texas and Louisiana comprised the Fifth Military District under the overall command of Gen. Philip Sheridan, who was then stationed at New Orleans. Sheridan officially took charge on March 19, 1867, and ordered both states, as military subdistricts, to keep their present military commanders. This meant that Texas remained under the immediate direction of Gen. Charles C. Griffin, a West Point graduate who, like Sheridan, stood ready to deal firmly with ex-Confederates. Within two months, the two generals made it very clear that the Throckmorton-led government of Conservative Unionists and secessionists established in 1866 had become strictly provisional in the eyes of Congress and the military. In mid-April Sheridan ruled that the governor could not appoint anyone to fill vacancies in elective offices or hold elections for any purpose. No elections will be held, the general said, until ordered by the military commander. Later that month, Gen. Griffin, in response to numerous complaints from Unionists about their treatment in Texas courts, issued an order requiring all jurors to swear the Test Oath of 1862 that they had never voluntarily supported the Confederacy. Obviously, this order made the great majority of white men in Texas ineligible to serve. Governor Throckmorton considered the Jury Order "outrageously wrong" and sent protests to General Griffin and President Johnson. District judges, knowing of the governor's attitude, reacted largely as they chose. Some complied as fully as possible with the order, and others simply closed their courts without making a genuine effort to find jurors.

Thus, the worst fears of conservatives (defined from 1867 onward as those who opposed the Republican Party nationally and in Texas) concerning Congressional Reconstruction began to come true from the outset. The first critical step, however, in repeating the process of reconstruction was the registration of voters according to guidelines established by Congress and interpreted by Generals Sheridan and Griffin. The Reconstruction Acts called for registering all adult males, white and black, except those who had ever sworn an oath to uphold the Constitution of the United States and then engaged in rebellion (and the very small number of men who had held high civil or military offices in the Confederacy or owned property valued at $20,000 or more and could not register until they received a special pardon from the President of the United States). Sheridan interpreted these restrictions stringently, barring from registration not only all pre-1861 officials of state and local governments who had supported the Confederacy but also all city officeholders and even minor functionaries such as sextons of cemeteries. In May Griffin divided the state into fifteen registration districts, each of which had two supervisors and included six to eleven counties designated as subdistricts. The general also appointed a three-man board of registrars for each county, making his choices on the advice of known Unionists and local Freedmen's Bureau agents. In every county where practicable a freedman served as one of the three registrars. Registration began in most counties during June or July, continued for several months, and resumed for a week in late September. On December 16, 1867, Gen. Winfield Scott Hancock, commander of the Fifth Military District beginning in November, ordered an election on February 10–14, 1868, to choose delegates to the constitutional convention. Hancock also directed the boards of registration in all counties to reopen their books from January 27–31, 1868, for a revision of the existing rolls and the addition of newly eligible voters. Final registration amounted to approximately 59,633 whites and 49,479 blacks. It is impossible to say how many whites were rejected or refused to register (estimates vary from 7,500 to 12,000), but blacks, who constituted only about 30 percent of the state's population, were significantly overrepresented at 45 percent of all voters.

While they directed registration in preparation for the election of a constitutional convention, military commanders of the Fifth Military District and the District of Texas further demonstrated the provisional nature of state and local government by the wholesale removal of officials elected in June 1866. Congress gave the military virtually unlimited powers of removal and appointment on July 19, 1867, and Sheridan waited less than two weeks before removing Governor Throckmorton as an "impediment to the reconstruction" of Texas. The general's order of July 30 named former governor and unsuccessful Radical Unionist candidate in 1866, Elisha M. Pease, to replace Throckmorton. Soon, Sheridan began to remove state district judges, and on August 27, he authorized Gen. Griffin to replace all county officials judged disloyal. Griffin took command of both the Fifth Military District and the District of Texas when Sheridan left the former command on September 5, 1867, and removed all five justices of the Texas Supreme Court and three more district judges before he died of yellow fever on September 15. His replacement in Texas, Gen. Joseph J. Reynolds, took at least an equally dim view of former secessionists and Confederates as officeholders and within two months replaced more than five hundred county officials. Governor Pease gathered information and made recommendations to the general, who in turn ordered the removals and appointments. By late November 1867, when Gen. Winfield Scott Hancock, a Democrat who had little use for the Radicals, took over the Fifth Military District and exerted a restraining influence on his subordinate in Texas, military authority had substantially altered the personnel of state and local government elected in June 1866.

The election of a constitutional convention on February 10–14, 1868, resulted in a near-total victory for Texas's fledgling Republican Party, which had organized during the previous year and held its first state convention in Houston on July 4, 1867. Encouraged by chapters of the Union League, an organization pledged to oppose Confederates and support only loyal men, more than four-fifths (82 percent) of the newly enfranchised blacks went to the polls. In spite of widespread threats and reprisals, they voted overwhelmingly for the convention (36,932 to 818) and Republican delegates. By contrast only 31 percent (18,379) of registered whites voted, probably because conservative leaders had given contradictory and confusing advice before the election. At first, because the Reconstruction Acts required participation by at least half of all voters registered at the time of the election, conservative spokesmen urged whites to register and then refuse to vote. Just before the election, however, they became uncertain of the Republicans' strength and changed tactics, advising whites to vote "no" on the convention but to support conservative candidates in case the meeting won approval. Of the whites who voted, 10,622 opposed the convention, and 7,757 voted "yes." The latter group probably represented the extent of white support for the Republican Party in 1868 and indicated that conservatives, if they organized and turned out their vote, still could control Texas.

When the constitutional convention assembled in Austin on June 1, 1868, seventy-eight of its ninety members were Republicans. Southern-born whites or "scalawags" made up the bulk of these delegates. Only twelve, counting six whose state of birth could not be determined, may be classed as "Carpetbaggers," Northerners who came south after the war. Nine blacks, the first African Americans elected to public service in Texas, served as delegates. The best known among them was George T. Ruby, a native of New York who came to Galveston as a Freedmen's Bureau teacher in 1866. Others such as Shepherd Mullins of McLennan County and Benjamin F. Williams of Colorado County had been slaves and were well versed in the survival skills learned in bondage. Williams had served as the supervisor of registrars in his district, traveling at night for safety and acting, he wrote, "as wise as a surpent and as harmless as a dove."

Obviously, the seventy-eight Republicans could dominate the twelve conservatives in the convention and write any kind of constitution they wished, so long as they remained unified. From the outset, however, factionalism disrupted their efforts and threatened the future of their party almost as much as the strength of the white conservatives. The most important division among Republicans in the convention involved a split between moderates, led by former provisional governor A. J. Hamilton, and radicals, led by Edmund J. Davis. A native of Florida, Davis came to Texas well before the war, lived at various times in Corpus Christi, Laredo, and Brownsville, and was a state district judge in 1860. He opposed secession to the extent of forming the First Texas Cavalry (USA), which served with Union forces in Texas and Louisiana. Davis ended the war as a brigadier general and returned to Corpus Christi, where he was elected a delegate to the constitutional conventions of both 1866 and 1868–1869. When the latter convention organized, he became its presiding officer.

Moderate and radical Republicans fought most bitterly over three issues: a provision called *ab initio* that would have declared the ordinance of secession null and void and, as a result, voided all acts by the state government from 1861 until 1867; the disfranchisement of former Confederates; and the division of Texas to create a new western state. *Ab initio* had great importance because its passage would invalidate measures such as an 1864 act allowing six Texas railroads to pay part of their debts to the state school fund in depreciated wartime paper rather than in specie as originally required. Disfranchisement raised the emotional issue of punishment for secession and, of course, promised to strengthen the Republican Party. The creation of a new state in West Texas would probably have benefited Republicans even more, because Unionism was much stronger there than in East Texas. Radical Republicans favored all three measures, while moderates opposed them. Only one issue—the violence that had plagued Texas since June 1865—unified all members of the new party. The convention's Committee on Lawlessness and Violence compiled a report showing that 509 whites and 468 blacks had been murdered since the war and suggesting that most of these killings involved conservatives' hatred of loyalists of both races. Two Republican leaders, Colbert Caldwell and Morgan Hamilton, took the report to Washington to support their appeal for greater federal intervention on behalf of Unionists and freedmen.

The convention settled only the *ab initio* question, by rejecting the radical position, before it ran out of funds after three months. It then ordered the collection of a tax to fund another session and recessed from August 31 until December 1, 1868. During the second session, which ended in February 1869, moderate Republicans, aided by the conservatives, defeated the radicals on the other major issues and completed the new constitution. Texas was not divided, and the Constitution of 1869, often referred to as the "radical constitution," had no significant provisions for disfranchisement. Adult male blacks and virtually all adult white men could vote, once a voter registration system was created. (The convention, in response to a petition from a small group of women, considered but rejected a resolution enfranchising both sexes, thus beginning a fifty-year battle for woman suffrage in Texas.) Male freedmen also were promised other rights never enjoyed before—the opportunity to hold office, to serve on juries, to testify against whites, and to attend public schools. One more striking change brought by the constitution involved the centralization of power in Austin, especially in the hands of the governor. Elected to a four-year rather than two-year term as under previous constitutions, the governor would appoint the secretary of state, attorney general, and all the judges of the supreme court and state district courts. County government changed notably, too, in that the commissioners court composed of the chief justice and four county commissioners was replaced by a five-man county court composed of five justices of the peace elected by precinct. The justice residing in the precinct containing the county seat town would act as the presiding officer.

The conflict between moderate and radical Republicans carried beyond the convention and into the election to ratify the new constitution and choose officials under its terms. Both sides sought aid from U. S. Grant, winner of the 1868 presidential election, in which Texas had not participated, and Congress. A. J. Hamilton and the moderates, hoping to continue the advantage they held at the end of the convention and appeal to white conservatives as well, sought an early election and quick readmission to the Union. Davis and the radicals, needing time to solidify their hold on the black vote through the Union League and also to prevent an alliance of moderates and conservatives, urged delay in the vote. Congress put the decision in Grant's hands, and the president wound up supporting the radicals. He delayed until July 15 in calling the election and then set the voting for November 30–December 3, 1869. This, plus the decision by Gen. J. J. Reynolds, a personal friend of Grant and commander of the Fifth Military District, to support Davis rather than Hamilton, greatly improved the chances of a radical victory.

In the meantime, a second round of removing local officials and replacing them with military appointees affected many county governments across the state. The first round of removals, which took place in late 1867, generally saw officials replaced because they were disloyal or "impediments" to Reconstruction. This second course of dismissals was in response to an act of Congress on February 18, 1869, requiring all governmental officials in states still not restored to the Union—Texas, Georgia, and Virginia—to swear the Test Oath of 1862 that they had never voluntarily supported the Confederacy. Many local officeholders who had served to the general satisfaction of Unionists, blacks, and the military could not swear such an oath and had to be replaced in April and May 1869, further upsetting conservatives at the whole process of Congressional Reconstruction. Indeed, most whites found little to be pleased with in public life during this period except the closing of all local offices of the Freedmen's Bureau in the state at the end of December 1868.

The gubernatorial campaign between A. J. Hamilton, who had announced his candidacy on March 18, and Davis, the nominee of a Radical Republican convention in Houston held June 7–8, got underway in September 1869. Hamilton received an important boost on September 30 when Provisional Governor E. M. Pease, seeing that Gen. Reynolds was likely to replace moderates who held local offices with radicals friendly to Davis, resigned and publicly attacked the military's continuing interference in local government. Pease's action stung Reynolds to the point that he made few removals in late 1869 and at the same time let informed voters know that his friend Davis stood for military involvement and delay in ending Reconstruction. The general did not appoint a replacement for Pease, choosing instead to handle the functions of the office himself until after the election.

A final revision of voter registration lists, made on November 16–26, added more whites than blacks to the rolls, probably because more whites had refused to register earlier. When the election was held on November 30–December 3, whites constituted 58 percent of the eligible voters, but only slightly more than one-half went to the polls. By contrast, about two-thirds of the 56,905 registered blacks voted. Whites may have stayed away rather than vote for a moderate Republican, or they may have, as some claimed, thought that Texas would not be allowed to return to its proper constitutional relationship with the Union unless Davis won. In any case, their absence from the polls allowed blacks in eastern and central counties and white voters in the western part of the state to make the difference. The new constitution easily won approval by a vote of 72,466 to 4,928, but the contest for governor was very close. According to the returns certified by General Reynolds, Davis defeated Hamilton 39,901 to 39,092, a margin so thin that the loser would always believe that he had been cheated. Fortunately for Davis, radicals also would have working majorities in both houses of the new state legislature, the Twelfth. Republicans also won three of Texas's four congressional seats; the fourth went to a Democrat who, ironically, was a Carpetbagger.

On January 8, 1870, General Reynolds appointed E. J. Davis and all the other state officials elected the previous month to act as a provisional government while the final steps for restoration to the Union were taken. The general also called a provisional session of the Twelfth Legislature to ratify the Thirteenth, Fourteenth, and Fifteenth Amendments and elect United States Senators. At a brief session on February 8–24, 1870, the legislature ratified the amendments and elected two radical Republicans, James W. Flanagan and Morgan Hamilton (A. J. Hamilton's brother) to the senate. Congress then passed a bill that President Grant signed on March 30, ending Military Reconstruction in Texas. On April 16, 1870, General Reynolds turned over all authority to civil officers. The Twelfth Legislature met in a called session for the inauguration of Davis on April 28, and the slightly more than three years of Congressional Reconstruction in Texas came to an end with a call by the new governor for "a fresh departure in political affairs." The Republican Party had survived factionalism and conservative opposition to win control of the state; however, a glance at election results in 1868 and 1869 showed that the new party's reign would be very short-lived unless it found a way to appeal successfully to more white Texans. How many were ready for a "fresh departure" that meant accepting the supremacy of the national government and equal rights for blacks?

Republican State Government, 1870–1874

Immediately after his inauguration, Davis outlined an ambitious program that called for the government in Austin to play a much larger role than ever before in solving the state's problems. The foremost issue was law and order, which everyone agreed had broken down in many areas. Bands of outlaws operated most notoriously in the Big Thicket and the swamps and woodlands of northeastern Texas. Led by killers such as Cullen Baker and Bob Lee, these gangs often attacked U.S. troops and freedmen, thereby gaining a measure of support from some whites. Baker, for example, won acclaim as the "Swamp Fox of the Sulphur" (and Louis L'Amour eventually romanticized his career in a novel), but in reality he stole and murdered with political impartiality. Much of the violence, however, did have racial and political implications. The infamous Ku Klux Klan, which began in Tennessee in 1865 and played a major role in the opposition to Congressional Reconstruction across the South, did not operate as a unified organization in Texas, but groups with names such as the Knights of the White Camellia and Knights of the Rising Sun carried out Klan-type activities—night riding, threats, whippings, and murder—especially in eastern counties.

To deal with lawlessness, the legislature, at Governor Davis's prompting, took several actions in 1870. A bill passed in late June created a state militia composed of all able-bodied men aged eighteen to forty-five. The governor as commander in chief could call the militia into state service to police any county in which regular law enforcement could not be handled by constituted civil authorities. A second law-and-order measure, passed in June, established a state police force of 258 men headed by a chief of police. All local law enforcement officers had to aid the state police in their activities. Both the militia and state police were under the ultimate control of the governor, but the state adjutant general directed their everyday operations. Individuals accused of felonies by the state police or regular law enforcement officials were tried in state district courts, and there, too, the legislature increased the power of the governor. The Constitution of 1869 provided that the chief executive would appoint district judges but made no provision concerning the number of judicial districts. So, on July 2, the legislature increased the number of districts from seventeen to thirty-five, giving Governor Davis an opportunity to appoint thirty-five loyal Republicans to key positions in the state's justice system.

Governor Davis also called the special session's attention to the constitutional mandate that the state create "public free schools" for all children aged six to eighteen in Texas. The legislature passed a public education act in August 1870, but it called for a decentralized system, which quickly proved ineffective. So, on April 24, 1871, during its regular session, the Twelfth Legislature passed a new public school law that created a highly centralized system more to the liking of Governor Davis. Under the new law all supervisory power rested in a state board of education composed of the governor, superintendent of public instruction, and attorney general. The superintendent of public instruction appointed supervisors for each state judicial district, who in turn designated the counties in their districts as school districts and appointed five supervisors for each. County supervisors could levy a 1 percent property tax for building and maintaining schools in their districts. Overall, this centralized school system gave great power to the governor, especially since he appointed the attorney general and the first superintendent of public instruction, who served on the state school board. Public schools grew rapidly, peaking in 1872–1873 with an enrollment of more than 125,000, but they caused taxes to rise and drew opposition for educating blacks as well as whites.

The special session of the Twelfth Legislature in 1870 also passed three other pieces of legislation aimed at enhancing the position of the governor and maintaining Republican control of the state. First, an enabling act of June 28 permitted Davis to appoint replacements to most state, district, and local offices that were vacant at that time or became vacant before the next regular election. Second, the legislature gave the governor control of the voter registration system by empowering him to appoint a registrar and a three-man board of appeal for each county in the state. Third, the legislature passed a law postponing midterm congressional elections that should have been held in the fall of 1870 and state elections due in the fall of 1871 until November 1872. This allowed Republican congressmen elected in 1869 to go unchallenged in 1870 and local officials, such as sheriffs, who had won two-year terms in 1869 to hold their offices for at least an extra year.

The Twelfth Legislature met in regular session from January 10 to May 31, 1871, and passed several important pieces of legislation dealing with education. In addition to the new public school bill, it provided for the organization of Texas Agricultural and Mechanical College, the first public institution of higher education in the state. Proposals for a state university dated to 1839 when at the urging of President Mirabeau B. Lamar the Congress of the Republic of Texas donated fifty leagues of land (221,400 acres) as an endowment for two institutions of higher education. In 1856, the state legislature provided for selling university lands and creating a Permanent University Fund from the proceeds. Nothing more was accomplished, however, until after the Civil War when the Constitutional Convention of 1866 added a million acres to university lands in Texas and voted to build a school under the terms of the Morrill Land-Grant College Act of 1862, a federal law that donated public lands to states as a subsidy for new agricultural and mechanical colleges. Since Texas had no federal lands within its borders, it received title to 180,000 acres in Colorado, which it sold at seventy-five cents per acre. The new school thus became both a federal and state land-grant college. In April 1871, the legislature passed a bill creating Texas A&M College and providing funds to build the school. A committee appointed by Governor Davis located the college near Bryan, having been influenced no doubt by a donation of 2,416 acres by local citizens. Financial and political difficulties slowed building the school, but it opened in October 1876 with 106 students and 6 faculty members. By that time, of course, the administration that took the initiative in creating the school was only a bad memory for most of the people who benefited from it.

During the early 1870s, Governor Davis and the legislature faced a rising tide of criticism from conservatives and moderate Republicans such as A. J. Hamilton. This attack utilized the themes of tyranny and taxes and contained a strong element of racism. The militia law and state police force gave the governor dictatorial power, the conservatives said; moreover, some 40 percent of state policemen were black. State and local taxes had risen to unprecedented levels due to the expenses of an enlarged central government, efforts to improve roads and bridges, and the costs of establishing the public school system. Moderate Republicans, conservative Unionists, and former secessionists called a Tax-payers' Convention in Austin for September 22–25, 1871, at which representatives of ninety-four counties approved a report condemning virtually every action of the Davis administration to that date. Faced with an increasingly organized opposition and having failed to build a large constituency among the state's whites, virtually all of whom could and would now vote, Republican government in Texas had a very limited life expectancy by the fall of 1871.

The first important Republican defeats came in special congressional elections called for October 3–6, 1871. Originally delayed until 1872, these elections had to be held in 1871 because the Forty-first Congress—to which representatives had been elected in 1869—expired on March 4, 1871, and the Forty-second Congress would meet in December of that year, well before the date Republicans in Texas had hoped to choose new congressmen. The Democratic Party organized on a statewide and district level and took all four seats in Congress. During the election Governor Davis responded to a riot in Limestone County by declaring martial law and sending in state militia, who had to be paid by means of a special tax on local property holders. This action may have been necessary, but it only added to the conservative charges of tyranny and taxes.

The Twelfth Legislature held a relatively short and uneventful session from September 12 to December 2, 1871, and the two parties spent most of the next year preparing for a general election on November 5–8, 1872. In the presidential race, the first for Texas voters since 1860, the Democrats endorsed the Liberal Republican candidate Horace Greeley in opposition to the incumbent Republican U. S. Grant. The state also had to elect United States Representatives for the Forty-third Congress, one-third of the state senate (state senators under the Constitution of 1869 served six-year terms staggered so that one-third faced reelection every two years), and a new state house of representatives. Finally, the election had to fill the positions of local officials, such as sheriffs, who were limited to two-year terms under the constitution but had held office since winning in 1869. Candidates and campaigners for both parties worked hard across the state, and, as in 1871, the Democrats won overwhelmingly. Greeley carried the state in the presidential election, and Democrats won all six congressional races, including two at-large seats that had been awarded to Texas by redistricting after the Census of 1870. State legislative races were even more damaging to the Davis administration as Democrats won control of both houses of the Thirteenth Legislature. As 1872 ended, Davis suffered yet another blow when Adjutant General James Davidson, who had used the state police aggressively to attack lawlessness, fled the state with more than $30,000 in public funds. Thus, by 1873 Republicans still had strongholds in the governor's office and the judiciary, but conservatives confidently expected the next gubernatorial election to bring total "redemption" (their word for salvation from Republican government) to Texas.

The Democrat-controlled Thirteenth Legislature met from January 4 to June 4, 1873, and rejected all efforts at reconciliation by Governor Davis. Over his veto, it repealed the state police act, limited his use of the militia, and reduced the appointive powers of the governor's office. A new public education law, also passed over Davis's veto, decentralized the system and placed strict limits on the power of local boards to raise taxes for schools. Finally, the legislature called a one-day general election for state and local officials to be held on December 2, 1873, at the various precincts in each county rather than at the county seat, the scene of all elections since 1867.

The Republicans nominated Davis for reelection in 1873 and pointed out that the Thirteenth Legislature, controlled by Democrats, had increased taxes, added to the state debt, given eighty thousand acres of public lands to railroads, and destroyed the school system. Democrats, however, needed only to remind most white voters that Republicans were the party of Congressional Reconstruction, blacks, centralized "tyranny," and taxes. Their nominee, Richard Coke of McLennan County, a captain in the Fifteenth Texas Infantry throughout the war, overwhelmed Davis at the polls by an official total of 85,549 to 42,663. Black voters, due in part to intimidation, did not turn out as in earlier elections, but even if they had, Coke would have won easily.

Davis accepted defeat and prepared to leave office at the end of his term on April 28, 1874 (four years after his inauguration), but some Republican partisans raised a constitutional question that the governor felt obligated to pursue. The issue arose over the provision in the constitution providing that "all elections . . . shall be held at the county seats of the several counties until otherwise provided by law; and the polls shall be open for four days." Those who wanted to challenge the election argued that the semicolon made the two clauses independent; hence the legislature had no constitutional power to change the length of the election from four days to one. The Texas Supreme Court, which was composed of Davis appointees, ruled the election unconstitutional in *Ex Parte Rodríguez,* a decision known as the Semi-colon Case. In the meantime, Democratic leaders demanded that Davis resign on January 8, 1874, four years to the day after General Reynolds had made him provisional governor following the election of 1869, and when he refused, decided to have the legislature meet, inaugurate Coke, and take power until the federal government intervened. On January 11 Davis asked President Grant for aid in holding his office and preserving peace until the problem could be solved but received a curt refusal. The president pointed out that Davis had signed the election law in question and disregarded the governor's argument that he could not ignore a decision by the state supreme court. A local militia unit called the Travis Rifles took control of the legislative chambers in the capitol, and Coke was inaugurated on January 15. Davis, with no federal support forthcoming and unwilling to resort to force, had no choice except to resign from office four days later.

With Davis's resignation, the judiciary was the only branch of state government remaining in the hands of Republicans. However, a constitutional amendment adopted at the election on December 2, 1873, increased the membership of the supreme court from three to five justices and allowed Coke to appoint an entirely new court in January 1874. The governor also filled the positions of fourteen district judges, most of whom resigned or were removed by the state legislature, during 1874–1875. In all cases, of course, Coke appointed Democratic replacements, bringing virtually the entire state government of Texas under the control of "Redeemers."

A "Redeemer" Constitution, 1875–1876

Not satisfied with having removed Republicans from government, conservatives also believed it necessary to replace the "radical" Constitution of 1869 with a more appropriate fundamental law. In early August 1875 voters approved a convention and elected ninety delegates, three from each senatorial district. Seventy-five of the delegates (more than 80 percent) were Democrats, whereas only fifteen, including six black men, were Republicans. Forty delegates belonged to the Grange, an organization of farmers dedicated to "retrenchment" in government and therefore in complete sympathy with the conservatives' view of the existing constitution. A majority believed so strongly in economy that they did not hire anyone to take minutes and would not publish their proceedings.

The new constitution, which was completed by late November 1875, totally reflected the "Redeemer"/Granger dislike for centralized, activist, expensive state government. Governors would serve two-year terms and have no control over other elective state officers and local officials. Even the salary of the chief executive was reduced—from $5,000 a year to $4,000. The legislature would meet biennially, rather than annually as under the 1869 constitution, and legislators would be paid five dollars a day for the first sixty days of a session and two dollars a day thereafter. The legislature could not incur indebtedness greater than $200,000. Courts and judges would have much less power than under the Republicans. The supreme court would hear appeals on civil cases only, and a new court of appeals had jurisdiction in all criminal cases. The number of district courts was reduced from thirty-five to twenty-six. All judges were to be elected—district judges for four-year terms and higher-court judges for six-year terms. Constitutional provisions concerning public schools also reflected the conservatives' attitudes in that they decentralized the system and left support largely up to local government. The constitution abolished the position of state superintendent of education, authorized legislative support amounting only to a one-dollar poll tax and not more than one-quarter of property taxes, and had no provision concerning local school taxes. The convention approved its handiwork by a vote of fifty-three to eleven on November 24, 1875, and, as a final act before adjourning, adopted an address to the people of Texas. We, the convention said, make no pretense that this is a perfect constitution, but having "so recently recovered the right of self-government after years of misrule and misfortune," we "all agree that it is a vast improvement on the present one, and will bring great relief to the people."

Voters went to the polls on February 15, 1876, to ratify the new constitution and elect state and local officials under its terms. The Democratic state convention took no official position on the document while renominating Coke for the governorship, whereas the Republican convention unanimously opposed it and nominated William M. Chambers, an ex-Confederate turned Republican, to oppose the incumbent governor. Coke won easily by an official total of 150,581 to 50,030, a much greater margin of victory that he had over Davis in 1873. The constitution was somewhat less popular than the governor, probably because conservatives in counties with large black populations wanted it to include a poll tax limitation on the suffrage, but it won approval by a vote of 136,606 to 56,652. On April 18, 1876, the new constitution went into effect, sweeping away the last vestiges of congressional directives, military rule, and Republican leadership from the state government. In the words of the *Dallas Herald,* "Today [April 18] without a single murmur every single officer known to the State Government of Texas quietly surrenders up his position. Today the organic law which for four years has controlled the destinies of Texas is buried with the eternity of years that are no more, and the new Constitution, fresh from an overwhelming revolution by the people, takes its place."

Conservatives did not take absolute control of political life at the local level in 1876 because the constitution did not disfranchise blacks. This allowed counties with large populations of freedmen to continue to elect Republican officeholders. For example, in Fort Bend County, where blacks outnumbered whites two to one, Republicans controlled county government until the late 1880s. In Colorado County, where sizable populations of African Americans and Germans often cooperated politically, the Democrats did not elect a county judge until 1890. Cicero Howard, an African American Republican, served five two-year terms on the Colorado County commissioners court between 1878 and 1894. Most of these local pockets of Republican power disappeared by the turn of the century, often thanks to Democrats in the state government who winked at intimidation of voters or election chicanery, but for a while they served as a reminder of the changes attempted by Reconstruction.

The Legacy of Reconstruction

Reconstruction returned Texas to a normal constitutional relationship with the United States, but otherwise it left a very mixed legacy. In the case of political power, little changed. At the end, the government in Austin returned largely to the hands of the same men who had controlled it before disunion and during the Civil War. Richard Coke and Oran M. Roberts perfectly symbolized the ultimate victory of secessionist Confederates. Coke participated in the secession convention, served as a captain in the Fifteenth Texas Infantry, and became the state's "Redeemer" governor in 1874. Roberts, who chaired the secession convention and commanded the Eleventh Texas Infantry in 1862–1863, became chief justice of the Texas Supreme Court in 1874 and then served as governor from 1879 to 1883. Thus, the most bitter political struggles in the state's history to that time did not bring any basic change in its government.

Reconstruction provided African American Texans a legacy of both hope and despair. It gave rights and opportunities to the freedmen that allowed them to make remarkable progress in a short time. As soon as federal intervention opened the way, freedmen eagerly sought to demonstrate that they were capable of exercising the responsibilities of citizenship. A large proportion of adult males registered and voted, those chosen served on juries, and some held appointive and elective offices. Blacks, it seems from the reports of Freedmen's Bureau agents and military officers, rarely if ever met violence with violence. However, those who lived in counties where they enjoyed some strength from their numbers did not always submit quietly to violence or even rumors of violence.

While exercising basic political and civil rights for the first time, freedmen also worked with some success to improve their economic status and stabilize basic social institutions. For example, in Jefferson County, a coastal area that had not developed a cotton-based economy, most blacks lived in Beaumont where the men worked in the lumber industry or as laborers and the women as cooks and laundresses. They were poor, but the increase in blacks as a proportion of the population after 1865 suggests that town life and wage labor had an attraction for them. In largely agricultural counties such as Colorado, Harrison, and McLennan, most blacks wound up as landless sharecroppers or farm laborers, However, according to the 1880 census, approximately 20 percent of those who gave their occupation as "farmer" in those counties owned land, an impressive achievement for people who had emerged from slavery generally owning nothing but their own bodies. This census also showed that freedmen generally lived in families composed of a man, his wife, and their children. Moreover, one-third or more of the families having children aged six to sixteen had at least one of those children attend school within the past year.

Clearly, then, Reconstruction allowed at least one generation of freedmen to make notable political, economic, and social progress. Nevertheless, when the era ended, black Texans faced an extremely uncertain future. Nothing they had done, or could do, would destroy most whites' belief in their inherent inferiority or persuade most whites to accept any semblance of black equality. The rights and opportunities enjoyed by freedmen during the late 1860s and early 1870s would be very insecure in a state governed by conservative "redeemers."

Once Reconstruction ended, it very quickly entered the history and mythology of Texas as the darkest period in the state's past—and that may be its most important and lasting legacy. Conservatives insisted on interpreting the era as follows: Texans successfully reconstructed their state under the direction of President Andrew Johnson, but then Radical Republicans in Congress, without any justification, interfered and forced the state to repeat the process under military supervision. Congressional Reconstruction allowed Carpetbaggers, voted into office by illiterate blacks just out of slavery and propped up by Federal bayonets, to institute a tyrannical and corrupt regime that threatened to ruin a majority of white Texans. Worst of all, the Carpetbaggers ran an activist government that imposed outrageously high taxes and permitted blacks to participate on an equal basis. Thankfully, however, conservative Democrats "redeemed" the state and brought responsible leadership back to Austin.

This conservative interpretation of Reconstruction became a tightly held article of faith with most white Texans from the 1870s onward. In 1991, for example, an editor of the *Dallas Morning News* wrote that Reconstruction policies "lined the pockets of many a carpetbagger. And . . . left more than a few Texans broke and bitter." The following year a state senator referred to Carpetbaggers who "came in the dark of the night, looted the liberties of Texans for a number of years, then finally . . . were kicked the heck out of Texas." The popular view even showed up in a scholarly 1990 biography of Lyndon Johnson by Robert Caro. According to Caro, Richard Coke, the namesake of Coke Stevenson (whom Johnson defeated in a 1948 contest for the U.S. Senate), "in 1873 wrested the government of Texas from the Carpetbaggers and freed the state from the injustices of Reconstruction."

Reasons for the development of this interpretation of Reconstruction are not difficult to find. Congress, using the army as a means of enforcement, did indeed act in ways that most white citizens of the Lone Star State saw as arbitrary, radical, and even revolutionary. Some whites were disfranchised, and numerous officeholders were removed from positions to which they had been duly elected in 1866. Moreover, when Republicans gained control of the government, they took actions, such as establishing a public school system, that required significant increases in taxes. They also encouraged blacks to participate in the political and legal systems and set up a state militia and a state police force that enlisted blacks as well as whites. This course of events clearly provides "facts" to support the popular view that Reconstruction was imposed from outside the state and was often arbitrary and expensive.

Overall, however, the traditional interpretation of Reconstruction is replete with factual errors. For example, claims that Carpetbaggers ran Reconstruction in Texas and that the era ruined the fortunes of a great many whites are completely unfounded. Carpetbaggers held fewer than one-quarter of the seats in the Constitutional Convention of 1868–1869 and the major offices in state and county government between 1867 and 1874. Instead, a majority of the men who led Texas during Congressional Reconstruction and the administration of E. J. Davis were "Scalawags," that is, natives of the South who supported the Republican Party. The popular view blames them far less for Reconstruction, however, probably because it is easier and more satisfying to put the onus on Yankee outsiders. In any case, to speak of these years as a time of "Carpetbagger rule" is simply wrong. The impact of Reconstruction policies on the economic fortunes of Texans is difficult to measure, but it is clear that most of the wealthy did not have to relinquish their position in society between 1865 and 1876. They lost their slaves at the close of the war, of course, but they did not lose their lands or other forms of property. Thus, in spite of a general decline in absolute wealth, the economic elite remained where they had been before the war—richer than other Texans.

These factual errors amount to "red herrings" in the popular story of Reconstruction—smelly distractions that draw attention away from the basic issue—and once they are corrected, the essence of the traditional argument is clear. Stated directly, the popular interpretation argued that Texas did not need to give equal political and civil rights to all its citizens after 1865, that the national government should not have forced the state to do so, and that the Davis administration, which sought to provide equal rights and opportunities, deserved to be destroyed. "Redeemers" saw Reconstruction this way, and for the remainder of the nineteenth and much of the twentieth century a majority of white Texans tended to agree. Reconstruction alone did not shape the future of political life in Texas, but the era contributed heavily to the popular opposition to taxing and spending for public purposes and to the general lack of concern for civil rights that characterized the state's politics after the 1870s.

Chapter 12

OLD WEST AND NEW SOUTH, 1865–1890

Texas enjoys a fabled past as part of the Old West—a land of bold ranchers, courageous women, heroic cowboys, and legendary gunfighters. Somewhat ironically, this image is based on a very short span of time in the state's long history—the twenty-five years or so following the Civil War—and even then represents the experience of only a minority of Texans. While soldiers and buffalo hunters closed the Indian frontier and ranchers expanded the cattle frontier, most of the state's people continued to farm for a living. Publicists pointed to new railroads, growing cities, and developing industries as evidence that a prosperous and progressive New South had arrived in Texas as in other states of the old Confederacy, but in ever-increasing numbers farmers found themselves, like their counterparts across the Old South, in debt and working someone else's land. Moreover, conservative Democrats generally turned a deaf ear to their complaints and pleas for help. Thus, by the close of the 1880s, Texas had changed in important ways. Texans had secured a place in the romantic story of conquering the Old West, but many, having far more in common with southern farmers than western frontiersmen, stood on the verge of political revolt.

Many of the men and women who settled the frontier, raised cattle, or worked farms during these years were recent arrivals, participants in a new "Gone to Texas" enthusiasm. The state's population, which rose only 36 percent during the Civil War decade, grew from 818,579 in 1870 to 2,235,527 by 1890, an increase of 173 percent in twenty years. Most of the immigrants came from states of the Old South to escape the ruin and stagnation left by the war. They helped Texas recover more rapidly than did the older states and made its population more southern than ever. Germans also arrived in larger numbers than before the war. The number of residents having German ancestry increased from 41,000 in 1870 to 125,262 in 1890, a gain of more than 200 percent in two decades. In 1890 Texas-Germans outnumbered Texans of Mexican ancestry, whose total population stood at 105,193. African Americans remained the state's largest minority, increasing their numbers from 253,475 in

1870 to 488,171 in 1890, but the white population grew much faster. Blacks declined from 32 percent of all Texans in 1870 to 22 percent by 1890. Overall, Texas attracted so many immigrants as it became a part of both the Old West and the New South that it rose from nineteenth to seventh among all states in total population.

Closing the Indian Frontier

The defeat of the Confederacy provided new encouragement for Comanche and Kiowa raiders in northwestern Texas. Defenders sent to the frontier by Confederate and state authorities during the war went home in 1865, and the United States, busy with numerous postwar responsibilities, did not rush to reoccupy the forts evacuated in 1861. Seizing the opportunity, the Indians struck settlements along a line from Gainesville to Waco with murderous effect. Governor James W. Throckmorton reported later that between May 1865 and July 1867 raiders killed 162 Texans, captured 43, and wounded 24. The Federal government responded first with its traditional Indian policy—treaty negotiations—which had the usual limited success. In October 1867, the Treaty of Medicine Lodge Creek provided a large reservation for the Comanches and Kiowas in western Indian Territory and promised that in return for giving up their land claims and ending raids in Texas the Indians would receive food, blankets, clothing, and farming supplies. Most chiefs signed, but some, including the influential Kiowa leader Satanta, did not and continued to raid south of the Red River. Then, later in 1867, the U.S. Army began to reoccupy its old frontier posts and construct new ones, the most important being Fort Richardson near present-day Jacksboro, Fort Griffin in Shackelford County, and Fort Concho at the site of present-day San Angelo. (See map: U.S. Army Forts in Texas, 1866–1890.) The presence of troops in these forts helped, but as always, forces in widely separated posts had little success defending against raiders on horseback, who usually attacked on nights lighted by the full moon—the "Comanche Moon," settlers called it.

The administration of Ulysses S. Grant, which began in 1869, brought a change in Indian policy, although probably not one that might be expected from a former general. Instead of applying greater military pressure, Grant appointed Quakers to implement a peace policy based on fairness and understanding. Lawrie Tatum, who served as agent of the new Comanche/Kiowa reservation, sincerely attempted to apply Quaker principles. He soon found, however, that many of the Indians ignored admonitions about peacefulness but took advantage of his rule that the army could not enter the reservation in pursuit of raiders.

In the spring of 1871, a band of 150 Kiowas led by Satanta launched a raid that undermined the peace policy and led to aggressive use of military force against the Indians. Gen. William T. Sherman, the famed Civil War commander, and Gen. Randolph B. Marcy, the noted explorer, who were touring the Texas frontier, traveled along the road from Fort Griffin to Fort Richard-

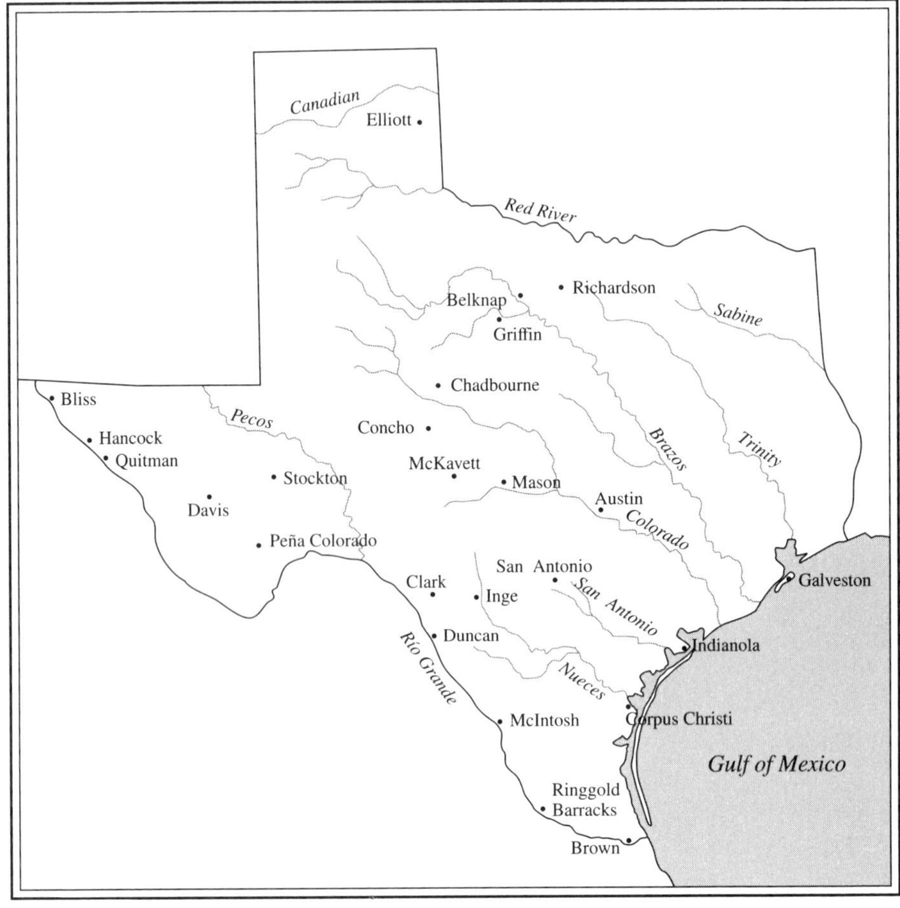

U.S. Army Forts in Texas, 1866–1890

son only a few hours before Satanta's band attacked a supply wagon train on the same route. The Kiowas killed and mutilated seven of the twelve teamsters in what became known as the Salt Creek Massacre, sending a graphic message to the generals of what might have happened to them and their party. Sherman had Satanta and two other chiefs arrested by Tatum when they returned to the reservation and brought to Texas, where they were convicted of murder and sentenced to hang. Governor E. J. Davis, however, gave in to pressure from officials in Washington who still believed in the peace policy and commuted the sentences to life in prison. Two years later, he granted parole to the chiefs, leading Sherman to write, "if they are to take [more] scalps, I hope yours is the first. . . ." Satanta soon began raiding Texas again, but he was rearrested in 1874 and returned to prison. He committed suicide in the penitentiary at Huntsville in 1878 by jumping from a window.

The Salt Creek Massacre and the narrow escape of two famous generals convinced even the Quaker agent Tatum that only military action could con-

Satanta, the White Bear (ca. 1820–1878). A chief of the Kiowas, Satanta, shown here in an 1870 photograph, led the Salt Creek Massacre in 1871 and eventually committed suicide by jumping from a window in the state penitentiary at Huntsville. Credit: Western History Collections, University of Oklahoma Library

trol the Indians—and Texas already had just the officer to do the job, Col. Ranald Slidell Mackenzie. An 1862 graduate of West Point, Mackenzie suffered six wounds and earned three brevet promotions in only three years of the Civil War. In 1871, he took command of the Fourth United States Cavalry and moved its headquarters to Fort Richardson on the northwestern frontier. The next year he campaigned across the Llano Estacado, the last stronghold of the Comanches, letting them know that they had no haven outside the reservation. Mackenzie left northwestern Texas in 1873 to deal with Indian raiders along the Río Grande and at one point crossed into Mexico to destroy the villages of Kickapoo and Lipan Apache marauders. Crossing the river without approval from the Mexican government raised questions of legality, but it proved effective and did not cause an international incident. Mackenzie then moved back north in 1874.

Just as military pressure on the Indians began to intensify during the early 1870s, white hunters started to inflict an equally serious blow by destroying the great buffalo herds. The Civil War had taught officers like Sherman and

Sheridan that victory came not only from defeating an enemy's armies but also from breaking the will of an enemy's people by destroying their sources of food and other vital supplies. In the case of the plains Indians, this meant exterminating the buffalo. The Indians themselves had begun to increase their annual kill in order to meet the demand for hides that could be made into robes. Therefore, some historians argue that hunters such as the Comanches eventually would have decimated the herds anyhow, especially since most Indians believed buffalo were supernatural beasts that bred in unendingly huge numbers under the ground and sprang out each spring. It seems unlikely, however, that Indians could have destroyed the great herds as quickly as white hunters did. Whites had hunted buffalo for meat and sport for many years, but shortly after 1870 in response to the demand for hides to tan into leather, the slaughter began.

Buffalo depended primarily on their sense of smell to detect danger, so hide hunters approached herds from downwind and, after getting to within 150–250 yards, used .50 caliber Sharps Rifles to shoot the bull that appeared to be the leader. The herd would begin to run but stopped when the leader fell and the rest scented blood. Hunters then shot other animals until the herd recovered and moved on. A skilled hunter might kill fifteen or more buffalo in an hour or two. Skinners then moved in to take the hides, which were taken to camp, staked out and dried, and then sold to traveling buyers. Within ten years, a few thousand hunters killed at least 3.5 million buffalo on the Southern Plains, exterminating the animals except for a few herds on private ranches or government property. The Indians watched with growing anger and fear. In the words of the Kiowa chief Kicking Bear, "They loved [buffalo] just as the white man does his money, and just as it made a white man's heart feel to have his money carried away, so it made them feel to see others killing and stealing their buffalo."

In the midst of the slaughter in 1875, the Texas legislature considered several bills designed to protect the buffalo. General Sheridan responded to these proposals with classic bluntness. Hunters, he said, "have done more in the last two years and will do more in the next year to settle the vexed Indian question than the entire regular army has done in the last 30 years. They are destroying the Indian's commissary. . . . Send them powder and lead, if you will, and for the sake of lasting peace let them kill, skin, and sell until they have exterminated the buffalo. Then your prairies will be covered with speckled cattle and the festive cowboy, who follows the hunter as the second forerunner of civilization." Rather than stop the slaughter, he concluded, you should strike a bronze medal for the hunters, depicting a dead buffalo on one side and a downcast Indian on the other. What brutally frank advice about the sad realities of the frontier.

The Comanches and Kiowas quickly recognized that the buffalo slaughter combined with military pressure threatened to force them permanently onto the reservation. Moreover, the government did not deliver rations as promised to those in the Indian Territory or prevent white encroachments on their property. These circumstances, coupled with the rise of a new Comanche spiritual leader, brought on a war in 1874–1875 that closed the Indian frontier in northwest Texas. The medicine man, Isa-tai, gained prominence as a prophet and healer in 1873. He claimed that a visit above the clouds had given him the power to bring the dead to life and to make bullets from white men's rifles fall harmlessly to the earth. At his instigation, the Comanches held a sun dance, a new ritual to them, in May 1874 and decided to strike at buffalo hunters in the Texas Panhandle. On June 27, a war party of seven hundred Comanches, Kiowas, and Southern Cheyennes led by Quanah Parker, the son of Peta Nocona and Cynthia Ann Parker, attacked a buffalo hunters' camp at Adobe Walls, an abandoned trading post near the Canadian River in Hutchinson County. The Indians hoped to surprise the hunters at dawn, but most of the twenty-eight men and one woman in the camp were awake because a ridgepole in one of their shelters had broken. They took cover in several houses and met the charging Indians with deadly fire from their buffalo rifles. Four hunters were killed, and the attackers lost about fifteen dead and a large number wounded before stopping their charges. The Indians maintained a siege for the next four days, suffering a few more casualties such as the famous shot by Billy Dixon that knocked a Cheyenne warrior off his horse at seven-eighths of a mile, and then withdrew. The battle discredited Isa-tai, who had watched from a truly safe distance, and thereby crushed the Indians' recently found spiritual strength.

The fight at Adobe Walls was not decisive militarily, but it led to the Red River War, which destroyed Indian resistance in Texas. After the battle, thousands of Comanches, Kiowas, and Southern Cheyennes, realizing that their attack would bring retribution, left the reservation and set up camps on or near the Llano Estacado. The U. S. Army then sent five thousand troops into the area during the summer of 1874, entering from five directions with the intention of leaving the Indians no escape. Soldiers and warriors fought several minor engagements, and a decisive fight came in September when troops commanded by Mackenzie attacked the Indians' main hideout in the upper Palo Duro Canyon. Moving down the steep wall at sunrise, the cavalry killed only a few Indians, but they destroyed five villages and captured 1,400 horses, most of which were then killed. The warriors, without food or mounts, had little choice but to return to the reservation. Fighting ended in the spring, and on June 2, 1875, Quanah Parker arrived at the reservation with 407 followers. The Comanches and their allies would never again create a military threat to the Texas frontier.

One last flurry of Indian raiding took place in far western Texas from 1877 to 1880 when an Eastern Chiricahua Apache chief named Victorio led several hundred of his people off an Arizona reservation and into Mexico. Victorio's band frequently raided in the area between Fort Davis and El Paso and managed to stay just ahead of pursuing United States Cavalry outfits. Finally, however, in August 1880, Lt. Col. Benjamin Grierson's unit of black cavalrymen defeated the Indians at Rattlesnake Springs north of present-day Van Horn and forced them to retreat into Mexico. A Mexican militia force killed Victorio and all his warriors in October of that year. Thus, by 1881, with the ex-

Quanah Parker (ca. 1845–1911). The son of Peta Nocona and Cynthia Ann Parker, Quanah Parker led a band of Comanches during the Red River War in 1874–1875. Following defeat and the subsequent move to a reservation in Oklahoma, he gained recognition as leader of all the Comanches and worked effectively to promote the self-sufficiency and self-reliance of his people. Credit: Western History Collections, University of Oklahoma Library

ception of the Alabama-Coushattas in the southeast and the Tiguas on the Río Grande below El Paso, Indians were, in a sadly ironic twist on the immigrant's slogan, "Gone from Texas."

Expanding the Cattle Kingdom

Soldiers and hunters, by defeating the Indians and slaughtering the buffalo, opened the way for Texans to cover the prairies and Panhandle with cattle and cowboys. Of course, the groundwork for turning much of the state into a cattle kingdom was in place well before the Civil War. Defeat of the Indians and near-extermination of the buffalo simply permitted explosive growth on the basis of existing foundations.

Spanish missions and settlers began open-range cattle raising in the region south of San Antonio during the eighteenth century; indeed, beef from Texas fed Spanish armies that fought the British during the American Revolution. Later, Anglo cattle raisers from the Old South, such as James Taylor White, brought their operations into southeastern Texas. Marketing difficulties, however, restricted the growth of early Texas cattle ranching. During the antebellum years, some Texans drove cattle to New Orleans and towns in the Midwest (even Chicago in one case), and after the 1848 gold strike in California, a few truly hardy individuals made drives to the Pacific coast. Exports by ship from Indianola and Corpus Christi became possible during the 1850s. Overall, however, before 1860 the state's cattle, especially those in South Texas, were worth more for hides and tallow than for their meat.

The Civil War brought increased demand for Texas beef, which was met by drives to shipment points on the Red and Mississippi Rivers. But this market closed when the United States took control of the Mississippi in 1863. Some cattlemen maintained their herds in the face of lost sales. For example, Robert King and Mifflin Kenedy continued to expand the famed King Ranch, and John Chisum and his partners from Denton County moved their operation to Coleman County and soon had eighteen thousand head grazing along the Colorado River. Others, however, allowed rapidly multiplying cattle to run unbranded on the open range. By 1865 thousands of mavericks roamed free in the region west and south of the farmers' line of settlement. Texans with ambition and energy could become cattlemen simply by rounding up all the unbranded cattle that they could find and hold as a herd on the open range.

When the war ended, the northern states—their livestock depleted by feeding the Union armies—had a huge appetite for Texas beef. A longhorn costing as little as three to six dollars could be sold at northern slaughterhouses for thirty to forty dollars. Demand, of course, did not reduce the distance to market, but it provided all the incentive necessary for Texans to try almost anything to overcome the problem. In 1866, Texas drovers moved some 250,000 head of cattle north, most of them along a trail from South Texas past Austin, Fort Worth, and Denison to a railhead at Sedalia, Missouri. (See map: Cattle Trails from Texas.) This Sedalia Trail proved unsatisfactory, however, because drovers had problems handling cattle in the timbered country from Fort Worth north and because farmers along the route knew that the herds carried Texas Fever. Although no one knew its cause, this disease came with Texas cattle, which seemingly it did not affect, and spread rapidly with nearly always fatal results among non-Texas livestock. (Actually, ticks transmitted the disease. Texas calves inherited enough resistance to withstand a mild case of the fever shortly after they were born and thereby built up enough immunity to survive it for the rest of their lives. However, they carried the disease in their blood, which allowed ticks to spread it from them to uninfected non-Texas animals with deadly results.) Violent opposition by farmers turned back whole herds at times and made the Sedalia trail unusable.

In 1867, an Illinois cattle buyer named Joseph G. McCoy solved the marketing problem for Texas cattlemen by making Abilene, a Kansas town on the Union Pacific Railroad, into a shipping center. He built the necessary facilities and marked a trail from the Red River to Kansas originally blazed in 1865 by an Indian trader named Jesse Chisholm. Soon known as the Chisholm Trail,

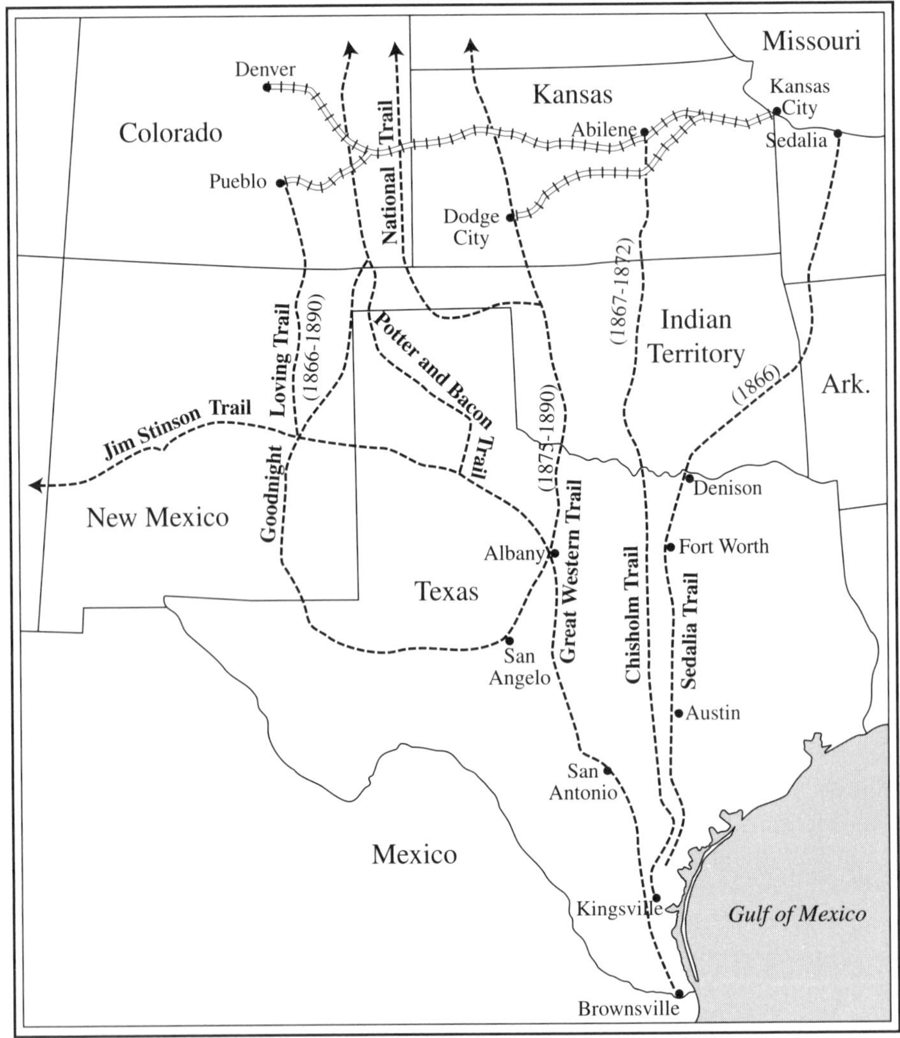

Cattle Trails From Texas

this most famous of all the cattle-drive routes ran through largely treeless plains and prairies and was far enough west to avoid areas settled by farmers. Shipping the cattle by rail directly from Abilene to slaughterhouses in the East greatly reduced problems with Texas Fever. An estimated 35,000 cattle reached Abilene in 1867, and the number doubled each year until 1871, when it reached approximately 600,000.

During the mid-1870s, Texas drovers began to find farms in the way of the Chisholm Trail, and a quarantine against herds possibly carrying Texas Fever kept them out of Abilene, forcing them farther west to Hays, Kansas. Fortunately for Texas cattlemen the removal of Indians and buffalo at about this time made it possible to open a new route that became known as the Western Trail. Beginning in the region south of San Antonio, this trail ran through the Hill Country, past Fort Griffin, across the Red River at Doan's Crossing, and on to a new railhead at Dodge City, Kansas. Within ten years, it was the route north for at least three million Texas cattle.

Not all Texas cattlemen sought connections to markets in the north and east; instead, some looked west and sold beef to feed Indians on reservations in New Mexico, soldiers at army posts, and miners in Colorado. In 1866 Charles Goodnight and Oliver Loving pioneered the first cattle drive to these western markets, taking a herd from the area of Fort Griffin southwest to San Angelo and the Pecos River and then north along the river to Fort Sumner, New Mexico. The Goodnight-Loving Trail, as it became known, was soon extended northward to Denver, and the Texans even made a few drives to Cheyenne, Wyoming. Loving died in a fight with Indians in 1867, but Goodnight continued driving cattle along their namesake trail for another ten years.

Texas drovers created numerous feeder trails and cutoffs, but the Chisholm, Western, and Goodnight-Loving Trails remained the best known and most used in the expanding cattle kingdom. Typically, the herds that moved along these routes consisted of about three thousand head handled by a trail boss and ten cowboys. A cook drove the wagon carrying food and supplies, and a wrangler tended the *remuda* of extra horses. The trail boss rode ahead of the herd, usually near the wagon and the *remuda,* while cowboys worked on all sides to keep the cattle together and moving. Those who were the youngest and least experienced drew the unenviable task of riding "drag" behind the herd, which grazed along at a leisurely pace of ten to fifteen miles a day, taking six weeks or so to reach market.

Cowboys, especially those who rode the cattle trails, became mythic folk heroes in Texas and across the United States. The reality of their lives, however, did not quite fit the image. Most were under the age of twenty; two-thirds of them Anglo whites and the others Mexican or black. They received lower pay than the trail boss, cook, or wrangler—forty dollars a month or less—and for the most part simply plodded along with the herd. Violent weather, stampedes, and river crossings brought excitement, of course, but with a high price in terms of danger. Also, contrary to the popular image, most did not carry pistols because trail bosses, fearing that gunshots would cause stampedes, did not permit it. When one trail ride ended, there was little to show for it except the experience and no certainty of employment on another. One cowboy summarized his career by saying "All . . . I got out of cowpunching is the experience. I paid a good price for that. I wouldn't take anything for what I have saw but I wouldn't care to travel the same road again, and my advice to any young man or boy is to stay at home and not be a rambler, as it won't buy you anything." These were the words of an old man, of course, and in all likelihood he would have paid no attention to them himself when he was young. The life of a cowboy, regardless of the reality, had mythic appeal even then.

Establishing Ranches and Making Cattle Raising a Business

By the mid-1870s, the success of trailing cattle to market, combined with the elimination of Indians and buffalo from northwestern Texas, encouraged the establishment of ranches in that region. Whereas many of the early cattlemen rounded up and herded mavericks without locating in a particular place or buying land, ranchers in the seventies set up headquarters where water was available and planned to stay. Generally they ran their stock on public land at first, but when the state opened those lands to sale they acquired title to as many sections as possible around their headquarters. At times, they built corrals or dugouts on unsold sections in order to discourage claims by would-be settlers. Charles Goodnight established the first large ranch in the Panhandle in 1876 by moving 1,600 longhorns into the Palo Duro Canyon. The following year he formed a partnership with an English investor named John G. Adair and began purchasing land in and around the canyon. In 1878, the JA Ranch, as it was called in honor of Adair, sent its first trail herd northward to Dodge City. At one point in the late 1880s, the ranch had 1,325,000 acres in parts of six counties and ran a herd of more than 100,000 head.

Goodnight's wife, Mary Ann, or Molly as everyone except her husband called her, became the unofficial first lady of the Panhandle. A native of Tennessee who had moved with her family to Fort Belknap at the age of fourteen, she married Goodnight in 1870 and moved to the JA Ranch in 1877. The couple's first home was a dugout topped with cottonwood logs, but within a few years they moved into a small home built of cedar logs and eventually into a nineteen-room ranch house. For a time, she was the only woman on the ranch, and her nearest female neighbor was Molly Bugbee, the wife of Thomas S. Bugbee, owner of the Quarter Circle T Ranch in Hutchinson County. They did not see each other or anyone off their own ranches for more than six months at a time, but both claimed not to mind. Of course Molly Goodnight, even though she had no children, had her hands full serving as, in the words of one historian, "doctor, nurse, homemaker, spiritual comforter, sister, and mother to the hands who worked for her husband."

Elizabeth (Lizzie) Johnson Williams demonstrated that the role of women in the cattle business was not necessarily limited to that of a helpmate. The daughter of a teacher and a teacher herself in Austin, Johnson learned about the money to be made in cattle by keeping books for several prominent ranchers. In 1871, at the age of thirty-one, she registered her own brand and began to acquire land and longhorns. She married Hezekiah Williams in 1879, but only after signing a prenuptial agreement that allowed her to retain control of her own financial affairs. When she and her husband drove cattle north on the Chisholm Trail, beginning in 1879, her herd remained separate from his, making her the first Texas woman to drive her own cattle to Abilene. Lizzie Johnson Williams, as a shrewd judge of cattle and investment opportunities, built a personal fortune that amounted to $250,000 at her death in 1924. A tall, striking woman, she was an interesting combination of the southern lady and western cattle queen, wearing silks, satins, laces, and diamonds for social occasions and switching to calicos, cottons, and a bonnet while on trail or at the Hays County ranch she shared with her husband.

Cattle ranching in Texas even attracted the interest of absentee British investors. One famously successful venture began in 1878 when a Texas cattleman, Henry H. Campbell, formed a partnership with a Chicago banker, A. M. Britton, and bought a small herd and grazing rights from Joe Browning, a free-range rancher in central Motley County about sixty miles to the northeast of present-day Lubbock. Within a year the partners brought in several other investors, including Spottswood W. Lomax of Fort Worth, and incorporated as the Matador Cattle Company. Lomax, a lover of Spanish literature, named the operation. The ranching enterprise prospered, and the investors decided to cash in on their success by attracting venture capital from Great Britain. Britton traveled to Dundee, Scotland, in 1882 and sold the entire property for $1,250,000 to the Matador Land and Cattle Company, a new Scottish corporation. The Matador Ranch, which eventually controlled well over a million acres, began to pay dividends in 1885 and successfully withstood all the ups and downs of the cattle business for more than fifty years before finally being sold to another company in 1951. A second ranching venture organized by Britton and Lomax, the Espuela Cattle Company, enjoyed far less success. Incorporated in 1883 to operate in the region southeast of Lubbock, the Spur Ranch, as it became known, had more than 500,000 acres. Two years later Britton convinced investors in London to create the Espuela Land and Cattle Company and buy out the original organizers. The Spur Ranch, however, struggled financially to the point that the British investors sold out shortly after the turn of the century.

The largest ranch in Texas, the famous XIT, also originated in the early 1880s, although in a notably different way than any other. In 1879, when the state legislature looked for ways to finance a new capitol building in Austin, it turned to the public domain (in yet another example of how the state benefited from owning its public lands) and used 3,025,000 acres to pay the contractor, Mathias Schnell of Rock Island, Illinois. Schnell soon transferred the land to a group of businessmen known as the Chicago Syndicate, who decided to use it for ranching until they could sell it to farm settlers. The Syndicate raised five million dollars from British investors and hired B. H. Campbell of Wichita, Kansas, to manage buying cattle and opening ranching operations on the land, which extended 220 miles north to south along the Texas Panhandle border with New Mexico. Eventually, the legend grew that XIT stood for "ten in Texas," because the ranch covered all or part of ten counties, but it is more likely that Abner P. Blocker, who drove the first herd of longhorns from Central Texas to the new ranch, sketched out the mark in the dust when Campbell asked for a brand that could not easily be altered. Within a few years the ranch had more than 100,000 cattle, and at its peak during the 1890s employed 150 cowboys who branded 35,000 calves in a single year. By the end of that decade, however, investors, especially those in Britain, wanted to sell out, so the Syndicate began to make large portions available to other ranchers. The last parcel of the XIT sold in 1963, but memories of the largest ranch in Texas history remain alive to this day in Panhandle towns such as Dalhart.

While ranching boomed in northwestern Texas after 1875, the state's most famous ranch, the King Ranch in South Texas, continued to expand. Created during the 1850s, the ranch was owned jointly by Richard King and Mifflin Kenedy from 1860 until 1868, when the partnership dissolved with King retaining control of the 53,136 acre Santa Gertrudis Grant. During the next ten years, King added more than 100,000 acres in southern Nueces County and, at his death in 1885, employed some 300 men on approximately 640,000 acres. More than half of the land he bought between 1875 and 1885 belonged originally to Mexicans, an indication of their continuing displacement by Anglos as landowners in South Texas. The King Ranch operated much like a Spanish or Mexican hacienda, with King as the *patrón* and those who worked the ranch as *peóns.* King provided housing, food and water, and small wages that *kineños* spent at the ranch store on their other needs. In return his workers practiced a Mexican style of ranching and made it pay. Upon King's death in 1885, his widow Henrietta Chamberlain King, the Missouri-born daughter of a Presbyterian missionary to Texas, took over ownership and management of the King Ranch. She personally supervised its affairs, and with the assistance of her son-in-law Robert J. Kleberg, paid off some $500,000 in debt while adding additional land. By the time of Henrietta King's death in 1925, the ranch had reached 1,173,000 acres, and she had also played a major role in promoting the economic and cultural growth of the entire region from Corpus Christi to Brownsville.

The development of ranches made cattle raising into more of a business than an adventure. Large ranchers began to acquire rights to pasture lands in Wyoming, Montana, and even Canada that were used to fatten Texas cattle before marketing. Through the early part of the 1880s, instead of stopping at railheads in Kansas, drovers on the Western and Goodnight-Loving Trails kept their herds moving even farther north. Also, ranchers made an effort to improve their basic longhorn stock. Goodnight and Adair, for example, brought one hundred Durham (shorthorn) bulls to the JA Ranch in 1877. In 1876 William S. Ikard introduced Hereford cattle on his ranch in Clay County, and Christopher Columbus Slaughter, the "Cattle King of Texas," built a prize herd of purebred Herefords at his Long S Ranch on the headwaters of the Colorado River. The XIT was among the first to use Aberdeen Angus bulls, and the King Ranch imported Brahmans, which were well suited to the South Texas climate. Crossing these animals with shorthorns produced a new breed—the Santa Gertrudis—special to the Lone Star State.

Cattle raisers, as they became more business-like and sought to protect the pastures and water sources used by their herds, brought an end to open-range ranching. Mifflin Kenedy and Richard King, innovative and concerned with ownership rights as always, were probably the first to fence their lands. After dissolving their partnership in 1868, they went to Louisiana and bought creosoted cypress posts and pine planks to use as fencing. Kenedy took advantage of the fact that one of his 131,000 acre grants was bounded on two sides by water (the Laguna Madre), leaving only two land boundaries to fence, and created the first fully enclosed range of any size west of the Mississippi River. King had a larger task, but he followed suit.

Ranchers elsewhere in Texas, of course, found wooden fences impractical and far too expensive, but for them the answer appeared in an 1874 invention—barbed wire. Patented by Joseph F. Glidden of Illinois, barbed wire eventually had many variants in design, but essentially it amounted to a strand of wire with barbs wrapped around it and held in place by twisting another strand around the first. According to legend, a salesman named John W. Gates made Glidden's product popular in Texas in 1878 by building a barbed-wire corral in San Antonio's Military Plaza, filling it with longhorns, and showing how the new wire turned the cattle. This story cannot be documented, but, one way or another, the wire, which Gates advertised as "light as air, stronger than whiskey, and cheap as dirt," found a huge market in Texas. Charles Goodnight fenced the boundaries of the JA Ranch along the Palo Duro Canyon, and other large ranchers followed suit, enclosing their water sources first and then all the land that they owned or leased. Fencing made it feasible and necessary for ranchers to use another improvement in their business—the windmill. Few water sources in western Texas were truly reliable, but the windmill, which used natural energy to bring water from wells to the surface, solved that problem. Some ranchers built windmills and protected them with fences; other found that they had to use windmills because fences kept their cattle away from surface water sources. In any case, windmills dotted the landscape after the 1880s. The XIT alone had 335 in operation by 1900.

As is the case with any notable economic change, turning ranching into a business and closing the open range exacted a price from some Texans that they did not pay without protest. In the early years of cattle raising, for example, cowboys often received part of their pay in calves or mavericks and even ran small herds on their employers' land. Corporate ranches, however, insisted on wages as the only form of compensation and kept pay at forty dollars per month. Angry at this treatment, in 1883 a group of cowboys demanded higher wages and went on strike against five ranches, including the T Anchor in the Palo Duro Canyon region. The Cowboy Strike, which may have involved as many as three hundred men, lasted more than two months but failed primarily because the ranchers had no trouble hiring replacements. Widely dispersed and highly mobile cowboys had little chance of organizing and bargaining successfully with large ranchers.

A second problem—fence cutting—proved far more difficult to handle. Brought on when ranchers fenced landless cattlemen off large areas of pasture, fence cutting became a serious issue in 1883, when a drought put special pressure on sources of food and water. Most of the ranchers had fenced only land that they owned or leased, but some had enclosed the property of others and even blocked public transit routes. Soon, indiscriminate use of wire cutters became widespread, especially along a north-south line down the middle of the state, and cost an estimated $20 million in damages. Conflicts between ranch hands and fence cutters erupted into violence that killed at least three men. Finally, in January 1884, a special session of the state legislature dealt with the issue by making fence cutting a felony punishable by one to five years in prison and ordering anyone who had enclosed lands belonging to the public or another individual to tear down the fences within six months. Those who built fences across public roads were to provide gates and keep them in repair. These laws ended all but a few sporadic incidents of fence cutting and secured the closing of the open range.

Thus, by 1890 the cattle kingdom had become a businessman's world. Even the most romantic of all cowboy adventures—the trail drive—was no more, having been ended by drought, quarantines, barbed wire, and the railroad. Several terribly dry years beginning in 1883 ruined the water sources and grass necessary to herds moving north. In 1885 Kansas and other northern states and territories enforced quarantines against cattle that might carry Texas Fever. Indeed, ranchers in northern Texas such as Charles Goodnight, arguing that their cattle did not carry the fever but would be infected by those moving up from the south, threatened to use rifles to enforce their own "Winchester Quarantines" against trail herds. Barbed wire fences closed off trails. Finally, railroads offered an efficient replacement for the long drive north. By 1890, as will be explained below, even western and southern Texas had rail access to the rest of the United States. Cowboys still might have to move herds a hundred or more miles to the railhead, but that paled in comparison with the great drives to Kansas and beyond.

Old West Lawlessness and Violence in Texas

Antebellum Texas was hardly a law-abiding, nonviolent society, but after the war the state became notorious for lawlessness and violence. In part a result of the brutalizing effect of the war itself, this breakdown in social order actually affected all Texans, particularly during Reconstruction. However, thefts and killings resulting from conditions on the Mexican and cattlemen's frontiers added greatly to the state's identification with the Old West.

Cattle rustling plagued the lower Río Grande region for nearly ten years after the Civil War. Mexicans crossed the river to round up unbranded mavericks, which Anglo cattlemen claimed as theirs, and on occasion to steal from the herds at established ranches. Anglos retaliated by forming vigilance committees, chasing the thieves, and raiding ranches owned by Mexicans. The so-called "Cattle Wars" continued until 1875–1876 when a forty-man company of Texas Rangers under the command of Capt. Leander H. McNelly, a former scout in the Confederate Army, arrived in the Nueces Strip. McNelly, a native of Virginia described as a "tallish thin man of quiet manner, and with the soft voice of a timid Methodist minister," brought an end to raids from Mexico and Anglo vigilance activities. His Rangers' methods, however, involved several illegal crossings into Mexico and extreme violence against raiders: At one point, after killing more than twelve rustlers in a fight that cost the life of one of their members, they stacked the dead Mexicans in the square at Brownsville. McNelly quieted the border before his death in 1877 at the age of thirty-three, but his tactics earned the Rangers undying hatred among many Texans of Mexican descent.

McNelly's Rangers operated as a special force authorized by the governor, but in 1874, the legislature created a more permanent Ranger force, the Frontier Battalion of six companies of seventy-five mounted men each. Commanded by Major John B. Jones, an ex-Confederate officer, this battalion saw more action than McNelly's force. It assisted the U.S. Army in fighting the Comanches and Kiowas in 1875 and then turned its attention to bandits and rustlers along the frontier. In 1877, for example, Jones and his men broke up one of the state's most infamous nests of outlaws by arresting forty men in Kimble County. The Frontier Battalion remained in existence until 1900 and created a far more positive image for the Texas Rangers as a law enforcement body than did McNelly's unit. Their reputation for individual daring and success in restoring order gave rise to the slogan "one riot, one ranger."

During the 1870s and 1880s, the Rangers also had to deal with Texas's most famous "wild west" outlaws—men such as Sam Bass and John Wesley Hardin, who gained the strange sort of awestruck admiration that Americans reserve for truly notorious thieves and killers. Bass, a native of Indiana, drifted into North Texas in 1870 and worked for several years at odd jobs. He helped organize a trail drive to Dodge City in 1876, but gambled away all his earnings and then recruited several other "hard characters" and turned to holding up stagecoaches. In 1877, he and his gang began robbing trains. Their greatest coup came in September when they held up a Union Pacific train in Nebraska and took $60,000 in newly minted gold coins. Bass then returned to Texas and continued to rob trains in the Dallas area before going south in July 1878 to hold up a bank in Round Rock just north of Austin. Informed on by one of his gang, Bass found Texas Rangers waiting at the bank and was fatally wounded in the gun battle that followed. He was twenty-seven years old. Texans immortalized Bass in poems and songs as a sort of Robin Hood "of the type you scarcely ever see."

John Wesley Hardin, born in Bonham in 1853, began his career as a killer at age fifteen by shooting a freedman in East Texas and continued it on an 1871 drive on the Chisholm Trail, killing seven men en route and three more in Abilene. Back in Texas, he killed another four men, surrendered to lawmen in Cherokee County in 1872, but broke out of jail and shot a former state police officer and a deputy sheriff. Hardin then left the state, but Texas Rangers arrested him in Florida. Convicted of murder in 1878, he received a twenty-five-year sentence, which he put to good use (when not trying to escape) by directing the prison Sunday School and reading law. He received a pardon in 1894, was admitted to the bar (surely one of the earliest lawyer jokes), and moved to El Paso. The next year, after having an affair with the wife of a client, he was murdered by a man whom he had hired to kill the husband/client and then refused to pay. Hardin insisted that he always fought in self-defense and that he "never killed a man who didn't need killing." Somehow, a good many people were willing to overlook the more than thirty notches on his gun and believe him.

Texas and the New South

While Texans living west of the 98th meridian (in modern terms, west of Interstate Highway 35) closed the Indian frontier and expanded the cattle kingdom, thereby giving the state its place in the legend of the Old West, those east of that line—the great majority of the total population—remained clearly a part of the South. The Old South, however, had passed with the war, and publicists soon began to tell Texans in the more settled part of the state that they were living in the "New South." Those who preached the New South creed emphasized economic growth—railroad building, urbanization, and industrialization—and the sort of progress that would remake their region into a replica of the North. The editor of the *Dallas Herald* perfectly captured the feel of New South thinking as early as 1868. "The live town of Dallas," he wrote, "seems determined to do all it can in the way of improvement. Several large, substantial, tastefully designed buildings are steadily going up, others in contract, and in almost every direction is heard the inspiring music of trowel, saw, forge, foundry and mill." He needed only to add the sound of a train whistle to have completed a New South symphony.

In some respects—railroad construction being the best example—Texas made great progress toward attaining the New South ideal during the 1870s and 1880s. The state had fewer than five hundred miles of railroads in 1860, and the war so interrupted construction and disrupted the few lines the state had that in 1870 only 486 miles of track were operative. (See map: Texas Railroads in 1870 and 1890.). During the next twenty years, however, builders added exactly eight thousand miles of rails and linked every city of four thousand or more residents, except Brownsville, with two or more railroads. One of the first major roads to resume building after the war was the Houston and Texas Central, which had begun construction in 1856 and reached Millican, eighty miles north of Houston, by 1860. The H&TC built into Dallas by 1872 and on to Denison the next year. There it connected with the Missouri, Kansas and Texas Railroad, giving Texas its first rail connection to St. Louis and the eastern United States. The Texas and Pacific Railway also deserves specific mention in that it, alone among railroads in the state, operated under a charter granted by the United States government. Chartered in 1871, the T&P acquired the tracks built in Harrison County before the war and linked to Shreveport during the war and then began to build west. It reached Dallas in 1873, Fort Worth in 1876, and Sierra Blanca, ninety-two miles east of El Paso in 1881. There it met the Southern Pacific, giving Texas a connection to San Diego, California.

By 1890, several other major roads—the International and Great Northern; Galveston, Harrisburg & San Antonio; Gulf, Colorado, and Santa Fe; and Fort Worth and Denver City—combined with the H&TC and T&P to tie the state together and give access to the rest of the United States. Texans knew that these railroads provided transportation and communication links unavailable by any other means, so state and local governments showered them with favors. The state had begun in 1854 to grant companies sixteen sections

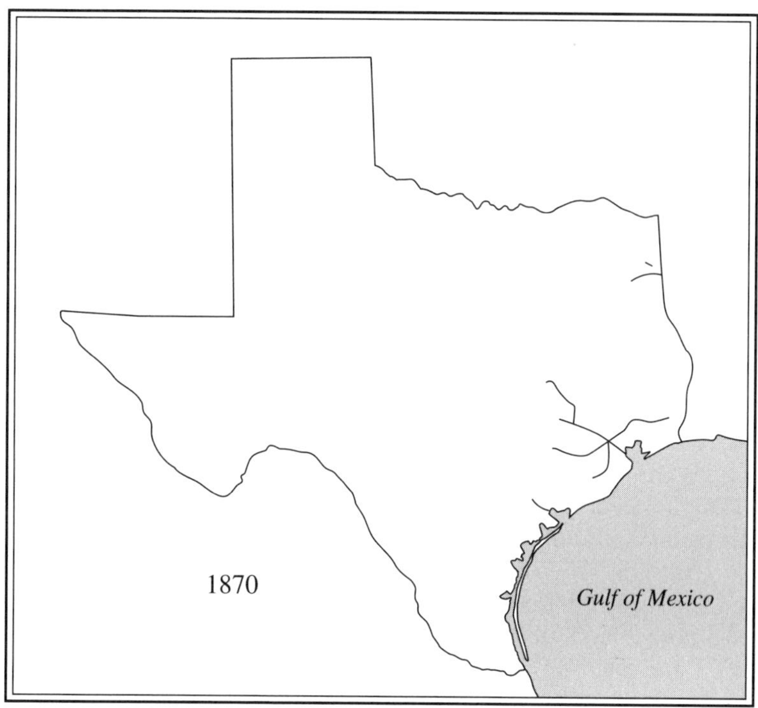

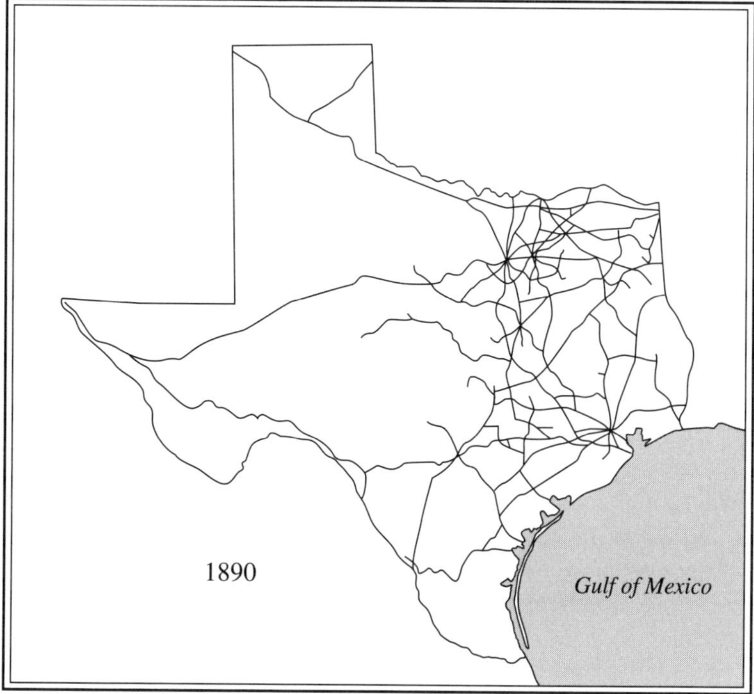

Texas Railroads in 1870 and 1890

of land (10,240 acres) for every mile of track completed, and that practice continued after the war except for a brief period from 1870 to 1874 when such grants were prohibited under the Constitution of 1869. An amendment in 1874 again permitted grants, as did the Constitution of 1876. The Land Grant Law of 1876 gave effect to these constitutional provisions, and the state continued to provide sixteen sections for every mile of main-line track built. By 1882, when so little available acreage remained that the legislature repealed the land-grant provision, Texas railroads had received more than 32 million acres in compensation for track built, most of it in the postwar years. Local efforts to attract railroad builders were exemplified by voters in Harrison County on the Louisiana border in East Texas. In 1872 they approved giving the Texas & Pacific $300,000 in thirty-year bonds bearing 7 percent interest payable in gold if the railroad would establish its Texas offices and shops in Marshall, the county's seat of government. Although the railroad upheld its end of the bargain, the county's taxpayers soon found their tax burden unbearable and, after a complex legal battle, managed to negotiate a scaled-down payment plan.

Railroads made urbanization, a second key element of New South progress, possible. In virtually every case any boom in a town's population between 1870 and 1890 can be traced to the arrival of a railroad. Dallas, for example, more than doubled the number of its inhabitants in 1872–1873 when the H&TC and the T&P arrived. From an estimated population of 3,000 in 1870, it grew to 38,067 in 1890, making it the largest city in Texas at that time. Marshall grew from 1,960 to 5,624 during the decade that the T&P located its offices and shops there. Laredo had only 3,521 people in 1880, but, following the arrival in 1881 of the Texas Mexican Railroad from Corpus Christi and the International and Great Northern from Austin, it grew to 11,319 by 1890. By contrast, Brownsville, which had a larger population in 1880 (4,938) but did not get a railroad until 1904, increased only to 6,134 over the decade. Finally, Fort Worth, bolstered by the arrival of the T&P in 1876 and the building of the Fort Worth & Denver City during the 1880s (both of which contributed to the town's position as a shipping center for the cattle industry), increased from a population estimated at 500 in 1870 to a census count of 23,076 in 1890.

Urban residents enjoyed technological progress well ahead of their rural counterparts. When the London Circus toured Texas in 1879, it advertised its lighting system of electricity and carbon filament bulbs as "A MIRACLE, A WONDER . . . worth traveling FIVE HUNDRED MILES to witness." Within a year, Galveston had installed a generator, and soon other towns began to follow suit. By 1891, Galveston, Houston, Austin, Dallas, Fort Worth, Waco, San Antonio, Laredo, and Sherman had built electric street railways. A. H. Belo, publisher of the *Galveston News,* saw Alexander Graham Bell's new invention, the telephone, at the Philadelphia Exposition in 1876 and two years later had a line installed between his office and home. By the mid-1880s telephone exchanges operated in all sizable Texas towns. Growing use of the telephone provided a new employment opportunity for women, because boys, who worked the exchanges at first, made too many rude remarks to customers and had to be replaced by more courteous and dependable operators.

From one perspective, urban growth was truly impressive during these years. In 1870 Texas had only nine towns or cities with populations of 2,500 or more (the usual definition of an "urban" place); by 1890 the number stood at forty-two. Five—Dallas and Fort Worth, plus San Antonio (37,673), Galveston (29,084), and Houston (27,557)—surpassed 20,000 people each. Austin (14,575) and Waco (14,445) were the next largest. The total number of Texans in these towns and cities, many of them recent arrivals in the state, rose from 59,521 to 349,511. Impressive as this urban growth was, however, it barely made a dent in the overwhelmingly rural nature of Texas. In 1890, 84 percent of Texans lived in rural areas, a change of less than 10 percent in the two decades since 1870.

Industrial development followed the same pattern as urban growth from the Civil War to 1890. In 1870, the state had only 2,399 manufacturing establishments, which produced goods valued at $11,517,302. Most industrial producers operated on a small scale because they could draw on only a local area for raw materials and markets. During the next twenty years, the number of factories and mills increased 120 percent to 5,268, and the value of their output rose to $70,433,551, a spectacular gain of more than 500 percent. The tremendous increase in value of products relative to number of establishments reflected the role of the railroad in allowing manufacturers to build larger plants at one location, have raw materials brought to them, and ship their products to distant markets.

Most of the growth between 1870 and 1890 took place in industries such as milling, lumbering, and mining that simply processed the state's agricultural products and natural resources. Flour milling, which was concentrated in North Texas, was the state's largest industry through the 1870s and most of the next decade. Dallas County alone milled flour valued at $2,750,000 in 1877, sending it to markets as far away as Shreveport, Louisiana, and San Antonio. By 1890, however, lumbering replaced milling in the top spot statewide. Based at first in the region east of Houston and then spreading over most of East Texas, the lumber industry enjoyed a symbiotic relationship with the railroads. Lumbermen depended totally on the railroad to move their product to waiting markets in places such as treeless West Texas, and after 1875 the railroads depended on lumber for most of the tonnage that they carried. Henry J. Lutcher and G. Bedell Moore, who moved from Pennsylvania to Orange in 1877, began the "bonanza era" in Texas lumbering by building a mill that produced 80,000 to 100,000 board feet of pine per day. Coal mining developed when railroads began to burn coal rather than wood in their locomotives. Texas coal, located mostly in north-central counties, was generally of inferior quality and had a high sulphur content, but veins could be mined at low costs. For a few years in the early 1880s, miners simply dug coal out of a hillside at a place called Coalville in Palo Pinto County. After a labor dispute closed this operation, a shaft mine was opened a few miles away in Erath County and the miners, many of whom were natives of Italy and Poland, moved there. In 1888 a group of investors that included a New Yorker named H. K. Thurber bought the mine, built a company town, and made it the largest operation of its kind in Texas. Thurber, a ghost town today, flourished to the point of having a population of at least eight thousand by 1920.

Texas experienced enough railroad and industrial growth during the 1870s that sizable labor unions appeared for the first time in the state. A few workers' organizations existed in Texas before 1880—most notably the Galveston Screwmen's Benevolent Association, a union formed in 1866 by skilled longshoremen who used screwjacks to pack cotton into the holds of ships—but efforts to create a national labor movement were restricted to the northeastern United States. That changed, however, in 1882 when the Knights of Labor organized their first assembly in Texas. Welcoming all working men, skilled and unskilled and blacks as well as whites, into their "one big union," the Knights pursued basic objectives such as shorter hours and better pay, although one Texas newspaper accused them of favoring "socialism and communism." By 1886, the union had thirty thousand members, but then it made the mistake of taking on Jay Gould, one of the greatest financial pirates in an age of "robber baron" industrialists. The firing of a foreman for union activities at the Texas and Pacific shops in Marshall began a walkout by the Knights that became known as the Great Southwest Strike when it spread to all of Gould's railroads in the region. Unfortunately for the Knights, events then followed the pattern typical of strikes in that age: the railroad refused to negotiate and hired strikebreakers, some strikers resorted to violence, public opinion turned against the striking workers, the government sent in state militia and Texas Rangers, the strike was broken, and the union ruined. As the Knights of Labor faded after 1886, they were replaced, albeit very slowly, by an association of trade unions affiliated with the new American Federation of Labor. The AF of L, however, never matched the Knights in terms of the percentage of Texas industrial workers who belonged to its locals.

While railroads and extractive industries flourished, even to the point of creating labor organizations and actions, more complex forms of manufacturing generally did not. Even cotton textile manufacturing, seemingly a "natural" in a state producing vast quantities of the fleecy staple, had virtually no success in Texas. Efforts at developing an iron industry also came to nothing. Longstanding problems such the absence of a source of power and the lack of capital continued to prevent the development of manufacturing. Overall, in spite of all the expansion during the twenty years after 1870, Texas lagged far behind the United States as a whole in industrialization. Consider this comparison: nationwide in 1870, the value of manufactured goods was nearly twice as great as the value of farm products, whereas in Texas as late as 1890, manufactured goods had a little more than half the value of farm products. Industrialization was gaining, but the state remained overwhelmingly agricultural.

Agriculture: Expansion and Ruin

Agriculture in Texas suffered serious setbacks during the Civil War, but it soon recovered and forged ahead to new heights of value and productivity. The following table indicates the gains made from 1870 to 1890:

Statistics on Texas Agriculture, 1870–1890

	Number of Farms	Number of Improved Acres	Value of Farms, Tools, & Livestock	Value of Farm Products	Bushels of Corn Produced	Bales of Cotton Produced
1870	61,125	2,964,836	80,777,550	49,185,170	20,554,538	350,628
1890	228,126	20,746,215	552,127,104	111,699,430	69,112,150	1,471,242

These spectacular increases—more than 300 percent in the cotton crop, for example—resulted primarily from bringing much more land into production, thanks to population growth and the railroad. Whole areas, barely settled in 1865, were covered with productive farms by 1890. "Farmers are pouring into western Texas so fast," claimed a New Orleans newspaper in 1886, "that ranchmen have just enough time to move their cattle out and prevent their tails being chopped off by the advancing hoe." Regions such as the Blackland Prairie that had everything necessary to join the cotton kingdom except transportation grew tens of thousands of bales a year once farmers there could reach markets by rail. Dallas County, for example, increased its cotton crop from 3,834 bales in 1870 to 21,649 ten years later, a gain of 465 percent.

Impressive overall agricultural statistics, however, masked increasingly serious distress for thousands of individual Texas farmers during these years. Prices fell, debts rose, and farm tenancy increased dramatically. During the decade of the 1880s, the number of Texas farms worked by landless tenants rose by more than thirty thousand. Some of the tenants paid an annual cash rent to the landowner, but most farmed as either share tenants or sharecroppers, paying rent with portions of the crops they produced. Although arrangements varied from place to place, share tenants generally provided their own seed, work animals, and equipment and paid the landlord one-fourth of the cotton and one-third of the corn as rent, whereas sharecroppers provided only their own labor and received the proceeds of one-half of the cotton crop. Share tenants had more control of their farming operations than did sharecroppers, and therefore enjoyed higher status. Still, one basic characteristic united all tenants—they owned no land.

Having few if any cash resources, most tenant farmers began each year by borrowing from a local merchant in order to pay for supplies and necessities such as food and clothing. This loan, which was secured by a chattel mortgage on the crop that the farmer intended to grow plus his other possessions such as a mule or cow, came in the form of credit at the store rather than cash. Goods bought with this credit line had much higher prices than those paid for with cash. And, of course, the merchant kept the ledger of transactions. At the close of the year, when crops were sold and debts paid, farmers generally broke even and could only begin the cycle again.

Most black farmers, coming out of slavery with no land and having little opportunity to acquire it, became tenants. For example, by 1880 in Harrison

County, 80 percent of all black families lived as tenant farmers, most of them as sharecroppers. However, increasing numbers of whites joined blacks in tenantry every year. New arrivals who could not afford land had no choice, and small farmers who mortgaged their land to buy supplies lost it to foreclosures when their crops did not return enough to pay their creditors. By 1890, 42 percent of all Texas farms were worked by tenants, and the percentage continued to rise year by year. The notion of an "agricultural ladder" by which young men moved from sharecropper to share tenant to landowner became more and more of a myth than a reality, and Texas farmers by the tens of thousands seemed doomed to live endlessly in near-poverty—working someone else's land.

Reasons for this decline in the fortunes of Texas farmers are complex and debatable, but to a large extent it happened because of a move from semi-subsistence farming to market-oriented agriculture based on cotton. During the antebellum years slaveholding planters produced cotton as a cash crop, but most smaller farmers practiced a safety-first agriculture that concentrated on feeding and clothing their families before attempting to make money. After the war, they generally abandoned this subsistence approach in favor of planting cotton and using the proceeds to buy necessities. Critics railed against this trend toward specialization and saw cotton as a destructive monster, but in fact the move away from subsistence made perfect sense in many ways. For one thing, cotton produced more value per acre than any other crop the farmer could plant, so once the railroad came to transport the money crop away and bring in foodstuffs such as flour at cheap rates, he could grow more cotton and use the proceeds to buy necessities. Also, cotton rarely failed completely as a crop, and it did not deplete the soil quickly. And finally, cash brought a better life. What farmer and his wife would not want "store bought clothes," fresh coffee, oranges and lemons, and canned foods to break the monotony of a corn and pork diet, especially if they saw that their neighbors had those things?

Thus, Texas farmers had compelling reasons to forsake the drab life of subsistence and enter the marketplace, and that step, in itself, was not the problem. Ruin came because of several conditions affecting the production and marketing of cotton in Texas. First, the rapidly expanding population increased the demand and prices for land, which in turn made farms smaller and therefore unable to grow enough cotton to meet expenses and leave a surplus. Farmers on smaller units were less productive also because they could not afford machinery. Second, and far more important, the price of cotton fell from an average of 15.5 cents per pound of lint (ginned cotton) in 1869–1871 to 8.1 cents per pound in 1889–1891. In part this fall in prices resulted from overproduction of cotton in Texas and across the South, but it also reflected a general deflationary trend that affected the whole nation during this period. An index of wholesale prices for farm products nationwide shows a fall of 37 percent between 1870 and 1890. (This deflation resulted to a large extent from the limited supply of money in the United States at that time. In 1879, the nation went on a de facto gold standard, which meant that the treasury stood ready to redeem every dollar of currency in gold. Adoption of the gold standard thus tied the amount of money in circulation to the amount of gold in the country and, since the supply of gold was very limited at that time, limited the supply of money. Limitations on the money supply meant that as the population and volume of business increased, more and more goods and services had to be priced in terms of relatively fewer dollars. Naturally, prices declined. Deflation affected everyone—even railroad rates fell—but farm prices generally fell faster and farther than costs.) Third, the rising tenancy rate meant that farmers had to try to grow more cotton, regardless of its price, because landowners insisted that share tenants and sharecroppers pay their rents with a cash crop. Overall then, cotton in itself was not the problem, but cotton farmers faced ruin.

Texas agriculture needed fewer farmers and larger, more mechanized farms, but such change would mean massive displacement of tenants, who at that time had nothing else to do and nowhere else to go. Obviously, since Texas did not have a dictatorial government that could order a transformation in agriculture, basic change would not come until the state's economy actually attained the New South ideal of industrialization and urbanization. Then, families that had for generations eked out a living growing cotton would find different jobs and better lives. Suffering farmers, of course, were not likely to accept an explanation of their problems that blamed impersonal economic forces beyond anyone's control; nor were they willing to sit quietly and wait philosophically for change to come sometime in the future. Instead, they focused on immediate contributors to their economic woes such as monopolistic railroads, "middlemen" (the merchants with whom farmers had to deal in selling produce and buying supplies), and the nation's inadequate monetary system. The relief measures that they sought were totally reasonable—for example, railroads did gouge the farmers and regulations would help—however, only basic changes that reduced reliance on agriculture would end the problem.

Farmer Organizations

Farming is a notoriously individualistic enterprise, but Texans saw that they had no hope of dealing with their problems unless they organized. The Grange, or Patrons of Husbandry, a fraternal order created in 1867 by Oliver H. Kelly, a clerk in the U.S. Department of Agriculture, provided the first means of bringing Texas farmers together. Focusing originally more on education and social interaction than on economic matters, the Grange became during the 1870s a major vehicle of farmer protest. An organizer from the national Grange formed Texas's first chapter at Salado in July 1873, and the movement grew quickly enough that a meeting in Dallas created the Texas State Grange in October. By 1875, the Grange claimed forty thousand members in more than one thousand lodges statewide.

The Grange's political agenda, which heavily influenced the convention that wrote the Constitution of 1876, included holding down the cost of government, restricting taxation, and giving the state government authority to regulate the railroads. Where the railroads were concerned, Grange members soon learned that constitutional provisions needed legislative "teeth" and began to demand laws prohibiting discrimination in rates and the creation of a state regulatory commission. The Grange also emphasized the creation of marketing and consumer cooperatives that would allow farmers to bypass the hated middlemen. Cooperatives sold shares of stock to individual farmers to raise money to begin operations. Then they assisted in marketing by grading, storing, advertising, and selling cotton and also purchased goods and supplies at wholesale prices and passed on part of the savings to consumers. Cooperatives charged small commissions for their marketing services and had minor markups on their goods, but any profits beyond those necessary to stay in business were returned to investors. Essentially then, cooperatives created marketing and purchasing operations that were large enough to bypass merchants, thus lowering middleman costs to the farmers.

Some of the Grange's cooperatives had a degree of success. For example, in 1883 the Texas Cooperative Association, which was established in 1878, handled more than sixteen thousand bales of cotton and showed a net profit of more than $20,000. Ultimately, however, attempts to bypass the middleman failed. Few farmers had capital to invest in such ventures, and virtually none knew how to manage them. As one leader said, "We are farmers, not merchants." Moreover, instead of sticking to a cash-only approach as originally intended, the cooperatives extended credit to their customers and then had to go into debt themselves in order to continue operations. The Grange ran into so many bankruptcies and such opposition from merchants and their allies that by 1890 it had only about five thousand members and little or no importance. At least it demonstrated that farmers could organize to work on their common problems.

As the Grange faded, a new organization called the Farmers' Alliance, which originated in 1877 in Lampasas County, took its place. During its early years, the alliance, like the Grange, focused on forming cooperatives, but by 1886, some leaders began to call for political action to bring economic relief. After all, they reasoned, cooperatives did not help the poorest farmers, who could not afford to join, and did nothing about falling cotton prices or abusive railroad practices. These "insurgents" took over the 1886 convention in Cleburne from more conservative members and adopted a series of demands that turned the alliance into a protest movement no one in Texas could ignore. After denouncing the "shameful abuses" heaped on farmers and workers by "arrogant capitalists and powerful corporations," the Cleburne demands called for the regulation of railroad rates, quick sale of public lands to settlers, and the use of silver as well as gold as a basis for money. This call for unlimited coinage of silver—a practice generally termed "free silver"—came because silver was very plentiful in the United States at that time. Using it as currency would create more money, which in turn would bring higher prices and stop the deflationary trend in farm prices.

The stir created by the Cleburne demands quieted in 1887, thanks to the efforts of a new leader, Charles William Macune, but the call for political action would soon return, stronger than before. Macune, a native of Wisconsin who had come to Texas in 1871 and worked at many odd jobs before becoming a doctor, joined the alliance in 1886 and almost immediately became chair of the state executive committee. In January 1887, wishing to avoid a split over the Cleburne demands, he proposed the creation of a statewide cooperative to market members' cotton crops and act as a central purchasing house as well. The Farmers' Alliance Exchange of Texas opened in Dallas later that year but tried to do far too much far too fast. Although only $20,000 of a projected $500,000 in capital was actually paid in, the Exchange's directors decided to construct a $45,000 building to house its operations. Moreover, the Exchange tried to relieve farmers of the chattel mortgage system by extending credit itself through a joint-note plan. Under this plan, landholding farmers and their poorer neighbors would jointly sign mortgages on the latter's crops, which the Exchange would accept as collateral for goods and supplies. The Exchange would then, in turn, use the joint notes as collateral to obtain loans from banks so that it could buy goods and supplies. Banks regularly made such loans to merchants who took crop liens, which may explain why the Exchange directors failed to ask in advance if they could make the same arrangement. By early 1888 the Exchange had taken $200,000 in joint notes and issued supplies on credit, only to discover that banks would not advance money on that kind of paper. Unable to recover, the Alliance Exchange closed its doors in 1889.

The exchange plan created a burst of enthusiasm that carried Alliance membership from 75,000 in 1887 to at least 150,000 the next year. "I am glad," wrote a Lavaca County woman, "that the farmers have awoke from their slumbers and see that it is high time that they were up and doing something that will break the yoke of bondage which they have so patiently carried for so many years." Women joined the Alliance and participated in its meetings. "I will say to the sisters," one wrote in 1888, "attend every meeting of the Alliance. If you become disinterested you need not expect your brothers, fathers, and husband to be very interested." Growth slowed in 1888, however, and Macune responded the next year by directing the organization's attention back to the issues raised in the Cleburne demands, especially the lack of an adequate national currency. However, he went well beyond the call for free silver and led in developing a new proposal—the subtreasury plan. This plan called for the United States government to create warehouse storage centers for nonperishable crops such as cotton. At harvest time, when these crops normally would flood the market, farmers could store them at the government warehouses and receive loans of up to 80 percent of their current market value. The loans would be in the form of legal tender paper money—currency without backing in silver or gold—and would carry an annual interest rate of only 2 percent. When they wished, farmers could redeem the crops from storage and sell them. In short, the subtreasury plan called on the national government to assist farmers with two of their major problems—overproduction and low prices—by allowing them to spread out the marketing of their crops and inflate the currency (and prices) at the same time.

Thus, by 1890, the Texas Farmers' Alliance largely gave up on self-help ventures such as cooperatives and concentrated on a political agenda that emphasized strong railroad regulation, expansion of the money supply, and the subtreasury plan. Its newspaper, the *Southern Mercury,* regularly ran educational pieces on those subjects and began to make support for the Alliance program a "litmus test" for Texas politicians. This was a test, however, that the conservative Democrats who ran Texas from 1874 onward did not want to take and were unlikely to pass if they did.

Conservative Politics in the New South

Once conservative Democrats "redeemed" Texas from the E. J. Davis administration in 1874 and wrote the Constitution of 1876, they maintained control with relative ease until 1890. Most of the tremendous influx of immigrants from the Old South during these years agreed with the "Redeemer" view of Reconstruction and strengthened Democratic control of the state. The Republican Party, which was limited essentially to areas with large numbers of black voters, could get no more than one-third of the vote statewide. Davis remained its leader until his death in 1883, when he was replaced by Norris Wright Cuney, a talented politician who might have accomplished a great deal under more favorable circumstances. The mulatto son of a Washington County planter and a slave mother, Cuney attended a school for blacks in Pennsylvania in 1859–1861 and returned to Texas after the war. He supported E. J. Davis, took over leadership of the state party in 1883, and held a variety of elected and appointed positions, including collector of customs at Galveston. Well connected in the national party, he fought off efforts to make the state Republican organization "lily white" throughout the 1880s. Nevertheless, no leader, regardless of his talent, could have convinced significant numbers of white Texans to vote Republican. Indeed, conservative Democrats were so invincible that they could afford to fight among themselves over personalities and shadings of conservatism. In general, however, they offered the least government possible—one that did what was necessary to protect property and preserve law and order and otherwise kept spending and taxing to a bare minimum.

The first "redeemer" governor, Richard Coke, resigned in December 1876 to take a seat in the United States Senate. Lieutenant Governor Richard B. Hubbard, a solid three-hundred pounder called "Jumbo" by his friends, served out Coke's term with reasonable success and then sought the Democratic nomination in 1878. He was opposed, however, by James W. Throckmorton, a hero to many because of his removal from the governorship by the military during Reconstruction, and the two deadlocked, leading the convention to turn to Oran M. Roberts, the former secessionist and ex-Confederate.

No Republican could beat the "Old Alcalde," as Roberts was called, but the appearance of a third party threatened to take votes from the Democrats and at least make the election interesting. This new organization, the Greenback Party, focused on monetary policy, an issue that became increasingly important to farmers from the 1870s onward. During the Civil War, the United States had issued legal tender paper money—greenbacks—that had no backing in gold or silver, but then in 1875 as part of legislation intended to put the nation back on a gold standard, Congress provided that as of 1879 the value of greenbacks in circulation would be limited to $300,000 and those would be redeemable in gold. This made greenbacks "as good as gold" and meant that they could not be expanded to bring inflation. In response, the Greenback Party called for the issuance of fifty dollars in paper money per person and sought to increase its appeal to ordinary Texans by advocating railroad regulation and public education. The party nominated William H. Hamman, a native of Virginia and ex-Confederate, and urged the Republicans to join them in opposing Roberts. E. J. Davis supported Hamman, saying, "The best thing that can be done for the future of Texas is to break down the Democratic party," but his party rejected fusion and nominated A. B. Norton. Democrats were bothered enough by the Greenbackers that Roberts took to the campaign trail, accusing the new party of being a northern import that appealed to blacks and Republicans. That fall, the "Old Alcalde" swept to victory, getting 158,302 votes to Hamman's 55,002 and 23,172 for Norton. Conservative Democrats thus had the support of two-thirds of Texas voters; the opposition did well only in areas with large black populations or groups of old Unionists.

Roberts's first administration (1879–1881) concentrated on fiscal conservatism aimed at balancing the budget and eliminating debt. The governor demanded a reduction in the state's already meager spending on public schools and vetoed two 1879 appropriation bills before the legislature gave in and cut school spending from one-fourth to one-sixth of general revenues. He also successfully insisted that the remainder of Texas's public lands be sold, in part for the revenue and in part to increase tax revenue once they were in private hands. The so-called Fifty Cent Law of 1879 made all unreserved public land available for sale at fifty cents per acre. Even after paying for surveying and patenting the acreage, ranchers and speculators acquired huge tracts at the cost of only about one dollar per acre. Roberts also worked to cut the taxes paid by landholders.

In 1880, Governor Roberts won renomination, and the Greenback Party ran Hamman again. This time, however, the Republicans not only refused to join the new party but hurt them even more by nominating E. J. Davis, their best-known leader. Roberts again won nearly two-thirds of the vote (166,101), and Davis far outpolled Hamman (64,382 to 33,721). During his second term (1881–1883), Roberts continued to emphasize the strict fiscal conservatism favored by most voters. The one truly important achievement of these years—creation of the University of Texas—came largely because it could be accomplished at a very limited cost to the public.

Proposals for a state university dated to 1839 when the Congress of the Republic set aside fifty leagues for two colleges, but no effective action to create a public institution of higher learning took place until after the Civil War. Once the war ended, the state, prompted by the offer of federal land subsidies through the Morrill Land-Grant College Act of 1862, created Texas Agricultural and Mechanical College, which opened its doors in 1876. The writers of the Constitution of 1876, however, saw the fledgling A&M campus as a branch of a larger "university of the first class" that would be dedicated to the study of literature and arts and sciences. To support both schools, the constitution added one million acres of West Texas land to the fifty leagues donated in 1839. In March 1881, the legislature called an election to decide on a location for the university and created a board of regents to direct its operation. Voters selected Austin as the site, and the school formally opened on its forty-acre campus in September 1883 with 8 professors and 221 students. A medical branch at Galveston, although approved in 1881, did not open until ten years later.

Texas A&M College, although seen in the constitution as a branch of the University of Texas, operated under its own board of directors as an essentially separate institution. Both schools struggled for funding from the legislature and the Permanent University Fund. The legislature appropriated no maintenance funds until 1889, and the PUF, which drew proceeds from the fifty-league donation of 1839, the million acres provided in the Constitution of 1876, and another million acres given in 1883, did not generate significant income until the twentieth century. Thus, the Roberts administration, thanks to the blessing of state-owned public lands, presided over the creation of a university that, along with its preexisting and absolutely distinct "branch" at College Station, eventually would attain the financial resources to become first-class.

Texas's first two public "normal" schools dedicated to the training of teachers also were created while Roberts served as governor, although they, too, owed their inception in part to funding from sources other than state taxes. In 1876 the legislature created an "Agricultural and Mechanical College for the Benefit of Colored Youth" as part of Texas A&M College, and the school opened near Hempstead in 1878. It had few students, however, and in 1879 Roberts suggested closing it. Fortunately, at that point, an agent of the George Peabody Fund offered the state financial assistance in establishing schools for educating teachers, and the legislature chartered Prairie View Normal Institute, the first public black college in Texas. That same year, also with the Peabody Fund's encouragement, the legislature established Sam Houston Normal Institute in Huntsville.

Roberts refused to be considered for a third term in 1882, and the Democratic convention chose John Ireland, yet another secessionist, ex-Confederate officer, as its candidate. Ireland, a lawyer whom railroad men had dubbed "Oxcart John" because of his opposition to their subsidies, agreed with Roberts on low taxes but took less conservative stances on several other issues. For example, he favored greater support for public schools, land sales to settlers only, currency expansion, and some degree of railroad regulation by the state. Greenbackers and Republicans, although appearing still hopelessly outnumbered, mustered some enthusiasm when George W. "Wash" Jones announced that he planned to run as an Independent, anti-Democratic candidate for governor. Jones, a native of Alabama who had opposed secession but then commanded the Seventeenth Texas Infantry, CSA, had won two terms in Congress (1878 and 1880) as a Greenback/Republican candidate. His district in south-central Texas contained numerous German and African American voters, and he had openly campaigned for support from blacks as well as whites. Jones received nominations from both the Republicans and Greenbackers and ran on opposition to the Democrats' record, especially on public education and land sales. Jones and Ireland campaigned hard and even met in a face-to-face debate in Houston, which "Wash" had the better of with his kindly and humorous approach. For the most part, however, Ireland and other Democratic speakers stayed clear of their opponent and reminded voters that an Independent victory would in effect bring back Republican government and "the horrors of ten years ago." In November 1882, Jones ran a little stronger than opposition candidates in the previous two elections; nevertheless, Ireland won easily with 60 percent of the vote (150,809 to 102,501).

Governor Ireland's first term (1883–1885) marked a few notable changes, such as repeal of the Fifty Cent Law and an effort to market the state's remaining public lands according to their resources and value. He also struggled with and presided over a settlement of the fence-cutting issue. Support for public education improved slightly following adoption of a constitutional amendment in 1883 and passage of a new law in 1884 that gave the state a larger role in the schools. The law required an elected state superintendent, county school districts run by the county judge, teacher certification, and compulsory education from ages eight to sixteen. Independent school districts run by their own officials were exempt from this law. Overall, Ireland's moderation of Roberts's brand of Democratic conservatism proved successful enough to win reelection by an overwhelming margin in 1884. "Wash" Jones ran again, but the Republicans, rather than supporting him as they had in 1882, nominated a candidate of their own—A. B. Norton. Of course, whether the opposition ran one candidate or two made no difference when Ireland gained 65 percent of the vote.

Jones's second defeat at the hands of Ireland sapped what little strength remained in the Greenback movement. By the mid-1880s, however, two new movements greatly complicated Texas politics. The Farmers' Alliance, which had grown rapidly in the decade's early years, turned to politics in 1886, and a movement demanding the prohibition of alcoholic beverages appeared on the scene at about the same time. Prohibition was hardly new in Texas, having been a major reform before the Civil War, but the arrival of the Women's Christian Temperance Union in 1883 energized the movement. The Constitution of 1876 allowed local-option "wet-dry" elections, but the prohibitionists wanted the manufacture and sale of alcoholic beverages outlawed statewide. Important Democrats such as the state's United States Senators, John H. Reagan and Samuel Bell Maxey, supported prohibition, but others opposed. Faced with reform demands from farmers and a divisive issue such as prohibition,

Democrats would find it increasingly difficult to maintain control by promising limited government and reminding voters how they had "redeemed" the state from rule by corrupt black Republicans. Fortunately for the party, however, it had Lawrence "Sul" Ross, one of the most personally popular men in the state, as their candidate in 1886 and 1888.

Ross, following his service against the Indians and in the Confederate Army, had been a member of the constitutional convention in 1875 and the state senate from 1881 to 1885. As a candidate for governor, he took positions that leaned toward moderation rather than old fashioned "Redeemer" conservatism. For example, he supported the sale of public land to actual settlers and said that the Farmers' Alliance only wanted "fair legislation and impartial administration." He argued that competition among the railroads eventually would solve the problem of unreasonably high rates, but that in the meantime the roads should be prevented from working "against the public interest." Almost certainly, Ross, who had a railroad lawyer, George W. Clark, as his campaign manager, regarded state regulation as a last resort, but his statements did not rule it out. On the prohibition issue, Ross favored local option rather than statewide action, a stance that made him nothing more than a "saloon stump speaker" in the eyes of dry leaders. The Republican Party candidate, A. M. Cochran of Dallas, also opposed prohibition. Disgusted at the lack of choice, the prohibitionists formed a third party and nominated Ebenezer L. Dohoney of Lamar County for the governorship. The Kentucky-born Dohoney's political interests had run the gamut from Unionist to Confederate to Greenbacker, but he consistently opposed liquor. He tried, with little success, to broaden the appeal of his cause by calling attention to the problems of labor. In November 1886, Ross's personal popularity and moderate inclinations utterly overwhelmed his opponents. He received 78 percent of the vote (228,776) to only 65,236 for Cochran and 19,186 for Dohoney.

In spite of its poor showing in the election, the Prohibition Party pushed for a constitutional amendment to prevent the production, sale, or exchange of alcoholic beverages in Texas. And in the spring of 1887 the legislature decided to let the wets and drys have it out in a nonpartisan contest. Both sides organized and campaigned hard. Those who opposed prohibition did not take a pro-alcohol position, of course, but argued against state interference with personal freedom and called for temperance through private and religious efforts. Black Texans tended to see prohibition as an attempt to take away one of their rights, and many German Texans could not imagine life without beer. Prohibitionists presented themselves, in the words of John H. Reagan, as the champions of "virtue, thrift and prosperity . . . right, justice and humanity." During one campaign confrontation before 7,500 people in Waco, B. H. Carroll, a Baptist minister, called Congressman Roger Q. Mills, "Roger the Dodger . . . [who] finally would not dodge the devil," and Mills replied that hell was "full of better preachers" than Carroll. The election drew more voters than had the contest for governor in 1886, and the wets won convincingly—220,627 to 129,270.

This crushing defeat did not destroy the prohibition movement in Texas, but it forced the issue into the background of state politics for the next twenty years. However, the election's significance may not have ended there. Supporting or opposing prohibition was such a personal matter that years later voters remembered the 1887 election as a time "when friendships were severed and family ties subjected to the keenest trial." Almost certainly, then, the bitter campaign loosened party ties as well among all those involved—Democrats, Republicans, and third-party men. This meant that divisions would appear more easily in the future over other political issues, such as economic reform.

The second year of Ross's term was highlighted by the dedication of a new state capitol in Austin. Construction of such a magnificent building would have seriously challenged the "no spend/no tax" philosophy of Texas's post-Reconstruction leaders had they not been able to finance it largely from the state's public lands. But again that unique blessing came into play. The Constitution of 1876 set aside three million acres to fund construction, and in 1879 the legislature provided for surveying this capitol land in the Panhandle (the acreage that eventually became the XIT Ranch) and using it to pay a builder. A Chicago firm handled the construction, using red granite from a quarry in nearby Burnet County. The 392-room building, modeled on the national capitol and topped by a Goddess of Liberty, was dedicated in a week of ceremonies during May 1888.

Ross easily won renomination in 1888. His opponent, Marion Martin, ran on a nonpartisan Union Labor ticket put together by a mixed assortment of old Greenbackers, Farmers' Alliance men, and workers. Martin, a native of Kentucky and former Confederate officer, had served as Lieutenant Governor under Ireland, sought the Democratic nomination in 1886, and campaigned for prohibition in 1887. The Republicans and Prohibitionists endorsed his candidacy, but even this combination of all the reformer/opposition groups in the state had no chance against Ross and the Democrats, especially since the governor had behaved as a moderate during his first term. Although a believer in limited government, Ross attempted to be, in the words of one observer, "up with the urgent need of the times." For example, he presided over a notable expansion in public services for orphans and the disabled, and his administration took steps to help Texas farmers help themselves. The Texas Agricultural Experiment Station, established in 1887, researched every aspect of agriculture in the state in an effort to give farmers and ranchers information on how to increase production, lower costs, and expand markets. Bolstered by personal popularity and a good record, the governor won reelection with 72 percent of the vote.

A Threat to Democratic Conservatism

Sul Ross was the fifth consecutive Democrat to serve as governor following "redemption" in 1874. In general he and his predecessors—Coke, Hubbard, Roberts, and Ireland—although varying from utterly conservative to moderate on issues such as railroad regulation and public education, believed in keeping the government as small, inactive, and inexpensive as seemed reasonable. "A plain, simple government, with severe limitations upon delegated powers, honestly and frugally administered," said Ross in 1889, is "the noblest and truest outgrowth of the wisdom taught by its founders." When Texans undertook major ventures such as establishing public universities and building a new capitol, the financing came largely from public land, so that taxpayers' obligations remained minimal. Even the Texas prison system operated on the principle, as one historian put it, of "penology for profit." From 1871 until 1883, the state leased the penitentiary at Huntsville, along with its inmates, to business firms that ran the prison and used the prisoners as laborers on their own ventures or hired them out to work for others. At times the push for profit led to horrifying treatment of the inmates, but some of the lessors made so much money that the legislature decided to reserve the profits of convict labor for the state alone. Accordingly, beginning in 1883, the prison system leased inmates directly to businessmen on an individual basis or put them to work on state-owned farms. This system continued until 1912, earning much of the money necessary to operate the prison system but often leaving leased convicts to the not-so-tender mercies of guards at work camps.

The essentially conservative approach to government remained popular with many voters, especially since Democrats regularly contrasted it with the "horrors" of Republican rule, but it proved a good deal more beneficial to railroads, corporations, large ranchers, and wealthy merchants than to ordinary farmers. In 1888, the state Farmers' Alliance, pointed out that an "alarming destitution" was pushing "the masses of the people . . . nearer a condition of serfdom and tenantry" that only "legislative remedies" could correct. Some Texans, of course, had called for reforms from the 1870s onward, but they could not agree on a specific program and often wound up associated with the Republican Party, which the great majority of whites hated. By the late 1880s, however, worsening economic conditions, the passage of time since conservatives had "redeemed" the state, and the moderation of leaders such as Sul Ross began to alter the dominant philosophy in the Democratic Party. James Stephen Hogg, a reform-minded Democrat from East Texas, personified this change.

Hogg, a native Texan born in 1851 and therefore too young to fight in the Civil War, represented a new generation of Democratic politicians. Orphaned at an early age, he worked in a print shop and as a sharecropper before becoming a self-taught lawyer at Quitman in Wood County in 1875. A huge man, standing more than six feet tall and weighing 250 pounds, Hogg had a tremendous voice and knew how to shed his coat and appeal to Texas audiences with homespun humor. He held a variety of local offices during the early 1880s and then ran successfully for attorney general in 1886. Serving as attorney general during the Ross Administration, he demonstrated that long-standing southern doubts about the federal government, which he shared with most Texans, would not prevent his using the power of the state to meet the needs of the public. Most important, he quickly made a reputation for determined attacks on railroads and other corporations that abused their power. He demanded that the roads obey laws requiring them to sell their land holdings to settlers within set time limits and managed to break up the Texas Traffic Association, which the railroads used to fix rates and limit competition. Hogg's office also forced underfunded "wildcat" insurance companies out of Texas and helped write an antitrust law in 1889 prohibiting price fixing and other monopolistic practices that was the second such state act in the nation. Indeed, Texas had an antitrust law a year before the U. S. Congress passed the famed Sherman Anti-Trust Act.

By 1890, Hogg became convinced that the attorney general's office did not have the resources necessary to carry out laws regulating the railroads and began to advocate the creation of a Railroad Commission. He sought the Democratic nomination for governor that year on a platform calling for the passage of a constitutional amendment, which the legislature had put before the voters, permitting the creation of a commission and for the actual creation of a commission. "By Gatlins," he told friends, "I'll make the race and I'm in it to stay." In spite of heated opposition from the railroads and their political allies, one of whom warned Texans that Hogg represented "communistic and agrarian rapacity," he won the nomination and overwhelmed his Republican opponent Webster Flanagan and token opposition from the Prohibition Party in the general election. When Hogg (the state's first native-born governor) took office in 1891, he would deliver on his mandate to make changes, especially where railroad regulation was concerned. Many Texas farmers, however, thought that their desperate situation required drastic steps that even the reform-minded Hogg would not take. In the early 1890s, the Democratic Party, in spite of the way its "redeemer"-era conservatism had given way to greater moderation and even reform, would face a serious challenge from a movement called Populism. A good many Texans had found the "New South" an empty promise and wanted something better.

Chapter 13

AN ERA OF REFORM, 1891–1920

James Stephen Hogg took over the governorship of Texas just as farmers across the southern and midwestern United States rose in revolt against the nation's two major political parties. Suffering from low prices, high costs, and rising tenancy rates, and tired of waiting in vain for help from the government, farmers organized the People's Party (more commonly called the Populist Party) in 1891 and challenged Democrats and Republicans in state and national elections the following year. The Populists thoroughly frightened politicians in the two major parties by calling for radical changes, such as public ownership of the railroads, and appealing for support from black as well as white voters. Like all third-party movements, Populism soon disappeared—much of its energy drained off when the national Democratic Party adopted parts of its platform in 1896—but it enlivened politics in Texas for a few years and provided impetus for reform that outlived the movement.

Around 1900, a broader and more successful movement called Progressivism followed Populism onto the reform stage and remained there for nearly two decades. Whereas the Populists rose in agricultural regions and called primarily for changes to aid farmers, the Progressives appeared nationwide and sought to reform the many accumulated evils of industrialization and urbanization. Too diverse to follow a single creed or agree on one set of issues, these reformers generally attacked railroad and business monopolies, emphasized the need for social legislation such as child labor laws, and called for the development of greater efficiency in government and society. They also championed the primary system of nominating candidates for political offices, popular election of United States senators, woman suffrage, prohibition, and the conservation of natural resources. (These reforms were not new. Men and women with a reformist or progressive frame of mind supported such measures before and after the first two decades of the century, but the intensity of concern during these years earned reformers at that time the title "Progressives.") Many Progressive reforms can only be considered positive, but others such as prohibition are questionable, and some clearly were negative. Most strikingly, Progressivism in the South, although generally similar to the movement across the nation, had a large "For Whites Only" sign on it and brought suffrage restriction and a hardening of the segregation of blacks. One Progressive reform or another affected virtually every Texan, and the prohibition issue gained so much attention in the Lone Star State that it helped change attitudes toward the role of government, at least a little.

Emphasis on Progressive reform largely ended when the United States entered World War I in 1917, although the push for prohibition and woman suffrage continued until both became effective a few years later. Then, in 1920, the entire nation, worn out from years of crusading to clean up evils at home and end all wars abroad, decided, in the words of Republican presidential candidate Warren G. Harding, to "return to normalcy." For Texans by this time "normalcy" in politics meant flamboyant leaders and constant controversy, and that continued during the twenties. The push for major social and economic reforms, however, died away.

Texas remained remarkably unchanged in many basic ways during these years of Populism and Progressivism. Although the usual influx of migrants helped push the state's population from 2,235,527 in 1890 to 4,663,226 in 1920, an increase of 109 percent in thirty years, most Texans continued to live agricultural and rural lives. Cotton, according to the *Texas Almanac* in 1910, sat "on the throne as the money crop in Texas." (Cotton remained king in spite of the arrival from Mexico in 1894 of the boll weevil, an insect that caused a steady drop in yields per acre over the next thirty years.) The state also led the nation in cattle raising and the total value of crops. Industry lagged far behind. As befitted an agricultural people, as late as 1920 two of every three Texans lived in places having populations of less than 2,500. And they gloried in rural life, insisting that cities "could not exist but for the man who plows, sows and reaps"—the farmer who stood as a rock of stability in a world moving too fast.

Also, Texas maintained its close identity with the South. "So many Texans have come out of the South, including Missouri and Kentucky and Tennessee," two scholars wrote in 1916, "that Texas is predominantly Southern in thought and feeling." This meant, unfortunately, that the practices associated with white supremacist beliefs across the South during these years marred the history of Texas as well. Blacks lost ground numerically—declining from 22 percent of the total population in 1890 to 16 percent in 1920—and their social and political status declined appreciably, too. Segregation, the physical separation of the races in all public places, became commonplace during the nineties, and disfranchisement came in the aftermath of the Populist challenge. Physical intimidation occurred regularly, and too often ended in the horror of lynching. Between 1890 and 1920, Texans lynched 309 men, 249 (81 percent) of whom were black. Lynchings generally followed the accusation of an assault on a white woman and involved sickening torture as well as hanging and burning the victim. In 1893, for example, members of the family of a murdered girl in Paris burned the accused all over his body with hot irons, even thrusting them into his eyes and throat before finally burning him to death. Crowds gathered to watch lynchings and gathered souvenirs of the occasion. After another accused murderer was burned while tied to an elm tree near Whitesboro in 1901, a newspaper reported that "Visitors came pretty near dismantling the little elm tree. . . . Nearly everybody tried to get a twig or limb, and the popular boutonaire . . . is a smoke-stained elm leaf." Texans not immediately involved were likely to condemn such savagery as "barbarous," but they also insisted that it "set a good example." The underlying psychology and sociology of lynching is exceedingly complex, but one thing is clear—in the Texas of that day nothing limited what was done in the name of white supremacy.

Even while Texas remained essentially agricultural, rural, and southern into the early twentieth century, certain developments pointed toward a very different future. The first can be summarized in one word: oil! Texans had known for years that crude petroleum seeped from their state's soil, and Lyne T. Barret (sometimes called Lynis T. Barrett) actually drilled a producing well near Nacogdoches in 1866. However, significant commercial production did not begin until 1894, when well drillers seeking water near Corsicana struck oil instead. The Corsicana field, developed primarily by Joseph S. Cullinan, a Pennsylvania oilman, produced more than 800,000 barrels at its peak in 1900. Then in 1901 a single well drilled in a salt dome formation near Beaumont began to flow at the unbelievable rate of 75,000–100,000 barrels per day. The strike at Spindletop, a small hill supposedly named for a cypress tree that stood on it, was due primarily to the persistence of Pattillo Higgins, a native of southeast Texas who became interested in oil and gas as a source of energy for manufacturing brick and glass. After becoming a near-laughingstock for his many failures to find petroleum in the salt domes south of Beaumont, Higgins interested an Austrian-born engineer named Anthony F. Lucas in the project. Lucas obtained funding in 1900, and on January 10 of the next year his drillers, using a new type of rotary bit, brought in a gusher that blew through the top of the drilling derrick. During the nine days before the well could be capped, a sea of oil collected in the area around it. Eventually, a passing train set fire to the oil and sent clouds of smoke northward where, in the words of one observer, "rain coming down through this black smoke ruined the paint on most of the houses in Beaumont." Pollution, the flip side of the coin of industrial growth, had come to Texas.

Production in the Spindletop field, which reached 17,500,000 barrels in 1902, created the state's first great oil boom. Thousands of oil-crazed newcomers crowded into the Beaumont area—snapping up every available hotel or boarding-house room, buying and selling places in lines at restaurants, and bribing operators to place telephone calls. Soon, however, the boom diminished due to the drilling of too many wells. Other fields in southeast Texas such as Sour Lake (1902), Humble (1905), and Goose Creek (1908) also flourished at first and declined almost as rapidly. Many of the new companies failed in a year or two, although one, the Texas Company founded by Cullinan and others in 1902, expanded into all facets of the petroleum industry and eventually became famous as Texaco. Overall, in spite of the major dis-

Oral History of Texas Oil Pioneers
The University of Texas
Lucas Gusher, Spindletop, January 10, 1901

Spindletop gusher, 1901. Reportedly, the well flowed at 100,000 barrels a day for nine days before workers could cap it.

coveries, Texas stood only sixth in the nation in oil production in 1909, and petroleum products ranked only fifth in value among the state's products. The industry continued to grow during the next decade when it advanced into North Texas with discoveries at Electra, Burkburnett, Iowa Park, Ranger, and Breckenridge. Oil obviously held the key to fabulous wealth for Texas and many Texans, but that potential remained only partially realized during the Progressive Era.

A second development that held important implications for the future involved the state's largest urban areas. Little more than major towns in 1890, they began to develop into cities capable of exerting great influence on their surrounding areas. In 1890, Texas had no urban area with a population of 40,000, but by 1920, four cities—Dallas, Fort Worth, Houston, and San Antonio—boasted more than 100,000 residents each. Houston was growing more rapidly than the others, thanks in large measure to the completion of a ship channel from the city to Galveston Bay in 1914. Financed jointly by the federal government and the City of Houston, the twenty-five-foot-deep channel allowed Houston to become the leading cotton port in the United States and a major oil-refining center as well. El Paso, with 77,560 people, stood as the fifth-largest city in the state in 1920 and by far the largest in West Texas.

The third new development involved the revival of an old variant of "Gone to Texas." Around the turn of the century, immigrants from Mexico began to arrive in significant numbers for the first time since the Texas Revolution. Pushed out before 1910 by the repressive regime of Porfirio Díaz and then for the next ten years by the violent upheavals of revolution, their population in Texas rose from an estimated 71,602 in 1900 to 251,827 by 1920. Texans of Mexican descent, immigrants and native-born combined, amounted to only about 10 percent of the state's population in 1920; nevertheless, a key trend had appeared. Most new arrivals lived in South Texas and the El Paso area, but others dispersed across the state. In Central Texas, for example, thousands of Mexicans entered the cotton economy as wage laborers and sharecroppers. White tenant farmers objected to this intrusion and generally refused to accept the new workers as "white," placing them on an ethno-racial middle ground between Anglos and African Americans. Although not as rigidly segregated as blacks, Mexicans generally lived in separate neighborhoods and attended separate schools and churches. As a resident of Caldwell County (just south of Austin) put it in the 1920s: "If a Mexican bought a lot among the whites, they would burn him out. We are just old, hard-boiled southerners in this county."

Mexicans generally bore their less-than-equal status with few complaints, but in South Texas the influx of immigrants and border disturbances created by the Mexican Revolution that began in 1910 brought challenges to existing political and social arrangements. In September 1911, members of the Idar family in Laredo—Nicasio, editor of the newspaper *La Crónica,* and his son, Clemente, and daughter, Jovita—organized El Congreso Mexicanista, the first meeting to oppose discrimination against Mexicans in Texas. Delegates called for the protection of basic civil rights and an end to school segregation. Soon, however, some Mexicans rejected cooperative and protest activity and endorsed a far more revolutionary proposal that appeared in January 1915 in San Diego, a town in Duval County. The "Plan de San Diego," actually the work of Mexican nationals in Monterey, called for a "Liberating Army of Races and Peoples" to "free" Texas and the other southwestern states from the United States and form an independent republic, which might later seek annexation to Mexico. Made up of members of "the Latin, the Negro, or the Japanese Race," the Liberating Army would fight an all-out race war, summarily executing all white males over the age of sixteen. Beginning in July 1915, raiders from Mexico robbed stores, destroyed property, and killed more than twenty Anglos in the lower Río Grande Valley. Retaliation by U.S. Army troops, Texas Rangers, local law enforcement agencies, and armed citizens' groups took the lives of at least three hundred Mexicans, generating even greater ethnic antagonism than already existed.

Overall, then, the years of Populism and Progressivism are a deceptively complex period in Texas history. The state accepted only limited parts of these reform movements and remained essentially unchanged in the way most of its people lived. Political and social beliefs and values seemed to change little, also. Members of the state's two largest minority groups, blacks and Mexicans, found themselves generally treated as second-class citizens at best. The Anglo Texan majority clung to their Confederate past as never before; the twenty years or so from 1890 to 1910 were the heyday of building monuments to the memory of Civil War soldiers. And yet, the state obviously could not, and did not, stand still. Perhaps Anglo Texas should be depicted in 1890 as a man fifty to sixty years of age, wearing a gray uniform and looking to a Confederate past. Then, twenty to thirty years later, the state could be personified by a son of the older man; still youthful, he would have grown far larger than his father but remain awkward and uncertain. The young man would have much of the father in him, of course, but he would never see life in exactly the same way. Indeed, for his past he might begin to look more to the glories of the Texas Revolution and the cattle kingdom than to the defeated Lost Cause.

Hogg Democrats and the Populists

When James Stephen Hogg became governor in January 1891, he had a clear mandate to bring meaningful railroad regulation to Texas. Overcoming mild opposition from railroad lawyers and representatives from areas in South and West Texas that still needed rail connections, his administration quickly pushed through legislation creating the Railroad Commission, a three-man regulatory body with jurisdiction over rates, operations, terminals, and express companies. To head the commission, Hogg chose long-time Democratic leader John H. Reagan, who demonstrated his commitment to railroad regulation by resigning a seat in the United States Senate to take the position. In spite of a petition from the Farmers' Alliance that one of their leaders be placed on the commission, the governor's other two appointees, L. L. Foster and William P. McLean, also were well-known Democrats. Alliance men, although many were Democrats, began to believe that they had been betrayed by Hogg and the Democratic Party.

The Railroad Commission was hampered in its early years by inadequate funding and a legal challenge by seven railroads. However, the United States Supreme Court upheld its constitutionality in *Reagan v. Farmers Loan and Trust Company* in 1894, and it played a role in holding down railroad rates during the rest of the decade. Even then, rates in Texas remained above the national average. This happened because Hogg and Reagan always intended to use the commission more as a weapon against non-Texas railroads than as a means of ensuring fair competition within the state. They wanted Texas-owned railroads to charge rates that would allow all towns in the state to ship local products on equal terms and grow at an even rate. Eventually, the commission would be given the power to regulate Texas's oil and gas industry and become one of the most important agencies of its kind in the entire nation. Of course, no one in the early nineties could have guessed at what the legislature had wrought while dealing with the long-standing issue of railroad regulation.

During the next few years, Governor Hogg led in the passage of at least four other pieces of reform legislation—known collectively with the Railroad Commission act as the "Hogg Laws." One forced the railroads to state the actual value of their stock rather than issuing inflated ("watered") values as a basis for setting their rates. Two dealt with land, ordering land corporations to sell their holdings to settlers within fifteen years and stopping grants to foreign corporations. The fifth measure restricted the amount of bonded indebtedness that counties and cities could acquire, thus limiting giveaways to corporations. Hogg also increased state support for public colleges and universities and presided over the creation of a state archives division.

In spite of all his successes as a reformer, Hogg could not keep a sizable proportion of the Farmers' Alliance men in the Democratic Party. Part of the reason lay in a basic difference—Hogg opposed cutthroat business methods because out-of-state corporations used them to hurt Texas; he did not really mind the practices themselves. Reform-minded farmers disliked sharp corporate practices no matter who used them. Moreover, Hogg wanted to keep the role of government as limited as possible. Problems began when the governor did not put one of the Alliance leaders on the Railroad Commission, and the developing rift grew wider during the summer of 1891 over the subtreasury plan. This plan, which called for the United States government to build warehouses and loan legal tender paper money to farmers who stored major perishable crops there until putting them on the market, became a test of faith for Texas politicians. Most Alliance men thought it necessary, but many Democrats, even reformers such as Hogg who certainly were not anti-farmer, objected to it as a violation of states' rights by the federal government. When the governor and other Democrats made it clear that anyone who supported the subtreasury plan was not welcome in their party, Texas Alliance leaders had little choice but to join the rapidly developing Populist Party.

The Farmers' Alliance movement, which had begun in Texas and grown much larger as the Southern Farmers' Alliance under the leadership of Texan Charles W. Macune, largely provided the impetus for the new party, although it was officially created at a convention of several reform organizations in Cincinnati in May 1891. William R. Lamb, a leader of the Union Labor Party in 1888, represented the Texas Alliance at the convention and was chosen to the new party's national executive committee. Back home, he arranged for the first convention of the People's Party in Texas to meet in conjunction with a meeting of the state Alliance scheduled for August in Dallas. Only about fifty delegates attended, most of whom were there for the Alliance meeting as well, but they made up in fiery rhetoric what they lacked in numbers. Led by Lamb, the first state chairman, and H. S. P. "Stump" Ashby, a one-time Methodist minister turned Alliance speaker, the Populists promised "to enact radical reforms of the abuses and usurpations of power" by the major parties. Democrats and Republicans alike, the platform continued, allow corporations "to oppress and enslave the people," but "refuse to aid or assist the laborers . . . by just and wholesome laws. . . ." Accordingly, the Populists called for a great variety of reforms including creation of the subtreasury plan; free coinage of silver; a progressive income tax; direct election of the president, vice president, and U.S. Senators; and the eight-hour day for city and state workers. Their most radical proposal dealt with the railroads: "We demand the most rigid, honest, and just national control of the means of public communication and transportation, and if this . . . does not remove the abuses now existing, we demand the government ownership of such means of communication and transportation." Populism thus threatened to go beyond reforming capitalism to supporting a major socialist proposal.

The Populist movement was "radical" in another way as well—its inclusion of black Texans. When some members of the Dallas convention proposed limiting the party to whites only, "Stump" Ashby responded, "We want to do good to every citizen of the country, and [the Negro] is a citizen just as much as we are, and the party that acts on that fact will gain the colored vote of the south." He urged "full representation" of blacks in the party, and the convention elected two African Americans to the state executive committee. The Populist position on race stood in total contrast to that usually taken by the Democratic Party, which had no black leaders and only tolerated black participation in politics.

Populist organizers spent the next year, in the words of the *Dallas Morning News,* going "out into the hills and down into the valleys preaching their new gospel of political salvation." Indeed, they even held camp meetings similar to religious revivals. And their message, coming during economic hard times and based on traditional American beliefs in democracy and equality before the law, reached many willing believers. In less than a year after the party's organization in Texas, the state had more than two thousand local Populist clubs and a statewide newspaper, the *Dallas Southern Mercury.* Blacks, in the words of one organizer, came "into the new party in squads and companies." On June 23–24, 1892, a thousand Populists gathered in Dallas and nominated Thomas L. Nugent, a Louisiana-born ex-Confederate and former Democratic politician/district judge, for governor. The candidate perfectly personified the somewhat otherworldly, revivalistic nature of Populism. Recognizing that he had no chance to win, Nugent made the race for the purposes of education and moral instruction. He taught the beliefs of the Swedenborgian faith—that the Kingdom of God would come on earth through human endeavor—and criticized capitalism for substituting "the 'rule of gold for the golden rule.'" The government, he said, should restrain capitalistic avarice and encourage Christian brotherhood. His sincerity impressed even those who disagreed with his views. "It would be supreme folly," wrote the *Morning News,* "to despise and belittle a movement that is leavened with such moral stuff as this."

Nugent may have been correct about the chances of victory for the People's Party in 1892, but its rise put tremendous pressure on Governor Hogg by taking away many of his farm supporters just as he had to face an attack from the conservative wing of the Democratic Party. Angered by Hogg's early reforms, especially the Railroad Commission, conservatives rallied around George Clark, the railroad lawyer who had served as campaign manager for

Sul Ross, and called for an end to "the reign of King James I." Clark announced as a candidate for the Democratic nomination in February 1892, criticizing Hogg for restricting the state's economy and offering the slogan "Turn Texas Loose." Clark waged a nasty campaign against Hogg for the nomination during the spring and summer of 1892, but the governor had a clear lead when the state convention assembled in Houston in August. Clark's supporters tried to take control anyhow by packing the convention hall—the city's streetcar shed—and electing the chairman by voice vote. Texas Ranger Bill McDonald, a Hogg man, kept nondelegates out of the shed, however, and after a brief dispute over electing the chair, Clark's people gave up and withdrew. Hogg's supporters then renominated the governor on a platform that endorsed some of the Populist reforms—free silver and the income tax, for example—but specifically rejected the subtreasury plan and government ownership of railroads. The Hogg Democrats also called for electing members of the Railroad Commission, a change favored by the Farmers' Alliance.

Clark's conservative forces, after withdrawing from the "street car barn convention," held their own meeting and nominated their man on a platform that denounced Hogg for "keeping capital from the State." Then, in another twist on the old adage about politics and "strange bedfellows," Norris W. Cuney, the state's leading black Republican, convinced his party to endorse Clark. The basis for this alliance lay in the belief by national Republican leaders that Clark's pro-business views made him the best for their party among the three Texas gubernatorial candidates. They were correct on that point, and Cuney did what his party wanted.

The national presidential campaign in 1892 further enlivened the contest for governor in Texas, especially since the Populists ran their candidate on the so-called "Omaha Platform," which called for the reforms already endorsed by the movement in Texas. One of the Populists' most effective campaigners was a Texan, James H. Davis, a northeast Texas lawyer, who campaigned for Democrats, including Hogg, before joining the Populist movement in 1891. Standing six feet, three inches tall, Davis mounted the speaker's platform wearing a long Prince Albert coat and carrying the collected works of Thomas Jefferson under his arm. Then, using a voice that could be heard blocks away with no visible effort on his part, he preached the Populist message with a vocabulary drawn largely from the Psalms and the Gospels. Known early in his career as "Methodist Jim" for the fervency of his delivery, Davis eventually won the nickname "Cyclone" for the way he devastated an opponent in debate. He campaigned all over the South in 1892, but he also ran for attorney general of Texas on the Populist ticket.

All three candidates for governor took potshots at each other during the fall of 1892. Nugent said that Clark represented only the laissez faire conservatism of the national Democratic Party and its candidate Grover Cleveland while Hogg's platform was "quite meaningless." Clark called Hogg a "false Moses" who had simply stolen his platform from the Populists. Hogg attacked the Clark men as "boltercrats" and "calamity howlers" and described the Populists as "poisoned from disappointed ambition, mad with the world in general, chimerical in political convictions, shifting in party name." All three parties sought African American votes with one promise or another, but the Hogg forces set a record for hypocrisy by organizing clubs of black supporters in some counties while reminding white voters in other places to vote against the "Three C's—Clark, Cuney, and the Coons."

Hogg retained the governorship, winning 44 percent of the vote (190,486) to Clark's 31 percent (133,395) and Nugent's 25 percent (108,483) and a handful of votes for minor candidates. The governor won with the support of more productive white farmers, a few important businessmen who did not object to the Railroad Commission, workers in the cities, and a good many black voters. Clark had the support of most businessmen in the cities, large ranchers in the south and west, and blacks loyal to the Republican Party. Nugent's strength lay, as expected, with white small farmers. Given Populist support for the economic interests of poor blacks, he received disappointingly few votes from them, probably because the party had made no specific mention of their other needs. Nothing was said, for example, about the Hogg Administration's endorsement of an 1891 Jim Crow law that mandated segregation on railroad cars in Texas. In one sense, then, the Populists ran very well—convincing 25 percent of the electorate to support a third party that had virtually no chance to win was impressive—but in another way the results were not promising. The Populists needed black votes, but to get them would have to offer more to blacks, an action that in turn would alienate whites in their own party and allow the opposition to accuse them of undermining white supremacy.

Populism also received virtually no support from Mexican American voters in South Texas. In 1892, Nugent did not get a single vote in Cameron, Hidalgo, Starr, Webb, and Duval Counties, an interesting failure in light of the movement's attempt to appeal to the poor and dispossessed. The explanation lay primarily in the boss-rule system of politics in South Texas personified by James B. Wells of Brownsville. Wells, a native of the coastal bend region, began his rise as a law partner of Stephen Powers, a leading South Texas politician, and by the late 1880s built a machine that controlled the whole region. He and local bosses, such as Archie Parr of Duval County and Manuel Guerra of Starr County, organized voters; determined the winners in local, state, and national elections; and dispensed political patronage. Wells and his associates maintained power by promoting the interests of ranchers and merchants and by taking care of the poor Mexican American voters. The wealthy received low taxes, promotion of railroad development, and strong support for law and order on the border. The lower class, which formed a sizable majority, received help with their everyday problems that no governmental agency existed to give. Wells was, according to one observer, the "Father Confessor" for "a people . . . whose notes he has endorsed and paid, whose babies he has played with, whose tangles he has untangled, and whose troubles he has made his own for more than thirty years." This approach, which was much the same as that followed by big-city bosses in the northeast, worked especially well with people who had no tradition of independence in politics and were accustomed to relying on the advice and assistance of *patrones.* Wells, a conservative Democrat, did not particularly like Hogg or any other reformer, but he never pursued political ideology within the party at the expense of his machine. He could, however, draw the line at Populism, and that he did, especially since in doing so he supported a likely winner.

Hogg's second administration had some success with reform—in 1894, for example, the Railroad Commission was made elective—but many Texans faced even harder economic times due to a national financial panic in the spring of 1893 that touched off a four-year depression. Worse-than-ever conditions for farmers promised to strengthen the Populists, and therefore the Democrats were compelled to hold a successful "Harmony Meeting" in Dallas early in 1894. The reunified party then nominated a Dallas lawyer, Charles A. Culberson, for the governorship and prepared to withstand another challenge from the radical agrarians. Culberson, the son of a congressman and a graduate of Virginia Military Institute and the University of Virginia Law School, did not have Hogg's common touch with rural Texans, but he had served two terms as attorney general and successfully defended the Railroad Commission. Moreover, he had an especially adept political manager in the person of Edward M. House, a wealthy Texan who had managed Hogg's campaign in 1892. House liked the process of politics rather than the substance, which gave him the flexibility necessary to manipulate issues and men with great success. He could not control a strong politician such as Hogg, but Culberson proved more malleable. As one politician put it, "Charley would be all right if he had a little more iron down his backbone." Culberson's platform did not call for any major reforms, although the candidate himself spoke for free silver.

The Populists nominated Nugent again and continued to push the subtreasury plan and other reforms. They also worked harder to win support from blacks, particularly through the efforts of John B. Rayner, the mulatto son of a North Carolina planter who became the party's best known African American spokesman by 1894. He traveled all over the state, organizing Populist clubs that invited in "all who favor justice, liberty, a higher price for labor, and a better price for products." When drunken Democrats threatened Rayner, he made jokes about how they wanted to run him out of town. Increasing support from blacks, coupled with Culberson's personal limitations as a candidate and the depression, helped the Populists in 1894, although not nearly enough to bring them victory. Nugent received 152,731 votes (36 percent of the total, compared to 25 percent in 1892), but Culberson won with 206,141 (49 percent). More than likely, fraud and intimidation in heavily black counties helped put the Democratic total to that level. The Republican and Prohibitionist candidates ran far off the pace.

Although none of them won, Populist candidates for Texas's seats in Congress ran strongly in 1894, and the new party elected twenty-two members of the state house of representatives and two state senators. It still seemed to stand on rising ground, counting forty thousand subscribers to the *Southern Mercury* alone in 1895 and many other readers of the state's one hundred other "reform" weeklies. Populist organizations such as the Young People's League of Texas and local glee clubs attracted popular support. John B. Rayner and other blacks worked hard among their people, doing work that, in the words of state chairman "Stump" Ashby, "no white man can do." The next election, however, would undo the People's Party and mark the beginning of a quick end to the Populist movement.

The Culmination of Populism

Across the United States in 1896, three years of depression hung like the infamous albatross around the neck of Grover Cleveland, the Democratic president who had been unfortunate enough to take office just before the economy collapsed. Even southern and western Democrats, already unhappy with Cleveland's laissez faire politics and determined support of business interests and the gold standard, had turned against him. After the Republican national convention nominated William McKinley on a conservative, pro-northeastern platform, farm state Democrats took over their party and reoriented it to support reform. The 1896 Democratic platform called for free and unlimited coinage of silver, direct election of senators, and the income tax—all of which the Populists favored—but, significantly, it did not endorse the subtreasury plan or government ownership of the railroads. To head their ticket, the Democrats chose an exciting young orator, thirty-six-year-old William Jennings Bryan of Nebraska. Bryan had held only one elective office, having served two terms in Congress, but he compensated for a lack of experience with the evangelical fervor of his spellbinding oratory. The speech at the Democratic convention in which he defended free silver and warned against "crucifying mankind on a cross of gold" still stands as one of the most effective (although hardly learned or analytical) orations in American political history.

The Democrats' nomination of Bryan presented the Populists with a dilemma. On one hand, they could endorse Bryan and have a chance to win the presidency with a candidate who supported much, but not all, of their program. On the other, if they fused with the Democrats, their party would likely disappear, win or lose, but especially if they lost. Texas Populists stood solidly against fusion, believing in the words of a telegram sent from Dallas County to the national convention: "Bryan means death." The Texans were in a hopeless minority, however, and the national Populist Party voted to fuse with the Democrats, at least to the extent of endorsing Bryan. Unable to accept the Democratic convention's choice for vice president, Arthur Sewall, a businessman from Maine, the Populists named Tom Watson from Georgia for second place on their ticket. This created a great deal of confusion, as some states ran Bryan-Sewall tickets and others paired Bryan and Watson.

Texas Populists, who held their convention a week after the national meeting, endorsed the Bryan-Watson ticket with some reluctance and nominated Jerome C. Kearby for governor. Kearby, like many Populist leaders, had a Confederate and Democratic background. He enlisted in the Twenty-ninth Texas Cavalry as a fifteen-year-old "boy soldier" in 1862 and ended the war as a major. Then, after beginning a career in the law and politics, he became disgusted with the Democratic Party's economic policies, supported all the reform movements of the 1880s, and ran for Congress twice as a Populist during the early 1890s. A handsome man with the flair for oratory so admired in that age, he made a strong candidate.

The election contest then became incredibly complicated in Texas. Democrats renominated Culberson for governor, of course, and insisted on a Bryan-Sewall national ticket. Thus, Democrat-Populist fusion extended only to the support of Bryan, and even then with separate sets of electors. Some Populists were so disgusted with fusion of any kind that they talked of supporting the Republican McKinley in the presidential election in return for that party's votes in the contest for governor. The Republicans made no gubernatorial nomination and in effect endorsed Kearby. Democratic newspapers then accused the Populists of selling out to the Republicans, a charge that aggravated many who were inclined to support the People's Party. Chaos ruled as the Democrats attacked Kearby as both a prohibitionist and a heavy drinker; "gold Democrats" criticized Bryan on the money issue; Populists accused the largely inactive Culberson of excessive spending; and a rising black Republican leader, William "Gooseneck Bill" McDonald, campaigned for the Democrats.

When it was all over, Democrats once again demonstrated their mastery of Texas. Their Bryan-Sewall ticket easily carried the state with 234,298 votes to 158,863 for McKinley. The Populists' Bryan-Watson ticket ran a distant third with only 78,926 votes (17 percent). Kearby had 238,325 votes for governor, by far the highest percentage (44 percent) ever won by a Populist candidate. Many of those, however, came because the Republicans did not have a candidate, and even at that Culberson, still managed by House, convincingly won reelection with 55 percent of the vote (298,643). Democrats attained that margin in part by employing fraud and intimidation, particularly against blacks. In John B. Rayner's home county (Robertson), for example, forty men with rifles ringed the courthouse to turn away black voters, and the Democratic county judge personally saw to the result in his home precinct. "I went down to the polls and took my six-shooter," he said later. "I stayed there until the polls closed. Not a negro voted." Concerning his violent role in restoring white supremacy in his county, he explained years later, "I only shot when I thought I had to. I know God pulled me through."

Fusion and defeat led to a rapid decline by the Texas Populists. "The opportunity was lost," said the defeated Populist candidate Kearby in 1896. "I trust it may appear again. I fear not." His fears proved correct. Reform-minded farmers found it easy to return to the Democratic Party once it adopted parts of their program such as free silver. Whites who had never been comfortable with the Populist appeal to black voters happily returned to racist politics. Moreover, farm prices recovered to some extent, thanks to poor harvests in other parts of the world and to the discoveries of gold in Alaska, Australia, and South Africa. Some of this newly produced gold found its way to the

United States and provided a basis for expanding the nation's money supply. After all the fuss over free silver, inflation came through gold.

State elections in 1898 and 1900 demonstrated the rapid decline of Populism. Barnett Gibbs, a late convert to the party, ran for governor in 1898 on a platform calling for building a state-owned railroad from the Red River to the Gulf and received only 28 percent of the vote. Joseph D. Sayers, yet another safe Democratic candidate under the management of E. M. House, won easily with support from 71 percent of the voters. A native of Mississippi and veteran of the Confederate Army, Sayers oversaw strengthening the antitrust law and accomplished little else. Nevertheless, House managed him to reelection in 1900 with 69 percent of the vote, while the Populists, with only 6 percent, passed from the political scene. The next Democratic governor, Samuel W. T. Lanham, ran essentially without opposition in 1902 and 1904. Lanham, a South Carolinian by birth, fought in a Confederate unit from his home state and moved to North Texas after the war. He entered politics as a conservative Democrat, served eight terms in Congress during the eighties and nineties, and had ideal credentials for a House-sponsored candidate. Winning with 76 percent of the vote in 1902 and 74 percent two years later, he ran a moderate, pro-business administration.

Even as Populism disappeared under a wave of resurgent conservatism, it contributed heavily to a movement intended to reduce the voting strength of blacks and poor whites in Texas. Those who supported disfranchisement after 1900 had an incredible tangle of motives, but most related in some way to the Populist revolt. A majority of whites—conservative Democrats, reform-minded Hogg Democrats, and Populists alike—had only limited acceptance of black suffrage under any circumstance, and many remained angry over the way both sides had appealed to and used the black vote during the recent political battles. They agreed that disfranchisement of blacks would mean fairer fights between whites. Moreover, Hogg Democrats saw disfranchisement as a means of convincing white Populists to return to their old party and help in the fight against conservatives. Disfranchisement was complicated by the fact that any measure to take the vote from blacks legally (that is, one that did not violate the Fifteenth Amendment by singling out blacks) would likely disfranchise some poor whites as well, but leaders among both the reform Democrats and Populists accepted that possibility and hoped to keep its impact to a minimum. Overall, proponents of limiting the franchise presented it as a Progressive reform. Many prohibitionists, remembering how blacks tended to vote against their cause, readily agreed.

Interest in disfranchisement after 1900 resurrected the idea of requiring payment of a poll tax as a requirement for voting, an electoral "reform" first proposed shortly after "redemption" in the 1870s. The tax, although only a dollar or two, was large enough to discourage the poor regardless of race, and it had to be paid early in the year and the receipt kept until elections were held, usually months later. In 1879, State Senator Alexander Watkins Terrell, a native of Virginia and former Confederate officer, introduced a poll tax bill in the Texas legislature. "Unless some *flank* movement can be made on the mass of ignorant negro voters," he wrote Oran Roberts, "we will soon be at Sea in Texas." Terrell's bill passed the senate but failed in the house where it was attacked as an attempt to disfranchise the poor. The issue then remained dormant until the threat of Populism, plus the example of black disfranchisement in Mississippi and South Carolina, revived interest among Democratic politicians in Texas. In 1902, the legislature submitted to Texans a constitutional amendment permitting use of the poll tax as a requirement for voting. Political bosses such as Jim Wells of South Texas, labor groups, and the State Brewers Association—all of whom depended on the votes of the poor and minorities—opposed the poll tax, as did poor Populist farmers in North Texas. However, they could not overcome the combination of conservatives, Hogg Democrats, Populist leaders such as "Stump" Ashby and "Cyclone" Davis, and prohibitionists who supported it. The amendment passed by nearly a two-to-one margin.

Following adoption of the poll tax requirement, A. W. Terrell sponsored additional election-law reforms that passed during the Lanham administration in 1903 and 1905. The Terrell Election Laws established a direct primary system of nomination for all state, district, and county elective offices. Not so incidentally, the election law reforms also permitted parties to put specific limitations on membership, thus giving not-so-subtle encouragement to the white primary, which some counties had already adopted, as another means of restricting black suffrage. The Terrell laws ended the convention system, making Lanham the last Texas governor nominated in convention (as well as the last Confederate elected to that office), and reduced the role of political manipulators such as E. M. House in the nomination of candidates. Since winning the Democratic nomination guaranteed victory in the regular election, the primary opened the way to members of that party to go as far as their personal appeal, ideas, and financial backing would take them without having to win the approval of established leaders. Perhaps, then, the election-law reforms that passed in the aftermath of the Populist revolt, while anything but beneficial to blacks and poor whites, at least had the merit of permitting greater competition within the dominant Democratic Party during the Progressive era that followed.

Progressive Reform from Disaster: The Galveston Hurricane of 1900

On the morning of September 8, 1900, Galveston was a prosperous city of more than 37,000 residents; twenty-four hours later more than half of its buildings were gone and at least 6,000 people were dead. The hurricane responsible for this devastation is still regarded a century later as the greatest natural disaster ever to strike the North American continent. Galvestonians had advance warning—the Weather Bureau in Washington, D.C., sent daily notices beginning on September 4—but no one could imagine a storm of such magnitude until it was too late. As winds increased and the tide rose on the morning of the 8th, Isaac M. Cline, the bureau's official in Galveston, drove around the island urging residents to move to stronger buildings located in the center of the city. Evacuation was not an option because bridges to the mainland fell early. Any movement out of doors became dangerous as wind-blown pieces of wood, bricks, and roof slate flew along the streets. During the afternoon, Cline helped forty or fifty people into his own home at Rosenberg Avenue and Q Street and then watched as the water rose steadily around it. At 7:30 P.M., he wrote later, "there was a sudden rise of about four feet in as many seconds. I was standing at my front door, which was partly open, watching the water, which was flowing with great rapidity from east to west. The water at this time was about eight inches deep in my residence, and the sudden rise of 4 feet brought it above my waist before I could change my position." Over the next hour the tide rose another five feet, reaching a total of twenty feet above sea level.

The rushing water pushed buildings ahead of it that acted as a battering ram against Cline's house so that, in his words, "at 8:30 P.M. my residence went down with about fifty persons who had sought it for safety, and all but eighteen were hurled into eternity. Among the lost was my wife, who never rose above the water after the wreck of the building. I was nearly drowned and became unconscious, but recovered though being crushed by timbers and found myself clinging to my youngest child, who had gone down with myself and wife." Fortunately for Cline, another man saved his other two children, and they, plus several other survivors, managed to float on pieces of debris for the next three hours before landing on a standing building. "While we were drifting," he wrote, "we had to protect ourselves from the flying timbers by holding planks between us and the wind, and with this protection we were frequently knocked great distances." By morning the Gulf had receded to normal levels. The monster storm continued north through Oklahoma and Kansas, turned northeastward across the Great Lakes and Canada, and moved into the North Atlantic.

Martial law was declared on Monday, September 10, and collection of the dead began. Finding it impossible to bury so many bodies on the island, authorities decided to take them to sea. A Houston reporter described the scene: "Center street wharf was used for the loading, and every wagon, dray, boat, or cart to be found was impressed into service, and the bodies carried to the wharf. There was no time to stop for identification. Decomposition had set in, the town was full of stench, and at once every one began to think of the pestilence which would follow unless the dead were disposed of. . . . The day I was there the barge was loaded with 1000 bodies and was towed out to sea. Weights were attached to each and they were buried in the Gulf." The full death toll will never be known, although the usual estimate is six thousand. Property damage estimates ranged from twenty to thirty million dollars.

Galveston struggled to recover. Ten years after the hurricane it had fewer residents than on September 8, 1900. The city, however, was too rich and important to go the way of Indianola, the second largest port in Texas until it was devastated by storms in 1875 and 1886. A town of five thousand located

Survivors on the beach at Galveston following the great hurricane of September 1900. Only a few partially ruined buildings remain standing. Credit: Courtesy of the Rosenberg Library, Galveston, Texas.

on Matagorda Bay, Indianola rebuilt on a smaller scale after the first hurricane destroyed all but eight buildings and then was abandoned after the second. Galveston's leaders, rather than giving up, built a six-mile-long seawall rising seventeen feet above mean low tide and pumped sand from the Gulf to raise the level of the city by seventeen feet. An incredible engineering challenge, elevating the city required raising more than two thousand buildings, plus water pipes and streetcar tracks. A three thousand-ton church was lifted five feet off the ground with jacks so that fill could be pumped under it.

Rebuilding Galveston led to a new form of city government widely hailed as one of the first important progressive reforms. Local businessmen, fearing that the existing mayor-council government lacked the efficiency to oversee the recovery program, devised a plan to have the governor appoint a five-man commission to run the city. Critics charged that this plan, which went into effect in 1901, created an undemocratic system of appointive government, and the legislature soon modified it by requiring at-large election of the commissioners. Even then, the at-large system reduced the voice of the poor and minorities who tended to concentrate in one or two wards of the city. Commissioners as a group made all general governing decisions such as establishing the tax rate, and each commissioner as an individual had charge of a particular aspect of city government such as public works. The plan worked so well in Galveston that other cities, beginning with Houston in 1905, copied it. Progressive leaders including Theodore Roosevelt and Woodrow Wilson endorsed the commission form, and by 1920 about five hundred cities nationwide adopted it. Eventually, the council-city manager form of government supplanted the commission, primarily because executive leadership was necessary to prevent bickering among commissioners heading specific departments. For the time, however, Galveston's invention provided a classic case of creating progress out of disaster and also a demonstration of how the Progressives tended to value efficiency even at the expense of democracy.

Progressivism and Prohibition

Reform took a brief vacation following the defeat of Populism, and Americans enjoyed distractions such as their nation's "coming out party" as a world power—the Spanish-American War of 1898. Texans could take special pride in the exploits of the "Rough Riders," the famed volunteer unit recruited at the Menger Hotel in San Antonio by Leonard Wood and Theodore Roosevelt. Soon, however, demands that politicians deal with the accumulated evils of industrialization and urbanization returned in the form of Progressivism. The Progressive movement drew energy from national leaders, particularly Theodore Roosevelt, the "madman" (according to Republican boss Mark Hanna) who took over the presidency in 1901, but it would have accomplished little without the support of important state groups as well. In Texas, the Farmers' Union, which was organized in 1902 as a group much like the Farmers' Alliance of the 1880s, claimed 100,000 members by 1906 and called for additional railroad regulation and higher cotton prices. The State Federation of Labor, although it grew to only about nine thousand members between its birth in 1898 and 1906, added another voice to reform. Prohibitionists began to gather strength again with the formation of the Texas Local Option Association in 1903. Groups of Texas businessmen also wanted new laws to improve city government—the best example being the commission idea that appeared in Galveston—and to give them advantages in dealing with out-of-state competition.

Texas women played a role in supporting Progressivism that in some respects amounted to a reform in itself. The state's women had never been locked away at home to quite the extent that is often pictured. They worked in the temperance movement of the antebellum years, for example, and were highly visible in prohibitionist activities and the Farmers' Alliance. Jenny Bland Beauchamp of Denton served as president of the Woman's Christian Temperance Union (WCTU) in the mid-1880s and on the platform committee of the Prohibition Party in 1886. Mary M. Clardy of Sulphur Springs served on the same platform committee and two years later was elected assistant state lecturer of the Texas Farmers' Alliance. Frances Leak, a physician and WCTU activist from Austin, became secretary-treasurer of the Texas Farmers' Alliance in 1895. She and Clardy were two of only three women elected to state offices in Alliance organizations anywhere in the South. During the Progressive Era, women participated in public life even more effectively, primarily through voluntary associations, and their work as reformers led them to greater interest in changes affecting themselves.

Women's organizations, regardless of their original purposes, often wound up supporting reforms that protected public health, children, and working women. For example, during the 1890s middle- and upper-class women across the state formed numerous literary study clubs as part of a general popular education movement. In 1897 representatives of these organization met in Waco and formed the Texas Federation of Women's Clubs, which by 1903 had 232 clubs and more than 5,000 members. Although the state had relatively few middle-class African Americans, a similar organization of black women, the Texas Association of Colored Women's Clubs, appeared in 1905 and began to grow slowly. Club women's interest in learning moved them to work for the establishment of public libraries and from there to support improvements in public education and health. Such activism, justified as "social motherhood," led women in larger numbers than ever to recognize just what they could accomplish in public life, especially if they had equal rights with men. Even the Texas Division of the United Daughters of the Confederacy, organized in 1896 with the anything-but-forward-looking purpose of honoring the memory of southerners in the Civil War, showed many of its members what they could accomplish in public life if given an opportunity.

The desire for greater equality was hardly new—for example, a discussion of giving the vote without regard to gender occurred at the constitutional conventions of 1868–1869 and 1875; the Woman's Christian Temperance Union endorsed woman suffrage in 1888; and a short-lived Texas Equal Rights Association appeared in 1893—but the role of women in Progressivism brought renewed emphasis on their rights. One success came in 1913 when the Texas Federation of Women's Clubs led in convincing the legislature to amend the state's married women's property laws to give wives not only ownership of their separate property, which had been their right since the 1840s, but control as well. That victory raised an obvious question: If a woman could control her own property, why should she not have her own ballot? Woman suffrage, an issue raised hesitantly several times before, especially by the Texas Equal Suffrage Association after its formation in 1903, returned in 1913 as a focal point of the movement for the remainder of the decade. Of course, the women who worked for the vote made it yet another "for whites only" reform. Black women in their own federation had to struggle against prejudice and at the same time work to improve the lives of their people. Mexican-American women, organized in La Liga Femenil Mexicanista, faced a similar situation.

Progressivism gained momentum in 1906 when the succession of quietly conservative governors managed into office by E. M. House came to an end with the election of Thomas M. Campbell. A native of Rusk in East Texas, Campbell became a lawyer and from his work with one of Jay's Gould's railroads developed a dislike for monopolistic practices. He had the support of former governor Jim Hogg and drew an endorsement from "Cyclone" Davis as "the nearest approach to old-time Populism that is now before the country." Once he captured the Democratic nomination in a fight with three candidates from North Texas, he brushed aside the Republicans and several minor parties and won 81 percent of the vote. Campbell gave Texas a reform-minded executive like those in other southern states at the time and compiled a record of considerable achievement. Under his leadership the legislature created a state department of agriculture to provide useful information to farmers, revised the property tax system to include full valuation of railroad property, and increased restrictions on corporations issuing securities in Texas. The Robertson Insurance Law of 1907 smacked of Governor Hogg's dislike of "foreign" corporations by requiring companies to invest at least 75 percent of the reserves devoted to life insurance policies on Texans in Texas real estate and securities. Legislation provided increased funding for public schools, lengthened the school year from four to seven months, and raised teachers' minimum annual pay to $390.

In 1908 conservative Democrats ran Robert R. Williams, the "Village Blacksmith of Cumby," against Campbell in the primary, but the incumbent easily won renomination and reelection over token opposition in the general election. Two important reforms passed during his second term. The first had to do with state-chartered banks, which had been constitutionally prohibited in Texas from 1876 until 1904. Within a few years of their legalization, state banks outnumbered those with national charters in Texas and fears arose concerning their stability—and therefore the safety of depositors' money—in times of financial crisis. Campbell asked for the creation of a guaranty-fund system for state banks in 1909 and, when the legislature did not act, denounced it as "a sham and a fraud" and threatened to keep it in special session as long as necessary to have the law passed. The Bank Guaranty Law of 1909 required all state banks to contribute a percentage of their average daily deposits during the previous year to a fund that could be used to pay off depositors in the event of a bank failure. This system worked well into the 1920s as the number of state banks increased to more than one thousand, but then a large number of failures, plus the tendency of bankers to seek national charters and thus avoid guaranty-fund payments, destroyed it. The other major reform of Campbell's second term, a law passed in 1910, called for an end to the convict lease system in 1914. Working prisoners only "within prison walls, and upon farms ownd by the state," assured somewhat more humane treatment for prisoners. Many concerns of Progressives across the nation remained untouched in Texas under Campbell—for example, the state still did little for its blind, deaf, and mentally ill citizens—nevertheless, he encouraged a truly impressive array of twentieth-century reforms.

Campbell's administration marked the reemergence of prohibition as an issue that took center stage for the remainder of the Progressive era. The impact of this dry crusade on Progressivism in Texas is easily underestimated. From the vantage point of later years, outlawing the manufacture, sale, and consumption of alcoholic beverages seems more reactionary than forward looking. In Texas, however, where there were relatively few of the abusive corporations, struggling industrial workers, and boss-ridden cities that took the attention of Progressives elsewhere in the United States, the manufacturers and purveyors of liquor made perfect targets for reformers wishing to protect basic American values and build a better nation. Prohibition promoted Progressivism, too, because "demon rum" could be destroyed only if the government passed and enforced laws against liquor. In using the state to bring prohibition, drys helped erode the traditional antigovernment philosophy of conservatives and create support for other reforms as well. "I believe," Thomas B. Love of Dallas, a Democratic politician and ardent prohibitionist, told an audience of bankers in 1908, "that the best vindication of State's rights will be brought about by the State's governments doing as thoroughly and wholesomely and effectively the things lawfully within their spheres as the National government does those things lawfully within its sphere to do." Love probably was not prepared to accept an activist national government, but when leading Texas Democrats agreed to reforms emanating from Austin they were a step closer to approving progressive proposals from Washington as well.

This transition from conservative to more progressive views among leaders, with prohibition playing a major role, is illustrated by the careers of Joseph Weldon Bailey and John Morris Sheppard, two of Texas's United States Senators during this era. Bailey, a native of Mississippi who moved to Gainesville in 1885 after his part in a raid on Republicans and blacks ruined a budding political career at home, won a seat in the United States House of Representatives in 1890. After ten years in the House, where he became known as a champion of free silver and strict construction of the United States Constitution, he won election to the Senate. One of the best in a long line of handsome Texas orators, Bailey never missed an opportunity to show off his verbal brilliance. His actual accomplishments, however, led a Houston newspaper to compare him to a perpetually blooming tree, "all flower and no fruit." Also, his erratic temper caused trouble, especially in 1902 when he physically assaulted Senator Albert Beveridge of Indiana after a debate, and a shadow hung over his career from the beginning because in 1900 he took a personal loan from Henry Clay Pierce, the president of the Waters-Pierce Oil Company, while representing that corporation in legal proceedings in Texas. He also made large sums of money as an advisor to John Henry Kirby, the lumber baron of southeast Texas. Bailey denied any wrongdoing and won reelection in 1906, but many Texans saw him as a man who valued his clients more than his state. The rise of Progressivism left the senator increasingly alienated from his party, especially on issues such as prohibition. Use the power of government to solve social problems, he predicted, and reformers will step in to end racial segregation and bring miscegenation. National prohibition, he warned on one occasion, will mean that "there will not be a square foot of territory in the United States where it will be unlawful for negroes and white people to intermarry." In 1911, unhappy with his party and facing a strong challenge for reelection to a third, the senator announced that he would retire at the end of his term in 1913. "Baileyism" provoked strong feelings for another decade, however, and he continued to be a hero to Texans who opposed change.

Morris Sheppard, Bailey's successor in the Senate, took a significantly different approach to Democratic politics. A native of northeast Texas whose father served in Congress from 1898 to 1902, Sheppard held bachelors and law degrees from the University of Texas and a master of laws from Yale University. He won the congressional seat previously occupied by his just-deceased father in 1902 and held it until the state legislature chose him to replace Bailey. Like Bailey, Sheppard won fame as an orator who thrilled Texans with speeches on the history and character of the South. "Words are inadequate to describe it, human language is too lame, the mind cannot conceive of it," wrote one reporter after a 1909 oration in East Texas. Yet Sheppard did not let love of the Lost Cause create a total commitment to states' rights and opposition to the federal government. He supported national antitrust laws, child labor legislation, woman suffrage, and above all, prohibition. Liquor, he said when elected to the Senate, "is a source of danger to posterity because the alcoholic taint foredooms the unborn millions to degeneracy and disease. I shall oppose this scourge from hell until my arm can strike no longer and my tongue can speak no more." More generally, he promised "to place my energies and my devotion at the call of progressive Democracy." Sheppard would remain in the Senate until his death in 1941 and never go back on his word. He gave no indication of any desire to challenge white supremacy, but thanks in no small part to the prohibition issue, he was a far cry from Joe Bailey.

Prohibitionists, from their defeat in 1887 until the Campbell administration, concentrated on local option elections and met with enough success, particularly in North Texas, that alarmed liquor interests formed the Texas Brewers Association in 1901. In response, drys organized the Texas Local Option Association in 1903 and a state chapter of the Anti-Saloon League in 1907. These two antiliquor groups merged in 1908 and demanded that the legislature call a referendum on a statewide prohibition amendment, the first such proposal to be placed before voters in twenty years. Legislators rejected this call in 1909, but voters in the 1910 Democratic primary strongly endorsed the referendum and elected a majority of dry representatives and senators, thereby virtually ensuring that it would win approval once the legislature met in 1911. Curiously, this prohibitionist success did not carry over into the governor's election, which was won by Oscar B. Colquitt, a Georgia-born wet politician who had served on the Railroad Commission since 1902. Colquitt overcame several weak dry opponents by appealing to antiprohibition sentiment in South Texas and winning over conservatives with a promise of "political peace and legislative rest."

Prohibitionists quickly put aside their disgust at Colquitt's victory because early in 1911 the legislature lived up to their expectations and submitted a constitutional amendment to voters. The campaign, which culminated in July, took on more the air of a moral crusade than a political contest. Drys and wets raised money, held rallies and torchlight parades, and sponsored speakers to take their message to the people. Evangelical Protestant churches "locked shields" against the liquor interests and led the campaign. Drys drew strength from racial prejudice in that blacks were identified with the wets. According to Thomas B. Love, "[T]he Negro ought not to be permitted to vote on the question or whether or not liquor shall be sold in Texas any more than the Indian should be permitted to vote on the question of whether or not liquor shall be sold in Indian country." Texans of Mexican and German descent came in for their share of criticism also, as did the big cities for their "temptations and allurements." Antiprohibitionists argued that the drys constituted a threat to personal freedom that knew no bounds. "Civil liberty," said Governor Colquitt, "will give way to military despotism to appease fanaticism on this subject." On July 22 more than twice the number of voters who had gone to the polls in the previous year's gubernatorial election turned out and defeated the amendment by a narrow margin of 6,297 votes (237,393 to 231,096). Drys insisted that the manipulation of black voters had produced the wet victory and vowed to fight on. The issue could not be killed simply by one defeat.

Governor Colquitt toned down the Campbell administration's emphasis on reform but proved somewhat less conservative than his campaign slogan about peace and rest suggested. He ended the convict lease system in 1912, two years earlier than projected in the act passed under Campbell, and signed laws that restricted child labor, promoted factory safety, and limited the work week for women to fifty-four hours. Colquitt also sponsored a conference of southern governors in 1912 to consider means of stabilizing the cotton market. The governors' recommendation—acreage reduction—was endorsed by the Texas Farmers' Union, and two million fewer acres were planted in 1912. Prices rose, and Colquitt naturally took credit, overlooking the possibility that worldwide conditions may have made the difference.

For prohibitionists, of course, Colquitt could do no right while refusing to support their cause, so they made a major effort to deny him renomination in the Democratic primary in 1912. Their candidate, Texas Supreme Court Justice William F. Ramsey, ran a campaign of personal vituperation, charging, for example, that in 1911 the governor had chosen the daughter of a leading Republican to christen the battleship *Texas* in return for a guarantee of 35,000 black votes against prohibition. Colquitt did not respond in kind, and that, plus the tradition of giving governors two terms to prove themselves, allowed him to defeat Ramsey and gain renomination.

The 1912 general election was especially interesting to Texas Democrats, not from any concern that Colquitt might lose, but because their party had a chance to win the presidency for the first time since 1892. Former President Theodore Roosevelt, after unsuccessfully challenging the more conservative incumbent President William Howard Taft for the Republican nomination in 1912, bolted and created the Progressive Party, taking many reform-minded voters with him. Meanwhile, the Democrats managed with considerable difficulty to unite behind Woodrow Wilson, a native of the South, who supported Progressive causes such as antitrust, lowering the protective tariff, and banking reform. Wilson relied heavily on the advice and money of E. M. House, who after retiring in 1906 from making governors turned to making a president. Thanks to House and a few other leaders, he received consistent support from the Progressive and prohibitionist Democrats who made up Texas's delegation to the national convention, and in the fall easily carried the state with 221,000 votes to only 28,000 for Taft and 26,000 for Roosevelt. Once in office he knew that he could count on Texas's U.S. Senators Morris Sheppard, who also came to Washington in 1913, and Charles A. Culberson, the former governor and a senator since 1899.

President Wilson repaid Texans for their political support by appointing two to his original cabinet—Albert Sidney Burleson as postmaster general and David Franklin Houston as secretary of agriculture—and naming Thomas Watt Gregory as attorney general in 1914. Born in San Marcos in 1863, Burleson served in Congress from 1899 to 1913 and developed such a reputation for political intrigue that Wilson called him the "Cardinal." Immediately upon taking office he demonstrated the "for whites only" nature of Progressivism, especially under Wilson, by segregating the black employees in his department. Houston, a native of North Carolina, built his career as a professor of political science and had the unusual distinction of serving as president of both Texas A&M University (1902–1905) and the University of Texas (1905–1908). Gregory grew up poor in Mississippi (his father was killed in the Civil War) before graduating from the University of Texas and becoming a lawyer in Austin. He built a reputation as a Progressive mainly by attacking Senator Joe Bailey and serving as the prosecutor in a case charging the Waters-Pierce Oil Company with violating the state's antitrust law. None of these men were advanced Progressives who pushed for the most important reforms of the Wilson Administration. Houston, for example, only went along with agricultural reforms such as the Warehouse Act of 1916, which put into place a version of the Populists' subtreasury plan. Nevertheless, the presence of three Texans in the cabinet, plus the roles of House, Sheppard, and Culberson, provided highly visible evidence of how much Wilson relied on the South. More important, it marked the emergence of Texas as a powerful force in the national Democratic Party, a development of tremendous importance to the state for much of the twentieth century.

The first two years of Wilson's presidency, coinciding with Governor Colquitt's second administration, largely overshadowed politics within the state. Politically aware Texans, for example, celebrated the creation of a badly needed new banking, currency, and credit system by the Federal Reserve Act in December 1913, and were especially delighted the next year when Dallas was chosen as the home of a Federal Reserve district bank. Most of the state's leaders were so happy with Wilson that they backed him rather than Governor Colquitt in dealing with disturbances along the Río Grande resulting from the revolution that began in Mexico in 1910. A good many Mexican Americans and Mexicans in Texas supported the revolt against the dictatorial government of Porfirio Díaz, often allowing rebels to gain financial aid and weapons in the area from El Paso to Brownsville and even in San Antonio. At times, fighting just south of the border threatened the lives of Americans visiting in Mexico and created greater-than-usual lawlessness along the river.

Colquitt argued for doing whatever was necessary to protect Americans along the border, even if it meant sending Texas Rangers or U.S. troops into Mexico, but President Wilson favored "watchful waiting" and a hands-off policy. Senator Sheppard insisted in 1914 that the people of Texas were "almost unanimously in sympathy with Woodrow Wilson" and "not in sympathy with the Governor of Texas on this question." As Colquitt's term ended, however, Texans did not view either Wilson's reforms or policy toward Mexico as key issues in the 1914 gubernatorial election. Instead, drys and wets looked forward to a contest over prohibition that would prove decisive on the liquor question and mark an important victory for the Progressives' positive approach to government as well. At that point, however, James E. Ferguson arrived on the political scene, and any semblance of clarity in the Democratic Party's philosophy and policies disappeared.

"Fergusonism"

Ferguson, who had never before held an elective office, came out of nowhere politically to win the governorship in 1914 and dominate state government for the next three years. He called himself a "Hogg Progressive Democrat" and drew primarily on the discontent of Texas's poor farmers for his success, but he practiced a far more personal than principled brand of politics. Barely skirting the raw edges of demagoguery, Ferguson abused the powers of his office to such an extent that he became the only governor of Texas to be impeached and convicted. His is a spectacular but largely unproductive chapter in the state's political history.

Born near Salado in 1871, Ferguson grew up poor, although probably not quite like "Job's turkey," as he liked to claim later. He had to work on the family farm after the death of his father when he was four, but at age twelve he entered a local preparatory school called Salado College. Four years later he was expelled for disobedience and then spent some time wandering the western United States working at odd jobs. Returning to Texas, he worked on the railroad briefly and then turned to the law. He studied two years, gained admittance to the bar in 1897, set up a practice in Belton, and married Miriam A. Wallace in 1899. An intelligent man who continued to educate himself, Ferguson soon branched out into real estate and banking. In 1907, he moved to Temple and with other investors established the Temple State Bank.

Ferguson became active in local politics, working for Colquitt in 1912, for example, and consistently opposing prohibition even on a local-option basis. He had no statewide experience, however, and surprised everyone in late 1913 when he announced as a candidate for governor the following year. At that point, the leading contender for the Democratic nomination was Thomas H. Ball, a Houston lawyer and former congressman. A well-known Progressive and ardent prohibitionist, Ball had a major liability that he tried to meet head on when his campaign began. "I belong to the Country Club of Houston," he said. "Drinks are sold there, but I do not indulge there or elsewhere." Unfortunately for Ball, disclaimers of this sort could not deflect the charges of hypocrisy that were certain to follow. Ferguson, by contrast, believed that voters had tired of wet/dry disputes and took an unequivocal position in his first campaign speech. "If I am elected Governor," he said, "and the Legislature puts any liquor legislation up to me, pro or anti, I will strike it where the chicken got the axe."

Ferguson drew attention away from the prohibition issue by focusing on the problems of Texas's tenant farmers and sharecroppers. Rising every decade since the 1880s, the proportion of tenants among the state's farmers reached 50 percent in 1900 and continued upward. By 1910, at least 200,000 Texas families—whites, blacks, and a rising number of Mexicans—were caught in the trap of working someone else's land while suffering from inadequate food, shelter, and clothing. Everyone suffered. Men wore out physically before their time from unending labor in a punishing climate. Women bore and reared child after child while working constantly to meet their families' needs. "Show me a housewife with eight or ten children," wrote a journalist in 1918, "all of them ragged and dirty, with her own dress drabbled and frayed, with her back bent over with toil, . . . and the chickens on the front porch—and nine times out of ten you are showing me the wife of a tenant farmer." Children had little chance to improve their lives because they had to work in the fields rather than attend school. After the turn of the century, landlords made life even harder by demanding a bonus payment from their tenants in addition to the usual shares of crops. Tenants, who were generally uneducated, on the move, and disfranchised, received little attention from politicians, but they could not be ignored indefinitely. "One of these days," the *Houston Chronicle* argued in 1912, "this issue is going to fly up and hit our lawmakers in the face; they'll know they have met it." Ferguson made it "fly up" by proposing a law to fix rentals at one-third of the grain and one-fourth of the cotton (for tenants who furnished teams and tools) and prohibiting the requiring of bonuses. He also proposed to improve public schools.

Ball had numerous advantages in the campaign, including endorsements from President Wilson, Senator Sheppard, former Governor Campbell, and even Joe Bailey (who called the tenant proposal "socialistic"). But he could not match Ferguson's energy or appeal to ordinary Texans. Ball delivered two or three speeches a week, often to audiences filled with women and children, whereas "Farmer Jim" spoke daily to "the boys at the forks of the creek." Farmers, said one observer, took "to his land proposal like a hungry cat would to a piece of fresh beef liver." At the same time, Ferguson pounced on Ball's membership in the Houston Country Club. He visited the club himself, he told voters, and the "first thing that greeted my eyes was about three billiard tables and two pool tables." Men were playing cards and drinking liquor "after the hours when saloons were closed and on Sundays when you fellows can't get a smell." Ferguson even turned Wilson's endorsement of Ball into a negative, arguing that the attempt by the president to "cross a State line and interfere with the sovereign right of a sovereign people to elect a Governor" was an insult to the "sacred principles for which the gallant Confederate soldiers fought and bled on so many Southern battlefields." When it ended on

July 25, 1914, voters turned out in the largest numbers ever to that date in a Democratic primary and gave Ferguson a 237,062 to 191,558 victory. He won by keeping the usual wet support from Germans and South Texans and by using his tenant proposal to cut deeply into North Texas counties that generally voted dry.

Conservative Democrats attempted to turn the primary result into a rejection of Wilsonian Progressivism, but when Joe Bailey tried in August to have the party's state convention endorse antiprohibition and anti–woman suffrage resolutions, Ferguson countered successfully by insisting that the real issue was keeping campaign promises and giving the people of Texas a "business-like administration." He mended fences with the national administration, easily won the perfunctory general election in the fall, and took office in January 1915. His inaugural address emphasized harmony with legislators—if you want to talk, he said, "just come right in, sit right down, and make yourself at home"—and they responded by passing several of his campaign proposals, including a bill to limit rents charged farm tenants. Although seldom enforced and later declared unconstitutional by a state court (1921), this act at the time of its passage appeared to be a notable victory for Ferguson. The new governor also secured a special appropriation of $1 million for rural schools and legislation that in effect forced localities themselves to provide greater financial support for their schools. A compulsory-attendance education law passed over objections that it violated the sanctity of the family, and funds for the University of Texas were increased. Several other Progressive advances, although not emphasized by Ferguson, came in 1915. These included the creation of an institution for the mentally retarded (known now as the Austin State School) and the establishment of the Texas Department of Forestry (later renamed the Texas Forest Service) as a nonpolitical conservation agency.

Ferguson's legislative successes enhanced his popularity and added to his belief that he should and could run all state agencies and institutions as he pleased. In 1915, for example, he packed the governing board of Prairie View Normal and Industrial College in order to secure the removal of the school's principal, Edward L. Blackshear, who had made the mistake of supporting Ball in the primary. "A negro," the governor argued, "has no business whatever taking a part in the political affairs of the Democratic party, the white man's party." A few newspapers complained at this highhandedness, but Ferguson ignored them, an easy thing to do given that Blackshear was an African American. Soon, however, the governor took on the University of Texas, an institution with many friends and considerable retaliatory power. The battle began in the spring of 1915 when Ferguson questioned the acting president of the university, classics professor William J. Battle, about the school's budget and insisted on treating it as a payroll rather than a financial plan requiring flexibility in the use of funds. That dispute passed, but Ferguson continued the attack by demanding that Battle be replaced and that six faculty members who had angered him be fired. In response to a question about his reasons for these demands, he replied: "I don't have to give any reasons. I am Governor of the State of Texas." In the spring of 1916, the university's regents, without obtaining Ferguson's approval, named Robert E. Vinson, the head of Austin Presbyterian Theological Seminary, as the new president. Reportedly "red hot" at the news, the governor became even angrier when Vinson also refused to fire the faculty members in question. Unless the professors were terminated, he warned Vinson, you will face "the biggest bear fight that has ever taken place in the history of the State of Texas."

Ferguson had to delay his "bear fight" in the summer of 1916 to run for reelection in the Democratic primary. As expected, he had no difficulty in winning, but his opponent, Charles H. Morris, a wealthy East Texas banker and devoted prohibitionist, made charges during the campaign that caused serious trouble later. Most damaging potentially were the claims that Ferguson had deposited $100,000 of state money in his Temple bank and kept it there without paying interest and that he owed the same bank more than $150,000 that he had taken in overdrafts. Morris also accused the governor of taking $30,000 from a Houston brewery during the 1914 campaign. Ferguson denied or ignored all the charges and defeated Morris by nearly seventy thousand votes; still, his total increased only slightly from two years earlier. One observer commented that the governor needed to be on "good behavior" thereafter, but Farmer Jim had no intention of dropping his attack on the educational elitists at the university, especially since in October 1916 the board of regents refused to fire the faculty members whom he had targeted.

Ferguson's second administration, which began in January 1917, had one important achievement, the creation of a state highway commission in recognition of the arrival of the automobile as the most revolutionary change in transportation since the railroad. The previous year, the first for registration of motor vehicles in the state, Texans owned 194,720 autos. The 1917 act charged the commission with granting financial aid to counties for road building and, incidentally, set Texas's first speed limits—eighteen miles per hour in rural areas and fifteen miles per hour in cities. Positive accomplishments ended at that point, however, because of the governor's ongoing battle with the university. In his January message to the legislature Ferguson promised that he opposed higher education when it "becomes either autocratic or aristocratic in its ways or customs and begins to arrogate to itself an unwarranted superiority over the great masses of the people. . . ." Accordingly, following the close of the legislative session in May, he vetoed the appropriation bill for the university. "If the University cannot be maintained as a democratic University," he told the regents, "then we ought to have no University."

The veto touched off a storm of protest across the state. Friends of the university led the attack, and all of Ferguson's old prohibitionist enemies eagerly joined in. The governor took his case to the ordinary people with some apparent success at first, but he had very little support from the press in turning opinion in his favor. Instead, newspaper reports of his angry comments—"I do not care a damn what becomes of the University," he told the *Dallas Morning News*. "The bats and owls can roost in it for all that I care."—only hurt him more. The noose that Ferguson had fashioned for himself then began to tighten in late July 1917. On the 23rd, Speaker of the House Francis O. Fuller, a prohibitionist, issued a call for a special session to meet in early August and consider impeachment of the governor. Four days later the Travis County grand jury indicted Ferguson on nine charges of misuse of public funds and embezzlement. Apparently unfazed, he posted a $13,000 bond and announced plans to run for a third term so that the people could decide "whether we shall have a democratic University or an autocratic University."

Ferguson believed that constitutionally only the governor could call a special session but decided against a risky attempt to prevent the legislators from assembling. Instead, on July 30 he gave in and called the session himself, ostensibly to consider the university's appropriation. The special session made the appropriation quickly and turned to impeachment proceedings. After sweltering through several weeks of testimony, including an appearance by the governor in which he refused to disclose the source of a personal loan of $156,500 received earlier in the year, the house of representatives voted a twenty-one article bill of impeachment. Fourteen of the charges dealt with Ferguson's finances, and one charged him with contempt for refusing to disclose the source of his loan. Others resulted from the university fight. Once impeachment was formally voted, Lieutenant Governor William P. Hobby took over Ferguson's duties, and the governor prepared to defend himself before the senate. He insisted in five days of testimony and a summary statement that he had done no wrong and that the people would support him, but on Friday September 22 the senate by the necessary two-thirds majority found him guilty on ten charges, most of which involved violations of the law in handling his personal finances. The Senate adjourned for the weekend before fixing a penalty, giving the governor an opportunity to resign on the 24th and claim that the judgment did not apply to him. Ignoring the resignation, the senate on the 25th removed Ferguson from office and disqualified him from holding any public office in the future.

Lieutenant Governor Hobby, a native of East Texas who had entered politics following a career in journalism as managing editor of the *Houston Post* and publisher of the *Beaumont Enterprise and Journal,* completed Ferguson's term. The ex-governor raged that he had not been given the same chance "of securing an impartial jury as is given to a 'nigger' crap shooter or a 'nigger' bootlegger," when in fact he had been the architect of his own ruin. His enemies rejoiced that he was as politically dead as a "salt mackeral," but they were wrong. The Ferguson smell would linger in Texas politics for another twenty years.

World War I

While the Ferguson "circus" occupied the center ring in Texas, an event of far greater importance took place nationally—the United States entered World War I against Germany. The war had begun in August 1914 over European issues that did not concern the United States, so most Texans, although interested in the conflict, were happy not be involved. They generally supported

President Wilson's policy of neutrality, but some became dissatisfied when his definitions of American rights set up potential conflict with Germany. Wilson insisted that Americans had a neutral right to travel in safety on unarmed ships belonging to nations at war, and when German submarines sank British and French ships with losses of American lives, he threatened to break diplomatic relations unless such attacks stopped. This position, which obviously could draw the United States into the war, drew criticism from Congressman Atkins Jefferson ("Jeff") McLemore of Austin, who introduced a resolution in early 1916 to keep Americans from traveling on ships of nations at war. Wilson persuaded the House to table McLemore's resolution, but eight Texans voted to support it, leading some newspapers to raise fears of undue German influence in the state. Germany made concessions to Wilson's demands until the end of 1916, then, deciding to make an effort to win the war at all costs, announced a return to unrestricted submarine warfare on February 1, 1917. Believing that this would bring the United States into the war, Germany began to sink American ships and sent the famous Zimmermann Note to the government of Mexico proposing an alliance against the United States. Mexico, the Germans said, could regain all the territory stolen by its northern neighbor, including Texas. Texans, for the most part outraged, supported the declaration of war on April 6, 1917.

Texas mobilized for war in 1917–1918 as never before. More than 988,000 men registered under national draft laws, and 197,389 either volunteered or were drafted, mostly into the army. Some 450 Texas women served in the Nurses Corps. More than five thousand men and one nurse died while in the service, most losing their lives in the great influenza epidemic of 1918. Texans on the home front were organized by the State Council of Defense and similar county councils at the local level. These councils sold Liberty Bonds—"Give Till It Hurts," they urged—and worked in numerous ways to support the troops' morale. Following the lead of national food administrator Herbert Hoover, Texans cooperated in conservation efforts by planting war gardens and having wheatless Mondays, meatless Tuesdays, and porkless Thursdays and Saturdays.

Because of its warm and dry climate, Texas became the location of numerous training camps. San Antonio, continuing its tradition as a military city, had an older base at Fort Sam Houston, the nation's largest new camp, Camp Travis, and three fields for the newest weapon in warfare, the airplane. Many Texans saw airplanes for the first time at Kelly Field, where pilots and mechanics trained. Brooks and Wise Fields trained instructors, aerial observers, and army balloonists. Across the state, in addition to older posts such as Fort Bliss at El Paso, army training bases included Camp Bowie at Fort Worth, Camp MacArthur at Waco, and Camp Logan at Houston. Air bases were also established at Ellington Field near Houston, Taliaferro Field near Fort Worth, Love Field in Dallas, Rich Field at Waco, and Call Field at Wichita Falls.

This enlarged military presence benefited the state through increased federal spending, but it also created tensions between soldiers and civilians that in at least one case had tragic results. While Camp Logan was under construction at Houston, soldiers in a black United States infantry regiment sent there to guard the site were angered at the discrimination they faced from streetcar operators, police, and the public in general. Black soldiers, most of whom were southerners, knew about segregation, but expected equal treatment due to their military service. Local whites believed that the soldiers could cause other blacks to get "out of their place." On August 23, 1917, Houston police arrested a black soldier and then fired at and arrested a black military policeman who went to inquire about the first serviceman. The men still in camp, upset by all sorts of rumors, decided to march on the police station to secure the MP's release, but as they were organizing, a soldier yelled that a white mob was approaching the camp. Grabbing rifles, the soldiers fired wildly toward the supposed mob and then, disobeying their white officers, moved toward downtown Houston under the leadership of a black sergeant, killing fifteen whites and wounding twelve others. Four of the soldiers also died, two killed accidentally by their own men. Finally, the sergeant in command told the soldiers to slip back to camp and killed himself. The army quickly moved the black unit out of Houston and eventually found 110 men guilty of mutiny and riot. Nineteen were hanged, and sixty-three received life sentences. The Houston Riot stood as yet another ironic comment on the state of race relations in a nation fighting for freedom and democracy in the world.

Texas did not escape the hysterical fear of all things German that accompanied wartime patriotism across the United States in 1917–1918. A special session of the state legislature, following the lead of Congress, passed espionage and sedition laws that made it a crime to criticize the U.S. government, its officials, the flag, or soldiers, or in any way to impede the war effort. Governor Hobby vetoed the appropriation for the German department at the University of Texas in 1918, and high schools dropped German from their course offerings. The University's regents fired a well known antiwar professor (doubtless making Ferguson wish that he had been able to use wartime patriotism in his fight with the intellectual elite). A town in Stonewall County called Brandenburg changed its name to Old Glory. Some of the county councils of defense turned into vigilante groups and intimidated or attacked Texans of German descent who were suspected of not fully supporting the war. This hysteria subsided slowly once the war ended with victory over Germany on November 11, 1918.

World War I, in conjunction with the Ferguson fiasco, gave renewed vigor to the prohibition movement. The drys had begun a comeback in 1914 by restructuring the state Anti-Saloon League and choosing a new leader, the Reverend Arthur James Barton, a gifted speaker and debater. Two years later, the prohibitionists backed U.S. Senator Charles A. Culberson for reelection against the challenge of the wet former governor Oscar B. Colquitt. Although many factors determined the outcome, including Colquitt's tendency to be pro-German and anti-Wilson, Culberson's victory in 1916 encouraged the drys. The war then gave new momentum to their cause by providing an argument that recruits at the new military bases had to be protected from the evils of liquor.

In early 1918 the legislature in Austin prohibited the sale of alcohol within ten miles of any base, a step that one wit protested would dry up 90 percent of the state. Legislators also made Texas one of the first states in the Union to approve national prohibition by ratifying the recently proposed Eighteenth Amendment. The amendment received ratifications from three-quarters of the states by January 1919 with the result that nationwide prohibition was scheduled to become effective in January 1920. Texas drys, however, would not wait a year "to make an end of old John Barleycorn." They pushed through yet another proposed dry amendment to the state constitution, and a referendum was scheduled for May 24, 1919.

Voters in this referendum also had to decide the fate of a woman suffrage amendment, a progressive reform that, like prohibition, had received encouragement during the war but faced even tougher opposition in Texas. Western states gave women the vote first, followed by some eastern states, but as late as 1917 no southern state had followed suit. The former Confederate states may simply have been more old-fashioned in their views of "womanhood," but they also were especially sensitive to matters of equal suffrage. Give women the vote, many southerners feared, and "Negro rule" will follow. Faced with such obstacles, the movement stirred slightly in 1903 with formation of the Texas Equal Suffrage Association, but soon went dormant and remained so until revived in 1913 by Mary Eleanor Brackenridge of San Antonio. Brackenridge, the sister of the wealthy businessman and philanthropist George W. Brackenridge, was seventy-five at the time, a veteran of the woman's club movement and the struggle for prohibition. She became involved in the suffrage issue in 1913, she said, because the public was ready, and events proved her correct. Drawing on their web of contacts within the club movement, suffragists by 1916 formed eighty local chapters and claimed 9,500 members for their statewide organization.

In 1915, the Texas Equal Suffrage Association came under the leadership of Minnie Fisher Cunningham, an intelligent and aggressive young Texan who pushed her cause ahead with great skill. Born near New Waverly in 1882, the daughter of a planter/politician, she studied at the University of Texas Medical Branch at Galveston and in 1901 became one of the first women pharmacists in the state. She worked one year in Huntsville where unequal pay, she said later, "made a suffragette out of me," and then married Beverly J. "Bill" Cunningham, a lawyer and local politician. After moving to Galveston in 1907, Cunningham joined the suffrage movement there, gained the recognition that made her president of the state organization in 1915, and opened a headquarters in Austin in 1917. U.S. entry into the war then gave her and other women leaders an opportunity to prove their patriotism by activities such as selling war bonds and supporting the Red Cross and at the same time point out that their nation was fighting to make the world safe for democracy while denying half its own population the right to vote. Persuaded by political pressure to support a reform that he had never before championed, Governor Hobby took the lead in having the state legislature pass an act in 1918 allowing women to vote in primary elections. This could be done without a constitutional amendment, and in a one-party state such as Texas, giving the vote in the Democratic primary amounted to full enfranchisement.

Some Texas women opposed equal suffrage. Pauline K. Wells, the wife of boss Jim Wells of Brownsville, led an association that distributed material contending that woman suffrage meant black domination and socialism. More women, however, wanted to vote, and they probably had little difficulty in choosing a gubernatorial candidate when they went to the polls for the first time in the 1918 Democratic primary. Hobby ran for reelection, and Ferguson, an inveterate opponent of woman suffrage, entered the contest against him after obtaining a court order to place his name on the ballot. Hobby enjoyed repeating Ferguson's reply to suffragettes in 1916: "Women's place is in the home." But the contest became vicious as Ferguson called Hobby a "political accident," and the incumbent's friends went over all the old charges about the ex-governor's finances. Wartime hysteria played a part. Some Hobby supporters even claimed that the loan that Ferguson revealed during the impeachment proceedings had come from the Kaiser himself. Farmer Jim fired back with charges that Hobby had put "full-blooded Germans" in positions of trust in Texas, only to have those charges backfire because the men in question were well-respected patriots.

Naturally, women across the state formed "Hobby Clubs" and helped reelect the governor with 461,479 votes to 217,012 for Ferguson. (These returns are especially impressive in light of the fact that only 177,355 men bothered to vote in the general election that fall.) Women voters in 1918 also had a chance not just to cast ballots for the first time but also to vote for a woman candidate, Annie Webb Blanton. Born in Houston in 1870, Blanton taught public school in Austin before graduating from the University of Texas in 1899 and serving on the English faculty of the college that is now the University of North Texas from 1901 to 1918. She became a strong believer in equal rights for women and in 1916 was elected president of the Texas State Teachers Association. Her role there led the suffragists to ask her to run for state superintendent of public instruction in 1918. Supporters of the incumbent, Walter F. Doughty, called Blanton an atheist and a tool of others, but she fired back with charges that he had a close relationship with Ferguson and the brewers. Victorious by a large margin, she won easily in the fall and became the first woman to hold statewide office in Texas.

In January 1919, Governor Hobby recommended a constitutional amendment to enfranchise women in all elections, but unfortunately he also proposed that aliens not be allowed to vote until they had completed the naturalization process. At this time, "first paper" aliens who had begun the process were fully enfranchised. The legislature paired the issues so that voters could not give women the vote unless they disfranchised aliens. And, to make matters worse, while women could not vote in the referendum, aliens could. The referendum, which included the prohibition amendment as well, took place on May 24, 1919. Minnie Fisher Cunningham and Jane Yelvington McCallum of Austin, the state manager of press and publicity, led the campaign, but

Annie Webb Blanton (1870–1945). This photo shows Blanton in 1918, the year she became the first woman to win statewide office in Texas. Credit: Center for American History, UT-Austin.

while prohibition won by about 25,000 votes, woman suffrage lost by a nearly equal margin, primarily because of strong opposition in South Texas. Antisuffragists naturally claimed that the result was a mandate for their view, but suffragists insisted that the issue of alien disfranchisement determined the outcome. Fortunately for the latter, the U.S. Congress submitted a constitutional amendment enfranchising women to the states in June 1919. Hobby called the legislature into special session immediately, and Texas became the ninth state overall, the first in the South, to ratify the Nineteenth Amendment. The legislature also adopted an act written by Senator W. Luther Dean of Huntsville providing for the enforcement of prohibition beginning in October 1919. Under the Dean Law, the manufacture or sale of any beverage having 1 percent or more alcoholic content was a felony punishable by one to five years in prison.

Close of the Progressive Era

Even though Texas Progressives pushed on in 1919–1920 to achieve prohibition and woman suffrage, other developments during those years indicated that the spirit of reform could not last much longer. For one thing, the "menace of Bolshevism" associated with the Russian Revolution allowed conservatives to identify social problems and reformers with "Reds" who threatened the American way of life. When workers, facing higher prices without matching wage increases and rising unemployment, sought to organize and bargain collectively, they were considered part of the radical menace. Texas newspapers denounced unions, and businessmen formed "Open Shop Associations" that refused to hire union workers. A dockworkers' strike at Galveston turned violent, confirming popular suspicions and leading Governor Hobby to declare martial law in June 1920. Race relations, although never a focus of Progressivism, also contributed to the reaction. Some returning black servicemen questioned segregation, leading whites to say that they had been infected by Bolshevism. A major race riot in Longview in July 1919 increased tensions. Sparked by an article in a Chicago newspaper about a relationship between a black man from Longview and a white woman from Kilgore that had led to the man's murder by a mob, the riot resulted in one death and the burning of the homes of blacks before Governor Hobby sent in national guardsmen to end it. When an official of the National Association for the Advancement of Colored People visited Austin in August, a group of men beat him unconscious on the street near the Driskill Hotel. The national office protested, to which the governor replied: "Your organization can contribute more to the advancement of both races by keeping your representatives and their propaganda out of this state than in any other way."

Conditions seemed ripe for a conservative reaction, and former Senator Joe Bailey rose to lead it. In 1919, Bailey denounced the "growing tendency to regulate everything by law" and early the following year announced as a candidate for governor. He promised to "lead Texas back into the straight and narrow path of the time-honored principles of the old Bailey Democracy" and away from national prohibition, woman suffrage, socialism, monopoly, and class legislation. As the campaign went on, Bailey attacked labor unions and added to his reputation as the foremost race-baiter among Texas politicians of that age. "I have no prejudice against the negro, mind you," he told one audience. "I like the negro in his place. But the marriage altar of white people is not his place. It's all right if Massachusetts wants to permit negroes to intermarry—that is a matter of taste. No, not altogether matter of taste either. It's partly a matter of smell."

Three candidates opposed Bailey in the Democratic primary. All were Wilsonian Progressives, but one stood out as a model of personal probity. Pat Neff, a Waco lawyer and former Texas legislator, was a devoutly religious prohibitionist who proudly accepted a boast by one of his friends that he had "never shot a gun, baited a fish hook, used tobacco in any form, nor drunk anything stronger than Brazos water." Admitting to such a past probably would doom any candidate for office in Texas before or since 1920—as one critic said, even Christ made wine and fished—but in this particular case Neff benefited from the personal contrast with Bailey. Neff also showed imagination by campaigning from an automobile, the first Texas politician to do so, and by advocating a huge highway building program, a system of state parks, and water conservation policies. With three candidates splitting the progressive vote, Bailey ran first in the primary but did not get a majority. Neff, who trailed by fewer than three thousand votes, ran second and then swamped Bailey with 59 percent of the vote in the runoff.

Bailey's failure marked a final defeat for old-style Texas conservatism. In spite of all the frustrations and tensions upsetting the state in 1920, a sizable majority of voters refused to reject the reforms of the Progressive Era or return to an almost totally negative view of the role of the state and national governments. On the other hand, Progressivism had begun to decline in intensity, and Texans still faced an array of economic and social problems. Thousands upon thousands of farmers continued to live in destructive poverty as tenants and sharecroppers. Giant corporations still wielded monopoly power because antitrust and regulatory laws had always aimed more at "foreign" businesses than at the abuses of bigness in and of themselves. Laws protecting women and children in industry either went unenforced or were repealed. The doctrine of white supremacy ruled race relations, and in South Texas Anglo bosses exploited Texans of Mexican descent politically and economically. Progressivism was not dead in 1920, but most Texans, rather than worry about their state's problems, wanted a rest from reform and an opportunity to enjoy the business prosperity of the new decade.

Chapter 14

THE "PROSPERITY DECADE" AND THE GREAT DEPRESSION, 1921–1941

The words *prosperity decade* summarize the United States during the 1920s. Across the nation, basic economic activities such as residential and commercial construction boomed, and new industries—the manufacture of automobiles, radios, and synthetics, for example—grew with unimaginable speed. Businessmen and politicians called the twenties a "New Era" and spoke confidently of ending poverty in America, all the while paying little attention to weaknesses in agriculture and several other key industries and ignoring the overconcentration of income and wealth in the hands of a relatively few people. In 1929, it all came crashing down in the worst financial panic and economic depression in the history of the United States. Republican President Herbert Hoover, the chief architect of the "New Era," fell with the economy, and Americans turned in 1932 to Democrat Franklin D. Roosevelt and his promise of a "New Deal." Under Roosevelt's leadership during the thirties the United States survived but did not escape the Great Depression. Full economic recovery came only with World War II.

Texas experienced these years in generally the same way as the rest of the nation, of course, but differed in important details. For example, rather than growth in manufacturing, the production of oil, an extractive industry, joined cotton and cattle as the keys to prosperity in Texas. Also, one of the underlying weaknesses of the "New Era"—a struggling agricultural sector—affected many Texans. The farm tenancy rate, continuing its steady rise since the 1880s, reached 61 percent by 1930. When financial panic and depression hit, many Texans barely recognized the difference. As the song remembers it, "They say the stock market fell, but we were so poor that we couldn't tell." Most welcomed New Deal programs that provided relief and hope; still, they saw only limited economic improvement during the thirties.

Population growth mirrored economic trends during these years, showing a large upsurge in the twenties and a sizable slowdown in the thirties. Totals rose from 4,663,228 in 1920 to 5,824,718 in 1930, an increase of more than one million during a decade for the first time in the state's history. Then, not even the appeal of "Gone to Texas" could withstand the deadening effects of the Great Depression. From 1930 to 1940 the state added only 590,109 residents, the smallest numerical increase in any ten-year period since the 1860s, and its total population in 1940 (6,414,824) marked a decline of one spot, from fifth to sixth, among the most populous states in the nation.

Urbanization followed exactly the same pattern. The proportion of Texans living in urban areas of 2,500 or more residents rose sharply from 32 percent in 1920 to 41 percent ten years later. Houston became the state's largest city with a population of 292,352, followed by Dallas (260,475), San Antonio (231,453), and Fort Worth (163,447). Then, depression, which made city jobs scarce and put a premium on growing food, slowed urbanization to a crawl. During the next ten years, the urban population increased at less than half the rate of the twenties, reaching only 45 percent of the total by 1940. Texas thus remained a more rural than urban state at the close of the Great Depression.

As in every decade since the 1870s, the number of black Texans continued during these years to increase at a slower pace than whites. A good many African Americans left the state in the 1920s, and overall their population grew only 25 percent between 1920 and 1940 (741,694 to 924,391) compared to a 38 percent expansion of the total. By 1940 blacks represented just 14 percent of all Texans. The number of Texans of Mexican descent reached almost 684,000 in 1930, but then declined markedly during the Great Depression, and the total in 1940 stood at about 484,000. Some of the approximately 250,000 who moved to Mexico did so under the pressure of economic hard times, but many left because they were denied access to government relief programs or fell victim to an intense federal repatriation program. The census of 1940 may have undercounted Texans of Mexican descent, but almost certainly a significant decrease occurred.

Overall, then, when Texans celebrated the centennial of their state's birth in 1936 they badly needed something positive in their lives. The depression threatened to wipe out all the progress of the previous decade, stem the usual influx of immigrants, and leave their state nearly as rural, agricultural, and poor as it had been in 1920. Small wonder that they organized commemorative events statewide and a central exposition at Fair Park in Dallas and harkened back to the triumph of 1836 with so much enthusiasm.

The Prosperity (for Some) Decade

Texas's role in the economic boom of the 1920s depended heavily on expansion of the oil industry. Following the Spindletop strike in 1901, the production of oil and gas increased at first in southeast Texas, then moved after 1910 into the north-central part of the state. Major discoveries at Electra (1911), Ranger (1917), Desdemona (1918), Burkburnett (1918), and Breckenridge (1919) produced tens of millions of barrels in a few years and created boom towns to match those of the fabled gold rush era. Ranger's population, for example, rose within one year from 1,000 to 30,000, mostly male oil-field workers who were somewhat less than refined in their social pursuits. Gambling houses and brothels flourished, and killings occurred regularly. Even with such growth and excitement, the oil industry remained relatively small in 1920. Texas had 8,749 wells employing 13,599 wage earners and producing oil and gas valued at $143 million at the beginning of that year, but Oklahoma had 44,735 wells, 21,180 workers, and nearly $250 million in products. This situation was about to change, however, thanks particularly to discoveries in the Panhandle and West Texas.

In the early twenties, drilling began in earnest in a 115-mile-long producing zone centering on Carson, Potter, Hutchinson, and Moore Counties in the Panhandle. In 1927 production in that area peaked at nearly 40 million barrels. Amarillo in Potter County grew from fewer than 16,000 residents in 1920 to more than 52,000 in seven years, but for spectacular growth and sheer spectacle as well, the town of Borger in Hutchinson County outdid them all. Founded in 1926 by Asa P. Borger, a Missouri-born promoter, the 240-acre town site, purchased for $12,000, sold out in six months for more than a million dollars. An estimated twenty thousand men and women, attracted by advertisements playing on the riches of "black gold," arrived within ninety days, making "Booger Town" a haven for criminals and tricksters as well as honest working people. Eventually violence became so prevalent that, following the murder of a district attorney in 1929, the governor declared martial law and sent in Texas Rangers to clean up the town. Law and order returned, but not before the founding father, "Ace" Borger, was shot to death in 1934.

Midway through the decade, oil production began in the Permian Basin region of West Texas. Centering on Reagan, Upton, Crane, Midland, and Ector Counties, the basin produced oil that created growth in the entire region, most notably in Midland and Odessa. Some of the area's ranchers and farmers profited from selling leases to the point that they bought a "town house" in addition to their original homestead. Development of the Permian Basin also made the University of Texas and Texas A&M University rich. The two million acres of land donated to the Permanent University Fund (PUF) in the nineteenth century had generated little income during the years since—grazing leases earned $40,000 in 1900, for example—but then in 1923 drillers brought in the Santa Rita well on university lands in Reagan County. Other discoveries followed so that by 1925 the PUF was growing at a rate of $2,000 per day. In 1931 the legislature arranged a division of the fund, with the University of Texas receiving two-thirds of the income and A&M receiving one-third. By 1990 the PUF amounted to more than $3.5 billion and generated more than $250 million a year to support two great universities.

In 1928 Texas for the first time led all other states in oil production with 256,888,000 barrels, nearly 20 percent of the total for the entire world. Actual exploration and production did not require huge numbers of workers, but the broader impact of the industry can hardly be exaggerated. Moving oil required the building of thousands of miles of pipelines, providing work for men and demand for steel. Refineries were constructed and operated, particularly in cities and towns along the crescent-shaped border from El Paso to Beaumont. Between 1919 and 1928, the number of Texas refineries more than doubled, and their capacity increased from 277,200 barrels per day to 750,000. Income generated by the oil and gas industry wound up in Texas banks and insurance companies, financed new office buildings, and paid for goods sold in stores. The industry also contributed to the state as a main source of tax revenue, paying more than $1 million on the value of production in 1919 and $5.9 million in 1929.

No other industry or business approached oil and gas in importance to the 1920s boom, but highway construction and manufacturing promoted economic growth as well. The federal government began in 1921 to offer matching funds for road-building efforts, the money going at first to counties. In 1923, however, the state imposed a gasoline tax of one cent per gallon to raise money for roads, and soon the Texas Highway Department took responsibility for building and maintaining a state system. At the end of the decade, Texas had 18,728 miles of main highways, 9,271 miles of which were hard-surfaced. Manufacturing in the state continued to concentrate on processing the products of forests, farms, and ranches. Lumber mills turned out paper and newsprint; meatpacking plants processed hogs and cattle. Although the number of manufacturing establishments of this sort did not increase during the decade, they employed 26 percent more workers in 1929 than 1919, and the value added to their products by the manufacturing process increased 56 percent over that decade. Texas was hardly an industrial giant as the twenties came to a close, but gains in transportation and manufacturing during the decade supplemented the boom fueled by oil.

Agriculture presented something of an anomaly during the twenties, expanding production to record levels but experiencing hard times as well. Between 1920 and 1930, the number of farms rose 14 percent, acreage planted in cotton increased from 11.5 million to 16.8 million acres, and cotton production grew from 2.9 million to 3.8 million bales. Most of this increase took place on the southern High Plains around Lubbock, an area turned from cattle pastures into productive farmland by irrigation water from the giant Ogallala Aquifer. Once wells began to pump from the aquifer, farmers could use machinery—tractors with gang plows, two-row planters and cultivators, and mechanical pickers and harvesters—to produce huge crops of cotton, wheat, and sorghum. The boll weevil, a scourge to cotton farmers in other parts of the state, could not survive the cold High Plains winters. Cotton production in the region jumped amazingly from 50,588 bales in 1918 to 1.1 million in 1926. An important new development came to South Texas, too, in the form of citrus fruit trees. Once their potential was discovered in the early twenties, investors rushed in, and by 1925 the Lower Río Grande Valley had 750,000 fruit trees.

Agricultural expansion obviously benefited some Texas farmers during the twenties, particularly new arrivals on the High Plains, but relatively few enjoyed notable prosperity. Prices for crops fell sharply in 1920–1921, thanks to surpluses after the war, and struggled to recover for the remainder of the decade. Cotton, for example, sold for forty-two cents a pound in April 1920 but dropped to less than ten cents by March 1921 and hovered between ten and twenty cents for the rest of the decade. Between 1920 and 1930, the total value of farm lands and buildings actually decreased from $3.7 to $3.6 million (without significant deflation as a cause), and the farm tenancy rate, which had stabilized at an unhealthily high 53 percent in 1910 and in 1920 rose to 61 percent. Tenants who managed to rent sizable acreage made money, but the majority had to work relatively small farms and did not prosper. "It is impossible," wrote an agricultural expert in 1924, "to build a prosperous and progressive rural civilization with more than half the farmers cultivating the land on some basis of cash or share tenancy." The economic boom of the 1920s left a majority of Texas farmers—and that was still most Texans—behind.

African American and Mexican American Texans generally participated even less than whites in the expanding economy. Blacks moved to towns and cities in increasing numbers, but most found work only in relatively low-paying jobs such as janitors and day laborers. An urban middle class of professionals and businessmen developed, but it remained small. Among the state's more than 800,000 blacks in 1930, only 205 were doctors, 99 were dentists, and 20 practiced law. There were fewer than two thousand black-owned retail establishments and only four banks. Most blacks continued to live in rural areas and farm for a living, more than 70 percent of them throughout the decade as tenants. Opportunities for blacks to advance through education were limited by the segregated, underfunded public schools they attended. Mexican Americans, depending on the location of their homes, experienced a variety of changes in their work lives, none of which meant prosperity. Some of those who lived in South Texas counties such as Kenedy and Brooks that were suited only to stock raising managed to hold on to their land and continued to ranch as they had for years. Poorer Mexicans in those counties still earned a living as ranch hands. However, in the Lower Río Grande Valley, where commercial farms owned by Anglo newcomers had largely replaced cattle ranches, people of Mexican descent often had to work as day laborers. Farther north, in Central Texas, they depended on tenant farming, primarily as sharecroppers. Also, a new mode of support identified particularly with Mexican Americans—migratory labor—developed during the twenties. Every year entire families followed the cotton harvest from South Texas northward, ending in the Panhandle before returning south for the winter. Many of these migrant families used cities such as San Antonio and El Paso as their home bases. There they joined permanent residents, who generally worked as day laborers, in segregated barrios noted for poverty, malnutrition, and disease. As was the case among African Americans, Mexican Americans had only a small middle class of proprietors, managers, and professionals in the cities. In a few communities, Mexican children attended classes with Anglos, but local officials generally placed them in separate buildings or in separate classes within Anglo schools, a form of segregation that usually meant inadequate facilities and poorly prepared teachers. The 1920s truly did not bring prosperity or opportunity to all Texans.

Social Tension and the Ku Klux Klan

During the decade or so following World War I, change swept over the social lives of Texans, striking some as modern and exciting, while bewildering and angering others. Joseph Weldon Bailey sounded a warning in 1920, complaining that "the stately old dances have been supplanted by the fox-trot and the bunny hug" and expressing displeasure over songs such as "I Love My Wife, But Oh You Kid." Music and dance only grew more "risque," however, with the rising popularity of jazz and the advent of the Charleston and Black Bottom. Clothing styles became less modest. "Flappers," for example, wore short skirts and, to make matters worse, cut their hair short, used makeup, smoked, and drank. Young men and women attended lewd movies and took late-night automobile rides together. Sexual promiscuity increased, or at least critics were certain that it did.

Only a minority of Texans, of course, had the time and money to be fully "modern," and few fit the stereotypes of "flappers" or college boys in racoon coats. However, most knew of these extreme cultural changes and had some experience with the things that tore down the traditional and brought in the new. Increasing urbanization put more people together in limited areas, allowing the rise of a popular culture impossible to create when rural isolation was the rule. The automobile provided the easy and rapid means for Texans to reach and move about in cities and towns and enjoy what they had to offer. Radios made the newest music widely available, advertised the latest fashions, and took the city's culture to rural areas. Motion pictures allowed Texans to see how the sophisticated world outside dressed and behaved. They loved the movies, seeing on the average twenty a year by 1920, and undoubtedly felt the influence of lifestyles depicted on the screen.

Changes in popular culture during the twenties were accompanied by new trends in more basic social institutions such as the family. For one thing, although birth control did not gain wide acceptance until the Great Depression, the size of families decreased dramatically, from 4.6 persons in 1920 to 3.5 in 1930. Married women worked outside the home in ever-increasing numbers. The state's divorce rate more than doubled between 1916 and 1929. All these trends were most pronounced in urban areas, and added to the concerns of traditionalists about the decline of society.

In the eyes of a good many white Texans, the lifestyles of blacks and Mexican Americans in the cities also constituted a threat to proper social order. Clubs in the black districts of Houston and Dallas, for example, offered music and dancing, at times to racially mixed customers. Black musicians, writers, and poets traveled across the state and sold their works. Some black Texans achieved national recognition for their contributions to cultural movements. For example, Melvin B. Tolson of Wiley College in Marshall became known as Texas's poet of the Harlem Renaissance. Texans of Mexican descent became numerous enough in the cities of South Texas to form lasting organizations aimed at cultural unity and equal rights. By 1930, for example, San Antonio was home to 33,146 natives of Mexico and a great many more Tejanos. In 1929, a meeting in Corpus Christi created the League of United Latin American Citizens (LULAC), an organization destined to play a major role in the story of Mexicans in Texas. Founded by business and professional people, LULAC worked to integrate Mexican Americans as "the best, purest, and most perfect type of true and loyal citizen[s] of the United States of America." At the same time, LULAC opposed any form of discrimination "on account of race, religion, or social position as being contrary to the true spirit of Democracy, our Constitution and Laws."

Texans were on the periphery of several other developments that created social tension in the twenties, particularly the fear of "Reds" and the anti-evolution crusade. The Red Scare of 1919–1920 did not hit Texas especially hard, largely because the state had relatively few of the unionized workers and foreign-born radicals that so frightened Americans elsewhere in the nation. Antiradicalism, however, had an underlying appeal that never disappeared. The anti-evolution movement rose in the 1920s for all the reasons that made it so strong in Tennessee and other southern states. Above all, fundamentalist Christians insisted that Darwinism contradicted Genesis and thereby undermined morality. Proposals to prohibit the teaching of evolution in the state's public schools came up in every meeting of the legislature from 1923 to 1929, but no law ever passed.

The final straw, it seems, for Texans made fearful and angry by social change was a decline of law and order. Violence in oil-field boom towns such as Ranger and Borger forced the imposition of martial law, causing decent folk to wonder what had gone wrong with their state. And then there was prohibition, surely one of the greatest incentives to lawbreaking in the history of the United States. Thousands of Texans at all levels of society—from the elite in their country clubs to the poorest white tenant farmers and blacks in urban ghettos—simply would not obey the law against the production, sale, and consumption of alcoholic beverages. Their demand for liquor provided the impetus for illegal distilleries at home and smuggling from Mexico. Bootleggers made fortunes in the underground alcohol industry and, ironically, teamed with prohibitionists to see that the state did not legalize liquor again. Although federal enforcement authorities were notoriously understaffed, making it relatively easy to laugh at the law, 22 percent of all arrests in Texas from 1925 to 1931 were for violations of prohibition. No wonder the public had a perception of widespread lawlessness abroad in the state, particularly in connection with alcohol.

Discontent over the breakdown of traditional ways in everything from popular culture to law enforcement led many Texans in the early twenties to join the Ku Klux Klan and make that organization a potent factor in the state's cultural and political life. A revival of the KKK that practiced intimidation and terror against freedmen during Reconstruction, the new secret order of hooded "knights" was created in a ceremony on Stone Mountain, Georgia, in 1915. The born-again Klan grew slowly until 1920 when William J. Simmons, the one-time Methodist minister who revived it, formed a partnership with publicist Edward Y. Clarke to promote the organization's growth. Clarke advised field organizers called "kleagles" to begin membership drives by contacting leading citizens in each community and then working down through the middle class to what might be called the "lower orders." That approach assured prestige at the outset and a cross-section of society at the end. Members had to be white, Protestant, and native-born—and have the ten dollar initiation fee, four of which went to the kleagle. The Klan appealed to them on the basis of law and order, 100 percent American patriotism, antiradicalism, anti-Catholicism, anti-Semitism, and white supremacy. By the end of 1922, the Klan had 700,000 members nationwide.

The KKK arrived in Texas in September 1920 when a kleagle came to Houston and recruited one hundred men into the state's first local chapter. "The initial roster represented literally a glossary of Houston's *Who's Who,*" wrote one observer. "The charter members were silk-stocking men from the banks, business houses, and professions." Simmons and Clarke joined the successful kleagle for an installation ceremony, which was held in conjunction with the annual reunion of the United Confederate Veterans. When the veterans held their parade through downtown Houston on October 8, they were accompanied by a line of marchers and horsemen in Klan regalia. That night an initiation ceremony replete with flaming crosses was held in suburban Bellaire, completing the creation of "Sam Houston Klan No. 1." (Poor Sam! Although he owned slaves and flirted with Know-Nothingism during the 1850s, his name should never have been associated with such bigotry.)

From its Houston beginnings, the Klan spread rapidly across the state, even forming chapters in such heavily Catholic towns as Brownsville, Edinburg, and McAllen. In January 1922, when membership reached more than 75,000, Texas was organized as a realm of the "Invisible Empire" under its own grand dragon, A. D. Ellis, an Episcopal priest from Beaumont. That same year women, who had begun to create their own local chapters, obtained a Texas charter as the Women of the Invisible Empire of America. In June 1923, 1,500 masked and robed klanswomen held a parade through Fort Worth. Eventually male membership alone stood at approximately 150,000.

The appeal of Klan ideology accounted in part for its rapid growth in Texas, but its success also depended on economic relationships and other more personal considerations. Klansmen and women were told to practice "Vocational Klanishness," meaning that they were to patronize each other in preference to nonmembers. Merchants and professionals joined for fear of a boycott or to increase their trade. As a writer for the *El Paso Times* put it, up-and-coming salesmen, realtors, bankers, and contractors "joined the Klan for the greater glory of Protestantism and Better Business." Protestant ministers generally supported the Klan because it promised to uphold Christian morality and help guard against the menace of Catholicism. In some cases, criminals such as bootleggers, the very antithesis of law and order, sought protection under Klan robes. One woman professed shock upon learning the identities of some of the Klansmen who had sworn to protect the purity of women because, she said, "I found on reliable authority that when womanhood was in their presence, it had all it could do to protect itself." Indeed, as one historian has written, "the white sheets covered some strange bedfellows."

Although much of the Texas Klan's terror—whipping, tarring and feathering, maiming, and murder—had to do with maintaining white supremacy, the focus was on crime and immorality rather than on blacks as such. For example, whipping victims in 1921 included a Houston merchant accused of bothering high school girls, a Beaumont doctor who supposedly performed abortions, a Bay City banker charged with adultery, and two Goose Creek oilfield workers described as undesirable citizens. Blatantly racist incidents also occurred, however, such as the castration of a black dentist in Houston because he allegedly associated with a white woman. In May 1922 alone, nine blacks were killed by unmasked mobs of white men. The Klan always denied involvement in murderous terrorism, but it seems certain that Klansmen, often acting without officials present, usually were responsible. Proof is unavailable, in large measure because the law enforcement officials who should have investigated and prosecuted such criminal acts often belonged to the Klan themselves. According to a Dallas newspaperman, "the Klan's control of the police force was the main influence in the city because it scared the people." Similar circumstances existed in Austin, Waco, Houston, and Fort Worth. If lawmen did try to stop the Klan, grand juries often refused to indict the accused. For example, when the sheriff of McLennan County attempted in October 1921 to break up a parade of Klansmen in Lorena and an ensuing riot left one man dead and several others, including the sheriff, wounded, the grand jury totally condemned his actions.

Within a year of its appearance some Texans began to resist the Klan. Blacks, Catholics, and Jews had disliked it from the start, of course, but only white native-born Protestants, people with the same qualifications as the Klansmen, could mount an effective opposition. Those who opposed secret societies and terror tactics viewed the Klan itself as a sower of social discord, and thought that the organization gave Texas a bad name. "I am 75 years old," wrote one former legislator in 1921, "but I stand ready to take up my shotgun and go out in defense of civilized and lawful government. The time has come for us to speak out as to whether we favor a visible government or an invisible government." The Texas Chamber of Commerce condemned the Klan as did the Texas Bar Association. A few leading newspapers, especially the *Houston Chronicle, El Paso Times,* and *Dallas Morning News,* crusaded against it as well. The *Morning News* called the Klan's claim that it guarded the community's social and moral welfare a "slander on Dallas," and ran a cartoon showing "Father Texas" with a black eye created by tar and feathers. The paper lost advertising and circulation, but continued the attack.

In November 1922, Hiram Wesley Evans, a dentist from Dallas who had begun as cyclops of the local chapter and quickly worked his way up the Klan's chain of command, was elected Imperial Wizard, or national leader, of the entire organization. Evans sought to change the Klan's image by placing strict controls on terror by members of local chapters and emphasizing instead the election of Klan candidates to state and local offices. Recognizing the special futility of third-party action in a one-party state, he sought to back friendly candidates in the Democratic primary. This approach made the Klan a serious threat to take over the government of Texas in the early twenties.

Business Progressivism and the Klan in Politics

Pat Neff was the first of several 1920s governors in Texas and across the South who are best called "business progressives." They were progressive in their willingness to support administrative reorganization, better roads, and improvements in education, but they favored business on matters of labor-management relations, the protection of women and children in industry, and worker's compensation. Such leaders emphasized efficiency and order but had little concern for the problems of tenant farmers or ethnic minorities.

Disfranchisement provides a good example of just how limited business progressives were when it came to minority rights. In 1923, Neff signed an act putting the force of law behind the white primary, a method (along with the poll tax) of disfranchising most blacks and many Mexicans that had been in use since the turn of the century. Dr. Lawrence A. Nixon, a member of the El Paso chapter of the NAACP, challenged the constitutionality of this act, and the United States Supreme Court ruled in *Nixon v. Herndon* (1927) that it violated the equal protection clause of the Fourteenth Amendment. Unfazed, the legislature passed an act, this time with the approval of Dan Moody, another business progressive governor, allowing the executive committee of each party to decide who could vote in its primaries. Nixon challenged this law as well, and won again when the court ruled in 1932 *(Nixon v. Condon)* that state law could not give party executive committees the power to exclude blacks. At that point, the Democratic Party, with a supporting opinion from one of the state's most progressive politicians, Attorney General James V. Allred, simply acted on its own to prevent blacks from voting in its primary. In *Grovey v. Townsend* (1935), the Supreme Court upheld this practice on the grounds that the party was a private organization not subject to the Fourteenth Amendment's limitations on state action. Thus, even the most progressive Texas politicians of this era resorted to any legal subterfuge necessary to disfranchise blacks and Mexicans.

Unfortunately for Governor Neff, the state legislature had little interest in even his limited brand of progressivism and obstructed his program at every turn. When he called in 1921 for stricter law enforcement, consolidation of several government agencies, improvements in rural schools, water conservation, and better public health programs, virtually nothing happened. The legislature, resenting his high moral tone and thinking that the state had too many laws already, passed only two hundred of more than one thousand bills introduced and had to meet in two special sessions before agreeing to an appropriation measure. One of its provisions cut the salaries of faculty at the state's colleges and universities by 20 percent of the amount over $2,000.

Governor Neff's critics began in 1921 to plan a challenge in the next year's Democratic primary. Their leading contender, a farmer and labor leader from

Bonham named Fred S. Rogers, attacked the governor's record in dealing with the legislature, but voters seemed to pay little attention. Rogers then added the more sensational charge that Neff sympathized with the Ku Klux Klan, an accusation that may have had some basis in truth. The governor often condemned lawlessness, but he never attacked the Klan by name. When the publisher of the *Houston Chronicle* urged him to issue a "ringing message . . . denouncing that order or any other order which went out under cover of darkness and behind masks to take the law in its own hands," he received a cryptic reply assuring him that "[y]ou and I are working to the same end. We may travel at times, very different roads, but the goal, I am sure, is the same." Perhaps Neff saw the Klan as it saw itself—as a bulwark for law and order. In any case, the issue did not hurt him in the 1922 primary. He never mentioned Rogers by name and defeated all of his opponents combined by about fifty thousand votes. The general election was, as usual, no contest.

Texans did have one exciting election in 1922, however: the choice of a new United States Senator. Charles A. Culberson, the incumbent since 1899, announced for reelection in spite of poor health and chronic alcoholism. Culberson had not visited Texas in the past ten years, having won reelection in 1916 without setting foot in the state. He was challenged by none other than "Farmer Jim" Ferguson, whose impeachment conviction did not extend to federal offices, and Earle B. Mayfield, a native of East Texas with ten years of service on the Railroad Commission. The latter admitted to membership in the Ku Klux Klan and ran with the backing of the Invisible Empire, but that issue played a minor role at first. Culberson did not campaign, of course, and Ferguson sought as always to win the votes of poor tenants and working people. Mayfield talked mostly about the regulation of freight rates by the Railroad Commission. Unified Klan backing gave Mayfield a large plurality on July 22, 1922, but Ferguson finished second, some 30,000 votes behind, and forced a runoff. Texans then had to choose an impeached and convicted former governor or a Klansman for their next United States senator.

During the runoff campaign, Mayfield drew endorsements from many prohibitionists and progressives largely because they despised Ferguson. Senator Morris Sheppard supported him as did former Governor Hobby; Jessie Daniel Ames, president of the League of Women Voters; and Lily Joseph, head of the Federation of Women's Clubs. Ferguson made the Klan the central issue in his attack on Mayfield, asking Texans if they wanted a senator by order of "the imperial palace in Georgia" or "the sovereign voice of the people of Texas." Personal vituperation followed as Mayfield called Ferguson a "perjurer," and Ferguson described his opponent as a "hypocritical wet pro." When it was all over, Mayfield prevailed by a vote of 317,591 to 265,233. Perhaps a candidate without Ferguson's past would have won—the defeat of Klan-backed candidates for lieutenant governor and other positions suggests this—but Mayfield's victory, coupled with victories by Klansmen in local elections, allowed the Invisible Empire to claim Texas as its banner state politically in 1922 and eagerly anticipate 1924.

Relations between Governor Neff and the legislature did not improve appreciably during his second term. He asked in vain for a state board of education, larger appropriations for public schools, a nine-month school year, and a fixed amount of support for colleges and universities in order to avoid the "biennial political wrangling for funds." The governor also got nowhere with his suggestion that a convention write a new state constitution to replace the 1876 document that had been turned into a piece of "patch-work" by thirty-eight amendments. One of his few victories came when the legislature created a State Parks Board in 1923 and authorized it to solicit donations of land for parks, a step made necessary by the fact that the state had long since given away all its public lands. Eventually, Texas built a system of more than fifty parks, the first fittingly enough being Mother Neff State Park in Coryell County. The governor also advanced higher education in West Texas by signing a measure in 1923 that created Texas Technological College in Lubbock.

Neff's second administration also brought some legislative successes engineered largely by the Women's Joint Legislative Council, an organization created in 1922 by a coalition of women's groups. Condescendingly called the "Petticoat Lobby" by some politicians, the Council supported measures intended to improve public education and welfare. In 1923–1925, aided by Representative Edith Wilmans, a Dallas lawyer and the first of four women to serve in the state legislature during the decade, the lobby successfully supported a six-point program, including an emergency appropriation for public schools and matching funds for a federal maternal- and child-hygiene program. This "audacious piece of Bolshevism," in the words of one old-time lawmaker, was in fact only one of several reflections of the increasing political importance of women following their enfranchisement. Governor Neff, for example, had recognized women's new political role in 1921 by appointing at least one to all state boards, including the boards of regents at colleges and universities.

Neff retired after the traditional two terms, eventually to become president of Baylor University, and the Klan sought to follow up its victory in the 1922 senatorial race by electing the state's next governor. Its chances looked good, especially since Klansmen now numbered as many as 170,000 and controlled the Texas delegation to the Democratic national convention in 1924. Early in 1924, the Klan held a statewide elimination vote to choose a candidate and settled on District Judge Felix D. Robertson of Dallas. The son and grandson of Confederate generals, Robertson had served in World War I before beginning a career in public life. He promised to prevent tax increases and at the same time improve schools and enforce the laws. Also, he introduced his faith and a hint of the Klan directly into the race, saying that "America and Texas have forgotten God" and can stop their drift into ruin only by returning to "the rugged cross of Christianity." Robertson appeared on his way to victory over several Democratic opponents, but in June, less than two months before the primary, a new challenger named Ferguson appeared. "Farmer Jim" had hoped to run, but in June when the Texas Supreme Court upheld the ban resulting from his impeachment conviction, he entered his wife in the contest. The primary turned into a fight between Robertson's Klan hood and Mrs. Ferguson's womanly bonnet.

Forty-nine-year-old Miriam A. Ferguson, "Farmer Jim's" wife, had shown no previous interest in politics, preferring to remain in the background and raise the couple's two daughters, and at first most political pundits laughed at the idea of "Ma" as governor. But they underestimated the skill of "Pa," as he soon came to be called, and rising discontent with the Klan. Mrs. Ferguson played a minor role in the campaign, opening rallies with an appeal to Texas women to help her clear her husband's name and otherwise admitting that she had no political expertise and simply trusted that "my Redeemer [will] guide my footsteps in the path of righteousness for the good of our people and the good of our State." "Pa" then took over and attacked Robertson as the "Klan Klandidate" a tool of the "Grand Gizzard" who stood for hooded terrorism. When asked if "Ma" would be only a figurehead, he came up with the slogan "Two Governors for the Price of One." Meanwhile, several other candidates aimed their fire at the Klan and each other, allowing the Fergusons to escape relatively unscathed.

On July 26, 1924, more voters than ever before in Texas history went to the polls, giving Robertson an easy plurality with 193,508 votes. "Ma," however, came in second with 146,424 votes, and then the real fight began in the runoff. Robertson called Jim Ferguson a "traitor" and the biggest crook in the country. A victory for "Ma," he said, would be a slap in the face of those who had impeached "Pa." Ferguson supporters countered with the slogan: "Me for Ma, and I aint got a durn thing against Pa." The Ferguson campaign received a tremendous amount of publicity simply because "Ma" had a chance to be the first woman elected governor of any state. Newsmen insisted on photographing the candidate feeding chickens, hoeing the garden, and standing beside two mules while wearing a sunbonnet that belonged to a neighboring farm woman. The Klan issue, however, overshadowed all others and swung many people who could never imagine supporting anyone associated with Jim Ferguson over to "Ma's" camp. Most probably agreed with the endorsement editorial in the *Dallas Morning News* on August 17: "Soon or late we shall be compelled, as a means of saving the principles of popular government, to rid ourselves of the klan as a political power. We can do it now by electing Mrs. Ferguson. Her election will sound the death knell of the klan as a political power in this State." The turnout in the runoff on August 23 was even greater than in the first primary, and Ferguson won—or perhaps the Klan lost—413,751 to 316,019. Opponents of the Klan across the nation celebrated a defeat that, in the words of the *New York Times*, "ought to be a signal to start a war against it all over the country."

Texas Republicans, hoping to capitalize on anti-Ferguson sentiment, nominated George C. Butte, dean of the University of Texas Law School, to oppose Mrs. Ferguson in the general election. Butte announced his opposition to the Klan and attracted some Democrats with his insistence that his real opponent was "Pa" rather than "Ma." He had no chance to overcome the state's

James E. "Pa" Ferguson (1871–1944) and Miriam A. "Ma" Ferguson (1875–1961). Following his impeachment and conviction, "Pa" (on the left) could not hold public office in Texas, but he stood closely behind "Ma" (seated) during her two terms as governor. Credit: c02902, Austin History Center, Austin Public Library.

loyalty to one-party rule, however, especially after "Pa" called him "a little mutton headed professor with a Dutch diploma." The Republicans made their best showing in a gubernatorial election since Reconstruction but still lost 422,528 to 294,970. Texas voters took a risk in sending the Fergusons to the governor's mansion, but at least in the process they put the Klan on the path to destruction. By the end of 1924 prominent members of the Invisible Empire in Texas began to desert the cause, and the state no longer held first place in Klan affairs. It remained to be seen, however, what price Texans would pay for using the bonnet to rid themselves of the hood.

Mrs. Ferguson occupied the governor's office, but "Pa," who had his own office next door, ran her administration. She fought him successfully on a few things—his insistence, for example, on having a milk cow at the executive mansion—but generally he made the decisions. Indeed, at times he referred to himself as the governor of Texas. The Fergusons achieved one legislative success in 1925 with the passage of a law prohibiting the wearing of masks or disguises in public places. Although the Klan was already on the wane, the measure symbolized continuing public disapproval. In most other respects, "Ma" and "Pa" ran a penny-pinching, negative administration that cut funds for free textbooks, refused to improve the prison system, and hit at the University of Texas by eliminating funding for the departments of journalism and music and the School of Library Science. Most Texans had no problem with this approach, especially since it cut the state budget by $15 million, but just as in 1915–1917, Jim Ferguson's behavior raised the issue of corruption.

The Fergusons believed that Texas courts often sent poor people to the penitentiary for minor offenses, particularly violations of prohibition, while the rich committed the same crimes and escaped punishment. Accordingly, Mrs. Ferguson initiated an extremely liberal pardon policy, releasing more than two thousand convicts during her two years in office. This wholesale granting of pardons quickly led to charges that financial favors were involved. No evidence exists to prove that the Fergusons accepted money for pardons; nevertheless, numerous anecdotes to that effect circulated in the state. The best known involved an exchange between "Pa" and a man seeking clemency for his convicted criminal son. Ferguson supposedly kept switching the conversation back to a horse that he wanted to sell for $5,000. Finally, the man asked, "What on earth would I want with a $5,000 horse?" "Well," replied the former governor, "I figure your son might ride him home from the penitentiary if you bought him." Many also questioned the way Ferguson used his own newspaper, the *Ferguson Forum*, for personal gain based on public office. Companies doing business with the state, especially those building highways, were expected to buy expensive advertising space in the *Forum*. Once they did, they received highly favorable treatment in the granting of contracts. In the second year of the Ferguson administration, Dan Moody, the state's thirty-two-year-old attorney general, brought suit against two highway construction companies on the grounds that they had been promised $7 million in payment for roads that would cost less than $2 million. The resulting cancellations and modifications of contracts saved the state millions and added to the disrepute of the Ferguson family.

The Fergusons' antics soon made Texas a joke to many observers. When the governor, seeking to promote a "cheerful, happy outlook" among Texans, declared January 1926 "Laugh Month," the *Fort Worth Star-Telegram* commented: "We can expect the Fergusons to laugh just as long as Texas stands for it; and we can expect the nation to laugh as long as we stand for it." Voters were ready for a candidate who could restore respect to state government, and early in 1926 the perfect one emerged, Attorney General Moody. Announcing his candidacy in March 1926, Moody offered an end to "Fergusonism" and a return to business progressivism in government. Mrs. Ferguson sought reelection, and the contest quickly turned personal. As usual, "Pa" handled the campaigning, calling Moody an inexperienced "upstart" and "contemptible demagogue" (surely an exceptional example of the famed pot and kettle). Moody replied that even if he had "no peculiar qualifications for the office of governor . . . at least I have never been forbidden by any court of impeachment from holding any office of honor, trust, or profit in Texas." Moody led Ferguson in the first primary 409,732 to 283,482 and scored an even more convincing victory in the runoff, 495,723 to 270,595. Once more the Ferguson family left the governor's mansion, but again, not for the last time.

Dan Moody, at thirty-three the youngest governor in the state's history, gave Texas four years of competent, business-oriented, progressive leadership. He overhauled agencies such as the state highway department and appointed capable officials to make them work honestly and efficiently. The legislature increased the gasoline tax to three cents a gallon, providing funds for hundreds of miles of better roads. He also stopped the wholesale granting of pardons and convinced the legislature to authorize the office of state auditor to review public accounts on a regular basis. Modern fiscal controls in state government date from this measure. Moody, however, much like Neff in the early twenties, suffered many setbacks in dealing with the legislature. For example, he sought in vain to establish a state civil service system and to overhaul the antiquated court system.

Moody announced as a candidate for reelection in February 1928 and faced only a mild challenge from L. J. Wardlaw, a Fort Worth lawyer and good friend of Jim Ferguson. Although he actively campaigned only during the last two weeks before the July primary, the governor won renomination without a runoff. A much more interesting race occurred for the U.S. Senate nomination. The incumbent, Klansman Earle B. Mayfield, faced challenges from Tom Connally and four other candidates, including the suffragist Minnie Fisher Cunningham. Connally, a six-term member of the U.S. House of Representatives from McLennan County, urged voters to "turn out the bedsheet-and-mask candidate" and ran second in the first primary. Cunningham ran a distant fifth because, the state's leading men told her, "you are a woman." During the runoff campaign, Jim Ferguson, the one-time foe of Mayfield and the Klan, endorsed the incumbent, allowing Connally to gain support from opponents of both the Klan and Ferguson. He defeated Mayfield and went on to the Senate.

Moody's reelection and Mayfield's defeat in 1928 were important, but the most significant development for the future of Texas politics that year took place in the national election. Within the Democratic Party during the twenties, a bitter contest occurred between the older states' rights, rural conservatives who dominated the South and the younger, urban-oriented labor and immigrant leaders who controlled the Northeast. The two sides deadlocked in 1924, finally settling on the virtually unknown John W. Davis as the party's candidate, but as 1928 approached it appeared that Governor Alfred E. Smith of New York, leader of the northern Democrats would win the nomination. Texans as varied as Governor Moody, the Fergusons, and the Klan all found Smith, a second-generation son of Roman Catholic Irish immigrants who opposed prohibition, thoroughly unacceptable and did their best to block his nomination at the party's convention, held ironically enough in Houston. (Natives were dumbstruck apparently when delegates from New York called it "Howston.") Once Smith became the party's candidate, Moody remained loyal and asked Texans to support the ticket from "top to bottom." Many others, however, followed the lead of former governor Colquitt, who created "Texas Democrats for Hoover," and voted for the Republican nominee. Hoover carried the state with 52 percent of the vote, thus becoming the first presidential candidate of his party to receive Texas's electoral vote. Texans voted against Smith for many personal reasons, including his "wet" stance and his religion, and too much should not be made of the result. Nevertheless, in some respects the election of 1928 foreshadowed a significant decline in the state's support of the national Democratic Party.

Stock Market Crash and Onset of the Great Depression

The year 1929 opened on an auspicious note in Texas and across the nation. Prosperity was the watchword of the day, and good, solid men such as Governor Dan Moody and President-elect Herbert Hoover promised dependable leadership in the future. Few would have predicted that within less than twelve months a massive decline of prices on the nation's stock market would lead into an unparalleled economic disaster. But the unexpected happened, and the prosperity decade disappeared into the Great Depression.

Prices of shares in American corporations rose steadily from 1921 to 1927 and then soared upward, rising an average of more than 40 percent in 1928–1929. Earnings had virtually nothing to do with this rise; it was essentially a buy low/sell high, capital gains affair fueled by a get-rich-quick psychology. Most Americans, and certainly most Texans, were not "players" in this wild bull market, but the speculative activities of those who bought and sold came to symbolize the nation's prosperity. Banks encouraged the speculative mania by lending money to buy stock on margin. Those who bought stocks on margin paid as little as 25 percent of the price in cash and used the stock as collateral for a high-interest bank loan covering the other 75 percent. All went well so long as prices increased and margin buyers could sell for enough to cover their loans, but in September 1929, several large investors decided that the market would soon fall and began to sell. Their sales caused a fall in prices and helped burst the psychological bubble of speculation. Panic set in, particularly among margin buyers, and took over the market completely on October 29, 1929, "Black Tuesday." Stock prices fell irregularly for the next four years, wiping out some $40 billion in value.

The stock market crash did not destroy the productive capacity of the United States or Americans' need to consume goods and services; nevertheless, it provided the spark that touched off a general economic depression. For one thing, it greatly weakened confidence among investors and consumers alike, so that businesses, many of which already had large unsold inventories, cut back on hiring and production, and individuals, many of whom had shared too little in the good times of the twenties, reduced their spending. Reductions in investment and consumer spending fed on each other in creating a downward spiral in the economy. One way businessmen reduced investment, for example, was to fire workers; and increased unemployment, in turn, meant less purchasing power for consumers. The crash in stock prices also ruined banks when they were left holding worthless paper as collateral for loans. Depositors, panicked at news and rumors of banks with no money, demanded their funds, which even stable banks did not have on hand. "Runs" on banks closed literally thousands of financial institutions by the early 1930s, further destroying investment and consumer spending.

The immediate reaction among Texans to the stock market crash is difficult to gauge. A good many had only the slightest awareness that such an institution existed, let alone that it had crashed. The better informed probably worried over what it meant, but newspapermen and business leaders dismissed the fall in prices as something affecting only a few speculators and rich people in the Northeast. The real economy, they said, is strong, and there is no reason for pessimism. The *Dallas Morning News* of October 30 quoted a leading local merchant to the effect that "much of the losses chalked up were 'paper profits' that will make the burden seem much less than at first glance. Business thus far has not been affected and no damaging result is expected." Even agricultural journals, which reported on an activity already suffering depressed conditions, insisted that the market crash had little meaning for future cotton prices.

This "whistling-past-the-graveyard" optimism continued through 1929 and into the next year. Newspapers across the state denied the seriousness of the collapse, insisting that only a few Wall Street speculators had been hurt. At the same time, however, articles in labor journals published in Dallas and San Antonio spoke of widespread unemployment, and stories in major newspapers belied some of the rose-colored editorializing. For example, the *Houston Post-Dispatch* carried an account in March 1930 of a six hundred-person march organized in protest of the firing of city employees. "Houston," it concluded, "is relatively free of discontent due to economic conditions." Later that year, a Houston man left a suicide note that read: "This depression has got me licked. There is no work to be had. I can't accept charity and I am too proud to appeal to my kin or friends, and I am too honest to steal. So I see no other course. A land flowing with milk and honey and a first-class mechanic can't make an honest living. I would rather take my chances with a just God than an unjust humanity." While unemployment took its toll on urban workers, farmers saw already low prices for their products plummet. Farmers, the *El Paso Times* wrote in late 1929, would appreciate "more cash and less optimistic conversation."

Some looked to oil for economic salvation, and the industry did help in some ways—generating the construction of refineries in Houston, for example. In October 1930, however, Texas began to experience too much of a good thing when Columbus M. "Dad" Joiner and A. D. "Doc" Lloyd brought in the Daisy Bradford No. 3 in Rusk County and opened up a huge new oil field that stretched through East Texas from Upshur County in the north to Cherokee County in the south. The oil that poured from wells in this field created a brief boom as land prices rose, employment increased, and new refineries were built in East Texas, Dallas, and Fort Worth. Kilgore gained more than ten thousand residents in a few years and turned into a boom town reminiscent of Ranger and Borger. Imaginative entrepreneurs made money in every imaginable way; one even set up six privies on a lot in town and charged ten cents per visit. Soon, however, overproduction drove the price of oil down from a dollar a barrel in 1930 to as little as eight cents a barrel in 1931, and this drop added to the deepening ruin of depression statewide.

During the second half of 1930 and through 1931, conditions worsened. The construction industry began to wane in Dallas, so that by the close of 1931 the city had eighteen thousand unemployed. San Antonio, in spite of its military installations, had an estimated twenty thousand people in "dire circumstances" by February 1932. The state's most industrial city, Houston, apparently was hit the hardest, showing an unemployment rate of 23 percent at the beginning of 1931. Austin, cushioned by the presence of state government employees and the University of Texas, probably suffered the least among major cities, but even there business fell below normal levels during 1931. Thousands of unemployed, homeless "tramps" began to roam the countryside and show up around the state's largest cities. Farmers faced steadily worsening conditions as the price of cotton fell from nine to ten cents a pound when the 1931 crop was planted to a little more than five cents at harvest time. Prices for corn and cattle were more than 50 percent lower than in 1929. Under these circumstances, Texas newspapers and business leaders had to face reality. In July a professor of economics at Texas Christian University summarized the new consensus: "We must frankly admit that we are in a depression of no small consequence; in fact, said by some to be the most severe in 100 years. The depression is industrial and not simply financial. The depression is agricultural as well as financial and industrial."

The professor was correct, of course, but no one could have guessed how deep and lasting the depression would become. The value of farms in Texas would fall from $3.6 billion in 1930 to $2.6 billion in 1940, a loss of more than $.5 billion even when allowances are made for deflation during the decade. Cotton acreage, which stood at 16.8 million acres in 1930, declined to 8 million acres ten years later. The value of livestock on farms fell $100 million during the decade. The state had fewer manufacturing establishments in 1939 than in 1929, and workers in those industries received less in wages and salaries than they had ten years before. The oil and gas industry provided some cushion by expanding to make Texas the largest producer in the United States by 1939 and giving roughly 250,000 Texans jobs in everything from drilling for crude to retailing petroleum products, but even this growth could not offset the overall economic collapse. Unemployment stood at near-catastrophic levels throughout the thirties; indeed, as late as 1940 more than 300,000 Texans had no employment in private enterprise. Women who had jobs, especially those were married, came under pressure to give the work to men. As would be expected, poor people suffered the most. Unemployment among blacks was higher than among whites, and those who had jobs earned less. Average family income for blacks in 1935 stood at $942 per year. More Mexicans Americans than ever followed the cotton season, but their earnings

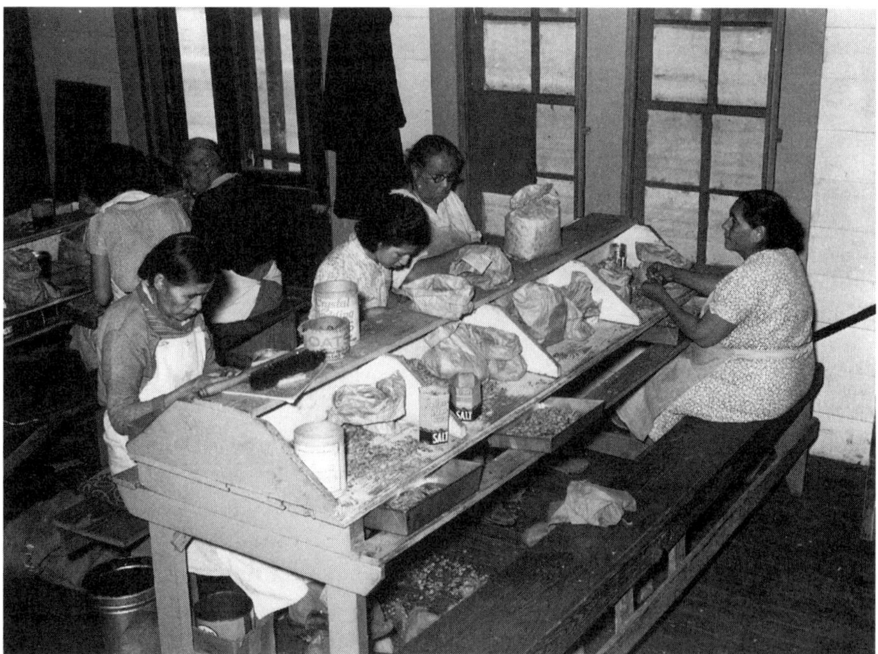

Mexican Pecan Shellers, Nonunion Plant in San Antonio, 1939. Workers such as these shelled more than half of the nation's commercial pecans at wages as low as five or six cents an hour. Credit: Library of Congress, Prints & Photographs Division, FSA/OWI Collection, LC-USF34-032671-D.

hardly offset travel costs. One study in 1938 placed the average migrant's income for the six-month harvest period at $37.50. Urban-dwelling Mexican Americans also suffered greater poverty than ever. Thousands, most of them women, worked as pecan shellers in San Antonio, earning only two to three dollars a week while laboring in uncomfortable and unhealthy shelling factories. In 1938, some twelve thousand pecan shellers went on strike, creating probably the largest labor stoppage in Texas history. Led by Emma Tenayuca, the workers forced the factory owners to agree to arbitration and won a pay increase. Their success proved largely illusory, however, because within a few years, cracking machines replaced ten thousand hand shellers.

Early Reactions to the Depression

Even as leading Texans admitted the reality of depression, they claimed that it would soon end and that, after all, Texas had not been hurt nearly so badly as other parts of the nation. Some actually seemed to enjoy seeing the northeasterners get their comeuppance. Also, a good many of those who finally recognized the depression insisted that it had numerous beneficial effects. It will teach us thrift, they said, make us more considerate of others, and bring us back to

God. Moreover, people will eat plain, more healthful food and wear less showy clothing. In 1932, an Amarillo newsman published a summary of these arguments entitled *I Like the Depression.* Exactly how many Texans accepted this point of view cannot be determined, but a woman from Levelland offered a stinging reply: "I can safely say any one who says he likes the depression has not had starvation staring him in the face. I don't like to see others go hungry while I have plenty, therefore, I DON'T LIKE THE DEPRESSION."

Those who agreed with the woman from Levelland needed someone or something to blame for the depression, and attention soon focused primarily on President Hoover and the Republican Party. This was not entirely fair, of course, but it amounted to poetic justice in that Hoover and his party had taken full credit for the prosperity of the twenties and therefore should have received the blame when it collapsed. The president became the symbol of dissatisfaction. Homeless Texans built shanty towns of packing crates and flattened tin cans outside major cities and called them "Hoovervilles." Cottontail rabbits and armadillos became "Hoover hogs," and newspapers that covered transients on park benches were called "Hoover blankets."

The question of blame, of course, was far less important than the problem of what to do next. How could the distress and suffering be relieved and economic recovery created? Until 1932 Hoover insisted that relief was the job of individuals and private charity organizations rather than government and that the economy should be left alone because recovery was "just around the corner." Many Texans, still imbued with antigovernment beliefs, agreed, and relief efforts at first were handled by the Red Cross, Salvation Army, Community Chest, and local relief committees. However, as this approach proved inadequate in combating hunger and the depression deepened, a majority of Texans turned to action by the state and national government. "It is a reflection upon civilization to permit welfare institutions to be supported by private purses," a Houston Jewish newspaper wrote. "No self-respecting nation should permit such an intolerable condition to exist."

Texans who wanted public action turned as would be expected to the state government first. Dan Moody, who began his second term in January 1929, largely escaped having to deal with relief because so many leaders denied the existence of depression that year and the next. Then, unfortunately, the Democratic primary in 1930 attracted eleven candidates, including "Ma" Ferguson and the old Klansman Earle Mayfield, and turned into more a contest of personalities than of policies. The only new face among the serious contenders was Ross Sterling, a Houston businessman who helped found the Humble Oil Company and served the Moody administration as State Highway Commissioner. Sterling's wealth—a total worth of more than $50 million—became an issue as did his proposal for a $300 million bond issue to pay for highway construction. However, he, like the other candidates, gave no indication of what he would do about conditions in the state. Thanks to Jim Ferguson's campaign efforts, "Ma" ran first in the primary, but Sterling took second place and then gained enough votes from supporters of the eliminated candidates to win the runoff with 55 percent of the total.

As governor, Sterling dealt with the depression much as Hoover did at the national level. He, too, pointed to a key problem—the loss of popular confidence—but had no success in restoring it with words. The problem, he told a conference on unemployment in October 1931, is that "our people seem to have lost faith, that quality of heart and mind so essential to the solution of those grave problems that sometimes appear to threaten the perpetuity of our institutions." The governor held most state expenditures to a minimum, and when he did want to spend, as in the case of a highway bond issue, the legislature rejected the proposal. Also, like Hoover, Sterling did not want the government to provide relief directly to individuals for fear that it would sap self-reliance and weaken the work ethic. Finally, in 1932, faced with overwhelming numbers of the unemployed, the president had to offer some help, and Texans benefited accordingly. Congress, with Hoover's approval, created the Reconstruction Finance Corporation, a federal agency that existed primarily to loan money to help businesses weather the depression but that also had the authority to loan $300 million to the states for relief purposes. Texas's share, which was distributed in the counties through local chambers of commerce, was not nearly adequate, but, obviously, any help was better than none.

Sterling's administration also had a miserable time dealing with two of Texas's key products, oil and cotton. Overproduction in the East Texas field drove prices so low (two cents a barrel on one occasion in 1931) that the governor sought to empower the Railroad Commission to enforce production restrictions. When the legislature refused to act, he declared martial law in August 1931, and national guardsmen shut the field down completely. Six months later the state Supreme Court ruled that Sterling had exceeded his powers and forced removal of the troops, but by then legislators had approved production restrictions by the commission. State regulation gradually stabilized the oil industry in East Texas, but "hot oil"—that is, oil produced in excess of commission restrictions—continued to be a problem. The governor also sought to raise the price of cotton by convincing the legislature in September 1931 to mandate a 50 percent reduction in acreage planted in that crop the following year. However, in February 1932 Texas courts struck down the law as a denial of citizens' rights to use their property as they chose. Cotton prices remained disastrously low.

Sterling faced reelection in 1932, and Jim Ferguson, mindful of the governor's difficulties and all the financial misery across Texas, decided that it was a "Ferguson year." In announcing as a candidate, Mrs. Ferguson promised to lower taxes but offered no other antidepression program. Sterling found himself on the defensive about his record over the past two years, but the emphasis was on the declaration of martial law in East Texas rather than his lack of success in bringing relief. Moreover, "Pa" constantly repeated the absolutely untrue charge that the state highway fund had accrued a $100 million shortage during the past five years. Just as in 1930, Mrs. Ferguson led the first primary, and Sterling forced a runoff. This time, however, "Ma" prevailed by less than four thousand votes in a total of nearly one million. Sterling and his friends pointed out that nearly one hundred, mostly Ferguson counties had more votes cast in the runoff than there were poll tax receipts issued, but neither the legislature nor the Democratic Party did anything to investigate the seemingly obvious corruption.

In the November general election, Mrs. Ferguson swept to victory with 62 percent of the vote over her Republican opponent, Orville Bullington, a lawyer from Wichita Falls. But her margin of victory looked insignificant in comparison to that of the Democratic candidate for president, Governor Franklin D. Roosevelt of New York. Roosevelt, who had outmaneuvered several other contenders for the nomination, including long-time Congressman John Nance "Cactus Jack" Garner of Uvalde, Texas, defeated Hoover with 89 percent of the vote. He took office owing a heavy debt to Texans, particularly Garner, who became his vice president, and Sam Rayburn of Bonham, a congressman since 1913 who played a key role in securing the New Yorker's nomination. When nominated, Roosevelt had pledged a "New Deal" for the American people, and Texans in Washington would wield great influence as the government sought to deliver on that promise.

Texas and the New Deal

Opening with a special session of Congress in March 1933, Franklin D. Roosevelt's New Deal brought a flood of innovative legislation aimed at providing relief for victims of the depression, recovery to the economy, and reform to prevent such disasters in the future. Pursuit of these "three Rs"—relief, recovery, and reform—brought the national government into the lives of Americans as a regulator of the economy and provider of basic welfare in ways made possible politically only by the collapse of the "New Era." Texans in Washington had a tremendously influential part in shaping the New Deal. John Nance Garner served as vice president for eight years; seven Texans held the chairmanships of committees in the House of Representatives; and both senators chaired important committees. Jesse H. Jones, a Houston businessman, headed the Reconstruction Finance Corporation (RFC), an agency Roosevelt inherited from the Hoover Administration and made into the primary investor in the American economy. Between 1933 and 1939, Jones was one of the most powerful men in Washington as he directed the loaning of $10 billion to aid businesses of all sorts in surviving the depression.

Governor Miriam A. Ferguson, whose second term began in January 1933, anticipated, of necessity, Roosevelt's first New Deal action. Faced with a panic that threatened to ruin all the state's banks, she ordered them all closed on March 2. Fortunately for the governor, since she probably had exceeded her constitutional powers, Roosevelt declared a four-day national banking holiday beginning on Monday, March 6, and called Congress into special session. Lawmakers quickly approved an Emergency Banking Act that called for immediate inspection of all banks and provided funds to aid the financially stable ones. Roosevelt reassured the American people about their banks in the first of his famous "Fireside Chats," and the system survived. Later that year Vice President Garner and Jesse Jones promoted creation of the Federal Deposit Insurance Corporation as an instrument to secure deposits and maintain public confidence. National banks had to join the FDIC, and state banks, which were encouraged to belong, generally responded positively in Texas.

Once the banking crisis eased, relief for the unemployed became a New Deal priority. The Reconstruction Finance Corporation continued to make loans to states for that purpose, but the problem required much larger and more imaginative programs. First, the Federal Emergency Relief Act of May 1933 (FERA) provided funds to the states on a matching basis ($1 from the national government for every $3 from the state) for direct assistance to those in need. To distribute these monies, the state legislature created the Texas Rehabilitation and Relief Commission, which was to work through a system of county boards. True to form, "Pa" Ferguson saw relief spending as an opportunity to gain political advantage. He chaired (without legal authority) the first meeting of the commission and arranged to have the county relief boards filled with his supporters. Then, needing more funds to distribute, the Fergusons convinced the legislature to submit a $20 million relief bond issue to the voters, which passed in August 1933. Local relief administrators pressured the unemployed to vote, even paying their poll taxes in some cases, and then frequently mismanaged the funds when they became available. The Bexar County board, for example, approved spending more than $18,000 a month on administrative salaries. Finally in 1934 a change in directors of the relief commission cleaned up the worst abuses, but by then the public was outraged. Once again, the Fergusons discredited a worthy cause by using it for personal advantage, but at least some of the approximately $50 million that came into Texas from the RFC and FERA in 1933–1934 found its way to those truly in need—white, black, and Mexican American. Because relatively few were in a strong financial position in 1929, a larger proportion of blacks than whites wound up on relief rolls.

Direct-relief payments, often called the "dole," went against the grain of American belief in individual self-reliance, and, except in emergency situations, New Deal leaders preferred programs that required the unemployed to work for pay. The Public Works Administration, created in 1933, hired skilled workers to construct large-scale projects such as bridges, schools, sewage plants, and other buildings of permanent value. During the remainder of the decade, the PWA initiated 922 projects in Texas and spent nearly $110 million that provided relief and produced worthwhile construction at the same time. Another program for the unemployed begun in 1933, the Civilian Conservation Corps (CCC), targeted unmarried men aged seventeen to twenty-five whose families were on relief. Those who enrolled in the CCC lived in camps supervised by the U.S. Army and worked primarily on soil and forest conservation projects. They received $30 a month in pay, $25 of which went home to their families. Technically, the CCC could not discriminate on the basis of color, but camps in Texas, like those across the South, were segregated, and only about four hundred black Texans enrolled. At its busiest, the CCC in Texas had room for 19,200 men in its camps, and from 1933 to 1942 some 50,000 Texans enrolled. An unmitigated success, the CCC, while providing relief, fostered conservation and contributed greatly to the building of the state's system of parks. Finally, as the winter of 1933–1934 approached with many thousands still in need of assistance, the Roosevelt Administration turned to work relief in the form of the Civil Works Administration. Work relief differs from public works in that the jobs assigned to the unemployed are often in the nature of "make work," that is, a task that does not accomplish anything of lasting value but is one for which men can be paid. Raking leaves on courthouse lawns became perhaps the best-known example of such work at the time. The point, of course, was to keep the work ethic alive regardless of the job being done, but many in the public (who had employment) saw it as the height of New Deal foolishness and waste. More than 239,000 Texans found employment with the CWA that winter, but the program ended under a torrent of criticism in the spring. The concept, however, did not disappear.

The New Deal also had to do something for agriculture, and do it quickly, because Texas farmers, who generally had not prospered during the twenties, faced absolute ruin by 1933. Roosevelt's administration responded with the Agricultural Adjustment Act (AAA), a measure that sought to increase farm income by limiting the production of key crops. Farmers were promised subsidies if they accepted acreage limitations and marketing quotas on field crops such as cotton, wheat, and corn as well as on hogs and dairy products. Money to pay the subsidies came from taxes on the processors of agricultural products. By the time the AAA passed in May 1933, spring crops had been planted, so the government paid Texas farmers nearly $43 million to plow under more than four million acres of cotton. In 1934 Texas farmers took more than five million acres of cotton, wheat, and corn out of production. Paying farmers to limit their crops when so many Americans were hungry and poorly clothed struck some observers as strange. (It truly perplexed Texas farm mules who had been conditioned for years to avoid stepping on cotton stalks and then in 1933 were whipped into pulling plows down the rows of young plants.) Crop limitation, however, was the most feasible way to raise farm income and preserve agriculture as a private enterprise in the hands of thousands of Texans. Roosevelt's administration also sought to keep farmers in business by creating the Farm Credit Administration in 1933 to loan money to aid in producing and marketing crops and preventing foreclosures.

Just as the New Deal offered Texas farmers a helping hand, nature dealt those in the western part of the state another blow in the form of a prolonged drought. Dry weather, coupled with the removal of native grass by grazing and plowing, turned much of the region into a so-called "Dust Bowl" after 1932. Massive storms of blowing dirt blacked out the sun for hours at a time, making life miserable and driving farmers off their land. In Amarillo, visibility fell to zero seven times between January and April 1935. More than a third of farmers in the region left during the next two years. The AAA offered short-term aid to drought-stricken farmers and ranchers by purchasing more than four million cattle, sheep, and goats in 1934–1935. Nearly 1.75 million were destroyed, and the rest given to relief agencies. On a more long-term basis, the AAA and other federal agencies such as the CCC worked on soil conser-

Dust Storm in Amarillo, 1936. Note the metal signs blowing in the wind. Rainfall in the Panhandle matched the annual average only three years between 1928 and 1940, resulting in storms of blowing dust dark enough to block out the sun. Credit: Library of Congress, Prints & Photographs Division, FSA/OWI Collection, LC-USF34-004058-E.

vation projects. The state also sought to help in 1935 by establishing conservation districts in the Panhandle and allowing local authorities to force farmers to take steps to prevent their soil from blowing away.

The New Deal's farm program did not end the depression in Texas agriculture, but it did bring appreciably higher prices (cotton sold for ten cents a pound at the end of 1933) and keep many people on their farms. Of course, these benefits went primarily to landowners. Although tenants were supposed to receive a share of the payments commensurate with their interest in the crop, landlords, who received the checks, often kept a grossly disproportionate portion for themselves. One AAA inspector called the situation in the Brazos River Valley "scandalous" and urged action "to protect the weak and ignorant from the greed and imposition of stronger and cunning fellows," but nothing was done. After the initial plow-up campaign in 1933, tenants often found themselves pushed off the places that they were working because owners received millions of dollars annually from taking their land out of production. Also, landowners began to create larger and larger farms that relied

Panhandle tenant farmers displaced by mechanization, June 1937. Credit: Library of Congress, Prints & Photographs Division, FSA/OWI Collection, LC-USF34-017265-C.

on mechanization and wage labor, thus eliminating the need for tenants. Having been "tractored out," one-time tenants had to find work as day laborers or go on relief or leave the state. Poor whites suffered intensely, but blacks and Mexicans seem to have been hit even harder. The number of black farm owners remained stable at about 20,000 during the thirties. Black tenants, however, decreased in number from 65,000 to 32,000, and farm laborers increased by 25,000. Unemployment among black farm laborers probably ran as high as 90 percent by 1935, forcing them to find relief or move. It is estimated that 20,000 left Texas. Mexicans increasingly found wage labor as their only option. For example, a Caldwell County ranch that employed nearly fifty Mexican sharecropper families in 1933 had only ten at the end of the decade. Small wonder that an estimated 250,000 Mexicans, given an additional push by federal repatriation programs, left the state between 1929 and 1939. In short, New Deal policies helped preserve farming in Texas, but in the process, eliminated many farmers.

In the case of manufacturing, the administration's efforts to bring recovery, primarily the National Industrial Recovery Act of 1933, affected fewer Texans because the state was not heavily industrialized. This act called for the drafting of codes to regulate all industries. Written by representatives of business, labor, and government, these codes would in effect reduce competition and fix prices with the intention of encouraging industrialists to keep their factories operational. The part of code writing that most interested Texas workers was the requirement that they specify minimum wages and the right to organize and bargain collectively. Those concerned with the oil industry had to take note that the act authorized the federal government to stop the shipment of "hot oil" in interstate commerce, thus increasing the likelihood that Railroad Commission regulations on production would be obeyed.

One other legislative measure passed in the first year of the New Deal, the Home Owners Loan Act, bears mentioning for its benefits to Texans. This law created a Home Owners Loan Corporation (HOLC) with the power to refinance mortgaged homes in urban areas. The agency "paid" off the original mortgage holder with government bonds and then arranged longer payout periods, often as long as thirty years, thus lowering payments and allowing thousands of home owners to keep their property. By 1936, the HOLC spent more than $100 million on refinancing homes in Texas. It remained in operation until after World War II and by 1946 collected enough in mortgage payments to retire the bonds used in refinancing.

While the New Deal produced a flurry of legislation in 1933–1934, the government in Austin took few actions of significance that did not originate in some way in Washington. The $20 million relief bond issue, for example, came in response to federal programs. Also, pressure from the federal government put prohibition on the run in Texas. In February 1933, Congress sent to the states a proposed Twenty-first Amendment to repeal the Eighteenth Amendment and directed that special conventions rather than state legislatures act on ratification. Drys vowed to fight to the end, but wets, arguing that repeal would aid in economic recovery, won over many people who had greater problems than demon rum. In August Texas voters approved a change in the state constitution permitting local choice on the sale of 3.2 beer and elected a slate of pro-repeal delegates to the ratification convention. The convention unanimously approved the Twenty-first Amendment, which received the requisite number of ratifications in December 1933. Texas still was dry except for 3.2 beer on a local-option basis, but statewide repeal was just a matter of time. It came two years later.

Mrs. Ferguson attempted to take the initiative in having the state adopt a sales tax or an income tax, but the legislature would not act. Lawmakers wanted only to cut appropriations, which they did. A proposal to reorganize 129 existing state bureaus and agencies into twenty new ones and to combine and consolidate some of the state's colleges came to nothing in spite of the fact that it would have saved between $4 and $6 million annually. The legislature also cut funds for the Texas Rangers, but the Fergusons had given an excuse in that case by once more engaging in partisan misuse of the governor's office. In the election of 1932, the Rangers made the mistake of supporting Sterling, and Mrs. Ferguson retaliated by firing the entire forty-four-man force. The legislature then limited the force to thirty-two men and slashed salaries, helping create a situation in which killers such as George "Machine-Gun" Kelly and Clyde Barrow and Bonnie Parker terrorized parts of the state.

To make matters worse, the governor handed out 2,344 special ranger commissions to political supporters. By 1934 the agency had become a joke.

Mrs. Ferguson honored the two-term tradition in 1934, and six candidates entered the Democratic primary with the hope of replacing her. The best known was James V. (Jimmie) Allred, a thirty-five-year-old from Wichita Falls who had served as attorney general for four years. Clean-cut and personable, Allred ran on support of the New Deal, the creation of a public utilities commission, and stronger law enforcement. Although he was forced into a runoff by Tom F. Hunter, an oilman from Wichita Falls, Allred won the governorship and began a largely successful two-term administration. Like other recent occupants of his office, he could not persuade the legislature to levy the taxes necessary to meet the state's financial needs, but he had a major success in August 1935 with the creation of the Texas Department of Public Safety, which modernized law enforcement. The DPS, as it would become known, included the Texas Highway Patrol and the Texas Rangers under the overall supervision of a Public Safety Commission appointed by the governor. Governor Allred also delivered on his promise of identifying with the New Deal and bringing federal money to Texas. His administration could not have begun at a better time for that purpose because it coincided with a new burst of legislative activity in Washington.

The New Deal, after its crisis-induced outburst of new laws in 1933, slowed considerably in 1934, and President Roosevelt found himself under attack from both ends of the political spectrum. Once the worst had passed, conservatives feared that the New Deal would make the national government too big and expensive and would bring too much regulation of business and social welfare legislation. Left-leaning liberals on the other hand argued that the administration had not done enough for the elderly, the poor, and the unemployed. Midterm elections in November 1934 gave Roosevelt an overwhelmingly Democratic Congress and provided the impetus for him to respond to the continuing depression and his critics by having the government do more rather than less. In 1935, to name only the most important new initiatives, Roosevelt created the Works Progress Administration (WPA), the National Youth Administration (NYA), and the Rural Electrification Administration (REA), and Congress passed the Social Security Act and the National Labor Relations Act. All had important implications for Texas.

The WPA, which kept the same acronym when renamed the Work Projects Administration in 1939, provided work relief (an approach that proved highly unpopular when first used in 1933) on a lasting basis. Between 1935 and 1943, it employed some 600,000 unskilled Texans without regard to gender or race at wages of $45 to $75 per month. WPA projects, which usually cost less than $25,000, included building sidewalks, parks, swimming pools, bridges, and stadiums; writing travel guides; surveying the state's historical records; painting murals in public buildings; and organizing groups of musicians and actors. The agency produced many things of value, but above all, it allowed thousands of families to subsist while keeping alive the work ethic. The NYA provided jobs and counseling for young men and women aged sixteen to twenty-five with the dual purpose of giving relief and encouraging youths to complete high school and college. For example, high school students received six dollars a month to perform part-time clerical or maintenance duties. Twenty-six-year-old Lyndon Baines Johnson, a native of the Hill Country who had begun his political career as secretary to Congressman Richard M. Kleberg from 1931 to 1935, served as the first director of the NYA in Texas. He strictly enforced the rule that financial need was the only criterion to determine eligibility for NYA assistance, and as a result within two years 40 percent of those who qualified in Texas were black. Between 1935 and 1943, the NYA aided 175,000 students in completing their educations and employed another 75,000 youths in out-of-school programs.

The REA offered long-term, low-interest loans (2 percent) to cooperatives organized by rural residents for the purpose of building systems to distribute electrical power. This was especially important to Texas because in 1935 only 2.3 percent of the state's farms had central-station electricity. Farmers and ranchers immediately began to form cooperatives that took the numerous advantages of electricity to areas that to this day do not have enough customers to produce the profits necessary to attract private energy companies. By 1965 only 2 percent of the state's farms did not have electricity.

The Social Security Act of 1935 had three major provisions, two of which put pressure on the state government to increase social-welfare services. Its best-known feature, the transfer-of-payments system that provided a pension fund for retired people, was essentially a federal program that began collecting payroll taxes in 1937 and making small monthly payments to retirees in 1940. However, the act also provided federal funds on a matching basis for state-administered programs of assistance to people who were elderly and poor at that time. Texas voters quickly approved a constitutional amendment authorizing an old-age assistance program (statewide prohibition was repealed at the same election), but Governor Allred had to call two special sessions of the legislature before gaining approval of a plan to put this program into effect. Texas mailed its first old-age pension checks in July 1936. Last, the Social Security Act mandated a joint federal-state unemployment compensation program. The legislature did not act on this program until October 1936 but finally passed the necessary law, largely because refusal would have cost the state federal dollars.

The National Labor Relations Act protected the right of workers to organize and bargain collectively with their employers. Unions, never strong in Texas, did not grow rapidly even after the passage of this law, but it did encourage unionization by the new Congress of Industrial Organizations (CIO) of workers in oil and sugar refining and the steel, telephone, and shipping industries. These not-always-successful efforts were marked by strikes, which antagonized many Texans, although perhaps not as much as militant union actions elsewhere. In the midwest, auto and rubber workers successfully sat down at their jobs in 1936–1937, refusing to work or to vacate the plants until their employers obeyed the National Labor Relations Act and engaged in collective bargaining. Many leading Texans, such as Vice President Garner, viewed the "sit-down strikes" as violations of property rights and were angry with President Roosevelt for not taking action to stop or prevent them. East Texas Congressman Martin Dies established the House Un-American Activities Committee in 1938 and spent the next six years engaged in highly publicized attacks on CIO unions as purveyors of communism and treason.

The New Deal, in spite of the continuing depression, received a ringing endorsement from ordinary Texans in 1936. A small group of disgruntled politicians, frightened businessmen, and lawyers with corporate connections worked with a national group called the Jeffersonian Democrats and argued that Roosevelt was a "red" determined to destroy the Constitution. They also played on racism, contending that the New Deal meant legalized marriage between whites and blacks. Texans refused to listen, however, and gave the president 88 percent of the vote over his Republican opponent, Alfred Landon. Governor Allred, who sought reelection the same year, clearly benefited from identification with the national administration as well as his generally successful record. Only a month before the Texas primary, he entertained President Roosevelt at the state's Centennial Exposition in Dallas, and he had the honor of renominating Vice President Garner at the Democratic convention. Four men challenged the governor in the primary, but he won without a runoff and then outdid Roosevelt in the general election, defeating his Republican opponent with 93 percent of the vote.

Allred's second administration had some successes—the creation of a teacher retirement system being the best example—but as before he could not convince the legislature to approve the taxes necessary to pay for increased services. The governor's political problems amounted to little, however, compared to those President Roosevelt stirred up for the New Deal, particularly among Texans, with his "court-packing" plan in 1937. This controversy originated in a series of decisions by the Supreme Court of the United States in 1935–1936 that declared New Deal legislation, such as the National Industrial Recovery Act and the Agricultural Adjustment Act, unconstitutional. Losing these laws caused Roosevelt little concern—they were not working well anyhow—but he worried that the Court's conservative justices would move on to invalidate the Social Security Act and National Labor Relations Act as well. Therefore, immediately upon beginning his second term, he proposed a reorganization of the federal court system that allowed the president to appoint an additional justice up to a total of six to the Supreme Court for every member of the court who reached the age of seventy and did not retire. Not so coincidentally, six of the current justices happened to be seventy or older; so the proposal would allow Roosevelt to appoint the maximum number immediately and raise the court's membership from nine to fifteen. The president apparently expected little opposition and had not prepared for the battle that followed.

A majority of ordinary Texans probably would have gone along with the reorganization plan, but many of the state's key political and business leaders opposed it. Governor Allred was unenthusiastic, but the killing opposition came from Vice President Garner, Senator Tom Connally, and Congressman Hatton Sumners, all of whom insisted that Roosevelt was going too far and threatening constitutional government. Garner, already angry over Roosevelt's refusal to denounce sit-down strikes, unsuccessfully sought some sort of compromise and then went fishing for six weeks rather than help the president. Garner had never before left Washington during a legislative session. Congressman Maury Maverick, a liberal Democrat from San Antonio, and Senator Morris Sheppard loyally supported the president, but they faced pressure from home in the form of a resolution passed by the Texas Senate requesting all the state's representatives in Washington to oppose the bill. The Texas Bar Association, organizations of businessmen, and most of the state's big-city newspapers also condemned it. Obviously Texans alone could not have defeated Roosevelt's plan, but they played a leading role as the struggle came to a close in the fall of 1937 without any change in the federal court system. (Incidentally, the Supreme Court changed its stance during that year and upheld both the Social Security Act and the National Labor Relations Act. Apparently several of the moderate justices learned, as one wit put it, that "a switch in time saves nine.")

Texas Democrats also played a key role in defeating another administration initiative in 1937 when Congress considered the passage of an antilynching bill. Ironically, one of the major proponents of the bill—Jessie Daniel Ames—was also a Texan. Born in Palestine in 1883, Jessie Daniel earned a degree at the Ladies Annex of Southwestern University in 1902 and three years later married Roger Ames, an army doctor. She became a protégée of the suffragist Minnie Fisher Cunningham and served in 1919 as the first president of the Texas League of Women Voters. In 1930, after moving to Atlanta, Georgia, Ames acted on her developing interest in preventing racial violence and founded the Association of Southern Women for the Prevention of Lynching. Hers was one of many groups that demanded a federal antilynching bill of the sort introduced in Congress in 1937. Congressman Maury Maverick supported the bill, but Hatton Sumners of Dallas fought it in the House and Senator Tom Connally led a filibuster that killed it in the Senate.

These defeats did not end the New Deal. In 1938 Congress passed a second Agricultural Adjustment Act that operated with essentially the same purpose as the first and a Fair Labor Standards Act that created the federal minimum wage and established maximum hours for workers. However, the court fight, and to a lesser extent the antilynching bill, brought many important Texans who already disliked the New Deal into open opposition, and antagonized influential newspapers such as the *Dallas Morning News.* An indication of the administration's fading strength in the Lone Star state came in the midterm congressional elections of 1938 when Roosevelt attempted to "purge" members of the U.S. House of Representatives who opposed him. He targeted several Texas representatives in the primary, but they won reelection over pro-administration candidates. Making the message even clearer, Congressman Maury Maverick of San Antonio, probably the president's strongest supporter in the Texas delegation, lost his seat. Most Texas voters still liked Roosevelt personally, but they no longer cared as much for his programs.

Overall, the people and political leaders of Texas had a curious relationship with the New Deal. Roosevelt's programs clearly helped the state survive the Great Depression and improved the quality of life for most of its people, but those successes did not bring lasting acceptance of federal economic regulation and welfare legislation. In spite of their influential position and the virtual worship of Roosevelt by millions of Texans, many of the state's political and business leaders had misgivings about the New Deal practically from the beginning and grew increasingly disenchanted as it developed. They were, as one congressman put it, "Democrats first and New Dealers second." Wanting relief and recovery for their state, they took federal aid but tended, with some notable exceptions such as young Lyndon Baines Johnson, to reject the underlying philosophy of big government and collective social responsibility. They spoke more and more often of threats to states' rights, disliked the increased spending necessitated by social welfare programs, objected to legislation that favored labor unions, and opposed even the discussion of civil rights and antilynching laws. The state government never fully endorsed the New Deal, not even when Jimmie Allred occupied the governor's office. In the long run, the political and social conservatism of most leading Texans could not fully accommodate the New Deal and its increasingly liberal, big-city leadership. Once Roosevelt's death cost the Democrats their popular leader, more and more ordinary folk would turn against the party of the New Deal as well.

The "Pappy" Lee O'Daniel Era

In addition to handing the president a resounding defeat at the polls in 1938, Texas voters treated themselves to a colorful governor who, although he offered no sensible way of dealing with the continuing depression, at least took their minds off the economy. In a manner reminiscent of "Pa" Ferguson, "Pappy" Lee O'Daniel burst onto the political stage, and once again personality overrode policy considerations across Texas.

Among the thirteen men who filed for governor in the 1938 Democratic primary, Wilbert Lee O'Daniel seemed the most unlikely candidate of all. A native of Ohio who grew up in Kansas, he moved to Fort Worth in 1925 at the age of thirty-five and became sales manager for a flour milling company. Soon, as an advertising ploy, he became the master of ceremonies on a radio show featuring a western band, the Light Crust Doughboys. (At one time the famed Texas musician Bob Wills played with this band.) The show, which aired daily at noon over the most powerful stations in Texas, always opened with a woman saying, "Please pass the biscuits, Pappy," and listeners loved it. O'Daniel created his own company in 1935 and continued the radio program, selling "Hillbilly Flour" while playing western and religious music interspersed with talks on religion, morals, and Texas heroes. His own efforts at songwriting included "Beautiful, Beautiful Texas" and "The Boy Who Never Got Too Big to Comb His Mother's Hair."

On Palm Sunday in 1938, O'Daniel told his listeners of numerous letters that he had received urging him to run for governor and sought their advice.

He claimed that 54,449 responses begged him to enter the contest, whereas three said that he was "too good to waste on the job." O'Daniel announced as a candidate on May 1, promising that the Ten Commandments would be his platform and the Golden Rule his motto. When pressed for something a little more specific, he promised a pension of $30 a month for every Texan over sixty-five and came up with the slogan: "Less Johnson grass and politicians, more smokestacks and businessmen." In deriding politicians, O'Daniel, who had never paid a poll tax or voted, struck a note that played well with many voters, then and now. Texans, and Americans in general, love to elect "non-politicians" to political office, a decision often akin to visiting a "non-doctor" for a medical problem or a "non-lawyer" for legal advice.

O'Daniel toured the state with his hillbilly band, holding outdoor rallies—"basking in God's sunlight," he said—that drew huge audiences. Reportedly, crowds of twenty thousand or more Texans gathered along highways just to glimpse his entourage. Few knew that "Pappy" was actually worth half a million dollars, had the advice of a professional public relations expert, and had entered the race primarily at the urging of wealthy businessmen. One of his closest advisers, Carr P. Collins of Dallas, had made a fortune in insurance and by selling Crazy Crystals, a laxative eventually outlawed by the Pure Food and Drug Administration because it had originated as a treatment for horses. O'Daniel's opponents sought to question the cost of his pension proposal and the lack of any other program, but they had no chance against a campaign so perfectly in tune with the state's evangelical traditions. He won the primary without a runoff and received 97 percent of the vote in the November general election.

Some 100,000 people crowded into Memorial Stadium in Austin for O'Daniel's inauguration in January 1939, and then the new governor soon demonstrated his lack of political experience. After first arguing that the state's tax laws would provide sufficient income if they were enforced, he proposed a 1.6 percent tax on all business transactions. The legislature recognized this as a sales tax in disguise and rejected it. Then, when the lower house proposed taxes on natural resources and utilities, the governor helped kill that idea. Short of funds, O'Daniel cut funding for state hospitals and asylums, the State Highway Department, and the Department of Public Safety. A story circulated that Texas Rangers were having to borrow ammunition from highway patrolmen. O'Daniel's appointments to state offices ranged from the unwise to the ridiculous. He nominated James M. West, an oilman from Houston, to the State Highway Commission in spite of the fact that West was known for bitter opposition to the Roosevelt Administration. The legislature, fearing a loss of federal highway funds, rejected the nomination. For state labor commissioner, he chose a desk worker at Southwestern Bell Telephone Company whose only apparent qualification was a letter praising one of his radio speeches. In the meantime, he made no effort to pursue the one specific promise of his campaign—pensions for elderly Texans.

"Pappy" O'Daniel's failures in Austin did not hurt him with the voters. In the 1940 Democratic primary he faced challenges from several capable men, including Highway Commissioner Harry Hines and Railroad Commissioner

Jerry Sadler, and from "Ma" Ferguson as well. Virtually every newspaper in the state opposed his reelection. "The highest office in the state has been the laughingstock of the United States for a year and half," said the *Dallas Morning News*. "If you have traveled out of Texas you know that is true; if you haven't you have a new experience in shame ahead of you." Nevertheless, "Pappy" defeated his Democratic challengers without a runoff and in the 1940 general election became the first gubernatorial candidate to receive more than a million votes.

The 1940 election also held special interest for Texans because, if Roosevelt honored the two-term tradition, Vice President Garner had a chance to become the first Texas-born nominee for the presidency. Even when it became clear that Roosevelt intended to seek a third term, Senators Sheppard and Connally and many other leaders insisted on sending a Garner delegation to the Democratic national convention. Roosevelt, of course, won the nomination, and Garner wound up "purged" from the ticket. The vice president spent the campaign in Uvalde, "sulking among the goats," in the words of one newspaper, and Governor O'Daniel also refused to endorse Roosevelt. Texans, however, gave the president 81 percent of the vote.

O'Daniel's second administration had no more success than the first in dealing with the state's tax laws. The governor still wanted a tax on business transactions, whereas the legislature favored increased taxes on the oil industry and new levies on the sales of automobiles and the receipts of insurance and utility companies. A deadlock ensued, and nothing happened. Even as his attempts to deal with finances failed, "Pappy" turned to a new and more popular target—"labor leader racketeers"—who, he said, were taking over Texas. Disregarding the weakness of unions in the state and the virtual nonexistence of strikes, the legislature listened to the governor and passed an antistrike law making it a crime to threaten violence to prevent anyone from working or to hold an assembly anywhere near the site of a labor dispute. Picketing strikers could go to the penitentiary, but strikebreakers who committed violent acts were not mentioned.

"Pappy's" anti-union law boosted his political fortunes just as a new electoral prize caught his eye in the spring of 1941. United States Senator Morris Sheppard died in April, necessitating the appointment of an interim senator until a special election could be held to choose a replacement for the rest of his term. Wanting the position himself and therefore having to be careful to choose an interim appointee who could not mount a serious challenge later, O'Daniel selected Andrew Jackson Houston, the only surviving son of Sam Houston. Eighty-seven years of age and suffering from senility, the interim senator, in the uncharitable words of one observer, "probably couldn't tell you whether the sun was up or had gone down." Houston entered the Senate on June 2, 1941, then the oldest man ever to serve in that body, and died on June 20. Thus, O'Daniel had no incumbent to worry about in the June 28 special election to choose Sheppard's successor.

"Pappy" ran his usual campaign in 1941—creating a circus-like atmosphere and threatening to "twist the tails" of Washington politicians. He promised to help "that boy" (President Roosevelt) who was surrounded by men incapable of running a peanut stand and offered an antistrike bill as his most important specific policy initiative. The strongest challenge to O'Daniel came from Lyndon Baines Johnson, the former director of the NYA who had served in the House of Representatives since 1937. Johnson ran as a supporter of the New Deal and stressed the need for unified support of the administration. Early results on June 28 appeared to give Johnson the victory, but returns from remote, rural counties trickled in for four days and gave the governor victory by about 1,300 votes. Almost certainly fraud played a role in the outcome, but Johnson did not contest the election, probably because his supporters' methods could not stand careful inspection either. "Pappy" resigned in August 1941 to enter the U.S. Senate where he continued to play the hillbilly buffoon, breaking Huey Long's record by making a speech on only his second day there. While speaking for twenty-five minutes against extending the draft, he informed his new colleagues: "I do like hillbilly music. I also like popular music, church songs, and grand opera; but unfortunately I do not play or sing any kind of music." Not surprisingly, his antistrike bill and other proposals failed by overwhelming majorities, but hundreds of thousands of Texas voters overlooked his ineffectiveness and continued to give their support.

When O'Daniel left for Washington, Lieutenant Governor Coke R. Stevenson succeeded him as Texas's chief executive. Born in a Mason County log cabin in 1888, Stevenson worked his way up as a banker, lawyer, and rancher and served five terms in the state house of representatives before winning the lieutenant governor's office in 1938. Strongly conservative, he had no use for the New Deal and would have cooperated even less than did O'Daniel with the Roosevelt administration. However, the Japanese attack on Pearl Harbor, coming only a few months after Stevenson took office, brought the United States into World War II and pushed domestic politics into the background. On December 8, 1941, the day following the sneak attack, thousands of military-age Texans lined up at recruiting offices, and most others prepared to focus their energies on defeating the nation's enemies. Doubtless some understood the sacrifices likely to be demanded of them, but none could have guessed just how great the impact of the next four years would be on virtually every aspect of life in their state. World War II would bring Texas out of the Great Depression, breathe new life into "Gone to Texas," and change the state as nothing had since the Civil War.

Chapter 15

WORLD WAR II AND THE RISE OF MODERN TEXAS, 1941–1971

World War II brought economic recovery to the United States and left the nation in 1945 a productive giant possessing military power on an unprecedented scale. Obviously, the war unsettled virtually every aspect of life across the United States, but nowhere was its effect more dramatic than in Texas. The state's economy recovered and never looked back as diversification increasingly became the rule. Population growth, slowed notably by the Great Depression, resumed, and a gain of more than 1.2 million residents during the war decade brought the total to 7,711,194 by 1950. This increase came in spite of the fact that a good many black Texans left the state for work in California and northern cities during the 1940s. By 1950 the state's 977,458 African Americans represented only 13 percent of all Texans. Departing blacks were replaced, however, by a rising Mexican American population that reached approximately one million in 1950. More and more Texans moved into towns and cities, and the urban population rose from 45 to 60 percent, the largest increase during any decade in the state's history. Essentially, then, Texas entered World War II a largely impoverished, rural, agricultural state and emerged from the war decade thriving and far more urbanized and industrialized than ever before. The foundation for these changes was in place prior to 1941, of course, but the war provided the impetus for spectacular growth.

World War II—The Military Effort

The December 7, 1941, attack on military installations at Pearl Harbor caught United States forces by surprise and shocked most Americans, but the onset of hostilities, somewhere, was hardly unexpected. After all, aggression by Germany and Italy in Europe and Japan in the Far East had thrown much of the world into war by 1939, and the United States, although technically neutral, had in several ways come to the aid of the victims of the Axis powers, as the aggressors called themselves. Most important, in the spring of 1941 Congress, at the urging of President Roosevelt, passed the Lend-Lease Act, which in effect simply gave war material to nations fighting the Axis. At first this meant only Great Britain, France having been knocked out of the war in 1940, but then when Germany attacked the Soviet Union in June 1941, lend-lease material went to that nation as well. Lend-lease obviously ended all pretense of neutrality and, coupled with other forms of assistance to the British and to China in its fight against the Japanese, created a strong possibility that the United States would enter the war. Recognizing this, the Roosevelt administration sped up the rebuilding of the nation's military that had begun in 1940 with measures such as the selective service act to draft men into the armed forces.

Texans, like most Americans, did not want direct involvement in the war, but they generally supported the administration's efforts to strengthen the military and aid nations under attack by the Axis. Only two Texas congressmen, Martin Dies and Hatton Sumners, did not vote for the selective service act. Senator Tom Connally, as chair of the Foreign Relations Committee, played a key role in passage of lend-lease, and with one exception Texas's entire congressional delegation supported the measure. Undoubtedly patriotism keyed this support—a Texas cartoon of the day showed a powerful armaments workman with the caption "When Do We Call In The Big Boy?"—but the state also benefited economically from the military buildup. The federal government spent more than $500 million on military hardware and supplies in Texas during 1941 and once again, as in World War I, took advantage of the state's relatively level terrain and clear weather to build training facilities. For example, Fort Hood near Killeen became the training ground for tank forces that could compete with German Panzer units (and even to this day remains a center for training in armored warfare).

The attack on Pearl Harbor led immediately to a declaration of war with Japan. Senator Connally of Texas introduced the necessary resolution on December 8, and several days later offered similar resolutions for war with Germany and Italy after those two nations joined their Axis ally against the United States. Governor Coke Stevenson denounced the "cowardly Japanese attack" and correctly predicted that Texans would support the war enthusiastically. Volunteers lined up immediately at induction centers and continued to come throughout the course of the war. Overall, Texas, which had 5 percent of the nation's population, provided 7 percent of those who served in the armed forces. The state's total came to approximately 750,000, including 12,000 women. Most served in the army and air force, but about one-quarter were in the navy, marines, and coast guard. While they were away, their families dreaded the receipt of a telegram from the military, and terrible news came too often as 22,022 Texans died or suffered fatal wounds in battle. Texas suffered a greater loss of life proportionately during the Civil War, thanks to the diseases that ran rampant through armies of that era, but World War II battles were the deadliest ever faced by the state's soldiers.

Several units composed largely of Texas soldiers served with particular distinction. The Thirty-sixth United States Infantry Division, a national guard unit that also served in World War I, was called into national service in November 1940. Nicknamed the "Texas Division" or "*T*-Patchers" for the distinctive T on their shoulder patches, the Thirty-sixth trained in Texas and Louisiana during 1941. In November one unit—the Second Battalion, 131st Field Artillery—was detached and sent to the Far East. This unit, comprising mostly men from north-central Texas, reached Pearl Harbor a week before December 7 and was continuing west when the Japanese attacked. They proceeded to Australia and in early 1942 joined British, Australian, and Dutch troops in a futile defense of Java in the Dutch East Indies. Forced to surrender on March 10, the unit became known as the "Lost Battalion" because the Japanese did not reveal the prisoners' location for more than a year. Most of the Texans wound up in 1943–1944 as laborers building a railroad from Burma to Bangkok, Thailand, a project that included the bridge made famous in the book and film *Bridge on the River Kwai.* Moving tons of earth by hand in a tropical climate, having inadequate food and virtually no medical attention, and suffering brutal punishments from their guards, only the strongest and luckiest of prisoners survived. Roy Offerle of Wichita Falls, one of the survivors, later described how he and his older brother Oscar developed tropical ulcers from small rock cuts on their legs. The younger Offerle managed to keep his ulcer clean by standing in a stream and letting minnows eat away the decaying flesh, but his brother's ulcer went to the bone. Late one afternoon, Roy remembered, he found Oscar running a high fever and semiconscious. "I put his head in my lap," he said, "and he died."

Other units of the Thirty-sixth Division escaped the horrors of Japanese prisoner of war camps, but they faced murderous fighting in North Africa and Europe from 1943 until 1945. After participating in the invasion of Algeria in April 1943, the division led the amphibious assault on Salerno, Sicily, in September and had a key part in the offensive that led to the capture of Rome in 1944. It then participated in the invasion of southern France in the late summer of 1944 and served as part of the force that occupied Germany in 1945. The Texas Division suffered one of the highest casualty rates of any in the army—3,717 killed, 12,685 wounded, and 3,064 missing in action.

The Ninetieth Division, a Texas unit also known as the "Tough 'Ombres" and the "Alamo" division, took part in the D-Day invasion at Utah Beach and fought across France and Germany into Czechoslovakia before the war ended. It suffered nearly 18,500 casualties, including 2,963 killed, many of the deaths coming in close fighting in the hedgerow country of Normandy. Like the Thirty-sixth, the Ninetieth provided occupation troops in Germany until late 1945.

The list of individual Texans who served with special distinction fills pages; a few must serve as examples. Admiral Chester W. Nimitz, a native of Fredericksburg and graduate of the United States Naval Academy, took over command of the Pacific Fleet after Pearl Harbor and coordinated the effort that brought the Japanese to unconditional surrender in September 1945. Colonel Oveta Culp Hobby, a native of Killeen and the wife of former governor William P. Hobby, organized and commanded the Women's Army Auxiliary Corps, which in 1943 became part of the army and dropped the word

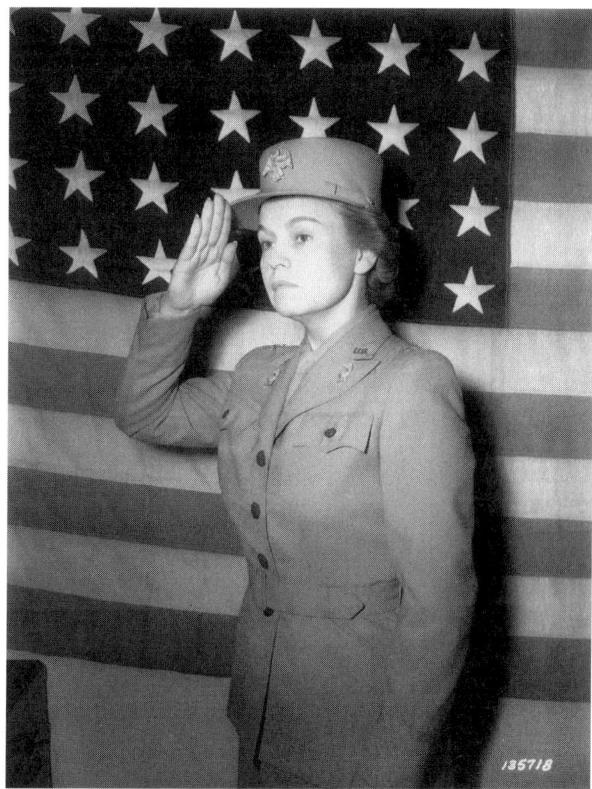

Oveta Culp Hobby (1905–1995). Hobby, commander of the Women's Army Corps during World War II, was the first woman to attain the rank of colonel in the United States Army. National Archives, #111-SC-135718.

Auxiliary. Some 200,000 WACs, as they became known, handled 239 different army jobs encompassing secretarial work to motor-vehicle maintenance to folding parachutes. The first woman to hold the rank of colonel in the army, Hobby received the Distinguished Service Medal in 1945.

Samuel D. Dealey and James Earl Rudder stand out among Texans who held commands in the field and actually engaged the enemy. Born in Dallas and educated at the Naval Academy, Dealey commanded a submarine, the USS *Harder*, that sank sixteen Japanese ships before being destroyed itself in August 1944. His exploits made him the most highly decorated man in the U.S. Navy during the war and earned a Congressonal Medal of Honor, awarded to his widow in 1945. Dealey Plaza in Dallas permanently honors his memory. Rudder, born in Eden, a small Concho County town, graduated from Texas A&M and became a second lieutenant in the army reserves. Called to active duty in 1941, he commanded the Second Ranger Battalion at the Normandy invasion. His unit scaled 100-foot cliffs to knock out German gun batteries, suffering more than 50 percent casualties in the fight. Rudder, although wounded twice himself, continued in command after the battle and emerged from the war as a colonel. Eventually, he became a general in the army reserves and served as a highly effective president of Texas A&M University.

The only difficulty in describing Texans who fought heroically as enlisted men is choosing those to mention. Doris (Dorie) Miller grew up near Waco, joined the navy in 1939, and on December 7, 1941, was serving as Mess Attendant, Second Class, on the USS *West Virginia* at Pearl Harbor. As an African American, Miller had to serve in the segregated steward's branch of the navy and did not receive training in gunnery. When the Japanese attack began, Miller helped remove the ship's fatally wounded captain from the main deck and then ran to an unattended deck gun and began firing at the enemy planes. News stories credited him with as many as four kills, but none were confirmed. Miller himself said that he thought he hit one plane. In any case, he received the Navy Cross in 1942 and died in 1943 when the ship on which he was serving as a cook was torpedoed and sunk near the Gilbert Islands. Eventually, the navy named a destroyer escort vessel in his honor. Macario García, a native of Mexico whose family moved to the Houston area in 1923, singlehandedly attacked two German machine-gun emplacements in November 1944. Although wounded in the shoulder and foot, he crawled forward and destroyed the two nests, killing six enemy soldiers and capturing four in the process. This display won García the Medal of Honor, one of five awarded to Tejanos in the war.

Audie L. Murphy, a poor boy from Hunt County who stood five feet seven inches tall and weighed 130 pounds when he volunteered on his eighteenth birthday in 1942, became the most decorated soldier in the history of the U.S. Army to that time. Near Holtzwihr, France, on January 26, 1945, already seasoned by fighting in the invasions of North Africa and Sicily, Murphy gave probably the greatest display of courage under fire of any single soldier in the entire war. As a second lieutenant (thanks to a battlefield promotion) ordered to hold a position with about thirty men and two tank destroyers under his command, he faced an attack by two hundred German infantrymen supported by six tanks. One of his tank destroyers had to be abandoned when it ran into a ditch, and the other took a hit from a German 88-millimeter shell. Ordering his men to take cover in nearby woods, Murphy fired at the advancing Germans with his carbine until he ran out of ammunition; then he jumped on the disabled tank destroyer and began using its .50 caliber machine gun. American artillery fire closed in on his position to the point that a fire control officer called on the field telephone to ask how close the German troops were. "Hold the phone," Murphy replied, "I'll let you talk to one of the bastards!" A forward artillery observer who saw the action later wrote "With the Germans 100 yards away . . . he was completely exposed to enemy fire and there was a blaze under him that threatened to blow the destroyer to bits. Machine gun, machine pistol, and 88-shell fire was all around him. . . . His clothing was riddled by flying fragments of shells and bits of rock. I saw that his trouser leg was soaked with blood. He swung the machine gun to where 12 Germans were sneaking up a ditch in an attempt to flank his posi-

Audie Murphy (1924–1971). Murphy entered the U.S. Army on his eighteenth birthday in 1942 and emerged as the most decorated soldier in World War II. This photo, taken shortly after the end of the war, shows Murphy wearing some of the medals he earned for valor in battle, including the Congressional Medal of Honor. Bettmann/ CORBIS.

tion, and he killed all of them at 50 yards." In about thirty minutes, Murphy killed fifty of the enemy, forcing them to pull back. When he was discharged from the army in San Antonio in 1945, Audie Murphy wore thirty-seven decorations, eleven of them for valor in battle. He eventually became an actor, playing himself in the autobiographical movie *To Hell and Back,* and died in a plane crash in 1971.

Most Texas soldiers trained in their home state, which became the largest military training ground in the world between 1941 and 1945. Twenty combat divisions numbering 1.2 million men prepared for war at the state's fifteen major army bases, and an estimated 200,000 airmen trained at forty military airfields. Texas also was the training home for a group of women pilots whose contribution to the war effort received little acknowledgment until years later. In 1941 facing a shortage of male fliers, the armed forces began several programs to attract women pilots. One of these, the Women's Flying Training Detachment (WFTD) directed by aviator Jacqueline Cochran, began operations at the Houston Municipal Airport in November 1942. Women trainees lived in motels and private homes in the area and were driven to the airport each day. Early in 1943, the WFTD moved to more adequate quarters at Avenger Field near Sweetwater, and in August of that year it merged with the other women pilots group, the Women's Auxiliary Ferrying Squadron (WAFS), to form the Women's Airforce Service Pilots (WASPs) under the direction of Cochran. The 1,074 WASPs ferried 12,650 planes of all types, including B-17 bombers, from manufacturers to airbases and also towed targets and flew simulated strafing and bombing missions. Although these women fliers who trained in Texas obviously were part of the war effort, they remained civilians without military benefits, and an attempt to militarize the program failed in 1944. In 1977, thirty-five years after their deactivation, the surviving WASPs received honorable discharges and veterans benefits from the government.

Texas military installations maintained segregated facilities for black soldiers, including the eighty-thousand African American Texans who entered the service. Even then whites near the bases sometimes complained about the presence of black soldiers, and blacks grew angry at their separate and unequal treatment. Black and white soldiers at Fort Bliss attacked each other in 1943, but fortunately no serious outbreak, such as the Houston Race Riot during World War I, occurred. The thousands of Mexican Americans who served in the military also faced discrimination, but generally in less obvious ways than blacks. When the war ended, Mexican Texan veterans would demand equality and, in 1948, organize the American G.I. Forum to work toward that goal.

Ironically, while millions of American soldiers began the war at Texas training bases, more than fifty thousand Axis soldiers ended the conflict in the state's prisoner of war camps. Texas had twenty-one permanent camps, the largest located at Mexia, Hereford, Hearne, and Huntsville, and more than twenty temporary camps. The prisoners, mostly Germans, lived under tight security at first, but this gradually eased as thousands were put to work on Texas farms and even as replacements for American skilled craftsmen such as carpenters and electricians at military bases. Far from home and generally well treated, the prisoners of war made few escape attempts. Texas also had internment camps at Seagoville, Kenedy, and Crystal City to house citizens of the Axis powers, most of whom were Japanese sent to the United States from Latin American countries. Held to prevent possible internal sabotage and to provide bartering pawns for American civilians taken by the Axis, some five thousand of these interns remained in the camps until the close of the war.

World War II—The Home Front

When the war began, Texans, especially those in the cities along the Gulf of Mexico, had to face the possibility of an attack by air or sea. Galveston and several other cities practiced blackouts and air-raid drills in early 1942, but fortunately German submarines in the Gulf represented the closest threat mounted against Texas by the Axis. This left Texans at home free to concentrate on supplying the food and materials necessary to support "our boys overseas." Rationing became a way of life as the national government set limits on the consumption of items such as sugar, meat, coffee, shoes, rubber, auto parts, and gasoline. Local rationing boards distributed coupons and oversaw the program. Rationing created a great deal of anger—Governor Stevenson, for example, opposed limitations on gasoline, arguing that fuel was as necessary in Texas as "the saddle, the rifle, the ax, and the Bible"—but generally Texans accepted it as essential to the war effort.

Just as in World War I, Texans sought to remedy shortages in food supplies by growing their own. "Victory gardens" sprang up in flower beds and back yards across the state. Efficiency became an exercise in patriotism, too. Whole communities held scrap-metal drives, collecting tons of reusable material under slogans such as "Bury a Jap with Scrap." To conserve gasoline, speed limits were lowered to 35 miles per hour. This drastically slowed travel by personal auto and, in combination with rationing, encouraged thousands of Texans to use buses and trains. The state's bus systems reported 17 million passengers in 1941 and 88 million two years later.

American agriculture had to feed the nation's civilians and soldiers and those in allied countries as well, and Texas farmers did their part. Mechanizing rapidly with the aid of federal guaranteed loans, they focused on the production of meat and food crops such as wheat, corn, vegetables, and citrus fruits. The amount of land devoted to cotton decreased notably, and many East Texas farmers turned from their traditional crop to cattle raising. One-time cotton fields became pastures to the extent that by 1945 East Texas had more cattle than West Texas. Labor shortages became a problem as farm boys entered the service, requiring greater involvement than ever by the entire family. Work was nothing new to farm women, but during the war they had to do more of the jobs usually reserved for men such as plowing and cultivating with tractors, hauling grain, and working cattle. Farmers, particularly in South Texas, also relied on undocumented Mexican labor. The possibility of legally obtaining the labor of Mexican nationals existed, thanks to the Bracero Program negotiated by the United States government and Mexico in 1942. This agreement allowed Mexican farm workers to enter the United States with the promise of a thirty-cent-an-hour wage and humane treatment. Texas, however, refused to participate, and in 1943 Mexico banned "braceros" from the state because of the unfair treatment often given Mexicans and Mexican Americans there.

Oil production, the key activity in Texas's nonagricultural economy before the war, received less of a boost from the conflict than might be expected. The outbreak of war in Europe in 1939 reduced the market for American petroleum, so by early 1942 Texas fields were producing at less than 60 percent of their potential. Once the United States entered the conflict, demand increased, but German submarines seriously threatened tankers moving oil products by sea to the northeast. To solve this problem, the federal government built two pipelines called the Big Inch and the Little Big Inch. The former, which carried crude oil in its twenty-four-inch diameter pipe, ran from

Longview northeast across the Mississippi River, through southern Illinois, and on to New York City and Philadelphia. The latter, carrying refined products in a twenty-inch diameter pipe, ran from the Houston-Port Arthur area to Linden, New Jersey. Both were completed by early 1944 and, together, moved more than 350 million barrels of Texas petroleum products to the east. Even with the encouragement provided by these pipelines, however, the oil industry lagged because trained personnel had to enter the service and military equipment required all available steel.

The most dramatic economic changes brought by war came in manufacturing rather than agriculture or oil production. Along the coast from Beaumont and Port Arthur southwestward to Corpus Christi, the petrochemical industry that produced fuel and synthetic rubber for the allied military effort grew into the largest of its kind in the world. Steel mills opened in Daingerfield and Houston; a giant tin smelter began production in Texas City; and the paper and wood-pulp industry flourished again in East Texas. Shipyards at Port Arthur, Beaumont, Houston, Galveston, and Corpus Christi turned out naval vessels, and huge aircraft factories were built at Garland, Grand Prairie, and Fort Worth. The largest of these, the Consolidated Vultee Aircraft Corporation plant near Carswell Air Force Base outside Fort Worth, was a mile-long structure that at one time employed up to 38,000 workers. Texas plants also manufactured powder and ammunition. For example, the Lone Star Army Ammunition Plant, which was built near Texarkana in 1941, produced artillery shells and bombs as well as small-caliber ammunition throughout the war.

The growth of industry, coupled with the demand for men in the military, created a labor shortage that worked to the advantage of unions in Texas. Under the auspices of the National War Labor Board, organizers unionized most of the state's industries by 1945. Labor shortages also brought thousands of Texas women into the workforce for the first time. Encouraged by government advertisements, especially those playing on personal relationships—"Longing won't bring him back sooner," said one poster that showed a woman holding a letter to her breast, "take a war job and help him come home"—women worked at "male" jobs such as riveting and operating punch-presses. "Rosie the Riveter" became the symbol of these female workers in military industries. Most Texans, male and female, expected them to give up their jobs to men and return to more traditional roles when the war ended, and whether or not their employment had any long-term impact on society is a matter of debate. Some of the long-time legal disabilities placed on women, such as the denial of service on juries, would be changed within ten years after the end of the war, but those changes might have come anyhow. No one can say with certainty. The only absolutely clear point is that the World War II generation of Texas women contributed immeasurably to victory.

The need for labor also led to a doubling of the number of African Americans (from 150,000 to 295,000) who worked in wartime manufacturing. Discrimination continued, however, in many ways. The Consolidated Vultee plant segregated its assembly line, and Baytown oil refineries paid blacks less

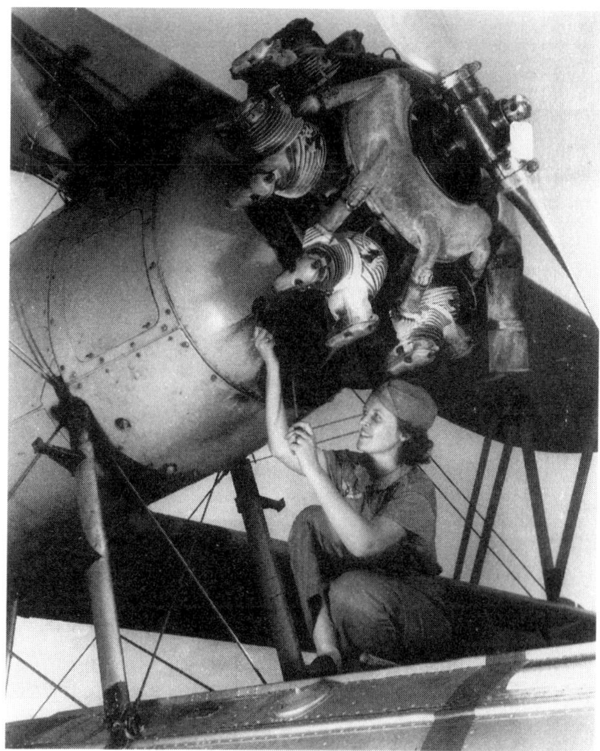

Mary Josephine Farley, Airplane Mechanic, Corpus Christi Naval Air Base, 1942. Farley, at the age of twenty, had a private pilot's license and had made several cross-country flights. National Archives, #208-AA-352-00-1.

than whites for the same work. Mexican Americans did not fare even that well. Relatively few found work in industry, and those who did were in unskilled, low-wage jobs.

Regardless of their gender or ethnicity, Texans seeking work in the booming wartime industries had to move into or near cities to find it. As a result, during the 1940s the state finally completed the transition from its overwhelmingly rural past to a predominantly urban present. By 1950, for the first time a majority (60 percent in fact) of Texans lived in towns and cities of more than 2,500 population. Houston, having grown 55 percent since 1940, was the largest with 596,163 people, followed by Dallas (434,462) and San Antonio (408,442). Fort Worth, in spite of new defense industries, was a distant fourth in size (278,778). Three other cities—Austin, Corpus Christi, and El Paso—grew to more than 100,000 residents during the decade. Corpus Christi experienced the most spectacular rise, a 90 percent gain from 57,301 in 1940 to 108,827 in 1950.

The war effort, accompanied by economic recovery and boom, meant that political conflict on the home front was limited during the early forties. Governor Coke Stevenson used the return of prosperity to the fullest advantage, eliminating the $42 million state debt created during the depression and then, without an increase in taxes, raising state spending on highways and education. "Calculating Coke," a nickname given the governor because of his quiet, unruffled manner, became so popular that he won reelection in 1942 and 1944 virtually without having to campaign. However, the 1942 senatorial election and 1944 presidential election gave a foretaste of a new tone that would dominate postwar Texas politics.

In 1942, former governor Jimmie Allred challenged the recently elected incumbent W. Lee O'Daniel for one of Texas's seats in the U.S. Senate. Allred had support from the Roosevelt administration and New Dealers in general as well as from labor leaders, servicemen, and local bosses. Some liked his progressivism, and others knew that he could deliver New Deal projects to their regions. O'Daniel responded by insisting that Allred had the support of "Communistic labor leader racketeers" who had offered him $200,000 to run for the Senate and another $200,000 if he won. To improve his support among ordinary Texans, "Pappy" praised Roosevelt to the skies. One observer in Dallas explained that O'Daniel "has the support of the leading figures of business and industry, including the dominant oil industry. They are for him because he hates Roosevelt and labor, and is clever enough to deceive his rural followers . . . into believing that he is a friend and supporter of the President." Allred forced O'Daniel into a runoff in the Democratic primary, where "Pappy" prevailed by a vote of 451,359 to 433,203. His victory first demonstrated the full potential of anticommunism and anti-labor as political issues in modern Texas.

The presidential election of 1944 brought the strongest opposition yet to Roosevelt and the New Deal from within the Texas Democratic Party. Conservatives had expressed disagreement in 1936 and 1940, but in 1944 they rebelled openly. Their grievances included Roosevelt's "dumping" Garner from the ticket in 1940 in favor of the liberal Henry Wallace, the myriad regulations imposed on business during the depression and the war, the administration's friendship with organized labor, and the tendency of the national government to support minorities. They were particularly upset at the 1944 Supreme Court decision in *Smith v. Allwright* that reversed *Grovey v. Townsend* (1935) and struck down the white primary. When Texas liberal Democrats who remained loyal to Roosevelt and the New Deal managed to commit the state party to support the president once he won renomination in 1944, the conservatives broke away and formed a third party, the Texas Regulars. Hoping to draw off enough Democratic votes to prevent a Roosevelt victory, the Texas Regulars offered a platform that included calls for the "Return of state rights which have been destroyed by the Communist-controlled New Deal" and the "Restoration of the supremacy of the white race, which has been destroyed by the Communist-controlled New Deal." Senator O'Daniel served as the Regulars' primary campaigner, but leadership and financial backing came from a who's who of the state's wealthiest businessmen and their lawyers. The Regulars could not destroy Roosevelt's popularity with rank and file Texans, and certainly O'Daniel's claim that the president was a greater threat than Hitler did not help. Roosevelt carried Texas with 72 percent of the vote, while the Regulars (who had a program but no actual candidate), gained only 12 percent. "Gentlemen," said one Regular, "the yokels discovered that they can outvote us." Nevertheless, defeat did not undermine the conservatives' convictions. Their revolt against the national Democratic Party would continue in postwar Texas.

Postwar Economic Expansion: The Fabulous Fifties and Soaring Sixties

"Texans Manufacture A Boom," read a headline in the December 1956 issue of the usually staid *Texas Business Review*. "Texas industrialization is an exciting, fast-paced story of giant aircraft plants covering the prairies and vast petrochemical complexes webbing the Gulfwater plain," the article explained. "It started with Spindletop at the turn of the century, gathered momentum as new fields came in and large refineries were built along the coast, and hit its stride with World War II. Since then, plant expansion has become one of the most dynamic factors in the nation's economy, moving with all the swiftness of a Roy Bean trial." Pointing to the Gulf coast's advantages in cheap transportation and access to resources, the author ticked off a list of plants that used heavy raw materials to create bulk finished products: Reynolds Aluminum at Corpus Christi; Dow Chemical in Brazoria County; Sinclair Oil, Hughes Tool, Champion Paper, Cameron Iron, and Sheffield Steel in Houston; Shell Oil at Deer Park; Carbide & Carbon Chemicals and American Oil at Texas City; Humble at Baytown; DuPont at Orange; Gulf Oil and Texaco at Port Arthur; and Magnolia Oil at Beaumont. Manufacturing in North Texas, he explained, depended on truck and rail transportation and therefore tended to focus on the production of consumer goods such as clothing, household supplies and furnishings, food products, and printed matter. Of course, the automobile and airplane industries were very large exceptions to this rule. The Convair plant in Fort Worth, which originated as Consolidated Vultee during the war and was then bought by General Dynamics Corporation in 1954, had more than twenty thousand employees. General Motors and Ford had assembly plants in Tarrant and Dallas Counties respectively. "A half-century ago," the article concluded, "Texas had practically no manufacturing. Today the state has changed from an agricultural province to one of the country's most important manufacturing centers and is seriously challenging the positions of long-established industrial regions. . . . Texas's ten-thousand-plus industries are manufacturing one of the most spectacular booms in the nation's history."

Statistics to back up these claims about postwar industrial growth in Texas are readily available. In 1947, the state had 7,128 manufacturing establishments that added $1.7 billion dollars in value to the raw materials that they fashioned into finished products. By 1973, the comparable numbers were 14,431 plants and $15.2 billion in value added. The increase in value, even when adjusted for the more than 100 percent inflation rate between 1947 and 1973, amounted to more than 300 percent in a little more than two decades. During the same period, employment in manufacturing more than doubled, from fewer than 300,000 workers in 1947 to more than 730,000 in 1972.

Oil refining and chemicals production dominated Texas manufacturing during this period, but a new industry—electronics—grew faster than any other, an indicator of its great importance to the state's economic future. Producing consumer goods, such as televisions sets, phonographs, radios, calculators, and computers, and military equipment, such as navigation and guidance systems, the early electronics industry flourished in Houston. However, Texas Instruments (TI), a corporation created originally by two physicists working on advanced oil exploration technology in Oklahoma, gave Dallas the lead in the 1950s. Called Geophysical Services, Incorporated until 1951, TI was the first company to take full advantage of the recently invented transistor, a tiny device that controls the flow of electricity in electronic equipment. Engineers at TI developed transistors that used silicon as a semiconductor and paved the way for Jack S. Kilby, one of their co-workers, to invent an entire circuit made of silicon in 1958. This integrated circuit or "computer microchip" provided the brains for TI's hand-held calculator, which was patented by 1971, and eventually for nearly all electronic devices from computers to cell phones to garage-door openers. Thanks to the integrated circuit and aggressive expansion, TI built its sales to more than $200 million a year during the 1960s. Another Dallas-based corporation, Electronic Data Systems, became highly successful in the use of computers to manage data for other businesses, insurance companies, and financial institutions. Incorporated by H. Ross Perot in 1962, EDS signed long-term contracts with its clients—the Frito Lay Corporation, for example—and put its founder on the road to becoming a billionaire.

While the boom in manufacturing captured most of the headlines in postwar Texas, the state's economy became more dependent than ever before on the production of oil and natural gas. The nation's demand for energy, which became so great after the war that it turned the United States into a net importer of oil by 1948, did wonderful things for Texas producers. Although the industry suffered the usual instability during the fifties and sixties, expanding too rapidly when prices rose and contracting when recessions hit, the overall trend was upward. New wells were drilled in old fields, and production began in the tidelands along the Gulf of Mexico. In 1972, Texas wells produced more than 1.2 billion barrels of oil (a new record) and nearly 8 billion cubic feet of natural gas. More than 75,000 Texans found work in the oil and gas industry.

Texas agriculture took something of a back seat to manufacturing and the oil industry after World War II, but this decline in relative importance should not obscure vital steps toward modernization in the production of crops and livestock. Indeed, these years marked the transition from farming to agribusiness. Between 1945 and 1974, the number of farms decreased by more than half—from 384,977 in 1945 to 174,068 in 1974—while their average size more than doubled, rising from 367 to 771 acres. Farm tenancy decreased to 14 percent in 1974, a far cry from the 62 percent rate of 1930. Larger farms depended on mechanization as never before. Machines combined wheat and small grains, picked or stripped cotton from the plants, baled hay, and harvested a variety of other crops such as spinach, potatoes, peanuts, and pecans. Irrigation became the rule in much of South and West Texas, watering millions of acres by the 1970s. Farmers made increasing use of fertilizers and herbicides and planted higher-yielding varieties of crops developed by researchers at state and federal experiment stations. They also developed greater diversity in their crops, reducing the traditional reliance on cotton. Corn made a comeback, largely because of its use in another new aspect of Texas agriculture—the fattening of cattle in feedlots. The idea of concentrated feeding to put weight on cattle developed in the 1960s and by early in the next decade three million head were marketed annually from feedlots, most of which were located in the High Plains. Overall, the modernization process completed the re-centering of Texas agriculture from the state's eastern and central regions to the Lower Río Grande Valley and the plains around Lubbock. It also resulted in greater productivity and a rise in the value of crops and livestock sold from a little more than $1 billion in 1945 to $5.6 billion in 1974. Even allowing for steep inflation, this increase indicates that agriculture also had its place in the postwar boom.

"Gone to Texas," Postwar Style

The economic boom that followed World War II brought renewed population growth to Texas and a continuation of the movement from rural to urban areas within the state. As an encore to the impressive 20 percent gain during the 1940s, the population rose 45 percent in the twenty years from 1950 to 1970, reaching a total of 11,196,730 and moving Texas from sixth to fourth among the most populous states in the nation. Black Texans increased their numbers 43 percent to nearly 1.4 million over the same period, but their percentage of the total population still declined slightly—from 13 to 12 percent. By contrast, the Latino population, defined as Texans who spoke Spanish or had Spanish surnames, doubled to more than 2 million, some 18 percent of the total population. Mexican Americans, of course, constituted the overwhelming majority of those defined as Latino. Texans of Mexican descent probably surpassed African Americans as the state's largest minority as early as 1947.

Regardless of its growth, Texas continued in 1970 to have a largely southern population. Nearly 8 million of the state's slightly more than 11 million residents in 1970 were native Texans, the great majority of whom, other than those of Mexican descent, had southern roots. And among those born elsewhere, more came from states in the South (1,238,981) than from all the rest of the United States combined (1,092,596). Even when some 2 million Texas-born Latinos are subtracted from the population as non-southerners, nearly two of every three Texans in 1970 had ties to the South.

Urbanization, which had slowed notably in the 1930s but then raced ahead to take over the state during the 1940s, continued to advance nearly as rapidly in the two postwar decades. By 1970 eight of every ten Texans lived in a town of 2,500 or more residents. Houston, the state's largest city, increased in size 107 percent in twenty years and became the first to reach a population of more than a million (1,232,802 in 1970). Dallas nearly kept pace, growing 94 percent to a total of 844,401.

Population growth and rapid urbanization indicated boom times in postwar Texas; yet several million of the state's people shared a small and inadequate part of the rising prosperity. A report prepared by the Texas Office of Economic Opportunity showed that in 1970 approximately 2,028,000 Texans had an average of less than three dollars a day to meet their physical needs. This amounted to a poverty rate of more than 18 percent and ranked Texas twelfth among the states in that category. The highest incidence of poverty existed among blacks (39 percent), followed by Mexican Americans (36 percent) and Anglos (10 percent). Geographically, the poorest sections were South Texas (47 percent) and the Brazos River Valley (31 percent). The report concluded by recommending that the state government do more to improve education, aid workers in advancing their qualifications and finding work, and provide health care assistance. Being poor was hardly new in Texas—for many years laborers and tenant farmers by the hundreds of thousands had lived on the margin of subsistence—but modernization and rapid population growth increased the gap between rich and poor Texans and brought new dimensions to poverty in the state.

Postwar Politics: Democratic Factionalism and Republican Opportunities

In 1945 traditional Texas conservatism—defined as insistence on limited government, low taxes, minimal social services, and the denial of equal rights to minorities—maintained its hold on the state's Democratic Party. Texans had voted time after time for Franklin D. Roosevelt, sent New Dealers such as Lyndon B. Johnson to Congress, and twice elected James V. Allred as governor, but as the postwar period opened Governor Coke Stevenson and like-minded state legislators had firm control in Austin. Moreover, many of the party's leaders had indicated their dislike for the New Deal and, now that Roosevelt was out of the way, stood ready to insist that the national Democratic Party return to the principles that it generally followed before 1933. They had no use for liberals—people who favored a larger government that regulated business, promoted social welfare, levied higher taxes, and tended to support civil rights for minorities. Over the next decade, however, conservative Democrats in Texas faced a twofold challenge: one from continuing liberalism within the national party and another from an emerging group of liberals in their own party at home. The resulting factional disputes did not destroy conservative Democratic control of Texas, but they offered the Republican Party opportunities to make greater gains than at any time since Reconstruction.

Texas's liberal Democrats, a fledgling coalition of urban and professional progressives, former suffragists, labor, minorities, and low-income voters, had to wage an uphill battle under the best of circumstances. The average voter's ingrained distrust of the national government, dislike of taxes, and lack of concern about civil rights would not change easily. Moreover, during the postwar years, Texas liberals faced an additional obstacle—the Red Scare. Many Americans had felt threatened by communism since the Russian Revolution of 1917, and this general dislike turned into genuine fear in the late 1940s when the Soviet Union expanded its influence across Eastern Europe and exploded its first atomic bomb. Communism's successes in Europe, coupled with the "loss" of China to red forces, raised questions about internal security and the loyalty of American citizens. Was the United States losing the Cold War because some of its people were "soft" on Communism and permitting spies to operate in their midst? The 1948 indictment of Alger Hiss, a former State Department employee, on charges of lying under oath about his espionage activities during the 1930s seemed to give an answer. By early 1950, when Senator Joseph McCarthy of Wisconsin took the headlines with spectacular charges that the State Department still employed "card-carrying Communists," many Texans stood ready to take action and ferret out the reds. Liberals obviously made the best targets as the Red Scare grew, and their efforts to gain political strength suffered accordingly.

The budding split between conservative and liberal Democrats in postwar Texas appeared first during the 1946 campaign to choose a successor to Governor Stevenson. A fight over governing the University of Texas lay in the background. During the war years, the university's board of regents, most of whom were appointed by Governors O'Daniel and Stevenson, sought to increase their control over courses and faculty. The regents fired four untenured economics professors who spoke in defense of federal labor laws at an antiunion meeting in Dallas, weakened tenure, eliminated funding for social science research, and banned John Dos Passos's *U.S.A.* trilogy from an English department reading list because of its "obscene" and "perverted" content. (The novel won the Pulitzer Prize soon thereafter.) Homer P. Rainey, president of the university since 1939, regarded the regents' actions as violations of academic freedom and fought them at every step. Finally, after the banning of *U.S.A.*, Rainey made a statement of all his grievances to the general faculty, and the regents responded by firing him on November 1, 1944. Students held a funeral march to mark the burial of academic freedom in Austin, and the American Association of University Professors censured the University. Regents fought back with charges that the school taught communism, had a "nest of homosexuals," and that Rainey wanted to admit blacks.

Rainey took his case to the people in numerous speeches and radio broadcasts during 1945 and then announced as a candidate for governor in 1946. The professor-turned-politician outlined a program of social improvement, including advances in education, health, and old-age pensions. Funds to pay for his plan were to come from increased taxes, particularly on the oil and gas industry. This moderately liberal program gained significant support from the newspapers in middle-sized cities such as Austin, Waco, and Corpus Christi and appealed to those who had endorsed the New Deal and to organized labor. Rainey had the support of suffragists such as Minnie Fisher Cunningham and Jane Y. McCallum and also earned the votes of African Americans recently allowed to participate in the Democratic Primary by the decision in *Smith v. Allwright* (1944).

Because of his high profile and liberal stance, Rainey served as a lightning rod for the four conservatives who sought the Democratic nomination in 1946. The early favorite, Lieutenant Governor John Lee Smith, played on fears of racial integration and communist-infiltrated labor unions such as the Congress of Industrial Organizations (CIO). Rainey, he told one East Texas audience, will replace portraits of Jefferson and Wilson with "pictures of some kinky-headed ward heeler of the CIO-PAC." As the campaign developed, however, Smith's extremism alienated many and opened the way to victory by a more shrewd campaigner, Beauford Jester. The son of a Corsicana politician who had served as lieutenant governor in the 1890s, Jester graduated from the University of Texas and became wealthy as an oil industry lawyer before taking a seat on the Railroad Commission in 1942. As a candidate for governor he promised to fight the CIO but avoided personal vilification and placed special emphasis on a pledge to oppose any increase in taxes. Thanks to this approach, which seemed middle-of-the-road with Rainey and Smith in the race, Jester ran first in the July primary with nearly 444,000 votes. Rainey came in second with 291,282 votes and faced Jester in a runoff. The professor campaigned hard, arguing that Texas needed to continue the New Deal approach, but Jester countered with the argument that the state did not need a "new, radical, and expensive form of government" imposed on it. Most well-known Texans, including Governor Stevenson, endorsed Jester, and he swept to victory with 66 percent of the vote.

Issues related to labor unions took center stage during Jester's first term. The CIO organized plant after plant across Texas in 1946–1947, and strikes cost the state's corporations millions in lost goods and services. Most of the state's newspapers furiously denounced the unions involved and, with the *Dallas Morning News* in the forefront, crusaded for legislation to break their momentum. The legislature and Governor Jester responded in early 1947 by passing a right-to-work law that prohibited requiring union membership as a condition of employment. Antiunion spokesmen saw this as a matter of protecting workers' freedom; union leaders viewed it as a way of undermining their organizations by allowing workers to benefit from union efforts to improve wages and working conditions without bearing any of the cost of those efforts. The legislature also passed other antiunion laws, including one that prohibited pickets at strikes from being within fifty feet of each other or the entrance of the plant being picketed. Proponents of this legislation enjoyed their victory but did not rest. One group circulated a poster with photographs of legislators who had voted against the right-to-work law with the label "Communists in the Texas Legislature."

Jester's antiunion legislation proved generally popular, and he managed to obtain greater state spending without any new taxes. His call for increases in the salaries of teachers went unheeded, but the legislature sent to the voters a constitutional amendment (which later passed) providing more funding for construction at state colleges and universities. In 1948 he faced no significant opposition in the July Democratic primary and won renomination without a runoff. Voters probably found Jester's easy victory boring, but another contest taking place at the same time more than compensated for any lack of excitement. In fact, the 1948 Democratic senatorial primary was the most disputed and controversial election in Texas history.

"Pappy" Lee O'Daniel's senate term drew to a close in 1948, and he, in what a Lubbock newspaper called "the one most constructive act" of his political career, decided to retire. The race to succeed him turned into essentially a two-man contest between former governor Coke Stevenson and Congressman Lyndon B. Johnson. Stevenson supplemented his well-known views on limited government and taxation with condemnation of American communists, whereas Johnson ran on his record as a New Dealer who supported programs such as rural electrification and aid to the aged. Johnson's stance attracted the support of Texas liberals, but he had maintained ties with conservatives by condemning the civil rights initiatives of the Truman administration, championing the interests of oil companies, and voting for the antiunion Taft-Hartley Act of 1947. The two ran very different campaigns. Johnson attacked Stevenson's lack of experience outside Texas, stressed his own eleven years in Congress, and traveled across the state by helicopter to reach as many as sixty thousand people a week. Stevenson largely ignored his opponent, drove around in an old Plymouth, and took weekends off to tend cattle on his ranch. The older man ran first in the primary with 477,077 votes, but Johnson came in a close second (405,617) and forced a runoff.

Before beginning the runoff campaign, Stevenson spent two days in Washington talking to those responsible for U.S. foreign affairs—the shortest course of its kind on record, Johnson remarked—and then returned to Texas and tore into the congressman personally. Johnson concentrated on the state's urban voters and gained an endorsement from Miriam A. Ferguson that proved very helpful in East Texas. "Ma" had not forgotten that when "Pa" died in 1944 Stevenson failed to attend the funeral, whereas Johnson had shown great concern for the former governor and his family. Johnson received endorsements from many large city newspapers, but the *Dallas Morning News* condemned him as a New Deal leftist.

The election proved so close that no one will ever know which candidate actually won. Four days after the polls closed, the Texas Election Board announced that Stevenson had won by 362 votes, but then amended returns began to come in, primarily from counties in South Texas, and the results changed. Straining credulity beyond all reasonable limits, Box 13 from Alice in Jim Wells County reported 203 uncounted ballots—202 of them for Johnson. Poll lists showed that the voters had signed their names in alphabetical order and all had identical handwriting. Johnson wound up the winner by eighty-seven votes. The State Democratic Executive Committee certified this result by a 29 to 28 vote, and after a few fistfights between delegates, the state convention agreed with the committee. Stevenson then challenged the most obviously fraudulent returns from South Texas in the federal courts. He did not dare seek relief in state courts because they could have inquired into all the returns and would have found obvious fraud on his behalf in several East Texas counties. A federal district court issued a restraining order keeping Johnson's name off the general election ballot, but then the circuit court set aside the injunction on the grounds that federal courts had no jurisdiction in state elections. In October, the U.S. Supreme Court accepted this ruling, allowing Johnson to run in the general election. Stevenson endorsed Johnson's Republican opponent, but, as usual, the Democratic nomination amounted to election. The final challenge came in the Senate after Johnson took his seat there in 1949, but that body agreed with the courts that primary elections were state business alone. For several years *Time* magazine derisively referred to the new senator as "Landslide Lyndon," but he eventually became a highly productive leader of the Senate.

The presidential election of 1948 generated less excitement than the senatorial contest, but it marked yet another example of how a good many conservative Texas Democrats found their party's nominee unacceptably liberal. In 1948, President Harry Truman infuriated much of the South by ordering an end to racial discrimination in federal hiring and to segregation in the armed services and by calling for an antilynching law, elimination of the poll tax as a suffrage requirement, and the creation of a Fair Employment Practices Committee. Truman also angered Texans in particular by supporting a 1947 U.S. Supreme Court decision that denied California's claim to ownership of the oil-rich land off its shores from low tide to three leagues (10.35 miles) out into the Pacific Ocean. Texas, which obviously stood to benefit tremendously from leasing drilling rights in the tidelands along its Gulf coast, considered itself exempt from this ruling because it had established ownership while an independent republic from 1836–1845. Nevertheless, the threat of federal claims by the Truman Administration alarmed many.

Some leading conservative Democrats, who as the "Texas Regulars" had opposed Roosevelt in 1944, wanted to bolt their party if it nominated Truman. Governor Jester, not wanting to be involved in such a revolt, disagreed and argued for remaining loyal and fighting Truman from within. The Democratic national convention nearly ruined his strategy by placing a strong civil rights plank in its platform. "The time has arrived," said Hubert Humphrey of Minnesota, the plank's author, "for the Democratic party to get out of the shadow of states' rights and walk forthrightly into the bright sunshine of human rights." His words earned a ten-minute ovation from the convention and caused delegates from Alabama and Mississippi to walk out. The Texas delegation remained seated, however. Conservatives from the Deep South then formed a third party called the States' Rights Democratic Party, quickly nicknamed the "Dixiecrats," and nominated Governor J. Strom Thurmond of South Carolina for the presidency. Some Texas Democrats fought furiously to have their party support the Dixiecrats rather than "Truman and his Commiecrats," as one put it, but loyalists maintained control. Thurmond, who offered no positive program, received only a little more than 100,000 votes in Texas, and Truman easily carried the state over Republican Thomas E. Dewey. This victory, however, owed more to tradition and the lack of viable opponents than to support for Truman's policies in Texas. The more liberal the national Democratic Party became, the greater the opportunity for personally appealing Republican candidates to win in Texas.

Jester's second term began in 1949 with a legislative session that became the longest in state history and the first to pass an appropriations bill calling for more than a billion dollars in spending. Meeting from January 11 to July 6, the Fifty-first Legislature modernized the prison system and improved supervision of state mental hospitals and schools for handicapped children. Most important, it passed the landmark Gilmer-Aikin laws (named for long-time champions of education reform Representative Claud Gilmer of Rocksprings and Senator A. M. Aikin of Paris) that provided the framework for modern public education in Texas. These statutes replaced the appointed nine-person State Board of Education and elected superintendent of public instruction with an elected twenty-one member board having the power to appoint a commissioner. Overall direction of the system then lay in the hands of the board, commissioner, and their support staffs, known collectively as the Texas Education Agency. Gilmer-Aikin guaranteed children nine months of education for twelve school years, each year consisting of a minimum of 175 days. Smaller school districts were encouraged to consolidate into more efficient units, and the state provided money to supplement local taxes and equalize funding. Increases in pay attracted more teachers to the classroom and encouraged professional preparation. This reform, which in retrospect seems so necessary, drew an amazing amount of opposition. Friends of the incumbent superintendent of education objected to his removal from office. School officials pointed out that paying teachers according to their academic qualifications could mean that some blacks would earn more than whites. Oil and gas producers feared that additional expenses for education would mean taxes on their industry. When the bills finally came to a vote in the house of representatives, opponents absented themselves in an effort to prevent a quorum. However, the house's sergeant-at-arms tracked them down—finding three hiding behind the bar in an Austin tavern—and the reforms passed. Even after Gilmer-Aikin, Texas public schools remained seriously underfunded, but at least the system had a more sound organizational structure.

On July 11, 1949, a few days after the legislature ended its marathon session, Governor Jester died of a heart attack and Lieutenant Governor Allan Shivers took over leadership of the state. Shivers, a relatively poor native of East Texas, worked his way through the University of Texas, became a lawyer, and in 1934 won a seat in the state senate, all by the time he was twenty-seven. Three years later he married the daughter of a wealthy Río Grande Valley businessman and gained financial security for the remainder of his political career. Service in the U.S. Army from 1943 to 1945 interrupted his rise, but he ran successfully for lieutenant governor in 1946 and again in 1948. After serving the remainder of Jester's term, he easily won the governorship in

1950. Caso March, his most serious opponent, was a young Baylor law professor, who toured the state in a car decorated with steer heads and fox tails. In many respects, Shivers mirrored Jester's approach to state politics—favoring antiunion laws, education reforms, and increased consumer taxes to provide better funding for public services—but he did not maintain his predecessor's loyalty to the national Democratic Party. Like most white Texans, Shivers disliked the Truman Administration's tendency to support civil rights and was infuriated in May 1952 when the president vetoed a bill that would have guaranteed state ownership of the tidelands. The presidential election that fall gave the governor a chance to respond, but first he had to face a liberal challenger for his own office.

In the 1952 Democratic primary, Shivers drew opposition from Ralph Yarborough, an East Texan who had graduated from the University of Texas law school with honors in 1927, worked for the attorney general's office during the early 1930s, and earned a Bronze Star while serving in the U.S. Army during World War II. Yarborough called himself a "liberal-conservative," but he was known as a supporter of the Truman Administration's efforts to continue the New Deal and soon would become the most important liberal Democrat in the state. Voters also had a choice between conservative and liberal candidates in the contest to replace Tom Connally, who retired from the United States Senate after twenty-four years in office. Price Daniel Sr., an East Texan who as attorney general from 1946 to 1952 led the defense of his state's claims to the tidelands, accused the Truman Administration of extravagant spending, corruption, and socialism. His opponent, Congressman Lindley G. Beckworth of Gladewater, had a record of cooperation with the national Democratic Party. Shivers and Daniel teamed up to run a conservative campaign in opposition to "Trumanism," the "mess in Washington," and the "Tidelands steal." On July 26, 1952, both won convincing victories, although Yarborough showed some political promise, even in defeat, by gaining nearly half a million votes.

In the meantime, Shivers led a revolt against the Democratic presidential ticket, which was headed by Adlai Stevenson, an Illinois liberal who would not guarantee Texas ownership of the tidelands. The governor refused to pledge his support during the national convention and then when the state party held its meeting in Amarillo—the airport, one source noted, was "choked with oil company planes"—he orchestrated an endorsement of the Republican nominee, Dwight D. Eisenhower. "Ike," the popular military leader from World War II, promised to "return" the tidelands to Texas and respect states' rights in general. Thus, for the first time in Texas history, the state Democratic Party, although it reluctantly put Stevenson on the ballot, officially supported a Republican candidate for the presidency. To make their position even clearer, every Democratic nominee for state office except one took advantage of a 1951 law that allowed one party's candidates to cross-file as candidates of another and put their names on the ballot as Republicans also. This meant that Shivers and Daniel had no opponents in the November general election (Shivers, for example, received 1,375,547 votes as a Democrat and

468,139 as a Republican) and could devote full attention to carrying the state for Eisenhower. The "Texas Democrats for Eisenhower" ran a campaign focused on the tidelands issue, making it a matter of federal stealing of royalty money that would benefit the state's school children, and also regularly brought in charges of corruption and communism. This approach, coupled with a popular candidate, gave Eisenhower victory with 53 percent of the more than two million votes cast. Soon after taking office, the new president signed a bill guaranteeing state ownership of the tidelands to their "historic limits," an action that guaranteed significant revenue for Texas and benefit oil companies even more. He also appointed a conservative Texan, Oveta Culp Hobby, to his cabinet as the first Secretary of the Department of Health, Education, and Welfare. Hobby, commander of the WACs during World War II, served four years and established herself as, in the words of Secretary of the Treasury George Humphrey, "the best man in the Cabinet."

Republicans owed their victory in the 1952 presidential election to conservative Democratic voters who otherwise remained loyal to their party. Shivers and his fellow leaders continued to support the traditional one-party system and to control government at the state and local level. Liberal and loyalist Democrats, however, did not forget the betrayal of Stevenson and looked for ways to pay back the conservatives even if it cost their party at the polls. In 1954, for example, liberals refused to support Wallace Savage, the Democratic nominee for a congressional seat in Dallas, because he had chaired the "Texas Democrats for Eisenhower." Their action helped the conservative Republican candidate, Bruce Alger, win the seat and become only the second member of his party to represent Texas in Congress in more than fifty years.

Liberals also demonstrated rising strength in the governor's race in 1954. Shivers ran for an unprecedented third term that year and again faced a challenge from Ralph Yarborough. The governor preempted many of Yarborough's issues early in 1954 by having the legislature increase taxes on gas pipelines, corporation franchises, and beer in order to provide money for higher teacher salaries and more spending on education and public services. However, the challenger focused on corruption under the Shivers administration, particularly in the largely unregulated insurance industry, and made headway until he ran afoul of the Red Scare.

The outcry against communists reached a crescendo in 1953–1954, particularly in Houston, where the Minute Women, a group pledged to eliminate red influence from government and schools, led the charge. This group, which had no bylaws and prohibited motions from the floor during meetings for fear that they, like the garden clubs, might be infiltrated by communists, had a major success in July 1953 when the Houston school board voted to fire George Ebey, the deputy superintendent of schools who had only recently arrived from Oregon. A lengthy investigation had not provided evidence that Ebey was a communist or had engaged in espionage; nevertheless, the board found his background and personal views unacceptably liberal. Later that year, after a CIO-led strike in Port Arthur, Governor Shivers sent in investigators who found a "clear and present danger" of communist-dominated

Ralph W. Yarborough (1903–1996) is questioned by a voter. Credit: Center for American History, UT-Austin; CN #11502.

unionism in the state. Shivers then called a special session of the legislature in the spring of 1954, which passed a bill making membership in the Communist Party a felony punishable by a fine of $20,000 and twenty years in the penitentiary. Although disappointed by the refusal of lawmakers to accept his suggestion that communists receive the death penalty, Shivers signed the law and campaigned against Yarborough as the leader who had saved Texas from communistic unions. "We're going to crush them under the heel any way we can," he said. Although "my opponent is not a Communist," he asserted, "I feel that he is a captive of certain people who do not approve of being tough on Communists."

If the Red Scare did not doom Yarborough, a decision by the United States Supreme Court in May 1954 completed the ruin of any chance that he had against Shivers. In *Brown v. Board of Education of Topeka,* the court ruled that segregation of public schools violated the equal protection clause of the Fourteenth Amendment. The governor, knowing that most white Texans bitterly opposed integration, announced that "[a]ll my instincts, my political philosophy, my experience, and my common sense revolt against this Supreme Court decision." By contrast, he said, Yarborough's "closest political advisors are working hand-in-glove with the NAACP." Texas, he said, will not change the way it conducts its public schools. Yarborough tried to evade the issue but finally spoke against "forced commingling" in the schools. On the other hand, he did not denounce the Supreme Court or promise to fight integration. This vacillation did little to win conservative support and cost him votes among liberals of both races. Yarborough forced a runoff, gaining 645,994 votes to Shivers's 668,913, but the same issues bedeviled him in the second primary. Teams of businessmen from Port Arthur toured the state to tell the untrue story of how union activity had made their city a ghost town and to warn that only Shivers could prevent a spread of unionism. Newspaper cartoons showed Shivers prying up a rock labeled "public indifference" to show the "labor racketeers," "pinkos," and "commies" underneath. Ninety-five of the state's one hundred daily newspapers endorsed the governor. Under the circumstances, Yarborough did amazingly well to receive 47 percent of the primary runoff vote.

Thus by the mid-1950s, liberalism seemed to be on the rise in the Democratic Party, and the resulting factionalism provided opportunities to Republicans in state as well as presidential elections. Witness Bruce Alger's victory in the 1954 congressional race in Dallas. The most liberal of Texas's Democrats welcomed the developing division in their party and hoped that eventually their conservative opponents would move to the Republican Party. This, some theorized, would give the state a two-party system similar to that in many other parts of the nation. A Democratic Party of urban and professional progressives, blue-collar and low-income workers, and minorities would oppose a Republican Party of businessmen and the economic elite in contests fought primarily over economic issues. Such essentially class-based elections, liberals believed, gave them a reasonable chance of victory. Their theory, however, underestimated the conservatism of middle- and lower-class Texas Anglo voters and failed to take into account the way issues related to race could reinforce the traditional support for conservative candidates of either party.

Integration and Civil Rights in Postwar Texas

At the close of World War II, individuals in Texas's two large minority groups—African Americans and Mexican Americans—remained largely submerged, second-class citizens. The poll tax still worked to disfranchise large numbers of the poor, and gerrymandering diluted potential minority voting power as well. Democratic Party officials often tried to disregard the U.S. Supreme Court's ruling in *Smith v. Allwright* (1944) and prevent black participation in primary elections. Anglo political bosses and farmer/businessmen in South Texas generally blocked Mexican Americans from doing more than voting for hand-picked candidates. Educational opportunities for minorities were restricted—in the case of blacks by strict segregation into supposedly "separate but equal" systems and in the case of Mexicans often by de facto separation into inferior "Mexican schools" or separate classes within Anglo districts. Public accommodations such as restaurants, movie theaters, barber shops, and swimming pools also denied equal access to minorities. After 1945, however, all these forms of discrimination came under attack, and changes came, albeit slowly and grudgingly.

Mexican Americans faced fewer obstacles than blacks did in the assertion of their political rights, primarily because Anglos traditionally had accepted them as "whites" politically and never insisted on total disfranchisement. Thus, there was relatively little resistance in the early 1950s when Anglo leaders in cities with large Mexican American populations, wishing to create a favorable climate for business expansion, began to include Tejanos in local government. This participation opened the way to the election of Mexican Americans to positions of greater importance. In 1956, Henry B. González of San Antonio became the first Tejano in the twentieth century to win a seat in the Texas Senate, and the following year Raymond Telles won the mayor's office in El Paso. By 1960 six Tejanos served in the state legislature, and in 1961 González again broke new political ground by winning a seat in the United States House of Representatives. Three years later, Eligio "Kiki" de la Garza of South Texas, joined González in Congress. Greater political partici-

Henry B. González (1916–2000). González achieved numerous political "firsts" for Mexican Americans in Texas—first elected to the Texas Senate (1956), first to run for governor (1958), and first elected to the U.S. House of Representatives (1961). Credit: Courtesy of the Institute of Texan Cultures.

pation and representation by no means solved all the problems facing Mexican Americans in Texas, but obviously it marked an advance that could bring improvement in education and everyday life as well.

African American voters met considerable resistance even after the U.S. Supreme Court outlawed the white primary. Congressman Wright Patman from northeast Texas vowed, for example, that blacks would vote in his district "over my dead body," and several counties attempted to ignore the ruling. This attitude on the part of whites, plus the blacks' generally low educational level, fifty years of experience with legal disfranchisement, and belief that white politicians had no interest in their needs, slowed but did not prevent the increase of African American political participation after 1945. The 1946 contest between Jester and Rainey attracted 75,000 black voters, at least one-third more than in any recent election. Still, that number represented less than 20 percent of voting-age African Americans in the state. The proportion of potential black voters actually prepared to vote did not pass 50 percent until the early 1960s. Blacks generally voted for liberal Democratic candidates in state and national races, a trend that began during the New Deal and continued after World War II. In 1948, the Progressive Voters League, which originated in Dallas during the 1930s as one of the first black political organizations in the state, placed the word *Democratic* in its title and committed to the support of that party locally and nationally. Ralph Yarborough received the support of African American voters by an eight-to-one margin over Shivers in 1954, and in the closely contested 1960 presidential race between John F. Kennedy and Richard M. Nixon, Texas blacks provided the votes that put their state in the Democratic column.

Slowly, as their political importance rose, African Americans began to move into positions of leadership in the Democratic Party and run for offices themselves. William J. Durham of Dallas, one of the most effective black lawyers in the state, became a member of the State Democratic Executive Committee in the late 1950s. Barbara Jordan, a graduate of Boston University Law School in 1959, entered politics in Houston, her native city, by campaigning for John F. Kennedy. Bitten by the political bug, she ignored a Rice University professor who told her—"You've got too much going against you. You're black, you're a woman, and you're large. People don't really like that image"—and ran for a seat in the Texas House of Representatives in 1962. She lost that race and another in 1964, at least in part because Harris County voters elected all twelve of their state representatives on an at-large basis, an approach that diluted the electoral strength of blacks, who amounted to about 20 percent of the total population. After Jordan's second defeat, however, several Supreme Court decisions turned the tide in her favor. First, in *Baker v. Carr* (1962) and *Reynolds v. Sims* (1964), the Court ruled that members of both houses of state legislatures had to be elected from districts with approximately the same number of voters. This "one-man, one-vote" rule ended the at-large system and increased the chances of blacks to win in largely minority districts. Second, in 1966 the Court decided that the poll tax, which the Twenty-fourth Amendment (1964) already had abolished as a requirement for voting

Barbara Jordan (1936–1996). Pictured here with her parents in 1972, Jordan won a seat in the Texas Senate in 1966 and six years later became the first African American woman from the South to win election to the United States House of Representatives. Credit: Houston Chronicle photograph.

in federal elections, was illegal in state and local elections as well. Bolstered by these developments, Jordan ran for the state senate in 1966 from a newly drawn single-member district and won. This victory, coming in a district in which half of the voters were minorities, made her the first black since 1881, and the first black woman ever, to serve in the Texas Senate. Adopting the role of a pragmatist with a keen sense of detail, Jordan avoided confrontation and won the respect of her white colleagues to the point that they unanimously elected her president pro tempore of the senate in 1972. That same year she set another precedent by becoming the first black woman from the South to win a seat in the U.S. House of Representatives.

Two other African American candidates, Curtis Graves of Houston and Joseph E. Lockridge of Dallas, won seats in the state house of representatives in 1966. When Lockridge died in an airplane crash in 1968, he was replaced by Zan Wesley Holmes Jr., a Methodist minister who had graduated from Southern Methodist University. Blacks also began to win offices in local and city government. At the beginning of the 1970s, forty-two African Americans served at the local level, and others held city council seats in Austin, Bryan,

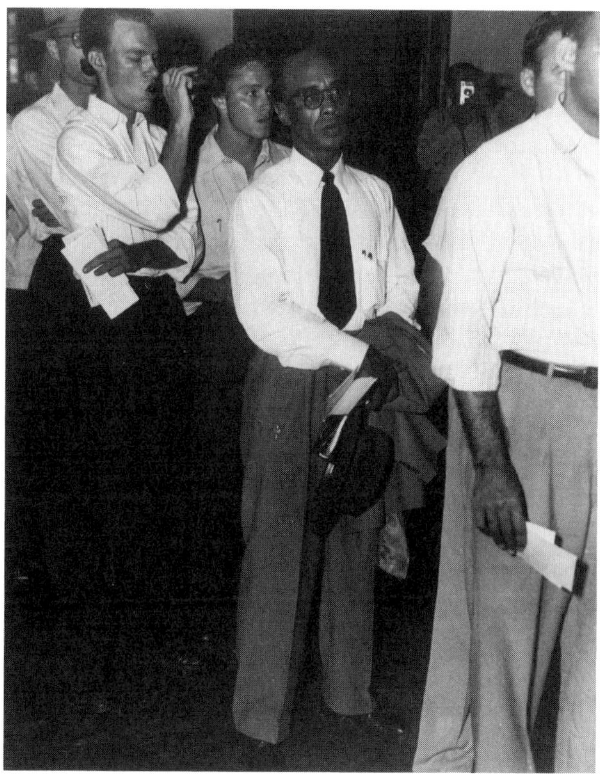

Heman M. Sweatt (1912–1982). Sweatt, shown here standing in a registration line in 1950, brought the legal action that forced integration of the University of Texas School of Law. Credit: Center for American History, UT-Austin.

Fort Worth, Galveston, Hearne, Houston, Huntsville, Malakoff, Port Arthur, San Antonio, Waco, and Wichita Falls.

While they pushed successfully for the right to vote and hold public office, African Americans in postwar Texas also sought equal access to higher education. Brushing aside claims that the underfunded Prairie View A&M University (as the legislature designated it in 1945) offered "separate but equal" education for black students, the state NAACP decided to mount a legal challenge to segregation at the University of Texas. At the urging of Dallas lawyer William J. Durham and Houston activist Lulu White, Heman M. Sweatt, a Houston postal worker, applied for admission to the university's law school in 1946. President Theophilus Painter rejected the application, touching off four years of legal and political maneuvering. Sweatt brought suit in a Texas district court, which ruled that the state had six months to provide an "equal" law education to the plaintiff. The government reacted by setting up a temporary law school for blacks that operated first in Houston and then moved to the basement of a building near the state capitol in Austin. Also, the legislature provided an appropriation to take over the Houston College for Negroes and expand it into the Texas State University for Negroes (later Texas Southern University). Sweatt, however, refused to attend the obviously inferior temporary school or wait for a new segregated school, and his lawyers, including Durham and Thurgood Marshall of the national NAACP, decided to challenge not only the lack of "equal" facilities but segregation itself. After losing at every level in Texas state courts, they took their case to the United States Supreme Court in 1949. In the meantime, Sweatt received encouragement from students at the University of Texas, who founded the largest all-white NAACP chapter in the country in his support, but he also had to endure threats to himself and his wife, vandalism to his home, and an ulcer attack that required hospitalization. In June 1950, the Court gave Sweatt and his lawyers a significant victory by ruling that the state had failed to provide equal facilities. This opened the way for Sweatt to enter the University of Texas's law school and for other blacks to enter its graduate schools and schools of medicine and dentistry in 1950–1951.

The court's ruling in *Sweatt v. Painter* did not destroy the doctrine of "separate but equal," but it left the courts only a short step from deciding that separate was inherently unequal—thereby ending segregation. Sweatt paid a considerable personal price for this success. Worn out emotionally and physically by the struggle, he gave up law school in 1952 before finishing his degree. The strain also broke up his marriage. Later in the 1950s, he earned a master's degree in social work from Atlanta University and began a career with the NAACP and National Urban League that lasted until his death in 1982. The University of Texas now holds an annual Heman Sweatt Symposium on Civil Rights.

Integration of college and university undergraduate education began during the early 1950s and continued into the following decade. At times violence threatened to break out, as at Texarkana Junior College in 1955 when a crowd of whites prevented blacks from enrolling. Overall, however, desegregation advanced quietly. Rice University was among the last to admit black students because the will of its founder, William Marsh Rice, established a whites-only policy. A court order in 1964 broke that part of Rice's bequest. Black professors joined the faculties of the University of Texas and Rice in the mid-sixties. Smaller state institutions such as North Texas State College in Denton and Texas A&I in Kingsville integrated their athletic teams in the late 1950s. Their success with players such as Abner Haynes, who led North Texas to an appearance in the Sun Bowl in 1959 and then became a star with Houston in the American Football League, helped convince the major schools that belonged to the Southwest Athletic Conference to follow suit to a limited extent beginning in 1965. The conference's first black player, Jerry LeVias, had a key role in Southern Methodist University's championship season in 1966, but as late as 1969 the University of Texas won a national championship with an all-white team.

African Americans could not have integrated higher education in Texas without the rulings of the U.S. Supreme Court in cases such as *Sweatt v. Painter,* and the same is true of desegregating public schools. At the beginning of the

1950s, blacks across the state attended separate elementary and high schools that were grossly unequal in every way to those provided for white children. Then, in 1954 the court handed down its decision in *Brown v. Board of Education of Topeka,* and segregation began to topple—very slowly. Accepting the argument made for the plaintiffs by Thurgood Marshall, Chief Justice Earl Warren wrote: "We conclude that in the field of public education the doctrine of 'separate but equal' has no place. Separate educational facilities are inherently unequal." Warren's words angered a majority of whites across the South, and some leaders immediately threatened to close public schools rather than integrate. Governor Shivers took a less extreme stand at first, saying that a solution could be found, but soon he found it politically expedient to use the issue in meeting a challenge by Ralph Yarborough in the 1954 Democratic primary. "We are going to keep the system that we know is best," he said. "No law, no court, can wreck what God has made." Texas officials did nothing to integrate the state's schools in 1954–1955, especially since the Supreme Court had not yet issued an implementation order for its decision. That order, when it came in May 1955, called for desegregation "with all deliberate speed," a phrase that encouraged white conservatives. "I think that is good," said Governor Shivers. "I have always advocated that these matters be handled by local agencies of government."

Some Texas school districts that had relatively few African American students chose to heed the Supreme Court's decision almost immediately. Friona, a town of about 1,500 in the Panhandle, became the first in the state to comply with the Brown decision by quietly admitting five black students to its elementary school in the fall of 1954. Seventy-three more districts, located mostly in West and South Texas, began desegregation during the 1955–1956 school year. These districts, which included El Paso, San Angelo, Harlingen, and San Antonio, had no difficulty bringing at least a token number of blacks into white schools. In Central and East Texas, however, integration faced much stronger resistance. White Citizens Councils, an anti-desegregation group organized first in Mississippi, appeared in Texas during the summer of 1955 and soon claimed a membership of twenty thousand. "Negroes," said Ross Carlton of Dallas, the first chairman of the group's executive committee, "have . . . become unwitting and dumb tools of the Communistic propagandists in the NAACP."

In 1956, as integration inched ahead in West and South Texas but drew strong opposition elsewhere, Shivers decided to use the issue as a political rallying point. His third full term, which drew to a close that year, had suffered from scandals involving the insurance industry and the veterans' land program, and his position as party leader faced a challenge from Senator Lyndon B. Johnson, who wanted the state's favorite-son nomination for the presidency. Therefore, in an effort to hold on to power and perhaps even win a fourth nomination, the governor sought to use the segregation question, in the words of one advisor, "to weld together conservative forces." His effort focused on placing a proposal called "interposition" on the Democratic Party's primary ballot in July. This idea, essentially a revival of the Old South's doctrine of nullification, called for states to interpose themselves between the national government and their citizens in order to block integration dictated from Washington. Shivers managed to get it, along with a proposal exempting children from compulsory attendance at integrated schools and another calling for stronger state laws against racial intermarriage, on the primary ballot. However, the popular support that the governor hoped to gain never materialized, forcing him to drop any hope of running for a fourth term and to relinquish control of the state party to Democrats who supported Lyndon Johnson.

With Shivers out of the picture in 1956, the governor's race turned into a contest between U.S. Senator Price Daniel Sr. and Ralph Yarborough. Daniel, having settled the tidelands issue in Texas's favor, had lost interest in national office. I would "rather be governor of Texas," he said, "than president of the United States." Neither candidate hit the race issue hard—in part because Yarborough, as in 1954, refused to endorse desegregation completely—but Daniel, as the more conservative of the two, had an advantage. He regularly linked labor unions and integrationists, telling voters that the CIO financed the NAACP. Any such charges paled into moderation, however, when compared to those by two lesser candidates in the race. J. Evetts Haley, a West Texas rancher and writer, called integration a communist plot to destroy the white race, and "Pappy" Lee O'Daniel claimed that the communist-inspired Supreme Court would cause blood to run in the streets. Daniel ran well ahead in the first primary vote, but Yarborough managed to force a runoff. The race issue appeared more prominently in the runoff because Governor Shivers endorsed Daniel and, in the words of Yarborough, "said I was a 'nigger lover' . . . the vilest term you could give anybody in Texas at that time, traitor wasn't that bad." However, in a classic case of politics making strange bedfellows, "Pappy" O'Daniel, one of the chief race-baiters in the first primary, endorsed Yarborough. Thus, many Yarborough voters were anything but racial liberals, and Daniel's narrow runoff victory (698,001 to 694,830) did not truly indicate how Texans viewed integration. Instead, results of the three-question referendum on the primary ballot provided a more true indicator. All three—interposition, exemption from attending integrated schools, and a stronger ban on racial intermarriage—passed by margins of at least four to one and were written into the party platform that fall.

The first test of Texans' ability to handle a truly contested school desegregation case came in the fall of 1956 at Mansfield, a small town seventeen miles southeast of Fort Worth. Mansfield, which had about sixty school-age African Americans, segregated younger children in an inferior elementary school and required those wishing to attend high school to ride public buses to Fort Worth, where they were dropped about twenty blocks from the school. In 1955, T. M. Moody, a local leader and one of the founders of the Mansfield branch of the NAACP, organized the filing of a court suit asking that three African American high school students be admitted to Mansfield High School. The U.S. Federal District Court in Fort Worth denied the petition, but the Fifth Circuit Court of Appeals in New Orleans reversed the lower court's decision.

In August 1956, Mansfield became the first school district in Texas ordered to desegregate its schools. The situation then turned ugly. Moody received telephone threats, and crosses were burned in the black section of town. An effigy, hanged from a wire stretched above a main intersection, bore the words: "This Negro tried to enter a white school." When registration began on August 30–31, mobs of three hundred to four hundred whites ringed the high school and prevented the three black students from entering. Local residents roughed up outside observers and prevented cars carrying anyone suspected of sympathizing with the integrationists from entering the town. A lawyer for the black students appealed for help from Austin, but Governor Shivers called the crowd's actions an "orderly protest against a situation instigated and agitated by the National Organization for the Advancement of Colored People." He sent Texas Rangers to keep the black students out of Mansfield High and authorized the school board to transfer them to Fort Worth. President Eisenhower, facing a reelection contest in which he needed Texas votes, held to his "hands off" philosophy and permitted the state to defy federal law. Several weeks after the Mansfield incident, Shivers again crossed party lines and endorsed Ike; a "bigger and better man," he said, "by any and all the political, moral and spiritual standards by which we judge men, than his opponent. . . . " Eisenhower once again carried Texas, this time with 55 percent of the vote. The parents of African American students in Mansfield, not wishing to subject their children to more intimidation and possible violence, gave up their fight.

The Texas Legislature, emboldened by the success at Mansfield, passed laws in 1957 that prohibited school integration unless local voters approved and provided a variety of pretexts—lack of space, inadequate transportation, a decline in morality, etc.—that local officials could cite as reasons for continuing segregation. Later that year, after violent opposition to integration in Little Rock, Arkansas, forced President Eisenhower to commit troops to protect black children, the Texas legislature voted to close public schools rather than accept such federal interference in their state. Governor Price Daniel, who tended toward moderation once he took office, signed these acts without enthusiasm, and the courts later declared them unconstitutional. Nevertheless, the state government's resistance and the creativity of local districts in drawing school zones ensured that integration advanced at a snail's pace. In 1964, a decade after the *Brown* decision, only about 18,000 of the state's 325,000 black students attended integrated schools. Major progress came only after the Civil Rights Act of 1964 permitted the federal government to withdraw financial aid from segregated schools. The Mansfield School District, for example, integrated in 1965 under the threat of losing federal funds. By 1970, more than 75 percent of Texas's black students attended schools that were integrated to some degree, and during the 1970–1971 school year, a federal judge combined the last nine all-black school districts in East Texas with adjoining white or biracial districts. Also in 1971, the U.S. Supreme Court approved busing of students to reduce de facto school segregation that resulted from racial separation in residential housing. Many whites angrily opposed busing, and nearly twenty years after the *Brown* decision, in spite of the obvious progress brought by desegregation, many blacks still attended inferior schools.

Mexican Americans in most South and Central Texas communities faced de facto school segregation until after World War II. However, the state's long-standing recognition of Mexicans as "white" gave them an advantage over blacks in the struggle for integration. In 1940 the state superintendent of education ruled that "under the laws . . . children of Latin-American extraction [are] classified as white and therefore have a right to attend the Anglo-American schools in the community in which they live." Even then, court challenges were necessary to bring integration. The first came in 1948 when the League of United Latin American Citizens (LULAC) encouraged a group of parents led by Minerva Delgado to charge that separate schools for Mexicans in several Central Texas school districts had no state constitutional or statutory authority and violated the equal protection clause of the Fourteenth Amendment. Almost immediately, the American G.I. Forum, a new organization of Mexican American veterans led by Dr. Héctor P. García, joined LULAC in the case, providing moral and financial support. The U.S. District Court in Austin ruled *(Delgado v. Bastrop ISD)* that segregating Mexican students did indeed violate the Constitution, but it left a tiny loophole by providing that school districts could maintain separate classes on the same campus and in the first grade "solely for instructional purposes." This proviso, made for the purpose of teaching English to Spanish-speaking beginner students, allowed Anglo officials to set up segregated "first grades" that lasted in some cases four years. In 1957, U. S. District Judge James V. Allred (a former governor of Texas) heard *Hernández v. Driscoll Consolidated School District* and issued an order against such an interpretation of the Delgado decision. Thus, by 1960 court rulings prohibited the practice of de facto segregation of Mexican school children, although residential separation and placing students in separate classes on the basis of language or academic ability still undercut the ideal of equal educational opportunity in many South and Central Texas districts.

Along with their advances toward greater equality in politics and education during the 1950s and 1960s, blacks and Mexicans began a push for other basic civil rights such as equal access to public accommodations. City and county governments, faced with the breakdown of the "separate but equal" doctrine and increasing pressure from the NAACP, integrated libraries, parks, golf courses, restaurants and restrooms in public buildings, and bus stations and airport terminals. Attention then turned to privately owned businesses, such as restaurants and theaters, that practiced segregation. In 1960 college students began to use direct action against this type of discrimination by staging nonviolent sit-ins and demonstrations like those held earlier that year in North Carolina. Black students at Bishop and Wiley Colleges in Marshall staged the first sit-ins; others from Prairie View and Texas Southern soon followed suit with boycotts of local merchants. A new organization, the Congress of Racial Equality (CORE), under the leadership of James Farmer, a native of Marshall, provided direction in the use of direct action. White students at several universities, including the University of Texas and North Texas

State College, lent support. These direct confrontations provoked some change, and the Civil Rights Act of 1964 completed the process by outlawing discrimination in all places of public accommodation.

The "Sixties": Civil Rights Activism and Antiwar Protest

American society came apart after 1965. Nonviolent civil rights groups found themselves challenged and overshadowed by new organizations, such as the Black Panthers, who spoke of "black power" and armed self-defense. Riots that cost dozens of lives and millions in property damage tore through black neighborhoods in major cities such as Los Angeles and Detroit. Mexican Americans created the "Chicano Movement" and mounted a militant, although nonviolent, attack on the conditions that hindered their people. The Vietnam War, which escalated rapidly from 1965 to 1968 and brought a rising death count but no apparent success, divided the nation into "hawks" and "doves." Thousands of college students who supported the civil rights movement and opposed the war became embittered critics of American society and joined a counterculture based, as the cliché went, on sex, drugs, and rock and roll. "Never trust anyone over thirty," became a campus motto. Long-haired demonstrators regularly held protest marches and taunted the police who sought to maintain order as "pigs." Older Americans, particularly those of a conservative bent, called for restoring "law and order" and put bumper stickers proclaiming "America: Love It or Leave It" on their automobiles.

Texas escaped the worst violence of the sixties—the state's major cities had no major riots—although Houston came close. In 1967, a meeting of African Americans at Texas Southern University turned violent when police arrived. Stone throwing escalated into gunfire, and one policeman was killed, possibly by a stray police bullet. A grand jury indicted five students for inciting a riot, but a lack of evidence prevented any trial. Three years later, a shootout between Houston police and a militant black group called the People's Party II resulted in the death of its leader, Carl Hampton. Several other Texas cities, including Midland and Lubbock, had lesser incidents of violence, and across the state African Americans accused the police of discrimination and brutality.

Greater militancy among Mexican Americans appeared first with a march of Tejano farm workers from the Río Grande Valley to Austin in the summer of 1966. Supported by LULAC, the G.I. Forum, and the more recently founded Political Association of Spanish-Speaking Organizations (PASO), the so-called "Minimum Wage March" contributed to the passage of the state's first minimum wage law shortly thereafter and energized the Mexican community in Texas. The next year José Angel Gutiérrez led in the formation of the Mexican American Youth Organization (MAYO), which challenged all forms of discrimination against Mexican Americans, especially inferior schools. MAYO appealed to young people who called themselves "Chicanos" as a way of harkening to a proud Aztec and Mayan heritage. The most important indication of this new militancy came in 1969 in a small Zavala County town called

Crystal City (or *Cristal,* as it is known in Spanish). Long under total domination by an Anglo minority, "mexicanos" in the Crystal City school district called for reforms such as bilingual education and more Mexican American counselors and, when the school board ignored their requests, staged a walkout. After more than a month of losing state funds because of 65 percent absence rates, school officials gave in and granted most of the students' requests. This success led Gutiérrez and others involved in the boycott to form La Raza Unida Party (RUP) and successfully challenge Anglo control of the Crystal City school board and city council during 1970. In October 1971, Raza Unida supporters from across Texas met in San Antonio and decided to run candidates in statewide elections the next year. The RUP platform in 1972 set out a variety of programs to help Mexican Americans and called for disbanding the Texas Rangers. Its candidate, Ramsey Muñiz, received only 6 percent of the vote, and the party faded away within the next few years. However, the new-found militance that it symbolized was part of a Mexican American awakening that did not subside.

Opposition to the war in Vietnam provided the center point for protest and a flourishing counterculture on Texas's college campuses. Opposition to the war escalated along with U.S. involvement after 1965. Students and liberal professors generally limited their response to "teach-ins" and peaceful marches, but the potential for violence always existed. The situation in Austin during early May 1970 provides a good example. When President Nixon ordered an invasion of Cambodia on April 30 and a resulting campus demonstration at Kent State University led to the killing of four students by national guardsmen, students at the University of Texas marched on the capitol and someone threw a rock through the etched glass in the front door of the building. Police reacted by firing tear gas in and around the building. State policemen and Texas Rangers then took up positions at the capitol for the following week, and officers armed with rifles were placed on rooftops of buildings between the university and downtown. Students at the university planned a protest parade but had difficulty securing a permit from the Austin city council. In the meantime, Frank Erwin, chairman of the University's board of regents, warned professors who encouraged the protests that in the case of violence "the blood will be on the faculty's hands." Finally, on May 8, a federal district judge issued an injunction against the city council's denial of a permit, and the parade took place. The marchers, estimated at between 10,000 and 25,000, proceeded without serious incident from the campus along Guadalupe Street into downtown and back. "I'm thankful that it did go off peacefully," said Austin's chief of police. Student militance soon declined as the war wound down to a close in 1973, and for all but a few truly committed "hippies" the counterculture of the sixties faded with it.

Politics, 1957–1970: The Democrats Hold On

The civil rights movement of the fifties and the coming apart of America in the sixties threatened to complete the process of destroying the Democratic

Party's hold on Texas. Traditionally Democratic white voters found the national party's increasing identification with minority rights and protest movements more and more unacceptable. Even many who had supported the New Deal turned against the sixties brand of liberalism. They had accepted government action to fight the Great Depression because in their eyes measures such as work relief and rural electrification represented an effort to help ordinary people and preserve decency and order. Militant blacks, rioting college students, and radical women, however, threatened every basic assumption in their lives. Conservative Texas Democrats also watched fearfully as the liberal wing of their state party continued to gain strength under the leadership of Ralph Yarborough. If the Democratic Party became too liberal for Texans at both the national and state levels, they would in all likelihood turn to Republican candidates for positions in Austin as well as Washington. Democrats maintained control through the 1960s, however, thanks especially to the role of Lyndon B. Johnson and a more moderate stance by state leaders.

Ironically, Price Daniel's victory over Yarborough in the 1956 gubernatorial race led immediately to a major success for Texas liberal Democrats. Daniel had to vacate his U.S. Senate seat when he became governor, necessitating a special election in April 1957 to choose a successor who would complete his term. In the special election, unlike a primary, there was no runoff. The candidate with the most votes won. This gave the liberals an unusual advantage in that conservatives could not, as they generally did, split on the first vote and then unite in the runoff. Yarborough, with strong backing from a recently formed liberal group called the Democrats of Texas (DOT), won the election with 38 percent of the vote because conservatives divided their support between Democrat Martin Dies (29 percent) and Republican Thad Hutcheson (23 percent). (Sixteen other candidates shared the remaining 10 percent of the vote.) The term Yarborough won expired in January 1959, and few observers gave him much chance of holding the seat longer than the next election. He was challenged in the 1958 Democratic primary by William A. "Bill" Blakley of Dallas, a wealthy director of Braniff Airways and a strict conservative. Blakley had the support of Shivers and other conservatives, but Yarborough stressed his opponent's wealth and promised to "put the jam on the lower shelf so the little man can reach it." Aided by a last-minute endorsement from popular Representative Sam Rayburn, he won with relative ease. Republicans vowed that they would defeat the "socialist Yarborough" in the general election, but a sharp recession reduced the Eisenhower administration's popularity that fall. Under the circumstances, Texas voters stuck to their traditional Democratic loyalties and gave Yarborough 75 percent of the vote.

Yarborough and Texas's other senator, Majority Leader Lyndon B. Johnson, went against the grain of southern conservatism by voting for the Civil Rights Acts of 1957 and 1960. These laws, which aimed primarily at protecting blacks' voting rights, were too weak to have much effect, but as the first of their kind since Reconstruction, they signaled another advance in the developing attack on racial discrimination. Before 1957, neither Yarborough nor Johnson had a notable record of support for equal rights. On the other hand,

Yarborough had never engaged in race-baiting politics, Johnson had seldom done so, and neither had taken positions totally at odds with the "Second Reconstruction" in race relations that developed in the postwar years. Yarborough's stance matched his consistent liberalism on other issues such as education and welfare. Johnson's position came from an honest belief in the ideal of equal rights and his desire to win the presidency. To win the nomination in 1960, he needed to build his reputation as a national statesman and appeal to minorities as well as southern whites. Thus, both senators had good reasons to support civil rights legislation, and both faced the real likelihood that a majority of Texas Democratic voters would not approve.

The administration of Governor Price Daniel, who followed his win over Yarborough in 1956 with relatively easy reelection victories in 1958 and 1960, also tended toward moderation rather than southern extremism. Daniel did not follow up on Shivers's idea of using state "interposition" to block integration, and no Texas official stood in a schoolhouse door to keep black students out. He also worked on a law requiring the registration of lobbyists and convinced the legislature to pass a plan for conserving water resources. Daniel's most significant defeat came on tax policy in 1961 when the legislature, rather than follow his call for raising revenue half from taxes on business and half from a sales tax, passed a 2 percent general sales tax. Food, drugs, and certain other necessities were exempt; nevertheless, a sales tax took a larger share of income from the poor than from the rich. Daniel let the bill become law without his signature, but it became a key part of his record, especially since store clerks as they rang up sales liked to say, "Now, let's have a penny for Price."

In 1960, after voting Republican in the last two presidential elections, Texas swung back to the Democratic column, primarily it seems because a native son, Lyndon B. Johnson, was on the ballot. Johnson, after losing his bid for the presidential nomination to Senator John F. Kennedy of Massachusetts, agreed to take second place on the ticket. Kennedy offered the vice presidency because he needed Texas's twenty-four electoral votes, and Johnson simply could not turn it down. He hedged his bets, however, by also running for reelection to the Senate. The Kennedy-Johnson ticket expected a tough fight in Texas against the Republican ticket of Richard M. Nixon and Henry Cabot Lodge III, especially since Eisenhower had carried the state twice and former governor Allen Shivers once again organized conservative Democrats in support of the Republican ticket. This expectation proved correct, as the Democrats prevailed by fewer than fifty thousand votes from a record total of more than 2.25 million cast. Mexican American voters organized in "Viva Kennedy" clubs and African Americans pleased with Kennedy's support of Martin Luther King Jr. provided the margin of victory. Johnson also won the senate race, although his opponent, John Tower, a young college professor from Midwestern State University in Wichita Falls, surprised everyone by polling more than 900,000 votes. Tower proved himself an able campaigner by focusing on Johnson's selfishness in running simultaneously for vice president and senator.

In spite of losing the election of 1960, Texas Republicans made notable progress during the next two years, partly as a result of the Kennedy administration's reputation for liberalism and partly because of the ongoing division between the liberal and conservative wings of the state Democratic Party. John F. Kennedy and his brother Robert, who served as Attorney General, irritated many Texans by using federal force to overcome resistance to integration in Mississippi and Alabama. Democratic factionalism cost the party victory in the April 1961 special election to choose a successor to Lyndon Johnson in the U.S. Senate. Liberals split their votes among three candidates including Henry B. González of San Antonio, while conservatives united behind Bill Blakley, the Dallas businessman who had lost to Yarborough in 1957. John Tower, having run so impressively against Johnson the previous year, again had the support of Republicans. He and Blakley received the most votes and faced each other in a runoff, which a new law required even in special elections. Liberal Democrats, arguing that the defeat of Blakley would encourage conservatives to switch to the Republican Party and create a true two-party system, either "went fishing" on election day or voted for Tower, allowing him to win by 10,343 votes in a total of 886,091. He went to the Senate

Senator John Tower (1925–1991), flanked by President Richard M. Nixon and future president George H. W. Bush in 1970. The first Republican to represent Texas in the United States Senate since Reconstruction, Tower held office from 1961 until his retirement in 1985 and played an important role in his party's rise to dominance in the state. Credit: From *Two-Party Texas: The John Tower Era, 1961–1984* by John R. Knaggs. Photo by Charles Pantaze. Courtesy of John Knaggs Collection, Special Collections, Southwestern University.

as the first Republican to win a statewide race in Texas since Reconstruction. Liberals, believing that in the future a Democratic Party under their control would defeat a Republican Party run by conservatives, looked on Tower's victory as a success. They could not have been more wrong, immediately or in the long run.

The Republican surge continued in the 1962 governor's election. Price Daniel, running for an unprecedented fourth term, faced opposition in the Democratic primary from liberal Houston attorney Don Yarborough (no relation to Senator Yarborough), Vice President Johnson's political ally John Connally, and three lesser candidates. One of the three, retired General Edwin Walker, flew a U.S. flag upside down at his home in Dallas as a warning that the nation was under attack from the federal government's support of integration. Daniel ran third, thanks in part to the new sales tax, and then Connally narrowly defeated Yarborough in the runoff. In the general election, Connally, whose views tended toward political moderation, faced a strongly conservative oilman Democrat-turned-Republican, Jack Cox. Connally won, but Cox, with 46 percent of the vote, ran far stronger than any Republican gubernatorial candidate in recent memory. His party also elected two U.S. Representatives and seven members of the Texas lower house.

Republicans eagerly anticipated the 1964 general elections, but their rising fortunes, and all of Texas for that matter, took a serious blow on November 22, 1963, when Lee Harvey Oswald assassinated President Kennedy and seriously wounded Governor Connally in Dallas. Vice President Lyndon Johnson took sure-handed control of the government, reassured the public, and used the prestige of his office to keep the liberal-conservative split in Texas to a minimum. Connally's near martyrdom made him virtually unbeatable so long as he wished to hold the office of governor. Johnson, the first true Texan to hold the presidency (Eisenhower was born in Denison but grew up in Kansas), pursued many of the initiatives begun under Kennedy. For example, he secured passage of the Civil Rights Act of 1964, which outlawed segregation in all places of public accommodation and created the Equal Employment Opportunity Commission. In the Senate Ralph Yarborough stood with Al Gore Sr. of Tennessee as the only southern Democrats voting for the bill, and John Tower joined southerners in a filibuster against it. "I think," Johnson said to a friend after signing the bill, "we just delivered the South to the Republican Party for a long time to come." The act did indeed hurt the Democratic Party across the region but not enough to take the president's own state away from him in the 1964 presidential election.

Republican fortunes suffered in 1964 not only from the presence of native son Lyndon Johnson on the Democratic ticket but also from the identification of Republicans with right-wing extremism that seemingly had taken over Texas politics, especially in the Dallas area, during the early 1960s. Whipped up by a steady barrage of propaganda from organizations such as Dallas oil billionaire H. L. Hunt's LIFE LINE, crowds of Dallas right wingers had threatened and jostled Lyndon and Lady Bird Johnson in 1960 and heckled, hit, and spit on U.N. ambassador Adlai Stevenson in 1963. Kennedy's assassination appeared to many as the logical progression of such political hatred. In 1964 Dallas, and for that matter much of Texas, needed to improve its image. Thus, when the Republicans nominated Senator Barry Goldwater of Arizona, a man easily painted as an extremist, the Democrats swept to victory. Johnson received 63 percent of the vote, even drawing the support of Democrats such as Allan Shivers and Oveta Culp Hobby, who had supported Eisenhower and Nixon in previous elections. Connally won reelection as governor even more impressively with 74 percent of the total. Senator Ralph Yarborough held his office against a serious challenge from George H. W. Bush, the Connecticut-born son of a U.S. Senator, who had built a career as an oilman in Texas before entering Republican politics. Bush attacked Yarborough's liberal record, particularly his vote for the Civil Rights Act, but the incumbent pictured his challenger as a "carpetbagger" and won with 56 percent of the vote. The Democratic sweep even removed the two Republican congressmen from Texas—Bruce Alger of Dallas and Ed Foreman of Odessa.

After the election of 1964, Governor Connally, working with Speaker of the House Ben Barnes, compiled a notably successful record, especially in improving higher education in Texas. The Texas College and University System Coordinating Board, created in 1965 and renamed the Texas Higher Education Coordinating Board in 1987, directed the planning and development of a comprehensive system of public colleges and universities. At Connally's urging, the legislature increased funding for construction and faculty salaries. Liberal Democrats complained that the governor's programs depended too heavily on increasing revenue from the sales tax, but he remained popular with his party's moderates and conservatives. In 1966 he won reelection without serious opposition.

In the meantime, Lyndon Johnson's administration began as a productive dream and turned into a nightmare. The president's vision of a "Great Society" resulted in the greatest burst of domestic reform since the New Deal. Measures to ensure voting rights, to aid public education, to protect the environment, and to provide medical care for the poor (Medicaid) and elderly (Medicare) poured from Congress after 1965. During the same years, however, the costly and divisive war in Vietnam built to a climactic moment—the Viet Cong's Tet Offensive in January 1968—that delivered a knockout blow to the American public's morale and led Johnson to announce in March that he would not run for reelection.

Going into the election of 1968, huge numbers of Texans had some reason to oppose the national Democratic Party. Conservatives blamed Johnson for not prosecuting the war more vigorously, whereas liberals denounced the president for escalating the war in the first place. Many traditionally Democratic voters, even those who supported New Deal–style liberalism, disagreed with the Great Society's welfare state measures and despised the counterculture of antiwar protestors. The Democratic nominee, Vice President Hubert Humphrey, mirrored his party's division and everything the conservatives opposed—being identified with liberal policies on one hand and the unsuccessful war on the other. Thus, the Republican candidate, Richard M. Nixon, a conservative who promised to end the war and restore unity to the nation, seemed certain to carry Texas, and would have but for the appearance of a third party. George Wallace of Alabama, a leader in the fight against integration and, at that point in his career, a blatant racist, ran on the American Party ticket. He received only 19 percent of the vote in Texas, but that represented 584,269 voters, many of whom would have supported Nixon had Wallace not run. This allowed Humphrey to carry the state over Nixon by one percentage point (41 to 40 percent), a difference of fewer than 39,000 voters.

State elections in 1968 demonstrated that traditional conservatism continued to rule the Democratic Party and that Republicans, regardless of their strength in national elections, still could not break through to control the government in Austin. Ten Democrats entered their party's gubernatorial primary; six received at least 150,000 votes; and the runoff pitted a conservative, Preston Smith, against the perennial liberal candidate Don Yarborough. Smith, a West Texan from Lubbock who served as lieutenant governor under Connally, capitalized on his strength among rural and small-town voters to win with 55 percent of the vote. Then, in the general election, he held enough of the usual Democratic voters to defeat his Republican opponent, Paul Eggers, by an even larger margin (57 to 43 percent). Smith's impressive victory paled to some extent, however, in comparison to the margin run up by Speaker of the House Ben Barnes in winning the lieutenant governor's office. Barnes, who was generally regarded as a rising star in the tradition of Johnson and Connally, received two million votes, the largest total ever to that point for a Texas politician. Smith appeared to some observers as simply an interim governor between Connally and Barnes, and his relatively few accomplishments added to that impression. Gus Mutscher, the new speaker of the house, bottled up any reform legislation, and some of the proposals Smith supported backfired on him. In 1969, for example, he endorsed the idea of extending the sales tax to food, only to have a "housewives' revolt" lead the legislature to kill the proposal.

Conservative Democrats handed liberals in their party and Republicans another defeat in 1970. In the primary Ralph Yarborough failed to win the nomination for a third full term in the U.S. Senate. His successful opponent, Lloyd Bentsen Jr., a Houston millionaire and former congressman, attacked the incumbent's liberal record and nonsupport of the Vietnam War. Bentsen then defeated Republican congressman George H. W. Bush in the general election. In a rematch with Paul Eggers, Preston Smith retained the governor's office, albeit by a smaller margin than in 1968. Thus, some twenty-five years after rising liberalism in the national Democratic Party and increasing factionalism at home seemed to offer such great opportunities for Republican success in Texas, the party held only one of Texas's U.S. Senate seats (John Tower, who won election to a full term in 1966), three seats in the U.S. House of Representatives (Jim Collins of Dallas, Bill Archer of Houston, and Bob Price of Pampa), and a few in the Texas Senate and House. Republicans could take comfort at least in the fact that Democratic liberals had even less power.

No doubt older Texans looking back from 1971 over the years since American entry into World War II shook their heads over the changes that had overtaken their state. Attracting immigrants from all over the United States as well as from Mexico, it had moved from sixth to fourth place among the states in the size of its population. Cities had grown beyond the imagination of most, and the economy had far greater diversification than ever before. Conservative Democrats still controlled the state, but Republicans had carried it twice in presidential elections and gained a seat in the U.S. Senate for the first time in nearly a century. The right-wing fanaticism of the fifties and early sixties and the wild counterculture of the sixties made the enthusiasm of prohibitionists or the demagoguery of "Pappy" O'Daniel seem very tame. If older Texans also reflected on the rate at which changes had come since 1941, they had to ask themselves if the next thirty years could possibly maintain such a pace. The answer in most respects would be "yes."

Chapter 16

MODERN TEXAS, 1971–2001

Few, if any, major historical changes occur decisively in a clearly limited period of time. Even a political revolution that on a particular day brings down one government and replaces it with another takes years to develop and even longer to run its course. Thus, historians always have room to debate exactly when great changes begin and end. The modernization of Texas is no exception. When did the state move from "old" to "modern," not just chronologically, but in terms of its economy, society, and political life as well?

"Old" Texas had a semicolonial economy that depended on the production of a few raw materials—cotton, cattle, and oil—and left the control of manufacturing, commerce, finance, and services largely to outside interests. Southern-born Anglo males, especially those living in rural and small-town settings, dominated socially. Their ideas and beliefs set the state's cultural standards. Politically, Democrats controlled the state, generally providing a conservative government that kept taxes low, gave business some help and little regulation, and offered only minimal social services. "Modern" Texas is far more diversified than "old" Texas in every way. The economy still draws support from agriculture and oil, but it depends more heavily than ever on manufacturing, commerce, and finance. Moreover, electronics and other high-tech industries, health-support enterprises, and service businesses have risen to positions of vital importance. Socially, women stand much closer to equality with men, and the once-dominant southern Anglos share the state on a more equal footing with African Americans, Mexican Americans, Asian immigrants, and many new arrivals from across the United States. Virtually all recent migrants live in cities, making Texas in 2000 as overwhelmingly urban (80 percent) as it was rural (83 percent) a century earlier. Political life in modern Texas is also dramatically different, at least on the surface. In 1978, Bill Clements, a Republican, won the governorship, giving his party its first such victory in more than a century and ushering in what many see as two-party government in the state. Democratic candidates for governor won in 1982 and 1990; Republicans in 1986, 1994, and 1998. The parties also shared other executive offices and achieved a fairly even balance in the legislature. Some observers think that rather than becoming a two-party state, modern Texas is actually in a period of transition from one-party rule by conservative Democrats to one-party rule by conservative Republicans and therefore remains "old" in its politics. That remains to be seen, however, and for the moment political life appears more competitive.

Texas's move from "old" to "modern" cannot be tied exclusively to a single event or time period, but certainly World War II and its aftermath brought notable steps in that direction. Then, rapidly accelerating change during the last three decades of the century nearly, although perhaps not totally, completed the process. Through it all, at least one thing is certain—Texas never lost its appeal to immigrants. "Gone to Texas" appeared in so many languages in so many places that in 1994 the Lone Star State passed even New York and took second place in population among the United States.

Women's Role in Modern Texas

After winning the right to vote in 1920, Texas women did not sustain the activism that carried them so far during the first two decades of the century. The atmosphere of the 1920s discouraged reforms of any kind, and the Great Depression of the thirties further dampened the aspirations of women to break out of traditional roles as wives, mothers, and housekeepers. In 1940 suffragist leader Minnie Fisher Cunningham saw the last two decades as an opportunity lost. "It was maddening to think," she wrote to her colleague Jane Y. McCallum, "that we somehow didn't carry on as vigorously as we could have done. . . ." Cunningham tried to remedy this lack of activism by running for governor in 1944, forming a Women's Committee for Educational Freedom to support Homer Rainey in his battle with the University of Texas regents, and offering to mortgage her property to found the *Texas Observer* as a liberal newsmagazine in 1954. For the most part, however, women's causes languished during the forties and fifties. Women received the right to serve on juries in 1954, but that change was long overdue. A promising step came in 1957 when Hermine Tobolowsky, a Dallas lawyer, persuaded the Texas Business and Professional Women to endorse a Equal Legal Rights Amendment (ELRA) to the state constitution. Actual passage, however, remained far in the future. As the best known suffragist leaders passed from the scene—McCallum died in 1957 and Cunningham in 1964—their success in attaining the vote appeared to have done little for the broader cause of equal rights.

The sixties brought the women's movement out of the doldrums nationally, but Texas activists did not keep pace. For example, five years after its founding in 1966, the National Organization of Women (NOW), which demanded the equal rights promised under Title VII of the Civil Rights Act of 1964, did not have a chapter in Texas. Only three of the six women who served in the state legislature during the sixties supported the proposed Equal Legal Rights Amendment. The others agreed with male critics that the proposal would take away special legal protections for women, and one argued that passage might lead her husband to stop acting like a gentleman. The amendment remained bottled up in the legislature in 1969. Even the one truly important legislative gain for married women during the sixties, the Marital Property Act of 1967, likely owed its passage to opposition to the ELRA. In an effort to deny the need for an equal rights amendment, the State Bar Association's Louise Raggio, a Dallas lawyer, drafted legislation to give married women an equal right to community property (that is, each spouse has an equal right to his/her earnings and to the earnings of his/her separate property). Tobolowsky, thinking that this measure would reduce the need for the ELRA, opposed it, and the desire to hand her a defeat helped gain approval. At least married women gained an important right.

The modern women's rights movement finally took hold in Texas during the early seventies. In March 1971 the state legislature agreed to submit the state ELRA, which was co-sponsored by Senator Barbara Jordan and Representative Frances "Sissy" Farenthold of Corpus Christi, to the voters in November 1972. Later in 1971, Liz Carpenter, the former press secretary for President Lyndon Johnson, led in forming the Texas Women's Political Caucus, an Austin-based organization dedicated to passage of a proposed national Equal Rights Amendment and the elimination of laws that infringed on women's "reproductive freedom." Congress passed the amendment in March 1972, and a special session of the Texas legislature gave its approval within less than two months. In November 1972, Texas voters approved the state ELRA by a 4 to 1 margin, and, as if to add an exclamation mark, elected six women to the legislature, more than had ever been seated at any one time to that date. Activists created a state chapter of NOW in 1973, and local chapters spread across the state.

During the early seventies, Texas women also played key roles in the landmark case, *Roe v. Wade,* which struck down a state law that made all abortions illegal (except those necessary to save the life of the pregnant woman). Sarah Weddington and Linda Coffee, two Dallas lawyers, filed a legal action in March 1970 on behalf of "Jane Roe" and all other women "who were or might become pregnant and want to consider all options." Their suit requested an injunction to prevent Henry Wade, the local district attorney, from enforcing the antiabortion statute. Weddington, sparked by memories of her own experience "as a scared graduate student in 1967 in a dirty, dusty Mexican border town to have an abortion," argued the case twice before the U.S. Supreme Court, which ruled in January 1973 that the Texas law violated a woman's constitutional right to privacy. The decision in *Roe v. Wade* proved to be more of an opening gun than a final victory in the battle for "reproductive freedom"—antiabortion forces have persuaded the legislature to prohibit abortion in the third trimester of a pregnancy and "right to life" conservatives insist that the Supreme Court will overturn the decision in the near future—nevertheless, it symbolized greater control for women over their own lives.

By the close of the seventies, the women's movement appeared to lose momentum. The ERA failed to win approval nationally, a sign of the times even though Texas had given its approval. Also, a backlash against "radical feminists" developed, especially among antiabortionists and conservative religious groups. Texas women, however, did not retreat to the 1950s. Instead, a steadily increasing proportion of married women worked outside the home, and women's issues received greater attention throughout society. Communities established rape crisis programs and shelters for battered women and concerned themselves with day care centers. Colleges and universities established women's studies programs of the sort virtually unheard of before the 1960s.

Finally, Texas women modernized their role in politics by running for and holding public office in unprecedented numbers. Literally thousands of women served on school boards, city councils, and as the mayors of towns and cities. By the end of the 1990s, all of the state's largest cities had elected at least one woman as mayor, Lila Cockrell of San Antonio being the first in 1975. The number of women in the state legislature grew from six in 1973 to thirty-two in 1999, and ethnic minorities shared in the gain. African Americans Eddie Bernice Johnson and Senfronia Thompson were among the state representatives elected in 1972, and Irma Rangel from Kingsville earned distinction as the first Latina representative in 1976. Frances "Sissy" Farenthold ran for governor in 1972, unsuccessfully, but Ann Richards won the state's highest office in 1990. Their stories, however, along with those of other women who distinguished themselves statewide during the 1980s and 1990s, are best told as part of the overall political history of the period.

Politics as Usual, 1971–1976

In January 1971 Texas politics seemed to hold little promise of anything new. Democrats gathered in Austin for a "victory gala" celebrating the reelection of Preston Smith as governor. Conservatives were especially happy, having dumped the best-known liberal in their party, Senator Ralph Yarborough, in the previous year's primary and yet maintained enough Democratic solidarity to elect the man who defeated him, Lloyd Bentsen Jr., of Houston, in the fall. Republicans, although they had built a strong grassroots campaign organization, had only one U.S. Senator, three U.S. Representatives, and a handful of state legislators to show for their efforts. Fewer than 20 percent of Texans considered themselves Republicans as opposed to 52 percent who identified with the Democratic Party. Even as the Democrats celebrated, however, and the landscape of Texas politics seemed so unchanged, the federal Securities and Exchange Commission exposed a scandal that ruined the careers of Governor Smith and Lieutenant Governor Ben Barnes, the party's rising star, and threatened to upset the entire traditional system.

The scandal developed from a complicated plot hatched in 1969 by Frank W. Sharp, a Houston businessman who controlled the Sharpstown State Bank and the National Bankers Life Insurance Company. In an effort to have the legislature pass a bill exempting state banks (such as his) from regulation by the Federal Deposit Insurance Corporation, Sharp arranged unsecured loans of more than $600,000 to Governor Smith, Speaker of the House Gus Mutscher, State Democratic Chairman Elmer Baum, State Representative Tommy Shannon, and several aides. The officials used the loans to buy stock in National Bankers Life, which Sharp promised to inflate in value once his bank bill passed. Smith then called a special legislative session at which Mutscher and Shannon pushed through the desired bill. At that point, as promised, Sharp inflated the value of the insurance company stock by advising a Jesuit group to make a large investment in it, allowing Smith and the other officials to sell for some $250,000 in profits. Curiously, Governor Smith, after taking his profit, talked to banking leaders and vetoed the bill on the ground that he had not understood it properly. An SEC investigation of Sharp's stock manipulations and other business shenanigans led to the politicians in early 1971, and the Sharpstown scandal became headline news.

Smith, Mutscher, and the other officials claimed that their business dealings with Sharp had no relationship to the banking bill, but political pressure mounted on them and on Lieutenant Governor Barnes as well. Barnes had no immediate part in the plot, but he also had received a loan from Sharp's bank. Most of the pressure came from a mixed coalition of Democratic and Republican, liberal and conservative, state representatives called the "Dirty Thirty." They demanded that Mutscher drop his heavy-handed control of the house and permit an investigation of the scandal. The speaker responded by appointing five of his cronies to an investigative committee, an abuse of power that further angered his critics. Continuing publicity, much of it coming from attacks by the "Dirty Thirty," led to a grand jury investigation that indicted Mutscher, Shannon, and the speaker's key aide for bribery. The Austin district attorney who led the investigation informed the press that Governor Smith was an unindicted co-conspirator. Publicity required a change of venue to Abilene, where in March 1972 a jury needed only a few hours to find the three defendants guilty. The judge sentenced each to five years' probation.

The Sharpstown Scandal created a demand for political reform and, since only Democrats were involved, should have opened the door to Republican victories. In the 1972 Democratic primary, Governor Smith ran a far-distant fourth in his bid for another term, and Ben Barnes, who had received more than two million votes in an earlier race for lieutenant governor, came in third with fewer than 400,000. The top two vote getters, Dolph Briscoe, a conservative banker/rancher from Uvalde, and Frances "Sissy" Farenthold, a liberal member of the "Dirty Thirty" from Corpus Christi, were untainted by the scandal. Farenthold employed women in key positions during her campaign and drew enthusiastic support from liberals and women across the state. However, Briscoe prevailed in the runoff with 55 percent of the vote. Democrats hoped that his image as a "clean" conservative would help them hold the governor's office that fall against the challenge of Republican Henry C. Grover, a state senator from Houston. Grover ran with several handicaps, including a lack of name identification with voters and his party's need to spend a great deal of its money on reelecting President Richard Nixon and Senator John Tower. Even then, he received more than 1.5 million votes and, with the help of Ramsey Muñiz, the La Raza Unida Party candidate, who had more than 214,000 votes, pushed Briscoe into the position of winning with only a minority (48 percent) of the vote. In addition to Grover's near-miss, Republicans could cheer a landslide win (67 percent of the vote) by Nixon over George McGovern, the reelection of Tower to the Senate in a tough contest with Harold "Barefoot" Sanders, the election of Alan Steelman of Dallas to join the three incumbent members of his party in the U.S. House of Representatives, and a gain of seven seats in the Texas House of Representatives. (These gains in the house came at least in part from a redistricting following the U. S. Census of 1970 that gave greater representation to heavily Republican urban areas.)

In addition to ruining the careers of several leading Democrats and improving the fortunes of Republicans, Sharpstown brought notable reforms in state government. The 1973 legislature passed laws requiring candidates for office to release details about their campaign finances and state officeholders to disclose their sources of income. Other new legislation gave the public increased access to government meetings and records and forced greater disclosure of activities by paid lobbyists. The scandal also gave impetus to a movement aimed at replacing the badly dated Constitution of 1876. At the 1972 general election, voters approved an amendment proposed the previous year designating the legislature scheduled to meet in January 1974 as a constitutional convention. Preparations for this convention began in 1973 with the appointment of a constitutional revision commission that worked throughout the year to develop a modernized frame of government. However, after meeting from January to July 1974, the convention failed by a three-vote margin to reach agreement on a document to submit to the public. The only change of significance to emerge from three years of discussion that cost more than $3 million in state appropriations was a 1973 amendment extending the terms of the governor and other state officials from two to four years.

Even before all the fallout from Sharpstown settled on the political landscape of Texas, a national scandal—Watergate—ruined Nixon's second administration and dragged down Lone Star State Republicans as well. The June 1972 break-in at offices of the Democratic National Executive Committee in the Watergate complex in Washington and the subsequent cover-up by the administration, which led to Nixon's resignation in August 1974, could hardly have come at a worse time for the president's party in Texas. Distrustful of Republicans, voters found comfort in the traditional politics offered by Governor Briscoe in 1973–1974. Briscoe took few initiatives, maintained satisfactory relations with labor and Mexican Americans as well as with businessmen and conservatives, and delivered on his promise of "no new taxes." In 1974 as his term came to an end, the political scene looked just like the "good old days" in that he faced only a mild challenge in the Democratic primary and none at all in the general election. Frances Farenthold, the "Dirty Thirty" representative from Corpus Christi who had forced Briscoe into a runoff in the 1972 primary, again offered the opposition. As a well-known woman—her name had been put into consideration for the vice presidential nomination at the 1972 Democratic convention—waging an aggressively liberal campaign, Farenthold received a great deal of media attention, but Democratic voters were no longer interested in change. Her vote decreased by more than half of the number received in 1972, and Briscoe won with 67 percent of the total. In the general election, the governor swept to an easy victory over Jim Granberry, the Republican mayor of Lubbock.

Following the elections of 1974, it appeared, in the words of a writer for the *Houston Chronicle,* that "the Republicans are wiped out state-wide for the foreseeable future." That prophecy seemed accurate two years later when Texas returned to the Democratic column in the presidential election won by Jimmy Carter. Careful observers, however, could detect indications of a quick Republican recovery built around the presidential ambitions of Ronald Reagan, the former governor of California. Reagan appealed strongly to the right wing of his party and attracted conservative Democrats and supporters of George Wallace as well. In the 1976 Texas Republican presidential primary, he ran against Gerald Ford, the vice president who had succeeded Nixon in the Oval Office, and helped draw in six times as many voters as had participated in the 1974 gubernatorial primary. Reagan defeated Ford by a two-to-one margin in Texas and likely would have carried the state had the national party made him rather than the incumbent its nominee. More important for the future, many of the conservative voters that he attracted, unlike those who had voted for Eisenhower and Nixon in general elections, switched party allegiances. As one journalist put it later, "Middle-class Anglos discovered they didn't get warts or become socially ostracized for having voted in the 1976 Republican presidential primary for Ronald Reagan, so they were willing to try it again."

While the Republicans' quick comeback from Watergate developed during the mid-1970s, Briscoe quietly served out the four-year term he had won in 1974. He "seemed to enjoy being governor," says one study, "but to care little about performing the functions of the office." Political leadership seemed to matter little at the time, however, because Texans found themselves in the midst of an economic and population boom almost beyond imagination. By 1980 Texas would stand as "the living, breathing symbol of prosperity to the entire Free World." Millions now learned what Texans had always known—the Lone Star shone on a truly special place. Eventually, of course, all would discover what economists could have foretold—booms end in crashes.

Boom and Crash, 1971–1987

The economy of the United States staggered into the 1970s, hit especially hard by double-digit annual inflation rates that led President Nixon to impose wage and price controls in 1971. Then, in 1973, as economic activity slowed to the point of recession, the Organization of Petroleum Exporting Countries (OPEC) added to the nation's woes by restricting the production of oil. Prices, which stood as low as $4 a barrel in 1972, soared upward toward $40 a barrel by the early 1980s, and the resultant increase in energy costs helped deepen the national recession. Texas largely escaped these economic problems, however, because it exported oil and in that respect at least bore more of a resemblance to the OPEC nations than to the rest of the United States. Higher oil prices brought fantastic prosperity to the state while economic hard times stalked most of the nation.

Somewhat ironically, oil production in Texas peaked in 1972, one year before the great boom began. The state produced a record 1,263,412,000 barrels that year and then began a steady decline that reached 725,029,000 barrels in 1987. Nevertheless, rising prices more than made up for declining production, and the industry boomed, pulling the state along with it. Statistics demonstrating the rate of expansion are truly impressive. Between 1973 and 1981, the state gained more than 2.2 million jobs (a 40 percent increase), and Texans' personal income tripled. In just four years, 1979–1982, while the United States as a whole suffered a loss of $26 million in gross national product and 200,000 jobs, Texas had a gain of $43 million in output and added 800,000 jobs. Oil production fueled this prosperity, but manufacturing and agriculture contributed as well. By 1985 more than a million Texans worked in manufacturing, a gain of 39 percent since 1971. The number of farms increased only a little during the seventies and eighties, but productivity showed marked improvement. For example, 174,068 farms produced a little more than 2.5 million bales of cotton in 1974, whereas the 1987 crop grown on 188,788 farms amounted to more than 4 million bales. Overproduction slowed the oil boom in 1982, but prices remained far higher than in the early 1970s; moreover, at that point the urban construction industry stepped in to help keep the economy moving. To the delight of developers, real estate wheeler-dealers, and the savings and loan operators who provided the financing, Texans seemingly needed an unending supply of new houses, apartment complexes, office buildings, and shopping malls. Favorable tax laws on real estate ventures and the reduction of regulations on savings and loans gave added encouragement. The boom hesitated in 1982 and then roared ahead again.

Fifteen years of spectacular economic expansion created yet another chapter in the story of "Gone to Texas." Between 1970 and 1980, new job seekers helped build the state's population from 11,196,730 to 14,229,191, a gain of 28 percent, and move it to the third-largest in the nation behind only California and New York. Then, over the next five years the number of Texans increased by another 2 million. New arrivals fleeing the recession-ridden "Frostbelt" cities such as Detroit concentrated in Texas's "Sunbelt" urban areas, particularly Houston. The only Texas city with more than a million residents in 1970, Houston grew by 29 percent during the next decade, reaching a population of nearly 1.6 million as the oil boom approached its peak in the early 1980s. "This is not a city," the *U.S. News & World Report* wrote of Houston in 1978. "It's a phenomenon—an explosive, churning, roaring juggernaut that's shattering tradition as it expands outward and upward with an energy that stuns even its residents." Dallas had a lower growth rate during the seventies, but it expanded rapidly with the development/real estate/finance boom and by 1990 became the second Texas city to have a million residents. San Antonio had a similar growth pattern and stood just below one million in 1990.

Texas's prosperity and growth in the midst of national economic stagnation caught the imagination of people everywhere and created a rage for all things "Texan." Boots and jeans became fashion statements; Southwestern art filled galleries; and Country and Western music grew in popularity. Hollywood contributed *Urban Cowboy,* the story of "Bud," a young man from rural Texas who moved to Houston for work in a refinery, met and married "Sissy," and proved himself the best country dancer and mechanical-bull rider at Gilley's honky-tonk. Television offered *Dallas,* a prime-time soap opera about the oil-rich Ewings. Millions of fans had to wait the entire summer of 1980 to find out who shot "J. R.," the family's leading scoundrel. The Dallas Cowboys, in spite of losing the 1975 and 1979 Super Bowls to the Frostbelt's Pittsburgh Steelers, became "America's Team." Most Texans loved all the attention, of course, and tended to think that their state was not only special but invulnerable and invincible as well.

The inevitable collapse did not come suddenly but instead arrived in increments. In 1982, an oil glut stopped the spectacular upward trend in prices that had recently reached $40 a barrel and led optimistic forecasters to predict "$85 in '85." Although prices remained far higher than when the boom began, the slowdown cost Texas some 200,000 jobs that year. This bursting of the oil bubble did not immediately destroy the Texas economic miracle, however, because real estate took up the slack, at least for a while. Bankers, flush with profits from loans to the oil business but also heavily committed to a now-weakening industry, looked to place their money elsewhere and found land deals, construction, and development. Operators of savings and loan associations also jumped into the real estate market. Once called "thrifts" because they only accepted individual savings deposits at regulated interest rates and made loans to residential homeowners, S&Ls sought to take full advantage of deregulation, which allowed them to pay higher interest rates and to make high-yield corporate and nonresidential real estate loans. Texas's economy boomed again in the mid-1980s, fired up this time by rampant speculation in real estate. Parcels of land were "flipped" two and three times in a matter of weeks or even days as developers, appraisers, and S&L directors worked together to approve and finance one sale after another, always at higher prices. By the close of 1985, some 6.7 million Texans had jobs, a million more than in 1980.

The prosperity of the mid-1980s, based largely on finance and real estate rather than on oil production and manufacturing, did not have the strength of the earlier boom. Thus, when oil prices suffered a dramatic fall in 1986, from more than $30 a barrel to less than $10, the good times ended. The collapse of the oil industry rippled through the entire economy, destroying public confidence, bankrupting businesses, and throwing workers out of their jobs by the thousands. The number of nonagricultural jobs, which had risen 14.5 percent between 1980 and 1985, fell 3.4 percent in one year from 1986 to 1987. Speculative real estate deals fell apart and took dozens of S&Ls down with them. Defaulting developers and speculators left "thrifts" holding so much property worth only a tiny fraction of the money loaned on it that by the end of October 1987 the combined value of all the state's S&Ls was a minus $5.1 billion. Investigations soon disclosed the role of fraud and conspiracy as well as bad loans in causing the losses. A few of the criminals went to jail, but ultimately the federal government called on taxpayers to replace nearly $500 billion lost by depositors.

As Texas's version of the American Dream turned into a nightmare, the state lost a good deal of its allure, especially since the rest of the nation did not suffer a recession. The population, which had increased by 585,097 people in 1981, added only 45,231 in 1987. Jokes abounded: "How do you get a Texas banker out of a tree? Cut the rope!" Even "America's Team" appeared caught in the malaise, fading to a horrible 3–13 record in 1988. The Cowboys changed ownership the next year, when Dallas banker H. R. "Bum" Bright and his partners sold out to Arkansas oil-and-gas investor Jerry Jones. Then, before Texans could adjust to an outsider owning "their" team, Jones fired the Cowboys' legendary coach Tom Landry and hired Jimmy Johnson in his place. In their first year under new management, the Cowboys sank even lower, finishing 1–15. The Cowboys would recover, of course, and go on to win three Super Bowls within four years during the mid-1990s, and the Texas economy would revive as well—in fact it regained strength ahead of the Cowboys' resurgence. The 1990s economy, however, would depend far less on oil and would move in step with the rest of the nation to a greater extent than ever before. In a sense, then, the boom that extended from the early 1970s to 1986–1987 marked the final stage in the evolution of Texas's economy from "old" to modern. Coincidentally, the same years saw political life in the state take a major step toward modernization as well. Genuine two-party competition appeared to develop.

Republican Victories, 1976–1988

Following his easy reelection in 1974, Governor Dolph Briscoe enjoyed the political benefits of holding office during an economic boom. He exerted little leadership, but there seemed to be no need for activism of any sort. After all, as *Texas Business Review* put it some years later, "The most difficult problem facing state government was what to do with the billion-dollar budget surplus caused by the unexpected rise in tax revenues precipitated by the increase in oil prices." Briscoe worked on highway improvements and otherwise took a conservative approach that favored the status quo. In 1978 he sought another four-year term, which would make him the longest-serving governor in Texas history, but, somewhat surprisingly, voters in the Democratic primary narrowly rejected him in favor of Attorney General John Hill. A moderate, Hill attacked Briscoe as a do-nothing governor, won the enthusiastic support of teachers by championing education, and also benefited from voters' unwillingness to let any one politician hold the state's top office for ten years.

Hill, having won the nomination, confidently expected victory in the fall. After all, no Republican had won the governorship since 1869. Indeed, after

William P. Clements Jr. and Rita Clements leaving the Texas Capitol following his inauguration as governor, January 16, 1979. Clements upset Democrat John Hill to become the first Republican governor of Texas since Reconstruction. The Ross Volunteers from Texas A&M University, the governor's official honor guard, provide the traditional arch of sabers. Credit: Texas State Library and Archives Commission.

the primaries in 1978, political pundits spent most of their energy on the senatorial campaign that pitted the Republican incumbent John Tower against Congressman Robert Krueger, an energetic Democratic challenger from New Braunfels. Few gave the Republican nominee for governor, William P. Clements Jr. of Dallas, much of a chance. An upset was in the making.

Bill Clements, the multimillionaire founder and chief executive officer of SEDCO, a giant oil-drilling company, entered politics in 1972 as co-chairman of the Nixon campaign in Texas. He then served as undersecretary of defense for four years, returned to Texas and announced as a candidate for governor in 1977, and easily defeated former state party chairman Ray Hutchison in the Republican primary. An aggressive, abrasive man—"fast-on-the-lip, shoot-from-the-hip," one writer said—Clements lacked experience in electoral politics, but his wife Rita, an experienced grassroots organizer, and friends such as George H. W. Bush more than made up for that deficiency. Moreover, Clements's campaign had other advantages that became apparent in retrospect. First, John Hill's attacks on Briscoe had so angered conservative rural

Democrats that many would drop their traditional support in the general election. Briscoe's wife, while promising to vote Democratic, said that Clements "would make a better governor than Hill." Second, the Republican Party's "southern strategy"—an appeal to white voters based on backlash against the civil rights movement and federal support of minority interests—had come into its own in Texas. Republican voters in the 1976 primary, for example, voted overwhelmingly against busing to achieve school integration, whereas the Democrats refused to place the question on their ballot. The Democratic Party continued along the road to becoming the refuge of minorities, a high percentage of whom did not vote, and Republican candidates such as Clements benefited from a steady influx of whites into their party. Third, the Clements campaign identified Hill as a liberal associate of President Jimmy Carter. Vowing to hang Carter around Hill's neck "like a dead chicken," Clements tossed a plastic plucked chicken at his opponent during a joint banquet appearance in Amarillo. Some of the candidate's advisers feared that the stunt would appear rough and insensitive. "Little did we know," said one, "it would be that part of his character that would be most appealing to voters." Finally, Clements spent millions, much of it his own money, and campaigned hard all over the state, especially in rural counties. His message of conservatism and straight-talking, "Texan to his toenails" personality won over Briscoe Democrats by the thousands.

Clements's all-out effort—he continued to push for votes to the very end while Hill complacently planned his administration—paid off in a razor-thin victory. After weeks of late returns and local recounts, Clements had 49.9 percent of the official vote to 49.2 percent for Hill. (Two third-party candidates accounted for the remaining .9 percent.) Tower retained his U.S. Senate seat, defeating Krueger by an almost identically narrow margin. "The Lord smiled on Tuesday," said State Republican Chairman Ray Barnhart. In actuality, Democrats still held all important statewide offices other than the governorship and sizable majorities in the legislature. The Republican victory in 1978 did not make Texas a true two-party state, but it marked the arrival of competitive politics in gubernatorial as well as presidential elections. "There would appear to be," said the *Houston Post*, "no turning back from the coming of age of Texas politics."

The new governor's promise to reduce the size of state government and cut spending led immediately to conflict with Democrats such as Lieutenant Governor Bill Hobby and Attorney General Mark White and members of the 1979 legislative session as well. Clements opposed "throwing money at education"and therefore sought to cut the level of appropriations proposed by Hobby for teacher pay raises and aid to public schools. He clashed with White over his power to veto the appropriation of constitutionally guaranteed funds for college construction. The governor's efforts to reduce the number of state employees failed, but there was no increase either, even though the population was growing rapidly. Clements also maintained a highly open and adversarial relationship with the media—"Intimidation was just his style," wrote a *Dallas Morning News* reporter. Overall, while a good many people in Austin disliked Clements's personality and politics, the public gave him a high approval rating for his first year in office.

In the 1980 presidential election, Clements led Texas solidly into the camp of Ronald Reagan and George H. W. Bush. This was hardly difficult, since the state's Republicans had long preferred the California conservative and regarded Bush as one of their own, but Clements brought his usual outspoken abrasiveness to the campaign. When interviewed by the *Texarkana Gazette* about President Carter's claim that his administration had strengthened the United States military, the governor accused the president of "lying." "I just can't say it any stronger," he said. "Well, I could say he is a goddamn liar." Democrats cried foul, but Clements refused to apologize, and the Reagan-Bush ticket raised millions of dollars in Texas and carried the state with 56 percent of the vote. Texans flocked to the inauguration, indicating that their state's influence in Washington increasingly operated through the Republican rather than the Democratic Party.

Clements worked more successfully with the legislature in 1981, obtaining a package of anticrime and antidrug laws that he wanted and agreeing to a pay increase for teachers. He and the legislature also had to face the need for changes in the state's prison system, which had a rapidly increasing inmate population housed in inadequate facilities and disciplined by antiquated methods. In some cases, for example, prisoners slept on floors, and inmates had the responsibility to maintain discipline in their cell blocks. Change came as the result of a handwritten brief filed by inmate David Ruiz in the United States District Court at Tyler in 1972 and ruled on eight years later. The decision in *Ruiz v. Estelle* provided for federal oversight of the Texas prison system and ordered the state to reduce overcrowding, provide recreation and rehabilitation for prisoners, and end disciplinary practices that threatened inmates' safety. After exchanging recriminations over Clements's veto of $30 million in prison funds two years earlier, the governor and Democratic leaders in 1981 appropriated nearly $160 million for the construction of new prisons and another $26 million for improvements in the state's parole and probation systems. These expenditures amounted to little more than a Band-Aid, however, and the prison system remained under federal oversight and an embarrassing issue to Democrats and Republicans alike for the next twenty-one years.

Clements ran for re-election in 1982 and suffered a defeat almost as surprising as his victory four years earlier. The incumbent had no opposition in the Republican primary, enjoyed financial backing far greater than any Democrat, and could boast of a scandal-free administration. On the other hand, Clements found it easier to focus a campaign as an "outsider" seeking office than as an incumbent. There were fewer negatives to hang on his opponent. Also, Texas's great economic boom staggered badly in 1982, and as always, the party in office received the blame. Finally, Clements did not have the luxury of running against a divided Democratic Party. Mark White, facing two opponents in the Democratic primary, did not win a majority, but Buddy Temple, the East Texas timber millionaire who ran second, withdrew rather than enter an expensive and divisive runoff. Lieutenant Governor Hobby, a popular moderate Democrat, ran for re-election, and the party united behind progressives Jim Mattox for attorney general, Ann Richards for state treasurer, and Garry Mauro for land commissioner. The re-election bid of popular U.S. Senator Lloyd Bentsen also drew voters into the Democratic column, in spite of an effort by the challenger, Congressman Jim Collins, to paint him as a liberal. White and other campaigners pounced on every incident demonstrating the governor's abrasive personality and shoot-from-the-hip style, while Clements made no effort to hide his personal dislike for White. "I am competent," the governor told a television personality, "and he's incompetent." On election day large turnouts in Mexican American and African American precincts pushed the total vote notably higher than in 1978 (nearly 3.2 million compared to 2.4 million) and helped White win with 53 percent of the total, a surprisingly large margin. Democrats won every statewide race, and Senator Bentsen easily retained his seat.

White's victory and other Democratic successes in 1982 seemed to indicate that once again Republicans had stumbled badly on the road to a two-party Texas. On this occasion, however, they quickly regained their balance, thanks in part to the tremendous popularity in Texas of the party's national leader, President Ronald Reagan. In 1984, Reagan ran for re-election against the avowedly liberal Democratic team, Walter Mondale of Minnesota and Geraldine Ferraro of New York, setting up an easy choice for Texas voters. Nearly two of every three (64 percent) supported Reagan, and the president's broad coattails helped his party improve its position in the state legislature and the U.S. Congress as well. Republicans took 52 of 181 seats in the Texas House of Representatives, 6 of 31 in the state senate, and 10 of 27 in the U.S. House of Representatives. They also held on to John Tower's seat in the U.S. Senate seat when he, having served since 1961, retired and set up a contest between Republican Phil Gramm and Democrat Lloyd Doggett. Gramm, a professor at Texas A&M University before winning a seat in Congress as a Democrat in 1978, had resigned after switching parties in 1983 and won re-election from the same district as a Republican. He took 59 percent of the vote in easily defeating Doggett, a liberal who had beaten moderate Bob Krueger in the Democratic primary. Clearly, Republicans had lost little strength as a result of Clements's defeat in 1982. In fact, the party continued to make gains, thanks especially to its "southern strategy" of appealing to whites by opposing federal actions benefitting minorities. The Mondale/Ferraro ticket received the votes of 95 percent of black Texas voters, but Reagan and Bush had the support of 74 percent of white voters.

Texas Republicans also made a quick comeback because Mark White proved to be an unpopular governor. Even though his administration passed laws providing health care for the indigent, unemployment insurance for farm workers, health insurance for retired teachers, tougher pesticide regulations, and other reforms, few Texans actually warmed to the new governor as a leader. Liberals thought him too conservative, and conservatives thought him too liberal. When he took the initiative on pressing issues, the results angered just about everyone in some way. Public education provides a good example. The state's scholastic population grew rapidly during the 1970s, reaching more than 3 million by the close of the decade and putting an additional burden on the perennially underfinanced public school system. A report by the U.S. Secretary of Education in the early 1980s showed that Texas ranked forty-ninth among the states in income-per-capita spending on public schools, forty-second in the percentage of students graduating from high school, and well below national averages in teacher salaries and standardized test scores. White responded by calling on H. Ross Perot, the wealthy founder of EDS in Dallas, to head a select committee on public education. Once the Perot committee reported, the governor called a special legislative session in June 1984 to respond to its recommendations. The resulting Educational Reform Act provided a significant salary increase for teachers but also established stricter guidelines for certification and initiated competency testing for those already employed. Students faced periodic competence tests, too, and a "no-pass, no-play" rule that prohibited those with an average below 70 on any subject at the end of a six-weeks grading period from participating in extracurricular activities until they scored 70 or above on all subjects at the end of a subsequent grading period. Finally, the law made an effort to deal with the problem of unequal funding that rose from the practice of depending heavily on local property taxes to finance public education. Obviously, school districts with wealthy populations had far more money than did those with mostly poor residents. Perot's reforms called for an increase in state funding for poor districts and a decrease for the rich.

These educational changes, no matter how necessary they seemed in the abstract, were met with angry disapproval from groups who opposed particular details. Parents disliked the pressure put on their children by standardized tests and argued that the schools spent too much time "teaching the tests." Teachers resented competency testing. Coaches and fans criticized "no-pass, no-play," contending that it penalized athletes and took away one of their reasons for staying in school. Districts with low property values argued that the law did too little to equalize funding.

Educational reform thus cost Governor White support in many quarters—teachers no longer supported him, and coaches actually organized a group to lobby against him—but his chances of reelection in 1986 suffered an even greater blow when oil prices totally collapsed that spring. In addition to ruining the industry and throwing many thousands out of work, the collapse dried up a key source of tax money. The state comptroller forecast a budget deficit of $2 billion, and White had to call a special legislative session to deal with the problem. Unhappy at the turn of events, especially in an election year, legislators passed a hodge-podge of measures that postponed state obligations, cut expenditures everywhere possible, revoked raises promised to government employees, and temporarily increased a variety of taxes. Through it all, the governor looked more indecisive and incapable than ever.

In spite of the nightmarish political conditions he faced in 1986, White overcame five opponents in the Democratic primary with relative ease. Then, he had to face a rejuvenated Bill Clements whose message perfectly fit the times. Return me to office, said the former governor, and I will create "jobs, jobs, jobs." The Republicans also had an unbeatable commercial featuring the question "Say, what's up with Mark White?" and an answer that ticked off "sales taxes, property taxes, gasoline taxes, franchise taxes, crime, tuition, utility bills, state spending, the budget deficit, unemployment, and small business failures." The "ding" of a cash register followed each item on the "up" list. "We dinged him to death," said one Republican campaigner. Clements won with 53 percent of the vote, but that was a surprisingly small margin under the circumstances. Moreover, Democrats continued to hold every other statewide political office.

Half a year into his new term, Clements probably wondered why he had wanted to win the job. The still-weakening economy created an even larger budget deficit, projected by the comptroller at $6.5 billion for the next biennium (1987–1989). Clements and the legislature could not agree on spending and taxes during the regular session, and only the threat of shutting down much of the state government led to agreement at the close of a special legislative session in July. To the dismay of hard-line Republicans, Clements approved $5.7 billion in tax increases, the largest such measure in state history. The governor's defenders argued that had someone else held the office, the increase would have been larger. Also in 1987 Clements also found himself, for the first time in his political career, entangled in a scandal. While he had served on the board of governors at Southern Methodist University between 1983 and 1987, supporters of the school's football program had paid $61,000 to thirteen players and violated numerous other National Collegiate Athletic Association rules. Clements had played no part in paying players or breaking rules, but when made aware of the problem, he argued that the payments, which he regarded as a commitment, should be continued. That story hit the press early in 1987, delighting commentators—"There is a certain twisted logic about having a moral obligation to continue an immoral contract," one wrote—and forcing Clements to make a public apology. A poll taken in August 1987 gave the governor a 68 percent disapproval rating.

Clements's problems, however, did not translate into losses for his party. In the 1988 presidential election, the Republicans ran George Bush, Reagan's vice president, and Senator Dan Quayle of Indiana against Michael S. Dukakis, the governor of Massachusetts, and Senator Lloyd Bentsen. Bush and Bentsen gave each party a Texas connection, but Democrats hoped that their highly popular senator would overmatch the Connecticut-born vice president, who had spent little time in the state during the past eight years. They were badly mistaken. Bush's friend and campaign manager James A. Baker III ran a campaign that pictured Dukakis as an unpatriotic liberal who favored gun control and tended to pardon dangerous criminals, especially blacks. Willie Horton, a black man imprisoned for murder who committed another serious crime while on a furlough given by Dukakis, became a symbol of the candidate's weakness. In the meantime, Dukakis campaigned ineffectively, especially in Texas where he did not call on Bentsen's people until it was too late. The

Bush/Quayle ticket carried Texas with 56 percent of the vote. Republicans also won their first "down-ticket" statewide races, electing three members of the Texas Supreme Court and a member of the Railroad Commission. Having swept three consecutive presidential races by landslide margins, won two of the last three gubernatorial elections, and begun to cut into Democratic control throughout state government, Republicans in 1988 could claim that they stood ready to replace their opponents as the majority party in Texas.

Economic Recovery and Modernization, 1988–2001

Texas recovered quickly from the sharp recession of 1986–1987. Although stories of economic doom and gloom dominated much of 1988—former governor John Connally auctioned off portions of his estate as part of a personal bankruptcy settlement and the famed Houston heart surgeon, Denton Cooley, also declared himself financially insolvent—several developments that year pointed to both recovery and a more modern economy. First, the Semiconductor Manufacturing Technology corporation (SEMATECH), a consortium of private manufacturers, universities, and the U.S. Department of Defense, located its headquarters in Austin. Formed to meet foreign competition and assure continued leadership by the United States in the semiconductor industry in particular and electronics in general, SEMATECH sponsored research, design, and development of advanced computer chips and manufacturing techniques. It located in Austin because of a multimillion-dollar incentive package offered by the city and state governments and the University of Texas. Another huge step into the world of "high-tech," with all its accompanying prospects for economic expansion, came in November 1988 when the U.S. Department of Energy announced plans to build the Superconducting Super Collider (SSC) near Waxahachie in Ellis County. Designed to crash subatomic particles into each other at very high speeds, the SSC was intended to promote pure research into the "building blocks of matter" rather than to achieve any immediately practical or commercial purpose. Congressional critics who saw the project as too theoretical and expensive (especially since it was located in a state other than their own) killed it in 1993, but when initially announced it gave Texas a lift and attracted other businesses to the state. For example, in late 1988 GTE and Fujitsu, a Japanese telecommunications company, both announced moves of large parts of their operations to the Dallas area.

By the spring of 1989, the "Great Texas Turnaround" had brought the state's economy back to early 1986 levels in terms of nonagricultural employment and opened the door to another period of rapid expansion. The boom of the 1990s, however, depended on diversification and consumer spending, the marks of a modern economy, rather than on one or two resource-based, export industries. While oil, cotton, and cattle remained extremely important, high-tech manufacturing, trade with foreign nations, and consumer services became vital as well. "Broad-based diversification is really the key to our staying power over the long haul," economist Ray Perryman wrote in 1990, and the next ten years certainly seemed to bear out his words. Growth was especially fast in the early nineties—more rapid in fact than in any of the other ten largest states—in part because the recession had lowered values and left a great deal of room for expansion.

Oil production declined steadily from nearly 700 million barrels in 1988 to fewer than 400 million in 2000; still, Texas ranked first or second among the states (depending on how offshore wells are counted) and had one-quarter of the nation's refining capacity. The wellhead value of petroleum produced in the state amounted to approximately $20 billion a year. More than 100,000 Texans found employment directly in crude-oil production, and the industry gave work to many thousands more in transportation, refining, and marketing. Agriculture, although somewhat overshadowed by higher profile activities, actually showed statistical increases in all major products during the 1990s. The cotton crop, for example, reached 4.8 million bales in 1997, an increase of nearly 800,000 bales over 1987. Throughout the 1990s, Texas led the nation in the production of cotton, cattle, sheep, goats, wool, mohair, and hay. Overall, at the end of the century agricultural commodities added about $14 billion per year to the state's economy.

Manufacturing employed only a relatively few more Texans in 1999 than in 1989 (955,235 opposed to 948,255). Many continued to find work in petrochemical plants and the production of oil-field machinery, but the decade saw a steady shift toward jobs in relatively new industries. For example, employment in the manufacture of computers and electronic equipment increased 55 percent. Overall, manufacturing in the 1990s, even though not employing a notably larger number of Texans, made large gains in worker productivity, much of the improvement coming from the application of computer technology. An increase in foreign trade, primarily with Mexico, also sparked the boom. In 1992 the United States entered into the North American Free Trade Agreement (NAFTA), a treaty that greatly reduced barriers to commerce among Canada, the United States, and Mexico. The potentially negative impact of NAFTA on industries and workers in the United States (as factories and jobs moved to cheap labor markets in Mexico) created a controversy that continued through the decade, but Texas began to benefit immediately from an increased flow of goods across the Río Grande. By 1994, the state's businesses reaped an estimated $25 billion from trade with Mexico. Finally, the services sector of the economy—everything from professional, scientific, and technical services to educational services to arts, entertainment, and recreation—grew at an amazing pace during the nineties. Health care and social assistance alone provided work to more than 900,000 Texans at the end of the decade. Overall, between 1989 and 1999, employment in services, allowing for some variation in counting and reporting methods by the U.S. Census Bureau, increased approximately 100 percent.

Texas's surging economy sparked yet another round of the "GTT" phenomenon. "We observe," said the *Texas Business Review* in August 2000, "that the Texas economy is again booming and people are again flowing into the state." Actually, the story should have said "pouring" rather than "flowing."

During the decade of the nineties, Texas's population increased 23 percent to a total of 20,851,820, making it second in size only to California by 2000. (Estimates indicate that it passed New York in 1994.) In absolute numbers, the gain of 3,865,485 residents—more than one thousand per day for ten years—was the largest during any decade in the state's history. One of every eight people added to the population of the entire United States between 1990 and 2000 lived in Texas.

The explosive growth of the 1990s made Texas's population more urban than ever. While some western counties such as Reagan, Upton, Winkler, and Yoakum actually lost residents, those having large cities in or near them grew at unbelievable rates. Dallas County, for example, increased its population 20 percent while the two counties immediately to its north, Collin and Denton, grew 86 percent and 58 percent respectively. In 2000, Texas had three of the ten largest cities in the United States—Houston (number four with 1,953,631 residents), Dallas (number eight with 1,188,580), and San Antonio (number nine with 1,144,646). The state also had three of the ten fastest-growing metropolitan areas in the nation—McAllen-Edinburg-Mission (fourth), Austin-San Marcos (fifth), and Laredo (ninth). One last statistic, perhaps the most impressive of all, summarizes urban growth in Texas by the year 2000: at that date the 5.2 million residents of the Dallas-Fort Worth Metroplex outnumbered the entire populations of thirty-one of the fifty states.

The population boom also brought greater diversity than ever before among the peoples of Texas. Texans of Latino descent increased their numbers 54 percent between 1990 and 2000, reaching a total of nearly 6.7 million. The Asian population grew even more rapidly, although in absolute numbers it reached only a little more than 500,000. African Americans matched the growth rate for the state as a whole, 23 percent, and numbered a little more than 2.4 million persons in 2000. People considered "white," not counting Latinos, increased at a much slower rate than others (8 percent), but still totaled 11 million. With non-Latino whites amounting to only 52 percent of all Texans, while Mexican Americans represented 32 percent, African Americans 12 percent, and Asians 3 percent, the state stood on the verge of having a majority composed of minorities. Houston could serve as a model, having had that situation since the 1980s. By 2000, the city's population was 39 percent Latino, 25 percent black, 7 percent Asian, and only 29 percent Anglo.

Thus, during the 1990s economic recovery turned into another boom, and the pace of modernization in Texas accelerated. Spectacular population growth accompanied this new economic expansion. Even as the good times rolled, however, the state faced stubborn problems—pockets of extreme poverty, unequal funding of public schools, lack of opportunity for minorities in higher education, and overcrowded prisons—to name a few of the most pressing. A true two-party political system would have responded to these circumstances by offering voters reasonably clear choices between competing ideas and programs. Meaningful competition would in turn spark party unity and a high level of voter participation. Whether or not Texas politics actually modernized along these lines in the 1990s remains a matter of debate.

Two-Party Politics (?), 1989–2001

"The enormous engines of the Texas economy are fired up once again," Governor Clements told the legislature in January 1989 as he began his last two years in office. According to the governor, returning prosperity meant that he could stick with traditional "no new tax" policies and still handle the state's needs. This proved largely true in the case of the prison system, which had faced federal pressure to relieve overcrowding since the 1980 decision in *Ruiz v. Estelle*. In March 1989 the legislature, continuing the building program begun earlier in the decade, appropriated $324 million to construct units with eleven thousand new beds for inmates. Federal oversight of Texas prisons terminated in 1990, and the entire legal action closed two years later. Just as the prison crisis eased, however, Clements had to face an even more difficult problem—the equalization of funding for public schools.

Prisons were solely the responsibility of the state, which meant that the governor and legislature fully controlled their funding and operations. When the courts demanded reform in the *Ruiz* case, the state could respond without fear of offending any local constituency. Public schools, by contrast, drew most of their financial support from local property taxes and had a large degree of local control. The tremendous variation in property values from one independent school district to another allowed some school boards to run systems that offered far greater educational opportunities than others could hope to provide. Obviously, any change in this funding system would likely draw opposition from voters in wealthy districts. Clements and the legislature certainly did not want to deal with such a potentially "messy" issue, but it landed in their laps in 1989 when the Texas Supreme Court handed down its decision in *Edgewood ISD v. Kirby*.

The *Edgewood* case originated in 1984 with the Mexican American Legal Defense and Education Fund (MALDEF), an organization incorporated in San Antonio in 1967 under the leadership of Pete Tijerina. MALDEF, in addition to bringing numerous legal actions against continuing segregation of Mexican American students, focused on the fact that local funding for public schools gave a huge advantage to children in rich districts over those in poor districts. Its first challenge to inequitable funding, *Rodriguez v. San Antonio Independent School District*, met defeat in 1973 when the United States Supreme Court ruled that the problem had to be solved at the state level. With that decision in mind, MALDEF encouraged plaintiffs in the *Edgewood* case to make it a state issue by arguing that inequitable funding violated the Texas Constitution's call for an efficient and free school system. When, after five years of legal maneuvering, the case finally reached the state supreme court, the justices unanimously agreed with the plaintiffs' contention. Noting that the Edgewood ISD in Bexar County had $38,854 in property wealth per student, while the nearby Alamo Heights ISD had $570,109 per student, the court in October 1989 ordered the state legislature to devise and implement a system of equitable funding by the 1990–1991 school year. The regular legislative session having ended, Clements called a special session to deal with the question. He favored providing more money to poor districts but wanted to couple any appropriation with a reduction of state regulation of public schools. The issue proved so controversial that legislators failed in three special sessions to produce any legislation before finally agreeing in a fourth special session to a bill that increased state spending on public schools by $528 million, much of it for poor districts. A small increase in sales taxes (one-quarter of a cent) and a rise in cigarette taxes provided the funds. The plaintiffs in *Edgeworth,* recognizing that this legislation did nothing about the property-tax advantage enjoyed by rich districts, continued their legal action. A Travis County District Court agreed that the new law had not solved the constitutional question, but Clements had the state appeal that ruling. By the time this newest appeal reached the Texas Supreme Court in 1991, he was safely out of office.

Clements's first term as governor had provided a landmark for Republicans simply because he was the first in more than a century to hold the office, but his second term probably did more to strengthen the party in Texas. He mellowed a little in his dealings with the legislature and media, and his work in promoting economic recovery through attracting new businesses to Texas earned widespread approval. Also, Clements and his wife played a key role in the restoration of the state capitol and the addition of an underground extension. Planning and fund raising began in 1987, and the project was concluded in 1993. Thus, as Clements prepared to leave office after the 1990 election, Republicans believed that they had a chance for another first—to hold the governor's office for consecutive terms—and several recognized leaders sought the nomination. Railroad Commissioner Kent Hance, Secretary of State Jack Raines, and Dallas attorney Tom Luce entered the Republican primary, but party voters rejected them in favor of Clayton Williams, a wealthy West Texas rancher. Williams took advantage of being an outsider—the "I'm not a politician" image that many find appealing—and spent $9 million on television ads pointing to his record as a successful rancher/businessman.

The 1990 Democratic primary attracted eight candidates, but only three—former governor Mark White, Attorney General Jim Mattox, and State Treasurer Ann Richards—could be considered serious contenders. White had too many political liabilities from his term as governor and loss to Clements and ran a distant third. Mattox, who had gained attention for tough enforcement of laws such as those requiring the payment of child support by divorced parents, appealed to liberals. Richards had not held a high-profile position in state government, but she was well known nationally for her keynote-address attack on George H. W. Bush at the 1988 Democratic convention. The first primary gave Richards a slight edge over Mattox, and she then won the runoff, a truly bad-tempered negative contest, with 57 percent of the vote.

Most observers thought that Williams, who led by 20 points in a poll taken early in the campaign, would win the governorship easily. As the contest developed, however, he made mistake after mistake and gave victory to Richards. A public comment comparing bad West Texas weather to rape—"When rape is inevitable," he said, "relax and enjoy it"—hurt him badly with many voters. Refusing to shake hands with Richards after a televised debate also cost support, as did admissions that he did not know about a proposed constitutional amendment on the ballot that year and that he had paid no income tax in 1986. In spite of all Williams's mistakes, Richards received only 50 percent of the vote to his 47 percent. (Three percent went to a Libertarian Party candidate.) Democrats, probably aided as well by the inept Williams campaign, also won several other important victories. Former State Comptroller Bob Bullock took the lieutenant governorship, and Dan Morales became the first Mexican American to hold statewide office by winning the race for attorney general. Republicans avoided complete disaster, however. Incumbent U.S. Senator Phil Gramm kept his seat by getting 60 percent of the vote against his Democratic challenger Hugh Parmer of Fort Worth, and Kay Bailey Hutchison, a rising Republican politician from Dallas, won the state treasurer's office.

"As governor of Texas," wrote one observer, "Ann Richards rose to national political stardom." She traveled extensively and appeared often on television, always singing the praises of her state, and in 1992 chaired the Democratic National Convention. Her successes seemed to epitomize the empowerment of women politicians in the nineties. On the other hand, she did not provide particularly effective leadership as governor. Perhaps her most important accomplishment was the appointment of unprecedented numbers of women and minorities to the state's various boards and commissions. The immensely complicated problem of equalizing school finance she left largely

Ann Richards. Photographed at her inauguration on January 15, 1991, Ann Richards was the second woman to serve as governor of Texas. She dramatically diversified the state's appointive officeholders and gained national prominence within the Democratic Party. Credit: Texas State Library and Archives Commission.

to Lieutenant Governor Bullock and the state legislature. After several false starts, legislators finally passed a bill in May 1993 that the courts found acceptable. This law provided five ways by which wealthy districts could provide funds to those with low property values; the simplest called for the rich districts to send money to the state for use in poor districts. Parents in wealthy districts objected to any "Robin Hood" plan, of course, and the whole matter remained controversial. Certainly, it did little for the popularity of the politicians who wrestled with it.

Governor Richards's national popularity did not translate into much success for her party in Texas. In the 1992 presidential election, George Bush, the Republican incumbent, faced a challenge from Governor Bill Clinton of Arkansas. Bush, whose popularity had risen spectacularly during the Gulf War in 1991, enjoyed a huge advantage over Clinton in his adopted state in spite of a minor economic recession that hurt him nationally in 1992. Then, H. Ross Perot, the billionaire founder of EDS in Dallas, entered the race and greatly complicated things. Running on the slogan, "United We Stand America," Perot hammered at the issues of government spending and the public debt. Polls taken in April 1992 showed him running ahead of both Bush and Clinton in Texas, and volunteer workers got his name on the ballot in twenty-four states. That summer, however, upset by the glare of personal publicity and criticism of his simplistic solutions to complex problems, he suddenly withdrew from the race, and then, having taken the steam out of his campaign, returned. In spite of this bizarre behavior, Perot won 22 percent of the 6.1 million votes cast in Texas, most of them coming from voters who otherwise would have supported Bush. Even then, Bush carried the state by more than 200,000 votes (41 percent to Clinton's 37 percent), giving Texas Republicans their fourth consecutive victory in presidential elections.

The Republican march to dominance continued in 1993, thanks at least in part to Governor Richards's difficulties as a party leader. President Clinton chose Senator Lloyd Bentsen to serve as secretary of the treasury, thereby creating a vacancy in one of Texas's senate seats. Needing to select an interim appointee who could hold the office against an expected strong challenge from the Republicans in a special election that spring, Richards wavered among several candidates, including Jim Mattox, before settling on Bob Krueger. Although Krueger had served in the U.S. House of Representatives and run well against John Tower in 1978, many Democrats considered him an ineffective candidate. He got 29 percent of the vote in the first round of the special election and was forced into a runoff with Kay Bailey Hutchison. Only 21 percent of the state's eligible voters bothered to go to the polls for the special election runoff, but those who went gave Hutchison an overwhelming 67 percent of the vote. Republicans now held both of Texas's seats in the U.S. Senate for the first time since the 1870s.

Governor Richards easily won renomination in 1994, but this time her Republican opponent, George W. Bush, did not hand her the election. Bush, the son of President George H. W. Bush, had spent his early years in the oil business in Midland and more recently participated as a financial junior partner

George W. Bush and his father, President George Herbert Walker Bush, walk toward the White House in April 1992. Two years later "W," as he became known, won the governorship of Texas. He was reelected in 1998, and moved on to the presidency of the United States in 2000. Credit: George Bush Presidential Library

but titular head of a combination of businessmen who bought the Texas Rangers baseball club. Achieving maximum publicity with the Rangers, especially when voters in Arlington agreed to underwrite the building of a state-of-the art ballpark for the team, Bush projected the image of a man of strong character who had succeeded in business. He ran a positive campaign, saying nothing more negative about Richards than calling her a "liberal," a charge that associated her with President Clinton and his failed ideas for a national health insurance program. Bush also emphasized the need for local control and accountability in public education. Richards had few achievements to run on, nor could she criticize the record of an opponent who had never held an elective office. Moreover, the Republicans' "southern strategy" again proved its validity. Richards held the Democrats' now-traditional minority support, getting more than 90 percent of the African American vote and 75 percent from Mexican Americans, but a majority of Anglo voters, even those with low incomes, opposed her. Bush won with 54 percent of the total.

Bush's victory heralded other major successes for his party in 1994. Kay Bailey Hutchison easily held her U.S. Senate seat against a seemingly half-hearted challenge from Richard Fisher. Fisher spent more than a million dollars to defeat Jim Mattox in the Democratic primary and then put only $300,000 into the race against Hutchison, which she won by a 61 percent landslide. Republicans also took eleven of the state's thirty seats in the U.S. House of Representatives and won a majority on the Texas Supreme Court (another first since Reconstruction). Democrats could take comfort only in the fact that Lieutenant Governor Bob Bullock, Attorney General Dan Morales, State Comptroller John Sharp, and Land Commissioner Garry Mauro, all of whom were incumbents, defeated Republican challengers and held their offices. The next two elections proved, however, that these "down-ticket" victories amounted to more of a last gasp for the Democrats than an indication of residual strength.

In the 1996 presidential election, Republican Bob Dole lost badly to Bill Clinton across the nation but easily carried Texas with 49 percent of the vote. Only the candidacy of Ross Perot, which took 7 percent of the vote, denied the Republicans a landslide victory in the Lone Star State. The 1996 campaign for the U.S. Senate seat held by Phil Gramm also indicated that Democrats stood on the verge of becoming noncompetitive in Texas. Gramm, having made an unsuccessful bid for the Republican presidential nomination, had some $20 million in backing from contributors who appreciated his consistent pro-business conservatism to use in seeking reelection to the Senate. To oppose him, voters in the Democratic primary chose Victor A. Morales, a high school civics teacher who entered the race on a dare from his students. Morales, who had virtually no funding and knew little or nothing of national issues, made headlines by driving around the state in an old Nissan pickup truck. Reporters, recalling the 1939 movie *Mr. Smith Goes to Washington,* the story of a plain, honest, nonpolitician who wins election to the Senate, called Morales "Señor Smith." The publicity hoopla hid the fact that fewer than 500,000 voters participated in the primary runoff won by Morales over State Senator John Bryant, an experienced Democrat, and that a good many voters prefer candidates who know something about the issues. Moreover, Morales placed so much emphasis on his ethnicity that he worried Anglo voters, especially after he referred to a leading Republican Mexican American as a "coconut"—a slur meaning "brown on the outside and white on the inside." Morales received only 30 percent of the Anglo vote in November and lost to Gramm by a landslide, 55 to 44 percent. More than likely no Democrat could have defeated a well-funded incumbent such as Gramm, but the nomination of a novelty candidate such as Morales indicated just how weak the party had become.

George W. Bush's first term as governor added a few more nails to the Democrats' coffin. Working successfully with key Democratic leaders Lieutenant Governor Bullock and Speaker of the House James M. "Pete" Laney, Bush achieved notable legislative successes for his conservative program. A pro-business tort reform measure reduced the chances for juries to make large awards in personal damages lawsuits against corporations. The state gave greater control to local school districts and watered down "no-pass, no-play" from the original six-week suspension from extracurricular activities to a three-week period that does not coincide with a set grading period and is largely unenforceable. A new law permitted the carrying of concealed handguns. Welfare payments were restricted. Bush failed only in his proposals for tax reform, but few Texans regarded that as a pressing issue anyhow.

By 1998, political commentators regarded Bush's reelection as such a certainty that they spent much of their time speculating on when he would announce a bid for the presidency two years later. Before the year began, Lieutenant Governor Bullock, rejecting all potential candidates from his own party, endorsed Bush, and Attorney General Dan Morales, one of the most promising young Democrats in the state, announced his retirement from politics. *Texas Monthly* commented that Morales's announcement "made December 2, 1997, the day the Democratic Party of Texas finally collapsed, not with a bang but a whimper." And the elections nearly a year later bore out that statement completely. George W. Bush defeated Garry Mauro 68 percent to 31 percent, and Republicans swept every other statewide race, many by similarly overwhelming margins, and gained a majority in the state senate. Democrats succeeded only in holding on to a tiny majority in the state house of representatives and maintaining a seventeen-to-thirteen edge in members of the United States House of Representatives.

Two years later George W. Bush did indeed win the Republican presidential nomination and defeated Al Gore in a controversial election settled ultimately by a decision of the United States Supreme Court concerning the vote count in Florida. Bush did not have a popular vote majority nationally, but of course he had no problem carrying Texas, getting 59 percent support to Gore's 38 percent and Ralph Nader's 2 percent. Senator Kay Bailey Hutchison easily defended her seat, defeating Gene Kelly, another novelty candidate known only for having the same name as the famous dancer, 65 percent to 32 percent. Thus, in 2001 Texas appeared almost as solidly Republican as it had been Democratic only some forty to fifty years earlier. A semblance of two-party balance existed in the state legislature and the Texas delegation in the U.S. House of Representatives, but redistricting after the Census of 2000 promised to give Republicans a majority in both houses of the legislature. "Republicans could control Texas as long as the Democrats did," said *Texas Monthly* in 1998, "and the Democrats will have nothing to do but learn, as the Republicans had to, just how long a century really is."

A Balance Sheet on Public Policy in Modern Texas

The presidential campaign of 2000 put the government and society of modern Texas under a microscope of partisan scrutiny. George W. Bush formed a "Proud of Texas Committee" to praise the values such as self-reliant individualism and the economic opportunities characteristic of the state he had governed for nearly six years. Al Gore, the Democratic candidate, sent out a "Texas Truth Squad" to tell voters how Bush's state stood near the bottom on virtually every indicator of social progress. Both sides exaggerated, of course, but each had a valid point. The tremendous economic gains of the 1990s translated into a better life for many Texans. Others, however, struggled far behind and received little or no public assistance with their problems. Median household income increased slightly more than 13 percent statewide from 1989 to 1999, but Texas ranked tenth among the states in the percentage of its people living in poverty. Texas had some of the finest medical facilities in the world, but 24 percent of Texans, the largest proportion of any state's population, had no health insurance. The state, in spite of its wealth, ranked at the bottom in spending on public and mental health and provided welfare benefits such as food stamps at a very minimal level. To some observers, income disparities and limited public support for the poor and unfortunate result simply from Texans' emphasis on self-reliance and personal freedom; to others, such conditions stand as an indictment of the state's brutally competitive economy and lack of social compassion.

Charges made during the Bush-Gore campaign also raised questions about how well modern Texas dealt with large issues of public policy that affected not only the state's present welfare but its future as well, issues such as protection of the environment and improvement of education at all levels. On these matters, also, defenders pointed to progress while critics found much to decry.

Until the mid-twentieth century, because their state had few cities and even less heavy industry, Texans had little or no concern about protecting the quality of their air and water. When modernization began to threaten the environment, the state's leaders reacted with predictable reluctance to the need for governmental regulation. The first legislation dealing with air quality did not come until 1965. It created a Texas Air Control Board, appointed by the governor, to control and limit air pollution, but the law also directed the board to consider the effect of its rulings on existing industries and economic development. By 1990, the agency had more than four hundred employees and a budget of nearly $16 million—a good deal of the growth coming as a result of the need to comply with federally mandated standards—and yet Texas ranked worst in the nation in the emission of carbon dioxide. The Air Control Board became part of a larger agency, the Texas Natural Resources Conservation Commission, in 1993, but conditions did not improve during the decade. By 2000 Houston had achieved the dubious distinction of having the worst air of any city in the United States, the Dallas-Fort Worth Metroplex regularly endured air-quality-alert days during the summer, and Texas ranked first in the release of ozone-producing chemicals and a variety of other air pollutants. The Bush campaign pointed with pride to an act that allowed Texas plants built prior to 1971 to reduce emissions voluntarily. His detractors replied that few polluters responded positively on a voluntary basis and called for stronger legislation. At the end of the century, air quality stood largely on the negative side of the balance sheet of modern Texas.

Water is an especially complicated environmental issue in Texas because it involves quantity as well as quality. The state has two water sources—surface water in rivers and man-made lakes and underground water in aquifers—and both face increasing demands from the growing population and expanding economy. Conservation of surface water has always been in the hands of the state, which holds it in trust for the people, and as early as 1905 legislation encouraged the creation of local water districts that would build lakes and maintain streams. Underground water, however, in effect "belongs" to the person who owns the land it flows under, and its use remained largely unregulated until the mid-twentieth century. In 1949, concern about the depletion of the huge Ogallala Aquifer in West Texas led the legislature to pass an act permitting the creation of local underground water districts that could regulate the amount of water pumped. Thirty-four of these local regulatory agencies existed by 1992, but they often became battlegrounds for conflicting interests and had only a mixed record of success. During the 1980s and 1990s, Texans pumped water from underground aquifers twice as fast as the recharge rate.

Local surface and underground water districts helped, but clearly Texas needed a comprehensive statewide water plan. The first effort to create a plan of this nature came in the Water Planning Act of 1957, which passed primarily in response to the drought conditions of that time, but every planning initiative bogged down due either to the impossibility of satisfying everyone in such a huge and diverse state or to seemingly insurmountable costs. By the end of the century, the Texas Water Development Board, an agency created originally in 1957 to provide loans to local surface water projects, took on the responsibility for planning and produced a report, "Water for Texas—2002." The board argued that its plan, which incorporated work already completed by sixteen regional groups with maximum participation at the grassroots level, would "if implemented, . . . meet the needs of all Texans, even during conditions of drought" until 2050. "Without implementation," the report states, "Texans clearly will not have the ability to meet their water needs." Unfortunately, the cost of implementation is estimated at more than $100 billion, and it remains to be seen how Texans will respond to this challenge of modernization.

The quality of Texas water rather than its quantity also drew some attention from state government by the middle of the twentieth century, but resulting attempts at regulation lacked consistency and coherence. The state established a Water Pollution Advisory Council in 1953, a Water Pollution Control Board in 1961, the Texas Water Commission in 1962, a Water Quality Board in 1967, a Department of Water Resources in 1977, and finally, the Texas Natural Resources Conservation Commission in 1993. This rapid turnover of agencies suggests a lack of effective regulation, and some waterways have indeed become terribly polluted at times—the Houston Ship Channel, for example. Overall, however, thanks in part to federal mandates for clean water and to the lack of heavy industry on major rivers, modern Texas has fewer problems with water pollution than with air quality.

Modernization puts a premium on education at all levels, and it is not easy to decide on which side of the balance sheet the state's support for schools should fall. Even most critics in 2000 admitted that public education had improved during the past decade thanks to the greater equalization of funding that resulted from the *Edgewood* case and to the emphasis on accountability under Governor George W. Bush that led to standardized tests such as the Texas Assessment of Academic Skills (TAAS). The "Robin Hood" funding plan remained controversial, however, test scores improved slowly, and only a few states had higher dropout rates. Moreover, in 2001, Texas ranked thirty-second in spending per student and thirty-sixth in teacher salaries. Even when allowances are made for a great deal of variation from district to district across the state, and when due recognition is given to the efforts of many committed administrators and teachers, a recent critic probably came closest to the truth when he described the public education system in modern Texas as "mired in mediocrity." And there is no evidence that turning education over to private enterprise ventures such as the Edison Project or to charter schools (public schools exempt from most state regulations) offers any likelihood of significant improvement. In 2002, the Dallas Independent School District canceled a contract with Edison on the grounds that performance promises were not being met, and a report indicated that students in Texas charter schools generally did not score as well on standardized tests as did those in public schools.

Higher education probably deserves a spot on the positive side of the balance sheet, in no small part because the two university systems funded by the Permanent University Fund—The University of Texas and Texas A&M University—have the resources to support numerous programs of high quality. Also, in 1985, funding improved for universities outside the two flagship systems when the legislature created a Higher Education Assistance Fund (HEAF) to provide money for capital improvements. Recognizing that all Texans needed access to higher education, the state implemented affirmative action plans as early as 1983 and significantly increased enrollment by African Americans and Latinos in Texas colleges and universities. Affirmative action suffered a setback in 1996 when the U.S. Fifth Circuit Court of Appeals ruled in *Hopwood v. The State of Texas* that the use of racial preferences in admitting students to the University of Texas Law School denied white candidates equal protection of the law. The legislature responded in 1997 with a bill that gave automatic admission to public universities to any student in the top 10 percent of his or her graduating class. Ironically, de facto segregation in public schools gave minority students greater access to higher education. More equal access came in a different way when LULAC sponsored a legal action arguing that the state did not provide adequate graduate and professional programs to the largely Latino population of South Texas. In response the legislature adopted the South Texas Initiative that resulted in millions in new funding for schools along and south of a line from Corpus Christi to San Antonio to El Paso. Also, the flagship universities brought regional schools into their systems—The University of Texas at Brownsville and Texas A&M Universities at Corpus Christi, Kingsville, and Laredo.

Problems and challenges abound in higher education, of course; most of them centering on the issue of funding. And that leads to the critical item on the balance sheet—taxation. Texas cannot pay for its schools, protect its environment, fund an adequate water plan, maintain its prisons, or meet the myriad other public obligations of a modern society without adequate sources of revenue. Texans, however, like people everywhere, do not like paying taxes; they never have and never will. The modern state has a hodge-podge of revenue measures, including the general sales tax, corporate franchise taxes, severance taxes on oil and gas production, "sin" taxes on alcohol and tobacco, gasoline and motor vehicle taxes, etc. In recent years, state government increasingly relies on the sales tax (55 percent of all state revenue in 1999), and local governments depend heavily on property taxes (although cities have sales taxes as well). Critics point out that the revenue system with its reliance on sales taxes hits lower-income Texans the hardest. A study in 1998 estimated that the poorest 20 percent of the population paid 16 percent of their income in state and local taxes, whereas the richest 20 percent paid less than 4 percent.

As the century drew to a close, leading Texans and special committees periodically pointed out that the state's antiquated tax system needed reform to make it more equitable and to generate adequate revenue for public purposes. However, the obvious solution, a personal income tax, is regarded as absolutely, to use a cliché, the "third rail" of Texas politics. Touch it and die. Two of the state's most respected Democratic leaders, Lieutenant Governor Bill Hobby and State Comptroller Bob Bullock, endorsed the idea in 1989, but virtually every candidate running for office the next year pledged to oppose it. Even the suggestion in 2002 by Republican Lieutenant Governor Bill Ratliff of a state property tax to solve the problem of equity in the funding of public education drew horrified gasps. So long as a majority of Texans are more interested in tax cuts than meeting the challenges of modernization, the balance sheet on public policy is likely to have a preponderance of checks on the negative side.

TEXAS IN THE NEW MILLENNIUM

Thanks to diversification during the 1990s, Texas entered the twenty-first century with an economy more like that of the United States as a whole than ever in its history. "For a long time Texas was different," said a noted economic analyst. "Well it ain't another country anymore." The recession of 2001–2002, which began following the bursting of the bubble in Internet company stock prices, affected Texas almost as soon as it hit other parts of the nation. The state also had its share of the latest scandals in corporate America—the reporting of false profits through a variety of manipulations involving subsidiaries and "creative accounting" in order to inflate the value of stock that insiders sold for fortunes and left other investors, especially those holding the stock in retirement accounts, with nothing when the nature of the corporation's activities came to light. Indeed, one of the earliest and best known of these collapses involved Enron, a Houston energy trading corporation widely regarded as a prototypical business venture of the new century. In 2001, the Houston Astros played their home games at Enron Field; a year later, the name disappeared from the ball park.

Regardless, however, of sagging stock prices, recession, and the Enron scandal, analysts pointed to the basic strength of the Texas economy and argued, in the words of an article in *Texas Business Review,* that the "general business situation in Texas in the 2000s shows prosperity and promise." The magazine's projections for the first two decades of the new century indicated tremendous growth, especially in areas of the economy that had played key roles in the diversification of the 1990s. Services, for example, which contributed approximately $150 billion to the gross state product in 2000, are expected to add more than $500 billion in 2020, and the amount contributed by trade is projected to increase from $125 billion to nearly $400 billion during the next twenty years. By contrast, the oil and gas industry and agriculture, once the mainstays of the Texas economy, will increase their contributions from $40 billion to $90 billion and $10 billion to $20 billion respectively. These amounts are significant, of course, but they indicate that the state is no longer dependent on oil, cotton, and cattle. In short, Texas's economy in the new millennium should remain modern and spectacularly productive.

The future of Texas politics in the early twenty-first century also appears reasonably clear, at least for a decade or so. Republican domination, established during the late 1990s and carried forward triumphantly with the election of George W. Bush to the presidency in 2000, faced a notable but unsuccessful challenge from Democrats in 2002. Senator Phil Gramm's retirement from the United States Senate led to a contest between Republican John Cornyn, the state's attorney general, and Democrat Ron Kirk, the former mayor of Dallas. In the race for governor, Tony Sanchez, a wealthy banker and businessman from Laredo, won the Democratic nomination over Dan Morales of San Antonio and opposed the incumbent Republican Rick Perry. The combination of Kirk, an African American, and Sanchez, a Mexican American, both of whom would be "firsts" in Texas to hold the offices they sought, led some to say that the Democrats had a "dream ticket" and others to complain that such a pairing represented an attempt to divide the state along ethnic lines. In the race for lieutenant governor, the Democrats also nominated a strong candidate in the person of John Sharp, a former state comptroller, to oppose Republican David Dewhurst, the incumbent General Land Office commissioner. Interest in these three races overshadowed the contests for seats in the state legislature, in part because most observers believed that, following redistricting, the Republicans would win control of both houses for the first time since Reconstruction.

The races for senator, governor, and lieutenant governor quickly became personal, but mud-slinging aside, the two parties offered significantly contrasting images. Cornyn, Perry, and Dewhurst, employing the theme that had played such a large role in realigning Texas politics during the second half of the twentieth century, pictured their opponents as "big-government, tax-and-spend liberals" closely aligned with those of similar ilk in the national Democratic Party. Kirk, Sanchez, and Sharp ran as moderates, trying to avoid alienating conservatives while remaining appealing to liberal voters. Sanchez, who had never held public office, pointed to his career in private enterprise, and the other two Democrats emphasized their records of successful cooperation with businessmen. Sharp won endorsements from most of the state's major newspapers and had campaign spots featuring the support of Nolan Ryan, a popular baseball hero and avowed Republican. Nevertheless, Democrats again lost every statewide office by landslide or near-landslide margins, and Republicans took control of both houses of the state legislature and a majority of seats in the U.S. House of Representatives. Cornyn easily defeated Kirk in the race to replace Gramm in the U.S. Senate.

The election of 2002 sent a clear message that Texans remains overwhelmingly conservative in their politics. Democrats regarded 2002 as a comeback year, and in spite of some optimistic post-election talk—the party faithful in Dallas County, for example, professed to be cheered by carrying one of twenty-four local judicial races—the results are likely to discourage any meaningful opposition in the near future. It seems certain that Texas politics in the new millennium will continue for some time in the state's long tradition of one-party government with competition occurring only within that party. Republican primaries will determine the winners of virtually all important political offices. The only exceptions are a few old-style conservative Democratic congressmen who will hold on until retirement and several congressional seats deliberately left to minority Democrats during the redistricting process.

On the other hand, given the state's modern economy and the increasing diversity of its people, it is difficult to imagine that political life can continue along the same path indefinitely. The following table based on data produced in the office of the state demographer presents population projections for Texas from 2000 to 2040, assuming rates of net migration one-half of those during the 1990s:

Texas Population in 2000 and Projected Population 2010–2040 by Race and Ethnicity

Year	Total	Anglo	Black	Hispanic	Other
2000	20,851,820	11,074,716	2,421,653	6,669,666	685,785
2010	24,178,507	11,494,673	2,730,659	8,999,827	953,063
2020	27,738,378	11,735,043	3,004,173	11,742,820	1,256,342
2030	31,389,565	11,701,065	3,191,230	14,900,692	1,596,578
2040	35,012,330	11,382,992	3,283,413	18,391,333	1,954,592

These projections show the state with a majority non-Anglo population by 2010 and the number of Hispanics surpassing Anglos by 2020. Even when it is assumed that net migration is zero (not shown in the table), Hispanic Texans will outstrip their Anglo neighbors in numbers by 2040. If and how a non-Anglo majority changes the state's politics remains to be seen, but modifications in traditional conservatism seem likely. Even now, some observers say that regardless of how Texans vote, polls indicate that they are not a great deal more conservative on social issues such as abortion, homosexuality, and race than are other Americans. Residents of Houston express a preference for investments in education and public services to tax cuts and support emissions controls on vehicles. Perhaps, regardless of the outcome of the 2002 election, Texas cannot long avoid the development of competitive two-party politics.

Thus, Texas, by virtue of its balanced economy, diverse population, and modernizing politics, may be on the verge of ceasing to be "another country." Texans, however, a sizable majority of whom according to a 1993 poll saw themselves as "particularly unique" in comparison to other Americans, will not gladly give up the special identity they have enjoyed for nearly two hundred years. What will become of the "Texas mystique" if the state becomes simply one of the United States?

An answer to this question depends first on asking another: In what sense has Texas ever been truly exceptional? Texas is not unique because it has so much land and such a harsh environment. There are many large states with climates and geography that challenge anyone attempting to live in them. Texas is not unique in its emphasis on liberty and boundless opportunity. All states in the United States provide freedom and opportunity. Texas is not unique in its emphasis on individualism. Texans are no more individualistic than, for example, residents of Vermont. Texas is not alone in producing fighting men of great courage and audacity. Stonewall Jackson and George S. Patton Jr., for example, were not Texans. Texans are noted for their easygoing friendliness, but Americans in general, especially those in the South, are known for the same quality. Texas, in spite of the image of the "cattle baron" and the "oil millionaire," is not special for its superrich with their ostentatious displays of wealth. Cornelius Vanderbilt was not from Texas, and neither is Donald Trump.

What, then, is the key to Texas's image of distinctiveness and its mythically appealing history? The answer lies in part in the way that the Lone Star State embodies in an exaggerated way so many of the ideals and emotions shared by citizens of the United States. Consider how Texas became a state in the first place. No other state had a revolution so like that by the thirteen original colonies (Vermont, California, and Hawaii do not come close) and existed for nearly ten years as an independent nation. This revolution, with its spectacular events such as the Alamo and San Jacinto, gave Texas an especially American point of departure. Then, Texas, the biggest state in the Union (forget a late arrival like Alaska), developed outsized emphasis on many of the qualities and characteristics regarded as being especially American—a fierce devotion to personal liberty, rampant individualism, and admiration for the superrich, for example. Thus Texas is seen as special and its history has become myth-encrusted, not because it is so greatly different from the other states but because it is such an exaggerated version of the United States.

Texas also is widely regarded as a special place simply because Texans insist that it is. John Steinbeck made this point in 1962 when he wrote: "Texas is a state of mind, but I think it is more than that. It is a mystique closely approaching a religion." Anglo Texans in particular virtually worship their state and take advantage of its outsized "Americanism" to convince themselves that the Lone Star State is indeed exceptional. Perhaps where the "Texas mystique" is concerned, what is believed is what matters most.

At least one thing seems certain—regardless of the extent to which Texas is truly a special place, its image and opportunities will continue to excite the imaginations of millions. Every indication is that the twenty-first-century version of "Gone to Texas" will appear on countless doors across the United States, throughout Latin America, and in Asia as well.

Appendix 1

Population of Texas at United States Census Years

Year	Total	African-American	Mexican Ancestry
1850	212,592	58,161/394*	
1860	604,215	182,566/355*	
1870	818,579	253,475	
1880	1,591,749	393,384	
1890	2,235,527	488,171	
1900	3,048,710	620,722	
1910	3,896,542	690,049	
1920	4,663,228	741,694	
1930	5,824,715	854,964	683,681**
1940	6,414,824	924,391	484,306**
1950	7,711,194	977,458	1,000,000***
1960	9,579,677	1,187,125	1,400,000***
1970	11,196,730	1,399,005	2,059,671
1980	14,229,191	1,692,542	2,985,824
1990	16,986,510	1,976,360	4,339,905
2000	20,851,820	2,421,653	6,669,666

**Slaves/Free Blacks*
***The 1930 and 1940 census statistics are probably undercounts.*
****The 1950 and 1960 statistics are estimates.*

Appendix 2

Chief Executives of Texas, 1691–2002

GOVERNORS OF SPANISH TEXAS

1691–1692 Domingo Terán de los Ríos

1694–1715 Texas unoccupied

1716–1719 Martín de Alarcón

1719–1722 Marqués de San Miguel de Aguayo (Texas and Coahuila)

1722–1726 Fernando Pérez de Almazán

1727–1730 Melchor de Mediavilla y Azcona

1730–1734 Juan Antonio Bustillo y Ceballos

1734–1736 Manuel de Sandoval

1737 Joseph Fernández de Jáuregui y Urrutia (Texas and Nuevo Leon)

1737–1740 Predencio de Orobio y Basterra

1741–1743 Tomás Felipe Winthuysen

1743–1744 Justo Boneo y Morales

1744–1748 Francisco García Larios (ad interim)

1748–1750 Pedro del Barrio y Espriella

1751–1759 Jacinto de Barrios y Jáuregui

1759–1767 Angel de Martos y Navarrete

1767–1770 Hugo O'Conor (ad interim)

1770–1778 Juan María, Barón de Ripperdá

1778–1786 Domingo Cabello y Robles

1787–1790 Rafael Martínez Pacheco

1790–1799 Manuel Muñoz

1799–1805 Juan Bautista de Elguezábal

1805–1808 Antonio Cordero y Bustamante

1808–1813 Manuel María de Salcedo

[1811 Juan Bautista de las Casas—revolutionary governor]

1813–1817 Cristóbal Domínguez, Benito de Armiñan, Mariano Varela, Ignacio Pérez, and Manuel Pardo (ad interim)

1817–1821 Antonio María Martínez

PROVINCIAL GOVERNORS OF MEXICAN TEXAS

1821–1822 Antonio María Martínez

1822–1823 José Félix Trespalacios

1823 Luciano García

GOVERNORS OF COAHUILA Y TEXAS

1824–1826 Rafael González

1826 José Ignacio de Arizpe

1826–1827 Victor Blanco

1827 José Ignacio de Arizpe

1827 José María Viesca (provisional)

1827 Victor Blanco

1827–1830 José María Viesca

1830–1831 Rafael Eca y Músquiz

1831 José María Viesca

1831–1832 José María de Letona

1832–1833 Rafael Eca y Músquiz

1833 Juan Martín de Veramendi

1833–1834 Francisco Vidaurri y Villaseñor

1834–1835 Juan José Elguezábal

1835 José María Cantú

1835 Marciel Borrego

1835 Agustín Viesca

1835 Miguel Falcón

1835 Bartolomé de Cárdenas

1835 Rafael Eca y Músquiz

PRESIDENTS OF THE REPUBLIC OF TEXAS

3/17/36–10/22/36 David G. Burnet (ad interim)

10/22/36–12/10/38 Sam Houston

12/10/38–12/13/41 Mirabeau B. Lamar

12/13/41–12/9/44 Sam Houston

12/9/44–2/19/46 Anson Jones

GOVERNORS OF TEXAS

2/19/46–12/21/47 James Pinckney Henderson

12/21/47–12/21/49 George T. Wood

12/21/49–11/23/53 Peter Hansborough Bell

11/23/53–12/21/53 J. W. Henderson

12/21/53–12/21/57 Elisha M. Pease

12/21/57–12/21/59 Hardin R. Runnels

12/21/59–3/16/61 Sam Houston

3/16/61–11/7/61 Edward Clark

11/7/61–11/5/63 Francis R. Lubbock

11/5/63–6/17/65 Pendleton Murrah

6/17/65–8/9/66 Andrew J. Hamilton (provisional)

8/9/66–8/8/67 James W. Throckmorton

8/8/67–9/30/69 Elisha M. Pease (provisional)

9/30/69–1/8/70 General James J. Reynolds (acting)

1/8/70–4/28/70 Edmund J. Davis (provisional)

4/28/70–1/15/74 Edmund J. Davis

1/15/74–12/1/76 Richard Coke

12/1/76–1/21/79 Richard B. Hubbard

1/21/79–1/16/83 Oran M. Roberts

1/16/83–1/18/87 John Ireland

1/18/87–1/20/91 Lawrence Sullivan Ross

1/20/91–1/15/95 James Stephen Hogg

1/15/95–1/17/99 Charles A. Culberson

1/17/99–1/20/03 Joseph D. Sayers

1/20/03–1/15/07 S. W. T. Lanham

1/15/07–1/17/11 Thomas M. Campbell

1/17/11–1/19/15 Oscar B. Colquitt

1/19/15–9/25/17 James E. Ferguson

9/25/17–1/18/21 William P. Hobby

1/18/21–1/20/25 Pat M. Neff

1/20/25–1/18/27 Miriam A. Ferguson

1/18/27–1/20/31 Dan Moody

1/20/31–1/17/33 Ross S. Sterling

1/17/33–1/15/35 Miriam A. Ferguson

1/15/35–1/15/39 James V. Allred

1/15/39–8/4/41 W. Lee O'Daniel

8/4/41–1/21/47 Coke Stevenson

1/21/47–7/11/49 Beauford H. Jester

7/11/49–1/15/57 Allan Shivers

1/15/57–1/15/63 Price Daniel

1/15/63–1/21/69 John Connally

1/21/69–1/16/73 Preston Smith

1/16/73–1/16/79 Dolph Briscoe

1/16/79–1/18/83 William P. Clements, Jr.

1/18/83–1/20/87 Mark White

1/20/87–1/15/91 William P. Clements Jr.

1/15/91–1/17/95 Ann Richards

1/17/95–1/17/00 George W. Bush

1/17/00– Rick Perry

Select Bibliography

CHAPTER 1 The First Texans

Anderson, Gary Clayton. *The Indian Southwest, 1580–1830: Ethnogenesis and Reinvention*. Norman: University of Oklahoma Press, 1999.

Aten, Lawrence E. *Indians of the Upper Texas Coast*. New York: Academic Press, 1983.

Dillehay, Tom D. "Late Quaternary Bison Population Changes on the Southern Plains." *Plains Anthropologist* XIX (August 1974): 180–196.

Jennings, Jesse D. *Prehistory of North America*. 2nd ed. New York: McGraw-Hill, 1974.

La Vere, David. *The Caddo Chiefdoms: Caddo Economics and Politics, 800–1835*. Lincoln: University of Nebraska Press, 1998.

Newcomb, W. W., Jr. *The Indians of Texas: From Prehistoric to Modern Times*. Austin: University of Texas Press, 1961.

———. *The Rock Art of Texas Indians*. Austin: University of Texas Press, 1967.

Perttula, Timothy K. *"The Caddo Nation": Archaeological and Ethnohistoric Perspectives*. Austin: University of Texas Press, 1992.

Ricklis, Robert A. *The Karankawa Indians of Texas: An Ecological Study of Cultural Tradition and Change*. Austin: University of Texas Press, 1996.

Schilz, Thomas F. *Lipan Apaches in Texas*. El Paso: Texas Western Press, 1987.

Sellards, E. H. *Early Man in America: A Study in Prehistory*. Austin: University of Texas Press, 1952.

Shafer, Harry J. *Ancient Texans: Rock Art and Lifeways along the Lower Pecos*. Austin: Texas Monthly Press (for the San Antonio Museum Association), 1986.

Smith, F. Todd. *The Caddo Indians: Tribes at the Convergence of Empires, 1542–1854*. College Station: Texas A&M University Press, 1995.

Stephenson, Robert L. "Culture Chronology in Texas." *American Antiquity* XVI (October 1960): 151–157.

Tunnell, Curtis D. *The Gibson Lithic Cache from West Texas*. Austin: Texas Historical Commission, 1978.

Wedel, Waldo R. *Prehistoric Man on the Great Plains*. Norman: University of Oklahoma Press, 1961.

Wendorf, Fred, and James J. Hester. "Early Man's Utilization of the Great Plains Environment." *American Antiquity* XVIII (October 1962): 159–169.

CHAPTER 2 Exploration and Adventure, 1519–1690

Chipman, Donald E. *Spanish Texas, 1519–1821*. Austin: University of Texas Press, 1992.

Chipman, Donald E., and Harriett Denise Joseph. *Notable Men and Women of Spanish Texas*. Austin: University of Texas Press, 1999.

La Vere, David. *Life Among the Texas Indians: The WPA Narratives*. College Station: Texas A&M University Press, 1998.

Morris, John Miller. *El Llano Estacado: Exploration and Imagination on the High Plains of Texas and New Mexico, 1536–1860.* Austin: Texas State Historical Association, 1997.

Newcomb, W. W., Jr. *The Indians of Texas: From Prehistoric to Modern Times.* Austin: University of Texas Press, 1961.

Weber, David J. *The Spanish Frontier in North America.* New Haven: Yale University Press, 1992.

Weddle, Robert S. *The French Thorn: Rival Explorers in the Spanish Sea, 1682–1762.* College Station: Texas A&M University Press, 1991.

———. *Spanish Sea: The Gulf of Mexico in North American Discovery, 1500–1685.* College Station: Texas A&M University Press, 1985.

———. *Wilderness Manhunt: The Spanish Search for La Salle.* Austin: University of Texas Press, 1973.

———. *The Wreck of the Belle: The Ruin of La Salle.* College Station: Texas A&M University Press, 2001.

CHAPTER 3 Spanish Texas, 1690–1779

Alonzo, Armando C. *Tejano Legacy: Rancheros and Settlers in South Texas, 1734–1900.* Albuquerque: University of New Mexico Press, 1998.

Chipman, Donald E. *Spanish Texas, 1519–1821.* Austin: University of Texas Press, 1992.

Chipman, Donald E., and Harriett Denise Joseph. *Notable Men and Women of Spanish Texas.* Austin: University of Texas Press, 1999.

De la Teja, Jesús F. *San Antonio de Béxar: A Community on New Spain's Northern Frontier.* Albuquerque:University of New Mexico Press, 1995.

Kavanagh, Thomas W. *Comanche Political History: An Ethnohistorical Perspective, 1706–1875.* Lincoln: University of Nebraska Press, 1996.

Newcomb, W. W., Jr. *The Indians of Texas, From Prehistoric to Modern Times.* Austin: University of Texas Press, 1961.

Smith, F. Todd. *The Caddo Indians: Tribes at the Convergence of Empires, 1542–1854.* College Station: Texas A&M University Press, 1995.

———. *The Wichita Indians: Traders of Texas and the Southern Plains, 1540–1845.* College Station: Texas A&M University Press, 2000.

Weber, David J. *The Spanish Frontier in North America.* New Haven: Yale University Press, 1992.

Weddle, Robert S. *The French Thorn: Rival Explorers in the Spanish Sea, 1682–1762.* College Station: Texas A&M University Press, 1991.

———. *The San Sabá Mission: Spanish Pivot in Texas.* Austin: University of Texas Press, 1964.

CHAPTER 4 Spanish Texas in the Age of Revolutions, 1779–1821

Almaráz, Félix D., Jr. *Tragic Cavalier: Govenor Manuel Salcedo of Texas, 1808–1813.* Austin: University of Texas Press, 1971.

Chipman, Donald E. *Spanish Texas, 1519–1821.* Austin: University of Texas Press, 1992.

Chipman, Donald E., and Harriett Denise Joseph. *Notable Men and Women of Spanish Texas.* Austin: University of Texas Press, 1999.

Everett, Dianna. *The Texas Cherokees: A People Between Two Fires, 1819–1840.* Norman: University of Oklahoma Press, 1990.

Jones, Oakah L., Jr. *Los Paisanos: Spanish Settlers on the Northern Frontier of New Spain.* Norman; University of Oklahoma Press, 1996.

Thonhoff, Robert H. "Texas and the American Revolution." *Southwestern Historical Quarterly* XCVIII (April 1995): 511–517.

Tjarks, Alicia V. "Comparative Demogaphic Analysis of Texas, 1777–1793." *Southwestern Historical Quarterly* LXXVII (January 1974): 192–338.

Weber, David J. *The Spanish Frontier in North America.* New Haven: Yale University Press, 1992.

CHAPTER 5 Mexican Texas, 1821–1835

Barker, Eugene C. *Mexico and Texas, 1821–1835.* Dallas: P. L. Turner Company, 1928.

Campbell, Randolph B. *An Empire for Slavery: The Peculiar Institution in Texas, 1821–1865.* Baton Rouge: Louisiana State University Press, 1989.

Cantrell, Gregg. *Stephen F. Austin: Empresario of Texas.* New Haven: Yale University Press, 1999.

Everett, Dianna. *The Texas Cherokees: A People between Two Fires, 1819–1840.* Norman: University of Oklahoma Press, 1990.

Green, Stanley C. *The Mexican Republic: The First Decade, 1823–1832.* Pittsburgh: University of Pittsburgh Press, 1987.

Henson, Margaret. *Juan Davis Bradburn: A Reappraisal of the Mexican Commander of Anahuac.* College Station: Texas A&M University Press, 1982.

Himmel, Kelly F. *The Conquest of the Karankawas and the Tonkawas, 1821–1859.* College Station: Texas A&M University Press, 1999.

Morton, Ohland, *Terán and Texas: A Chapter in Texas-American Relations.* Austin: Texas State Historical Association, 1948.

Smith, F. Todd. *The Wichita Indians: Traders of Texas and the Southern Plains, 1540–1845.* College Station: Texas A&M University Press, 2000.

Tijerina, Andrés. *Tejanos and Texans under the Mexican Flag, 1821–1836.* College Station: Texas A&M University Press, 1994.

Utley, Robert M. *Lone Star Justice: The First Century of the Texas Rangers.* New York: Oxford University Press, 2002.

Vigness, David M. *The Saga of Texas, 1810–1836: The Revolutionary Decades.* Austin: Steck-Vaughn Company, 1965.

Weber, David J. *The Mexican Frontier, 1821–1846: The American Southwest under Mexico.* Albuquerque: University of New Mexico Press, 1982.

CHAPTER 6 The Texas Revolution, 1835–1836

Campbell, Randolph B. *Sam Houston and the American Southwest.* New York: HarperCollins, 1993.

Cantrell, Gregg. *Stephen F. Austin: Empresario of Texas.* New Haven: Yale University Press, 1999.

Hardin, Stephen L. *Texian Iliad: A Military History of the Texas Revolution, 1835–1836.* Austin: University of Texas Press, 1994.

Lack, Paul D. *The Texas Revolutionary Experience: A Political and Social History, 1835–1836.* College Station: Texas A&M University Press, 1992.

Lowrie, Samuel H. *Culture Conflict in Texas, 1821–1835.* New York: Columbia University Press, 1932.

Poyo, Gerald E., ed. *Tejano Journey, 1770–1850.* Austin: University of Texas Press, 1996.

Reséndez, Andrés. "National Identity on the Shifting Border: Texas and New Mexico in the Age of Transition, 1821–1846." *Journal of American History* 86 (September 1999): 668–688.

Weber, David J. *The Mexican Frontier, 1821–1846: The American Southwest under Mexico.* Albuquerque: University of New Mexico Press, 1982.

CHAPTER 7 The Republic of Texas, 1836–1846

Campbell, Randolph B. *Sam Houston and the American Southwest.* New York: HarperCollins, 1993.

Connor, Seymour V. *Adventure in Glory, 1836–1849.* Austin: Steck-Vaughn, 1965.

Everett, Dianna. *The Texas Cherokees: A People between Two Fires, 1819–1840.* Norman: University of Oklahoma Press, 1990.

Friend, Llerena B. *Sam Houston: The Great Designer.* Austin: University of Texas Press, 1954.

Gambrell, Herbert P. *Mirabeau Bonaparte Lamar: Troubadour and Crusader.* Dallas: Southwest Press, 1934.

Haynes, Sam W. *Soldiers of Misfortune: The Somervell and Mier Expeditions.* Austin: University of Texas Press, 1990.

Nance, Joseph Milton. *After San Jacinto: The Texas-Mexican Frontier, 1836–1841.* Austin: University of Texas Press, 1963.

———. *Attack and Counterattack: The Texas-Mexican Frontier, 1842.* Austin: University of Texas Press, 1964.

———. *Dare Devils All: The Texan Mier Expedition, 1842–1844.* Edited by Archie P. McDonald. Austin: Eakin Press, 1998.

Schmitz, Joseph William. *Texan Statecraft, 1836–1845.* San Antonio: Naylor, 1941.

Siegel, Stanley. *A Political History of the Texas Republic.* Austin: University of Texas Press, 1956.

———. *The Poet President of Texas: The Life of Mirabeau Bonaparte Lamar, President of the Republic of Texas.* Austin: Jenkins, 1977.

Smith, F. Todd. *The Wichita Indians: Traders of Texas and the Southern Plains, 1540–1845.* College Station: Texas A&M University Press, 2000.

Weems, John Edward. *Dream of Empire: A Human History of the Republic of Texas, 1836–1846.* New York: Simon & Schuster, 1971.

CHAPTER 8 Frontier Texas, 1846–1861

Benner, Judith Ann. *Sul Ross: Soldier, Statesman, Educator.* College Station: Texas A&M University Press, 1983.

De La Teja, Frank Jesus, ed. *A Revolution Remembered: The Memoirs and Selected Correspondence of Juan N. Seguín.* Austin: State House Press, 1991.

De Leon, Arnoldo. *Mexican Americans in Texas: A Brief History.* 2nd ed. Arlington Heights, IL: Harlan Davidson, 1999.

———. *The Tejano Community, 1836–1900.* Albuquerque: University of New Mexico Press, 1982.

Graham, Joe S. *El Rancho in South Texas: Continuity and Change from 1750.* Denton, TX: University of North Texas Press, 1994.

Kavanagh, Thomas W. *Comanche Political History: An Ethnohistorical Perspective, 1706–1875.* Lincoln: University of Nebraska Press, 1996.

La Vere, David. *Life among the Texas Indians: The WPA Narratives.* College Station: Texas A&M University Press, 1998.

Montejano, David. *Anglos and Mexicans in the Making of Texas, 1836–1986*. Austin: University of Texas Press, 1987.
Schilz, Jodie Lynn Dickson, and Thomas F. Schilz. *Buffalo Hump and the Penateka Comanches*. El Paso: Texas Western Press, 1989.
Schilz, Thomas F. *The Lipan Apaches in Texas*. El Paso: Texas Western Press, 1987.
Smith, Thomas T. *The U.S. Army and the Texas Frontier Economy, 1845–1900*. College Station: Texas A&M University Presss, 1999.
Thompson, Jerry D., ed. *Juan Cortina and the Texas-Mexico Frontier, 1859–1877*. El Paso: Texas Western Press, University of Texas at El Paso, 1994.
Utley, Robert M. *Lone Star Justice: The First Century of the Texas Rangers*. New York: Oxford University Press, 2002.
Winders, Bruce. *Crisis in the Southwest: The United States, Mexico, and the Struggle over Texas*. Wilmington, DE: Scholarly Resources, 2002.
Wooster, Robert. *Soldiers, Sutlers, and Settlers: Garrison Life on the Texas Frontier*. College Station: Texas A&M University Press, 1987.

CHAPTER 9 Empire State of the South, 1846–1861

Campbell, Randolph B. *An Empire for Slavery: The Peculiar Institution in Texas, 1821–1865*. Baton Rouge: Louisiana State University Press, 1989.
———. *Sam Houston and the American Southwest*. New York: HarperCollins, 1993.
———, and Richard G. Lowe. *Wealth and Power in Antebellum Texas*. College Station: Texas A&M University Press, 1977.
Carroll, Mark M. *Homesteads Ungovernable: Families, Sex, Race, and the Law in Frontier Texas, 1823–1860*. Austin: University of Texas Press, 2001.
Fornell, Earl Wesley. *The Galveston Era: The Texas Crescent on the Eve of Secession*. Austin: University of Texas Press, 1961.
Friend, Llerena B. *Sam Houston: The Great Designer*. Austin: University of Texas Press, 1954.
Hogan, William Ransom. *The Texas Republic: A Social and Economic History*. Norman: University of Oklahoma Press, 1946.
Jordan, Terry G. *German Seed in Texas Soil: Immigrant Farmers in Nineteenth Century Texas*. Austin: University of Texas Press, 1966.
Lowe, Richard G., and Randolph B. Campbell. *Planters and Plain Folk: Agriculture in Antebellum Texas*. Dallas: Southern Methodist University Press, 1987.
Silverthorne, Elizabeth. *Plantation Life in Texas*. College Station: Texas A&M University Press, 1986.
Stegmaier, Mark J. *Texas, New Mexico, and the Compromise of 1850: Boundary Dispute and Sectional Crisis*. Kent, OH: Kent State University Press, 1996.
Wallace, Ernest. *Texas in Turmoil, 1849–1875*. Austin: Steck-Vaughn, 1965.

CHAPTER 10 The Civil War, 1861–1865

Ashcraft, Allan C. *Texas in the Civil War: A Resumé History*. Austin: Texas Civil War Commission, 1962.
Baum, Dale. *The Shattering of Texas Unionism: Politics in the Lone Star State during the Civil War Era*. Baton Rouge: Louisiana State University Press, 1998.
Buenger, Walter L. *Secession and the Union in Texas*. Austin: University of Texas Press, 1984.
Frazier, Donald. *Blood and Treasure: Confederate Empire in the Southwest*. College Station: Texas A&M University Press, 1995.

Gallaway, B. P., ed. *Texas, The Dark Corner of the Confederacy: Contemporary Accounts of the Lone Star State in the Civil War*. 3rd. Ed. Lincoln: University of Nebraska Press, 1994.

Johansson, M. Jane, ed. *Widows by the Thousand: The Civil War Letters of Theophilus and Harriet Perry, 1862–1864*. Fayetteville: University of Arkansas Press, 2000.

Kerby, Robert L. *Kirby Smith's Confederacy: The Trans-Mississippi South, 1863–1865*. New York: Columbia University Press, 1972.

McCaslin, Richard B. *Tainted Breeze: The Great Hanging at Gainesville, Texas, 1862*. Baton Rouge: Louisiana State University Press, 1997.

Marten, James. *Texas Divided: Loyalty and Dissent in the Lone Star State, 1856–1874*. Lexington: University Press of Kentucky, 1990.

Murr, Erika L., ed. *A Rebel Wife in Texas: The Diary and Letters of Elizabeth Scott Neblett, 1852–1864*. Baton Rouge: Louisiana State University Press, 2001.

Smith, David Paul. *Frontier Defense in the Civil War: Texas' Rangers and Rebels*. College Station: Texas A&M University Press, 1992.

Thompson, Jerry Don. *Vaqueros in Blue and Gray*. Austin: Presidial Press, 1977.

Wooster, Ralph A., ed. *Lone Star Blue and Gray: Essays on Texas in the Civil War*. Austin: Texas State Historical Association, 1995.

———. *Texas and Texans in the Civil War*. Austin: Eakin Press, 1996.

CHAPTER 11 Reconstruction, 1865–1876

Campbell, Randolph B. *Grass-Roots Reconstruction in Texas, 1865–1880*. Baton Rouge: Louisiana State University Press, 1997.

Crouch, Barry A. *The Freedmen's Bureau and Black Texans*. Austin: University of Texas Press, 1992.

Moneyhon, Carl H. *Republicanism in Reconstruction Texas*. Austin: University of Texas Press, 1980.

Pitre, Merline. *Through Many Dangers, Toils, and Snares: The Black Leadership of Texas, 1868–1900*. Austin: Eakin Press, 1985.

Ramsdell, Charles William. *Reconstruction in Texas*. New York: Columbia University Press, 1910.

Rice, Lawrence D. *The Negro in Texas, 1874–1900*. Baton Rouge: Louisiana State University Press, 1971.

Richter, William L. *The Army in Texas During Reconstruction, 1865–1870*. College Station: Texas A&M University Press, 1987.

———. *Overreached on All Sides: The Freedmen's Bureau Administrators in Texas, 1865–1868*. College Station: Texas A&M University Press, 1991.

Smallwood, James M. *Time of Hope, Time of Despair: Black Texans During Reconstruction*. Port Washington, NY: Kennikat Press, 1981.

CHAPTER 12 Old West and New South, 1865–1890

Barr, Alwyn. *Reconstruction to Reform: Texas Politics, 1876–1906*. Austin: University of Texas Press, 1971.

Benner, Judith Ann. *Sul Ross: Soldier, Statesman, Educator*. College Station: Texas A&M University Press, 1983.

Cotner, Robert C. *James Stephen Hogg: A Biography*. Austin: University of Texas Press, 1959.

Graham, Joe S. *El Rancho in South Texas: Continuity and Change from 1750*. Denton: University of North Texas Press, 1994.

Holden, William Curry. *Alkali Trails, or Social and Economic Movements of the Texas Frontier, 1846–1900*. Dallas: The Southwest Press, 1930.
Jordan, Terry G. *Trails to Texas: Southern Roots of Western Cattle Ranching*. Lincoln: University of Nebraska Press, 1981.
Kavanagh, Thomas W. *Comanche Political History: An Ethnohistorical Perspective, 1706–1875*. Lincoln: University of Nebraska Press, 1996.
La Vere, David. *Life Among the Texas Indians: The WPA Narratives*. College Station: Texas A&M University Press, 1998.
Pierce, Michael D. *The Most Promising Young Officer: A Life of Ranald Slidell Mackenzie*. Norman: University of Oklahoma Press, 1993.
Schilz, Jodie Lynn Dickson, and Thomas F. Schilz. *Buffalo Hump and the Penateka Comanches*. El Paso: Texas Western Press, 1989.
Schilz, Thomas F. *The Lipan Apaches in Texas*. El Paso: Texas Western Press, 1987.
Smith, Thomas T. *The U.S. Army and the Texas Frontier Economy, 1845–1900*. College Station: Texas A&M University Presss, 1999.
Spratt, John Stricklin. *The Road to Spindletop: Economic Change in Texas, 1875–1901*. Dallas: Southern Methodist University Press, 1955.
Utley, Robert M. *Lone Star Justice: The First Century of the Texas Rangers*. New York: Oxford University Press, 2002.
Walker, Donald R. *Penology for Profit: A History of the Texas Prison System, 1867–1912*. College Station: Texas A&M University Press, 1988.
Wooster, Robert. *Soldiers, Sutlers, and Settlers: Garrison Life on the Texas Frontier*. College Station: Texas A&M University Press, 1987.
Zlatkovich, Charles P. *Texas Railroads: A Record of Construction and Abandonment*. Austin: Bureau of Business Research, University of Texas at Austin, 1981.

CHAPTER 13 An Era of Reform, 1891–1920

Anders, Evan. *Boss Rule in South Texas: The Progressive Era*. Austin: University of Texas Press, 1982.
Barr, Alwyn. *Reconstruction to Reform: Texas Politics, 1876–1906*. Austin: University of Texas Press, 1971.
Barthelme, Marion K., ed. *Women in the Texas Populist Movement: Letters to the* Southern Mercury. College Station: Texas A&M University Press, 1997.
Buenger, Walter L. *The Path to a Modern South: Northeast Texas between Reconstruction and the Great Depression*. Austin: University of Texas Press, 2001.
Cantrell, Gregg. *Kenneth and John B. Rayner and the Limits of Southern Dissent*. Urbana, IL: University of Illinois Press, 1993.
Coerver, Don M., and Linda B. Hall. *Texas and the Mexican Revolution: A Study in State and National Border Policy, 1910–1920*. San Antonio: Trinity University Press, 1984.
Foley, Neil. *The White Scourge: Mexicans, Blacks, and Poor Whites in Texas Cotton Culture*. Berkeley: University of California Press, 1997.
Gould, Lewis N. *Progressives and Prohibitionists: Texas Democrats in the Wilson Era*. Austin: University of Texas Press, 1973.
McArthur, Judith N. *Creating the New Woman: The Rise of Southern Women's Progressive Culture in Texas, 1893–1918*. Urbana, IL: University of Illinois Press, 1998.
Martin, Roscoe C. *The People's Party in Texas: A Study in Third Party Politics*. Austin: University of Texas Press, 1933.
Olien, Diana Davids, and Roger M. Olien. *Oil in Texas: The Gusher Age, 1895–1945*. Austin: University of Texas Press, 2002.

Spratt, John Stricklin. *The Road to Spindletop: Economic Change in Texas, 1875–1901*. Dallas: Southern Methodist University Press, 1955.

Zamora, Emilio. *The World of the Mexican Worker in Texas*. College Station: Texas A&M University Press, 1993.

CHAPTER 14 The "Prosperity Decade" and the Great Depression, 1921–1941

Blackwelder, Julia Kirk. *Women of the Depression: Caste and Culture in San Antonio, 1929–1939*. College Station: Texas A&M University, 1984.

Brown, Norman D. *Hood, Bonnet, and Little Brown Jug: Texas Politics, 1921–1928*. College Station: Texas A&M University Press, 1984.

Foley, Neil. *The White Scourge: Mexicans, Blacks, and Poor Whites in Texas Cotton Culture*. Berkeley: University of California Press, 1997.

McCarty, Jeanne Bozzell. *The Struggle for Sobriety: Protestants and Prohibition in Texas, 1919–1935*. El Paso: Texas Western Press, 1980.

Patenaude, Lionel V. *Texans, Politics, and the New Deal*. New York: Garland Publishing, 1983.

Whisenhunt, Donald W. *The Depression in Texas: The Hoover Years*. New York: Garland Publishing, 1983.

———, ed. *The Depression and the Southwest*. Port Washington, NY: Kennikat Press, 1980.

CHAPTER 15 World War II and the Rise of Modern Texas, 1941–1971

Allsup, Carl. *The American G.I. Forum: Origins and Evolution*. Austin: Center for Mexican-American Studies, University of Texas, 1982.

Carleton, Don E. *Red Scare! Right-Wing Hysteria, Fifties Fanaticism, and Their Legacy in Texas*. Austin: Texas Monthly Press, 1985.

Cox, Patrick. *Ralph W. Yarborough, The People's Senator*. Austin: University of Texas Press, 2001.

Dallek, Robert. *Lone Star Rising: Lyndon Johnson and His Times, 1908–1960*. New York: Oxford University Press, 1991.

———. *Flawed Giant: Lyndon Johnson and His Times, 1960–1973*. New York: Oxford University Press, 1998.

Davidson, Chandler. *Race and Class in Texas Politics*. Princeton: Princeton University Press, 1990.

Green, George Norris. *The Establishment in Texas Politics: The Primitive Years, 1938–1957*. Westport, CT: Greenwood Press, 1979.

Hine, Darlene Clark. *Black Victory: The Rise and Fall of the White Primary in Texas*. Millwood, NY: KTO Press, 1979.

Knaggs, John R. *Two-Party Texas: The John Tower Era, 1961–1984*. Austin: Eakin Press, 1986.

Ladino, Robyn Duff. *Desegregating Texas Schools: Eisenhower, Shivers, and the Crisis at Mansfield High*. Austin: University of Texas Press, 1996.

Lee, James Ward, et al., eds. *1941: Texas Goes to War*. Denton: University of North Texas Press, 1991.

Olien, Roger M. *From Token to Triumph: The Texas Republicans Since 1920*. Dallas: Southern Methodist University Press, 1982.

Pitre, Merline. *In Struggle Against Jim Crow: Lulu B. White and the NAACP, 1900–1957*. College Station: Texas A&M University Press, 1999.

San Miguel, Guadalupe, Jr. *"Let All of Them Take Heed": Mexican Americans and the Campaign for Educational Equality in Texas, 1910–1981*. Austin: University of Texas Press, 1987.

CHAPTER 16 Modern Texas, 1971–2001

Barta, Carolyn. *Bill Clements: Texian to His Toenails.* Austin: Eakin Press, 1996.

Davidson, Chandler. *Race and Class in Texas Politics.* Princeton, NJ: Princeton University Press, 1990.

De Leon, Arnoldo. *Mexican Americans in Texas: A Brief History.* 2nd ed. Wheeling, IL: Harlan Davidson, 1999.

Jones, Nancy Baker, and Ruthe Winegarten. *Capitol Women: Texas Female Legislators, 1923–1999.* Austin: University of Texas Press, 2000.

Kinch, Sam, Jr., and Ben Procter. *Texas Under A Cloud.* Austin: Jenkins Publishing, 1972.

Knaggs, John R. *Two-Party Texas: The John Tower Era, 1961–1984.* Austin: Eakin Press, 1986.

Olien, Roger M. *From Token to Triumph: The Texas Republicans Since 1920.* Dallas: Southern Methodist University Press, 1982.

Perryman, M. Ray. *Survive and Conquer, Texas in the '80s: Power—Money—Tragedy . . . Hope!* Dallas: Taylor Publishing Company, 1990.

Index